P9-DIA-369

THE EARLY MALLARMÉ

The Early Mallarmé

BY

AUSTIN GILL

VOLUME 2

YOUTH AND YOUNG MANHOOD
EARLY POEMS

CLARENDON PRESS OXFORD
1986

Oxford University Press, Walton Street, Oxford OX2 6DP
Oxford New York Toronto
Delhi Bombay Calcutta Madras Karachi
Kuala Lumpur Singapore Hong Kong Tokyo
Nairobi Dar es Salaam Cape Town
Melbourne Auckland
and associated companies in
Beirut Berlin Ibadan Nicosia

Oxford is a trade mark of Oxford University Press

Published in the United States
by Oxford University Press, New York

British Library Cataloguing in Publication Data

Gill, Austin
The early Mallarmé.
Vol. 2 : Youth and young manhood : early poems
1. Mallarmé, Stéphane—Criticism and interpretation
I. Title
841'.8 PQ2344.Z/

ISBN 0-19-815790-8

Set by Wyvern Typesetting Limited, Bristol
Printed in Great Britain
at the University Printing House, Oxford
by David Stanford
Printer to the University

ACKNOWLEDGEMENTS

In preparing this volume I have been assisted by friends and colleagues too numerous to be named but whom I should like to thank. To one however I am specially beholden, to Hety Varty for resolving on my behalf the never-ending difficulties that the German language presents to the ill-equipped. (Will no one translate, for instance, into French or perhaps English, a work as indispensable as Kurt Wais's *Mallarmé*?) I have much appreciated also ready help given by members of the staff of two libraries in particular, the Bibliothèque littéraire Jacques Doucet and the library of Glasgow University. I have constantly been made aware also of two debts of a different kind, to benefactors no longer alive. Both take me back many years in memory and both are inseparable from private reminiscence. The first is to the distinguished scholar who first introduced me, with no intention of doing so, to the poetry of Mallarmé. The scene was the University of Grenoble, where in the early nineteen-thirties I was the *lecteur d'anglais* and (may I add in this context, with generous financial assistance from Manchester University) a student of French philology. I was present one day, quite by chance, at a conversation between one of the professors of French literature, Monsieur Henri Jacoubet, and a schoolmaster who was deputizing for the professor of English, absent abroad. The subject was modern French poetry, about which I knew very little, and the schoolmaster had asked: 'Est-ce que vous comprenez Mallarmé?' To this Monsieur Jacoubet replied: 'Non, je ne comprends pas tous les poèmes de Mallarmé, mais il a écrit ces vers.' He then quoted, quietly and simply, several lines from the poem 'Apparition', and made me a Mallarmé addict for the rest of my life. The second debt is less personal. Indeed, it seems to me to be owed by all the students of Mallarmé in my generation—to go no further. It is what we owe to Henri Mondor, also associated for me with a private memory. In 1943, after the 'Allied landing' in French North Africa, I was sent (by good fortune not as a soldier) to Algiers.

There, in a street along which I sometimes had occasion to pass, was a book-seller's shop that seemed to have been closed 'for the duration'. A display of books had been left in the window, and among them was one that bore the title *Vie de Mallarmé*, and the name of the author, Henri Mondor. It was a pleasing promise of appetizing reading when we should all be back in our own occupations. Only in the years that followed, when to the life of Mallarmé had been added the *Œuvres complètes* by Henri Mondor and G. Jean-Aubry, and the *Correspondance de Stéphane Mallarmé* had been launched, did it become clear that a new era of Mallarmé studies had been inaugurated, and the foundations for it laid, by the distinguished surgeon Doctor Mondor. A period of stimulating and rewarding research it has proved to be, shared in by many during the last forty years, and for which our thanks to that gifted predecessor are very decidedly due.

CONTENTS

ABBREVIATIONS

MALLARMÉ'S VERSE AND PROSE

O.c.—Stéphane Mallarmé, *Œuvres complètes*, texte établi et annoté par Henri Mondor et G. Jean-Aubry, Gallimard, Bibliothèque de la Pléiade, 1945. (Page references are to that edition. When there is disparity, the page reference to the 1951 edition is added in square brackets.)

Poésie—Stéphane Mallarmé, *Poésies*, Gallimard, 'Collection *Poésie*', 1966 edition.

Fl., i.—Stéphane Mallarmé, *Œuvres complètes*, édition critique présentée par Carl Paul Barbier et Charles Gordon Millan. I Poésies, Flammarion, 1983.

E.qu.m.—*Entre quatre murs*, presented by Carl Paul Barbier in *Documents Stéphane Mallarmé*, vol. vii, Nizet, 1980.

BAUDELAIRE'S VERSE AND PROSE

B., *O.c.* [vols. i and ii]—Baudelaire, *Œuvres complètes*, texte établi, présenté et annoté par Claude Pichois, Gallimard, Bibliothèque de la Pléiade, 1975–6.

BOOKS BY HENRI MONDOR

Vie—*Vie de Mallarmé*, Gallimard, 1941.

M.pl.i.—*Mallarmé plus intime*, Gallimard, 1944.

Lef.—*Eugène Lefébure*, Gallimard, 1951.

Propos—*Propos sur la poésie*, Éditions du Rocher, Monaco, 1953.

M.lyc.—*Mallarmé lycéen*, Gallimard, 1954.

Autres précisions—*Autres précisions sur Mallarmé et inédits*, Gallimard, 1961.

SERIAL PUBLICATIONS

Corr.—Stéphane Mallarmé, *Correspondance*. Recueillie, classée et annotée par Henri Mondor et Lloyd James Austin, vols. i to ix, Gallimard, 1959–85.

DSM.—Documents Stéphane Mallarmé présentés par Carl Paul Barbier, vols. i to vii, Nizet, 1968–1980.
MLR.—Modern Language Review.
NRF.—Nouvelle Revue Française.
RHLF.—Revue d'Histoire Littéraire de la France.

In page references to any of the above publications, the number of the page is given without the word 'page' or its abbreviation.

Chapter 1

The year 1860: pause for reflection, and *Glanes*

A convenient distinction adopted in an earlier chapter gives to all Mallarmé's schoolboy poems the status of 'juvenilia'.[1] The three latest of them to have survived (in *Entre quatre murs*) are dated respectively February, March, and April 1860.[2] The juvenilia, that is, straggle on as far as the fourth month of that year. On the other side of the division are the 'early poems', of which the earliest known to have survived, also three in number, are dated by their author simply '1861'. The intervening period lasted therefore at least eight months and quite possibly more than a year. Not until October 1861 is there evidence of its having ended. It was on the eighth of that month that Des Essarts arrived at Sens,[3] and he is not likely to have been there for more than a very few weeks when he was told of the young man who lived a somewhat secluded life, in his father's house, and 'wrote poetry when he was so minded'.[4]

We know that if, as seems to be the case, before his schooldays were over Mallarmé had ceased for a time to write verse, it was not because his interest in poetry was flagging. He appears rather to have indulged it more purposefully. During the summer and autumn of 1860, and probably a fair part of the winter months that followed, his hours of stolen leisure were spent in compiling the private anthology which he entitled, oddly, *Glanes*,[5] and which comprises some eight thousand lines of verse culled from the works of a variety of French poets past and present whose poems he did not himself possess. It was briefly described in an early chapter of this study,[6] but must now be scrutinized more attentively, and questions asked as to the circumstances that may explain its existence. The question that needs to be answered first, since a reliable answer will help to settle other controversial matters too, is chronological.

When was *Glanes* compiled? I have already ventured to answer the question confidently and must justify my reply. As so often happens, it is Henri Mondor who points the way. He provided without hesitation the approximate date when in *Mallarmé lycéen* he began as follows his chapter on *Glanes*:

Je crois devoir donner la table des matières de *trois autres cahiers* [additional, that is, to the one entitled *Entre quatre murs*, containing Mallarmé's own juvenilia] datés, sur chacun, de 1860, numérotés I, II, III, et calligraphiés élégamment, par le jeune poète de Sens.[7]

Had there been no reason for considering 1860 an unlikely period, Mondor's readers would no doubt have followed his example and accepted the date on the notebooks, without demur, as being the date of the anthology itself. There was, however, an impediment, clearly indicated in the first two items of Mallarmé's table of contents, at the beginning of his Notebook I: '1. Poésies choisies d'Edgar Poe. 2. Poésies choisies de Beaudelaire (*sic*).'[8] For it had hitherto been generally believed by students of Mallarmé that he did not read *Les Fleurs du mal* until 1861, and that it was his interest in Baudelaire that led him to the poems of Poe. To that belief the Pléiade editors, Mondor himself and G. Jean-Aubry, had lent their authority:

En 1859 même, il est fort douteux qu'il eût eu connaissance d'Edgar Poe dont la révélation dut lui être faite à travers Baudelaire dont il ne connut les œuvres qu'en 1861, avec la seconde édition des *Fleurs du Mal*, c'est-à-dire une fois sorti du lycée.[9]

Therein lay the main reason for interest in the correct dating of *Glanes*. Its importance was not simply academic. It would resolve another uncertainty, of some consequence for the poet's literary biography. For if we knew whether it was in 1861 or about the middle of the previous year that he first read *Les Fleurs du mal*, we should also know the nature of his first response to the challenge of Baudelaire.[10] Did he, as had been supposed, meet that challenge by writing poems so Baudelairian in theme and attitude that, as Guy Michaud puts it, 'l'imitation semble parfois tourner au pastiche'?[11] Or, on the contrary, did that first reading coincide with, and perhaps indeed help to motivate, a decision on Mallarmé's part to stop composing for a time, and busy himself gathering for careful study a selection of poems by masters of his art—beginning with Baudelaire—whose works he did not himself possess. In which case Mondor was probably right, on discovering that selection a century later, to see in its contents:

Des anthologies fort diverses—dites par lui *Glanes*—que le bachelier, pour éduquer son goût et enrichir sa science prosodique, avait scrupuleusement constituées avant de quitter le lycée de Sens, et pour éviter de se croire poète.[12]

As to the time of its compiling Mondor had no doubts. The date 1860 written on the first page of each of the three notebooks proved to his satisfaction that the poems they contained had all been copied there by the young anthologist during that year. To some students of Mallarmé however (or to one at least), it appeared that another possibility had to be considered. The '1860' might concern the exercise-books themselves, noting the year of their purchase, or issue, or distribution for use in the class-room or for private study. To be entitled like Mondor to make up one's mind on the subject, one must like him have examined the *carnets* and the date they all bore, for any clue they might provide as to the function of that date.

Pending this, it seemed prudent to test anew the previous dating, which placed the first reading of Baudelaire's poems early in 1861 but which was now clearly in doubt. And when this was done, it became quite apparent that the claims of this later dating were flimsy. They amounted, in fact, to nothing more substantial than two facile assumptions that soon proved to have little justification. One was that Mallarmé first read *Les Fleurs du mal* in the second edition, published in February 1861. This notion (which we may note gets no support from *Glanes*, since the poems by Baudelaire included there are specifically declared by the anthologist himself to be copied from the first edition)[13] had perhaps been instilled, inadvertently, by Mallarmé's son-in-law Edmond Bonniot when he made known the following fragment of family lore:

A dix-huit ans, en 1861, Mallarmé engageait avec sa famille une lutte courtoise, mais tenace et victorieuse, pour la possession de la seconde édition des *Fleurs du mal*: qu'il faisait ensuite relier, ensemble la copie des pièces interdites.[14]

The other rash assumption was that the obvious imitation of Baudelaire, in poems that Mallarmé was known to have written in 1861, must clearly be attributed to his enthusiasm on first reading *Les Fleurs du mal*. Its suspect character was suggested by an involvement in something very like a circular argument that gave it spurious support. When an obvious imitation of Baudelaire was detected in one of Mallarmé's early poems whose precise date was not known, it was deemed reasonable to suppose that he composed that poem in 1861. For instance, the Pléiade editors could comment thus on the poem 'L'Enfant Prodigue':

> Quoique aucune date ne figure sur ce manuscrit et que celle de 1862 ait été proposée, le caractère évident d'imitation baudelairienne que présente ce poème nous induit à penser qu'il remonte plus probablement à l'année précédente, au moment où Mallarmé est encore sous la première impression du choc intellectuel que lui a fait éprouver la découverte des *Fleurs du Mal*.[15]

This inference also has been proved mistaken. The date does figure on the manuscript, and that date is 1862.[16]

When, therefore, in *Mallarmé lycéen*, Henri Mondor abandoned his former opinion on this subject, and tacitly acknowledged that Mallarmé read Baudelaire's poems at some time in 1860, he was denying not a well-tried hypothesis but a supposition commonly but uncritically adopted. The new dating could be accepted if other relevant facts did not preclude it. It might seem that they did. Mondor himself pointed out, in admiration, how extraordinary it was that during a year in which he had to prepare for the baccalauréat examination—and to sit for it twice, in August and again in November—Mallarmé should have copied out with care not only the two thousand lines of his own verse that make up *Entre quatre murs*, but another eight thousand from the works of a variety of poets 'sans jamais cesser de les transcrire très lisiblement et en une soigneuse mise en page'.[17] Nevertheless, if the scriptory evidence of the manuscript of *Glanes*, the dating of the three carnets, was as compelling as Mondor thought, it could and must be accepted.

For my part, after having belatedly examined the documents, I do now fully accept it. It is true that in Notebooks I and II (more exactly, .1. and .2.) the date neatly entered, like the owner–pupil's name, could well apply to the notebooks themselves, not to the particular purpose to which they were put. But Notebook III shows clearly that such was not the case. Its opening page has more individuality than that of the other two, and all the appearance of a title-page every detail penned on which, including the date 1860, is visibly an integral part of it.[18] Furthermore, when one turns from these physical features to the contents of the anthology, an item in Notebook II is found to confirm that date as that of the anthology, in a very positive way. Mondor ventures a sibylline hint of its identity in one of his lists of contents, headed 'Poésies diverses'. It is represented there not by a title but by what appears to be a query: *Richard: Grand Concours 1860?* When identified, following 'Fragments des *Châtiments* de Victor Hugo', the poem proves to be, like them, a satire against the Bonaparte dynasty. One moreover that was well known, having acquired a certain notoriety in the late summer of 1860. The *Grand Concours* that Mondor's queried suggestion refers to is the competition whose official title was 'Le Concours général des lycées et collèges de Paris et Versailles' (as it then was, not of all France as it was later to be). One need look no further than the article *Concours général*, in Larousse's *Grand Dictionnaire universel du XIXe siècle* (Vol. IV, 1869), to find the meaning of Mondor's query, and confirmation of his suspicion, in the following story of student contestation in France under the Second Empire:

> En 1860, on [*i.e.*, the board of examiners for the *Concours*] proposa comme sujet de vers latins, en rhétorique, l'éloge du prince Jérôme [a brother of Napoleon I recently deceased]; c'était plus qu'une allusion, c'était une flatterie directe qu'on demandait aux élèves. La plupart obéirent, et, dans la langue de Virgile, comparèrent le prince défunt au héros de l'*Énéide*. Mais un élève de Charlemagne [*i.e.*, du lycée Charlemagne], tête chaude et généreuse, cœur de poète . . . s'indigna du rôle qu'on voulait lui imposer; et, au lieu de vers latins, il remit aux surveillants une satire inédite que le *Grand Dictionnaire* voudrait bien donner ici, car c'est du Juvénal dans la langue de Victor Hugo, mais . . . Cette pièce, les lycéens se la passèrent manuscrite; elle courut et elle court encore dans le quartier Latin, où la mémoire de Jacques Richard obtient un juste tribut d'honneur.[19]

The fact that Mallarmé was himself in the Latin Quarter as a

candidate for the baccalauréat and a member of the student throng, in August 1860,[20] while Richard's bold protest was still hot news, points to that month as the time at which he is most likely to have procured a copy of the poem and given it a place in his anthology.[21] For it is indeed that poem that is found there, without a title but with the author's name appended: 'Richard'.

A suggestion much more general in its scope, concerning not simply the date of *Glanes* but its general character and origins, is broached by Mondor in his 'Notes sur les *Glanes*' and clearly deserves careful consideration. He refers, suddenly and without further comment, as if expressing a passing thought about Mallarmé's choice of pieces from *Châtiments*, to an intriguing possibility that might apply to other important sections, and even the whole conception, of the anthology:

> Rien ne peut nous assurer, il est vrai, que le choix eût été fait par Mallarmé lui-même: ce ne fut peut-être que copie de copie.[22]

It was very soon pointed out, in a review of *Mallarmé lycéen*, that some parts at least of *Glanes* are indeed selections from previous selections, and in that sense 'copie de copie'. The most obvious example is found in the two considerable sections devoted to sixteenth-century poets. There, the texts transcribed are all taken from quotations in Sainte-Beuve's *Tableau de la poésie française au seizième siècle* and its appendices.[23] But of still greater interest is the more general underlying thought, that the idea itself of compiling a private anthology, and also the planning of its composition, may not have been entirely Mallarmé's own. Even in the abstract, the possibility makes the undertaking, and its result, more understandable, in the modern sense more 'credible'. For some aspects of *Glanes* appear to reflect a knowledge of French poetry and its history, and an attitude towards them, that Mallarmé cannot at that time have possessed.

It seems that he must have had generous and very competent assistance, and when the question is asked whence that assistance might come, it is almost embarrassingly easy to answer. In an article already referred to, and which we shall find invaluable, Des Essarts recalls that when he first met Mallarmé, in the late autumn of 1861, 'Stéphane ne connaissait encore parmi les lettrés qu'Émile Deschamps, le vieux maître,

gracieux patriarche, qui recevait les rythmeurs nouveaux avec une bienveillance coutumière mais pleine de nuances et de discernement.'[24] When he went on to attribute Mallarmé's acquaintance with Deschamps to their having 'des parents communs, habitant à Versailles', Des Essarts appears to have been mistaken.[25] But a connection did exist though of a different kind. Deschamps had once been employed in the Registry administration. He and André Desmolins had been colleagues, though no doubt of different rank, in Paris at the Ministry of Finance.[26] It was at an opportune time for their grandson, therefore, in March or early April 1860, that the Desmolins moved from Passy to Versailles, where Deschamps had lived in retirement for several years. The professional link on the one hand, and on the other the kindly, ultra-sociable disposition and habits for which Deschamps—a leading figure now among the intelligentsia of Versailles—was widely known,[27] fully explain how the young poet from Sens might be introduced to him and win his good opinion,[28] soon after his grandparents made Versailles their home. Why not, indeed, during the week after Easter which presumably, in 1860 as in previous years, Stéphane spent with them?[29] And if that was so, what more likely than that they should have further conversation during his two other annual stays, during the summer holidays and then in December, for the feast of Stephen.[30]

The indications to be found in *Glanes* itself, that Deschamps may have had a hand in its planning, seem to me in the circumstances fairly convincing. They can be summed up simply enough. First, the theoretical possibility that any other of Mallarmé's literary associates gave the assistance he appears to have had is virtually out of the question. They could only be found among his teachers, who would certainly not encourage him in an intention so contrary to his scholastic interests during that critical year.

Secondly, the whole purpose of Mallarmé's *Glanes* was plainly to supplement the limited resources of his own library. Its execution involved therefore his borrowing from a richer store, not only such works as Sainte-Beuve's *Tableau*, already mentioned, but the banned first edition of *Les Fleurs du mal* (which Mallarmé may have come upon, as he told Régnier, by chance in a second-hand bookshop,[31] but would hardly be

allowed by the bookseller to take away), and also a copy of the clandestine, 'unexpurgated' edition of Hugo's *Châtiments*, published secretly in Brussels at the same time as the official but expurgated first edition, with the imprint (proudly copied out at the head of this section of the anthology): '1853, Genève et New York, Imprimerie universelle, Saint-Hélier (Jersey Dorset-Street 19)'.[32] Such a library was Émile Deschamps's. We need not assume that he had a copy of *Les Fleurs du mal*, since we know that he received one from its author when it first appeared.[33] As to *Châtiments*, Hugo's comrade in the days of the romantic victory, a fellow-member of the 'Cénacle', who continued to correspond with him during his exile ('Cher Victor', 'Cher Émile')[34] would not only have his own copy but know where to obtain another whenever he wished.

Apart from these material considerations, the contents of the anthology reflect values and loyalties that we know to have been those of Deschamps. The prominent place given to Sainte-Beuve not only as the anthologist of French sixteenth-century verse, but also as a poet to be respected and studied, would be puzzling if we could not ascribe it in part at least to the close association of Deschamps with Sainte-Beuve in the romantic cause, and continuing friendship and occasional collaboration since.[35] In addition to which, few students of French poetic styles would be so sensitive as Deschamps to the affinities, from the point of view of the development of those styles, between Sainte-Beuve and Baudelaire, a relationship fully recognized today.[36] More generally, in the predominance usually given to qualities of form in the choice of poems, the anthology follows the known tendency of Deschamps's poetic taste and doctrine, as well as the example of Sainte-Beuve, not only in his *Tableau* but also in his *Œuvres choisies de Ronsard* (of which Mallarmé presumably possessed a copy since Ronsard is completely absent from the three notebooks). It is interesting to observe that one of the footnotes to *Glanes*—they are few, and oddly out of place in so private a collection—designates explicitly 'les beaux vers' as the qualification for inclusion. It is appended to the short section near the end of Notebook III which carries the heading (itself insisting on that qualification) 'Quelques-uns des plus jolis vers de Théophile de Viau qui ne se trouvent pas

dans les *Grotesques* de Théophile Gautier' (also presumably on Mallarmé's own shelves). The footnote reads:

C'est à ma paresse, plutôt qu'au manque de beaux vers, qu'on doit le nombre restreint des pièces qui se trouvent ici: cependant, bien que peu nombreuses, je crois qu'elles le sont assez pour effacer le fameux "Il en rougit le traître!" et permettre qu'on puisse

O Malherbe, à Racan préférer Théophile . . .[37]

Clearly, if the labour of love that the schoolboy's anthology represents had its due reward, it would take its share of credit for the superiority, from the point of view of poetic form (felicitous phrasing, strength and subtlety in rhythms and rhyme) that the best among Mallarmé's early poems were to show over the rather glib formal competence already achieved in the later juvenilia.

Further comment on *Glanes* must be brief. I shall confine it to the most unexpected section, the first. It consists of a word-for-word translation of eight poems by Edgar Poe. That in 1860 Mallarmé had already started translating Poe's verse is interesting new knowledge. One wonders however why his first attempts should find a place in his private anthology of French verse. Once more, a footnote may provide the answer. The section, the reader of that footnote is given to understand, is a contribution (Mallarmé's own, or his English master's, or one from that experienced translator Émile Deschamps?) to the study of poetic form. Thus perhaps it establishes the right of Poe's poem 'The Raven' to be included in *Glanes*—as providing an opening lesson:

La traduction littérale n'est à l'américain que ce que serait le squelette d'une jeune fille à la fille fraîche et rose. Le squelette montre seulement qu'elle n'était ni bossue ni bancale: des lignes françaises, de même, révèlent que la pièce ne manque d'aucune qualité de fond. En voyant l'un, on ignore comment furent fraîches et roses les chairs qui le recouvraient, en lisant l'autre, on ne se doute pas de la beauté du rythme lugubre. Le "jamais plus" est un effet immense en américain: il dit "never more" qu'on prononce "néveur môre" [;] c'est un des plus beaux mots anglais par son idée si triste, et c'est un son lugubre qui imite admirablement le croassement guttural du sinistre visiteur. Voici pour les mots; chacun juge du cœur.[38]

NOTES

1 See above, vol. I, p. 77.

2 My own account of the juvenilia referred to only two poems dated 1860, 'Réponse à une pièce de vers' and 'Pénitence' (ibid. 150 and 239). Carl Barbier, however, in his edition of *Entre quatre murs*, saves from oblivion a third, 'Au bois des noisetiers', whose text is crossed out in the manuscript but still legible; see *DSM*. vii, 82, and *Fl.*, i, 43.

3 *DSM*. v, 63.

4 In his obituary article on Mallarmé (see above, vol. I, p. 31, n. 22) Emmanuel des Essarts wrote: 'A ma sortie de l'École Normale, en octobre 1861, j'étais envoyé au lycée de Sens. Peu de temps après deux de mes collègues me parlèrent d'un jeune homme qui vivait assez solitairement dans sa famille et faisait des vers à ses heures.' The young man was Stéphane Mallarmé.

5 'Glanes' seems inappropriate, even if it is taken to mean 'gleanings'. The title had been used by Louise Bertin for a volume of poems: *Glanes* (1842); she was to use it again for a second volume: *Nouvelles Glanes* (1876). Sainte-Beuve, in his review of the former, remarks that the word is incorrectly used: '*Glanes* (j'aimerais mieux *Glanures*)' (*Portraits contemporains*, Calmann-Levy, 1889, vol. III, p. 310).

It is possible that Mallarmé, using the word like Louise Bertin in the sense of 'gleanings', referred to the special purpose of his anthology, which was to increase his store of poetry by adding to the poems of poets whose works he possessed a selection picked out of volumes he had not yet acquired.

6 See vol. I, pp. 81–2. A careless mistake is made there for which I take this opportunity of apologizing. 'On Mondor's reckoning' the three notebooks of *Glanes* contain not *four* thousand but some *eight* thousand lines of verse (*M. lyc.*, 295: 'plus de *huit mille*', and 325: 'près de huit mille').

7 Ibid. 295.

8 Mallarmé's spelling of the poet's name, 'Beaudelaire', leads one to suppose that his discovery of *Les Fleurs du mal* was recent. (*Note*: The correct form of the title of Baudelaire's volume appears to be the one I have just used, and I shall continue to use it as a general rule. But even among students of Baudelaire usage is curiously divided as between 'Mal' and 'mal'— the Garnier edition has 'Mal' on the title-page and 'mal' on the cover. When quoting, I shall as far as possible adopt the form used in the text I am quoting from.)

9 *O.c.*, 1510 [1516]. One of the two editors had written earlier: 'De ce dernier [*i.e.* Baudelaire], Stéphane Mallarmé, qui le découvre en 1861, est enthousiaste. La rencontre a été décisive' (*Vie*, 28).

10 His own recollection of the experience of reading *Les Fleurs du mal* for the first time, as recounted to Henri de Régnier, was quoted above (vol. I, p.

88): 'l'étrange fascination', he called it, 'une possession, quelque chose à rendre fou'.

11 *Mallarmé*, p. 11 [1971 edition: p. 14].

12 *M. lyc.*, 113. In a later chapter, Mondor repeats this most likely purpose of Mallarmé's anthology: 'étudier de près la poésie et d'abord en artisan' and again: 'pour compléter ses connaissances techniques et assurer son goût' (ibid. 277 and 323). This is hypothesis, but most likely.

13 The heading of the section of *Glanes* devoted to *Les Fleurs du mal* states explicitly the date of the edition used: 'Paris 1857'. Also, the selection of poems includes one that was expunged from the 1861 edition ('*Femmes damnées*: Comme un bétail pensif') and none of those that in 1857 were not yet included.

14 *Le Manuscrit autographe*, May–June 1926, p. 14. Mondor (*Vie*, 29) quotes Henry Charpentier's rather more detailed version of this conflict, recounted in the article 'De Stéphane Mallarmé' that he contributed to the special 'Mallarmé' number of *NRF* (1 November 1926): 'Il était bien jeune encore lorsqu'il acheta cette deuxième édition des *Fleurs du mal*, que lui confisquèrent, à deux reprises, son père et sa belle-mère, et dont il ne conserva, lecteur obstiné, qu'un troisième exemplaire, qu'il compléta en y ajoutant, de sa main, les six pièces condamnées et qu'il garda toute sa vie.' Charpentier presumably owed the added details to Dr Bonniot, whom he declares at the beginning of his article to be 'celui de ses familiers [i.e. Mallarmé's] qui, en dehors de toute préoccupation littéraire personnelle, subit peut-être le plus profondément son influence et garde fidèlement sa mémoire.'

15 *O.c.*, 1386 [1388].

16 Re-editing, in 1971, Mallarmé's *Vers et Prose d'enfance et de jeunesse*, Carl Barbier pointed out that 'malgré ce qu'en dit Mondor, (. . .) le manuscrit [de 'L'Enfant Prodigue'] est bien daté "1862"' (*DSM*. iii, 87). Dr Bonniot's facsimile of the manuscript (itself since lost?) shows faint traces of the date, written so small that it is not surprising if Mondor did not recognize it as writing. Of the four digits, the second and third are illegible in the photograph, but the first is 1 and the fourth just recognizable as 2.

17 *M. lyc.*, 295.

18 The numbering of the three notebooks is not precisely as Mondor states. They are not 'numérotés I, II, III', but '.1., .2., III.' This is the most conspicuous detail in which the third notebook shows a singularity that seems to include the date, and with it its purpose.

19 The poem was published in 1863 and again in 1868, then in 1885 included in the collected works of Jacques Richard, with an introduction by A. Dietrich; see the catalogues of the Bibliothèque Nationale and the British Library. Henri Mondor appears to have known of the affair and guessed that the poem transcribed by Mallarmé (with no other indication than the name 'Richard') was the one that gained Jacques Richard a celebrity he was not, alas, to enjoy for long. He died in 1861, 'de la poitrine'. In the meantime, his audacity had cost him his place at the École Normale.

20 The result of the *Concours général* was announced on 1 August, and the Richard episode would probably be known about earlier. The date of Mallarmé's examination (or the first of its two days) is stated in Madame Desmolins's letter to Mélanie Laurent of 21 June 1860: 'Stéphane travaille à force, pour passer son examen le 10 août' (*DSM*. v, 335). As to the place, candidates had some choice between University towns; see *Programme pour l'examen du Baccalauréat ès-Lettres*, Dezobry et E. Magdeleine, 1852, p. 6, n. 1. It was not possible for Mallarmé to sit at Sens or Auxerre; the *Bulletin administratif de l'Instruction publique* for June 1860 published the text of a ministerial order dated 8 June which declared: 'Dans les Académies de Paris, de Besançon, de Lyon, de Strasbourg, de Clermont, de Dijon et de Poitiers, il n'y aura d'examens de baccalauréat ès-lettres (. . .) qu'au siège des Facultés.' Although Sens was in the Academy whose seat was Dijon, Paris was much nearer as well as more attractive. Mallarmé certainly chose Paris for his second attempt, in November, since his baccalauréat certificate was signed by the Rector of the University of Paris; see *DSM*. v, 63. There is no reason to think that in August he had done otherwise. On both occasions he would probably have been expected to pay a short visit to his grandparents at Versailles.

21 Another circumstance tends to confirm the vague chronological sketch that the inclusion of Richard's poem at that place in the anthology suggests. Mondor notes in *Histoire d'un Faune* (p. 25) that Mallarmé purchased the works of Mathurin Régnier in September 1860. The transcription of the first section of Notebook III—'XVIe siècle (suite)'—was probably performed later, since it includes satires by D'Aubigné but none by Régnier. Such indications are uncertain however; the numbering of the notebooks may itself be deceptive. It is by no means sure that Notebook III was started on when Notebook .2. was full. It is quite likely that it began earlier, to complete the study of the sixteenth-century poets started at the end of Notebook .1.

22 *M. lyc.*, 315.

23 The review was L. J. Austin's 'Les "Années d'apprentissage" de Stéphane Mallarmé' in *RHLF*., Jan.–Mar. 1956. He drew attention also to the fact that several poems, including all those in the section 'Poésies amoureuses modernes', are to be found in Julien Lemer's *Les Poètes de l'amour* (1850 and 1858), presumably borrowed also. Another example of the need for a generous lender, to make such borrowing possible, is the section of poems composed by Théophile; the edition used was probably that of Alleaume, published in 1855.

24 On this article, see above, vol. I, pp. 7 and 31 (n. 22); also, n. 4 of the present chapter.

25 In his biography, *Un Bourgeois dilettante: Émile Deschamps* (1921), p. 525, Henri Girard writes: 'Un hommage auquel le vieux poète dut être particulièrement sensible fut celui d'un jeune homme dont il appréciait la nature exquise, une originalité d'esprit plus rare encore, et auquel s'unissait un même culte pour les poètes anglais, il s'agit de Stéphane Mallarmé: nous le rencontrons sans cesse auprès d'Émile Deschamps,

dans les derniers temps de sa vie, mais nous n'avons pu découvrir comment ils étaient entrés en relations.'

Pierre Breillat, however, in a very interesting article entitled 'De Chateaubriand à Mallarmé: Versailles et les lettres françaises au XIXe siècle' (*Revue de l'histoire de Versailles*, 1954, p. 67), notes the Registry connection: 'Mallarmé comptait à Versailles au moins un ami de choix. Il est probable que des relations littéraires communes l'ont présenté à Émile Deschamps. Il est plausible aussi qu'il vint chez lui, amené par ses grands-parents. M. Desmolins pouvait fréquenter Émile Deschamps: ils étaient voisins, de même âge, ils avaient fait carrière dans l'Enregistrement, tous deux, l'Enregistrement, cette administration si chère à la famille Mallarmé.'

No family relationship with Deschamps figures in Carl Barbier's genealogy of Mallarmé, appended to *DSM*. v.

26 H. Girard states (op. cit., p. 472) that he has not been able to find out whether Deschamps held his post at the Ministry of Finance (which was not a sinecure) until the retirement age (i.e. until 1861). There is evidence however that he did not. Baudelaire, in an anonymous letter written from Versailles and published by *Le Figaro* on 14 April 1864, under the heading 'Anniversaire de l'année de Shakespeare', has occasion to mention him and does so in these terms: 'Ici, à Versailles, à quelques pas de moi, habite un vieux poète qui a marqué, non sans honneur, dans le mouvement littéraire romantique; je veux parler de M. Émile Deschamps, traducteur de *Roméo et Juliette*.' He continues: 'M. Émile Deschamps a été pendant longtemps un des principaux employés du ministère des Finances. Il est vrai qu'il a, depuis longtemps aussi, donné sa démission' (B., *O.c.*, ii, 226). This information must have come from Deschamps himself. He probably retired when he went to live at Versailles, in 1845. (For this date, see H. Girard, op. cit., p. 469.)

27 His readiness to appreciate the efforts of young would-be poets, and give them his advice, was an important part of his reputation. 'Vieillard infiniment affable', Catulle Mendès calls him, in his *Rapport sur le mouvement poétique français* (1903), p. 77. In *La Légende du Parnasse* (1884), p. 35, he had written: 'Il avait été une des lueurs douces de la farouche aurore romantique. Maintenant, il vivait à Versailles, (. . .) accueillant les jeunes hommes avec une clémente courtoisie d'aïeul, les encourageant, les louant (. . .) S'il leur trouvait à tous du talent, c'était qu'il aurait tant voulu qu'ils en eussent.' Paul Juillerat, after regretting that Deschamps had often wasted his own talent on 'cette société dont il s'est laissé faire le poëte officiel', admits that there is another side to such sociability: 'Ne faut-il pas lui tenir compte de tant de fructueux conseils donnés avec une paternelle indulgence aux jeunes poëtes qui viennent frapper sans relâche à sa porte si libéralement ouverte?' (introduction to the poems of Deschamps in Eugène Crépet's *Les Poètes français* (1862), p. 177). In the opening chapter of Book IV of his biography of Deschamps, headed 'Les dernières années d'Émile Deschamps à Versailles' (op. cit., pp. 469–70) H. Girard sums up the rôle he had come to play in the shaping of modern French poetry as follows: 'Nous verrons à peu près

tous les adeptes de la jeune école parnassienne, Glatigny, Mendès, Verlaine, Coppée, faire dévotement le pèlerinage de Versailles pour recevoir des mains du vieux sachem romantique les signes sacrés de la Muse.'

As a poet, Deschamps appears to have been regarded, above all, as a master of verse form. Hugo wrote to Aloysius Bertrand, in the heyday of the Romantic school: 'Je lis vos vers en cercle d'amis (. . .) Il est impossible de posséder à un plus haut point les secrets de la facture. Notre Émile Deschamps s'avouerait égalé' (quoted by H. Girard, op. cit., p. 277). In his advice to young poets, he appears to have laid particular stress on the paramount importance of form, insisting that 'dans les arts, *si la forme n'est rien toute seule, il n'y a rien sans elle*' (ibid. 50–3). It was a belief that he shared with a younger generation, and partly explains, no doubt, his particularly good relations with Banville.

28 The quality of the affection shown by Mallarmé, in his twenties, for Deschamps in the last years of his life would be hard to understand without supposing a debt of gratitude for exceptional kindness; see *Corr.* I, 139, 345 and 355. The fact that Deschamps and Mallarmé's grandfathers had been colleagues in Registry would no doubt make the Desmolins less conscious than they should have been of the fact that from their point of view the influence of Deschamps on their grandson in the early days of their acquaintance was much to be feared.

29 I find no direct reference to Stéphane's Easter visit that year in Fanny Desmolins's letters, for instance the one she wrote to Mélanie Laurent on 24 March, a week before Easter Sunday, full of grief and sympathy for Numa's family, and prayerful hopes for his recovery (*DSM.* v, 328). But it may well have been in preparation for his stay that her housekeeper (?), Christine, was ready to put off her marriage till after Easter and help in the moving in (letter of 8 February to Mélanie, ibid. 329). The bad news from Sens was a reason for, not against, Stéphane's spending the usual week with his grandparents. Later that year, writing to Mélanie of his August–September stay, she said as much: 'je sais très bien qu'à Sens, on est assez embarrassé de lui, par suite de l'état de son père, toujours assez malade et affaibli'; see above, vol. I, 65. From Stéphane's point of view, the change from Passy to Versailles would be a welcome novelty.

30 For Stéphane's three weeks' stay at Versailles in August and September 1860, see above, Vol. I, p. 265. To the ritual December visits for the feast of Stephen (or Boxing Day), Stéphane himself bears witness in his letter to his grandfather of 17 January 1862, quoted below, p. 20.

31 See above, vol. I, p. 88, n. 14.

32 The elaborate manner in which this 'unexpurgated' edition (the true first edition) was prepared in Brussels for clandestine circulation in France, at the same time as an 'expurgated' edition for regular commercial channels, is described in two articles by Pierre de Lacretelle (*Le Bulletin du Bibliophile*, 1933, pp. 36–46 and 96–111). For the application of the ban, see Pierre Angrand, *Victor Hugo raconté par les papiers d'état* (1961), ch. 6.

33 H. Girard, who describes Deschamps as 'ce lettré de l'ancienne France qui

fut dans sa vieillesse un des premiers admirateurs de Baudelaire' (op. cit., p. 85), quotes the letter he sent to the author of *Les Fleurs du mal* on receiving from him a copy of the first edition, a letter so full of praise that it served the publisher as an advertisement in his presentation of later editions. It hailed 'les prodiges de poésie et de versification qui sont manifestés par votre œuvre . . . Votre verve, votre coloris, votre harmonie à part ont pu seuls en venir à bout, et que de secrets de forme, comme de cœur, s'en échappent! Que de vers trempés d'une vigueur étonnante et d'un enchantement inaccoutumé! Que de tours elliptiques et nouveaux, que de rythmes dociles et fiers!' (ibid. 508).

35 Ibid 358–9, 522–3, and 538–9, for instance.

35 See ibid. 405–23.

36 See for instance Robert Vivier, *L'Originalité de Baudelaire* (1952), *passim*, and Jean Prévost, *Baudelaire* (1953), pp. 22–6.

37 *M. lyc.*, 327. The final quip takes up the defence of Théophile by Gautier in *Les Grotesques*: 'On voit que sa destinée de malheur a été complète (. . .) Il serait complètement oublié sans les deux ridicules vers de Nicolas Boileau dans l'*Art poétique*:

A Malherbe, à Racan préférer Théophile,
Et le clinquant du Tasse à tout l'or de Virgile.

et sans une mauvaise pointe tirée de sa tragédie de *Pyrame et Tisbé*:

Le voilà ce poignard qui, du sang de son maître,
S'est souillé lâchement;—il en rougit, le traître,

que l'on cite dans tous les traités de rhétorique comme un monstrueux exemple de faux goût.'

Mallarmé seems to have been impressed by Théophile, and for his additions to Gautier's choice he probably had the use of Alleaume's 1856 edition, of which Deschamps would almost certainly possess a copy.

38 *M. lyc.*, 324.

Chapter 2

Youth has its way

From late December 1860, when Stéphane Mallarmé, *bachelier ès lettres*, entered the Registry service at his family's bidding, provisionally, very reluctantly,[1] and with gloomy forebodings, he disappears almost completely from our ken for very nearly a year. When news does begin to reach us again, however, it is quite substantial thanks to two main sources. One of them has already been mentioned.[2] It is the article published in 1899, some ten months after Mallarmé's death, by Emmanuel des Essarts, once his close companion and most intimate friend though three years his elder. It provides a sympathetic witness's account, from long memory but well-informed, of young Stéphane's background and habits, and family situation, at Sens during the closing months of 1861. The other source is a succession of some dozen letters, dated from 17 January to 11 February 1862 and exchanged between Stéphane on the one hand, discreetly supported by his stepmother, and on the other hand M. and Mme Desmolins his grandparents. This correspondence records, stage by rapid stage, Stéphane's determined and completely successful bid, within those three weeks, radically to change direction with a view to becoming a man of letters.

The general picture at the start is supplied by Des Essarts, of all the friends of Mallarmé's youth the one best qualified to depict him as he had appeared at that critical moment, in the middle of his twentieth year:

J'ai sur mes camarades du groupe parnassien le douloureux avantage d'avoir été le premier à connaître Stéphane Mallarmé. A ma sortie de l'École Normale, en octobre 1861, j'étais envoyé [sent, that is, to a first teaching appointment] au lycée de Sens. Peu de temps après, deux de mes collègues me parlèrent d'un jeune homme qui vivait assez solitairement dans sa famille et faisait des vers à ses heures, étudiant en droit pour la forme, essentiellement lettré. C'était mon futur ami;

car une prompte amitié suivit nos relations premières fondées sur la communauté des goûts, l'amour passionné de la poésie. (. . .) un second mariage de son père lui avait donné une belle-mère aussi distinguée que sympathique, un frère et trois sœurs, enfants alors et destinés à devenir pour leur grand aîné des parents affectueux et sûrs.

Mallarmé voyait fréquemment quelques amis, anciens camarades ou professeurs du lycée.[3]

In the state of affairs then recollected by Des Essarts, however, one very important feature is glossed over and indeed almost totally concealed behind the vague description 'étudiant en droit pour la forme, essentiellement lettré'. The reference thus discreetly veiled[4] was to the issue on which Mallarmé was seriously at odds with his family, and in whose resolution Des Essarts, his new ally, was to play an important part.

By that time Mallarmé was largely neglecting his Registry duties, and disregarding the hopes his relatives still cherished concerning his career. He was giving his attention to activities that they feared (and he knew) were irreconcilable with their fond desires. A few poems that he composed at that time have survived in manuscript and will be identified in due course. Diverse articles that he published during the winter months of 1861–2 will be commented on in the next chapter. Only one of them bore his signature, however, a review, in the Paris magazine *Le Papillon*, of a collection of poems by Des Essarts, *Les Poésies parisiennes*.[5] Three other prose writings published at about the same time, unsigned, are certainly from his pen. They are pieces of dramatic criticism that appeared in the twice-weekly local newspaper *Le Sénonais* ('Journal de l'Yonne'), respectively on 7, 14, and 21 December 1861.[6]

These first three articles, as well as opening Mallarmé's career as a writer, testify to the birth of another literary friendship, with the actor–playwright and poet Léon Marc. He was thirteen years older than the young Sénonais but when they met, at the beginning of a season spent in and about Sens by the itinerant company in which Marc served as actor and occasionally as author, they soon became good friends.[7] The warmth of the understanding that developed between them owed much to the first of Mallarmé's articles in *Le Sénonais*. It contains an eloquent tribute to Marc, the key passage of which reads:

Mme. Léon-Marc a commenté et rendu avec ses élans passionnés la belle pièce de Léon-Marc. Voici une chose noble et grande: dans un art—j'allais écrire un métier, et j'aurais dit juste, car trop souvent le métier envahit nécessairement l'art, en province,—où le malheur et le découragement brisent les uns, le gaspillage de la vie de Bohème énerve les autres, M. Léon-Marc a servi de son talent un vin généreux, le travail. Noble exemple, et rare! Entre le devoir de créer—et vous savez avec quel soin—chaque jour un rôle nouveau dans une pièce qui ne tiendra l'affiche qu'une seule fois, et les obligations du ménage—ne riez pas à ce mot, car ce coudoiement perpétuel de l'idéal et de la réalité, ces contraintes ironiques qui interrompent l'Hamlet de province dans son monologue pour lui dire: Pense demain, il te faut vivre aujourd'hui, sont tristes et navrantes,—entre ces deux nécessités, dis-je, M. Léon-Marc a compris que le loisir de l'artiste ne doit pas être la paresse, comme l'ont chanté des poètes et se le sont imaginé des badauds: il a su faire une pièce poignante en vers énergiques. Je sais bien qu'on pourrait faire quelques observations de détail, mais la critique n'ose élever la voix que pour louer, devant une telle victoire remportée sur le temps et toutes les fatalités.[8]

In writing thus, the young critic was not only expressing a natural fellow-feeling for a struggling artist, but acknowledging a personal debt to that artist for the example he gave. It would seem strikingly relevant to his own situation when Marc told him, as he could not fail to do, that the office he had left at the age of twenty, in order to follow the Muse, was the Registry, the *Bureau des Hypothèques* at Cambrai, his native town.[9] Marc's gratitude, on the other hand, was for the encouragement and stimulus the article in *Le Sénonais* gave him. On two occasions, three years and ten years later, he was to thank its author for writing it as for a good deed shining in a naughty world. He expressed himself privately on the subject in a letter from Paris dated 12 April 1865:

Je me répète les paroles que vous avez dites dans le temps au sujet d'une de mes productions dans un bienveillant article de journal: "C'est une victoire remportée sur le temps et toutes les fatalités".[10]

The same sentiment was given more public expression in the dedicatory preface ('A Stéphane Mallarmé') to Marc's first volume of verse, *Oiseaux des tempêtes*. The terms were very similar:

Depuis longtemps, d'ailleurs, j'attendais l'occasion de m'acquitter d'une dette de reconnaissance, d'abord envers vous, cher critique (. . .)

Vous avez écrit quelque part, dans un journal, en rendant compte d'une pièce de moi, jouée en province, une phrase se terminant ainsi: "Cette victoire remportée sur le temps et toutes les fatalités . . . "

Vous ne pensiez peut-être pas avoir si bien deviné et dire si juste.[11]

Thus the second of the friends that Mallarmé frequented, to our knowledge, at the end of 1861, and intermittently during the greater part of 1862, was a poet like the first, Des Essarts. Like him also, he was one whose influence and example might strengthen the younger man's resolve when the question of his career came up—as it was about to do when they met—for final settlement at last. The question, that is, whether Stéphane was to continue his apprenticeship in the Registry service, as his family intended he should, or to be a schoolmaster and man of letters, as he desired.

That it had been left for too long virtually in abeyance was no doubt due largely to the state of his father's health. For Numa Mallarmé was now incapable of taking any active part in determining his son's future.[12] The parental responsibility had to be borne by the subrogate guardian André Desmolins,[13] himself ailing and weary, and perhaps where his grandson was concerned no more than the mouthpiece of his wife. It was fortunate for Stéphane that when the moment for decision came he had his stepmother Anne Mallarmé by his side, to represent a tolerant sanity and bring practical common sense to bear on the very emotive issue. How far the legal authority of the subrogate guardian went in such circumstances does not emerge clearly,[14] but Stéphane appears not to have questioned the family's assumption, which was that in practice if not in law his grandfather's permission must be obtained if he was to leave the Registry service and prepare himself for a very different occupation. The inevitable wrangle, in which crabbed age put up an ill-managed and ineffectual resistance to the carefully laid and well-founded plans of confident youth, was conducted by post between the Mallarmés at Sens and the Desmolins at Versailles. The pressure to end the uncertainty came from Stéphane himself. During the month from mid January to mid February 1862, eleven letters were dispatched from Sens; all have been published. The replies were fewer and only three appear to have survived.[15]

The matter was brought to a head in the letter that Stéphane wrote to his grandfather on 17 January, formally submitting his own proposals:

Le cœur était dans tout ce que je vous ai dit, à ta fête, à la Saint-Étienne, au jour de l'an. Je voulais prendre courage, et tenter de persévérer dans l'Enregistrement. Décidément, cela m'est tout à fait antipathique.

Quand je sortis du lycée, j'avais exprimé le désir d'entrer dans l'université. C'est ce qui convenait le mieux à mon tempérament. L'Enregistrement, à moins qu'il ne vous plaise réellement, ne se contente pas d'absorber du temps, il absorbe de l'individu aussi: tandis que dans l'université, plus le professeur travaille et apprend, plus l'homme a de valeur intellectuelle.

Et parmi les chaires qui mènent le plus loin, il faut compter celle des langues étrangères.

Un examen se passe à Paris tous les ans: je le passerais cette année uniquement pour bien voir ce que c'est et m'y présenter l'an prochain sérieusement, pour l'Anglais.

Reçu, l'on est nommé professeur avec deux mille francs de fixe, sans compter l'éventuel ou les répétitions. Dans l'Enregistrement je n'aurais seize cent francs que dans cinq ans et à condition de les gagner dans quelque village. Mon père va avoir sa retraite, ce serait bien long d'attendre cinq ans, en dépensant, et sans rien gagner.

Professeur je prépare ma licence ès-lettres, uniquement pour pouvoir subir ma thèse de doctorat. Une thèse à faire sur un auteur étranger, cela serait autant une distraction qu'un travail.

Une fois docteur, l'avenir s'ouvre. Avec quelques éléments d'italien et d'espagnol, on peut arriver professeur de littératures étrangères en une faculté.[16]

Stéphane's letter was followed up four days later by one from Anne Mallarmé to Mme Desmolins, giving her an account of his situation as she saw it:

En effet, bien chère madame, nous avons causé en famille de l'avenir de Stéphane qui nous a paru tout à fait compromis dans l'enregistrement.

Puisque cette carrière lui est tout à fait antipathique, d'après quelques mots que j'ai pu recueillir comme lui étant échappés, t[ô]t ou tard il y aurait renoncé pour suivre ses goûts, je suis à me demander si sa froideur, son peu d'abandon ne serait pas le contre-coup de l'ennui qu'il éprouve dans un travail qui ne lui pla[î]t pas? Je ne puis obtenir de lui de longues heures au bureau, c'est toujours à regret qu'il y va, et ne cherche pas du tout à s'instruire. Nous aurions donc bien des inquiétudes à avoir pour un nouvel examen. Je comprends bien toute la peine qu'a dû vous faire sa lettre, cette nouvelle décision ne me laisse pas sans inquiétude (. . .). J'ai causé de cela avec Mr Desessarts,[17] ce jeune professeur, qui sait toute la répugnance de Stéphane pour son emploi, et son désir d'une autre carrière, il en a aussi causé bien sérieusement avec mes frères qui le verraient avec regret végéter comme il le fait depuis un an.[18]

In the exchange thus opened, the Desmolins were to show no appreciation of Stéphane's point of view. They could see no sense in his wish to quit, for a career of which they knew nothing,[19] one in which he would have the benefit of their guidance and influence; 'l'enregistrement, où tu as tant de chances de réussite', his grandfather wrote, 'avec les bonnes amitiés qui t'y soutiendraient'.[20] Their family pride was wounded too. When Desmolins upbraided Stéphane for what he called 'le profond dédain que tu professes pour un état qui a fait vivre honorablement toute ta famille, et où ta place était marquée d'avance',[21] his grandson replied: 'Je ne dédaigne pas du tout l'Enregistrement, seulement je le crois moins en rapport avec mes aptitudes que l'université'.[22] But his grandfather was referring to the less diplomatic terms in which he had made the comparison ten days before: 'tandis que dans l'université plus le professeur travaille et apprend, plus l'homme a de valeur intellectuelle'.[23]

The most striking feature of Stéphane's letters is his cool imperturbability. He would have his way simply by rationally proving his case. He firmly rebuts charges of insincerity and duplicity. Taunting references to his callow youth, lack of perseverance, fond illusions, even his imperfect grammar and over-ornate handwriting, are simply ignored as irrelevant. It is apparent that he sensed the disarray that such insulting disparagement betrayed. He knew that the opposition was largely his grandmother's, and told her so: 'Comme (. . .) la lettre de bon papa n'est que la tienne, répétée d'un ton moins affable, c'est à toi que je réponds'.[24] Knowing her as he did, he no doubt realized that there was more distress than anger behind the harsh brow-beating. He knew also the sacred nature of the trust in which she feared she might fail. In a letter addressed to his grandfather but intended also explicitly for her, Stéphane wrote:

Sois certain que mon travail et un jour mes succès te feront revenir des regrets que tu éprouves en ce moment en songeant, comme eût fait ma pauvre mère que vous remplacez, à mon avenir, et que tu n'auras jamais à te repentir de ma décision. Tout ce que je te dis, je le dis aussi à ma chère bonne maman que je confonds avec toi dans mon amour et ma reconnaissance.[25]

That peace-making message was sent at a point in the discussion at which Stéphane believed the fight was over, and bygones could be bygones. His main requests had been conceded. He would leave the Registry, and begin his preparation for a career as a teacher of English. Also, if it was really necessary (as he was given to understand it was) he would go to England for a year. He did not yet know of the unreasonable condition that was to be attached to the latter concession, either as a last attempt to thwart his plans or, more likely, as a genuine though forlorn effort by the Desmolins to guard their grandson against 'les dangers de toute sorte qu'offre ce pays à la jeunesse trop confiante'.[26] The new stipulation was that if Stéphane did spend a year in England it should be as a boarder in a Catholic school. The letter in which this ultimatum was delivered is apparently lost, but as Stéphane's answer to his grandparents was simply an expression of incredulity they repeated its terms with peremptory bluntness a few days later:

Nous avons donc arrêté que tu n'irais pas en Angleterre, s'il le faut absolument, que dans un collège ou une pension *catholique*, où tu serais admis comme *interne*; sans quoi tu ne peux espérer notre autorisation.[27]

The letter continued in the same tone of authority:

Ainsi donc, si tu es réellement de bonne foi dans tes idées de travail et que tu songes *sérieusement* à te créer un avenir, tu dois comprendre nos sollicitudes, et te soumettre de bonne grâce aux seules conditions qui peuvent nous présenter quelque sécurité. Si au contraire tu essaies de résister, ce sera nous prouver que ton arrière-pensée *est seulement d'être libre*, et de t'affranchir de tout contrôle. Auquel cas, notre *devoir* sera de t'empêcher, par tous les moyens en notre pouvoir, de faire de nouvelles sottises.

Je suis fâché d'avoir à te parler ce langage sévère, ton peu de sincérité m'y force; et il faut que tu sois bien convaincu, que malgré ton étude sur tes droits prétendus, les familles ont aussi les leurs, et sont toujours soutenues par la loi, quand il s'agit d'arracher leurs enfants à ce qui serait leur perte. Un peu plus de réflexion sur tes devoirs, mon cher ami, te fera comprendre nos motifs; si tu nous aimes réellement tu n'ajouteras pas à nos chagrins par des résistances inutiles, et tu nous éviteras d'en venir à des mesures toujours pénibles. J'attends donc ta soumission *formelle*.[28]

Stern language indeed, but Stéphane must have realized that it was bluff, or little more. There was little likelihood that the law or even a family council would support Desmolins in an attempt to prevent his grandson and ward from pursuing a course so reasonable and respectable, recommended as suiting his ability and temperament by the headmaster of the lycée and at least one of his colleagues, Des Essarts. A course moreover which he would in any case be free to follow a year later, when he came of age. As to their final condition concerning the Catholic school, even before the Desmolins reiterated it Stéphane had disposed of the strongest argument in its favour, which was that it would make the stay in England less expensive. In the letter that is lost, Desmolins must have stressed this advantage, since Stéphane replied to his grandmother:

Tu me parles aussi de dépenses qui ne sont pas à ma charge, mais le code—si je le cite, c'est dans les bureaux d'Enregistrement que je l'ai lu—ne dit-il pas qu'à partir de 18 ans, les parents doivent compte des intérêts de la fortune de l'enfant, mais prélèvent ce qu'il a dépensé (de cet âge à 21 ans) de la somme totale, en cas que ses dépenses excèdent les in[té]r[ê]ts?[29]

In other words, as Anne Mallarmé was careful to make plain:

Il sait pour s'en être informé qu'à partir de l'âge de 18 ans il a la jouissance de ses revenus, et m'a ajouté que ce qu'il dépenserait au-delà serait à retrancher du capital qui lui sera donné aux r[è]glements de ses comptes.[30]

It would seem that this point of law to which Stéphane drew his grandparents' attention with quietly ironic satisfaction destroyed their case, and put an end to their resistance. If he could himself finance the stay in England, their most plausible objection to it disappeared.[31] Stéphane had won his case. The last document we possess on the contestation is Anne Mallarmé's letter of 11 February to his grandmother, assuring her that he would never accept their stipulation, and adding that on the other hand, 's'il se remet à l'enregistrement il ne fera absolument rien'.[32] Perhaps the suggestion she then made that he might go to Versailles and discuss the matter orally, was taken up, and the subrogate tutor's permission given by word of mouth or tacitly.[33] It appears to have been agreed that he would go to London in January 1863,[34] under no humiliating conditions and with a regular allowance.[35] He would study the English language, with a view to passing, the following August, the examination for the Certificate of fitness to teach English in state secondary schools (*lycées* and *collèges*).[36] In the meantime he was to begin his preliminary preparation at Sens, with a private tutor recommended by the headmaster of the lycée.[37]

There is no evidence that he set about that preparation with the promised diligence,[38] and much to show, on the contrary, that he gave considerable time and attention to literature and in particular to literary productions of his own. In the negotiations about his future, little had been said of his literary ambition, but the one passing reference to it is an admission that it was at the root of the disagreement. In replying to Stéphane's objections to a Registry career, as stated in his first letter, André Desmolins pointed to the material advantages it offered, and added: 'le tout avec un travail qui n'est pas tellement assidu qu'on ne puisse encore, avec de la bonne volonté, trouver du temps pour se livrer à des goûts littéraires, puisque c'est là, malheureusement, ce qui l'emporte chez toi sur la raison.'[39] But Stéphane had not said that the Registry service would leave him no spare time. His objection was fundamental, as has been seen: 'L'Enregistrement, à moins qu'il ne vous plaise réellement, ne se contente pas d'absorber du temps, il absorbe de l'individu aussi.'[40] In the context, this was probably another way of saying that it pulled one down to the level of a brutish existence.[41] He had not rebelled simply against work of a dreary, humdrum kind. He did indeed find it unbearably so, but there were other aspects of a Registry career that seemed to him appalling. A glimpse of one of them is provided in his opening letter to his grandfather on the subject: 'Dans l'Enregistrement je n'aurais seize cents francs que dans cinq ans et à condition de les gagner dans quelque village'.[42] Not simply 'en province', as for instance at the Bureau des Hypothèques of a cathedral town, within easy reach of Paris, but as drudge to a *receveur* in some benighted canton of a remote department, and no kindred spirit within a hundred miles.

Now that he had eluded that fate he could show himself to his fellow-citizens in his true colours. On 19 and 22 March respectively he published in *Le Sénonais*, signing them 'S.M.', another review of '*Les Poésies parisiennes* par Emmanuel des Essarts' and an appreciation of '*La Milanaise et l'Autrichien*, Drame en trois actes et en prose par M. Léon Marc', performed by M. Besombes's company at Sens three days before. Both are friendly, of course, but it was for Marc that the reviewer had most praise. He showed himself already, as he would remain, prompt to admire and defend against bourgeois disapproval (though never tempted to emulate) poets of Bohemian disposition or way of life, careless of respectability.[43] Poets like the impecunious actor Glatigny of whom Des Essarts had told him and to whose experience that of his new friend bore some resemblance.[44] How frequently Marc and Mallarmé saw each other during the actor's several stays at Sens is a matter for surmise,[45] but one document has reached us that bears clear witness to the steady ripening of their friendship. It is a letter written by Marc from Auxerre on 12 May, a tardy but affectionate answer to one he had received from Mallarmé, unexpectedly, a week or two before. It reflects a comradeship that was confident and at the same time respectful, on both sides despite the difference in age:

Mon cher Stéphane

Une lettre de vous est comme un rayon de jeunesse et à la fois une brise fraîche et pleine des senteurs de mon passé déjà lointain . . . C'est une charmante et imprévue diversion aux bruits et aux soins vulgaires qui m'assaillent sans relâche. Aussi auriez-vous droit de vous étonner de ma lenteur à vous répondre. On a fait une vertu aux rois de ne point se faire attendre; mais les rois ont des ministres et une armée de secrétaires pour faire la besogne à leur place; et moi je n'ai que ma main droite et ma cervelle fatiguée pour défricher incessamment les broussailles sans cesse renaissantes des vulgarités qui obstruent ma route, et procurer de loin en loin une éclaircie pour la poésie et l'amitié.—Jugez-en!—rien que pour cette semaine deux aubaines[.] La *fille de l'air* féerie vaudeville, de la fabrique Cogniard frère et cie. Il y a dans cette machine 42 rengaines avec chœurs, ritournelles, trémolos etc etc, ad hoc (notez que notre directeur se garde bien de faire venir la musique toute faite de Paris . . . vadè retrò!)—Il faut donc établir un scenario d'après la dictée de mm. et dames mes collègues aux souvenirs et à l'intelligence musicale desquels il faut souvent suppléer par la divination;—seconde aubaine! . . . trois amateurs sont venus s'offrir pour jouer (. . .) ô Déception! que voyons-nous arriver à la répétition? . . . D'honnêtes et braves ouvriers faisant bien leur métier, style Béranger et Désaugiers (. . .)—quant à l'oreille musicale pour les couplets et surtout les ensembles . . . Tenez! Chantez la Marseillaise tandis que Roquier chantera Fleuve du Tage et Des Essarts Tantum ergò . . . et vous aurez une idée exacte de la justesse des sons. Voilà sur quoi nous travaillons et le régal que nous préparons pour jeudi au bon public d'Auxerre . . . ! qui le mérite bien! il faut être juste.

Vous vous plaignez du soleil mon cher Stéphane et vous vous proposez de passer la plus grande partie de l'été à dormir . . . Hélas! je voudrais bien pouvoir en faire autant, car moi aussi je me sens le cerveau malade . . . mais il faut aller toujours. Si quelque chose dort chez moi, c'est l'âme, ou plutôt la poésie . . . ne comptez donc pas, ou ne craignez pas ouïr à mon retour à Sens quelque nouvelle élucubration. Pour le moment je suis trop occupé à abattre les insectes filandreux ou gluants qui assiègent ma pensée sous la forme de rôles, couplets de vaudeville, soins de ménage et d'enfants. A mesure qu'ils se dressent je les écrase fièvreusement . . . mais il en revient d'autres . . . c'est comme les punaises dans un garni parisien.—Espérons qu'une fois parti d'Auxerre je pourrai respirer un peu et entrevoir quelques loisirs dont quelques-uns vous seront consacrés. (. . .)

Je me fais une fête de lire le volume du comte (*sic*) de Lisle que vous possédez. Je désire ardemment pouvoir le mettre au rang de mes rares amis poétiques, car quoique vous m'appeliez homme difficile, nul au monde ne recherche avec plus d'ardeur matière à aimer et admirer. Seulement j'ai une diable de logique qui ne s'accorde pas toujours avec celle de la nouvelle école. "L'art pour l'art, le beau pour le beau", dit-elle! Soit! C'est aussi mon avis . . . mais alors commencez par mettre cette maxime en pratique vous-mêmes . . . et que l'harmonie et la beauté de la forme remplacent au moins les idées . . . Ne faites pas tout consister dans la rime et comptez la musique, c'est-à-dire le rythme pour quelque chose.

Ma femme vous embrasse et j'en fais autant.—Répercutez cela sur Roquier et Des Essarts nos amis communs, nous attendons leur *revue*[46] avec impatience (. . .)

E. Léon Marc[47]

As well as affording a comprehensive impression of this second of Mallarmé's friendships, merging for a time it would seem with the first, Marc's letter contains indications of others he was entering or had entered into. Particularly conspicuous are the references to one Roquier. They are the only evidence we possess that Émile Roquier was one of Mallarmé's frequent companions at that time,[48] that is during the spring and early summer he spent at Sens, restless and with no firmer obligation than the undertaking he had given to study the English language, impatient for the independence that awaited him in London town.[49] Roquier was a Sénonais, Mallarmé's elder by three years, early examples of whose literary promise, as of Mallarmé's a little later, are preserved in the *Cahier d'Honneur du Lycée de Sens*.[50] He had continued to write poetry since leaving school,[51] and on the evidence of Marc's letter could well be one of the kindred spirits with whom, as Des Essarts remembered long after, Mallarmé consorted when they first met.[52] Carl Barbier thought (and it seems indeed very likely) that Roquier was the 'E. R.' to whom Mallarmé had addressed two of the most interesting of his schoolboy poems.[53] They were to keep up a cordial though fitful correspondence, and meet occasionally, during the next few years.[54]

One more acquaintance is referred to, though not named, in Marc's letter. Indeed, the form and context of the reference suggest that Mallarmé's particular purpose in writing to Marc at Auxerre may have been to ask for news of the person concerned.[55] But there was no news to report:

Je réponds maintenant et brièvement à vos questions.

1° Je n'ai pas vu le jeune homme en question; peut-être nous trouve-t-il un peu candides tous les deux, vous de me recommander à lui, moi de croire qu'on trouve un ami sur recommandation, comme les officiers trouvent, en changeant de garnison, un café et une pension léguée par leurs prédécesseurs. Du reste je m'en console . . . votre amitié m'attend à Sens.

Mallarmé too would be disappointed at the failure of his good offices. He would hardly be surprised, however, for he had had to wait several weeks, and then send a second letter, before eliciting a response to his own first approach, earlier that year, to the same young man. His identity is not in doubt, since his answer to Mallarmé's reminder is known. It is dated 'Auxerre, 9 avril 1862', and Mallarmé received it therefore, as it chanced, little more than a week before the itinerant company, again on its way to Auxerre, made a brief call at Sens and gave a courtesy performance there.[56] The reply Mallarmé had received was fresh in his mind, therefore, and no other reason than the cordiality of that reply need be sought to explain why Léon Marc, when the company resumed its journey south, was the bearer of a letter of introduction from Mallarmé to its author. He was Eugène Lefébure, a talented young poet of twenty-three years, Mallarmé's former schoolfellow and a classmate of Roquier's.[57] He was earning a modest livelihood as a post-office clerk at Auxerre. What better companion indeed for Marc, to relieve the tedium of a long stay there? His letter to Mallarmé reads:

Auxerre, 9 avril 1862

Mon cher ami,

Je reçois à l'instant votre lettre et comme je vois que vous tenez beaucoup aux poésies d'E. Poe, je m'empresse de vous répondre que je ne les ai plus; je les ai remises précisément hier au soir à Courtois qui part ce matin et doit vous les porter: je vous dis cela parce que je le sais au moins aussi paresseux que moi, et qu'il pourrait bien, comme moi, vous les faire attendre deux mois, ce qui ferait quatre.

Vous avez bien raison de publier ces poésies, elles sont fort belles, excepté peut-être *Al Aaraf*, dont je n'ai lu que la moitié mais qui ne m'a guère plu. Je crains que mon édition ne soit pas complète; je ne trouve pas vraisemblable qu'E. Poe ait fait aussi peu de vers: au reste Baudelaire qui a un E. Poe complet pourra vous renseigner là-dessus. A propos de Baudelaire, tâchez donc de savoir s'il croit au diable. (. . .)

J'ai commencé une pièce de vers, *les Asphodèles*, que je voudrais dédier à Baudelaire, auriez-vous la bonté de me donner son adresse? Voici la première strophe de mes vers:

Il est près de l'Hadès un pré plein d'asphodèles
Où viennent habiter les ombres des vivants:
Une humide clarté rôde et flotte autour d'elles,
Et la prairie ondoie où palpitent leurs ailes;
Les spectres et les fleurs se bercent dans les vents.

Puisque je fais quelques vers je suppose que vous devez en faire une foule, un poète doit être plus productif qu'un postier. Je vois de temps en temps des articles de vous dans le *Sénonais*, mais comme je ne vois ni le *Papillon* ni l'*Artiste*, il y a une éternité que je n'ai lu de vos vers, et encore, je n'en ai déjà pas tant lu. Je ne connais guère de vous que le rondeau des six Phillis, vous savez, et la charmante petite pièce de *l'Enfant à la rose*:

Des pas sur les pierres sonnèrent,
Un pauvre passait dans ces lieux,
Où les blancs lilas s'inclinèrent
Et les oiseaux des bois chantèrent,
Le pauvre étant l'ami de Dieu.

Il priait tout bas la madone, etc. . . .
L'enfant lui présente sa fleur.

J'ai demandé les *Poésies parisiennes* de des Essarts, mais je ne les ai pas encore reçues: je suis bien impatient de les lire. J'ai lu de des Essarts, il y a trois mois, une très jolie pièce de fin d'année dans la *Gazette rose*. Je serais très enchanté de faire sa connaissance, comme vous me le proposez, et aussitôt que je serai un peu libre, je tâcherai d'aller à Sens. Malheureusement il nous est si difficile d'obtenir un congé que je ne sais trop quand je pourrai le faire: N'auriez-vous pas de votre côté quelque occasion de venir à Auxerre?

Je viens de faire la découverte d'un poète de dix-neuf ans, barbu, du reste, et très bon caricaturiste [;] il illustre en ce moment les *Fleurs du Mal*, et fait une *Charogne* magnifique: il m'a dédié avant-hier son premier sonnet, j'aurais bien voulu vous l'envoyer mais il le corrige et je ne l'ai pas. Pour moi, si le soleil continue à faire éclore mes vers en petites pattes de mouche, je vous en dédierai quelques-uns—ô jeune Vacquerie.

En attendant, je ne veux pas laisser passer l'occasion de vous remercier de m'avoir tendu la main et d'avoir secoué ma vieille paresse, et je le fais de grand cœur.

Votre ami affectionné
E. Lefébure.[58]

Thus began what was destined to be, despite the loss of the greater part of Mallarmé's side of it, the most interesting and by far the most illuminating of Mallarmé's early correspondences.[59] The most intimate also, intellectually at least, of all his friendships and the strongest personal influence on his poetic development. But that was to come about later. For the time being, nothing appears to have happened beyond one or (more likely) two more letters from Mallarmé to Lefébure, which we do not possess, and Lefébure's answer, long awaited, like the previous one. It is dated 25 June and contains interesting reflections on Hugo's *Les Misérables* (concerning which, he said politely, he shared almost entirely Mallarmé's opinion), compliments on Des Essarts's volume of poems, and approval of Mallarmé's review of them in *Le Sénonais*. Also, some observations on more personal though still literary matters:

Auxerre, 25 juin 1862.

Mon cher ami,

J'ai autant de pardons à vous demander que de remerciements à vous faire. Vous me pardonnez ma paresse, n'est-ce pas? oui. Eh bien passons. Savez-vous que vous m'avez envoyé de charmantes photographies de vous-même? et que j'ai retrouvé dans vos vers l'artiste ferme et dédaigneux que je connaissais? et que vos tercets sont dignes de Théophile Gautier, et que Baudelaire, s'il rajeunissait, pourrait signer vos sonnets? Complétez le portrait, je vous en supplie, ou sinon, je suis capable de courir après le *Papillon* pour lui demander de vos nouvelles. Quant à la *Revue Fantaisiste* où vous avez écrit, je suis à la veille de me la procurer. (. . .)[60]

J'ai remarqué une ressemblance curieuse entre votre portrait et celui de Tennyson, le doux Tennyson, dont la poésie, je crois, est un peu le contraire de la vôtre. Seulement, il est beaucoup plus frisé que vous. (. . .)

Pour le moment, je me hâte de terminer cette vieille lettre, afin de vous prévenir, si vous ne le savez pas avant moi, qu'on vient de traduire une partie des poésies d'E. Poe, et plusieurs contes inédits du même auteur. Je vous envoie le volume.[61] Seriez-vous assez bon pour me copier les poèmes condamnés de Baudelaire, s'ils ne sont pas trop longs?[62] J'ai la nouvelle édition et ses *Paradis artificiels*. Vous devez les avoir lus. (. . .)

Plus j'y pense, plus je me reproche d'avoir tardé si longtemps de répondre à vos charmantes lettres, mais j'espère que vous ne m'en voudrez pas trop quand vous saurez combien j'ai travaillé. Je vous conterai cela bientôt. J'ai même fait des vers, et nous avons, à deux, improvisé une cinquantaine de sonnets que je vous enverrais bien, quand ils seront mis au net, s'ils en valaient la peine.

Adieu, mon cher ami. Léger qui couche avec moi, et qui vient d'acheter du bonheur pour trois francs, vous serre la main, et j'en fais autant, de tout mon cœur, en attendant votre réponse, que je n'ai pas le droit de vous demander prompte.

E. Lefébure.

Présentez, je vous prie, mes compliments et mes respects à M. des Essarts, qui a bien voulu penser à moi dans votre dernière lettre. J'ai lu les *riens* en vers de Germain, un recueil bien intitulé.[63]

Left to his own devices, Mallarmé might have responded to Lefébure's suggestion, gone to see him at Auxerre, and then hobnobbed with him by post through a lazy Burgundian summer. But Des Essarts had other plans for him, thanks to which before May was over exchanges in another quarter had quite dramatically enlivened his existence. The friendship with Lefébure was postponed, superseded for the time being by others, less lethargic.[64]

In the list of young writers cited by Des Essarts nearly forty years later as friends of his who became his protégé's friends too, the first named is Henri Cazalis, a former classmate of his at the Collège Henri IV (lycée Napoléon under the Second Empire) in Paris:

Un de mes premiers soins fut naturellement de mettre Mallarmé déjà causeur séduisant et charmant camarade en relations avec tous mes amis de la jeune littérature (. . .). C'est ainsi que de 1862 à 1864, j'eus le plaisir de lui faire connaître mon plus ancien compagnon Henri Cazalis, puis Catulle Mendès, Albert Glatigny, Léon Dierx, Armand Renaud, [et] notre chef à tous Théodore de Banville.[65]

Cazalis was a year younger than Des Essarts and so Mallarmé's senior by two years. He was the friend whose advent in the life of the young man of Sens did most to make him feel welcome to a place in the sun. Their friendship was decidedly of Des Essarts's making. Such was the enthusiasm with which he spoke to each of the other that they were already friends before they met. On 5 May 1862 Mallarmé wrote to Cazalis to thank him for a present Emmanuel had brought him.[66] The letter, though eagerly responsive in intention, begins in a formal, even ceremonious style. One senses that the writer is feeling his way in company that is inviting, but intimidatingly unfamiliar. It is the name of (and affection for) their mutual friend Emmanuel that helps him out of his diffidence:

Cher . . . ami,

Il y a longtemps que j'eusse dû vous remercier de l'exquise délicatesse avec laquelle vous m'avez destiné, dès son apparition, la prose d'un de mes maîtres les plus vénérés: mais je sors à peine d'une série de jours brumeux et stériles, et mon premier sourire est à vous. (. . .)

Il ['ce journal espéré'] est précieux en effet, trois fois précieux. D'abord, parce que vous avez pensé à moi; puis, parce que c'est une carte de visite qui annonce un petit voyage à Sens; enfin, parce que, de même que vous avez été *vous* en me l'envoyant, Baudelaire y est Baudelaire.[67]

Vous ne savez pas combien j'attends impatiemment le mois prochain, qui—Emmanuel me l'a promis, tenez son serment—doit vous ammener [*sic*] à Sens, ainsi que l'excellent Monsieur des Essarts [Emmanuel's father].

Je crois que le prisonnier de Béranger ne soupirait pas plus après ses hirondelles.

C'est égoïste, ce que je vous dis là, car je sais d'avance que le moins charmé de la rencontre sera vous. Emmanuel, dont l'imagination est pleine de cœur ou dont le cœur est plein d'imagination, a dû me peindre à vous, si j'en juge par le bon accueil que vous fîtes à mon nom chaque fois qu'il le prononça, sous des couleurs dont l'amitié rehaussait infiniment l'éclat. Que vous serez désillusionné quand vous verrez cet individu maussade qui reste des journées entières la tête sur le marbre de la cheminée, sans penser: ridicule Hamlet qui ne peut se rendre compte de son affaissement.

Je sais d'avance que ma surprise, éveillée il y a longtemps par le portrait que m'a fait de vous Emmanuel, changée en admiration fraternelle à la lecture d'une certaine *Lettre* imprimée par l'éditeur des *Misérables*,[68] grandira de jour en jour quand je verrai de mes propres yeux tout ce qu'il y a d'exquis et de généreux en vous.

On a des séries de bonheurs, de malheurs: on peut dire aussi, grâce au charmant proverbe: *Les amis de nos amis* . . . ,[69] que les amis ne viennent pas seuls. C'était déjà une bien grande joie pour moi de connaître ce cœur d'or et ce talent d'or qui s'appellent Emmanuel, et dont je ne vous parle pas assez longuement ici; je n'aurais pas osé espérer que cette amitié m'en r[é]v[é]lerait une autre aussi sincère que celle qui nous unira.[70]

This opening letter in a correspondence that was to continue with almost unbroken frequency for nearly ten years, and then intermittently till Mallarmé's death, is chiefly notable for the contrast it draws between the two correspondents. Mallarmé portrays himself as the morose, spleen-prone provincial and Cazalis as the active, charming, talented Parisian. The brief self-portrait framed in this antithesis may express on Mallarmé's part, rather than a sense of personal inferiority, an awareness of the difference between their social backgrounds. Twice in the following weeks he was at pains to depict in some detail his family circumstances as the obstacle that prevented him from joining Cazalis and his friends in their pleasures. It is thus, from two letters dated respectively 4 June and 7 July, that we may know how Mallarmé saw himself at the beginning of his twenty-first year, in his home setting at Sens:

Voici. Mon pauvre père est fort malade depuis longtemps, et, comme il ne sait plus guère le prix de l'argent, et me donnerait mille francs comme dix sous, j'ai une certaine pudeur qui fait que pour rien au monde je ne lui tendrais la main.

Du reste, la bourse est dans le secrétaire de ma belle-mère, assez jeune femme, qui n'a jamais compris ce que c'est qu'un jeune homme et n'a qu'un mot affreux sur les lèvres: [É]conomie.

Or, comme j'ai toujours peur de lui voir cracher cette souris rouge,[71] je ne lui parle que fort rarement.

Voilà comme je vis en famille. Emmanuel, du reste, a pu t'en parler jusqu'ici.

Oui, si je disais que j'ai besoin de courses vagabondes et d'air, elle me répondrait infailliblement: Le jardin a des allées, et, quant à l'air, nous respirons ici le plus sain qu'on puisse humer à Sens.

C'est, en partie, pour échapper à cet intérieur mesquin et étouffant que je donnerai un coup d'aile jusqu'à Londres, en Janvier.

Ici, je mène une espèce d'existence assez curieuse: regardé par tous comme un prodigue et honoré comme si j'avais trois maîtresses, moi qui n'ai jamais un sou dans ma poche, et qui ne couche même pas avec ma bonne. Je suis un bohême (*sic*) doré. (. . .)[72]

Pardonne-moi, toi, le papillon à travers l'aile de qui on voit le soleil, pardonne cette lettre maussade et ces détails stupides, mais entre vieux amis, ne doit-on pas tout se conter? [73]

Ah! certes, si ce n'était pas pour ne pas laisser Emmanuel seul dans ce désert qui s'appelle Sens; pour te voir aux vacances prochaines; pour vous que j'aime; je partirais dès aujourd'hui en Angleterre. Cela me peinerait fort de quitter mon pauvre père qui est malade: mais cette maison, quant au reste, me répugne tellement, j'éprouve à chacun de mes repas silencieux et taciturnes un tel malaise, j'y souffre d'une économie si sordide, moi qui ai pourtant quelques mille francs, que j'étouffe.

Et ce qu'il y a de fort, c'est que chacun d'ici me traiterait d'ingrat, s'il m'entendait.

Ma belle mère paraît un ange aux yeux du monde, et quand il y a quelqu'un au salon: un ange grippe-liard, soit, et ayant le front étoilé d'une pièce de deux sous.

Tout aboutit à la question d'argent, aussi ne puis-je plus souffler mot. (. . .)

Mais de quoi te parlé-je? Que t'importent ces niaiseries, ô mon poète?[74]

Meanwhile, the two had met in a manner that cemented their friendship (whence the 'tu' and 'toi'). Not at Sens however, nor after waiting as long as they expected. 'Le mois prochain', Mallarmé had said, but a few days later, on Sunday 11 May, they were together at a picnic in the forest of Fontainebleau, midway between Paris and Sens. This was the one outing he did take part in, and the joy it had given him explains his bitterness, on different occasions later, at having to refuse others, more distant and therefore more expensive. The party consisted of Des Essarts and several of his friends and acquaintances, all Parisians except Mallarmé. They were on the one hand three very young ladies, veritable 'jeunes filles en fleurs', chaperoned by the two mammas, and on the other hand Cazalis accompanied by his (and Des Essarts's) former classmate the painter Henri Regnault. Perhaps Mallarmé's letter of the 5th to Cazalis had brought him a late invitation to join the party, or the fact that Cazalis would be there had been kept from him, as a pleasant surprise. Be that as it may, and notwithstanding bad weather, the day was a great success.

For Mallarmé, this introduction to the carefree gaiety of bright young people, on the intellectual (and slightly bohemian) fringe of polite society, seems to have been an extraordinary experience, a further stage in his emancipation and the opening of another world. Never had he written with such enthusiasm as he did in extolling it to Cazalis. There is a new spontaneity in his letter, and a zest and liveliness that speak of the writer's confidence in his new-found friendships and as a consequence, in himself:

Ah! quel charmant souvenir je conserve aussi de notre délicieuse partie! Cela me semble déjà lointain, hélas! et comme vague. Si Henri ne les e[û]t écrasées de son talon, les fraises se confondraient avec les lèvres en une nuance rose et pourpre; et tout se mêle ainsi en demi teintes, déjà. Cette ville de Sens est si triste, tout ce qui y passe devient gris!

Ah! courses vagabondes de rocher en rocher! voiture où l'on était dix! chênes! pervenches! soleil aux yeux, au cœur, sans qu'il y en ait au ciel! et *scie* à trente-deux dents!—blanches. *All is over*, comme dit Byron. Ettie te traduira cela.

Tu me dis que j'ai plu à ces dames et j'en suis charmé.[75]

To a more soberly literary side of the day's pleasures, some reference will be made later. Stéphane read or recited some of his verse, and though he thought he had not read it well some of the ladies asked him for copies of the poems, which he was happy to send them.[76]

So exhilarating had the outing been that he spent the following Sunday finishing with Des Essarts the 'scie' mentioned in his letter, a string of mock-heroic verses improvised at Fontainebleau as their contribution to the fun. They called it, after the place in the forest where the day had been spent, 'Le Carrefour des Demoiselles'. Its seventeen four-line stanzas, or thirty-four (not thirty-two) couplets or 'teeth', were to be sung to the well-known tune and stuttering verse-pattern of 'Il était un petit navire'. It is not unjustly called a 'scie', a mere sing-song jingle, but when they had trimmed it they had copies printed at Sens to send to their friends, signed *Stéphane Mallarmé* and *Emmanuel des Essarts* and dated '18 mai 1862'.[77]

No less than Mallarmé and with a more precise reason, Cazalis too would look back on the day at Fontainebleau ('ce nom magique', Stéphane called it)[78] as one that changed his life. The recollections of it that they shared was a lasting bond between them. Five years later Mallarmé wrote to his friend, from Avignon where he was impatiently awaiting a long-promised visit:

Et puis, mon bon vieux, nous referons quelque *partie de Fontainebleau*! Tout a commencé là, notre amitié, et la vie de ton cœur que remplit une délicieuse enfant.[79]

The charming creature to whom homage was dutifully and so gracefully paid was an English girl, Harriet Yapp (Ettie to her friends). When her mother took her to Fontainebleau, with Madame Gaillard and her daughter Nina, to frolic with the gentlemanly Emmanuel Des Essarts and his friends, she was sixteen. She would be twenty-three when Cazalis, yielding to his family's disapproval and ending his own doubts and vacillations, jilted her most cruelly. In the meantime, the complaining, indecisive courtship to which he subjected her was, in its early days at least, part of Mallarmé's story too. Never so directly important or so private a part as has sometimes been suggested but considerable and quite intimate for a time, when Stéphane was Henri's confidant and Henri Stéphane's, each acting as the other's ambassador in their parallel suits.[80]

Back, after Fontainebleau, in his lawyer's office in Paris, Cazalis lost no time in telling his friends at Sens that he had indeed fallen in love. He seems to have expressed himself in extravagant terms, but his letter has not reached us. Emmanuel frowned over it, Stéphane only smiled.[81] He wrote to Cazalis on 24 May to tell him why:

Depuis, j'ai bien pensé à toi, cher heureux. Ce matin en me réveillant, ton souvenir a traversé mes rideaux avec le premier rayon de soleil; j'ai pris deux tasses de thé au jardin en ton honneur et je remonte t'écrire.

Emmanuel ni moi n'avons ri, non: seulement nous avons compris ta lettre chacun à notre manière. Emmanuel a froncé le sourcil, et moi j'ai souri. Ce que contenait ce froncement olympien, je crois que tu le sais déjà, car tu as dû recevoir la lettre qu'il a tournée immédiatement et qu'il m'a déclamée d'une voix foudroyante. Ce que contient mon sourire, écoute-le.

Je te dirai que je ne crois à un amour sérieux et véritable que quand il est consacré par le temps qui fait crouler bien des entablements sur la tête de leurs cariatides.

Jusqu'ici donc, bien que tu jettes feu et flammes, je considère ta passion comme une amourette. Mais cela ne la diminue en rien dans ma pensée. Le bonheur est fait d'amourettes comme d'amours; donc, je te dis ce que je dirai toujours à un ami que je verrai prêt à goûter des impressions nouvelles, "Bois le plus possible; on n'est heureux que lorsqu'on est fou, c'est-à-dire gris." (. . .) *Apprendre* et *jouir*, tout est là. Jouir, moralement pour les uns, et pour ceux qui ne savent pas, physiquement.

Donc, aime Ettie, et laisse-toi aller à la dérive.

Le fait est que les Anglaises sont d'adorables filles. Cette blondeur douce; ces gouttes du lac Léman, enchassées dans de la candeur et qu'elles veulent bien appeler leurs yeux, comme les autres femmes: cette taille si harmonieusement grecque; non pas une taille d'abeille prétentieuse, mais une taille d'ange qui reploierait ses ailes sous son corsage![82]

The release from long constraint that such passages betoken calls to mind the escape from routine that their author, when a schoolboy, had found in reading and composing verse, living in literature to escape from dull reality. The self-confidence displayed in the early letters to Cazalis was perhaps partly literary too. This friendship at a distance, to the cultivation of which those responsive, self-expressive, sometimes provocative letters were chiefly devoted, may have thrived to an unusual degree on the writer's satisfaction in writing them, showing the best of himself to himself as well as to his friend. They reveal an increasing degree of half-ironic dramatization which is of a literary nature, and inspired by specific literary examples. This is best seen by following the variations in the Cazalis–Mallarmé antithesis, which continues to be conspicuous. A hint of the new tendency is provided by the letter written on 4 June. The description there of Stéphane in his home setting, quoted above, is preceded by a playful conceit that places Henri-in-love in a decidedly literary convention and Stéphane his unromantic friend in another:

Hélas! tu sais combien je fus ravi de Fontainebleau, et, par cela, tu devines comme Chaville m'enchanterait.[83] Mais, pauvre hanneton, j'ai un fil à la patte: encore, si c'était, comme toi, un cheveu d'or d'Ettie.

Je le crois plutôt arraché à la perruque rousse d'Harpagon.[84]

This could be considered as no more than a rueful quip were it not that before a month had passed the whole antithesis had undergone a salutary change. Freeing itself from differences (real or supposed) of a social and cultural kind, consciousness of which can be irksome, it took on the shape of an opposition between two attitudes to love, the idealistic and the realistic.

The first stage in the transformation was Mallarmé's renunciation of his scepticism concerning the nature of his friend's passion for Ettie Yapp. The occasion for a declaration of this change of heart, and for the ceremonious instalment of Cazalis in the part of the ideal lover, was a letter dated 1 July, in which Mallarmé thanked his friend for sending him a likeness of Ettie Yapp by Henri Regnault (a copy of one presented to Ettie?)[85] The letter makes it clear that this new idealization of his friend's romance was inspired by a literary model. The day before the letter was written, the last instalment of *Les Misérables*, Parts IV and V, had appeared—had been released, it would be reasonable to say. Stéphane, like millions of his compatriots, was already reading 'L'Idylle rue Plumet'.[86] In his letter echoes of that romantic story make of Henri another Marius and of Ettie another Cosette, and like Hugo's pair the two of them are Romeo and Juliet too.

Et puis, nous parlons de toi et de celle dont le nom est un gazouillement, du matin au soir, avec Emmanuel, et je sors de ces entretiens si plein de vénération pour toi et pour elle que je n'ose plus t'invoquer, [ô] Dieu! Sais-tu que, bien que vous ayez encore dans le regard l'aube du commencement, vous êtes tous deux, enfants, bien loin dans la vie déj[à], et bien haut dans la gloire puisqu'il ne vous manque qu'un Shakespeare pour être les deux noms que tous les amants murmurent dans un baiser étant déj[à] aussi grand[s]![87]

Ah que l'amour est fort qui fait regarder l'avenir en souriant.

Et que nous sommes petits nous autres, nous les gens de plâtre, ou de Paros même! statues sans yeux dont l'aveuglement voudrait sottement se draper en sérénité!

Il y a un mot touchant et qui illumine toute ta lettre, le voici: "reçois, mon cher Mallarmé, le portrait de *notre sœur*." C'est simple, puisque nous sommes frères, et pourtant, c'est bien doux! Oui, elle se rangera dans mes rêves à côté de toutes les Chimènes, les B[é]atrices, les Juliettes, les Regina, et qui mieux est, dans mon cœur à côté de ce pauvre jeune fantôme, qui fut treize ans ma sœur, et qui fut la seule personne que j'adorasse, avant de vous connaître tous: elle sera mon idéal dans la vie, comme ma sœur l'est dans la mort.[88]

Stéphane wondered if he dared attempt the portrait in verse of Ettie that Henri begged him to write:

Seulement, je tremble. Vois-tu, c'est mon chef d'œuvre que je veux faire là. Comme je le ferai un jour pour ma pauvre sœur dont je n'ai point osé encore rythmer la vision. (. . .)

Je ne veux pas faire cela d'inspiration: la turbulence du lyrisme serait indigne de cette chaste apparition que tu aimes. Il faut méditer longtemps: l'art seul, limpide et impeccable, est assez chaste pour la sculpter religieusement.

Merci, ami, de me commander et de m'inspirer mes meilleurs vers.[89]

The adulatory idealization of the love born at Fontainebleau was resumed ceremoniously a week later, on 7 July, and its literary antecedents were now more ceremoniously acknowledged:

Je n'essuierai pas tes yeux parce qu'avec tes larmes je ne veux pas faire s'envoler le nimbe qui [presumably for 'que'] te met au front ton martyre.

De toutes les amertumes humaines, celle qui naît du départ, cette mort momentanée, est la plus affreuse (. . .)

Pauvre Roméo, et pauvre Marius, je te plains.

J'ai pensé à toi toute la semaine en lisant Marius, et à elle, en rêvant de Cosette.

Ce livre a dû être un baume pour toi. Vous y vivez, vous y aimez![90]

Meanwhile, the other term of the antithesis was also shaped. At the same time as the new version of Henri, a new Stéphane appears, attempting in the drab streets of Sens a much less starry-eyed approach to the experience of love. His amorous intentions were announced with a suitably casual air in the letter of 1 July:

Tu te plains, Cher, que je ne t'écris pas ces jours-ci; il est vrai, j'ai dressé des miroirs à alouette dans le champ de la galanterie et l'oiselle se contente de gazouiller de loin, invisible. Cela m'a distrait.[91]

The theme was pursued in the letter of 7 July, with an affectation of shame, a mischievous relish, and a discreet reference to Ettie-Cosette to keep in clear focus the contrast with Stéphane's chosen one.

Je suis ravi, heureux d'être aimé de vous deux. Vos pensées, ces palombes, apporteront peut-être un brin d'amour dans mon nid!

O comédie humaine! Quand je pense que, pendant que vous m[ê]liez vos larmes désespérées, moi, idiot saltimbanque, je prenais de l'eau dans ma cuvette pour en asperger un billet doux, et y feindre des pleurs!

Je ne te parle pas de cette gentille Allemande que je m'entête à avoir. Cela t'intéresserait vraiment bien, toi le sublime désolé, le martyr, de savoir que ce matin on m'a refusé un billet et qu'on veut me parler ce soir! Si je pouvais pourtant être pris à mon piège, et comme elle m'aimera, l'amouretter! Ce serait un rayon et un sourire.

Mais oublions cela, parlons d'Elle, toujours d'Elle.[92]

Stéphane's object in keeping Henri informed of his cynical designs on the honour of a nice German girl may have been partly to tease him, up there in his pale blue heaven, with news of goings-on in real life below. But his plan to seduce Marie Gerhard, a governess in a wealthy family at Sens, was no fiction. He was putting it in operation as methodically as he said. If he did not actually drip water for tear-drops on his paper when he wrote to his prospective victim, he used black ink to the same purpose, spicing the blandishments of a small-town Don Juan with a sprinkling of more refined love-lore, sardonically borrowed from the self-same source as so much of the homage he lavished on Ettie, when he wrote of her to his friend. In one of his letters to Marie he even mentioned that source, adding flattery to flattery:

Mon adorable adorée,

Quand vous m'évitiez tout à l'heure dans la rue, je lisais ces mots, dans l'œuvre nouvelle d'Hugo: "Vous qui souffrez parce que vous aimez, aimez plus encore (. . .)"

Je souffre, et vous adore.

Seulement,—vous allez en rire, n'est-ce pas, car c'est fort drôle en effet,—je souffre maintenant sans espoir.

Je suis désespéré.[93]

This overt reference to Hugo is made in the last of the three *billets doux* to Marie that have reached us. It is in the previous one, however, likewise dated by the editors '[juillet 1862]' that the love-story in *Les Misérables* is most deliberately exploited. It begins:

Mademoiselle,

Voici plusieurs jours que je ne vous ai vue.

A mesure qu'une larme tombait de mes yeux, il était doux à ma tristesse que je prisse une feuille de paper [et que] je m'efforçasse d'y traduire ce que cette larme contenait d'amertume, d'angoisse, d'amour, et, je le dirai franchement, d'espérance.

Aujourd'hui, elles ne sont plus faites que de désespoir. Ces lettres, je les gardais et je les entassais chaque matin, pensant vous les remettre et osant croire, non pas que vous les liriez toutes, mais simplement que vous jetteriez les yeux au hasard sur quelques phrases, et que de ces quelques phrases monterait à vous cette clarté qui vous enivre et qu'on ressent quand on est aimé.

Ce rayon devait faire ouvrir en votre cœur la fleur bleue mystérieuse, et le parfum qui naîtrait de cet épanouissement, espérais-je, ne serait pas ingrat.

Je le respirerais!

On l'appelle l'amour, ce parfum.[94]

Both the bright ray and the mysterious flower are recognizable as reflections from a chapter of *Les Misérables* (III. vi. 3,

'Effet du printemps') in which Hugo describes a fatal moment in Marius's early attentions to Cosette:

Qu'y avait-il cette fois dans le regard de la jeune fille? Marius n'eût pu le dire. Il n'y avait rien et il y avait tout. Ce fut un étrange éclair. (. . .)

Il est rare qu'une rêverie profonde ne naisse pas de ce regard là où il tombe. Toutes les puretés et toutes les candeurs se rencontrent dans ce rayon céleste et fatal qui, plus que les œillades les mieux travaillées des coquettes, a le pouvoir magique de faire subitement éclore au fond d'une âme cette fleur sombre, pleine de parfums et de poisons, qu'on appelle l'amour.[95]

The love-thoughts written down but never sent, on the other hand, figure in later episodes of Hugo's novel. During the period of their long separation, when Marius feared that he would never see Cosette again, he formed the habit of 'writing to' her:

De temps en temps, (. . .) il laissait tomber sur un cahier de papier où il n'y avait que cela, le plus pur, le plus impersonnel, le plus idéal des rêveries dont l'amour lui emplissait le cerveau. Il appelait cela "lui écrire".[96]

Later, Cosette did read these thoughts, not knowing whose they were:

Cosette n'avait jamais rien lu de pareil. Ce manuscrit, où elle voyait plus de clarté encore que d'obscurité, lui faisait l'effet d'un sanctuaire entr'ouvert. Chacune de ces lignes mystérieuses resplendissait à ses yeux et lui inondait le cœur d'une lumière étrange.[97]

Another detail in the letter to Marie, no less obviously borrowed from Hugo's romance, is the conceit with which it ends:

J'irai encore vous voir au Lycée, je suis heureux de vous voir, même de loin; il me semble, quand vous tournez la rue, que je vois un fantôme de lumière et tout rayonne.[98]

The phenomenon (the love-light again, but outward and visible) is one with which Marius was familiar. Hugo makes much of it, half-humorously as witness the opening examples:

Tout en approchant du banc, il tendait les plis de son habit, et ses yeux se fixaient sur la jeune fille. Il lui semblait qu'elle emplissait toute l'extrémité de l'allée d'une vague lueur bleue . . . Il s'y assit comme la veille, considérant de loin et voyant distinctement le chapeau blanc, la robe noire et surtout la lueur bleue (. . .) M. Leblanc et sa fille (. . .) se dirigeaient lentement vers le milieu de l'allée où était Marius. (. . .) Il tremblait. L'auréole venait droit à lui'.[99]

A strange use for a young poet to be making of the writings of his master, in so heartless an enterprise. But it may be that the consequences of that perversity countered his intention. It was perhaps the suavely idealistic romance of Marius and Cosette that converted Stéphane the would-be cynical deceiver to gentler thoughts and sentiments concerning Marie. For by the end of August the cynic was silenced, and even the philanderer much subdued. Mallarmé wrote to Cazalis to confess that his scheme had gone awry. He was hoist with his own petard, he explained, and 'quelque peu amoureux'. He continued:

Quand je vis cela, j'essayai de lutter, pressentant mille ennuis: sa position que je pouvais briser, car elle dépend tout entière de sa conduite, l'espionnage des petites villes, le temps perdu. La lutte ne fait qu'aiguillonner.

Elle est triste ici, et s'ennuie. Je suis triste et m'ennuie. De nos deux mélancolies nous pourrons peut-être faire un bonheur.

Il ne serait pas étonnant qu'elle commençat un peu à m'aimer.

C'est peut-être une sottise que je fais là.

Mais non, je serai moins seul ces vacances.[100]

The holidays referred to in this final pirouette were, presumably, the school holidays which deprived him of the company of Des Essarts. The fact that Emmanuel was still his closest friend, the one he saw continually and who for that reason was most immediately privy to his secrets, is easily lost sight of for lack of written correspondence. During the greater part of the year they were at Sens together. Though they exchanged letters when Emmanuel was elsewhere, few of them have been published. Our impressions of that first and best year of their friendship are consequently too much influenced by the flippantly burlesque manner in which Stéphane liked to describe Emmanuel's doings in writing to Cazalis.[101] There is one letter however which presents their friendship in a more natural and very different light. It was written on 23 August. The summer holidays had begun and Emmanuel was in Paris. He was confined to his room, undergoing treatment for an imprudent bachelor's ailment, and he needed sympathy and entertainment. Stéphane wrote with genuine, warm affection a letter full of good cheer, amusing gossip, and graceful fancy. There is even, as from one poet to another, an opening paragraph which (after the customary jest) reads very much like a draft for a prose poem in the style of *Gaspard de la nuit*:[102]

A quoi pense Dieu le père? Quel temps! Voici l'automne et l'hiver dans une même journée. L'automne. Ce matin des brouillards londoniens. J'ai fait un tour dans les champs avec Diane [the dog?] je ne voyais qu'herbes vert foncé et brumes. Diane gambadait dans les luzernes mouillées et faisait des orgies de crottes de chèvre. Voici qu'on met déjà des cordes aux potences des réverbères, et qu'au bout de ces cordes se balancent des pavés en attendant les luminaires ou les poètes enguignonnés.—L'hiver—J'ai froid aux mains, je ferais du feu. C'est à peine si j'écarte mes rideaux pour voir une averse de hallebardes et de pertuisanes, et trois pauvres hirondelles sur le pommier voisin, qui rêvent au pays de Garibaldi. Elles sont comme moi: il y a une fenêtre qui les retient. Elles, la croisée où coule en boue leur nid de terre: moi, celle par où Marie passe sa tête quand j'erre dans la Grande-Rue. Quels quatre volontaires nous ferions autrement![103]

And in a mood of easy intimacy he told Emmanuel what good sweethearts Marie and he had become:

J'ai fait hier l'emplette d'un album qui sera mon cœur relié en chagrin sans jeu de mots—et doré sur tranches. Tous mes amis y déposeront du sublime. Cambronne n'en est pas, heureusement. Depuis Marie qui y mettra un baiser jusqu'à Emmanuel qui y rimera une ballade et Cazalis qui y effeuillera un lys ou un ange, tous y laisseront un souvenir. Dans trente ans, ce sera divin à relire. "Je sais l'art d'évoquer les minutes heureuses." (. . .)[104]

Pour moi je savoure maintenant mon ivresse. Je suis certain que ma douce Marie m'adore et ne vit que pour moi. Donc, plus d'inquiétude. Cette semaine a été malheureuse. Deux ou trois baisers des lèvres, mais beaucoup du cœur. Je travaille tranquillement pendant qu'elle me regarde de son petit cadre en chêne sculpté qui ne quitte pas ma table. (. . .)

Les myosotis que je lui ai donnés pour sa fête—il y a huit jours—s'épanouissent et montent chaque jour, loin de se faner. C'est charmant de leur part.[105]

To Cazalis, Mallarmé still represented his courtship of Marie as contrasting with his friend's idyllic love. Henri and Ettie still dwelt in an ideal world on high, Stéphane and Marie on the earth below—though custom allowed him to call her an angel. The contrast was weakening, however, and losing its piquancy. Acknowledgements of Ettie's ideality were still made, but in a perfunctory tone. It was his own real Marie that now filled Stéphane's thoughts, and these were fast becoming more sentimental if not less earthly. After spending (it is thought) the first fortnight of September in Paris and at Versailles (where he saw Émile Deschamps and also Albert Glatigny),[106] he replied to a letter received a week before from Cazalis, just back from a visit to Ettie and her family in London, by sending him news from Sens of his own true love. And now he writes of it as gently and with as much respect, though less ceremonious sentimentality, as of his friend's:

Je relis encore ta lettre qu'illumine le souvenir d'un si beau Rêve! (. . .)

Quel Rêve, quel rêve, cher Cazalis! et que la réalité doit être pénible maintenant! Je suis sûr que tu ne peux croire que tu l'as vue comme avant tu n'osais croire que tu la verrais! Je connais cela.

Et elle a toujours été la même? Neige, hermine, plume de cygne—toutes les blancheurs.

Malheureux! Comment peux-tu maintenant griffonner dans une étude et respirer l'odeur nauséabonde du papier timbré! (. . .)

Oh! les voyages! les voyages!

Voici plusieurs jours que pour poème unique je lis un Indicateur des Chemins de Fer! Si tu savais quelles jouissances exquises je goutte à voir ces chiffres alignés comme des vers! Et ces noms divins qui sont mon horizon bleu: Cologne, Mayence, Wiesbaden. C'est là que je voudrais m'envoler avec ma douce sœur, Marie! (. . .)

Je suis fou, n'est-ce pas? La preuve, c'est que je vais faire un *poème en prose* sur ces projets de voyage.

Oh! ma pauvre Marie, je l'aime tant! Je la respecte tant, surtout, et je la plains!

Nous avons été bien malheureux pendant les quinze jours que nous avons passés loin l'un de l'autre. Que dis-je? Quinze jours, trois semaines, car elle n'est revenue à Sens que huit jours après moi. Comme elle a pleuré quand elle m'a revu, et comme nous sommes restés cinq bonnes minutes, le soir, à nous embrasser, elle pleurant, moi baisant ses larmes—sans nous dire un mot.

Je sais un ange. Il s'appelle Marie—est-ce *il* ou *elle* qu'il faut

dire?—Voilà une grande question grammaticale qui m'absorbe depuis ce matin.[107]

On an envelope containing a few dried flowers, found among Mallarmé's papers, two place-names and a date are written in his hand: 'Fontainebleau. Franchard. 29 7bre 1862'.[108] And a sentence in a letter written to Cazalis some months later, tends to confirm that it was on that day, spent in the romantic Gorges of Franchard,[109] that the lovers plighted their troth. At least, Marie agreed that when Stéphane went to London she would go with him, and he on his side promised to marry her—the exchange of vows appropriate no doubt to the situation.

The question of their marrying without delay came up for serious consideration between Stéphane and his friends. Des Essarts, the man of experience ('Emmanuel, qui a beaucoup vécu'), did not approve of it. When he returned to Sens early in October for the start of his second school year, exiled once more from his beloved Paris and the more disconsolate for Stéphane's impending departure, he voiced his own and perhaps some of Henri's objections. They had to do not so much with marrying too early as with the qualifications of the bride. Marie had neither good looks, nor social position, nor culture, nor money. Those at least were the arguments taken up by Stéphane in a letter he wrote forthwith to Cazalis, questioning the validity of each of them in turn, in an orderly manner but a style that probably echoed Emmanuel's oral eloquence. The letter (as well as illustrating the male chauvinism of the time) shows the ease with which a judicious selectivity and some rhetorical skill could make a fine scorn for bourgeois prejudice compatible with a convenient recourse to it.[110] The rhetoric did not however obscure the good sense with which Stéphane justified his choice of Marie. His final summary is as sober as one could wish:

J'admets que pour tout autre elle ne soit pas très-jolie, que ce ne soit pas une grande âme d'artiste—quoiqu'elle ait un grand charme sympathique répandu sur son visage et une intelligence très-délicate, et l'esprit du cœur—j'admets cela. Ce n'est pas ce que j'ai cherché en elle. J'ai voulu être aimé et je le suis plus qu'on ne peut l'être.

Ce qui m'attire vers elle, c'est quelque chose de magnétique et qui n'a pas de cause apparente. Elle a un regard à elle qui m'est une fois entré dans l'âme, et qu'on ne pourrait en retirer sans me faire une blessure mortelle.[111] Voilà tout. (. . .)

Si à Londres, notre amour va toujours en croissant, ce sera pour toujours, alors.[112]

It would seem from these closing words that Stéphane had perhaps not yet abandoned completely the part of a callous seducer for which he had originally cast himself. Cazalis must have received, perhaps from Des Essarts, more positive indications to the same effect, for in his answer to Stéphane's letter he took exception to a particularly cynical part of the elopement plan, not mentioned there. So preposterously cynical a part indeed that it can hardly have been intended as seriously as Cazalis supposed. It was the invention rather of an *enfant terrible* than a heartless deceiver. What Stéphane had apparently proposed was that on their arrival in London Marie and he should go through a wedding ceremony which would entitle them to live respectably together in England. The marriage would not be valid in France, and they could decide when they returned there whether to have it legalized. Cazalis was the more unhappy about the proposal as its ostensible purpose was to avoid the risk of their harming his standing with the Yapps. He disposed of this scruple:

Les Yapp, qui t'inquiètent, dans un mois, je l'espère, seront à Paris. Voilà qui peut-être va changer tous tes plans; et à vrai dire je le voudrais. Ce mariage à Londres, cette comédie, cette bouffonnerie, je ne l'aime pas, et elle et toi, j'en suis sûr, vous êtes comme moi: elle vous répugne, donc il faut l'éviter. Elle est noble et pure: elle t'a fait pur et noble. Et avoue-le, un noble ne va pas à un prêtre, anglican ou catholique peu importe, lui promettre dans les mains qu'on prend pour femme, devant Dieu, la jeune fille qui est là, rien, mon ami, que pour sauver les apparences et sans dire en son cœur ce que disent les lèvres. Cette comédie, crois-moi, tu la regretterais, et elle aussi. Maintenant, je te le répète, j'espère que les Yapp, dans un mois, seront ici. Tu partirais dans quelques jours, et tu les verrais quelques semaines à Londres, que sans peine, je crois, tu pourrais à Londres être à toute heure avec Marie, sans que les Yapp n'en connussent rien et ne pussent en rien soupçonner. Tu me demandes, ami, ce que je pense de Marie? Ce que tu penses d'elle: ma réponse est sincère, je te le jure. Marie est d'une beauté sublime,[113] puisque de toute son âme, elle t'aime Stéphane, et avec joie donnerait pour toi plus que sa vie—son honneur, son repos, le calme de sa virginité. Pour elle, comme pour toi seulement, avant le mariage, fais l'essai du mariage. (. . .) Les poètes sont des gentilshommes, Stéphane: la parole d'un gentilhomme, ce me semble, doit être, comme celle de Dieu, chose sacrée: ce qu'il a promis, il le fait, et laisse à la foule ces serments qu'on fait tout haut mais que tout bas on se promet bien de laisser là, le jour où le serment vous gêne. (. . .) Je ne te demande qu'une chose: attendre un an; j'aurais même le droit d'en demander deux. Ce n'est pas, je crois, t'outrager, ni outrager Marie: c'est vous sauver tous les deux. Aimez vous, soyez deux fiancés, qui sans cesse serez ensemble, et rêvez, vos deux fronts unis. Et puis dans un an, regarde ton cœur et si tu y trouves assez d'amour pour en verser encore, pendant des années sur la tête douce et pure de ta chère Marie, épouse la et je suis un de tes témoins: Des Essarts l'autre.[114]

And if not, what then of the pure sweet maid? The question was left unasked. The formula of the trial marriage without wedlock sounded reassuring, and Stéphane adopted it without demur. When due account is taken of his subsequent behaviour, however, it appears quite likely that the quieter, more thoughtful counsels of another friend were also influencing him in the conduct of his enterprise. He had sent news of his new situation to Léon Marc, who replied on 4 October in terms dictated by his own experience of the life the young poet must prepare for. He too was for caution, for less high-sounding but more enlightened and far-sighted reasons:

Il paraît mon pauvre cher Stéphane, que vous êtes bien et sérieusement pris? . . . Tant mieux et tant pis. Tant mieux si (comme je le crois) l'objet est réellement digne et n'est point examiné à travers le prisme d'un premier amour; tant mieux si vous êtes homme à savoir faire deux parts de la vie, si vous vous sentez la force (force rare et des plus supérieures selon moi) d'allier le mariage avec la poésie, et de faire vivre en bonne intelligence l'épouse et la muse.—Tant pis si vous êtes trop romanesque, si vous ne vous sentez pas cuirassé d'avance contre toutes les bassesses et tous les prosaïsmes de la vie. —Quelqu'un l'a dit avant moi. L'état de mariage ne convient qu'aux âmes vulgaires . . . et aux âmes tout à fait supérieures. Et ceci n'est point un paradoxe. (. . .)

Revers du dit conseil.—Jeune homme à l'âme poétique et exaltée, ne restez pas seul. La solitude mène à la folie, à la rêvasserie et finalement à l'impuissance. Une femme douce, intelligente et dévouée sera pour vous le meilleur gouvernail. Elle conservera la chasteté de votre muse; elle vous préservera de la bohême, de l'absinthe et des accouplements hybrides de la pensée et du corps. (. . .)

Suivez donc l'instinct de votre cœur. Aimez. Mais sondez le fond de l'amour. Pas de romanesque surtout, les amours suaves tout farcies de ballades à la lune, de couronne[s]de fleurs, d'extases perpétuelles, de rimes en ivresse, caresse, suprême, extrême, etc. ne se trouvent que dans les libretti d'opéras-comiques. Il faut être forts pour s'aimer sur la terre autre part que dans les soupers au champagne et dans les parties champêtres des premiers rendez-vous. Surtout, ô petit maître, ô jeune buveur d'idéal, ô jeune débridé toujours prêt à désarçonner la réalité par une ruade . . . surtout tâchez de ne pas avoir d'enfants.[115]

How Stéphane and Marie contrived their departure from Sens is not precisely known. It appears however from odd remarks in their first letters from London, that Marie left before Stéphane. She went to Paris and stayed there, presumably with her sister,[116] long enough to make herself known to Cazalis and be disappointed at not seeing him again before leaving, as he had promised she should. She seems to have gone on to Boulogne alone, there to await Stéphane. He on his side broke his journey for the inescapable duty visit to the Desmolins at Versailles,[117] and when he changed trains in Paris he had time to bid Cazalis farewell.[118] He crossed the Channel with Marie on 8 November.[119]

NOTES

1 The existence of *Glanes* is sufficient indication of an interest in the poetic art that would resist all his family's disapproval.

2 See above, ch. 1, n. 4.

3 This informative article ('*Souvenirs littéraires*: Stéphane Mallarmé', *Revue de France*, 15 July 1899), though included in bibliographies, seems to have been seldom read, partly no doubt because the Pléiade editors misnamed the journal 'Revue française'. Partly also, perhaps, because until fairly recently the run of the *Revue de France* at the Bibliothèque nationale was incomplete. Thanks to advice from the Taylor Institution, the courtesy of the New York Public Library, and some more private assistance for which I am no less grateful, I was able to procure a copy.

It might be interesting to know who the two colleagues were who spoke to Des Essarts of Stéphane Mallarmé. One was probably the headmaster of the lycée, M. Clément, who was to show himself, then and later, a good friend to his former pupil. The other may have been M. Buzy (or Busy), 'professeur de quatrième'; Carl Barbier (*DSM*. vii, 172) believed that he influenced 'tous les poètes en herbe dont les compositions figurent au *Cahier d'honneur* du Lycée impérial de Sens'. On his own poetic prowess, see *M. lyc.*, 88–9. There is another possibility however. A master nearer Mallarmé's own age and of whom he spoke warmly, as of a friend, had just left Sens when Des Essarts arrived. His home was at Auxerre, his new appointment at Versailles, and Sens on the main railway line between. It is not improbable that he kept up some of his Sens connections and so met Des Essarts quite early—perhaps even with the express intention of commending Mallarmé to him. He was a M. Motheré, for whose part in what was to follow, see n. 19 below.

When in the 1899 article Des Essarts referred to Mallarmé's friends as 'anciens camarades et professeurs du lycée,' he may very well have had Motheré particularly in mind. Anne Mallarmé, Stéphane's stepmother, referred to him in a letter to Mme Desmolins in these terms: 'Stéphane (. . .) a beaucoup vu ici Monsieur Moteret' (*DSM*. v, 365). He continued in the following year at least to take a friendly interest in Mallarmé as well as corresponding with Des Essarts. In a letter to Mallarmé which appears to have been written in the autumn or early winter of 1863, and which will be referred to again, Des Essarts names several friends he must write to, and concludes: 'Ajoutez-y Motheré qui m'a écrit pour me recommander un élève. J'ai eu de tes nouvelles depuis ta lettre de lui, pourtant fort en peine de tes destinées' (Bibliothèque littéraire Jacques Doucet, MS MVL 639).

4 Des Essarts is slightly less discreet in a shorter piece on 'Stéphane Mallarmé professeur d'anglais', which he wrote in answer to a query concerning Mallarmé's profession, in the journal *L'Intermédiaire des chercheurs et curieux*, 20 October 1906: 'Impatient de littérature, il se trouvait à l'étroit dans cette petite ville et dans un milieu familial d'ailleurs excellent et distingué.'

(Since the 'obituary' article, the more important of the two, is not easily available, it will be convenient to have at hand, for easy reference, those parts of it that are likely to be of interest here. They are: 'Mallarmé voyait fréquemment quelques amis, anciens camarades et professeurs du lycée. Il évitait les relations mondaines et ne comprenait pas nos ferveurs pour la danse. Cependant il faisait volontiers à ses débuts des vers coquets, sortes de tableautins à la Wat[t]eau, des stances en octosyllabes gracieuses et mignardes. La fantaisie devançait la poésie. Il me montra ses premiers vers et j'eus le bonheur de pouvoir en toute sincérité seconder de mes sympathies fraternelles la vocation d'un de nos poètes. Cependant Mallarmé n'était pas un humaniste accompli comme tel ou tel des Parnassiens: son esprit devait surtout se développer au contact des littératures étrangères ou des modèles qui s'en approchaient. Les poètes anglais, Edgar Poe, Charles Baudelaire, exercèrent alors sur lui la plus pénétrante influence. . . . Mes amis devinrent les siens. C'est ainsi que, de 1862 à 1864, j'eus le plaisir de lui faire connaître mon plus ancien compagnon Henri Cazalis, puis Catulle Mendès, Albert Glatigny, Léon Dierx, Armand Renaud, notre chef à tous Théodore de Banville.

A cette date de 1862 Stéphane ne connaissait encore parmi les lettrés qu'Émile Deschamps, le vieux maître, gracieux patriarche, qui recevait les rythmeurs nouveaux avec une bienveillance coutumière mais pleine de nuances et de discernement. Des parents communs, habitant Versailles, avaient montré quelques strophes du jeune poète à l'ancien lutteur romantique qui l'admit à sa correspondance . . . ')

5 It appeared on 10 January 1862.

6 For more details on the three articles, the earliest publications of Stéphane Mallarmé, see below, ch. 3, n. 1. The text of all three, and of related documents, is to be found in the first chapter ('Débuts critiques') of a very interesting doctorate thesis by Marilyn Barthelme, successfully sustained at the Sorbonne in 1959 but regrettably never published: 'Formation et mise en œuvre de la pensée de Mallarmé sur le théâtre'. Henri Mondor acknowledged her attribution of the articles to Mallarmé, in 'Léon Marc et Mallarmé', his contribution to the first number (July–September 1959) of *La Voix des poètes*. The three articles are republished and annotated in Carl Barbier's very substantial article on 'Mallarmé et Léon Marc', *DSM*. vii, 167–88.

7 For background information concerning Marc I am indebted to M. Michel Bouvy, Conservateur de la Bibliothèque municipale de Cambrai, who passed on my speculative request for enlightenment to Marc's grand-daughter. I am particularly obliged to Mme Quarré-Marc herself for sending me a photocopy of a biographical article on her grandfather, preserved among his papers. Attempts to identify the newspaper in which it had appeared have so far failed. It is reprinted ibid. 173–6.

8 *Le Sénonais*, 7 December 1861 (republished ibid. 179–80). The terms in which Marc referred later to this article suggest that when it was written he and its author were not yet close friends. But he and Mme Léon-Marc were already playing at Sens early in November and perhaps before.

9 This detail is recorded in the biographical article mentioned in n. 7 above: 'Concurremment [i.e. besides playing the bassoon in the theatre orchestra at Cambrai before he 'climbed on the stage'] Léon Marc griffonnait au bureau des hypothèques' (ibid. 174).

10 Ibid. 200.

11 Léon Marc, *Oiseaux des tempêtes* (1871), pp. 5–6. The preface is addressed 'A M. Stéphane Mallarmé, littérateur, professeur de langues étrangères au Lycée d'Avignon'.

Both documents, the letter and the dedicatory preface, are quoted from by the Pléiade editors, who note: 'La phrase: "Cette victoire remportée sur le temps et toutes les fatalités . . . ", que rappelle cette dédicace, ne figure pas dans l'article du *Sénonais* au sujet de *la Milanaise et l'Autrichien*. La mémoire de Léon Marc ne devait pourtant pas être en défaut (. . .). Il faut donc qu'il ait paru, vers la même époque (1862), un autre article de Mallarmé dont nous n'avons pas trouvé trace (. . .) sur un autre ouvrage ou sur le même, de Léon Marc' (*O.c.*, 1535 [1541–2]). This conjecture was corroborated by Marilyn Barthelme's identification of the series of three articles as being from Mallarmé's pen. The identification becomes certain when it is noted that the first of the three closely related articles, all on Léon Marc and the company he was a member of, contained the words twice quoted as Mallarmé's by Léon Marc himself.

12 In her letter of 19 April 1861 (*DSM*. v, 347) Mme Desmolins had reported: 'Son père est assez bien depuis quelque temps, et la famille se prépare à s'installer dans la propriété qu'il a achetée aux portes de la ville, et qu'il a rendue très agréable'. But by the end of the year he was on sick leave (ibid. 349 and 351). Forced retirement was inevitable and could only at best be delayed, as it was till June 1862; see Fanny Desmolins's letter of that date, ibid. 379. The negotiation about Stéphane's future had reached its final stage when Anne Mallarmé wrote to her, on 5 February 1862: 'Adieu, bien chère madame, qu'adviendra-t-il du projet de Stéphane quelle préoccupation. Mon mari ne sait rien encore' (ibid. 371).

13 See vol. I, ch. 1, n. 71.

14 André Desmolins began by advising his grandson against his idea of becoming a teacher of English: 'je sais, d'après ton caractère que [ces détails] auront peut-être peu d'influence, ton esprit étant monté d'avance; je dois donc te répéter que je ne peux pas te donner un consentement *positif*, mais seulement te laisser suivre, à tes risques et périls, une idée qui n'est pas m[û]rie par l'expérience' (ibid. 354). He said the same a few days later as to the stay in London (ibid. 363), dwelling however on the question of expense ('je m'en effraie pour la bourse de ton père'); for the idea that Stéphane could pay his way in England by teaching French, as the headmaster of the lycée had proposed, was not very seriously entertained. It was on the money question—the last resort perhaps of many a subrogate guardian—that he appears to have been relying when he threatened his grandson with the law.

15 The letters exchanged on this subject are published, and the circumstances explained, by Henri Mondor in a chapter ('Être professeur') of his *Mallarmé plus intime*. Mallarmé's letters to his grandparents, but not their replies, and not the letters Anne Mallarmé sent them, are published also in *Corr.* i, 15–24, with useful notes. Both sides of the correspondence are republished, complete and textually improved, in *DSM*. v, 348–77. It is to this edition that I shall continue to refer here.

16 Ibid. 348. The *Annuaire de l'Instruction publique* for 1860 shows that by that time there was a teacher of 'foreign literature'—a *professeur* or a *chargé de cours*—in nearly every Faculty of Arts in France. There was also a chair in 'littératures étrangères', occupied by Philarète Chasles, at the Collège de France. There was no *agrégation d'anglais* or *de littératures étrangères*.

17 The *Annuaire* for both 1862 and 1863 spells the name likewise, *Desessarts*. He was 'professeur de seconde', but for the time being, though *agrégé de lettres*, ranked as a *chargé de cours*.

18 *DSM*. v, 351.

19 They were loth to admit, however, that he, with members of the profession to inform him, knew more. The opening phase of the argument set the tone on both sides. To show how quickly a young man

might succeed as a teacher of English, Stéphane quoted the case of a lycée master who had left Sens the previous year to take up an appointment at the 'École spéciale militaire de Saint-Cyr' near Versailles ('the French Sandhurst'): 'Au dire d'un jeune homme de ma connaissance, âgé de 24 ans, qui était l'an dernier professeur d'anglais au Lycée et qui l'est maintenant à St Cyr avec cinq mille francs d'appointement ou de répétition, il y a dans ce moment, depuis que le ministre ne veut plus de ces vieux pantins anglais qui étaient la risée de leurs élèves, il y a, dis-je, pour de jeunes professeurs français et littérairement doués, un avenir réel' (ibid. 349). His grandfather did not reply till four days later because, he explained, 'je voulais prendre aussi mes renseignements sur tes nouvelles idées, et m'éclairer plus *positivement* que par les illusions de ton imagination montée, sur les véritables chances d'avenir que peut te présenter la carrière que tu nous vantes si bien, et qui fait, me dis-tu, l'objet de tes désirs'. His information, he said emphatically, was *very exact*. But what he asserted on the strength of it was not. Without being altogether false it was biased and sufficiently inexact to be easily contradicted. 'Les professeurs de langues vivantes,' he said, 'ne font pas, pour ainsi dire partie de l'université [i.e. of the teaching staff officially authorized to teach in the state system of secondary and higher education], ils ne remplissent que des fonctions *accessoires*, et n'y remplissent qu'une position *secondaire* (. . .) Dans les examens et les concours, les candidats anglais ont un avantage incontestable sur les français, à moins que ces derniers n'aient vécu un certain temps en Angleterre pour acquérir la prononciation si difficile de cette langue; et cela n'est pas possible pour toi, tu le sais bien. (. . .) Quant à l'exemple de Mr Lane, que tu me cites, d'abord il est probablement anglais, ce qui simplifie les choses, et détruit ta citation; puis, sa position à St Cyr est tout à fait unique et exceptionnelle, elle dépend du général, qui peut, s'il lui déplaît, le renvoyer d'un jour à l'autre; ce n'est pas là une autorité' (ibid. 352–4). To conclude, André Desmolins required his grandson to supply him with more details: 'fais-nous mieux connaître d'après quelles données tu crois devoir diriger tes nouvelles études, où, comment, et par quels moyens, ce que tu ne dis pas, et ce qui nous est important à connaître.'

By the time he received this letter Stéphane was in a position to supply these details, for his stepmother and he had seen the headmaster of the lycée. They were able to pass on to his grandfather the programme he advised: 'Étudier ici, à Sens, l'[a]nglais pendant un an avec un professeur, et aller passer une seconde année en Angleterre comme professeur de [f]rançais. Ce séjour d'une année entière me sourit peu mais il le juge indispensable, et dit que c'est une des conditions premières de l'examen' (ibid. 357–8). From this point on, that plan was the subject of the discussion, and the objections previously raised were laid to rest with diplomatic skill. How much the diplomacy owed to Anne Mallarmé's influence one can guess, but the cocksureness which it tempered was Stéphane's. Concerning the status of modern language teachers, for instance, he replied: 'Le proviseur [i.e. the headmaster] nous dit que les professeurs de langues vivantes qui ont pu subir l'examen font partie de l'université. Admettons qu'il se soit trompé: une fois professeur de langues, je passe ma licence. Licencié, je suis autant que mes collègues, et n'ai pas une position secondaire' (ibid. 360). As to the English master Stéphane had referred to, who had gone to Saint-Cyr and was earning good money, the Desmolins had thought to disconcert their grandson by finding out his name and declaring that he was English. But they had mistaken his identity, and Stéphane had the satisfaction of replying: 'Tu me parles d'un M. Lewis, Lowe, ou Lane? Je ne connais personne de ce nom. Mon ami, qui est aussi professeur de St Cyr n'est pas de Londres mais bien d'Auxerre, et [F]rançais comme moi, son nom le prouve' (ibid. 361). He did not add the name (mentioned in n. 3 above) *Motheré*. Anne Mallarmé told them about this other example, however, two days later: 'Il a beaucoup vu ici Monsieur Moteret, qui en ce moment professe à St Cyr et je ne sais dans quel lycée [;] sa place est avantageuse mais le but de Stéphane est d'arriver à une faculté' (ibid. 365). Meanwhile the Desmolins had written to their Mr Lane to check (and contradict) what Stéphane had said. Lane called on them courteously to apprise them of their mistake, and answered some of their questions, but the wind had been taken out of their sails by the failure of their shabby trick, and that matter was dropped (though they seized the meagre advantage of calling Motheré 'Matrey', and thus making him English).

In the *Annuaire de l'Instruction publique* 'M. Motheré' figures as the master in charge of English at Sens in 1860 and 1861. In 1862 he was temporarily replaced by a M. Fallet. He was presumably the J. Motheré who with one Marguerin published in 1864 a report presented to the Prefect of the Seine department: *De l'enseignement des classes moyennes et des classes ouvrières en Angleterre*. The catalogues of the Bibliothèque nationale and the British Library further record: 'J. Motheré, *Les Théories du vers héroïque anglais et ses relations avec la versification anglaise*. (Extrait de la *Revue de l'enseignement des langues vivantes*), Le Havre 1886'. Also, J. Motheré's editions of English (and Irish) authors, intended no doubt for use in schools: Maria Edgeworth, *Contes choisis*; Goldsmith, *The Traveller*, *The Deserted Village*; Pope, *Essai sur la critique*. The A. Motheré who published at Auxerre, in 1849, a translation of an Irish publication, *Histoire de la famine d'Irlande*, was perhaps his father, and perhaps of English or Irish descent.

20 *DSM*. v, 352.

21 Ibid.

22 Ibid. 360.

23 Ibid. 348.

24 Ibid. 374. The fact that the rough drafts of the letters from Versailles are all in Fanny Desmolins's hand proves no more than that she was her husband's amanuensis, but even as such she would obviously be in a position to speak her mind. My own strong impression is that she was mainly responsible for André Desmolins's letters to Stéphane as well as her own.

25 Ibid. 367.
26 Ibid. 372.
27 Ibid.
28 Ibid. 372–3.
29 Ibid. 369.
30 Ibid. 370.
31 Stéphane had himself, from the first, stressed the financial aspect of his proposals. See the fifth paragraph in his letter of 17 January, quoted above. At the end of the letter he insisted on the same point in these terms: 'pèse et examine surtout ceci: que, nos moyens étant réduits par [la] retraite imminente, je ne serais plus à charge que dix-huit mois au lieu de quatre ou cinq ans' (ibid. 349).
32 Ibid. 376. Stéphane's own letter, sent on the previous day, is conciliatory, but on the subject of the 'collège catholique' very firm: 'Je ne tiens pas à aller en Angleterre, mais je tiens à ne plus devenir un écolier' (ibid. 375).
33 A summary, selective account of what had taken place and of the upshot, as seen through the eyes of Fanny Desmolins, was sent to Eugénie Laurent a year later, on 14 February 1863: 'Tu sais peut-être, aussi, que notre pauvre Stéphane ne répond pas à nos vues et à nos espérances; sa carrière était toute tracée, mais il n'a pu s'habituer au travail administratif, et a désiré s'adonner à l'enseignement de la langue Anglaise, dans laquelle il se perfectionne en ce moment à Londres; cet éloignement est une cause de soucis présent[s], et nous redoutons aussi qu'il ne réussisse guères dans l'avenir; tout cela est bien triste, d'autant plus que son pauvre père est dans un état de santé qui lui ôte toute faculté de diriger son fils, et que mon cher mari ne se sent plus de force à prendre en main cette tâche, fatigué qu'il est de ses longs travaux' (ibid. 396).
34 In the letter to Henri Cazalis dated 4 June 1862, quoted in part below, Stéphane would declare, rather airily: 'C'est, en partie, pour échapper à cet intérieur mesquin et étouffant que je donnerai un coup d'aile jusqu'à Londres, en Janvier' (*DSM*. vi, 36). Two months later (4–5 August; ibid. 52) he wrote: 'Tu veux savoir quand j'irai à Londres. Je l'ignore encore, mais, selon toutes probabilités, ce serait en décembre ou au commencement de Janvier.' In the event he was to escape rather earlier, in November.
35 From London, on 23 January 1863, he wrote to Cazalis: 'je reçois à Londres de 3600 à 4000 Francs par an' (ibid. 120). That was nearly twice the amount he expected to be paid as a teacher, and probably represented most of the interest on the money inherited from his mother, to which he had asserted his right of access. (The editors of *DSM*. vi date this letter Friday 30 January, but Mallarmé says he spent the previous evening with Mrs Yapp, who was back in Paris by the 28th. 23 January is the likely date for a letter which replies to the one from Cazalis dated 16 January (ibid. 112).
36 When Stéphane told his grandfather that there were new opportunities for young French teachers of English 'littérairement doués' (see n. 19 above), he was referring to the reintroduction, after a period of suspen-

sion, of the *certificat d'aptitude à l'enseignement des langues étrangères* (i.e. German and English), by a ministerial order dated 27 July 1860. This diploma, together with the *baccalauréat* without which (or a foreign equivalent) he could not have applied for it, was the academic qualification on the strength of which Mallarmé was to teach English in state secondary schools (lycées or their equivalent) for thirty years. The nature of the examination which he had to pass to obtain it is therefore of some interest. The following are the relevant articles in the order of 27 July 1860:

Article 1er. Les candidats qui auront obtenu le certificat (. . .) pourront être appelés aux fonctions de chargés de cours des langues vivantes des lycées impériaux, et jouiront des avantages attachés à ce titre. (. . .)

Art. 4. Pour épreuve préparatoire, les candidats traduiront: 1° un texte français en allemand ou en anglais; 2° un texte allemand ou anglais en français.

Art. 5. Pour première épreuve définitive, chaque candidat devra corriger, après une heure de préparation, dans un lieu fermé, un devoir d'élève pris dans les classes supérieures des lycées de Paris et tiré au sort par le candidat. La durée de cette épreuve sera d'une demi-heure au moins pour chaque candidat.

Art. 6. Pour seconde épreuve définitive, chaque candidat devra traduire, à livre ouvert, un passage tiré au sort dans les auteurs allemands ou anglais, désigné par le Ministre. Il fera, en outre, la traduction, à livre ouvert, d'un texte français en anglais ou en allemand. Le candidat fera suivre son explication des remarques nécessaires pour la parfaite intelligence du texte. Ces remarques seront faites alternativement en langue française et en langue étrangère.

Art. 7. Pour troisième épreuve définitive, chaque candidat fera une leçon de trois quarts d'heure, après trois heures de préparation en lieu clos, sur une question de grammaire de la langue qu'il se propose d'enseigner. Les sujets seront choisis par le jury, tirés au sort par le candidat et délivrés par le président. (*Bulletin administratif de l'Instruction publique*, vol. XI (1860), pp. 208–9.)

It will be noted that André Desmolins was right in declaring that teachers of foreign languages were in an inferior position inasmuch as the *certificat d'aptitude* entitled them to the title and privileges of a *chargé de cours* (in theory appointed temporarily only), but not to those of a full *professeur*, to which an *agrégé* such as Des Essarts was promoted after a probationary period of five years.

For a detailed account of Mallarmé's teaching career, considered from an administrative point of view, see A. Gill, 'Mallarmé fonctionnaire', in *RHLF.*, January–February and March–April, 1968.

37 The headmaster, M. Clément, who had given Stéphane and his stepmother very valuable help in their tussle with the Desmolins, had also promised help later, as his ex-pupil informed his grandfather on 26 January 1862: 'Le Provise[ur] connaît beaucoup l'examinateur et se fait fort de me recommander à lui et de plus, de m'appeler comme professeur dans un lycée qui sera soit Sens, soit un lycée encore supérieur' (*DSM*. v, 358).

38 Writing at the beginning of February 1862 to Fanny Desmolins, Anne Mallarmé mentions 'le professeur dont il prend des répétitions chaque jour d'une heure pour 25 francs par mois', but without expressing any

confidence in this 'optional work'. (From the same letter we learn also that he was not interested in another idea for his future: 'Moi aussi, je l'aurais bien préféré dans le militaire. Je lui en ai dit encore un mot, mais ce n'est nullement dans ses go[û]ts'; ibid. 370.)

39 Ibid. 352. Stéphane's literary tastes seem to be regarded as an affliction. One is reminded of remarks like those of Dumas the Elder: 'La folie la plus épidémique de la jeunesse est celle de la littérature. Il n'y a pas d'écolier qui n'ait commencé sa tragédie romaine en seconde et qui ne l'ait achevée en rhétorique. Sorti du collège, et destiné à suivre la carrière de la médecine, du droit ou du commerce, ses rêves de classe le poursuivent dans les études de sa nouvelle profession. La vie dans laquelle il marche est pleine de lenteurs et de dégoûts; celle à laquelle il aspire retentit d'applaudissements, resplendit d'honneurs et rayonne de gloire.' (*Souvenirs dramatiques*, II, 1868). One remembers that Baudelaire had had to struggle for the right to live as a man of letters.

40 The distinction is made nicely in a contemporary English idiom by a young woman quoted in an article on working as a waitress (*The Observer*, 1 June 1980): 'What I do at work', she says, 'is mindless, but it doesn't take me over.'

41 See above, vol. I, p. 67, the pessimistic reflection: '26 Décembre 1860, premier pas dans l'abrutissement.'

42 *DSM*. v, 348.

43 At his age at the time, of course, not yet twenty, it may not have displeased him to have that reputation. We shall see him ridiculing 'les bourgeois', and in an early letter to Cazalis he complained somewhat boastfully of being considered a rake, 'un bohême (*sic*) doré' (*DSM*. vi, 36).

44 The comparison is made in Mallarmé's article on *La Milanaise et l'Autrichien* ('drame en trois actes et en prose par Léon Marc'), in *Le Sénonais*, 19 March 1862; see *O.c.*, 253, and below, p. 79.

45 A fairly precise statement of the periods spent by Marc at Sens is provided by periodic announcements in *Le Sénonais*, under the rubric *Théâtre de Sens*, of performances by 'M. Besombes et sa troupe'. From these one learns that in his first article, on 7 December, Mallarmé was not really introducing the company to its public. It had been performing at Sens at least since the middle of November. The last performance of that stay took place on 18 December. *Le Sénonais* of that day, echoed on the 21st, gave notice of the 'représentation d'adieux'. On the 21st it was also announced that on the following day 'M. Bruneton's company' would give its opening performances. M. Besombes and his colleagues seem to have been away during the whole of January and February, returning however at the beginning of March and staying for the greater part of that month. It was on 16 March that they played Marc's drama *La Milanaise et l'Autrichien*, reviewed in *Le Sénonais* by Mallarmé on the 19th. In April and May the company gave only one performance at Sens, breaking a journey from somewhere further north to Auxerre some thirty-five miles to the south (and Joigny the smaller town between). On 31 May *Le Sénonais* announced: 'L'excellente troupe de M. Besombes fait, à Sens,

sa rentrée la semaine prochaine'. It gave its opening performance on 4 June, stayed at Sens for a month, then left for richer pastures. So declared *Le Sénonais* on 5 July: 'La troupe nous quitte pour de plus fortunés rivages'. M. Besombes promised to return in November and kept his promise, but by that time the Léon-Marcs had left the troupe, and Mallarmé was also far away.

In Marc's letter is a phrase (*DSM*. vii, 191–2) which implies that when he was at Sens his leisure was less limited. He looked forward hopefully to 'quelques loisirs dont quelques-uns vous seront consacrés'.

46 There is no other reference to this 'review' in Marc's letters. It may have been the text for a theatrical entertainment, lightly promised to the actors by Roquier and Des Essarts.

47 Ibid. 189–93.

48 Marc again couples Roquier's name with Des Essarts's in a letter written a few months later, part of which is quoted and commented on by Mondor in his article 'Léon Marc et Mallarmé', mentioned in n. 6 above. (The letter is published in its entirety in *DSM*. vii, 194–7.) The context suggests that in the meantime Marc had kept up more continuous relations with Roquier and Des Essarts than with their younger friend. He was still seeing Roquier occasionally in April 1865, when they were both employees of the municipal authorities in Paris; see ibid. 201.

49 The Desmolins had not concealed their suspicion that the strongest motive behind Stéphane's plan to go to England was his desire to be free; see *DSM*. v, 372–3. A statement in a letter to Cazalis dated 4 June, and mentioned above, makes of the freedom to spend his own money an important part of that desire.

50 In January 1856, when Roquier was 'en rhétorique', his epistle in French 'de L'Hôpital à Charles IX' had the honour of being indited in the *Cahier d'Honneur du Lycée de Sens*. That was on the occasion of the feast of Saint Charlemagne, 'Students' Day', celebrated on 28 January. For the same feast two years later (when he would be in the Logic class, after opting for a second year of Rhetoric), he had the honour of writing the annual light-hearted poem in honour of its hero. Later that year, his epistle in French prose and verse, 'de La Fontaine à Patru', also gained a place in the school album. Clearly, his literary gifts were highly thought of by his masters.

51 In 1863 he published at Sens ('Impr. Ph. Chapu'), in collaboration with 'C. Pied-Guérin, limonadier à Sens', a volume entitled *Les Sénonaises, Chansons*. The individual poems are not signed, but one may presume that the Béranger-type poems and drinking songs are by the *cabaretier*, while Roquier contributed the grander compositions ('Les Maronniers du Mail de Sens' and 'Gloire à Béranger'—'couplets chantés sur le théâtre de Sens' on 10 February and 31 March respectively, 1859), and the gentle, rather wistful but not very poetical love and nature ditties.

52 See above, p. 17.

53 'Pan' and 'Causerie d'adieu' (*DSM*. vii, 111 and 131); see above, vol. I, pp. 173–94 and 234–5.

54 See Roquier's two affectionate letters to Mallarmé written in 1865 and

1866 (*DSM*. vii, 204–9); one of them is mentioned, and Roquier briefly placed, in *Corr*. i, 265, n. 1. The letters depict their author as a 'vieux célibataire', resigned to the life that Stéphane had eschewed, earning two thousand francs a year in a local government office doing 'work that any porter could do', but spending half his time there reading poetry and drama and trying to keep alive a wilting literary ambition. One is reminded of André Desmolins's picture (inspired perhaps by the example of his former colleague Émile Deschamps) of the time for literary pursuits his grandson might hope for in Registry employment; see *DSM*. v, 352. Henri Cazalis, who at the moment when Marc wrote of Des Essarts and Roquier was about to become Mallarmé's friend and for a time the friend he most admired, was in a not dissimilar situation before he quit the law for medecine. Mallarmé commiserated with him accordingly in August 1862: 'Ce pourquoi je te plains encore, c'est de sentir le papier timbré tout le jour et tous les jours, de griffonner là-dessus, . . . j'y ai passé, je sais ce que c'est' (*DSM*. vi, 52). There are other, more or less jesting references to 'le papier timbré' in later letters (ibid. 50 and 54).

55 It would seem from the words 'C'est une charmante et imprévue diversion', at the beginning of Marc's second sentence, that they were not in the habit of writing to each other during Marc's absences from Sens.

56 See above, n. 45.

57 In the *Cahier d'Honneur du Lycée de Sens*, for Saint Charlemagne's Day 1856, Lefébure's epistle in Latin ('De Jean-Jacques Rousseau à un jeune homme') is honoured alongside Roquier's epistle in French referred to in n. 50 above. The proofs given by Lefébure, as a schoolboy, of literary talent and dedication, are fully explored in Henri Mondor's invaluable *Eugène Lefébure*, Gallimard, 1951. The following excerpts from its opening chapter, 'Poète au lycée' (pp. 20–2), sufficiently account for Mallarmé's interest in him, even if he knew him only by repute:

> En seconde, en 1855, l'élève Lefébure eut un premier accessit d'excellence, un deuxième accessit de narration française et encore deux citations, en narration latine et version grecque. Le Proviseur, clairvoyant, nous instruit, dans ses notes de deuxième semestre, d'un penchant littéraire déjà décelable chez le jeune interne. "Élève intelligent qui promet d'être un esprit distingué. Il a beaucoup de goût pour la poésie française et a fait quelques pièces de vers assez remarquables." (. . .)
>
> L'année suivante, quand Eugène fut rhétoricien, son nom, dans le palmarès de fin d'année, brilla davantage, puisqu'il eut les premiers prix de discours français, de discours latin, de vers latin et de version grecque. (. . .)
>
> C'est en seconde, dans ce lycée de Sens, (. . .) qu'Eugène Lefébure, à seize ans, était devenu une sorte de rimeur lauréat, presque officiel; chargé, par exemple, d'une Ode pour saint Charlemagne et d'une Ode pour Monseigneur l'Archevêque de Sens.

In the same chapter, Mondor comments (pp. 22–6) on Lefébure's juvenilia, written between the same 'four walls' as Mallarmé's three years later.

58 *Lef.*, 169–71. It is not clear, either from the substance of this letter or its tone, friendly but a little formal, whether the writer and the recipient were fully acquainted. The fact of their being former pupils of the same lycée might justify, from a senior, the form of address 'Mon cher ami' and the formula 'votre affectionné ami'. But as former school-fellows, both boarders, though with Lefébure's three years of superiority between them, they cannot have been altogether strangers, and Mallarmé would be aware of his senior's academic and literary successes at school, more distinguished than his own. That they had at least one mutual acquaintance who shared their interest in literature, seems to follow from Mallarmé's knowing that Lefébure had a copy of Poe's poems, and on the other hand from Lefébure's precise references to Mallarmé's recent and unpublished verses. It is possible, for instance, that the obliging schoolmaster Motheré was a friend of Lefébure's too. It has been seen that he too lived at Auxerre; see n. 19 above.

59 On the non-survival of Mallarmé's eighty or so letters to Lefébure (as of those also that were sent to him by Des Essarts, Cazalis, and Villiers de l'Isle-Adam) see *Lef.*, 161–3. It is a serious loss. Fortunately, Lefébure's thoughtful answers often give a fair notion of the contents, or the more important contents, of the letters he was replying to. Lefébure's own side of the correspondence, consisting of the seventy-seven letters, were published by Mondor (ibid. 167–335), with five of Mallarmé's—most of them long or very long, and very substantial in content—that have fortunately been preserved (ibid. 339–58); a sixth was published, for the first time complete, in *DSM*. vi, 367–70.

60 The allusion is to poems that Lefébure seems to have known about (as witness his mentioning 'le rondeau des six Phyllis' in his first letter), which Mallarmé had sent to the editor of *La Revue fantaisiste* (Catulle Mendès), but which had not been accepted. See below, pp. 150–1.

61 Mondor's conjecture concerning this translation (*Lef.*, 59) is no doubt correct: 'Peut-être s'agissait-il de l'ouvrage paru chez Hetzel [i.e. in the Hetzel collection] en 1862, contes inédits d'Edgar Poe traduits par W. J. Hughes, et dans lequel neuf poésies étaient également traduites.'

62 It must be assumed that Mallarmé had told him he had the proscribed poems, but whether in a copy he possessed of the first edition, or transcribed from a borrowed copy, the terms of the request do not make clear: 'Seriez-vous assez bon pour me copier les poèmes condamnés de Baudelaire, s'ils ne sont pas trop longs?' (*Lef.*, 173). For the time being his plea went unheeded, since he had to repeat it two years later, on 13 May 1864 (ibid. 180): 'Envoyez-moi si vous le pouvez par la poste les poèmes défendus de Baudelaire.' Mallarmé obliged, and after a long silence, in November 1864, Lefébure wrote (ibid. 181–2): 'J'ai envoyé par la poste votre précieux Baudelaire, au risque d'avoir un procès-verbal.' The 'precious Baudelaire' was most probably a copy of the second edition of *Les Fleurs du mal* (February 1861), which Lefébure called 'la nouvelle édition', with Mallarmé's own manuscript copy of the proscribed poems bound in. This is the volume that Bonniot mentions

(in *Le Manuscrit autographe*, May–June 1926; it appears that it still exists, in a private collection; see *DSM*. vi, 166 n. 1. It may have been while his own copy was in Lefébure's hands that Mallarmé borrowed Des Essarts's. He still had it in December 1864, when its owner asked for it back: 'N'aurais-tu pas mon Baudelaire (poésies) que tu m'avais emprunté un jour?' (*Corr.* i, 144, n. 2).

63 *Lef.*, 171–4. The easy references to mutual acquaintances in Lefébure's two letters illustrate the kind of facility that their existence would lend to Mallarmé's approach, though they might also help on the other hand to dull any sense of urgency on the part of his correspondent. None of the young men mentioned would seem to have been friends of Mallarmé's, but some he certainly knew. The Courtois who brought Poe's poems to Sens for him was to be glimpsed in his story again the following year, once more as an intermediary between him and Lefébure; see below, p. 308. That they had anything much in common does not emerge. The same is true of Léger, who shared a room with Lefébure and added his handshake to the second letter. The Germain named in the postscript of the latter, on the other hand, is the Émile Germain who exchanged poems with Mallarmé at school. The disparaging comment, 'un recueil bien intitulé', is not undeserved. In *Riens mis en vers* (Sens, Imprimerie de Ch. Duchemin [the publisher, printer, and probably editor of *Le Sénonais*] Germain is far from heeding the exhortations of his erstwhile comrade to emulate Hugo's eagle flight (see above, vol. I, pp. 152–3). I have found no allusion to Mallarmé in his modest volume (though one poem headed '?—V. Hugo. Contemplations' could be a relic of their schoolboy exchanges). Since he still wrote verse and published it at Sens it is likely that they were still on friendly terms. It is doubtful whether Clément Privé, who was Lefébure's closest friend (see *Lef.*, 37–9) with whom he says in his letter he has 'improvised' some fifty sonnets, was known to Mallarmé. The anonymity of Lefébure's 'nous, à deux' suggests that he did not. On these *Sonnets Auxerrois*, see *Vie*, 134. Until a few years ago it seemed that the part he played in Mallarmé's life did not go beyond reporting to Lefébure, in April 1863, what Mallarmé had told Courtois (according to Courtois) of his experience in London (*Lef.*, 78–9). It now appears, however, that he may have some claim to the attention of students of Mallarmé. It is alleged that he was the author of a sonnet attributed to Mallarmé; see below, pp. 180–6.

64 Moreover, at the time of receiving Lefébure's second letter he was making his first moves towards another relationship, interestingly linked to his new friendships but of a different kind. His second clandestine letter to Marie Gerhard, his future wife (the first, written two days or so before, has not survived) was concocted on 26–8 June; see *Corr.* i, 32–4 and 33 n. 1, *DSM*. v, 380–1 and 380 n. 1.

65 '*Souvenirs littéraires*: Stéphane Mallarmé'; see above, ch. 1, n. 4. The exceptional situation enjoyed by Des Essarts as an animator in literary circles is abundantly demonstrated in Luc Badesco's *La Génération poétique de 1860*, Nizet, 1971; see in particular vol. II, pp. 819–40. Whether he personally introduced Mallarmé to all the poets mentioned

in his article is unimportant. Directly or indirectly, it was he who did most to make him known to, and put him in touch with, writers of the young generation.

66 Des Essarts had returned to Sens (or passed through Sens) for some reason on Easter Monday, that is on 21 April, 'voilà quinze jours', a week before the end of the Easter vacation. He had brought from Paris as a present from Cazalis, 'dès son apparition', a copy of the issue of *Le Boulevard* containing Baudelaire's article on *Les Misérables*, and bearing the date of Easter Sunday, 20 April.

67 It would seem from the circumstances that Cazalis had learned from Des Essarts of Mallarmé's interest in Baudelaire. Mallarmé understood his friendly gesture as referring to the author of the article in *Le Boulevard* more directly than to its subject. 'Baudelaire y est Baudelaire', he declared. I shall later have occasion to suggest that this is an odd remark unless it relates to some writing or incident in which Baudelaire had not fulfilled his expectations.

68 The recent editors of the letter to Cazalis (incomplete and inaccurate in *Corr.* i, 24–6) explain: 'Cazalis avait publié anonymement *Lettre aux Français sur l'histoire romaine, les idées impériales* (Bruxelles, A. Lacroix, Verboeckhoven et Cie, 1861), plaquette d'inspiration républicaine hostile au régime de Napoléon III. Le même Lacroix venait d'éditer *Les Misérables*' (*DSM*. vi, 30 n. 8).

69 'Les amis de nos amis', the saying goes, 'sont nos amis.'

70 Ibid. 27–30.

71 Mallarmé had probably been reading Baudelaire's 1859 article on Théophile Gautier (of which he would make liberal use in his own article 'L'art pour tous', probably written later that month. Baudelaire quotes there, as epigraph, a passage from Gautier's *Caprices et Zigzags*: 'Quoique nous n'ayons donné à boire à aucune vieille, nous sommes dans la position de la jeune fille de Perrault; nous ne pouvons ouvrir la bouche sans qu'il en tombe aussitôt des pièces d'or, des diamants, des rubis et des perles; nous voudrions bien de temps en temps vomir un crapaud, une couleuvre et une souris rouge, ne fût-ce que pour varier; mais cela n'est pas en notre pouvoir' (B., *O.c.* ii, 103). It is of this epigraph that Mallarmé was thinking, not of the fairy-story itself, in which there is no reference to a red mouse, only to 'un serpent ou un crapaud'. See below in ch. 3, p. 103 and nn. 96–7.

72 There were other explanations than these, so egotistical and unfeeling, for his inability to join various outings with Cazalis and his friends. On 25 May he wrote, perhaps more frankly: 'Je ne sais vraiment si je pourrai aller à Meudon. Il y a deux cornes diaboliques qui passent trop souvent à travers mon porte-monnaie' (*DSM*. vi, 34). This last remark probably explains one which he made later, in a letter to Cazalis dated 26 December 1864, and which has excited some curiosity: 'J'expie cruellement, par un r[é]el abrutissement, toi seul le sais, mon ami, le priapisme de ma jeunesse' (ibid. 247).

The financial situation resulting from his father's condition was summarized by Fanny Desmolins in a letter to Mélanie Laurent dated

21 June 1862: 'Son pauvre père, toujours aussi infirme, a dû se résigner à la retraite, qu'on lui a fait demander, pour rendre le coup moins amer. (. . .) Voilà donc à présent cette nombreuse famille réduite à vivre sur une pension de 3,000 f, bien modique revenu, comparé à ce que l'on perd, et Stéphane encore hors d'état même de se suffire à lui-même' (*DSM*. v, 379). That is, with four children to bring up and her sick husband to provide for, the pension Anne Mallarmé received amounted to less than Stéphane's allowance while he was in London. The 'interest' from the Desmolins probably sufficed to cover living expenses for the Mallarmé family, but one can well imagine that the cost of Sunday excursions for Stéphane with his well-to-do friends was more than the budget could stand.

73 *DSM*. vi, 35–6.

74 Ibid. 46–7.

75 Letter dated Saturday 24 May; ibid. 33.

76 See p. 35 above.

77 For the full text and critical introduction see *DSM*. iv, 25–35 and *Fl*., i. 122–6. Like *Les Sénonaises* by Roquier and Pied-Guérin the following year, it was printed by Ph. Chapu, rue Royale 45. Under the heading *Scies* I, which seems to promise other such frivolities to follow, it is prolifically entitled *Le Carrefour des Demoiselles ou l'Absence du Lancier ou le Triomphe de la Prévoyance, Fait en collaboration avec les Oiseaux, les Pâtés, les Fraises et les Arbres*. It was to be sung to the tune of 'Il était un petit navire, Qui n'avait *ja*mais navigué', the italic type indicating, here as in the text, the syllable that had to be twice (or if more convenient only once) repeated. The verses introducing the persons present are of some biographical interest. They read:

C'était une illustre partie/ De gens bien *vê*tus et bien nés.
Neuf Parisiens sans apathie/ Intelligents et *va*ccinés . . .
D'aimables mères de familles/ Qui se ré*jou*issaient de voir/
Du soleil aux yeux de leurs filles/ Et des messieurs *Sens* habit noir;/
Fort mal noté par les gendarmes/ Le gari*bal*dien Mallarmé/
Ayant encor plus d'arts que d'armes/ Semblait un *Jud* très alarmé;
Ettie, en patois Henriette,/ Plus agi*le* que feu Guignol,/
Voltigeait comme une ariette/ Dans le go*sier* d'un rossignol;/
Dans le sein de cette algarade/ S'idylli*sait* le Cazalis,/
Qui, comme un chaste camarade,/ Tutoyait *l'a*zur et le lis;/
Puis une Anglaise aux airs de reine/ A qui Di*ane* porte un toast,/
Qu'Albion envoie à Suresne/ Sous la bande du Morning Post;/
Piccolino, le coloriste,/ Qui pour par*fu*mer nos vingt ans
Pille comme un vil herboriste/ L'opulent *é*crin du printemps[.]/
Nina qui d'un geste extatique/ Sur le dol*men* et le menhir/
Semblait poser pour la Musique,/ La musi*que* de l'avenir;/
Puis des Essarts Emmanuelle/ Le plus beau-*det* jeunes rimeurs/
Offrait le fantasque modèle/ D'un poète *ay*ant gants et mœurs.

(*DSM*. iv, 31–3)

The 'nine Parisians' (including Mallarmé, Paris born and bred) are enumerated in plain prose by the editors of the Correspondence as follows: 'Participaient à cette expédition, outre Mallarmé, Des Essarts, Cazalis et Henri Regnault [his friend, a promising young painter], Mme Yapp, Ettie Yapp, une jeune Anglaise de leurs amies, Miss Mary, Mme Gaillard et Nina Gaillard' (*Corr.* i, 27, n. 1). Lawrence Joseph (art. cit.) points out that Miss Mary's presence makes it a group of ten, the ninth Parisian being Ettie's little sister Isabelle.

Attention was drawn to this composition by Fr. Ambrière, in 'Deux ouvrages inconnus de Stéphane Mallarmé', *Bulletin du bibliophile*, 20 November 1935. Cazalis had kept his copy, the only one known to have survived, and it was sold with the rest of the 'Collection Jean Lahor' (the pen-name Cazalis had adopted) on 24 June 1935. Two transcriptions were made before the sale, and from these is taken the text published by Lawrence Joseph in his very interesting article on 'Mallarmé et son amie anglaise' (*RHLF*., July–Sept. 1965). Another sale brought Cazalis's own copy of the printed text to the Bibliothèque nationale, where Carl Barbier transcribed it.

As a respected and respectable poet, Emmanuel's father disapproved of the publication; see *DSM*. vi, 38, and below, n. 81.

78 It was said in jest, when in early October 1862 Mallarmé invited Cazalis to Sens, and after all his disparagement of Sens and his home at Les Gaillons, did his best to make the latter at least seem enticing: 'Ah! que ne viens-tu grapiller! J'ai de si beau raisin. Du chasselas—de Fontainebleau. Ce nom magique va te décider' (*DSM*. vi, 60). For him too it was a most evocative name, and would remain so. He celebrated it in the prose poem 'La Gloire': 'ce nom connu pour déployer la continuité de cimes tard évanouies' (*O.c.*, 288).

(The letter to Cazalis lacks its first page or pages and therefore its date. It is dated by the editors of the Mallarmé–Cazalis correspondence simply 'October 1862'. But this can be narrowed to 'about 10 October' on the strength of a reference to Des Essarts: 'Emmanuel est ici depuis Lundi'. Since in 1862 the teaching year started on Monday 6 October the letter was written during the week following that date.)

79 *DSM*. vi, 374–5. On a very different, much later occasion, in November 1879, when Mme Gaillard and her daughter Nina sent him their condolences on the death of his little son Anatole, Mallarmé wrote to thank them for their letter, and the photograph of 'Tole' they had enclosed, and he added: 'Je pensais, il y a quelques jours, en revenant de notre triste forêt [that is, from the little house they rented at Valvins, near Fontainebleau], que nous nous y sommes connus aussi, bien inoubliablement autrefois, vous deux et moi' (J.-P. Richard, *Pour un tombeau d'Anatole*, 1961, p. 27).

80 Of the two, Mallarmé was the more interested in this reciprocity. In a letter written that summer (early July), he excused his own rather high-flown rhetoric and asked Cazalis to forgive him 'ce que cette lettre insensée a d'excessif en songeant à la première que tu nous écrivis après Fontainebleau' (*DSM*. vi, 44).

81 Caricaturing Des Essarts in writing to Cazalis was a pleasure that Mallarmé apparently relished, and Des Essarts seems not to have

objected. The game may have started in 'Le Carrefour des Demoiselles'. The undignified figure that friend Emmanuel cuts there may have been his father's reason for disapproving of the *Scie* (ibid. 38).

82 Ibid. 31–2.

83 The name Chaville is used to refer to the same excursion as (in another letter, ibid. 34) the name 'Meudon'. Chaville is a small town on the fringe of the Forest of Meudon.

84 Ibid. 35. Harpagon is of course Molière's 'Avare'. It may be that he wore, traditionally, an unsightly red wig to declare his poverty, contrasting with the fashionable *perruques* he so objects to his son's flaunting.

85 The original drawing, now in the possession of Ettie's grand-daughters, with Regnault's signature under the inscription 'Souvenir de sincère amitié' (see the photographic reproduction in *DSM*. vi, opposite p. 290), was presumably presented to Ettie herself. It may have been a photograph of it that Cazalis sent to Mallarmé, and later (on 24 December 1862; ibid. 94) asked him to return since he was still waiting for a new photograph of Ettie.

86 In Claude Gély's succinct study, *Les Misérables de Hugo*, pp. 219–20, the extraordinary success of Hugo's epic novel is admirably described, and neatly summarized by two quotations from critics, one favourable, the other inimical: 'Jules Janin, le 25 juin, dans un article de *L'Indépendance belge*, constatait le rayonnement populaire des *Misérables*: "A l'heure où nous sommes, M. Victor Hugo et son fameux livre ont accaparé uniquement l'attention de la France entière. On n'entend plus parler que des *Misérables*." Et Sainte-Beuve, non certes suspect de complaisance à l'égard de V. Hugo, écrivait dans ses *Poisons*: "*Les Misérables* tiennent le haut du pavé . . . Le succès des *Misérables* a sévi et continue de sévir au-delà de tout ce que l'on pouvait craindre."'

For the reasons why Monday the thirtieth of June was chosen for the launching of the final instalment, and the important commercial aspect of the whole enterprise, see the letter of 22 June 1862 from the publisher Lacroix to Victor Hugo and Hugo's reply, in Bernard Leuilliot's *Victor Hugo publie les Misérables*, pp. 374–7 and 381–2.

87 Cf. in IV. viii. 2 (i.e. Quatrième Partie, Livre huitième, chapitre 2) of *Les Misérables*: 'Donc ces deux êtres vivaient ainsi, très haut, avec toute l'invraisemblance qui est dans la nature; ni au nadir, ni au zénith, entre l'homme et le séraphin, au-dessus de la fange, au-dessous de l'éther, dans le nuage; à peine os et chair, âme et extase de la tête aux pieds; déjà trop sublimés pour marcher à terre, encore trop chargés d'humanité pour disparaître dans le bleu. (. . .) O léthargie splendide du réel accablé d'idéal!'

88 *DSM*. vi, 40. In the list of heroines, an obviously necessary correction is made here, of *Chimère* to *Chimène*.

89 Ibid. 41.

90 Ibid. 45–6; also, in the letter of 1 July (ibid. 41), 'l'alouette fatale'. Cf. *Les Misérables*, IV. viii. 1: 'Marius (. . .) avait fini par entrer dans le jardin de Cosette comme Roméo dans le jardin de Juliette'.

91 *DSM*. vi, 40. In the same letter, what appears to be a touch of impishness

appears in the praise of Ettie. A suggestion of a flaw in her beauty is disguised as a criticism of a detail in her portrait: 'Le menton ne serait-il pas un peu trop éloigné de la bouche: je sais que c'est une des particularités du type Anglais, mais je ne la crois pas si accentuée chez Ettie' (ibid. 39).

92 Ibid. 46. The reverential use of the capital in 'Elle', which from now on Mallarmé adopts from time to time in referring to Ettie, is also taken from *Les Misérables*. Cf. in III. viii. 8: 'C'était Elle. Quiconque a aimé sait tous les sens rayonnants que contiennent les quatre lettres de ce mot: Elle. C'était bien elle'; and in IV. ii. 4 ('Apparition à Marius'): 'Il songeait à "Elle"'.

93 *DSM*. v, 384.

94 Ibid. 382.

95 *Les Misérables*, III. vi. 3.

96 Ibid. IV. ii. 1.

97 Ibid. IV. v. 5.

98 *DSM*. v, 383. The editors of *Corr*. i remark (p. 38 n. 1) the presence of this conceit in the poem 'Apparition'; cf. below, ch. 5.

99 Other examples, equally conspicuous, can be quoted, such as these: 'C'était bien elle. C'est à peine si Marius la distinguait à travers la vapeur lumineuse qui s'était subitement répandue sur ses yeux'; 'Il contemplait non pas cette fille, mais cette lumière qui avait une pelisse de satin et un chapeau de velours. L'étoile Sirius fût entrée dans la chambre qu'il n'eût pas été plus ébloui'. The phenomenon is even given a place among the wise words that Marius 'wrote to' Cosette: 'Le jour où une femme qui passe devant vous dégage de la lumière en marchant, vous êtes perdu, vous aimez' (ibid. IV. iv. 4). Claude Gély makes some interesting comments on the symbolic aspect of this 'ange fait de rayons' (op. cit., pp. 67–9). But Mallarmé probably saw in this *leitmotif*, on first reading, no more than a charming and amusing fancy. A little later he was to give it more depth and refinement in 'Apparition'; see ch. 5.

100 *DSM*. vi, 51–2.

101 See above, n. 81. An example of this persistent teasing of Emmanuel is the use of the nickname Polichinelle and its variant Emmanuelcinella, and references to his supposed resemblance to Punch. It culminated in Mallarmé's sending to his friends, in August 1866, a photograph of his little daughter Geneviève with her doll Punch, and describing it as a photograph of Geneviève with her godfather Emmanuel, a very good one of the latter, who had kept quite still when it was taken. The photograph is reproduced in *DSM*. vi, plate 5, and commented on in *MLR*., January 1979, p. 214.

On the subject of Des Essarts's outward peculiarities, a description by his very good friend Maurice Dreyfous (in *Ce que je tiens à dire*) is quoted by L. Badesco (op. cit. II, p. 825): 'Il n'était pas d'aspect imposant, mon cher Emmanuel; il était de petite taille, trop gras pour sa hauteur et surtout pour son âge, il bredouillait en parlant. Sa réputation de poète commençait à poindre, et il lisait ou récitait volontiers ses poèmes, mais il les assassinait par des excès de cadence, par des roulements d'yeux imploratifs et mélancoliques, par une gesticulation d'escarpolette, par un retournement cocasse de ses mains accompagnant la courbe de ses bras trop courts. Une myopie excessive eût achevé de le rendre ridicule si on n'avait point su par avance quel homme de valeur, quel vaillant esprit et quel brave cœur on avait devant soi.'

102 This exercise may be an indication of the time at which Mallarmé read and (it would seem) studied Aloysius Bertrand's prose poems. The question of the date of that first reading is broached by the Pléiade editors (*O.c.*, 1544–5 [1551]) in relation to Mallarmé's prose poems. They quote his letter of 30 December 1865 to Victor Pavie, later published in Mallarmé's *Correspondance* (*Corr.* i, 188). It contains the following allusion to an early attachment to *Gaspard de la nuit* (first published by Pavie, at Angers in 1842): 'Exilé, pour un temps, dans une petite ville de province, je souffre beaucoup de voir ma bibliothèque, qui renferme les merveilles du Romantisme, privé de ce cher volume, qui ne m'abandonnait pas quand je pouvais l'emprunter à un confrère.' The editors comment: 'A cette époque, exilé depuis près de deux ans [two whole years in fact] à Tournon, il faisait allusion évidemment à une période de sa vie qui avait précédé cet exil, c'est-à-dire aux années 1862–1863, soit qu'à Sens il eût emprunté ce *Gaspard de la nuit* dès 1862 à Emmanuel des Essarts; à Paris, à Henri Cazalis; à Londres même, à ce chevalier du [*sic* for 'de'] Chatelain curieux de l'une et l'autre langue, et avec lequel nous savons qu'il se lia.' Cf. also *Vie*, 182 n. 1. Suzanne Bernard, in *Le Poème en prose, de Baudelaire à nos jours* (Nizet, 1959), p. 259 and n. 30, expressed her agreement with these observations: 'Il ressort de ces lettres [citées par H. Mondor dans sa *Vie de Mallarmé* (. . .) et dans les (. . .) *Œuvres*, p. 1544] que Mallarmé lisait Bertrand avant d'être à Tournon, sans doute à Sens vers 1862–1863.' Then, with respect to the years spent at Tournon and Besançon, she states this firm conviction: 'Toutes les fois que Mallarmé, à cette époque, est tenté de cadencer sa prose, (. . .) c'est donc certainement sous l'influence de Bertrand.' The paragraph of 'prose cadencée' (and whimsical fancy) in the letter that Mallarmé sent to Des Essarts on 23 August 1862 provides confirmation of the time of Mallarmé's first reading of *Gaspard de la nuit*. The paragraph is a delicate way of thanking his friend Emmanuel for lending him the volume. The fact that three days later *La Presse* began its publication of Baudelaire's prose poems with his tribute to Bertrand's example (in the dedicatory foreword 'A Arsène Houssaye'), underlines the likelihood that it was interest in Baudelaire that led Mallarmé to borrow Des Essarts's copy of *Gaspard*. Luc Badesco points out that the *Revue fantaisiste* had published in advance, on 1 November 1861, nine of the *Petits poèmes en prose*, and in its previous number an 'article retentissant' by F. Calmels on Aloysius Bertrand. See Badesco's comments on this (op. cit. II, pp. 796 n. 111, and 1269).

103 *Corr.* i, 47. 'Volunteers', that is, for Garibaldi's army. 'Le garibaldien Mallarmé', it may be remembered, figures in 'Le Carrefour des Demoiselles'.

104 Ibid. The album so aptly celebrated with a line from Baudelaire's 'Le

Balcon' has survived, and is described by Henri Mondor in *M.pl.i.* 120–9, under the title 'Album de province': 'relié, en effet, en chagrin vert très foncé, presque noir, doré sur tranches', it contains far fewer contributions than it was meant to receive, and few that are likely to have been indited that year. The honour of honouring it by occupying the opening page was reserved not for Des Essarts or Cazalis but for the elder poet Émile Deschamps. Sufficient reason for his occupying that place is suggested above in ch. 1. Messages he exchanged with Mallarmé from time to time, on appropriate occasions, will be referred to in the following pages.

105 *Corr.* i, 48.

106 The Pléiade editors state in their *Chronologie* (p. xviii): 'Octobre: Mallarmé passe quelque jours à Versailles et à Paris'. This is repeated in *Corr.* i, 369. But for October we must read September. The editors of Mallarmé's *Correspondance avec Henri Cazalis* point to one good reason why: 'C'est à Versailles qu'Émile Deschamps et Albert Glatigny copient deux poèmes dans l'album de Mallarmé. Celui de Glatigny est daté du 10 septembre 1862 selon Henri Mondor, *Mallarmé plus intime*, p. 122' (also *DSM.* vi, 53 n. 1). Deschamps's contribution too (a sonnet) is dated 'Septembre 1862'. Further evidence on this count is provided by a letter Mallarmé wrote to Cazalis on 25 September; from various remarks, put together, it appears that he had been back at Sens for a week and some days, after an absence of a fortnight. What does not emerge from these documents is how much of that fortnight was spent at Versailles, and how much (or how little) in Paris. His uncertain intentions in that regard were stated a month in advance, when he wrote to Cazalis on 4–5 August: 'Il est inutile de te dire que, dussé-je voler sur la grande route, je te verrai ces vacances à Paris. J'irai probablement passer huit jours près de vous [i.e. you and Emmanuel?], et huit jours à Versailles' (ibid. 52). Clearly, expense was an important consideration, but there is nothing to indicate that either Cazalis or Des Essarts invited him to be his guest. Cazalis indeed was in London during some part of the first half of September, as will be seen later, and on 23 August Mallarmé mentioned, in his letter to Des Essarts, one Ibouët with whom he had apparently expected to stay but probably would not: 'Cela fera probablement que je ne descendrai pas chez lui. Je lui écrirai délicatement à ce sujet' (*Corr.* i, 48). Perhaps this too was written 'délicatement'. Of other possibilities there was no mention. When Des Essarts's letters to Mallarmé are at last published, some of this uncertainty may be dispelled. Meanwhile, biographers must regret that Henri Mondor's article on the album does not tell us whether the entries that follow Glatigny's ('des poèmes courts d'Emmanuel des Essarts, d'Armand Renaud, et un beau fusain très appuyé d'Henri Regnault') are also accompanied by details of place and date.

107 *DSM.* vi, 53–5. The litany of place-names suggests that Marie had gone to visit her family in Germany.

108 See *DSM.* v, 386.

109 The night that George Sand spent there with Musset, as narrated by him in *La Confession d'un enfant du siècle* (1836), and by her in *Elle et Lui*

(1859), was doubtless famous, and Franchart (though not named by either) already a place of pilgrimage, literary and sentimental.

110 He was choosing a bride that the bourgeoisie of Sens would look down on, and justifying his choice by presenting her father, a school-teacher, in the same class as Cazalis and himself, because not employed in commerce. He continues to express himself with a noble disregard of their real situation: 'J'ai pour devise: *Rien de Louche*—et tout commerce est louche. Je méprise autant la veuve Cliquot que la mère Grégoire. On vole en grand, voilà tout. Ils sont nécessaires ces gens-là? Oui comme les laquais. Je donnerais mes bottes à mon laquais, mais pas la main de ma fille' (*DSM*. vi, 59).

111 It will be remembered that much is made of 'le regard' in *Les Misérables*.

112 *DSM*. vi, 61.

113 'Sublime' was a word they were to like using when they wrote about Marie.

114 Ibid. 62–4.

115 *DSM*. vii, 194–6. The letter was first published, incomplete, by Mondor in 'Léon Marc et Mallarmé' (*La Voix des poètes*, July–Sept. 1959). See above, n. 6.

116 Occasionally, the name of Marie's sister Anna is mentioned in Mallarmé's correspondence. Cazalis mentions her in a letter written on 14 January 1863, saying that he recognized her, which suggests that he had met her in Paris with Marie, on her way to London; see *DSM*. vi, 106. She appears to have been in some kind of domestic service, perhaps as a governess like her sister.

117 On 26 November 1862 his grandmother wrote to Mélanie Laurent: 'Nous avons eu le pauvre enfant quelques jours, avant son départ; (. . .) Il n'a pas manqué de nous faire beaucoup de bonnes promesses, espérons qu'il voudra les réaliser. Le pauvre garçon est parti il y a 15 jours, par le soleil, qui l'a quitté à Londres pour faire place à une atmosphère brumeuse, qui l'a désenchanté dès l'abord, et l'a fait réfléchir assez tristement, déjà, sur la solitude et l'isolement volontaire où il se trouve; attendu que cet épais brouillard ayant attaqué son gosier, en même temps que son esprit, il a dû se renfermer les premiers jours, pour soigner ce mal de gorge intense; il en a profité pour nous écrire très en détail, et nous mettre bien au courant de sa petite organisation de vie' (*DSM*. v, 388). If all Stéphane's letters from London to members of his family were known, they would make curious reading.

118 On 14 November he wrote to him: 'En te quittant, j'avais des larmes aux yeux' (in Mallarmé's first letter to Cazalis from London, *DSM*. vi, 65).

119 That is the date stated by the Pléiade editors (*O.c.*, XVIII), and also in *Corr*. i, 57 n. 2. On what evidence, is not revealed, but such details as can be noted in the correspondence tend to confirm that date.

Chapter 3

Fruits of the last year at Sens: prose

The student of Mallarmé's earliest writings as a practising man of letters is favoured by the existence, alongside the poems that have survived, of the seven articles he is known to have published between December 1861 and September 1862. They are all concerned with literature, and together sketch the general context of ideas, preoccupations, and intellectual attitudes within which his poems of that year took shape. They also provide useful guidance on some at least of the particular intentions behind individual poems, and even on their conceptual substance. Therefore, though in themselves the articles are of less literary interest than the poems, they are best examined first. That order is preferable for another reason too. Most of the articles are in some measure expressions of friendship, for either Léon Marc or Emmanuel des Essarts. They have thus a biographical aspect which links them closely to the previous chapter.

It is an aspect that is very obvious in the earliest group, the series of three articles of dramatic criticism published anonymously in *Le Sénonais* in December 1861.[1] Indeed the first of them, entitled 'M. Besombes et sa troupe'—a title which may be fairly understood as covering all three—was given prominence in the earlier, biographical chapter for the decisive part it played in its author's early relations with Léon Marc. When they are seen now in a more literary light, as Mallarmé's earliest published writings, it is again the first of the three that claims most attention, and the passage already quoted for its biographical interest is again outstanding. It is remarkable, in its substance and its tone, as a young poet's reflections on the vocation he is privately resolved to follow. If Mallarmé's tribute to Marc is read with his own future in mind the thoughts he expresses take on their full significance. The reflections on Marc are then seen to be an early attempt to bring into focus ideas that were later to occupy an essential part in his understanding not only of the situation of an artist in a hostile society, but of the human condition itself, as experienced by those humans he considers worthy of the name, 'les gens d'idéal' as he calls them. In his twentieth year he describes the modern artist's lot, as he observes it in the fortunes of his new friend, in these terms:

Ce coudoiement perpétuel de l'idéal et de la réalité, ces contraintes ironiques qui interrompent l'Hamlet de province dans son monologue pour lui dire: Pense demain, il te faut vivre aujourd'hui, sont tristes et navrantes. (. . .) M. Léon-Marc (. . .) a su faire une pièce poignante en vers énergiques. Je sais bien qu'on pourrait faire quelques observations de détail, mais la critique n'ose élever la voix que pour louer[,] devant une telle victoire remportée sur le temps et sur toutes les fatalités.[2]

Twenty-five years later, returning reluctantly from his solitude at Valvins to Paris, where he must review a performance of *Hamlet* ('la pièce que je crois celle par excellence') he would write:

avance *le seigneur latent qui ne peut devenir*, juvénile ombre de tous, ainsi tenant du mythe. Son solitaire drame! et qui, parfois, tant ce promeneur d'un labyrinthe de trouble et de griefs en prolonge les circuits avec le suspens d'un acte inachevé, semble le spectacle même pourquoi existent la rampe ainsi que l'espace doré quasi moral qu'elle défend, car il n'est pas d'autre sujet, sachez bien: l'antagonisme de rêve [*for*: du rêve?] chez l'homme avec les fatalités à son existence départies par le malheur.[3]

It is clear from the composition of his earliest article that Mallarmé intended his reflections on Léon Marc to occupy the place of honour in it, as if it was his main concern, and the review of the evening's performance in which it was inserted little more than a pretext. Far from attempting to conceal the fact that it is a digression from the task assigned to him, he is at pains to insulate it further. He begins his initial summary of the performances he has to review by setting Léon Marc's play apart from the rest:

D'abord, un charmant lever de rideau dont je parlerai tout à l'heure plus amplement. Puis, le *Capitaine Roquefinette*, une comédie où Dennery s'est permis de ne pas être Dennery, et où Dumanoir est resté triomphalement Dumanoir. Enfin, *Monsieur Garat*, une esquisse fine et pittoresque de l'auteur des *Intimes*, M. Victorien Sardou, ce triomphateur de la veille, doué d'une des plus heureuses originalités.[4]

The 'charming curtain-raiser' thus reserved 'for fuller treatment later' had been announced in the previous number of *Le Sénonais* as: '*La fin d'un Rêve*, pièce en un acte de M. Léon-Marc'.[5] For Mallarmé, its particular interest was that it was written in verse, and offered the opportunity therefore of honouring Marc as poet rather than as actor. The better to do so, and to rise to the level of discourse appropriate to that purpose, he employed a bold device. He simply brought forward into the body of his article the announcement of the following week's performances, which should have been the conclusion of his review. By this means, together with the delay in commenting on the curtain-raiser, he was able to speak of Léon Marc in the same breath as Victor Hugo. First, the performers in le *Capitaine Roquefinette* were dutifully praised;[6] then (after a laboriously contrived transition which he would have done much better to forego) the reviewer altered course, to proceed:

Jeudi, Ruy Blas! Voici un programme magique qui, affiché à Paris, signifierait salle comble.[7]—Espérons que ce n'est point une raison pour qu'il veuille dire salle vide à Sens.—Oui! l'on donne cette œuvre que nous, la génération nouvelle trop tard venue, nous reprenions chaque mois dans notre fauteuil, au coin du feu, en songeant mélancoliquement aux ardentes soirées du Théâtre de la Renaissance, et à ces glorieuses escrimes des Dorval et des Frédérick![8]

Et ce n'est pas la première fois, depuis l'arrivée de M. Besombes, que de beaux vers ont charmé notre scène. Jeudi, le lever de rideau qui fut si chaleureusement applaudi, était en vers, et Dieu le sait! souvent frappés sur la bonne enclume. A mon avis, il n'eut qu'un tort, celui d'être un lever de rideau. Je n'ai point parlé de M. et de Mme Léon-Marc, deux talents, l'un énergique et savant, l'une si émouvante et d'une passion touchante. Comme autrefois—si parva licet componere magnis—insinuerait Janin, La Béjart traduisant de sa verve franche la profonde pensée de Poquelin,[9] Mme Léon-Marc a commenté et rendu avec ses élans passionnés la belle pièce de Léon-Marc.

The passage already quoted, on the 'provincial Hamlet' Léon Marc, followed, virtually bringing the first article to a close.

From the point of view of the readers of *Le Sénonais*, in 1861, we may be sure that such indulgence in highly subjective digression was an unwelcome novelty. Nor was it the only indication of over-presumptuousness on the part of the unnamed substitute for 'Roberval', the paper's regular dramatic critic. There was, in addition, his liking for paradox and irony, and for using them particularly as spice for derogatory comment or innuendo regarding Sens and its citizens. For with praise for M. Besombes and his company of strolling players was associated dispraise, implicit or explicit, of Sens, unworthy of such visitors. Unworthy in particular, it appears, of the 'literary' character of their entertainments:

Nous avons à Sens une troupe qui offre la particularité inouïe qu'elle est une troupe. Un directeur qui donne ce spectacle étrange d'être un directeur. Jusqu'ici—depuis plusieurs années du moins,—notre scène voyait autour d'un talent ou deux, épars et dépaysés, se grouper quelques ombres chinoises. A ces fantômes évanouis ont succédé de vrais comédiens, s'il vous plaît, évoqués par l'intelligente magie de M. Besombes. J'ai prononcé le nom de celui que j'appelle un directeur, et non un négociant en denrées dramatiques; honneur à sa vaillance![10]
(. . .)
Ce fut un festin dont la carte était choisie avec un tact exquis, un festin littéraire. Prononçons ce mot bien bas; le crier trop haut serait à Sens, faire tort à M. Besombes. (. . .) M. Rivière montre une distinction rare en province, excelle dans des nuances insaisissables. M. Mauret a un comique achevé, non ce comique enfariné et épais, si facile à rencontrer, mais le fin, le spirituel, mais le littéraire.

It was with a jibe at the expense of his non-literary readers that the critic ended his article:

Voilà, dans l'espérance que mon feuilleton augure du passé, de quoi faire se remplir toutes les loges: d'où vient qu'elles étaient vides avant-hier? Que promettre de plus entraînant? Que raconter qui puisse séduire davantage?—Ah! tenez, voici une réclame la plus propre à vous attirer: 'La troupe a de charmants costumes.'

This mocking attitude towards the theatre-goers becomes very much bolder in Mallarmé's second contribution to *Le Sénonais*, on Saturday 14 December. The greater part of it is given over to deriding them. It is an ungainly composition, awkwardly cramped (perhaps in part owing to editorial cuts that the author was later to complain of),[11] disjointed and difficult to follow. For a publication of that nature it is altogether too ambitious in its scope and too elaborately contrived.

Its ostensible object is of course to review the performance of Hugo's play *Ruy Blas*, announced by Mallarmé a week before, and in a literal, narrow sense that assignment is scrupulously, even ostentatiously carried out. The review proper is as careful, as succinct and almost as well behaved as if it had come from the pen of 'Roberval'. But it occupies only about one-third of Mallarmé's article, the middle part, where he seems concerned to hive it off, aloof and self-sufficient, from what precedes and what follows. In a not dissimilar way the tribute to Léon Marc had been kept apart from the rest in the article of the previous week. Not however with the same intention. The critic does not now highlight his review in order to give prominence to its contents. He wishes, for the sake of the actors on whose performance it passes judgement, to keep it sober and conventional in tone, unaffected by the fooling at the audience's expense with which he plans to fill the other two sections. The better to protect its respectability, he has also hit on the device of formally disowning it, declaring it anonymous—while at the same time assuring his puzzled readers that to present it to them 'for the actors' sake' is the sole purpose of his *feuilleton*. The review consists, he says, of a few notes,

> griffonnées, j'ignore par qui, sur le dos du programme et ramassées dans ma loge, lesquelles, si on en excepte une admiration pour le poëte, sont toutes empreintes de la plus sévère vérité.

And he quotes them:

> "Monsieur Besombes fut splendide dans le personnage de Ruy-Blas, un rôle, du reste, qu'il avait joué à Jersey. De la scène où le valet, calme et pensif, ouvre une porte que lui commande d'ouvrir son maître, jusqu'à celle où l'amant, grandi de toute la hauteur de son amour, en ferme une autre sur le maître qu'il a tué, M. Besombes ne se démentit pas un instant. Il nous fit songer au mot d'Hugo sur Frédérick Lemaître: Cette soirée fut pour lui une transfiguration.—
> "M. Léon-Marc eut la raillerie froide et la haine sombre et concentrée de Salluste. Pour citer Hugo, il nous rappelait cette phrase de la préface:—Salluste est Satan grand d'Espagne.

"Mme Léon-Marc a été cet ange mélancolique que Dieu fit une femme, et le destin ironique une reine.
"Don Guritan est fort amusant, sans être peut-être assez grave."[12]

At this point the quotation comes to an abrupt end. The ingenious critic has decided that the programme is torn, and the remainder of the scribbled text lost. He must finish the review himself. This seems to mean in fact that notwithstanding his intention to keep his review immaculate he will perversely allow himself a satiric flourish, in the same vein as his parting taunt of the week before:

Ici le programme est déchiré. Je termine en deux mots: si l'acteur qui jouait Don César de Bazan ne plaisait pas généralement, cela vient de son rôle, sans doute. Quant à Casilda, dont le jeu fut approuvé de chacun, je prends sur moi de la juger littérairement: Elle est fort jolie.

So much for Thursday's performance. The rest of the article, that is the whole of the opening and closing sections, forms a two-scene burlesque satire directed against the audience. It exploits no less a subject than Hugo's rejuvenation of French drama in the 1830s. The satirist seems to have had in mind, rather vaguely, a scenario in which the public at Sens would be shown enacting, all unwittingly, a limp, Second Empire provincial version of two salient episodes in Hugo's career as a dramatist, the triumph of *Hernani* at the Théâtre Français in February 1830 and the performance of *Ruy Blas* at the Théâtre de la Renaissance in November 1838. The principal player in the parody is the critic himself, usually repeating the words, or playing the part, of another member of the audience, real or fictitious but consistent in expressing views hostile to Hugo. Such other characters as make an appearance are evanescent. Attempts to give one or other of them a semblance of personal identity come to nothing or very little.

This pedantic exercise in satiric antiphrasis, which is what the rigmarole soon turns out to be, was probably drafted at least in part before the play was performed. In its published state it nevertheless seems hastily botched. We shall learn with no surprise that it proved a failure. The author's ironic intention was not understood. His readers took the views expressed to be his own and not their opposite. Since a disproportionate degree of attention is required to follow the critic's moves in his humourless game, it will not I hope be taken amiss if the following account of his procedure is made painstakingly explicit.

The exercise starts immediately, in the opening paragraph, with a show of professional sarcasm undisguised, intended no doubt to set the tone and warn the readers of what is in store:

Il existe en France—hors de France, je crois—un poëte qui s'appelle Hugo (Victor), lequel n'a rien de commun avec M. Clairville, et exista un drame auquel il avait donné le nom de *Ruy-Blas* et qu'il ne faut pas confondre avec le *Voyage de M. Périchon*, ni avec les *Amours de Cléopâtre*. Ce poëte est né en 1802, à Besançon, et n'est mort encore que dans la mémoire des hommes: entre autres ambitions il eut celle de régénérer le théâtre moderne, comme s'il était jamais quelque chose qui eût besoin d'être régénéré!

The voice that comes in with this last remark speaks on. The histrionic critic has skipped into the part of a reactionary rather grumpy Philistine unnamed and unannounced. This individual is surprised in the act of preparing himself (like the critic his creator) for the performance of *Ruy Blas*. After much searching he has found in a history of literature a whole page on the forgotten poet Victor Hugo. He is reading it out to himself fragment by fragment, pausing after each to make his hostile comments. (These I have placed in brackets for greater clarity; the first readers were unfortunately given no such assistance.)

"A la première représentation d'*Hernani* . . .
(Hernani! Peut-on s'appeler Hernani quand la Grèce a inventé le nom d'Achille et M. Scribe celui d'Oscar!)[13]
"La jeunesse avait envahi le théâtre . . .
(Que la jeunesse était jeune en ce temps-là!)
"Fit du parterre un champ de bataille . . .
(Ah! je ferme le livre. Cela passe toutes les bornes! Se battre au théâtre!—Et les convenances? Se battre pour un poëme! Nous nous battons, nous, les beaux fils, pour une fille ou pour un cheval, si toutefois nous nous battons encore! Se battre pour un poëme!)"

The critic then takes over in his own person, to present his readers with the anonymous review so conveniently come by. Then, abruptly, we are in the theatre for the third section of the article, the subject of which is the play *Ruy Blas* itself. An elaborate move is made towards a dialogue between the critic (still as himself) and another member of the audience:

> Passons à la pièce: J'avais pour voisin un gros monsieur fort littéraire qui, pendant les trois premiers actes, ne cessait de me dire en ricanant: "Vous allez entendre ce vers—je crois qu'il est là-dedans—si baroque, outre qu'il a quinze pieds [in fact, eighteen 'feet' or syllables]:
>
> Affreuse compagnonne dont le menton fleurit et dont le nez trognonne."

The critic's ironical answer to the 'gros monsieur' was only mental, we are given to understand, but he divulges it to his readers. It consists of a few other lines quoted from *Ruy Blas* 'qui, pour être moins longs, ne sont pas moins ridicules'. These are of course lines that Mallarmé admires as being strong and dramatic, though they flouted traditional conventions. There the dialogue peters out. It is presumably the literary Philistine, but it could be the critic aping him, who is then heard misinterpreting Hugo's intentions:

> Voilà pour la forme. Et le fond! . . . Un valet se permet d'aimer, et qui? . . . Heureusement que cet impudent est remis à sa place par Don Salluste, le seul grand caractère de la pièce. Soyons justes: il y a une scène assez belle, c'est celle où ce laquais qui vient de chasser les ministres ramasse le mouchoir de son maître et sent qu'il n'est qu'un laquais, où l'orgueil reçoit le châtiment mérité! Cette scène rachète les mauvais vers et les sottises des autres.
>
> C'est une leçon pour M. Besombes: il veut faire de l'art! Nous prend-il pour des artistes? Nous avons bien le temps vraiment de l'être! Et n'y-a-t-il pas de sa part une ironie insultante à étaler sur son affiche ces deux mots: en vers. Est-ce qu'on lit des vers, maintenant? Et si l'on n'en lit plus, en veut-on entendre au théâtre où l'on va pour s'amuser?

With that the article ends, and as if to point the moral and acknowledge a return to a normal theatrical diet, the announcement of the programme for the morrow, that follows immediately, reads: 'Demain dimanche, pour la clôture, sans remise, *L'Ange de Minuit*, Drame en 6 actes; *Un bal à émotions*, vaudeville en 1 acte.'

The last of the three articles on M. Besombes and his company, which appeared on Saturday 21 December, should have been devoted to the performance of those two plays (by unnamed authors), on the eve of their departure from Sens on tour. But the critic accorded it very scant attention. One reason for this may have been that he had little to say in praise of either the performance or the plays. But another reason, much more in evidence, was that he preferred to return to his subject of the previous week. He began by explaining why:

> Ils l'ont cru! Voici trois jours que j'en ris! Ils ont cru que quand je leur disais: ne confondez pas Hugo avec M. Clairville, cela voulait dire: M. Clairville est le génie qu'on nomme après Homère et Shakespeare, et Hugo, le piètre vaudevilliste qu'on sait! (. . .)
>
> Ils n'ont pas compris que ce langage était le pastiche du leur et que le citer dans toute sa candeur, c'était le sûr moyen de le persifler! Ils ont vu dans leur caricature un portrait sérieux de l'auteur et lui ont tendu la main en lui disant: Merci, tu penses comme nous!
>
> Mais non, je ne pense point comme vous, messeigneurs! Voilà trois jours que je le répète du matin au soir à ceux qui viennent me complimenter, et leur procession ne discontinue pas. (. . .)
>
> Et j'ai beau leur crier: "Mais messieurs, je n'ai rien voulu dire de tout cela! Il est une façon de railler qui consiste à reprendre dans sa simplicité naïve tel argument qu'il vous plaît de persifler, et dont l'unique énonciation soulèvera une explosion de rire générale. J'ai plaisanté de la sorte, croyez-le. Gardez vos compliments, je les renie. Vous êtes mille fois trop bons et j'ai dit entièrement l'opposé de ce dont vous me félicitez. Au fond, je ne crois pas qu'il y ait dans Hugo un vers de dix-neuf pieds. Sincèrement, j'estime que dire: *Sommes-nous des artistes?* c'est dire: Nous sommes des crétins. Sérieusement, je pense qu'un laquais peut aimer une reine et que don Salluste est un démon. (. . .) Tout ce que j'ai dit, c'était par ironie: et vous l'eussiez mieux senti, du reste, si mon article n'avait pas été coupé en deux au moment d'être mis sous presse."

Well might he laugh, but his return to the fray was an admission that a good part of the joke was on him. Whatever he had intended his article on *Ruy Blas* to achieve, apart from the entertainment of his friends, whether he had expected it to anger the Philistines, or simply puzzle them, he had certainly not anticipated that it would cause them to hail him as their young leader and spokesman, and in particular as the arch-enemy of the poet he most admired. For Hugo's sake—as well as his own since his anonymity was apparently a fiction—he must clear up the misunderstanding and declare his opinions in plain language.

The penance he imposed on himself as part of that duty was severe. The posture of an ironist obliged to return to his irony and explain it is a mortifying one,[14] and the penitent made it more so by lecturing his readers on the mechanism of the rhetorical device he had so signally failed to manipulate competently. So at least it would seem, but Mallarmé nevertheless contrived to turn the situation finally to his advantage. The fault he so honourably confessed to lay, he confidently assumed, simply in his underestimating the depth of his readers' ignorance and the thickness of their skulls. (Similarly, when, in later years, his poems were found obscure, he would put the blame on his contemporaries who, he said, could not read.)[15] And to justify that belief he succeeded in making of a plain re-statement of the facts of the case better satire than the elaborate fiction of the previous week had proved to be. For in the end it was the procession of admiring callers, the mistaken Philistines, who came out of the incident worst:

> C'est en vain: ils ne croient pas qu'on ait pu les tourner en dérision, et voient leurs idées si délaissées qu'ils se jettent au cou de quiconque s'en déguise un moment, même pour en ridiculiser le masque, et l'étouffent de leurs embrassements plutôt que d'avouer qu'on s'est moqué d'eux!

On the other hand it was a further mistake, and a disappointment no doubt for M. Besombes and his company, to don the same disguise again for a farcical conclusion. They would be looking for a warmer farewell from Mallarmé than a gratuitous persistence in what must by that time seem a tedious, pedantic, rather childish game:

> Je ne dis rien de la soirée de dimanche et j'ai deux motifs de silence: d'abord je crains qu'un article trop long ne soit élagué comme celui de samedi, et puis . . . je ne sais vraiment de quelle façon m'exprimer pour être compris!
>
> Puisqu'on entend l'opposé de ce que j'ai l'intention de dire, et que si j'écris ironiquement l'on me lit sans sourciller, aujourd'hui que je n'ai plus à railler, le moyen d'être pris au sérieux, est d'être ironique.
>
> Essayons: Mme Léon-Marc a été détestable (on lira pleine de poésie, ce que je pense et ce qui est).
>
> M. Besombes n'a pas montré son talent habituel (ce qui signifiera qu'il l'a parfaitement montré).

Je ne dirai pas que M. Léon-Marc a été supérieur comme il l'est toujours, parce qu'on croirait qu'il ne l'a pas été.

Enfin, on n'a pas joué l'*Ange de Minuit*.

The opportunity to make amends to the actors was afforded some two and a half months later. The company were back at Sens and Mallarmé took up his pen again on their behalf. The fourth and last of his articles of dramatic criticism in *Le Sénonais* appeared on 19 March 1862, under the title '*La Milanaise et l'Autrichien*, Drame en trois actes et en prose par M. Léon-Marc'. It was signed 'S.M.' and since it figures therefore in the Pléiade *Œuvres complètes*[16] it is relatively well known. When compared with the earlier articles, written on what is in the main the same subject before the young author's life and prospects had so radically changed, it bears witness to altered social attitudes, less parochial than hitherto and to that extent more mature, less impudently self-assertive too, though hardly more modest. From the literary point of view the article is written more responsibly and with much more decorum than the second and the third. In comparison with the first, on the other hand, it suffers from too close a resemblance to it, in its substance and chief intention, without however the original eager impulse and consequent spontaneity and warmth of feeling. It is the opening theme of the article that invites us to suppose that it was written on the occasion of the company's return from a tour. The strolling players are hailed as wandering heroes in a society that denies art and artists their due recognition:

Un théâtre aujourd'hui: une grange, demain, après-demain: vingt planches sur quatre tonneaux. Il faut jouer, jouer toujours, et jouer partout: voilà la vie extérieure.

Pénétrez dans la vie intérieure. On essuie son fard, et l'on n'a pas le temps d'être soi-même avant d'en remettre de nouveau. Ruy Blas de demain, cours à la répétition.—J'étudie.—Ruy Blas de demain, pense à coudre du jais sur ton pourpoint noir.—J'étudie.—Ruy Blas de demain, n'oublie point ton inepte lever de rideau.—J'étudie.

Et voyez qu'il ne se plaint pas de ce que ce morcellement fatal de son existence le prive de vivre, mais de ce qu'il l'empêche d'étudier. Vivre, il a rayé ce mot du livre de ses espérances.

The 'provincial Hamlet' theme, so convincing in the earlier

version, is here much romanticized. The item 'Vingt planches sur quatre tonneaux' reminds one of the fairground stage of seventeenth-century engravings, and the reply 'J'étudie' would be recognized by M. Besombes and some of his companions as an allusion to their famous predecessor Fléchelles / Gaultier-Garguille, the *tragédien-farceur* of the 1620s. It was said of him that when some nobleman whose favour he enjoyed asked him to dine with him he would sometimes decline, saying that he was studying his part.[17]

This example from the heroic age of the French theatre had tempted the critic into a heightened eloquence that went beyond both the merits of its object and his own belief. It has a hollow sound, but it helps him to direct his readers' attention to his real subject, Léon Marc and his drama. Also one notes that the vagueness favoured by the turgid style allows him to pay homage to his fellow-poet without expressly praising his poetry. Mallarmé was already cultivating the art of so disguising a non-commital comment that it would be taken as the warmest praise. He had not however mastered it yet, and it is unlikely that Léon Marc himself would be altogether pleased with the passage in honour of his verse:

Il est pourtant des comédiens qui font plus que de vivre: qui rêvent. Oui, j'en sais qui pensent, qui chantent. Je n'examine pas leur pensée ou leur chanson: eussent-ils filtré la poésie de Legouvé ou souri du bout des lèvres la prose de M. Laya,[18] je leur dirais sérieusement: "Il est beau, quand tant d'êtres ont un feu et un fauteuil à eux, lesquels n'ont jamais pensé, qu'un de vous, chers errants, ramasse la lyre oubliée."

Que sera-ce donc si leur œuvre est une œuvre dont tout poëte à bon droit s'enorgueillirait? Et chacun sait qu'un acteur de Rennes s'appelle Glatigny, comme chacun saura qu'un acteur de Sens s'appelle Léon Marc. Nous sortons de voir le drame de ce dernier (. . .)

The account of the play is sober and clear, and aims perhaps at emulating some of the qualities praised:

La prose nerveuse, colorée sobrement et raisonnée à la façon de Vacquerie (. . .): les idées larges et libres, et bien que palpitant d'actualité, s'isolant dédaigneusement dans la sérénité de l'abstraction.

Then comes the audience's turn. The critic might have

refrained from returning to his quarrel with the public, but no. He does, however, avoid the scornful jeers that the young rebel had aimed at all and sundry in his earlier pages. His hope of an appreciative reception of the play had not been fulfilled and he complained: 'une illusion de plus émigrée au pays bleu des rêves'. But he acknowledged that the hope had been unrealistic. The pit knows what it wants and what it is capable of enjoying: 'O prodigieux esprit du peuple français, né intelligent!' Nor indeed had all those present at the performance been lukewarm. He was not alone in applauding the author and bidding him have confidence in his gifts.

Mme Léon-Marc received her share of homage—a very literary share. Her place was elsewhere than at Sens:

> Elle porte en elle et jusque dans les plis de ses vêtements, une poésie mélancolique et passionnée. Pauvre Ophélie, à qui l'on fait chanter, au lieu de la chère ballade:
>
> *And will he not come again?*
>
> ces chœurs merveilleusement rythmés qui battent des ailes dans les vaudevilles de M. Scribe!

In the meantime Mallarmé's other friend Emmanuel des Essarts had claimed a good share of his attention by publishing, a week after Léon Marc's departure from Sens at the end of 1861, *Les Poésies parisiennes*. The volume was very well received,[19] and among the early reviews in its honour was one signed 'Stéphane Mallarmé'. It appeared in *Le Papillon* on 10 January 1862.[20] The publication of a collection of Des Essarts's poems, by Poulet-Malassis the publisher of Baudelaire's *Fleurs du mal* (in 1857 and 1861) and Banville's *Poésies* and *Odes funambulesques* (both in 1857), was quite an important literary event for fellow-poets of the young generation. From Mallarmé's personal point of view, therefore, the publication of his review in a magazine held in good esteem was of some consequence too.[21] Such a promising Paris début augured well at that juncture, when with Emmanuel's help he was laying his plans to become a writer.[22]

In commending *Les Poésies parisiennes* to the literary élite of Paris the self-conscious provincial was no doubt anxious to claim that he was a member of it. Hence perhaps, and also in order to seize the opportunity of one more tilt at the Philistines, the dubious though well-intentioned compliment paid to his new readers in the second paragraph:

je prierai humblement les lettrés de l'ouvrir [the volume of poems, that is],—eux seuls,—estimant le succès qu'il peut obtenir en leurs rangs clairsemés supérieur à la vogue que lui décernerait la foule.

A further, more elaborate manœuvre was found necessary by the reviewer, to put him at his ease with both his public and his subject. For though the task assigned to him was very much to his taste, it had a delicate aspect, in view of all that he owed Des Essarts and the warm friendship that was forming between them. In view also, on the other hand, of the fact that they did not hold the same ideas on poetry, and those of Des Essarts must receive due attention in the review. For in the discussions on realism in literature that were then at their height, the ebullient Emmanuel had not failed to make his position known. His place was on the 'sincerist' flank of the realist school, which he would have liked to rename 'l'école sincère'.[23] It was to pay homage to these views that another reviewer of his poems would write: 'Sa douleur est vraie, ses larmes sont sincères, et la sincérité, dans l'art, c'est le grand créateur du beau.'[24] To focus attention on another aspect of his theoretical pretentions, his modernism, Des Essarts had placed his collection under a double epigraph:

L'Idéal des choses vivantes. PHILOXÈNE BOYER.
Il y a une beauté et un héroïsme modernes.
CHARLES BAUDELAIRE.[25]

Mallarmé could not therefore ignore those pretensions in his review. On the other hand he could not oppose to them his own uncompromising idealism, for that would detract from his praise of those qualities for which a well-disposed critic could honestly (if without enthusiasm) express admiration: technical skill above all, not always guided by good judgement; self-possession, emotional and intellectual, candour in portraying Parisian society.[26] The problem was solved by means of an ingenious introductory paragraph. With the help of a jocular literary allusion (again to a celebrity of the early seventeenth century) the reviewer declared himself quite frankly a friend of the poet's and at the same time vowed he would be moderate in his praise:

Quand le don Quichotte du Permesse, Georges de Scudéry, mit en tête des poésies de son cher Théophile l'adorable cartel au lecteur que vous savez, chacun dit admirer l'amitié chevaleresque, mais se méfier singulièrement d'un livre prôné flamberge au vent. Puisqu'à mon tour il m'est donné de dire ce que je pense des *Poésies parisiennes* de mon ami Emmanuel des Essarts, je n'imiterai point l'inimitable Georges, en insinuant à coups d'épée que c'est là un volume incomparable. (. . .) Aussi ai-je remis la réclame au fourreau et consacré à ces vers ce qu'il serait ambitieux d'appeler une étude.[27]

The comparison was far-fetched even as a jest, but served the critic's purpose admirably. Under its cover he could beg leave to judge the poems according to the poet's intention and not, more austerely, 'd'après les seuls principes de l'art'. Not, that is—what else could the expression mean?—according to principles to which the critic might himself subscribe. These he could set modestly aside, and so he did. Nowhere in the whole article are Mallarmé's views on poetry expressed, or even referred to as such. Des Essarts's 'intentions' on the other hand are carefully formulated, in a style that gives them a very theoretical ring. The style even seems a shade ironical. Its pat, glib abstractness may be a reflection not only on des Essarts's aims in this volume but on his fondness for theorizing in the jargon of the time:

Les sentiments de la vie parisienne pris au sérieux[28] et vus à travers le prisme de la poésie, un idéal qui n'existe point par son propre rêve et soit le lyrisme de la réalité, telle est l'intention des *Poésies parisiennes*.

For this definition of the poet's aim the critic relies, he says, on the title of the collection and its double epigraph. It must surely contain echoes also of conversations he had had with his friend, and a desire on Des Essarts's part that he should give prominence to these intentions in his review. Once he has provided his definition of the poet's aim, the critic turns away from aesthetic principles and without more ado begins his appreciation of the poems themselves.[29]

Once engaged in writing about poetry for a select public of literati he is very much more at ease than he was several months earlier deputizing for the dramatic critic of *Le Sénonais*. His pleasure at the change is reflected in the style of his article, cordial and easy-flowing, with an occasional flourish of urbane preciosity. In substance, his review of the poems is appreciative rather than admiring, and even that degree of approbation is not attained without some effort. Reticence is a very marked feature of the whole account. In the quite long systematic description of the characteristic features of the volume, there is no other praise of poetic merits than a suave tribute (not unqualified) to the mastery of versification that it displays:

Pour la forme, le vers racinien marié au vers moderne, et d'où naît une coupe originale et parfois dramatique, une langue plus sculptée que peinte, avec des hardiesses savantes. Généralement une ampleur à outrance, si bien qu'on pourrait avancer en plaisantant qu'il est peu de vers qui ne soient assez vastes et assez frappés pour terminer à merveille un sonnet.[30]

So faint are the references to poetic values in the rest of the description that were it not for the occasional mention of 'le poëte' what is described might almost be a volume of short stories, or prose portraits like those in Banville's *Esquisses parisiennes*, to which (perhaps pointedly) the critic refers:

"A Paris, derrière le million qu'on ambitionne, il y a toujours une figure de femme qui sourit et qui vous appelle avec le geste délicieux des sirènes," a dit dans ses excellentes "Esquisses parisiennes", Théodore de Banville. Aussi l'amour règne-t-il en maître dans deux parties du volume, la première et la dernière, qu'on pourrait intituler, la vie amoureuse et la vie galante, et se glisse-t-il toujours dans les deux autres, qui sont un reflet de la vie mondaine (high-life) et de la vie artistique. Rarement il vient avec l'arc et le rire moqueur de Cupidon: il y représente la passion moderne. Le poëte analyse les blessures plus souvent qu'il ne joue avec le carquois: il chante moins des péronnelles d'éventail que des femmes. Et ce n'est pas l'amour seul, mais tous les sentiments qui sont pris au sérieux. Partout éclate quelque chose de sincère, et qui se possède: rien en l'air, rien de vaporeux. (. . .) Ce n'est pas à dire pourtant que ce livre n'ait son côté frivole; il eût été incomplet si le poëte ne l'avait enrubanné de strophes en falbalas, et ne s'était fait parfois le Watteau de la mode. Pour que sa muse fût une Parisienne, elle devait savoir parler chiffons au besoin, et chanter la ceinture régente et les petits chapeaux de velours azuline.[31]

The one unfavourable comment in this section is an ironical innuendo in its last paragraph:

Si le volume entier pouvait se résumer en quelques pièces, je dirais que la *Danse idéale* révèle le mieux le procédé du poëte qui s'élève d'une mazurka à des théories platoniciennes, que la *Nuit d'hiver* en donne le ton, et la *Parisienne de Watteau*, la couleur.

This allusion, surely derisive,[32] to Des Essarts's theoretical preoccupations is not the earliest indication that though the self-effacing reviewer has avoided criticizing overtly the aesthetic aim defined so carefully at the beginning of his article, a challenge may yet be in store. Readers who are familiar with Mallarmé's early correspondence may have noticed one such indication, and observed also that the divergence between the two young poets goes deeper than the niceties of fashionable literary theory. I refer to the recurrent use of the phrase 'prendre au sérieux' ('les sentiments de la vie parisienne pris au sérieux', 'ce n'est pas l'amour seul mais tous les sentiments qui sont pris au sérieux'). The significance of this phrase for Mallarmé in such a context will be clear for any reader who remembers a striking sentence in a letter that he wrote a few months later to Cazalis:

Pour moi qui n'ai jamais pu comprendre ce que c'étaient que les réalités de la vie et pour qui les gens qui prennent la vie au sérieux sont de vils animaux . . .[33]

When the warning note is sounded again, in the reference to Plato and the mazurka, the challenge is imminent. It takes the form of a confrontation between Des Essarts's basic aesthetic principle and that of the anti-realists or 'fantaisistes', according to whom it is on the imaginary, not the real, that poetry thrives. The encounter is artfully managed:

Le livre a donc réalisé son rêve, et su choisir, au milieu des brillantes et diverses qualités de l'auteur, celles seules qui lui convenaient, ce qui est immense. Ajoutons qu'il est quelques craintes que le titre: *Les Poésies parisiennes*, eût pu faire naître chez ceux qui ne connaissent pas Emmanuel des Essarts et qui se dissipent dès qu'on entr'ouvre le volume. Ainsi l'on avait à s'attendre, dans cette fantaisie moderne, à quelques reflets involontaires de Théodore de Banville; mais, dans les *Poésies parisiennes*, ce n'est plus cet idéal étincelant et moqueur et harcelant la réalité de sa flèche d'or, qui vous enivre dans les vers de ce divin maître: c'est un idéal sincère, s'élevant au-dessus du réel et le prenant au sérieux.

It is significant that the critic draws his contrast not between one abstract formula and another but between an abstract formula on the one hand, defining Des Essarts's intentions, and on the other a poetic practice, Banville's, which puts such formulas to shame. The shaft was the more telling as Des Essarts (who was willing to serve many masters)[34] considered himself to be one of Banville's disciples.[35]

It may be noted that Mallarmé's praise of Banville in his review bears interesting witness to a new aspect of his own development. Banville was for Mallarmé, apparently, what he would thereafter remain, a 'divine master' whose example did not so much teach as inspire. He suggests as much here. He will explain further in 'Symphonie littéraire', some three years later.[36]

It remained for the critic, before giving his final blessing, to venture such adverse criticisms as had occurred to him (after much searching, he said) 'pour ne pas marcher sur les traces de Scudéry, et pour cela uniquement'. Of the three faults he could point to, one was serious, and so far from being hard to find that he had already commented on it. It was the 'ampleur à outrance', about which he was now a little more explicit—to the point of impinging on 'les principes de l'art':

Certains vers parfois ont plus d'ampleur que la pensée qu'ils revêtent, et pourraient faire songer les médisants à un certain amour du beau vers, la pire des choses.

To which can be related the neighbouring observations:

Emmanuel des Essarts doit être fier d'avoir trouvé sa forme. Et cela, je crois qu'il le doit à sa sincérité: il n'a glané nulle part, il a semé chez lui. Ses croyances sont dans son livre et sa jeune expérience aussi.

For the truth is that friend Emmanuel thinks to transform into poetry, to 'lyricize', simply by putting them into verse, the commonplace reality, everyday happenings, thoughts, imaginings, sentiments, and impressions which constitute his own conventional experience of life in Paris.

The second complaint on the other hand, that Pierrot in the poem entitled 'Le poème de la Pantomime' is made 'un peu trop charmant', seems perfunctory. The third is flippant, but not pointless:

Un dernier reproche, mais un grand: je n'ai jamais compris qu'un poëte médît des blondes. Je sais que la Muse d'Emmanuel des Essarts doit être brune: les brunes ont seules cette vivacité et seules peuvent inspirer ces vers frappés et nerveux. Mais l'idéal de la femme,— c'est-à-dire d'une des facettes de la beauté, ce diamant,—n'est pas la brune. Eve était blonde; Vénus blonde. La blondeur, c'est l'or, la lumière, la richesse, le rêve, le nimbe!

Mallarmé's readers would accept these observations as the ritual tribute to blond beauty expected from a new contributor to *Le Papillon*, in honour of its editor, the comely blond Madame Olympe Audouard.[37]

The general assessment of the poet's achievement with which the article ends probably refers back to the epigraph from Baudelaire: 'Il y a donc une beauté et un héroïsme modernes'. The critic recognizes, as the most manifest virtue of the poems, their modernity. But in this virtue is no glory: of beauty and heroism there is no trace. The poems are modern only in the tamest sense: the poet has chosen contemporary Paris as his subject. He has 'felt' that Parisian life could be idealized. So says the critic, but not that Des Essarts was right in that belief, much less that he has proved it true:

Il a senti que toute époque peut être *lyrisée*, et a compris qu'on pouvait chercher l'idéal hors de l'antiquité, du moyen âge, de la Renaissance ou du siècle Pompadour, dans la consciencieuse étude de son âme et dans la franche observation de son temps.

Thus is an article that is interesting above all as an exercise in critical diplomacy brought to a diplomatic conclusion.

Mallarmé followed up his review of Des Essarts's poems in *Le Papillon* with a revised version of it for a different public. It appeared on 22 March (four days after its author's twentieth birthday) in *Le Sénonais*, signed 'S.M.' like the article on *La Milanaise et l'Autrichien* in the previous number. It is not a rehash but an account of the poems written for less disinterested and also less practised readers. It also reflects new circumstances, very propitious to the friendship to which at Sens it would eloquently testify. Not only had the young schoolmaster's advice and support been crucial in his protégé's successful contest with the Desmolins, but already his sponsorship had introduced him to the public that an ambitious young poet needed to reach. *Le Papillon* had published his sonnet 'Placet', and *L'Artiste* another, 'Le Sonneur', together with a fragment of 'Le Guignon'.[38] The poet Stéphane Mallarmé was no longer unknown, and he could claim some part in the successful launching of Des Essarts's collection of poems.

There were good reasons therefore for the jubilation in the tone of the reviewer, when he exhorted friends and acquaintances at Sens to follow the example of the best people and enjoy the creations of the talented Parisian living in their midst:

Comme notre vie n'est qu'un désir permanent de tremper curieusement les lèvres dans la coupe de toutes les sensations,[39] après m'être enivré de cette volupté de proclamer des vers amis la veille de leur naissance,[40] je veux savourer celle de les applaudir au milieu de leur marche rayonnante, cependant que l'éditeur Malassis monnaie en écus leur étoile. Une troisième volupté serait de les défendre sous forme d'oraison funèbre:[41] malheureusement elle me sera refusée avec les *Poésies parisiennes*, car voici que ces Mabs et ces Titanias, vêtues en bridalines, font craquer triomphalement dans tous les sentiers du Tendre, leurs bottines à lacets rouges et tachent leurs gants Carimys à toutes les mûres du Permesse, folles de jeunesse et d'espérance. (. . .) Il y a des provinciales en la Chaussée d'Antin, comme il y a des Parisiennes à cent lieues de Paris, et nous ne sommes qu'à trente lieues. Ainsi ces Poésies peuvent sortir de la Chaussée d'Antin et du Faubourg Saint-Germain et prendre un billet de coupé pour tout pays où luit un coin de bleu. Elles se feront aimer à Sens aussi bien qu'à Paris, d'autant plus que, depuis l'extrême facilité des communications, les petits chapeaux de velours azuline, l'amour et la pantomime qu'elles chantent ont pu parvenir jusqu'ici.

The most notable difference from the early version, apart from the boisterous tone, lies in the marked change of emphasis, already apparent in the opening paragraph. The insistence on the poet's sincerity, reflecting a rather esoteric and perhaps too serious-sounding, theoretical preoccupation, has disappeared completely and with it the very word *sincère*. So on the other hand have the references to the predominance of love situations, 'la vie amoureuse et la vie galante', which might compromise the respectability by which the young schoolmaster set great store. Instead, the more frivolous aspects of Paris life are stressed, as witness the passage just quoted, and the literary quality that is featured now as outstanding in the collection is its originality. The reviewer appears to offer his apologies to the poet for saying too little on this subject in *Le Papillon*:

Les *Poésies parisiennes* sont évidemment le volume de vers le plus fort qui ait paru depuis les derniers chefs-d'œuvre du siècle, *les Fleurs du Mal* et *les Odes funambulesques*.[42] C'est, en outre, le plus original. J'insiste sur ce trait que je n'avais pas suffisamment éclairé dans le portrait que je fis d'elles autre part, il y a deux mois.[43]

Ironically, when he comes to 'sketch the most prominent features of that originality' he does not state in positive terms wherein it consists. He simply quotes from his previous 'portrait' the formal definition of the poet's intention, and that part of his critical analysis in the first article that is free from technicalities and also from all reproach. He does however reply to the opinions expressed in some reviews regarding Des Essarts's imitation of other poets. His defence is interesting, for two reasons. First, it allows Mallarmé to repeat, with a little clarification, the comparison with Banville:

Des esprits fort savants en choses poétiques annonceront, sans sourciller, qu'on y imite Gautier parce qu'on y rime merveilleusement: d'autres, qu'il y a là un reflet de Théodore de Banville parce que notre moderne Aristophane qui décoche contre la Réalité la flèche d'or de son arc divin, l'Idéal, fait juste le contraire d'Em. des Essarts, lequel prend le Réel au sérieux et le *lyrise*.

Secondly, he takes the opportunity also, instead of stoutly denying that Des Essarts ever imitates, to point out that critics are wrong who deny a young poet the right to imitate his masters. He expresses some ideas of his own on the subject:

Il eût fallu, sans doute, au gré de ces Messieurs, s'affranchir des formes de nos maîtres, et dédaigner leurs innovations; à ce compte, après le raisin, il n'était plus permis au lilas de fleurir, car le rythme de la grappe était inventé.

Pour le fond, ce livre est entièrement neuf. Je sais que les mêmes esprits, s'ils voient perler au bout d'une touffe de vers, ces douces larmes où luit un sourire, murmureront les noms de Musset, même de Murger (deux faibles sympathies de l'auteur, pourtant), et qu'ils découvriront ingénument que notre poëte, quand il s'élève, vole dans le lumineux sillage d'Hugo, toujours par cette même raison judicieuse qu'un homme ne pourra plus rire en pleurant, et donner un coup d'aile et être lui.

Tous les grands maîtres antiques et modernes sont des plagiaires d'Homère et Homère est un plagiaire de Dieu.

The fondness for sustained allusions to the literature of past centuries, of which examples have already been noted, prompts a graceful concluding paragraph on the *Poésies parisiennes*:

Mieux qu'un livre de Paris ou de Sens, je dirais qu'elles sont le livre du premier printemps. Ronsard, parfumé de roses sauvages, se lit le long des haies où gazouille Avril:[44] le volume d'Em. des Essarts autour duquel voltige l'odeur des fleurs citadines doit se lire quand vient mars, dans la chambre encore, en rêvant dans le fauteuil d'hiver qu'on a roulé jusqu'à la fenêtre ensoleillée.

Nous sommes en mars.

Between that month of March and his departure for London in November, Mallarmé published one other piece of prose, an article whose dual heading seems to promise others to follow in a series, though in fact none did: *Hérésies artistiques: L'Art pour tous*.[45] It appeared on 15 September in *L'Artiste*,[46] an honour it may have owed to the favourable opinion that Coligny the deputy editor had formed, earlier that year, of its author's promise as a poet,[47] and to the good offices of their mutual friend Emmanuel des Essarts. That Coligny was very favourably disposed towards Des Essarts's young friend is clear from the contents and tone of his letter of acceptance, preserved among Mallarmé's papers. When lightened of some indifferent and not altogether legible pleasantries, it reads:

Mon cher Poète et mon cher Ami, Vous êtes charmant de m'adresser votre portrait. Je vous rendrai cette très-affectueuse politesse aussitôt que j'aurai un nouvel exemplaire des miens. (. . .)

Vos *Hérésies artistiques* m'ont semblé justes et originales tout à la fois. Je les ai donné[e]s ès mains d'Arsène Houssaye, qui les a gracieusement accueilli[e]s; et nous allons les voir paraître instantanément.

Écrivez souvent, puisque vous écrivez bien.

Je suis bien content de savoir mon ami Emmanuel des Essarts à côté de vous. Il avait besoin d'un compagnon de cœur et d'esprit. Vous êtes celui-là. Je serai très flatté que vous soyez le mien de plus près: le temps en viendra.

Déjà cet été nous nous pourrions voir. Je m'en réjouis indiciblement.

Veuillez dire à Emmanuel que j'ai reçu ses vers ce matin. J'avais déjà placé son *André Chénier* dans le *prélecteur* [?] *tiroir* de *L'Artiste*, ce tiroir féerique qu'il connaît bien et où vous sommeillez aussi, mais pas pour longtemps. Il n'y a que les élus qui en franchissent le bouton.

Notre feuilleton de la *Presse* n'a pas eu de chance. Les affaires entre Arsène Houssaye et le sieur Peyrat sont au plus mal. J'expliquerai tout ce drame à Emmanuel, de vive voix, à sa prochaine venue dedans Paris. (.. . .)

Adieu mon cher poète. Tout à vous d'âme.

Charles Coligny.

Si vous avez quelques sonnets, envoyez-les-moi pour Dieppe.

Écrivez-moi souvent, mais veuillez m'excuser toujours si je reste huit jours sans prendre la plume. Emmanuel, défends-moi![48]

To critical readers of 'L'Art pour tous' today it may seem surprising that even with such editorial favour it was judged worthy of publication in that well-established and highly respected magazine. More surprising still, however, is the fate that awaited it there. For it was to remain undisturbed, escaping completely, it would seem, the notice of literary historians and critics, long after the name over which it appeared had become famous. It was not until 1940, nearly half a century after the poet's death, that Émilie Noulet came upon it and republished the complete text in the book that established her as a leading authority in her chosen field, *L'Œuvre poétique de Stéphane Mallarmé*.[49] Since when, 'L'Art pour tous' has attracted considerable attention as being (it seems to be fairly generally agreed) a precocious expression of ideas and intentions that were to be the basis of its author's poetic theory and practice during the years of his maturity. It was presented in that light by Mme Noulet:

Pour trouver dans un langage à découvert, préfiguré, tout Mallarmé, avec sa passion véritable, ses intentions et ses méthodes, c'est *l'Art pour tous*, c'est ce jeune texte qu'il faut interroger. Rendons-lui la lumière.

Hâtons-nous de surprendre, à l'état naissant, une pensée qui se voudra bientôt inaccessible; à l'état irréfléchi, une doctrine qui s'ignore en tant que doctrine.[50]

If allowance is made for an enthusiasm that was not unwarranted, this welcome to the document newly retrieved does not seriously overstate its interest for students of Mallarmé. The Pléiade editors, who in 1945 included it among Mallarmé's *Proses de jeunesse*, hailed it likewise as 'un précieux témoignage, et surprenant, de la précocité de ses convictions artistiques'.[51] It was clear that 'L'Art pour tous' was a document to which students of Mallarmé must pay serious attention, but its misadventures were not over. By the oddest coincidence, it has been treated as if it had been recovered in two parts, available for examination separately, rather than together. Two studies of 'L'Art pour tous', each by an eminent Mallarmé scholar, are at the disposal of students today. One, published in 1948, is by Henri Mondor.[52] The other, which appeared five years later, is by Guy Michaud.[53] Were it not that the earlier of the two appears to be little known, while the other has had far more interested readers than Mallarmé's article itself, they might be fairly regarded as complementary to each other. For while the one contains only a fleeting (though judicious) reference to the first part of the article and concentrates on the rest, the other deals exclusively with the opening paragraphs, ignoring completely the remaining four-fifths or so of the text.

In the new appraisal that I shall attempt of the whole, due account will of course be taken of the opinions of both these critics, as of others who have touched upon one aspect or another of the article. My own point of view will however be nearer to Henri Mondor's than to Guy Michaud's in one important respect. In accordance with the general aim of this volume, my concern will be to understand the document, and where necessary interpret it, as a product of Mallarmé's twenty-first year, written in the conditions of that time.[54] I shall not seek for a foreshadowing in it of what was to come later in his career. If I do on occasion make use of analogies with his more mature writings, it will be rather for the opposite purpose, of understanding the early texts better.

HÉRÉSIES ARTISTIQUES: L'ART POUR TOUS.—The title itself announces that the author approaches his subject from an 'art for art's sake' viewpoint, and with one of the leaders of that movement very particularly in mind. The literati who perused it in September 1862 might remember that *L'Artiste* had published, three years before, the first of Baudelaire's two essays on Gautier, the arch-priest of 'l'art pour l'art' in France.[55] It was there that Baudelaire, paraphrasing Poe's 'The Poetic Principle' and quoting from his own *Notes nouvelles sur Edgar Poe*, had proclaimed:

Des hérésies étranges se sont glissées dans la critique littéraire. Je ne sais quelle lourde nuée, venue de Genève, de Boston ou de l'enfer, a intercepté les beaux rayons du soleil de l'esthétique. (. . .) Il est permis quelquefois, je présume, de se citer soi-même, surtout pour éviter de se paraphraser. Je répéterai donc: "Il est une autre hérésie (. . .) (. . .) une erreur qui a la vie plus dure, [more resistant, that is, than 'l'hérésie de la longueur et de la dimension' or what Poe calls 'the idea that, to merit in poetry, prolixity is indispensable']

Baudelaire continues:

je veux parler de l'hérésie de l'enseignement, laquelle comprend comme corollaires inévitables, les hérésies de la *passion*, de la *vérité* et de la *morale*. Une foule de gens se figurent que le but de la poésie est un enseignement quelconque, qu'elle doit tantôt fortifier la conscience, tantôt perfectionner les mœurs, tantôt enfin démontrer quoi que ce soit d'utile . . . La Poésie, pour peu qu'on veuille descendre en soi-même, rappeler ses souvenirs d'enthousiasme, n'a pas d'autre but qu'Elle-même. (. . .) La poésie ne peut pas, sous peine de mort ou de déchéance, s'assimiler à la science ou à la morale; elle n'a pas la Vérité pour objet; elle n'a qu'Elle-même."[56]

There is no doubt, and ample confirmation will be found in Mallarmé's article, that its general heading refers to this passage on literary 'heresies'. It thus serves as a courteous bow in the direction of Baudelaire, the poetic theorist, from a young writer who had more than once expressed his admiration for *Les Fleurs du mal*, and was about to do so again in even more flattering terms.[57] For those readers of *L'Artiste* who enjoyed literary wranglings the heading would derive some piquancy (as indeed it acquires a sharper interest today), from its conjunction with the title 'L'Art pour tous'. For in this coupling, a clearly recognizable Baudelairian term is used to reject a doctrine generally known to have the blessing of Victor Hugo, the royalist turned republican, the prophet of Progress. It was a doctrine that had been propagated very effectively on Hugo's behalf by Auguste Vacquerie, particularly in his *Profils et Grimaces*, published six years before.[58]

The first section of the article thus heralded is written in a decidedly rhetorical style. It is, I have no doubt, the section that P. O. Walzer had in mind when he referred perceptively to 'L'Art pour tous' as 'cet intéressant morceau de bravoure'.[59] Not an earnest 'manifesto', to use Mme Noulet's term, but something rather more showy, a 'bravura'. (In quoting the article, I shall use italics, to distinguish it from other texts quoted.)

Toute chose sacrée et qui veut demeurer sacrée s'enveloppe de mystère. Les religions se retranchent à l'abri d'arcanes dévoilés au seul prédestiné: l'art a les siens.

La musique nous offre un example. Ouvrons à la légère Mozart, Beethowen [sic] *ou Wagner, jetons sur la première page de leur œuvre un œil indifférent, nous sommes pris d'un religieux étonnement à la vue de ces processions macabres de signes sévères, chastes, inconnus. Et nous refermons le missel vierge d'aucune pensée profanatrice.*

J'ai souvent demandé pourquoi ce caractère nécessaire a été refusé à un seul art, au plus grand. Celui-ci est sans mystère contre les curiosités hypocrites, sans terreur contre les impiétés, ou sous le sourire et la grimace de l'ignorant et de l'ennemi.

Je parle de la poésie. Les Fleurs du mal, *par exemple, sont imprimées avec des caractères dont l'épanouissement fleurit à chaque aurore les plates-bandes d'une tirade utilitaire,*[60] *et se vendent dans des livres blancs et noirs, identiquement pareils à ceux qui débitent de la prose du vicomte du Terrail ou des vers de M. Legouvé.*

Ainsi les premiers venus entrent de plein-pied dans un chef-d'œuvre, et depuis qu'il y a des poëtes, il n'a pas été inventé, pour l'écartement des importuns, une langue immaculée,—des formules hiératiques dont l'étude aride aveugle le profane et aiguillonne le patient fatal;—et ces intrus tiennent en façon de carte d'entrée une page de l'alphabet où ils ont appris à lire!

O fermoirs d'or des vieux missels! ô hiéroglyphes inviolés des rouleaux de papyrus![61]

This introductory passage, if my reading of it is correct, is characterized by an incongruity between form and content, deliberately sustained. What is asserted with such ostentatious eloquence is not written in good earnest. A close scrutiny will show, I believe, that the author is playing a game.

It starts quietly. The opening paragraph is rhetorically impressive enough and has sufficient vague plausibility to be read as a promising start to a serious argument. The first proposition, according to which everything that is holy covers itself in mystery, is not self-evident but would surprise none of the article's first readers. As the expression of a reasonable opinion or observation it would pass.[62] The less abstract statement to the same effect that follows would seem more dubious. Which religions does the writer refer to? Some such we know of, indeed, practised in far-off lands or past ages, but the one that he and they know best and which also tells of mysteries does not appear to hide behind them, and one wonders who the 'prédestinés' are to whom alone the holy secrets are revealed?[63] 'Art has its arcana': the implication is clear—'Art, that religion . . .' A common enough claim among believers in art for art's sake.[64] The general bias of the article, suggested in the title, is thus confirmed.

But the introduction has to play a separate part, and a curious part it proves to be. The case that it argues is nonsensical, and known by its exponent to be so. Music, painting, and statuary—the other arts—are hedged around (he says) by secrets that protect them from all but the predestined, which poetry is not. What is said of music, by way of sole illustration, sufficient it would seem for the 'other arts' in general, is absurd. In serried ranks the breves and quavers and demi-semi-quavers of a musical score may seem bizarre and even forbidding to unaccustomed eyes, but it surely cannot reasonably be maintained that they keep the art of music secret from all but the elect. They rather serve the opposite purpose of providing a language for its transmission that all who will, the world over, may learn to understand. And, just as the same black type, printed on a white page, is used for Baudelaire's poems as for those of Legouvé (which it was fashionable to refer to as the *ne plus ultra* of unpoetic verse), so the signs used to record a Beethoven sonata serve also to represent the melody and accompaniment of the most vulgar music-hall song. Also, and more to the point, the concert-halls of France (like the art-galleries) were no more closed to the public than Crépet's anthology *Les Poètes français* or a copy of *Les Fleurs du mal*—as is half-admitted later in the article.[65] And what a suspension of disbelief was required of the readers of *L'Artiste*, if they were to entertain for one moment the notion that only musicians or painters born and bred ever ventured to express an opinion on Wagner or discuss the latest Courbet.[66] On the other hand, the idea of a secret (international?) language known only to true poets, used only for true poetry and for ever immaculate, is patently, at best, a very idle fancy.[67]

What then? Were the readers of the article to enjoy this preliminary discourse as a kind of jester's paradox? Or to take it as an expression of emotion, after which reason would have its say?[68] The critic today is left in doubt, and wonders whether the author was not making in *L'Artiste* the mistake he had made in *Le Sénonais*, when he so misjudged the effect of his elaborate irony that he had to write another article to explain it.[69] But his purpose was this time more devious. For however much of the artful dissembling the readers were expected to see through, the main object of the introduction was intended to be hidden. It had to do with the title which, though well chosen to suit *L'Artiste*, had the defect of not being true. The author knew that his subject was not and could not be (because he was not competent to attempt it) an artistic heresy, art for all, but only a poetic heresy, poetry for all. The discrepancy had to be glossed over, and it is to that task that the opening paragraphs appear to be surreptitiously devoted. If the young poet declared that the other arts, 'music, painting, and statuary', were not subject to the interferences that were the bane of his own, this opinion might seem to entitle him to relegate them quietly to the background, and concern himself with poetry alone.

It is thus that I understand his declaration. The obvious weakness of my interpretation is that it is irreconcilable with the one so generally accepted, sketched by Mme Noulet,[70] adopted by Guy Michaud in his *Message du symbolisme* (vol. i, 1947),[71] and summarized by him succinctly in the following paragraph of *Mallarmé, l'homme et l'œuvre* (1953):

Article pourtant capital entre tous, puisqu'on y trouve comme la clef de son œuvre. Sous le titre *Hérésie artistique: l'Art pour tous*, Mallarmé, allant plus loin que les théoriciens de l'art pour l'art, part d'une idée fort ingénieuse, qu'il développe suivant une rigoureuse logique. "Toute chose sacrée et qui veut demeurer sacrée", constate-t-il d'abord, "s'enveloppe de mystère." Or, de même que la religion, l'art est sacré. Et, de fait, certains arts comme la musique emploient des signes sévères qui les rendent mystérieux au profane. La musique a ses arcanes. *Pourquoi donc la poésie n'aurait-elle pas les siens?* Il faut absolument, pense Mallarmé, ôter de l'opinion commune l'idée que la poésie authentique peut être lue par tous, sans préparation, sans culture, au même titre que les vers de M. Legouvé ou la prose du vicomte du Terrail. Il est indispensable de lui rendre sa dignité, de la préserver de toute admiration facile, vague et bête. Et, pour cela, il faut *en rendre l'accès difficile*. Or il y a des précédents.

O fermoirs d'or des vieux missels! ô hiéroglyphes inviolés des rouleaux de papyrus!

Pourquoi ne pas restituer à la poésie le caractère sacré qui, au Moyen âge, comme chez certains peuples antiques, n'en permettait l'accès qu'aux seuls initiés?

Il faut donc une poésie *fermée*, dont le sens se dérobe d'abord au lecteur.[72]

In large part, this is a more positive, more precisely explicit restatement of Mme Noulet's view on the contents of the article, and in that sense it has her backing. In one detail only is there a significant departure from the account she had given. It is the comment 'allant plus loin que les théoriciens de l'art pour l'art'. In an earlier work, M. Michaud had, like Mme Noulet, represented the ideas expressed in 'L'Art pour tous' as Mallarmé's own response to the situation ('à cet âge d'ivresse personnelle', insisted Mme Noulet).[73] But now he appears to take note of certain remarks, partly favourable to his own observations, in Paul Bénichou's searching study of 'Mallarmé et le public', first published in 1949:[74]

Il est remarquable que l'idée de la nécessaire obscurité apparaisse pour la première fois chez Mallarmé dans un texte où sont surtout en cause les relations du poète et du public. Il ne faudrait pas croire trop vite que l'obscurité mallarméenne soit le simple résultat d'un chiffrage destiné à écarter le vulgaire; (. . .). La poésie mallarméenne, si elle n'avait d'autre obscurité que celle d'un dédaigneux rébus, serait bien peu de chose. Si donc ce texte [i.e. 'L'Art pour tous'] a un mérite, c'est moins de définir la poétique de l'énigme que de la faire sortir d'un conflit entre le poète et la société, rétablissant par là un lien étroit entre l'œuvre de Mallarmé et des positions de pensée largement répandues au temps de sa jeunesse.[75]

In what direction Mallarmé may be said to 'go further' than the leaders of the art for art's sake movement is a question to be considered later. For the rest, the interpretation I have proposed of his introduction or prologue implies a rejection of

M. Michaud's. What he describes as a strictly logical argument I have explained as a rhetorical subterfuge. I have still to examine, however, the conclusion to which in his account the logic leads, the decision to fashion and practise a hermetic style of writing that will guard his future poems against the Philistines: 'Et, pour cela, *il faut en rendre l'accès difficile.* (. . .) Il faut donc une poésie *fermée* dont le sens se dérobe d'abord au lecteur.' It is of course possible that these ideas were in Mallarmé's mind (one notes the words: 'Il faut absolument, pense Mallarmé') but they are not expressed in his article—whose general contention will be found to be, more modestly, that poets should not make matters worse than they are. M. Michaud seems to extract the more radical conclusion from the double exclamation of nostalgic regret which brings the introduction to a histrionic end, and which he interprets thus: 'Pourquoi ne pas restituer à la poésie le caractère sacré qui, au Moyen âge, comme chez certains peuples antiques, n'en permettait l'accès qu'aux seuls initiés?'[76] In my judgement, to see in missals with their golden clasps, and in ancient impenetrable scrolls, a direct reference to ages in which poetry was (allegedly) revered as sacred, is not to read the text but to force it, and rearrange history to boot.[77]

This attempt to refute a widely held belief, concerning a question of such interest—the genesis of Mallarmé's obscurity—would be incomplete if it did not consider that belief briefly from the point of view of its adherents, retrospectively. If Mallarmé had indeed, in his later writings, given serious reason to suppose that he had made his poems obscure in order to protect them against the Philistines, the assertion that the intention to do so was formed and expressed in his twenty-first year would not in itself be implausible. But such is not the case. What he states in 'Le Mystère dans les Lettres', the essay of 1896 to which Mme Noulet refers us,[78] is something very different. It even includes explicit disapproval of deliberate obscurity such as the author of 'L'Art pour tous' is said by M. Michaud to have committed himself to, and planned. This is what, in his mid-fifties, Mallarmé declares:

Tout écrit, extérieurement à son trésor, doit, par égard envers ceux dont il emprunte, après tout, pour un objet autre, le langage, présenter, avec les mots, un sens même indifférent: on gagne de détourner l'oisif, charmé que rien ne l'y concerne, à première vue.

Salut, exact, de part et d'autre—[79]

A 'writing', that is—and the context makes it clear that what is referred to is an artistic writing, a poem whether in prose or verse—should be readable at two levels, corresponding to the 'double état de la parole, brut ou immédiat ici, là essentiel'. Serving, in other words, the practical function of communication on the one hand and the creation of poetic beauty on the other.[80] A poem should offer enough meaning at the common level to satisfy common readers, who can then go their ways and leave the poetic beauty undefiled. For it is the poet's art, the inner treasure, not the poem's surface meaning, that is sacred and should be kept secret from all but the elect. Thus the notion that to defeat the Philistines the poet can make his poems obscure 'at first sight' is found neither in 'L'Art pour tous' nor in 'Le Mystère dans les lettres'. It would be premature however to conclude that Mme Noulet was mistaken when she wrote: 'Sans doute retrouve-t-on trace des idées que "L'Art pour tous" contient dans *le Mystère dans les Lettres*'.[81] On the contrary, confirmation of that statement is not hard to find.

His equivocal prologue over and done with, and having duly whittled down his commitment in the course of it, from the arts in general to the art of poetry, Mallarmé seems ready to address himself to his subject, one that is not new to him, the Philistines. His style becomes markedly more sober, as analysis and sensible (if partisan) polemic argument take over from fantasy and show. The particular target chosen is the heresy 'poetry for all', seen in a concrete topical guise: Mallarmé's main purpose seems to be to answer the case made for the teaching of poetry at school by Auguste Vacquerie, under the heading 'L'Enseignement littéraire' in his *Profils et Grimaces*.[82] One may even suspect him of considering himself, in this enterprise, the mouthpiece for Baudelaire that Vacquerie was for Hugo.[83] If that was not so, if he was addressing the poets of France in his own person and as in his own right, on the strength of his sonnet 'Placet' published in *Le Papillon*, and in *L'Artiste* 'Le Sonneur' and a fragment of 'Le Guignon', his manner would be presumptuous to an improbable degree.

However, the narrow definition I have given of his aim does not do full justice to this, the main section of his article. Its reader needs to be receptive also to other preoccupations, expressed incidentally but of considerable interest. Henri Mondor is, I believe, the one critic to accord them the attention they deserve. He does so in the chapter of literary biography already mentioned, the fourth in his *Histoire d'un Faune*. The following fragments are picked out from his discursive account in that chapter of the early influence of Baudelaire on Mallarmé. Disjointed though they are, they will illustrate more faithfully than would a summary the aspect of 'L'Art pour tous' to which Mondor attributes the greatest importance. He assesses as follows the testimony it affords concerning the impression made by Baudelaire the critic and aesthetic theorist—as distinct from the poet—on the mind of his young admirer:

Avant de songer à secouer cette influence brusquement prédominante des *Fleurs du Mal*, Mallarmé, sans devoir jamais cesser d'en reconnaître le profit, subit plus encore, entre sa vingtième et sa vingt-troisième année, l'exemple de l'esthéticien remarquable qu'avaient révélé, à un petit nombre de lecteurs, trois ou quatre importants écrits de Baudelaire. (. . .)

Il est un livre, en particulier, que Mallarmé lut très attentivement, en ses études de début, et dont on peut retenir bien des lignes à son sujet; c'est le *Théophile Gautier*, publié chez Poulet-Malassis par Ch. Baudelaire en 1859.[84] (. . .)

Le petit ouvrage de Baudelaire sur Théophile Gautier est un véritable manifeste. Mallarmé ne s'y trompa pas et il n'est pas difficile de retrouver, dans les richesses accumulées du livre, les passages qui l'émurent, peut-être le dirigèrent. (.. . . .) Ce qu'avaient d'adéquat à son esprit les observations de Baudelaire les dotait, à ses yeux, d'une irrésistible évidence. (. . .)

En 1862, venait de paraître, chez Hachette, un beau recueil de vers publié sous la direction d'Eugène Crépet. Sept notices de Baudelaire, sur quelques-uns de ses contemporains, pouvaient apprendre, à leurs suivants immédiats, le grand critique qu'il était et les chemins grâce à lui entrevus. Qu'il parlât de Victor Hugo, de Marceline Desbordes-Valmore, de Gautier, de Banville ou de Leconte de Lisle, ses aperçus étaient à la fois profonds et lumineux.[85] (. . .)

Pendant plusieurs années, Mallarmé fit de l'auteur des *Fleurs du Mal* son inspirateur favori. (. . .) Sous cette influence, le jeune admirateur conquis prépara, pour *L'Artiste*, deux articles: l'un où l'étudiant de vingt ans allait déplorer, avec un juvénile emportement, que la Poésie ne fût pas mieux protégée contre certains sacrilèges par un langage plus secret ou même par d'inviolables hiéroglyphes; l'autre étude devait être ce qu'il appela finalement une *Symphonie littéraire*, court hommage à ses trois maîtres du moment: Baudelaire, Banville, Gautier.

En septembre 1862, parus, sous le double titre: *Hérésies artistiques—L'Art pour tous*, une sorte de ferme proclamation où le jeune poète, stimulé par sa lecture du panégyrique de Théophile Gautier dû à Baudelaire, faisait connaître l'une de ses convictions essentielles d'esthéticien. (. . .)

Si cet article *L'Art pour tous* révélait la place que Mallarmé faisait à son maître de poétique, et le rang aristocratique, parmi les artistes des vers, auquel Mallarmé voulait lui-même prétendre, le fragment de la *Symphonie littéraire* qui était consacré à Charles Baudelaire célébrait les *Fleurs du Mal*.[86]

How much in 'L'Art pour tous' is indeed borrowed from Baudelaire's first essay on Gautier, or may have been suggested by it, will be noted later in a detailed commentary on the text. So too will the possibility that his second essay on the same master may have made some contribution also.[87] But Mondor does not confine himself to identifying the Baudelairian content of Mallarmé's article. He also refers to the likelihood that the reading of Baudelaire's subtly revealing analyses, and eloquent praise, of the art and style of individual poets, his contemporaries, was for his disciple an inspiring experience. In using such forthright terms, I may seem to go beyond Mondor's discreet suggestions, but not I think beyond his intention. According to him, the reading of some of Baudelaire's critical essays after which and in reference to which Mallarmé wrote 'L'Art pour tous' marks an important phase in the formation of his aesthetic ideas, those 'principes de l'art' on which he had prudently held his peace when he reviewed *Les Poésies parisiennes*. I have no doubt that in this Mondor is right, and that the section of Mallarmé's article that he discusses should be read as the young poet's firm declaration, after his reading of Baudelaire's essays, of his adherence to the doctrine he found there.

That is not to say that this profession of allegiance was the result of a sudden *coup de foudre*. It was more likely to be the result of a gradual process of attraction. Mallarmé would know already some of Baudelaire's critical writings. Likely examples are those on Edgar Poe that serve to introduce the two volumes of his translation of Poe's tales. An article we know he had read quite recently and which may have re-kindled his interest was the review of Part I of *Les Misérables*, published by Baudelaire in *Le Boulevard* on 20 April 1862. The letter in which Mallarmé thanked Cazalis for sending it, as a pledge of friendship before they had even met, was quoted in the last chapter. His gratitude was expressed in the warmest terms, but about the article itself he was reticent. It was 'de la prose d'un de [ses] maîtres les plus vénérés', he said, and 'Baudelaire y est Baudelaire'.[88] However, he would surely find Baudelaire on the subject of Hugo intriguing, and if he did not already know the masterly 'Victor Hugo' contributed by Baudelaire a year before to *La Revue fantaisiste*,[89] he must have looked round for a copy. With Des Essarts to help him it would not be difficult to find. Mallarmé would be the more desirous to read the earlier article as it is quoted from and corrected at the beginning of the other, as a means of formulating a doctrinal aesthetic distinction of the first importance in the theory of 'l'art pour l'art'.[90]

Mallarmé also knew other versions than Baudelaire's of the art for art's sake theory. Of its boldest exposition, Gautier's *Mademoiselle de Maupin*, he had a copy of his own,[91] as also of his *Poésies complètes*, acquired in December 1859.[92] A sentence in Léon Marc's letter of 12 May 1862 from Auxerre may be remembered, that reads like a bluff reply to favourable comments made by Mallarmé on the subject of 'la nouvelle école'. Marc mentions them while at the same time expressing his eagerness to read what he calls 'le volume du comte de Lisle que vous possédez'.[93] Three weeks later, in a rather grandly casual manner, Mallarmé mentioned to Cazalis the article he was writing on that same poet, who had been honoured by one published by Baudelaire in his *Revue fantaisiste* series, a year before.[94] The 'new school' was evidently much in his thoughts.

As for the essay on Gautier itself, which we are asked to consider as the immediate source of the more important ideas in 'L'Art pour tous', a general indication of the time at which Mallarmé read it (or, who knows, re-read it) is provided by that imputed relationship on the one hand—the reading probably preceded immediately the writing, as indeed from the first the heading 'Hérésies artistiques' gave one to suppose—and on the other the near-certainty, founded on Coligny's letter, that Mallarmé's article was completed by about the end of June. The conclusion that he read Baudelaire's 'Théophile Gautier' not later than the end of May or early June, and started his article soon after (to the discomfiture of the one on Leconte de Lisle) seems safe, but rather vague. Strong confirmation and a little more precision are provided by as neat a textual clue as one could desire, which requires however a circumstantial explanation.

In the very confidential letter to Cazalis of 4 June, in which Mallarmé complained bitterly of his stepmother's constant reminders of the need for thrift, he used the cruel-sounding image already quoted: 'Elle n'a qu'un mot affreux sur les lèvres: Économie. Or, comme j'ai toujours peur de lui voir cracher cette souris rouge, je ne lui parle que fort rarement.'[95] Cazalis would probably recognize the reference to one of Perrault's fairy-tales, the one entitled 'Les Fées'. A fairy bestows contrasting gifts on two girls, according to their deserts. One is winsome and kind-hearted; to her goes the gift that henceforth, every word that falls from her lips shall be accompanied by a flower or a precious stone. The other, arrogant, selfish, and thoroughly disagreeable, receives the opposite gift, that her every word shall be accompanied by a toad or equally revolting creature. But if Cazalis remembered the story well the red mouse might surprise him, since it is not found in Perrault.[96] Mallarmé had found it in a corrupt version, aesthetically orientated, a passage in Gautier's *Caprices et Zigzags*, quoted by Baudelaire as an epigraph to one of his writings, none other than the 1859 essay itself, on Théophile Gautier.[97] Which makes it very likely indeed that Mallarmé had begun reading or re-reading Baudelaire's essay on Gautier by the fourth of June.

If, then, we accept Henri Mondor's view—and any uncertainty in that regard I shall try to dispel in the course of this commentary—Mallarmé's refutation of the slogan 'poetry for all' must be seen as having two main objects. To reply to Vacquerie's version of Hugo's doctrine on the subject appears to be the dominant aim,[98] but the desire to express approval, incidentally, for Baudelairian concepts concerning art for art's sake claims a good share of the author's attention. He opens his argument, however, with Vacquerie's thesis firmly in mind. He attacks it in relation to the Philistine attitude to poetry that it can be said to foster:

Qu'advient-il de cette absence de mystère?

*Comme tout ce qui est absolument beau, la poésie force l'admiration: mais cette admiration sera lointaine, vague,—bête, elle sort de la foule. Grâce à cette sensation générale, une idée inouïe et saugrenue germera dans les cervelles, à savoir, qu'il est indispensable de l'*enseigner *dans les collèges, et irrésistiblement, comme tout ce qui est enseigné à plusieurs, la poésie sera abaissée au rang d'une science. Elle sera expliquée à tous également, égalitairement, car il est difficile de distinguer sous les crins ébouriffés de quel écolier blanchit l'étoile sibylline.*

Et de là, puisque à juste titre est un homme incomplet celui qui ignore l'histoire, une science, qui voit trouble dans la physique, une science, nul n'a reçu une solide *éducation s'il ne peut* juger *Homère et* lire *Hugo, gens de science.*

The first proposition (after the rhetorical question has neatly asserted a link with the prologue) is an arresting one, the most interesting to my mind in the whole article. It defines what the author considers to be the root cause of Philistinism. The sense of the beautiful (Poe's 'immortal instinct, deep within the spirit of man', necessarily therefore universal)[99] is fully active only in the chosen few, and dim (perhaps dimmed by decadence)[100] in 'the crowd'. So essential to Mallarmé's aesthetic was this view of the modern poet's distance from the public that over thirty years later he would state it again. He did so in 'Le Mystère dans les Lettres', in terms that vindicate Mme Noulet's contention that ideas expressed in 'L'Art pour tous' are to be found also in that late essay.[101] It will be remembered that a method is proposed there by which a poet might elude the attention of the Philistines. But Mallarmé expressed at the same time a fear that the ruse he recommended might not be infallible. A Philistine's suspicion might be aroused by glints from the hidden treasure:

Si, tout de même, n'inquiétait je ne sais quel miroitement, en dessous, peu séparable de la surface concédée à la rétine—il attire le soupçon.[102]

Which can be recognized as a reiteration, though in Mallarmé's idiom of 1896, of an acknowledgement tendered in 1862, that the poetic incompetence of the interfering Philistine is not total, and that therein lies the poet's problem:

Comme tout ce qui est absolument beau, la poésie force l'admiration. Mais cette admiration sera lointaine, vague,—bête, elle sort de la foule.

In the sentence that follows this recognition in 'L'Art pour tous', it should be noted that the future tense, in '*germera*', '*sera abaissée*', and '*sera expliquée*', signifies the inevitability of the consequence referred to: it is a future morphologically, but not semantically, though from a stylistic point of view it may cloud a little the admission that the consequence was already installed in the French educational system. Mallarmé had himself experienced the manner in which poetry was taught, at least at the Lycée de Sens. We may suppose it was taught 'as a science' in the sense that prosody can be taught to all and sundry, whereas according to Mallarmé only the elect are capable of understanding the subtle art of poetry.[103]

As regards the passing sneer at egalitarianism in 'également, égalitairement', it will be observed that not only is it gratuitous, it is completely out of line with the rest of the author's argument. So far, it has been presumed that 'teaching poetry' means teaching pupils in general to read it—'poetry for all'. But now, to accommodate the stylistic inspiration of the moment and in despite of all logic, it is required to mean teaching future poets to write it. Mallarmé could hardly show more clearly how frivolous his reasoning is on this matter, and how shallow his concern for the issue involved. For the sake of a nicely balanced combination of incongruous images (whimsical? humorous? fanciful?) he gives up all claim to the reader's confidence in the seriousness and good faith of the case he is presenting.

What follows is almost as irresponsible. Whereas it is usual, in discussions on this subject, to distinguish between learning to read the ancients and learning to appreciate the moderns who write in our own language, he attempts to deal summarily with both together and so confuses the subject. For if in teaching Homer the aim is, as he appears to assert, to enable pupils to *judge* him, Homer is being studied not as a man of science but as a poet, with the idea (which of course Mallarmé considers vain for all but the predestined) of appreciating his poetry as art. On the other hand, to learn to *read* Hugo as a man of science is to expect his poems to instruct; thus we fall (like Hugo himself) into the major artistic heresy so emphatically condemned by Poe and Baudelaire, 'l'hérésie de l'enseignement'.[104] At this point Mallarmé's argument breaks off, and he returns suddenly, not without some jolting, to the theme of his introduction which we thought he had put firmly behind him:

Un homme,—je parle d'un de ces hommes pour qui la vanité moderne, à court d'appellations flatteuses, a évoqué le titre vide de citoyen,—un citoyen, et cela m'a fait penser parfois, confesser, le front haut, que la musique, ce parfum qu'exhale l'encensoir du rêve, ne porte avec elle, différente en cela des aromes sensibles, aucun ravissement extatique [? . . . ?]: *le même homme, je veux dire le même citoyen, enjambe nos musées avec une liberté indifférente et une froideur distraite, dont il aurait honte dans une église, où il comprendrait au moins la nécessité d'une hypocrisie quelconque, et de temps en temps lance à Rubens, à Delacroix, un de ces regards qui sentent la rue,—Hasardons, en le murmurant aussi bas que nous le pourrons, les noms de Shakespeare ou de Goethe: ce drôle redresse la tête d'un air qui signifie: "Ceci rentre dans mon domaine!"*

*C'est que, la musique étant pour tous un art, la peinture un art, la statuaire un art,—et la poésie n'en étant plus un (en effet, chacun rougirait de l'*ignorer, *et je ne sais personne qui ait à rougir de n'être pas un expert en art), on abandonne musique, peinture et statuaire aux* gens du métier, *et comme l'on tient à sembler instruit, on apprend la poésie.*

For other reasons as well as the sudden change of tack, the first of these paragraphs is disconcerting. It appears to be almost entirely taken up by a single bewildering sentence, a syntactical *tour de force*, until it is realized that both logically and grammatically the text is incomplete. What was intended was not one sentence but at least two. A printer's error or a too hasty editorial excision has resulted in an omission (represented in my transcription by the question marks in square brackets) which destroys the sense.[105] The mutilation only partly dims the other oddity, that the author has returned (but reasonably now) to the subject of the introduction, the difference of status that can be observed between poetry and the other arts. He explains it in terms that make the previous diatribe redundant as well as perverse, a mock-serious second version that should have been substituted for the first but was added to it instead, inserted at the head of the article. The straightforward (and as I suggest original) version makes it appear that the whole idea of contrasting poetry with music and the visual arts may have its origin in a piece of anti-Phlilistine satire met with in Baudelaire's first essay on Gautier. The passage was certainly in Mallarmé's mind since it is quoted from in his article, two paragraphs on, with formal acknowledgement. Baudelaire sketches a domestic scene of upper-middle-class life in Paris:

Je vous suppose *interné* dans un salon *bourgeois* et prenant le café, après dîner, avec le *maître* de la maison, la *dame* de la maison, et ses *demoiselles*. Détestable et risible argot auquel la plume devrait se soustraire, comme l'écrivain s'abstenir de ces énervantes fréquentations! Bientôt on causera musique, peinture peut-être, mais littérature infailliblement.[106]

A more trivial and very casual borrowing from the same source probably explains also why in 'L'Art pour tous' Shakespeare and Goethe are paired. Baudelaire had written:

Nos voisins disent: Shakespeare et Goethe! Nous pouvons leur répondre: Victor Hugo et Théophile Gautier![107]

The derisive treatment of the title 'citoyen' appears as gratuitous in this context as the scornful 'égalitairement' earlier. They are presumably intended as an inkling of the aristocratic posture about to be copied by Mallarmé from Baudelaire and maintained during the rest of his article. It is the subject broached next:

Il est à propos de dire ici que certains écrivains, maladroitement vaillants, ont tort de demander compte à la foule de l'ineptie de son goût et de la nullité de son imagination. Outre "qu'injurier la foule, c'est s'encanailler soi-même", comme dit justement Charles Baudelaire, l'inspiré doit dédaigner ces sorties contre le Philistin: l'exception, toute glorieuse et sainte qu'elle soit, ne s'insurge pas contre la règle, et qui niera que l'absence d'idéal ne soit la règle? Ajoutez que la sérénité du dédain n'engage pas seule à éviter ces récriminations; la raison nous apprend encore qu'elles ne peuvent être qu'inutiles ou nuisibles: inutiles si le Philistin n'y prend garde; nuisibles si, vexé d'une sottise qui est le lot de la majorité, il s'empare des poëtes et grossit l'armée des faux admirateurs—J'aime mieux le voir profane que profanateur. —Rappelons-nous que le poëte (qu'il rythme, chante, peigne, sculpte) n'est pas le niveau au-dessous duquel rampent les autres hommes; c'est la foule qui est le niveau, et il plane. Sérieusement, avons-nous jamais vu dans la Bible que l'ange raillât l'homme, qui est sans ailes?

This purple patch, of good rhetorical quality were it not for the inept hyperbolical (perhaps humorous) analogy with which it ends, is an interpolation. What the author is now to say is not 'à propos' of what he has just said. He is interrupting his argument against teaching poetry at school to offer his admiring approval of Baudelaire's attitude towards the Philistines, much more sophisticated than the view he has himself held hitherto. Once this tribute has been paid, the thread of the previous discourse is taken up again as if there had been no interruption: '*Il faudrait qu'on se crût un homme complet sans avoir lu un mot d'Hugo . . .*'. But the page of Baudelaire's essays that Mallarmé refers to and quotes from (incorrectly) will from this point on contribute more substantially to his own article than this overt reference reveals. The position he now takes up is largely determined by the salient passage that reads:

Or, le condiment que Théophile Gautier jette dans ses œuvres, qui, pour les amateurs de l'art, est du choix le plus exquis et du sel le plus ardent, n'a que peu ou point d'action sur le palais de la foule. Pour devenir tout à fait populaire, ne faut-il pas consentir à mériter de l'être, c'est-à-dire ne faut-il pas, par un petit côté secret, un presque rien qui fait tache, se montrer un peu populacier? En littérature comme en morale, il y a danger, autant que gloire, à être délicat. L'aristocratie nous isole.

J'avouerai franchement que je ne suis pas de ceux qui voient là un mal bien regrettable, et que j'ai peut-être poussé trop loin la mauvaise humeur contre de pauvres *philistins*. Récriminer, faire de l'opposition, et même réclamer la justice, n'est-ce pas *s'emphilistiner* quelque peu? On oublie à chaque instant qu'injurier une foule c'est s'encanailler soi-même. Placés très haut, toute fatalité nous apparaît comme justice. Saluons donc, au contraire, avec tout le respect et l'enthousiasme qu'elle mérite, cette aristocratie qui fait solitude autour d'elle.[108]

In accordance with this advice Mallarmé would now try, instead of jeering at the many as he had done at Sens in rowdier company, to pay homage to the few, that élite to which (as yet on slender authority, though by resolute choice) he presumed that he belonged. The penitent worker is not altogether successful however in putting the master's advice into practice. The disdain would have been more 'serene' and 'aristocratic' if it had been less volubly contemptuous.

Two details are noteworthy. First, the question 'qui niera que l'absence d'idéal ne soit la règle?' might well provoke the answer: Victor Hugo. For instance in the preface to *Ruy Blas*, that Mallarmé had certainly not forgotten: 'Nous savons fort bien que la foule est une grande chose dans laquelle on trouve tout, l'instinct du beau comme le goût du médiocre, l'amour de l'idéal comme l'appétit du commun.' Secondly, the device that allows the author of 'L'Art pour tous' to write as though in speaking of poetry he is not forgetting the other arts, 'le poëte (qu'il rythme, chante, peigne, sculpte)', may have been prompted by a detail in Baudelaire's *Notes nouvelles sur Edgar Poe*, section IV of which begins: ' "Genus irritabile vatum!" Que les poètes (nous servant du mot dans son acception la plus large et comme comprenant tous les artistes) soient une race irritable, cela est bien entendu.'[109]

Il faudrait que l'on se crût un homme complet sans avoir lu un vers d'Hugo, comme on se croit un homme complet sans avoir déchiffré une note de Verdi, et qu'une des bases de l'instruction de tous ne fût pas un art, c'est-à-dire un mystère accessible à de rares individualités. La multitude y gagnerait ceci qu'elle ne dormirait plus sur Virgile des heures qu'elle dépenserait activement et dans un but pratique, et que la poésie, cela qu'elle n'aurait plus l'ennui,—faible pour elle, il est vrai, l'immortelle,—d'entendre à ses pieds les abois d'une meute d'êtres qui, parce qu'ils sont savants, intelligents, se croient en droit de l'estimer, quand ce n'est point de la régenter.

Hugo: Such references illustrate the special situation occupied by Hugo in the esteem of former disciples committed to 'l'art pour l'art', which the master himself now denounces. When Mallarmé names a French poet in his article, as one of the very great, alongside Homer or Virgil, that poet is Victor Hugo still. The shift in allegiance to Baudelaire, Banville, Gautier, involved no great change in Mallarmé's poetic convictions. It was not he who had changed his mind but Hugo, when he declared himself the apostle of 'Progress, democratically achieved'.[110] It has been shown in an earlier chapter how vital and resilient the influence of an earlier Hugo was to prove on

Mallarmé's conception of poetry.[111] Nor was his fidelity in that regard exceptional. Albert Cassagne, in the chapter of his exemplary survey entitled 'Le sentiment aristocratique', shows that Hugo's prestige was unassailable in the eyes of poets whose leader he had once been. He summarizes it thus:

Bien qu'Hugo après *les Misérables* ait décidément tourné au démocrate et ne soit plus du tout des leurs, ils n'ont pas cessé de voir en lui le Maître et le Père:

> Gautier parmi ces joailliers
> Est prince, et Leconte de Lisle
> Forge l'or dans ses ateliers;
> Mais le Père est là-bas, dans l'Ile.[112]

Les abois d'une meute d'êtres. The barking pack are presumably the critics,[113] and in '*régenter*' there may be a prudent reference to Baudelaire's encounter with the law in 1857, his conviction for obscenity, and the banning of *Les Fleurs du mal* until the offending poems were expunged.[114] The admission in '*faible pour elle* [la poésie], *il est vrai*' is the one direct reference in the whole article to the possible consequences for poetry itself of what the author complains of. For the rest, his preoccupation concerns not what is good for poetry but what one young poet would like.

A ce mal, du reste, les poëtes, et les plus grands, ne sont nullement étrangers.

Voici.

Qu'un philosophe ambitionne la popularité, je l'en estime. Il ne ferme pas les mains sur la poignée de vérités radieuses qu'elles enserrent; il les répand, et cela est juste qu'elles laissent un lumineux sillage à chacun de ses doigts. Mais qu'un poëte, un adorateur du beau inaccessible au vulgaire, ne se contente pas du suffrage du sanhédrin de l'art, cela m'irrite, et je ne le comprends pas.

L'homme peut être démocrate, l'artiste se dédouble et doit rester aristocrate.

Et pourtant nous avons sous les yeux le contraire. On multiplie les éditions à bon marché des poëtes, et cela au consentement et au contentement des poëtes. Croyez-vous que vous y gagnerez de la gloire, ô rêveurs, ô lyriques? Quand l'artiste seul avait votre livre, coûte que coûte, eût-il dû payer de son dernier liard la dernière de vos étoiles, vous aviez de vrais admirateurs. Et maintenant cette foule qui vous achète pour votre bon marché vous comprend-elle? Déjà profanés par l'enseignement, une dernière barrière vous tenait au-dessus de ses désirs,—celle des sept francs à tirer de la bourse,—et vous culbutez cette barrière, imprudents! O vos propres ennemis, pourquoi (plus encore par vos doctrines que par le prix de vos livres, qui ne dépend pas de vous seuls) encenser et prêcher vous-mêmes cette impiété, la vulgarisation de l'art! Vous marcherez donc à côté de ceux qui, effaçant les notes mystérieuses de la musique,—cette idée se pavane dans les rues, qu'on ne rie pas,—en ouvrant les arcanes à la cohue, ou de ces autres qui la propagent à tous prix dans les campagnes, contents que l'on joue faux, pourvu que l'on joue. Qu'arrivera-t-il un jour, le jour du châtiment? Vous aussi l'on vous enseignera comme ces grands martyrs, Homère, Lucrèce, Juvénal!

'*A ce mal, du reste*'. Which evil? Surely not the teaching of poetry at school, nor the interference of critics. Readers who seek in what they have just read a precise antecedent for 'ce mal', or any mention of the ill for which they are asked to believe that poets themselves are partly to blame, will look in vain. It is named only when they have read on a few lines: '*cette impiété, la vulgarisation de l'art*'. Meanwhile, the identity of the poet to whom this homily is particularly addressed is darkly hinted at in the words '*et les plus grands*'. It is Victor Hugo, the aristocrat turned democrat, whence also the objurgation that soon follows, '*L'homme peut être démocrate, l'artiste se dédouble et doit rester aristocrate*'.[115]

'*Qu'un philosophe . . .*'. The visual symbol used to contrast the poet's situation with the philosopher's is a composite one. The philosopher that Mallarmé had in mind (and whose opinion he disagreed with on the issue in question) was Fontenelle. It was he who, according to Voltaire, 'disait que s'il avait la main pleine de vérités, il se garderait bien de l'ouvrir'.[116] But for the author of 'L'Art pour tous' the image had been made luminous, I believe by Victor Hugo. In one of the chapters of *Les Misérables* on which Mallarmé's correspondence had so thrived that summer, the fifth in Part IV, Book v, Cosette rereads the notebook left for her secretly by Marius, and is spell-bound:

Ce manuscrit de quinze pages lui révélait brusquement et doucement tout l'amour, la douleur, la destinée, la vie, l'éternité, le commencement, la fin. C'était comme une main qui se serait ouverte et lui aurait jeté subitement une poignée de rayons.[117]

The suggestion that Mallarmé had this passage fresh in his memory when he referred to the philosopher's '*poignée de vérités radieuses*' is made with proper caution, because if it is accepted it provides a corroborative clue to the date of Mallarmé's 'L'Art pour tous': it was not finished before early July. For Parts IV and V of Hugo's novel were published on 30 June 1862 and, as has already been noted, we know from Mallarmé's correspondence that on the following day he read the first book of Part IV.[118]

'*Le sanhédrin de l'art*' whose judgement is alone valid is no doubt composed of the confraternity of poets or perhaps of the leaders among them. Self-government was what mattered. When Guy Michaud says that Mallarmé went further in his article than the theorists of 'l'art pour l'art', I take that to mean that he separated poets from the rest of society more completely, so far as their art was concerned. And he does indeed appear to declare that poets alone are capable of reading poetry. In that regard he is more absolute than Baudelaire. Not to go beyond the two essays on Gautier, their author, referring to admirers of poetry who are not poets themselves, can use respectful expressions like 'les amateurs de l'art' (as opposed to 'la foule'), and 'quelque savant amoureux de la beauté'. He even writes admiringly of a poet's work 'préparé et mûri pour le public, pour l'édification des âmes amoureuses du Beau'. Only concerning very special insights does he declare that 'ceux qui ne sont pas poètes ne comprennent pas ces choses'.[119]

To express his disapproval of poets who are not content to be judged by other poets, Mallarmé uses an unlikely verb, '*cela m'irrite*'. It may be that he does so to claim a right accorded to poets by Edgar Poe, whose comments on Horace's 'Genus irritabile vatum' are paraphrased in a passage of Baudelaire's *Notes nouvelles sur Edgar Poe* already referred to.[120] The reproach concerning cheap editions must perhaps be considered authorized by this right, but addressed as it is by the erstwhile apprentice to the master whose fame had been the object of his constant admiration it was needlessly ungenerous. To introduce that subject was inevitably to degrade the argument, tainting the aspiration to glory—the eagle flight—with a suspicion of greed to which Hugo was particularly exposed.[121] The superfluity of the reproof, in the context, is admitted in the feeble semblance of a warning that accompanies it. The fate of Homer, Lucretius, and Juvenal as represented here, is glory in its clearest shape. Whether intended seriously or (for want of a better way out) as a wry joke, the paradoxical threat of martyrdom falls very flat. As to the unexpected reference to attempts made to vulgarize music (a danger from which that art had seemed secure at the beginning of the article), it is probably so much padding. It will be noticed that with the apostrophe '*ô rêveurs, ô lyriques*', Mallarmé has moved into a directly oratorical style. For the rest of the article he will harangue his fellow-poets and chide Hugo in would-be urgent tones.

Vous penserez à Corneille, à Molière, à Racine, qui sont populaires et glorieux?—Non, ils ne sont pas populaires: leur nom peut-être, leurs vers, cela est faux. La foule les a lus une fois, je le confesse, sans les comprendre. Mais qui les relit? Les artistes seuls.

'*Les artistes seuls*' means, we must suppose, 'Les poètes seuls', but a truthful answer to the question would have included: 'Les professeurs de seconde dans les lycées et collèges de France, et bon nombre de leurs élèves et anciens élèves, candidats au baccalauréat.'[122]

The author has one more warning to deliver, of the consequences that will follow if poets fail to change their ways. It is one that is unlikely to hold more terrors than the previous threat for those to whom it is addressed, particularly for the chief offender, now named:

Et déjà vous êtes punis: il vous est arrivé d'avoir, parmi des œuvres adorables ou fulgurantes, laissé échapper quelques vers qui n'aient pas ce haut parfum de distinction suprême qui plane autour de vous. Et voilà ce que votre foule admirera. Vous serez désespérés de voir vos vrais chefs-d'œuvre accessibles aux seules âmes d'élite et négligés par ce vulgaire dont ils auraient dû être ignorés. Et s'il n'en était déjà ainsi, si la masse n'avait défloré ses poëmes, il est certain que les pièces auréolaires d'Hugo ne seraient pas Moïse *ou* Ma fille, va prier . . . , *comme elle le proclame, mais le* Faune *ou* Pleurs dans la nuit.[123]

The poverty of the author's argument becomes ever more apparent. From the point of view he is ostensibly defending, a poet would surely have reason to rejoice, rather than despair, if his true masterpieces, accessible to none but the chosen few, were ignored by the vulgar, and only his less perfect creations sullied by popular praise. The case against Vacquerie is petering out, and the young élitist gives up all pretence of reasoning. The noble indignation of an 'artiste de race' against the notion of 'l'art pour tous' shows its true colour. It is the young gentleman of the cultured bourgeoisie who has the last word:

L'heure qui sonne est sérieuse: l'éducation se fait dans le peuple, de grandes doctrines vont se répandre. Faites que, s'il est une vulgarisation ce soit celle du bien, non celle de l'art, et que vos efforts n'aboutissent pas—comme ils n'y ont pas tendu, je l'espère—à cette chose, grotesque si elle n'était triste pour l'artiste de race, le poëte ouvrier.[124]

Que les masses lisent la morale, mais de grâce ne leur donnez pas notre poésie à gâter.

O poëtes, vous avez toujours été orgueilleux, soyez plus, devenez dédaigneux.

STÉPHANE MALLARMÉ

Critical readers of the article in *L'Artiste* might reflect ironically on reading this conclusion, that Baudelaire, a year before, had ended his article on Leconte de Lisle with this tribute:

Il lui suffit d'être populaire parmi ceux qui sont dignes eux-mêmes de lui plaire. Il appartient d'ailleurs à cette famille d'esprits qui ont pour tout ce qui n'est pas supérieur un mépris si tranquille qu'il ne daigne même pas s'exprimer.[125]

They would be justified in thinking that if Baudelaire himself read this article by one Stéphane Mallarmé, he would not recognize in its conclusion the thoughts of a member of that family of minds. The new adherent to the 'art for art's sake' movement would indeed seem to his elders a decidedly raw recruit. But a biographer may see in the bluntness of this ending another, no less interesting aspect. It may be that on reflection Mallarmé wished to withdraw the casuistic implications of his earlier claim, that '*l'homme peut être démocrate; l'artiste se dédouble et doit rester aristocrate*.' For now he appears to be conceding, with a curious degree of emphasis, that the aesthetic élitism he was preaching had indeed a political dimension.[126] Moreover, to support this conjecture, we know from his correspondence of a particular circumstance that is quite likely to have awakened or sharpened his awareness that this was so. It is revealed in the opening compliment of his letter to Cazalis dated 1 July 1862, which reads:

Frère, voici une journée pluvieuse qui a été traversée de deux rayons de soleil: l'un auroral et blanc, l'autre crépusculaire et flamboyant. Je parle de l'adorable portrait d'Ettie, et d'une centaine de pages philosophiques des *Misérables*.[127]

The pages referred to must be the hundred or so that make up the first book of Part IV, published on 30 June as was noted above. Hugo entitled it 'Pages d'histoire', but its six chapters are indeed philosophical in the main, in the sense that they are much less concerned with historical fact than with political philosophizing. If on the day following their publication Mallarmé perused those chapters with attention, he must have been struck and may have been jolted by a summary in historical terms of the choice with which French society was still faced, despite the succession of revolutions through which the country had passed. It concludes the fifth chapter, the subject of which is the political atmosphere in the poor districts of Paris in 1832, and it reads:

Ces hommes hérissés qui, dans les jours génésiaques du chaos révolutionnaire, déguenillés, hurlants, farouches, le casse-tête levé, la pique haute, se ruaient sur le vieux Paris bouleversé, que voulaient-ils? Ils voulaient la fin des oppressions, la fin des tyrannies, la fin du glaive, le travail pour l'homme, l'instruction pour l'enfant, la douceur sociale pour la femme, la liberté, l'égalité, la fraternité, le pain pour tous, l'idée pour tous, l'Édénisation du monde, le Progrès (. . .)

En regard de ses hommes, farouches, nous en convenons, et effrayants, mais farouches et effrayants pour le bien, il y a d'autres hommes, souriants, brodés, dorés, enrubannés, constellés, en bas de soie, en plumes blanches, en gants jaunes, en souliers vernis, qui, accoudés à une table de velours au coin d'une cheminée de marbre, insistent doucement pour le maintien et la conservation du passé, du moyen âge, du droit divin, du fanatisme, de l'ignorance, de l'esclavage, de la peine de mort, de la guerre, glorifiant à demi-voix et avec politesse le sabre, le bûcher et l'échafaud. Quant à nous, si nous étions forcés à l'option, entre les barbares de la civilisation et les civilisés de la barbarie, nous choisirions les barbares.

Mais, grâce au ciel, un autre choix est possible. Aucune chute à pic n'est nécessaire, pas plus en avant qu'en arrière. Ni despotisme, ni terrorisme. Nous voulons le progrès en pente douce.[128]

A tempting doctrine, but there were those for whom progress, even by the gentlest slope, would not be progress if its fruits were to be shared by all. 'Le pain pour tous', by all means, but not much more. Not, for instance, the arts. In the conclusion of 'L'Art pour tous' Mallarmé declared himself boldly to be one of their number: *'ne leur donnez pas notre poésie à gâter'*. It is not at all unlikely that the bluntness with which he chose to express himself was the effect of his reading the hundred philosophical pages. On his part, in the course of writing 'L'Art pour tous', it would be an understandable reaction to the 'bitter after-taste' that Hugo had foreseen would follow the reading of *Les Misérables*. Commenting on the revulsion that many readers did express, some publicly, and others (such as Flaubert and Baudelaire) privately, Claude Gély writes:

> De cette manière, l'"arrière-goût amer" pouvait être exorcisé; interprété, consciemment ou non, comme goût "trivial", c'est-à-dire comme "mauvais goût", il allait, par la connivence ou la confusion de la politique et de l'esthétique, s'abolir dans le recours aux codes rassurants de la critique dite "littéraire", laquelle était toute prête aux reniements. (. . .) *Les Misérables*, évidemment, déplaisaient, agaçaient les "positivistes", et heurtaient le "goût" des délicats, des raffinés, des religieux de l'Art . . .
>
> Ainsi reniés, ainsi honnis, semant le malaise chez les bien-pensants, la malédiction chez les intellectuels, la maladie chez les bourgeois, *Les Misérables*, écrits pour le peuple, devaient rester au peuple. Le peuple, une fois pour toutes, les adopta.[129]

It would be quite fitting that *Les Misérables* should leave its mark on the conclusion of 'L'Art pour tous', setting the seal as it were on Mallarmé's change of allegiance. For the significance of the article as a document lies chiefly in the witness it bears to a choice made by its author, at the beginning of his poetic career, between two conceptions of the poet's function in society, Baudelaire's and Hugo's. It makes clear his preference, and his enthusiasm for what Baudelaire has to say on the subject in certain of his critical writings, especially his two essays on Gautier. Mondor was right, I believe, to see in the expression of that enthusiasm the article's predominant interest, though he would have done well not to assume that the choice its author makes is total and undiscriminating. In the context of 'L'Art pour tous', it is misleading to call Baudelaire Mallarmé's 'maître de poétique',[130] and to make general assertions such as this:

Pendant plusieurs années, Mallarmé fit de l'auteur des *Fleurs du Mal* son inspirateur favori. Il le laissa, dans son propre esprit, exclure ou affadir, par l'irruption de son génie, d'anciennes admirations désormais délaissées.[131]

In its complementary object on the other hand, the purpose of proving that the proponents of the opposite, democratic conception are mistaken in their notions and their aims, the article is a signal failure. The attempt to present a convincing case has succeeded only in the sense, and in the measure, that the fine writing in which it is clothed appears to have hidden its defects from readers predisposed to admire.

Three other projects for writings in prose were mentioned by Mallarmé during the spring and summer of 1862. None of them reached the stage of publication. The article on Leconte de Lisle seems to have been put aside at an early stage to make way for 'L'Art pour tous'. It was taken up again a year or so later, with how little success will be seen. The intention, expressed on 25 September, of writing a prose poem, on plans for travel in Germany with Marie, was perhaps itself no more than a passing fancy, inspired by the publication of prose poems by Baudelaire in *La Presse*.[132] There was a little more substance, I believe, in the third venture which Mallarmé shared with Des Essarts, according to a letter about which he wrote to Cazalis on 24 April:

Quant à la For[ê]t-noire, cela dépendra de l'éditeur qu'Emmanuel rencontrera pour notre volume de *Contes [é]tranges*. Tu sais que nous le faisons à deux, fraternellement. Si l'éditeur paie de suite, c'est décidé et nous allons nous noyer dans les lacs de kirsch.[133]

Nothing more is known of this project, but certain coincidences make the following conjecture plausible. One 'strange story' by Mallarmé there is, which has survived in manuscript among his papers and is well known. It may well have been a candidate for a time, in the summer of 1862, for inclusion in *Contes étranges*. Indeed its existence may have been the only substance on which the ambitious notion of such a volume was founded. It is a narrative much discussed by Mallarmé scholars, none other than the story of Deborah's ghost, 'Les Trois Cigognes'. When in an earlier chapter this so-called *narration scolaire* was examined among the schoolboy compositions, reasons were given why the text as we know it could not be (even though a note in Mallarmé's hand asserts that it was) the exercise written in 1858 or 1859. My own opinion was that it was a revised version copied out carefully 'two or three years later, perhaps with a view to publication'.[134] In the conjectural case that I sketched for believing so, prominence was given to the presence in the text of passages which revealed (it seemed to me) a strong stylistic influence, that of *Gaspard de la nuit*, most unlikely before 1862. Later, I examined again, in the light of what seems to be new evidence, the general question of the date at which Mallarmé did read and study that work.[135] The conclusion reached was that the most likely date for the reading was the summer of 1862, which makes it a likely date also for the revision, under the influence of that reading, of the schoolboy composition 'Les Trois Cigognes'.[136] And the remaining question, which is why the revision took place, is answered by the reference to the project of publishing with Des Essarts a volume entitled *Contes étranges*.

That project provides also an adequate explanation of the fact that the maunuscript itself is prepared as if for publication. The publisher Des Essarts was looking for would want to see a sample of the tales he was asked to publish. 'Les Trois Cigognes' as it has reached us could well be that sample. Mondor remarks that 'Mallarmé a recopié sa composition, un peu comme il l'eût fait, déjà, d'une partition musicale'.[137] The same could be said, however, of copies of his poems that he prepared for his friends. It is in Carl Barbier's later, more technical description of the manuscript that more telling details appear: 'Encre bleue sur le recto de 31 feuilles blanches (15.5× 20.3 cm) numérotées au crayon rouge-orange.'[138] Why, if not with the printer in mind, does Mallarmé depart from his usual economical practice and write on one side only of his thirty-one sheets, and why does he number these in red if not to signify that the pagination is only the author's and provisional, restricted to one tale among several?

This whole argument is only valid, of course, even as conjecture, if the premiss is granted that Mallarmé does indeed imitate the style of *Gaspard de la nuit*, in such passages as the following which open sections I and III respectively of 'Les Trois Cigognes':

Il a neigé tout le jour. La terre est en blanc comme une mariée, et les constellations limpides diamantent un ciel lacté.

Deux gémissements sinistres traversent cette froide rêverie de la neige et du clair de lune.

Le premier est celui d'une porte tournant sur ses antiques ferrures, la porte de Nick Parrit qui sort de sa cabane,—un nid dans les broussailles. Nick Parrit ramasse le long du mur deux fagots d'aubépine, secoue ces grappes de neige dont l'hiver les refleurit par compassion avant qu'ils brûlent pour l'éternité, et rentre.

Le second gémissement, assez semblable au premier du reste, part des airs.

Est-ce le vent qui se plaint désespérément à travers les branches grises et mouillées?

Ou quelqu'oiseau passager qui pleure la mort des feuilles?

Ce n'est point le vent: car, pas un arbre ne tremble et le bois entier est immobile. Même, si vous regardez bien le toit de Nick Parrit, sur la pierre où séchait cet été une touffe de giroflées sauvages vous apercevrez non pas un oiseau, mais deux, mais trois, et blancs encore, et projetant une ombre pâle sur les tuiles moussues que baigne la pâle lune: trois cigognes mélancoliquement perchées sur une patte grêle, le bec enfoui dans leur jabot, à la fête des Rois qu'ont carillonnée les cloches matinales (. . .).

Aussitôt les cloches tintèrent à l'église du village voisin, et le séraphin extatique qui était sculpté sur le portail descendit silencieusement à terre. Il tailla un long voile dans la neige constellée à jour par les pas des bouvreuils, et le jeta sur sa robe azurée, si bien qu'il paraissait vêtu d'un linceul blanc semé d'étoiles bleues. Il cacha sa tête pensive dans ses bras, et, les cheveux dénoués sur ses ailes frissonnantes à peine, s'étendit dans la nuit, et plana.[139]

Quand l'oiseau se posa sur la cabane, l'ange s'arrêta et, pendant que les cloches carillonnaient follement, psalmodia sur un air lent et triste cette riante saltarelle (. . .).

Mallarmé appears to have had a particular purpose in mind when in writing 'Les Trois Cigognes' he sprinkled his earlier prose narrative with the spice of 'Gaspard' rhythms and rhetoric. It served to temper the too-strong impression that readers must otherwise have had, that this fantastic tale was in fact simply a children's story. It enabled him to withdraw most of the religious sentimentality of the *narration scolaire* into the intimacy of Nick Parrit's fireside, allowing the night outside to become a 'stranger', more imaginatively adult setting. The new rhythmic patterns and imagery sharpen a kind of insomnolent awareness of nocturnal sights and sounds, eerie goings-on in nature and beyond. It is not impossible that to sustain this effect Mallarmé also brought into his new version three storks not present before.[140] They could even be visitors from *Gaspard de la nuit*.[141] The fact that they do not go very far in the story is easily explained. Their activities rival inconveniently the ministrations of the angel, as can be seen in both the passages quoted.

This literary enrichment which is to my mind the most interesting feature of 'Les Trois Cigognes', did not suffice to make it suitable for publication in a volume of strange tales. Nor did the addition (perhaps) of the six six-line stanzas of the 'saltarelle'. The whole project can never have been realistic, and beyond Mallarmé's mention of it to Cazalis no other trace or echo of it is recorded than that which (if my suggestion is accepted) is found in 'L'Art pour tous'. It may be relevant to add that (prose poems apart) Mallarmé published no more narrative fiction, of his own composing, during the whole of his career.

NOTES

1 Referred to above, pp. 17 and 50. Quotations here are from the text of the three articles, as republished in *DSM*. vii, 177–80, 181–3, and 186–8 respectively. The page-references of other items first published in *Le Sénonais* will be given in separate notes.

2 *DSM*. vii, 180.

3 *O.c.*, 300.

4 *DSM*. vii, 178.

5 A copy of the text, as printed at Verviers in 1860, has survived; see ibid. 180 n. 3.

6 See quotation above.

7 That was probably so. The sixth chapter of André Maurois's biography of Hugo, *Olympio*, begins as follows: 'Depuis le coup d'État, les drames de Victor Hugo, ennemi du régime, n'avaient pas été joués à Paris. Vint 1867, année de l'Exposition universelle. On prétendait montrer au

monde ce que la France avait de plus beau. (. . .) La Comédie-Française pouvait-elle, en un tel moment, renier l'un de ses grands auteurs? Une reprise d'*Hernani* fut suggérée. Victor Hugo se méfiait. La police ne la ferait-elle pas siffler? Ses représentants à Paris, Vacquerie et Meurice, ne le croyaient pas. (. . .) On décida, pour ôter toute chance aux siffleurs, de modifier les vers jadis "emboîtés" (i.e., according to Larousse, "conspués"). Précautions inutiles. Ce qui choqua le public, ce furent les changements . . . ' (*Olympio*, 1954, p. 476.) It appears, however, that in one important respect the account of the situation given by Maurois is mistaken. Hugo's plays had not been banned in France during his exile. Pierre L. Horn, in an article on 'Victor Hugo's theatrical royalties during his exile years', published in *Theatre Research*, Spring 1982, shows that the authorities 'did not interfere with the performance of the Hugolian repertoire on the stage of Parisian theatres', and that the author's very considerable royalties continued to be paid.

8 The allusion is to the performance of *Ruy Blas* at the Théâtre de la Renaissance in 1838, with Frédérick Lemaître in the part of Ruy Blas. See R. Baldick, *The Life and Times of Frédérick Lemaître*, 1959, pp. 161–71.

9 Jules Janin's *Histoire de la littérature dramatique*, in six volumes, was published in 1853–8. 'La Béjart' was Madeleine Béjart, at one time Poquelin's (i.e. Molière's) mistress. But Mallarmé presumably meant Armande Béjart her daughter and Molière's wife, 'Melle Molière' on the stage. The analogy with Mme Léon Marc was an unfortunate one in either case.

10 See above, ch. 2, n. 6.

11 In the third article quoted above, p. 77: 'Vous l'eussiez mieux senti, du reste, si mon article n'avait pas été coupé en deux au moment d'être mis sous presse.' Also, p. 78: 'un article trop long . . . élagué'.

12 For Mallarmé's borrowings here from Hugo's own comments, see *DSM*. vii, 184, notes.

13 One of Scribe's plays, composed in collaboration with Duveyrier, is entitled *Oscar, ou le mari qui trompe sa femme*.

14 It may be that Mallarmé's interest in irony was awakened by Banville's praise of it in 'La Corde raide' (*Odes funambulesques*): 'Il [le poète] te prend tes masques railleurs / Et ton rire ô sainte ironie.'

15 In 'Le Mystère dans les lettres', published thirty-five years later, he gave his critics the answer: 'Je préfère, devant l'agression, rétorquer que des contemporains ne savent pas lire—Sinon dans le journal: il dispense, certes, l'avantage de n'interrompre le chœur des préoccupations' (*O.c.*, 386).

16 Ibid. 252–4.

17 The story is told in one of the seventeenth-century *Historiettes* of Tallemant des Réaux ('CDXXXV. Mondory ou l'histoire des principaux comédiens françois'). A second edition of Monmerqué's ten-volume arrangement of this collection appeared in 1861. Also, Édouard Fournier's 'Bibliothèque elzévirienne' edition of *Les Chansons de Gaultier-Garguille*, published in 1858, and more likely to be known

among the actors, repeats the story (p. 210, n. 1): 'Tallemant convient aussi que Gaultier Garguille menoit une vie on ne peut plus bourgeoise. (. . .) Il passoit de longues heures dans l'étude de ses rôles. "Il étudioit son métier assez souvent, dit encore Tallemant (. . .), et il arrivoit quelquefois que comme un homme de qualité, qui l'affectionnoit, l'envoyoit prier à dîner, il répondoit qu'il étudioit".'

18 Contemporary playwrights. Mallarmé was particularly fond of making satirical references to Legouvé's verse.

19 From this viewpoint, Luc Badesco singles out (op. cit. II, pp. 845–7) an anonymous review in the *Revue anecdotique*, t. V (première quinzaine de février, 1862), pp. 70–1. It reads: '*Les Poésies parisiennes* de M. Emmanuel des Essarts sont un grand succès de vente et un grand succès de mode. Précisément parce qu'il sait le grec mieux que Vadius et qu'il est sorti à vingt et un ans de l'École normale, agrégé des classes supérieures, le jeune poëte a su ne pas se barbouiller de grec et de latin, et son livre est de ceux que les reines de l'élégance peuvent tenir dans leurs petites mains blanches sans craindre de se barbouiller les doigts. Le titre de ce recueil fashionable est admirablement choisi; car si l'auteur est, comme tous les poëtes contemporains, un disciple de Victor Hugo, il a aussi cherché l'accent de l'art moderne chez Gavarni et chez Balzac. S'il a appris le rythme dans les poëmes de Baudelaire, de Brizeux, de Th. de Banville, il n'a pas dédaigné de vivre dans la vie, au bois, dans les salons, dans les boudoirs, et, à la façon dont il chante la valse, il est facile de deviner que là où l'on danse il ne se tient pas à l'écart comme un jeune savant maladroit et triste. La joie, la gaîté, la frivolité même, l'éclair du luxe élégant, les enchantements du *high life*, font des *Poésies parisiennes* une fête étincelante, quelque chose comme un bal masqué de nuit, sous les étoiles du ciel de juin, dans un parc de Watteau. La mélancolie, la tristesse, le drame n'en sont point absents; s'il rit en écolier railleur dans les triolets de *la Fortune de Lazare* ou dans *la Chanson du lundi*,—dans *le Délaissé*, dans *l'Idylle sur le quai*, dans *Mademoiselle Mariani*, M. Emmanuel des Essarts montre qu'il a le don de l'émotion et le don des larmes, et ses *Revenants d'Alice*, dans une expression lyrique exaltée, arrivent à créer la plus poignante terreur. Mais,—M. des Essarts est implacable sur ce point—il ne pactise nullement avec les *antres malsains*. Il veut bien à la rigueur nous montrer Marco, mais posant sur un tapis d'Aubusson un petit pied chaussé d'une pantoufle de soie blanche, et appuyant sa main d'enfant sur un guéridon d'ébène, incrusté d'ivoire et d'étain, de la première manière de Boule. D'ailleurs le goût du *bibelot* et des préciosités artistiques n'exclut pas chez lui les hautes visées; on sent qu'un poëte sérieux est caché derrière ce Valentin épris des premiers muguets, et qu'il *pelote en attendant partie*. Si nous avions un reproche à adresser à l'auteur des *Poésies parisiennes*, ce serait d'avoir un peu trop ménagé toutes les chèvres et tous les choux littéraires, comme le prouve l'implacable variété de ses dédicaces, qui réunissent des noms bien étonnés de se trouver ensemble; mais à quel âge serait-il permis de tout admirer, si ce n'est à vingt ans? A coup sûr, cela vaut mieux que de tout dénigrer; quoique M. des Essarts ait fait de fâcheux efforts pour imiter

un peu tout le monde, malgré lui et en dépit qu'il en ait, il n'est pas un de ses vers où n'éclate son originalité native; il y a là à coup sûr un tempérament qui, un beau jour, s'affranchira des livres et des comédies. M. des Essarts sera lui-même, on n'en peut douter en relisant *le Repentir de Paul* et *la Seconde enfance*. Ce jour-là, son verre n'en sera pas des plus petits, et il boira dans son verre.' Provided the reader is sufficiently aware of the avuncular indulgence, and consequently sceptical of a forecast that the rest of the review belies, here is an excellent account of *Les Poésies parisiennes*.

20 The Pléiade editors place it among the *Proses de jeunesse*. Since there are several minor and no doubt unintentional 'variants' in their reproduction (*O.c.* 249–52), I have gone back to the original text in the *Papillon* for my quotations.

In a second review, for *Le Sénonais*, examined below, Mallarmé refers to the pleasure he had in announcing the poems 'on the eve of their birth'. But the Poulet-Malassis edition, though dated 1862, figures in the *Journal de la librairie* of 28 December 1861. Badesco (op. cit. II, p. 820 n. 5) mentions a second edition, published by Dentu in 1862.

21 For the favour enjoyed by *Le Papillon* during 1861–3, and comments on Des Essarts's part in its success, see Badesco, ibid. 752–69. He writes (pp. 759–60): '*Le Papillon* a sa place ici grâce à son orientation esthétique, toute proche de la *Revue fantaisiste*, et à la collaboration assidue de Catulle Mendès et d'Emmanuel des Essarts, les deux hommes de liaison de la génération montante.' The much celebrated beauty of its editor Olympe Audouart was another reason for the magazine's success; see n. 37 below. Her editorial *alter ego* was (says Badesco, ibid. 753) Charles Coligny. For his sponsorship in his other capacity as the *alter ego* of Arsène Houssaye, the editor of *L'Artiste*, Mallarmé had also no doubt to thank, in the first place, Des Essarts; see above, pp. 90 and 91.

22 The pertinacity with which Des Essarts courted the support of the influential is illustrated by his letters to the critic Montégut, in 1860, 1864, and 1866, published by Burkhart Küster in his short article on 'Baudelaire et Montégut d'après les lettres inédites de Banville et Des Essarts' (*RHLF.*, July–August 1975). It may have served his purpose that his young friend should write a review of his poems for *Le Papillon*, but the advantage to Mallarmé is more obvious. That it helped to make him known and noticed is attested by the liberally but ambiguously barbed witticism published anonymously in the *Revue anecdotique* (April 1862), and quoted (incorrectly) by Badesco (p. 853 n. 82). As first published, and reproduced in *Le Parnasse satirique du XIX*[e] *siècle* (vol. 2, p. 31) over the signature of Catulle Mendès, it reads: 'Le poète très peu rassis / Auteur d'un livre mal famé / Est soutenu par Malassis / Et défendu par Malarmé.' In the version quoted by David Alston in the *Gazette des Beaux-Arts* (April 1978, p. 153 n. 18), the names of the editor and the reviewer are split (to explain the pun?): 'Mal assis' and 'Mal armé'. (The facile play on Mallarmé's name was particularly tempting when it could be paired with another, as in this case. Many years later, in 1889, Verlaine wrote a sonnet 'A Stéphane Mallarmé',

ending 'Vous n'êtes pas mal armé / Plus que Sully n'est Prud'homme.')

23 Des Essarts was for the time being a follower of Jules Levallois, whose campaign for a 'littérature engagée' is directed by the conviction that 'la mission de l'art contemporain est de concourir de toutes ses ressources, de toutes ses forces, à la reconstruction de l'édifice social' (quoted in the *Revue anecdotique*, première quinzaine de décembre 1861).

This was the area of 'artistic principles' in which Des Essarts and his friend the reviewer most decidedly disagreed, and it was presumably on account of this disagreement that Mallarmé preferred to judge Des Essarts's poems in relation simply to the poet's intention. Before the year was out he would declare his allegiance to the group of poets who held the opposite conviction, the movement of 'l'art pour l'art'. Since this difference was to remain, on Mallarmé's side at least, a source of disharmony, it is well to take note of Des Essarts's views. They are expressed in a review of Jules Levallois's *Études de critique militante* (*Revue bibliographique*, 20 January 1863, pp. 446–7): 'La vérité et la sincérité viennent au premier rang dans les exigences de l'art nouveau; ceux qui représentent ces tendances avec le plus de ferveur et de constance ne devaient-ils pas être mis en relief par un critique initiateur? Après les festins de Trimalcion que l'imagination s'est donnés, c'est la santé, c'est la vie qui président aux sobres repas que nous offre la vérité. Le réalisme ou, pour laisser ce terme équivoque et injurieux, l'école sincère est donc indispensable (. . .). En dehors de ses rangs, que voyons-nous dans les jeunes générations? Des imitations de toutes sortes, des oiseaux moqueurs du passé. C'est contre cet archaïsme servile que combat M. Jules Levallois en prêtant main-forte aux prétendus réalistes. Ainsi, il a porté sa défiance contre l'anarchisme jusqu'à la sévérité outrée à l'égard de Leconte de Lisle, dont il méconnaît les intentions philosophiques. (. . .) Selon M. Levallois, personne ne doit se désintéresser de son siècle. Il demande avant tout de l'art l'expression de nos douleurs, de nos passions, de nos joies. Rien de plus sage. Il faut que la critique agisse, et, certes, l'action de M. Levallois n'a pas été inutile aux progrès quotidiens de la littérature sincère. (. . .) C'est pour l'idéal moderne qu'il combat et qu'il veille, autant que pour les principes éternels de la raison et du goût.' In this tribute of the disciple to the master, who had welcomed the *Poésies parisiennes* and urged him to continue in the direction he had chosen, away from 'les derniers partisans de *l'art pour l'art*' (Badesco, op. cit. II, p. 858), the gesture of apology to Leconte de Lisle is characteristic. A common complaint was that Des Essarts was anxious to please everybody, as witness the shower of dedications that accompanied his poems.

24 Ernest Fillonneau, quoted by Badesco (ibid. 844). Again, Des Essarts is praised for his refusal of 'l'art pour l'art'.

25 By taking this sentence (doctored) out of its context, Des Essarts seems to ignore the poker-face inscrutability of the passage in which it occurs, in the conclusion of Baudelaire's *Salon de 1846* headed 'De l'héroïsme de la vie moderne'.

On the claim to modernity that Des Essarts makes in this epigraph,

David Alston (art. cit., pp. 150–1) comments: 'The result however is light-weight and nowhere does Des Essarts achieve an effect remotely comparable to the sharp modern twist of "J'aime le souvenir de ces époques nues". (. . .) Des Essarts's modernism rarely goes beyond the emotional compass of "vers de circonstance".'

26 Mallarmé is indulgent in that he refrains from expressing his opinion on the general poetic quality of the poems. In spite of the technical skill they display as verse compositions, considered as poetry they are mediocre at best. Situations, people, happenings, thoughts, sentiments are commonplace, and the attempts to dramatize or 'poeticize' them unavailing. Poetic imagination, whether in thought or language, is everywhere lacking.

27 Scudéry's edition of the works of Théophile was published in 1632, six years after the poet's death. The preface to which Mallarmé refers (and which I quote from Alleaume's 1856 edition vol. I, pp. 3–4) ends with the challenge: 'De sorte que je ne fais pas difficulté de publier hautement que tous les morts ny tous les vivans n'ont rien qui puisse approcher des forces de ce vigoureux genie; et si parmy les derniers il se rencontre quelque extravagant qui juge que j'offence sa gloire imaginaire, pour luy montrer que je le crainds autant comme je l'estime, je veux qu'il sçache que je m'appelle DESCUDERY.'

28 Cf. below, pp. 84–5.

29 It has been claimed that Mallarmé's own poetic intention, as he already understands it in 1862, is the exact opposite of Des Essarts's as defined in his review of the *Poésies parisiennes*: 'Or on ne peut imaginer une "intention" plus exactement contraire à la sienne propre et c'est pour cela sans doute que Mallarmé s'applique à la formuler si nettement. Aussi suffit-il d'en retourner les termes pour obtenir une parfaite définition de la poésie mallarméenne. Elle veut exprimer un idéal qui *existe* par son propre rêve et qui ne soit *pas* le lyrisme de la réalité' (Georges Poulet, 'Espace et temps mallarméens', in *Deucalion* 3, October 1950; included also in his volume *La Distance intérieure*, 1952). The claim is supported with enthusiastic eloquence by Henri Mondor, in *Autres Précisions*, 136. It can only be critically examined in relation to Mallarmé's later poems. Here, I must be content to point out that whatever his later development might be, the terms of his antithesis of 1862 did not contrast Des Essarts with himself but quite explicitly with Banville.

The praise of Banville as the poet 'qui n'est pas un homme, mais la voix même de la lyre', is further explained in 'Symphonie littéraire', composed two years later; see below, p. 349.

The preoccupation with the relation, in poetry, between the ideal and the real remained central in Mallarmé's aesthetic, and his ideas on the subject evolved with it. For his reflections and procedures at one stage of that evolution, a few years after the article in *Le Papillon*, see my paper '"Du fait à l'idéal": la transposition mallarméenne', published in the *Revue de linguistique romane*, July–December 1968.

30 The following fragments, taken from the three poems singled out by Mallarmé to 'summarize' the volume, are fairly representative: 'Il n'était

plus, le temps des rêves sous les chênes, / Des longs rêves bercés par les vagues de l'air; /Comme un spectre plaintif qui fait sonner ses chaînes, /Dans les noirs carrefours se lamentait l'hiver. /Il n'était plus, le temps des rêves sous les chênes. // Et pourtant nos regards s'égaraient, plus rêveurs, / Près du foyer paisible aux souriantes flammes: / Nos lèvres aspiraient de plus douces saveurs; / Un soleil inconnu pénétrait dans nos âmes; / Et nos regards unis s'égaraient plus rêveurs. (. . .) Soyez les bienvenus, morne Hiver, froid Décembre, / Geôliers discrets, merci de nous emprisonner. / Dans l'étroit horizon d'une petite chambre / Les yeux qui se cherchaient semblent mieux rayonner! / Soyez les bienvenus, morne Hiver, froid Décembre! / (. . .) La lampe à ton front blanc jette plus de douceur; / Et, si quelque motif lent et mélancolique / T'attire, je crois voir au piano, ma sœur, / Se pencher près de toi l'âme de la Musique. / La lampe à ton front blanc jette plus de douceur. // C'est l'instant de choisir un confident poète, / Sainte-Beuve ou Musset, ces blessés frémissants. / Dans l'assoupissement de la ville muette / La lyre laisse mieux entendre ses accents! // C'est l'instant de choisir un confident poète. // C'est l'heure où tout s'oublie, où tout semble mourir, / Hormis l'être adoré dont nous frôle l'haleine, / Les yeux ont un éclair et le cœur un soupir / Où passe l'infini dont notre âme est trop pleine. / C'est l'heure où tout s'oublie, où tout semble mourir. // Nuits d'hiver, nuits d'hiver, sombres enchanteresses, / Vous rapprochez les cœurs que Dieu fit pour s'unir; / Vous avez le secret des intimes tendresses, / Nous qui savons aimer, nous saurons vous bénir, / Nuits d'hiver, nuits d'hiver, sombres enchanteresses!' ('Nuits d'hiver', or 'Nuit d'hiver'—both titles are used as if indifferently, in the printed text—dated 1859). The five-line stanzas of this poem are perhaps modelled on those of Baudelaire's *Moesta et Errabunda*.)

'Un peu moins que les vers toujours j'aimai la danse, / Voyage d'un moment vers un pays meilleur! / Un sage me l'a dit tout bas en confidence: / "Ne vous y trompez pas, c'est l'âme qui s'élance / Et le corps obéit au maître intérieur." // (. . .) Il suit le mouvement des sphères éternelles, / Celui qui, s'enlaçant comme dans un réseau, / Glisse avec des langueurs tendres ou solennelles [.] / Ses pieds ont disparu pour se changer en ailes . . . / Il n'a qu'à se lancer dans l'air . . . il est oiseau! // (. . .) Et parmi les danseurs étonnés nous passions, / Légers comme des papillons / Ou comme l'alouette en rasant les sillons. // On aurait dit deux hirondelles, / deux chérubins unis, deux étoiles fidèles: / Tant nous allions à tire d'ailes! // (. . .) O souvenir qui me domine! / Furtive vision que l'extase devine! / C'était la Mazurke divine! // Parfois mes longs regards dans les siens confondus / S'arrêtaient, troublés, éperdus; / Car j'avais vu s'ouvrir des paradis perdus; // Et, dans la grâce sans rivale / D'une Psyché chrétienne à la splendeur royale, / Contemplé la Danse idéale!' ('La Danse idéale', Avril 1860).

'Vous agitez entre vos doigts, / Madame, une badine exquise, / Que le doux Lancret autrefois / Eût conseillé à Cydalise; // Et Boucher qui mène aux déserts / L'essaim coquet des inhumaines / Dans vos poses et dans vos airs / A reconnu ses Dorimènes! / Les Tyrsis ne vous manquent pas, / Et l'amour que Midas achète / Vous fournit à chaque repas / Des madrigaux à la brochette. // Hors les mouches, rien n'est changé! / Autre temps, mêmes aventures! / Sous vos traits, ô marquise, j'ai / Revu les belles des peintures; // Et, saisi d'un charme nouveau, / J'invite en parfait mousquetaire, / Une fille du grand Watteau / A l'embarquement pour Cythère ' ('Une Parisienne de Watteau', Juin 1860).

31 It is interesting to compare this passage with the anonymous review quoted in n. 19 above. They have much in common. (The word *azuline* is an anglicism, the name of a dye used as an adjective of colour. It is accepted by the *OED* in that sense (dated 1864), but not apparently by reputable French dictionaries, despite the pretty little velvet hats.)

32 Two very different documents confirm the privately satiric character of Mallarmé's references here: his poem 'Contre un poète parisien', discussed below, and a remark in Des Essarts's article written after Mallarmé's death. Of Mallarmé as he first knew him he noted: 'Il évitait les relations mondaines et ne comprenait pas nos ferveurs pour la danse.'

33 Letter dated by the editors October 1862, *DSM*. vi, 56.

34 See the later part of the review quoted in n. 19 above.

35 *Le Papillon* of 25 November 1861 contains a sonnet by Des Essarts: 'A Théodore de Banville', to be included in *Les Poésies parisiennes:* 'Le poète voudrait loin des bruits prosaïques, / Bercé dans les langueurs du ciel oriental, / Rêver aux doux pays parfumés de santal, / Dans des kiosques à jour pavés de mosaïques. // Voir avec le haschisch danser dans le cristal / Des houris, et glisser au loin, dans des caïques, / Des femmes au front pâle, aux splendeurs hébraïques, / Dont l'œil prit un rayon à leur soleil natal. // Le souffle du réel dissipe ses chimères, / Et, lassé de sculpter des châteaux éphémères, / Olympio se fait Gilles ou Pascariel! / Mais l'Idéal, tandis qu'il va souffler ses bulles, / Le suit, et le tréteau des libres funambules / N'est que le piédestal où se masque Ariel.'

It may be remembered that in the 1899 obituary notice quoted above (ch. 2, p. 31) Des Essarts hailed Banville still as having been 'notre chef à tous'.

36 Examined below, p. 349.

37 The poem 'Placet', published earlier in *Le Papillon*, was similarly interpreted. Des Essarts's compliment was paid in a poem on 'La Brasserie des martyrs', dedicated to 'Olympe Audouard', signed 'La Palférine' (one of his early pseudonyms, alongside 'Georges Marcy'), and published in the *Revue anecdotique* in 1861. The poem is built on a comparison between the fear inspired by 'Olympe la blonde' and the terrors of the *Brasserie des Martyrs* (a café frequented by aggressive young authors, realists and anti-realists; Duranty and Champfleury are mentioned, and also Banville and Baudelaire.) It reads: 'Là vit la tribu de l'absinthe / Ardente dès le saut du lit / A tomber son prochain sans crainte / A chaque angle on vous démolit, / Mais j'aurais moins peur seul au monde, / Dans cet antre aux jongles pareil, / Que devant Olympe la

blonde, / Dont les cheveux semblent de l'onde / Parfilée avec du soleil.'

Under the heading 'Sur des vers retrouvés de Stéphane Mallarmé' (*NRF.*, 1 May 1933), Auriant quotes the compliments to 'la blondeur' in Mallarmé's article and adds: 'Olympe Audouard, la belle directrice du *Papillon*, était blonde, elle aussi, blonde comme Ève, blonde comme Vénus. Coligny lui recommanda l'auteur. Elle agréa l'article comme un hommage à sa personne.'

38 See pp. 187–90 and 205–6.

39 This profession of 'pantheistic' amoralism reminds one of the similar declaration in the juvenile poem 'Causerie d'adieu' (see above, vol. I, p. 166), and a sentence in Mallarmé's letter to Cazalis of 24 May 1862 (see *DSM*. vi, 32): '*Apprendre* et *jouir*, tout est là.'

40 See above, n. 20.

41 This piece of facetiousness is presumably the ritual teasing of Emmanuel.

42 Both masterpieces were published in 1857. Presumably Mallarmé was forgetting that Leconte de Lisle's *Poésies complètes* (also published by Poulet-Malassis) appeared in 1858.

43 Badesco suggests that the second article was written to make amends for this defect in the first. It was a defect, he believes, that Des Essarts would regret. 'Le mot qu'il attend, n'y figure pas. Il cherche et ne trouve pas [in the first article] où est son "originalité". Mallarmé va essayer de se rattraper dans un autre article publié à Sens' (Badesco, op. cit. II, 851).

44 This reference to Ronsard confirms the supposition that the total absence of his poems from Mallarmé's manuscript anthology, his *Glanes*, is to be explained by his having them on his own shelves or permanently at his disposal. So it was, for instance, in the case of Gautier, Chénier, and (except significantly for some of the banned *Châtiments*) Hugo. When Sainte-Beuve published his *Tableau de la poésie française et du théâtre français au XVIe siècle*, in 1828, he also published as a companion volume, *Œuvres choisies de Pierre de Ronsard, avec notice, notes et commentaires par C.-A. Sainte-Beuve*. It was presumably to a copy of this anthology that Mallarmé had access.

A still more elogious tribute to Ronsard, as one of the greatest of lyric poets, is the place of honour that he occupies in the triumphal 'fête du poète' that Mallarmé imagines to conclude his prose poem in praise of Banville, the last movement of his 'Symphonie littéraire' (*O.c.*, 265).

45 It was probably from Des Essarts that Mallarmé borrowed this device (over-optimistic in the circumstances) of presenting an article as the first of a series. It will be remembered that when they published together 'Le Carrefour des Demoiselles' they labelled it '*Scies*. I'. Similarly, a review by Des Essarts of Léon Cladel's novel *Les Martyrs ridicules* had appeared in *Le Papillon* on 25 May 1862 as 'Sympathies litteraires (1)'; a footnote explained: 'Sous ce titre, notre collaborateur se propose de publier un certain nombre d'études.' Articles of the same nature by Des Essarts appeared under the same heading, numbered II, III, and IV, on 10 August, 10 September, and 25 September respectively, and another, not numbered, on 13 September of the following year. It may be with

those early articles in mind that Des Essarts headed his 1899 article on the friend of his youth '*Souvenirs littéraires*: Stéphane Mallarmé'.

In the case of Mallarmé's 'Hérésies artistiques', Henri Mondor (*Vie*, 70 and 103) and Guy Michaud (*Mallarmé, l'homme et l'œuvre*, p. 16; 1971 edition, p. 20) both eliminate the vain promise in the plural heading and quietly substitute *Hérésie artistique*. Mondor (*Vie*, 813) even amends the title in his index, thus: '*Hérésie artistique, l'art pour tous (une)*'.

46 *L'Artiste* was founded in 1831 and continued to appear until 1904. Paul Bénichou writes: '*L'Artiste* (. . .) se proposait seulement de faire connaître la vie des arts et de définir leur mission. Son titre dit assez le parti que ses fondateurs, en 1831, pensaient tirer de la vogue dont jouissaient depuis quelques années déjà, pourvus de majuscules, l'Art et l'Artiste. Toutes les écoles de pensée contemporaine s'étaient rencontrées sur ce terrain, toutes les perspectives convergeaient vers la magnification de l'art et de ses servants, quand fut fondée cette revue de luxe, qui devait durer trois quarts de siècle. *L'Artiste* était loin d'être, dans ses premières années, la revue désengagée et "fantaisiste" qu'elle devint, sous Houssaye et Gautier, dans les dernières années de la monarchie de Juillet et tout au long du second Empire' (*Le Temps des prophètes*, 1977, p. 403).

More precisely relevant to the publication of Mallarmé's article are the observations of Albert Cassagne on *L'Artiste* and 'l'art pour l'art': 'Il faut citer aussi le journal *L'Artiste*, dont Th. Gautier devint directeur en 1856. (. . .) "Nous croyons, disait Gautier dans l'Introduction qu'il plaça en tête du numéro du 14 décembre 1856, nous croyons à l'autonomie de l'art; l'art pour nous n'est pas le moyen, mais le but; tout artiste qui se propose autre chose que le beau n'est pas un artiste à nos yeux." (. . .) On reconnaît là les principes de l'art pour l'art. Avec la direction de Th. Gautier, apparaissent dans *L'Artiste* les signatures de Flaubert, d'Edmond et Jules de Goncourt, de Bouilhet, Baudelaire, Théodore de Banville, de tous les amis de Théophile Gautier, de tous les fervents de l'art pur' (*La Théorie de l'art pour l'art en France* (1906), Dorbon reprint, 1959, p. 137). Suzanne Damiron concludes a general account of the magazine, its aims, and its contributors, with the remarks: '*L'Artiste* n'a pas failli à la mission que cette revue tenait à remplir: elle a laissé toutes les tendances, toutes les idées se donner libre cours, elle a défendu ceux qui débutaient et, à travers son texte et ses illustrations, on peut suivre toutes les manifestations artistiques d'une époque' (*Gazette des Beaux-Arts*, vol. 44 (1954), pp. 191–202).

47 Luc Badesco observes (op. cit. II, 830 n. 33): 'Charles Coligny, lui-même poète et critique, avait un sens aigu des valeurs naissantes. Cela explique la protection efficace qu'il accordait aux tout jeunes poètes, non seulement à E. des Essarts si bien soutenu par ailleurs, mais à Glatigny, à Mallarmé, à Mendès.' Houssaye regarded his colleague and friend as completely devoted to Poetry and *L'Artiste*, but unpredictable. In *Mes Confessions* (1891), VI, p. 136, he wrote: 'Plus insouciant que La Fontaine, il était plus distrait que moi. (. . .) Je lui avais abandonné à première vue le gouvernement de *L'Artiste*. Ce journal qu'il aimait

comme Quasimodo aimait Notre-Dame, il s'y était incarné avec passion. (. . .) Par malheur pour lui, pour moi, et pour *L'Artiste*, il avait ses jours de nuées et ses jours d'éclipses. Le journal ne paraissait presque jamais à heure fixe, il avouait lui-même que sa montre retardait quelquefois de huit jours; pendant ces huit jours-là il était introuvable.' Drink was Coligny's weakness, particularly absinth. Houssaye depicts him going from café to café till midnight, 'éblouissant ses auditeurs par tous les flamboiements de l'esthétique.' This last predilection may have stood Mallarmé's article in good stead.

48 Doucet, MS MLV 411. Mondor quotes the most informative part of this letter (*Vie*, 70 n. 2). Some details call for comment: Arsène Houssaye was of course the editor of *L'Artiste*; Des Essarts's poem 'Les Visions d'André Chénier' appeared in the issue of 1 June 1863 and poems by him followed in October of that year and January, May, June, and September 1864; 'Dieppe' is shorthand for 'le Journal des Baigneurs, à Dieppe', the Sunday beach-magazine in which a sonnet by Mallarmé had been published on 6 July and another would appear on the 13th, as will be recorded.

On 10 July 1862 (the date of Coligny's letter) *Le Papillon* published the following note, under the heading *Le Journal des Baigneurs* and signed 'Ch. Helvéol': 'Dieppe est la plus belle océanide de la Manche; cela a été dit par tout le monde, mais surtout par le *Journal des Baigneurs*, qui est un journal moitié dieppois et moitié parisien. Tous les ans, cette charmante feuille apparaît trois mois de la belle saison des bains et des eaux, et voilà qu'elle compte douze ans de succès, douze étés glorieux. Le premier numéro de 1862 a paru avec une liste de collaboration qui est des plus brillantes: *Chronique parisienne*, par Charles Coligny; *Gazette du sport*, par Léon Gatayès; *Souvenirs parisiens*, par Roger de Beauvoir; *Voyages et Villiégiature*, par Louis Énault; *Comédies à la fenêtre*, par Arsène Houssaye; *Comédies normandes*, par Éliacim Jourdain; *Comédies des gazettes et des gazetiers*, par J. F. Vaudin; *Chronique musicale*, par Camille de Vos; *Variétés et Poésies*, par Émile Deschamps, Emmanuel des Essarts, Henri Cazalis, Stéphane Mallarmé, Victor Luciennes, Charles Monselet, Alfred des Essarts (. . .).'

Of the poets, Éliacim Jourdain (the pen-name of Étienne Séraphim Pélican, 'secrétaire de la mairie de Dieppe') was the most prolific contributor, as he was also to *Le Papillon*. He took his poetry seriously but was a figure of fun for his fellows. Auriant, in his short article 'Sur des vers retrouvés de Mallarmé' (*NRF*, 1 May 1933), says of him: 'Coligny l'avait découvert et lancé, histoire de se moquer du monde et de la publicité, qui dispense la gloire littéraire. (. . .) Le bonhomme avait la rime facile, et se croyait poète de génie parce qu'il rimaillait des lieux-communs. Sa fécondité était prodigieuse. (. . .) Coligny et ses amis flattaient sa marotte.' Des Essarts was one of these friends and Mallarmé was presumably invited to be another. The second of his two sonnets in *Le Journal des Baigneurs* is headed '*Soleil d'hiver*, à Monsieur Éliacim Jourdain'.

49 Published in 1940. The text of the article is reprinted there in its entirety

(pp. 37–41) and commented on at some length (pp. 41–5). Mme Noulet points out (p. 36 n. 1) that the article was known to exist. F. Montel and M. Monda had mentioned it (without identifying the review where it was published) in the appendix to their *Bibliographie de Stéphane Mallarmé* (i.e. in 1926). They included it among the early writings of Mallarmé that they believed Dr Bonniot was likely to make known soon. Perhaps a cutting of the published article had survived among the poet's papers.

50 Op. cit., p. 37.

51 *O.c.*, 1536 [1543].

52 In ch. IV ('Le péché pour parfum') of *Histoire d'un Faune* (1948), pp. 61–4.

53 In the compact volume first published under the title *Mallarmé, l'homme et l'œuvre*, in the collection 'Connaissance des lettres' (Hatier-Boivin). The revised edition published by Hatier in 1971 bears the shortened title *Mallarmé*, which will be used here. Page-references are to the first edition, but for the convenience of readers the reference to the revised edition will be added in square brackets. The account of 'L'Art pour tous' is found on pp. 16–17 [19–21].

54 A retrospective view of this early article may well be thought more generally interesting and, in itself, likely to be more immediately fruitful than the one that suits my present purpose. The most thoughtful retrospective account of 'L'Art pour tous' that I know is found in the second chapter of Norman Paxton's *The Development of Mallarmé's Prose Style* (1968), pp. 43–5. The opinions expressed there have been subjected to the test of the author's close examination of Mallarmé's later writings. They lead to the general conclusion that 'the view of literature given in this article was developed consistently and modified by no further literary influences, but only the impact on Mallarmé of other art forms—ballet, opera, concerts, and painting.'

55 "Théophile Gautier", *L'Artiste*, 13 March 1859; published also in booklet form by Poulet-Malassis, in November of that year.

56 B., *O.c.* ii, pp. 111–13. The *Notes nouvelles sur Edgar Poe*, from which Baudelaire quotes, had appeared in 1857, prefacing the second volume of his translation of Poe's tales; for the passage quoted, see ibid. 333. Baudelaire seems to have adopted easily Poe's use of the word 'heresy' to signify an error in literary theory. In his introduction to a selection of the poems of Pierre Dupont, for the Crépet anthology *Les Poètes français* (August 1862)—but published first in the *Revue fantaisiste*, 15 August 1861—he uses the expression 'l'hérésie renouvelée' to refer to 'cette nouvelle infatuation française pour la sottise classique' (ibid. 169). Too much should not be made of the use of this word in literary contexts. In Baudelaire's own usage it intruded into other fields also; the *Notes nouvelles* themselves provide an example: 'Le progrès, cette grande hérésie de la décrépitude' (ibid. 324). But in the heading of Mallarmé's article it probably still carried at least a reminder that art now claimed religious status.

57 In the fourth paragraph of his article.

58 In this collection of fragments from Vacquerie's own critical and literary-

polemical publications, published in 1856, several items preach the doctrine that Mallarmé directly opposes in 'L'Art pour tous'. Such are those numbered XXXIII, XXXIV, XXXVI-VIII and headed: 'Prospérité des lettres', 'L'Enseignement littéraire', 'L'Art pour l'art', 'L'Utilité de la Beauté', and 'L'Idée-Action'; see n. 98 below for a relevant example of his manner.

The expression 'l'art pour tous' had the merit of being a topical slogan. A magazine had been launched the previous year, attractively produced, and addressed to a fairly wide public under the title *L'Art pour tous: encyclopédie de l'Art industriel et décoratif*. The catch-phrase still serves, it appears, at least in English. In a recent issue of *The Guardian*, a letter from the association *London Entertains* was published under the heading 'Art for all'.

59 *Essai sur Stéphane Mallarmé* (1963), p. 25.

60 I see two possible explanations of this image, which is a striking though relatively simple example of the kind of obscurity that was to be a characteristic of Mallarmé's later prose. If '*d'une tirade utilitaire*' is a complement of the verb, giving the meaning 'to adorn the flower-beds with a utilitarian discourse', 'plates-bandes' is literal: the flower-beds (of parks and gardens) are bestrewn with news-sheets or notices distributed to the public at dawn and carelessly thrown away. This reading would seem very unlikely were it not that the image is similar to one that is found among the involuted conceits of the essay Mallarmé published in 1895 under the title 'Le Livre, instrument spirituel'. The poet is seated 'sur un banc de jardin' with a book and a newspaper, comparing their outward aspects as signifying their different functions, when 'libéré, le journal domine, le mien, même, que j'écartai, s'envole près de roses, jaloux de couvrir leur ardent et orgueilleux conciliabule: développé parmi le massif, je le laisserai, aussi les paroles fleurs à leur mutisme' (*O.c.*, 378–9). In the other interpretation, which I prefer, '*d'une tirade utilitaire*' qualifies the noun '*plates-bandes*', which is used figuratively. The whole expression is applied to the 'feuilleton' of a daily paper, which occupies the lower part of the page and usually consists of part of a serial story, or articles on literature or the arts. This would not be the first time that this ornamental border was celebrated in euphuistic terms. I note in Jules Janin's *Le Gâteau des rois*, mentioned in a previous chapter (vol. I, 98) as a probable source of 'Les Trois Cigognes', the following string of images: 'Au bas de chaque journal, tous les matins, (. . .) vous pouvez remarquer cette frêle parure, cette broderie gracieuse, ce galant mensonge placé là, comme une dentelle au bas d'un jupon court, comme un falbala autour d'une robe de bal, cette broderie, cette fête du journal,—ô bonheur! cela ne tient ni à la politique, ni à la littérature de chaque jour' (op. cit., 1847, p. 16). And again, ironic praise on the same subject, in highly figurative language, is to be found in one of Mallarmé's 1895 essays, this time 'Étalages': 'Plutôt la Presse, chez nous seuls, a voulu une place aux écrits—son traditionnel feuilleton en rez-de-chaussée longtemps soutint la masse du format entier: ainsi qu'aux avenues, sur le fragile magasin, glaces à scintillation de bijoux ou par la nuance de tissus

baignées, sûrement pose un immeuble lourd d'étages nombreux' (*O.c.*, 376).

61 The Pléiade transcription of the article (*O.c.*, 257–60) contains inaccuracies. Quotations here are from the original text in *L'Artiste*.

62 Norman Paxton (who notes that the ideas put forward in 'L'Art pour tous' are all derivative) comments on the assertion as follows: 'The notion that anything sacred must be esoteric is found in Ballanche, Fabre d'Ive and all the Fourierist movement' (op. cit., pp. 43–4).

63 The use of the word ***prédestiné*** in this context, to link the elect in art with the elect in religion, may have been suggested by a passage in Baudelaire's first essay on Gautier: 'La biographie d'un homme dont les aventures les plus dramatiques se jouent silencieusement sous la coupole de son cerveau est un travail littéraire d'un ordre tout différent. Tel astre est né avec telles fonctions, et tel homme aussi. Chacun accomplit magnifiquement et humblement son rôle de prédestiné' (B., *O.c.* ii, p. 104). The earliest text of the essay, published in *L'Artiste*, contained the expression 'les hommes de lettres prédestinés', omitted in the Poulet-Malassis edition to avoid a repetition; see ibid. 1130. (It is thought likely, however, that Mallarmé read the Poulet-Malassis edition, published a few months after the other, in booklet form.)

64 The claim is one to which Albert Cassagne gives much attention, in op. cit., pp. 205–12 and 347–450.

It was probably in reading the poems of Banville and Leconte de Lisle that Mallarmé had become familiar with the idea of poetry as holy, being the cult of 'la sainte Beauté'. But what an individual poet put into such words, so applied, is vague. Mallarmé's use of the word 'hérésie', and what he says in his first paragraph, is unlikely to signify anything more than comparability, in respect of the reverence and secrecy due, of art with religion.

For the conception of poetry as a continuing hymn to 'la sainte Beauté', see in Leconte de Lisle's *Poèmes antiques* the closing stanzas of the poem 'Hypatie', and for Leconte de Lisle's devotion to that conception Fernand Desonay, *Le Rêve hellénique chez les poètes parnassiens* (1929), pp. 298–303. That devotion is examined more critically, and comparatively, by Irving Potter in *Le Pessimisme de Leconte de Lisle* (1961), pp. 377–81.

The model for the religious attitude to art and beauty, so ardently expressed by Leconte de Lisle, is ancient Greece. But according to M. Michaud, Mallarmé's master in this respect was Baudelaire. The young poet owed to Baudelaire, he believes, 'non seulement son goût pour la densité, mais son culte de la création poétique et la conviction qu'il a de sa valeur religieuse et quasi-mystique' (op. cit., p. 16 [19]). I know of no evidence to support that view, and what we know of his ideas on religion in his teens makes it most improbable. On the contrary, he appears to have rejected the Christian–mystical conception of poetry found in Baudelaire's paraphrase of Poe's 'Poetic Principle' quoted below in chapter 4, pp. 193–4. And what follows would seem to Mallarmé a challenge to the artist: 'et quand un poème exquis amène les larmes au

bord des yeux, ces larmes ne sont pas la preuve d'un excès de jouissance, elles sont bien plutôt le témoignage d'une mélancolie irritée, d'une postulation des nerfs, d'une nature exilée dans l'imparfait et qui voudrait s'emparer immédiatement, sur cette terre même, d'un paradis révélé' (ibid.). Soon he would be opposing 'Art and Mysticity' to each other as alternatives between which seekers after the Ideal must choose, and deriding Des Essarts's—and Baudelaire's!—inability to see that the Ideal and the Real are separate and irreconcilable (see below, pp. 82–5, and for later developments, *Colloque Mallarmé (Glasgow)*, Nizet, 1975, pp. 148–9.

65 See the passage quoted on p. 106 above, from *O.c.*, 258.

66 With regard to music, Baudelaire's writings on Wagner show the absurdity of what his disciple said. After hearing the three concerts that Wagner had given of his own music at the Théâtre Italien, in January and February 1860, Baudelaire wrote to the composer, introducing himself as 'quelqu'un qui (. . .) *ne sait pas la musique* et dont toute l'éducation se borne à avoir entendu (avec grand plaisir il est vrai) quelques beaux morceaux de Weber et de Beethoven'. He apologized on his country's behalf for 'les articles indignes, ridicules, où on fait tous les efforts possibles pour diffamer votre génie', and added 'Enfin l'indignation m'a poussé à vous témoigner ma reconnaissance: et je me suis dit: Je veux être distingué de tous ces imbéciles'. (Many of the latter were no doubt critics who knew far more of music than is necessary to decipher a Verdi score.)

He then described in terms of the highest admiration the extraordinary sensations that he, though knowing no music, had experienced at Wagner's concerts. The letter, not published till 1922, is reproduced in B., *O.c.* ii, pp. 1452–3.

Interest in the Wagner furore among Mallarmé's friends is reflected in 'Le Carrefour des Demoiselles', where Nina 'Semblait poser pour la Musique, / La musique de l'avenir'.

In the case of the visual arts, Courbet's experience, also fresh in the minds of many of Mallarmé's readers in 1862, would dispose no less effectively of the notion of protective arcana. A contemporary account of the Salon of 1850 can be read in Pierre Larousse's *Dictionnaire universel du XIXme siècle*. There, in vol. V (1869), under 'Courbet (Gustave)', is sketched the career of 'le terrible novateur qui devait soulever tant de colères et tant d'enthousiasmes', and how at the Salon of 1850–1 'M. Courbet se posa véritablement en champion d'un art nouveau, et produisit sur le public un effet violent, profond, extraordinaire'. Charles Léger, in *Courbet et son temps* (1948), pp. 42–3, describes that effect briefly: 'Les tableaux de Courbet sont impossibles à caser dans un coin de la salle. Ses grandes toiles, bien en vue, déchaînent les rires du public en général. Pour certains visiteurs, c'est de la répulsion, de l'horreur. Ces paysans grossiers du *Retour de la Foire*, ces affreux *Casseurs de pierres*, et le comble: cet immense tableau: *Un enterrement à Ornans*, avec ses trognes rouges, bestiales, ne sont pas de mise à Paris, dans un Salon, qui est une exposition officielle. C'est intolérable, scandaleux. Journaux et

revues remplissent leurs colonnes aux dépens de cette peinture abominable.' How aware Mallarmé was of these happenings, and of their influence on literature and literary theory, there is no knowing, but in view of Des Essarts's interest in realism and 'sincérisme', already noted, it is unlikely that his protégé had been left without instruction on the subject. Besides which, Mallarmé had read with enthusiasm Banville's *Odes funambulesques*, in which realists in general and Courbet in particular receive a full share of mockery.

A lithograph by Daumier published by *Le Charivari* in June 1857 shows a top-hatted crowd of visitors waiting to enter the Salon. The accompanying comment reads: 'Aspect du Salon le jour de l'ouverture . . . Rien que de vrais connaisseurs, total soixante mille personnes.'

67 It is also alien to what Mallarmé would later declare to be the essential nature of poetry. If poets have their own separate idiom, what becomes (for instance) of their 'purifying the language of the tribe' ('Le Tombeau d'Edgar Poe'), the theory of 'le double état de la parole' (*O.c.*, 368 and 857), verse as the redeemer of languages, which in themselves are all imperfect ('lui, philosophiquement rémunère le défaut des langues, complément supérieur', ibid., 364), and the poet's pride in having, as material for his art, the means of communication that man has invented for everyday use (itself so nearly insubstantial, 'un frisson', an exchange of faint vibrations in the air we breathe, ibid. 857), 'les mots, les aptes mots, de l'école, du logis, et du marché' (ibid. 653). For the place of such notions in Mallarmé's theory of poetry, see A. Gill, '"Du fait à l'idéal": la transposition mallarméenne', *Revue de linguistique romane*, July–Dec. 1968.

Considered as fantasy, the notion of the unsullied language apart may have been inspired by a passage in Baudelaire's second essay on Gautier, first published in the *Revue fantaisiste* (15 July 1861), and serving to introduce the selection of Gautier's poems in Crépet's *Les Poètes français*: 'Figurez-vous, je vous prie, la langue française à l'état de langue morte. Dans les écoles des nations nouvelles, on enseigne la langue d'un peuple qui fut grand, du peuple français. (. . .) Si dans ces époques, situées moins loin peut-être que ne l'imagine l'orgueil moderne, les poésies de Théophile Gautier sont retrouvées par quelque savant amoureux de beauté, je devine, je comprends, je vois sa joie. Voilà donc la vraie langue française! la langue des grands esprits et des esprits raffinés! Avec quel délice son œil se promènera dans tous ces poèmes si purs et si précieusement ornés! Comme toutes les ressources de notre belle langue, incomplètement connues, seront devinées et appréciées!' (B., *O.c.* ii, 151.) And what a charming prospect to imagine for the fastidious young Sénonais!

68 The suggestion might come, here again, from Baudelaire's second essay on Gautier. It opens with a curious passage on the effect of absurdity when it is used, as in some of Gautier's poems, according to Baudelaire, it is, to express deep feeling: 'Le cri du sentiment est toujours absurde, mais il est sublime parce qu'il est absurde. *Quia absurdum!*' 'Sur le ton absolu du sentiment', absurdities may become sublime. In these

assurances Mallarmé may have recognized a grain of excuse that his readers might find for his planned unreason.

69 See above, pp. 76–7.

What the reactions of the first readers of 'L'Art pour tous' were we can only try to imagine, after placing the article in the literary and more generally cultural climate of the time. The one known contemporary pronouncement on it is Coligny's expression of approval on receiving it, quoted above. Mondor (*Vie*, 70 n. 2) quotes a fragment of another letter from Coligny to Mallarmé, undated but presumed to have been written about the same time. One of the sentences quoted, 'Votre article fulminant est tout composé', has been taken to refer to 'L'Art pour tous'; see Guy Michaud, *Message poétique du symbolisme*, p. 165. But this second letter was in fact written in 1864, and the article mentioned in it must be one of those that were never published, perhaps the one on Leconte de Lisle; see *Corr.* i, 29, n. 2.

70 Op. cit., pp. 44–5: 'Voilà donc ce que Mallarmé, dès ses vingt ans, a vivement senti: la souillure dont souffrait la poésie, à la merci de tous les yeux, et l'irrévérentieuse liberté de n'importe quel lecteur à son égard. Dès lors, ce qu'il a désiré pour elle par-dessus tout, c'est une protection, un mystère visible, un ensemble ou plutôt un système de moyens qui défende l'entrée du temple, rebute celui qui n'a pas assez d'amour et ralentisse le nombre des adeptes. Ce qu'il a cherché, c'est une clef d'or, un chiffre, un truc, un argot qui soit le secret de rares patiences. Tout l'effort de Mallarmé tend à combler cette choquante absence, à mettre au point une invention qui y remédie.'

71 P. 164. 'Ainsi, le lyrisme galvaude la poésie et la livre à l'admiration bête des foules. Cette poésie, il faut la protéger, la rendre difficile: il faut un mystère visible, un "système de moyens qui défende l'entrée du temple" et "rebute celui qui n'a pas assez d'amour" [E. Noulet]. Pendant deux ans, il va travailler à mettre au point cette poétique, à trouver les procédés de style, ellipses, inversions, qui deviendront peu à peu la substance même de son œuvre, et dont le *Pitre châtié* et *Aumône* nous offrent, ici et là, les premiers exemples.'

72 Pp. 16–17 [20]. Of scholars who appear to have adopted this reading of 'L'Art pour tous' the following are notable examples. Paul Bénichou, while warning against an over-simplification of Mallarmé's motives, does not question that in 'L'Art pour tous' is expressed 'l'idée de la nécessaire obscurité poétique' and also the need for a 'poétique de l'énigme'. 'Il ne faudrait pas croire trop vite', he remarks, 'que l'obscurité mallarméenne soit le simple résultat d'un chiffrage destiné à écarter le vulgaire', but he seems to imply that if we consider only what Mallarmé says in 'L'Art pour tous' we may well form that opinion (*L'Écrivain et ses travaux*, p. 78). M. Walzer (op. cit., p. 26) writes: 'Mallarmé devine d'emblée qu'il n'est qu'un moyen pour le poète de provoquer par son écriture le même "religieux étonnement" que suscitent les signes de l'écriture musicale, c'est d'utiliser les sigles du langage, c'est-à-dire les mots eux-mêmes, à la même fin, en leur donnant l'apparence du secret, en leur refusant la communicabilité immédiate.' For his chapter on Mallarmé's article he

chooses a maxim taken from the *Imitation of Christ*: *Non homini reveles cor tuum*; in which interpretation, as in M. Michaud's , what has to be kept secret is the meaning of the poem, not the poet's art. I am not sure that Georges Mounin is not agreeing with Guy Michaud, when he refers to Mallarmé's 'idéologie esthétique globale, qui est restée celle du terrible petit texte de 1862, "Hérésies artistiques. L'art pour tous", trop peu cité' ('Mallarmé et le langage', *Europe*, April–May 1976). John Weightman lends his support in a passing mention of a writing that is not named but can only be 'L'Art pour tous': 'An initial reason for his obscurity is the unashamedly highbrow intention of keeping the philistines or the *hoi polloi* at bay by creating a semi-secret language, a *trobar clus*, to mark the shift from the plane of humdrum speech to the aesthetic level of poetry. He says rather quaintly in *Divagations* that poetry, using a medium accessible to every one, is at a disadvantage in comparison with music, which is protected by its special notation' ('Mallarmé and the language obsession', *Encounter*, October 1978). Finally I have to record with regret, in a paper that I read in July 1962 to the Association Internationale des Études Françaises, a reference to 'l'article de 1862 dans lequel Mallarmé justifiait déjà l'hermétisme littéraire' (*Cahiers de l'AIEF*, March 1963, p. 93).

73 Op. cit., p. 41.

74 *Cahiers du Sud*, 2e semestre 1949. Included (pp. 69–98) in the collection of essays by Paul Bénichou published (Librairie José Corti) in 1967, under the title *L'Écrivain et ses travaux*, to which page-references here apply.

75 Pp. 78–9. The 'positions de pensée' are presumably those, or some of those, taken up by theorists of 'l'art pour l'art' (about which more will be said later). Georges Mounin took M. Bénichou's observations a bold step further, placing Mallarmé's pretensions firmly in a literary-historical context, when he wrote in *Poésie et Société* (I quote from the second, revised edition, published in 1968): 'Et l'individualisme romantique idéalisera cette coupure économique et sociale entre l'auteur et le public, en lui trouvant des justifications absolues: Gautier dans la préface à *Mademoiselle de Maupin*, Banville dans *Le clown*. Mallarmé codifie cette attitude historique dans son article du 15 septembre 1862: *L'art pour tous*.' The chief defect in M. Mounin's statement is the absence of any reference to Baudelaire.

76 *Mallarmé*, pl. 17 [20].

77 M. Michaud's mention of the Middle Ages may be understood as a reference to the *trobar clus*, cultivated by certain Provençal poets of the late twelfth century (on which subject see Paul Zumthor, *Histoire littéraire de la France médiévale* (1954), pp. 146, 174–5, 188, and 215, and for a very concise account—and an interesting comparison with Mallarmé's 'hermetic style'—Henri Davenson, *Les Troubadours* (1961), pp. 72–5). Paul Bénichou and John Weightman, in the publications referred to in n. 72 above, both use that term. But the *trobar clus* neither conferred on poetry in that style, nor signified a belief that poetry in general possessed, a religious character. It was as worldly or courtly as

euphuism in Elizabethan England, and there is no reason to suppose that Mallarmé thought otherwise, if indeed he knew anything about it.

Equally gratuitous is the assumption that some thirty years after the publication of Champollion's dictionary and grammar of the ancient Egyptian language a young French bachelor of letters might see in the hieroglyphs in which that language was preserved a cryptographic code, used by Egyptian poets to conceal the meaning of their compositions.

The exclamations that end the introduction seem to evoke symbols of the manner in which, by design or by chance, sacred writ has in the past been protected from prying eyes. It is probably not by accident that in form they remind one of the nostalgic closing lines of Hugo's poem 'Passé', in *Les Voix intérieures*: 'O temps évanouis! ô splendeurs éclipsées! / O soleils descendus derrière l'horizon!' They are quoted in part (not quite accurately) by Baudelaire in his first essay on Gautier (B., *O.c.* ii, 110).

78 Op. cit., p. 36. 'Le Mystère dans les Lettres' is indeed the writing in which Mallarmé comes nearest to stating precisely his position concerning obscurity in poetry. His odd remarks on the subject reported by fellow-writers or journalists are sometimes patently ironical and always suspect. Those that are likely to be authentic, on the subject of 'l'enigme' or 'le mystère en poésie', recorded for instance in Huret's 'Enquête' (*O.c.*, 869), or the *Journal des Goncourt* (23 février 1893), contain no suggestion, so far as I can see, that the enigma is needed as protection against the Philistines. It is much more likely that they refer to a feeling for mystery akin to that underlined by Baudelaire in *Fusées* (first published in 1887): 'J'ai trouvé la définition du Beau,—de mon Beau. C'est quelque chose d'ardent et de triste, quelque chose d'un peu vague, laissant carrière à la conjecture. (. . .) Le mystère, le regret, sont encore des caractères du beau' (B., *O.c.* ii, p. 657).

The tone of 'Le Mystère dans les Lettres', where obscurity and the Philistines is certainly the subject or one of the subjects, promises if not plain speaking—on that subject, in view of his reputation, how could such an ironist speak plainly?—at least seriousness and sincerity. So do the circumstances in which it was written and published. The Pléiade editors remark that among Mallarmé's contributions to *La Revue blanche* it stands apart: 'la précédente série des *Variations sur un Sujet* paraissait complètement abandonnée, lorsqu'elle reprit dans le numéro du 1er septembre 1896 avec ces pages sur *Le Mystère dans les Lettres*; mais ce ne fut qu'une reprise sans lendemain' (*O.c.*, 1569 [1576]). What they do not note is that a few weeks before, on 15 July, *La Revue blanche* had published an article by one Marcel Proust entitled 'Contre l'obscurité', attacking 'les Symbolistes'. There can be no doubt that 'Le Mystère dans les Lettres' is Mallarmé's answer.

79 *O.c.*, 382.

80 See the first paragraph of n. 67 above. Which of Mallarmé's poems could serve as examples would be an interesting problem to study.

81 Op. cit., p. 36.

82 See n. 58 above.

83 The idea that Mallarmé may have been conscious of playing the part of 'Baudelaire's Vacquerie' is not so far-fetched as it may at first seem. It is a use of the name which readers of Mallarmé's correspondence may have noted in a letter from Cazalis of February 1868: 'Dierx aujourd'hui en est venu à se faire arracher tous les cheveux qu'il avait sur le haut du crâne pour arriver à la sereine calvitie du Maître [Leconte de Lisle]. C'est son chien, son Vacquerie, hors de l'Eglise, pas de salut' (*DSM*. vi, 363–4).

In Lefébure's first letter to Mallarmé, dated 9 April 1862, there is a reference to Vacquerie which, since the letter from Mallarmé to which Lefébure's is a tardy reply has not survived, is unexplained. In his letter, Lefébure, à propos of Mallarmé's possibly translating the poems of Edgar Poe as Baudelaire had translated the tales, speaks of Baudelaire as if Mallarmé knew him personally and was on friendly terms with him: 'au reste Baudelaire qui a un E. Poe complet pourra vous renseigner là-dessus. A propos de Baudelaire tâchez donc de savoir s'il croit au diable. (. . .) J'ai commencé une pièce de vers, *Les Asphodèles*, que je voudrais dédier à Baudelaire, auriez-vous la bonté de me donner son adresse? (. . .) Pour moi, si le soleil continue de faire éclore mes vers en petites pattes de mouches, je vous en dédierai quelques-uns—ô jeune Vacquerie' (*Lef.*, 169–71). Might it not be that Mallarmé had spoken of his allegiance to Baudelaire and his aesthetic principles (those 'principes d'art' he had refrained from introducing into his review of *Les Poésies parisiennes*) in similar terms? That Lefébure regarded Mallarmé as a disciple of Baudelaire and the other poets of 'l'art pour l'art' is confirmed in his second letter, of 25 June 1862, 'Savez-vous que j'ai retrouvé dans vos vers', he wrote, 'l'artiste ferme et dédaigneux que je connaissais? et que vos tercets sont dignes de Théophile Gautier, et que Baudelaire, s'il rajeunissait, pourrait signer vos sonnets?' (ibid. 171–2.)

In replying to Vacquerie's arguments on the subject of 'l'art pour tous' Mallarmé was taking on a redoubtable adversary (and one whom as a prose-writer he admired; see *O.c.*, 253, and *DSM*. vi, 205). Luc Badesco has several times cause to emphasize his prestige with writers of 'the 1860 generation'. For instance: 'Pour les adeptes de cette position (. . .) l'art ou la poésie ne se conçoit que dans un mélange de rêve et d'action, d'idéal et de réalité. C'est la position défendue par Vacquerie, héros exemplaire de toute la jeunesse de l'époque, tout au long de ses *Profils et Grimaces*, un de ses livres de chevet' (op. cit. I, p. 274); '[la jeunesse] honorait en Vacquerie l'adepte fidèle, le représentant officieux de la pensée de Victor Hugo absent' (ibid. 292); 'Auguste Vacquerie le porte-parole officieux du grand exilé, s'était fait le champion de cette idée: l'unité de l'action et du rêve, de la vie et de l'idéal. Il en avait longuement parlé dans *Profils et Grimaces*, que toute la jeunesse avait lu. C'est dans un poème dédié à Vacquerie que Des Essarts avait affirmé, avec son emphase habituelle: "L'existence est un drame aux scènes grandioses / Où la Réalité, mêlée à l'Idéal / . . . "' (ibid. II, p. 857). (More exactly, in pessimistic mood Des Essarts looks back on those beliefs as youthful illusions: 'Aux yeux de cet enfant qui rêve apothéoses, / L'existence est un drame aux scènes grandioses, / Où la Réalité, mêlée à l'Idéal, / Accomplit dans ses jeux la

défaite du Mal.' The poem is 'L'éternel Gulliver', a tame treatment of the theme of Baudelaire's 'Le Voyage'.) The role of anti-Vacquerie, Baudelaire's mouthpiece, might well appeal to Mallarmé. Ironically, a few months later, à propos of his poem 'Les Fenêtres', he would be expressing privately his disagreement with both these elders on this same issue of the relation, for the artist, between the real and the ideal; see below, p. 355, n. 44.

84 See n. 55 above.

85 The Crépet anthology was published at the beginning of August 1862, too late for the author of 'L'Art pour tous' to have read it. The 'notices' on the poets included in it had, however, with one exception not relevant to Mondor's observation, appeared in *La Revue fantaisiste*, as a series under the general title *Réflexions sur quelques-uns de mes contemporains*, between 15 June and August 1861. It cannot be taken for granted that Mallarmé read them there, but since that ephemeral but important periodical was owned and managed by Catulle Mendès, and Des Essarts contributed to it, it would not be difficult for him to obtain a loan of the numbers he was interested in.

86 For the section (or movement) of the 'Symphonie littéraire' devoted to Baudelaire, see below, pp. 347–9.

87 In the series published in the *Revue fantaisiste* (see n. 85 above), it appeared on 15 July 1861.

88 *DSM*. vi, 27 and 28.

89 15 June 1861. It opened the series referred to in n. 87 above.

90 '"La morale n'entre pas dans cet art [du poète Hugo] à *titre de but*. Elle s'y mêle et s'y confond comme dans la vie elle-même. Le poète est moraliste sans le vouloir, par abondance et plénitude de nature."

'Il y a ici une seule ligne qu'il faut changer; car dans *Les Misérables* la morale entre directement à *titre de but*, . . .' ('*Les Misérables* par Victor Hugo', B., *O.c.* ii, 218).

91 See *Histoire d'un Faune*, p. 53. His possession of a copy explains the confident tone in which, by way of praising M. Besombes's company of actors, Mallarmé had declared in the first of his articles for *Le Sénonais*: 'Mlle Protin ferait regretter ses vingt ans à Déjazet, et rêver Gautier à Camille de Maupin' (*DSM*. vii, 178–9).

92 See *Histoire d'un Faune*, p. 25.

93 See above, p. 102.

94 See ibid.

95 For the context, see above, p. 33 and n. 71.

96 The fairy's gift was: 'A chaque parole que vous direz, il vous sortira de la bouche ou un serpent ou un crapaud', and its first effect: 'Eh bien, ma mère! lui répondit la brutale, en jetant deux vipères et deux crapauds.' The gift to the other girl was: 'A chaque parole que vous direz, il vous sortira de la bouche ou une fleur ou une pierre précieuse', and its first effect: 'et, en disant ces mots, il lui sortit de la bouche deux roses, deux perles et deux gros diamants.' See above, ch. 2, n. 71.

97 B., *O.c.* ii, 103. Theoretically, of course, the reference could be to *Caprices et Zigzags* (1852 and 1856): but how unlikely a coincidence.

98 It will help to situate Mallarmé's argument in its contemporary context, and to judge its worth, if the substance of the opposite case is known. It is summarized in the following extract from Vacquerie's article on 'L'Enseignement littéraire': 'Nous ne nions pas les dangers de l'éducation littéraire,—pas plus que nous ne nions le danger de l'eau ou du feu, dont nous ne demandons pas pourtant la suppression à cause des inondations ou des incendies qu'ils commettent tous les jours . . . Si de ces foules qui se pressent aux portes des lycées il résulte des inconvénients partiels, si les pères ne mesurent pas leur ambition à leurs ressources, si les fils, après être montés jusqu'à la contemplation de l'esprit, souffrent de redescendre au travail de la main, si des désordres sont produits dans la famille et dans la cité par la disproportion de la capacité et de la destinée,—ce sont des malaises dont il faut chercher le remède dans une plus équitable répartition du bien-être et du pouvoir, et non dans l'extinction de l'intelligence.

'Nous ne disons pas non plus que l'enseignement des collèges soit parfait; nous ne défendons pas l'Université, Dieu nous en préserve! Il serait, certes, possible de mieux concilier la littérature et la vie. Nous voudrions que tout collégien fût tenu d'apprendre un métier. Mais ce que nous refusons d'admettre, c'est que le positif et l'utile soient l'essentiel de l'instruction; c'est qu'il faille murer les cervelles humaines dans quelque spécialité étroite; c'est que, pour être un bon mécanicien, il soit indispensable d'être une brute; c'est qu'on ne doive rien apprendre à une créature de Dieu que les moyens de gagner son pain; c'est qu'il n'existe pas autre chose que le corps; c'est qu'avant de lâcher un homme dans les réalités grossières de la vie, il soit mauvais de l'avertir qu'il a une âme.

'L'éducation littéraire, qu'on trouve trop largement ouverte, est l'unique soupirail par où il entre un peu d'idéal dans le crâne des multitudes. (. . .) Laissez les enfants commencer par l'idéal et le désintéressement; les hommes auront toujours le temps d'être égoïstes et sensuels!'

For Vacquerie (ibid. 221) 'La question principale de ce temps, c'est l'enseignement du peuple (. . .)—et qu'est-ce qui répand plus de clarté que la littérature?' The debate on this subject seems to be unending. In the *Revue de France* of 15 May 1899, the case for 'l'enseignement littéraire' is argued again, very eloquently, by J. de Courty. In our own day, Georges Mounin defends it against the hostility it still encounters (op. cit., chapters 2 and 3). But none of these arguments are of much avail against the aristocratism preached by Baudelaire's disciple convinced, in the words of Derek Mossop (*Pure Poetry*, 1971, p. 110) 'that the greater the artistic value of a work the smaller the circle within which it will be understood and appreciated'. Only from a point of view very different from Mallarmé's can Georges Mounin's observation for instance have much validity: 'Et la gloire avant l'école obligatoire pour tous est autre chose que la gloire depuis l'école pour tous' (op. cit., p. 10). Mallarmé was choosing between two contradictory doctrines and (so far as these doctrines were concerned) two masters.

99 'The Poetic Principle'. It is true that in Baudelaire's account of this

principle (in *Notes nouvelles sur Edgar Poe*), 'deep within the spirit of man' appears to have been dispensed with.

100 Mallarmé entertained this idea later, for instance in 'Le Phénomène futur'; see above, vol. I, p. 206. It is found also in Banville, for whom the enemies of poetry are not 'the people' but 'la bourgeoisie'. In an article written seven years after the publication of 'L'Art pour tous' he expressed an opinion concerning poetry and the public nearer to Hugo's than Mallarmé's but founded on an observation similar to Mallarmé's on the universal response to poetry. He is concerned with poetry on the stage: 'Le Théâtre-Français actuel n'est plus la maison de Molière; il est surtout et avant tout celle de Scribe, vrai fondateur, vrai législateur du peuple heureux et riche qui vient là se pâmer d'aise aux banalités exprimées dans une langue banale. (. . .) Le public s'engageait à apporter fidèlement son argent; moyennant quoi le théâtre promettait de l'encourager dans son égoïsme et de lui prêcher la vanité des sentiments sublimes, l'excellence des métaux monnayés et le respect infini que tout citoyen prudent a le devoir de professer pour sa propre peau. (. . .)

Mais, après cela, était-il utile de dire que Racine, et Corneille, et Molière, et Hugo, n'étaient plus chez eux dans une maison d'où on avait chassé les hautes aspirations, les beaux vers, l'idée même de l'héroïsme et du devoir? Non, cela allait de soi; cela était de toute nécessité et de toute évidence. Mais quand on affirme que les chefs-d'œuvre sont impossibles partout et pour tous, on va trop vite, on dépasse le but, et la foule qui se presse chaque dimanche au théâtre de la Gaîté a, d'une puissance souveraine, cassé et réformé ce jugement inique. Elle sent battre ses mille cœurs en écoutant le demi-dieu Rodrigue raconter des exploits pareils à ceux dont elle se sent capable elle-même. (. . .) Chacun naît avec l'intelligence absolue de la poésie; pour perdre ces dons précieux, pour désapprendre ce qu'on savait par cela seul qu'on existe, il faut faire beaucoup d'efforts, dépenser beaucoup d'argent, voir jouer beaucoup de pièces charpentées, entendre beaucoup d'alexandrins de Ponsard. Le peuple n'a pas su se donner un tel luxe princier; ses moyens ne lui ont pas permis de désapprendre à si grands frais sa langue natale, et c'est pourquoi il comprend Corneille et Racine!' ('L'Art et le peuple', in the anthology of Banville's criticism, *Critiques* (1917), edited by V. Barrucand, pp. 34–5).

101 See Émilie Noulet, op. cit., pp. 36–7.

102 *O.c.*, 382. The visual image in 'miroitement' is characteristic of 'Le Mystère dans les Lettres'; the poet's linguistic artistry is described almost entirely in visual terms, for the reader (not the hearer or reciter) of poetry. The word 'miroitement' itself recalls a sentence in Baudelaire's *Notes nouvelles sur Edgar Poe*: 'Mais sa poésie est toujours d'un puissant effet. (. . .) c'est quelque chose de profond et de miroitant comme le rêve, de mystérieux et de parfait comme le cristal' (B., *O.c.* ii, 336). The verb is used by Mallarmé in the 'Bibliographie' appended to his *Divagations*, in a sense very near to that of 'miroitement' in 'Le Mystère dans les Lettres': 'les fragments obligatoires où miroita le sujet' (*Divagations*, Fasquelle, 1922, p. 373).

103 An example was given above (vol. I, pp. 105–7, and ch. 5, n. 15) of the use Mallarmé may have made of such tuition in his schoolboy poems. The master responsible was probably M. Buzy, 'professeur de quatrième', himself a competent and very willing writer of verse; see *DSM*. vii, 172. When Emmanuel des Essarts read 'L'Art pour tous' he may well have found parts of it decidedly ungrateful, and reflected that his protégé would not have had so smooth a passage into a literary career had it not been for the schoolmasters, who through the tousled hair of the schoolboy Mallarmé had detected the sibylline gleam; see above, ch. 1, p. 10 n. 4.

What in Mallarmé's opinion could not be taught at school and could only be learned by poets, from other poets, was presumably the kind of secret lore that Sainte-Beuve remembered learning, by great good fortune, from Victor Hugo, immediately after their first meeting in January 1827. He describes the experience thus: 'Hugo, au milieu de ses remercîments et de ses éloges pour la façon dont j'avais apprécié son recueil *Odes et Ballades* [reviewed by Sainte-Beuve for *Le Globe*,] en prit occasion de m'exposer ses vues et son procédé d'art poétique, quelques-uns de ses secrets de rythme et de couleur. Je faisais dès ce temps-là des vers, mais pour moi seul et sans m'en vanter: je saisis vite les choses neuves que j'entendais pour la première fois et qui, à l'instant, m'ouvrirent un jour sur le style et sur la facture des vers (. . .) Une seconde visite acheva de me convertir et de m'initier à quelques-unes des réformes de l'école nouvelle. Rentré chez moi, je fis un choix de mes pièces de vers et les envoyai à Victor Hugo, ce que je n'avais osé jusqu'alors avec personne (. . .). Hugo, en me répondant à l'instant, et en louant mes vers, sut très bien indiquer, par les points mêmes sur lesquels portait son éloge, quelles étaient tout à côté mes faiblesses. J'étais conquis dès ce jour à la branche de l'école romantique dont il était le chef' (*Portraits contemporains*, 1891 edition, Calmann-Lévy, vol. I, p. 469: Sainte-Beuve's own appendix to his essay of 1835 on Hugo). So far as I know, Mallarmé had no such lessons from older poets in person, only from the study of their works. But it may be that Émile Deschamps gave him the benefit of the technical skill for which he was famous.

It is anomalous that 'L'Art pour tous', so deferential to Baudelaire and so respectful in particular of the ideas he expresses in his essays on Gautier, is mainly concerned with flatly condemning a practice of which the second essay appears to express approval: 'Victor Hugo est enseigné et paraphrasé dans les universités; mais aucun lettré n'ignore que l'étude de ses resplendissantes poésies doit être complétée par l'étude des poésies de Gautier' (B., *O.c.* ii, 151–2).

'L'Art pour tous' tells us nothing of such study, but it does provide clear evidence that for the broad principles which were to govern his attitudes and practice (the 'principes de l'art' he refrained from referring to in judging *Les Poésies parisiennes*) Mallarmé was looking to poets of the art for art's school, particularly its least orthodox member Baudelaire. An illuminating account of the doctrines to be found in their writings is provided in the closing chapters 'Poetry as Art', 'From

Statement to Suggestion', and 'Imagination enthroned: Baudelaire' of Margaret Gilman's *The Idea of Poetry in France from Houdar de la Motte to Baudelaire* (1958). There is however no indication in Mallarmé's article that his reading of the theoretical writings of the elders he admired was either wide or thorough.

104 Cf. n. 56 above, and B., *O.c.* ii, 113 and 333.

105 What appears to be lacking, after the word 'extatique', is a description of the average man's behaviour at a concert, comparable and as it were symmetrical with that of the citizen in the art gallery. We may suppose that it brought the sentence to an end. 'Le même homme' presumably began a new sentence, perhaps with another (or more than one) between.

The hiatus will have robbed the long parenthesis that precedes it of whatever appositeness it may have had. It could not, however, be other than a digression, a reflection in elaborately precious imagery on music's inability to excite the sensibility of the common man. If the author entertains this thought 'with head raised high', it is no doubt from pride in the fact (which previously he deplored), that poetry does waken a vague response in 'the crowd'.

106 Ibid. 105.

107 Ibid. 125. In his article on Victor Hugo (*Revue fantaisiste*, 15 June 1861) Baudelaire again named Goethe and Shakespeare as the great poets of France's neighbours: 'Peut-être est-ce parce que l'Allemagne avait eu Goethe, et l'Angleterre Shakespeare et Byron, que Victor Hugo était légitimement dû à la France' (ibid. 133).

108 Ibid. 106–7. It will be seen that what Baudelaire wrote was 'injurier une foule', not (as in Mallarmé's quotation) 'la foule'. The disciple was less attentive than one would have expected.

109 Ibid. 330: I conjecture at p. 112 that the '*Genus irritabile vatum!*' may itself be echoed also in Mallarmé's article.

110 Baudelaire's reply to the prophets of Progress in 'Le Salon de 1859' is well known: 'La poésie et le progrès sont deux ambitieux qui se haïssent d'une haine instinctive' (B., *O.c.* ii, 618).

111 See vol. I, ch. 9.

112 Op. cit., p. 174.

113 The hostility between the artists of 'l'art pour l'art' and bourgeois critics is explored by A. Cassagne in the first chapter ('Le sentiment aristocratique') of the second part of the study referred to in n. 46 above; see in particular pp. 158–69. There are luminous passages also in the works of Paul Bénichou, for instance the following, with which the situation very inexpertly outlined in 'L'Art pour tous' is strikingly in accord: 'En fait, il n'y a jamais eu d'art pour l'art au sens où l'entendent les doctrinaux sociaux, c'est-à-dire poursuivant des fins gratuites, étrangères à tout intérêt humain; (. . .) Ce qui est en cause, c'est l'autonomie de l'art, la liberté de ses choix et de ses moyens. La dénonciation du soi-disant Art pour l'Art est pour la littérature militante un moyen d'esquiver le vrai problème. (. . .) "Si vous voulez conserver votre trône et vos couronnes, dit-on au poète, il faut qu'à l'âme de l'artiste vous joigniez la tête du philosophe, il faut que dans ces formes chéries et

tant caressées vous emprisonniez le secret de l'avenir, il faut que dans ce moule vous jetiez la statue du dieu que le peuple attend." "Il faut" toujours quelque chose à quoi le poète seul n'a pas assez songé. Heureux quand on ne le taxe pas d'extravagance et d'égarement' (*Le Temps des prophètes*, pp. 341–2).

Vacquerie, on his side, lavishes praise on the critics. Some there are, he agrees, who are not worthy of the name ('ces insulteurs qui crachent de l'encre sur le génie'). But: 'Ce siècle en a des critiques,—de bons serviteurs de la poésie, loyaux, dévoués, fiers de la célébrité des autres, admirant tous les talents, même les plus obscurs, même les plus glorieux. (. . .) Ils proclament les poètes et ils les expliquent, il les multiplient dans des milliers d'intelligences, ils donnent les chefs-d'œuvre à la foule et la foule aux chefs-d'œuvre, ils couronnent et ils éclairent, ils sont la gloire du génie et la lumière du peuple' (op. cit., pp. 155–6).

114 Of such harsh consequences of hostile opinions Mallarmé would be particularly mindful. He had reacted by restoring the banned poems to his own copy of *Les Fleurs du mal*; cf. above, ch. 2, n. 62.

115 In the 1853 preface to his *Odes et Ballades*, Hugo wrote: 'De toutes les échelles qui vont de l'ombre à la lumière, la plus méritoire et la plus difficile à gravir, certes, c'est celle-ci: être né aristocrate et royaliste et devenir démocrate.' His sober pride in this achievement contrasts with the aristocratic posturing of his untried critic.

116 The story ('the famous anecdote') is recalled in Robert Shackleton's edition of Fontenelle's *Entretiens sur la pluralité des mondes* (1952), p. 32.

117 *Les Misérables*, IV. v. 5.

118 See above, p. 37 and ch. 2, n. 86. In support of my suggestion I would point out that the image which I take to be Fontenelle's, poeticized by Hugo, certainly made a strong impression on Mallarmé and remained active in his imagination. In the closing lines of 'Apparition' (*O.c.*, 30) the Hugolian side of it is recognizable. The total image is used superbly in the lecture on Villiers de L'Isle-Adam: 'dans une frêle main, creuset de vérités dont l'effusion devait illuminer' (*O.c.*, 492). Paradoxically, it is stripped of its radiance and as it were restored to Fontenelle in 'Un coup de dés': 'ancestralement à n'ouvrir pas la main / crispée / par delà l'inutile tête' (*O.c.*, 464).

Mallarmé (and why not Hugo?) may have read the Fontenelle anecdote in Alphonse Karr's *Une Poignée de vérités* (1853), whose title the author explains as follows: 'Un sage disait: "Si j'avais la main pleine de vérités, je me garderais bien de l'ouvrir." Le titre de ce volume prouve que je ne suis pas du même avis . . . peut-être parce que je ne suis pas aussi sage.'

119 This statement occurs in Baudelaire's 1861 article on Victor Hugo. He criticizes Fourier who, he says, 'est venu un jour, trop pompeusement, nous révéler les mystères de l'*analogie*' (B., *O.c.*, II, 132). It is in that one respect, as gifted with the sense of universal analogy, that Baudelaire considered poets supremely intelligent. Mallarmé, in 'L'Art pour tous', sides with those writers for whom, in the words of Albert Cassagne (op.

cit., p. 213): 'seuls les artistes peuvent être bons juges de l'art'. He had no doubt observed that poets were beginning to live as though they believed that to be the case. To quote the same authority, the maxims that appear to have governed the relations within the art for art's sake group were these: 'Que votre orgueil soit double; qu'il soit à la fois individuel et collectif. Enorgueillissez-vous d'être Leconte de Lisle ou Flaubert, mais soyez fier aussi d'être du petit groupe des hommes qui ont voué leur vie à l'art. Ayez le culte du génie et le respect des maîtres: serrez-vous autour d'eux pour les protéger des contacts vulgaires et défendre leur gloire. Honorez quiconque, à sa manière, qui peut n'être pas tout à fait la vôtre, travaille pour l'art et crée de la beauté. Bien des divergences de détail séparent Gautier de Flaubert, Leconte de Lisle de Baudelaire, mais cela ne les empêche pas de se montrer unis, de se soutenir, de faire masse contre le philistin. Théophile Gautier apparaît à Théodore de Banville comme "exactement semblable à un Dieu"; les uns et les autres s'envoient ou se lisent leurs œuvres, se témoignent une admiration sincère et fervente' (ibid. 174).

It is not simply youth, or insufficient reflection, that leads Mallarmé (as it seems) to misinterpret Baudelaire's reference to 'cette aristocratie qui fait solitude autour d'elle'. Certainly he would experience later (witness the essay 'Solitude') the isolation that to Baudelaire is a danger, a noble fate that befalls the individual artist. But it was as a member of a different generation no doubt, that of *Le Parnasse contemporain*, that he saw the isolation of artists rather as their wilful withdrawal into a separate group or confraternity. In December 1865 he would gently upbraid Cazalis for being remiss in that regard: 'Tu négliges trop vraiment ta charmante connaissance des hommes qui dominent l'art que tu as choisi et de tes confrères: on respire parmi eux un air qu'il faut avoir respiré pour être un Poète' (*DSM*. vi, 303). Much later, how different the attitude of the Master of 'les mardis' would be, from Baudelaire's towards the poets of Mallarmé's generation. A letter that Baudelaire wrote to Jules Troubat on 5 March 1866, after reading Verlaine's eulogy of him in *L'Art*, is well known for the declaration it contains on this subject: 'Ces jeunes gens ne manquent certes pas de talent, mais que de folies! (. . .) Pour dire la vérité, ils me font une peur de chien. Je n'aime rien tant que d'être seul' (*Correspondance de Charles Baudelaire*; Conard, t. V, p. 305–6).

It may however be noted that if Mallarmé misunderstood Baudelaire's observations on the artist's solitude, his understanding did reflect a facet of the older poet's reputation. A brief review of *Les Fleurs du mal*, in Emile Belcour's column 'Causerie littéraire' (*Le Papillon*, 10 March 1861), contains the following remarks: 'A une époque où les secrets du style semblent sur le point de tomber dans le domaine public, M. Charles Baudelaire a pu se faire une place à part; avec Théophile Gautier et deux ou trois autres il s'est créé loin des profanes un petit sanctuaire où la foule n'entre point, car il n'écrit point pour elle, mais où les fidèles accourent, se prosternent et admirent.'

120 The passage paraphrased is found in Poe's 'A chapter of Suggestions'.

See *The Works of Edgar Allan Poe*, ed. Stedman and Woodberry, 1895, vol. VIII, pp. 337–8: 'Que les poètes (. . .) soient une race irritable, cela est bien entendu; mais le *pourquoi* ne me semble pas aussi généralement compris. Un artiste n'est un artiste que grâce à son sens exquis du Beau—sens qui lui procure des jouissances enivrantes, mais qui en même temps implique, enferme un sens également exquis de toute difformité et de toute disproportion. (. . .) Ainsi la fameuse irritabilité poétique n'a pas de rapport avec le *tempérament*, compris dans le sens vulgaire, mais avec une clairvoyance plus qu'ordinaire relative au faux et à l'injuste. Cette clairvoyance n'est pas autre chose qu'un corollaire de la vive perception du vrai, de la justice, de la proportion, en un mot du Beau. Mais il y a une chose bien claire, c'est que l'homme qui n'est pas (au jugement du commun) *irritabilis*, n'est pas poète du tout.'

121 The situation referred to is fairly represented by the following items recorded by Lorenz (*Catalogue général de la Librairie française* (1840–55), 1868, vol. II, pp. 625–6): '*Odes et Ballades*, Charpentier, 1841, 3 frs. 50 c.; Hachette, 1858, 1 fr.—*Les Orientales*, Charpentier, 1841, 3 frs. 50 c.—*Les Voix intérieures* et *Les Rayons et les Ombres*, Charpentier, 1841, 3 frs. 50 c.; Hachette, 1857, 1 fr.—*Les Contemplations*, Lévy frères, 1856–7, 13 frs.; Hachette, 1857, 7 frs.—*La Légende des siècles, première série*, Lévy frères, 1859, 15 frs.; Hachette, 1862, 3 frs. 50 c.'

122 Banville, in 'L'Art et le peuple', answers Mallarmé so precisely here, from the dramatic poet's point of view, that one is tempted to think that he must have read, and remembered, 'L'Art pour tous'; see above, n. 100.

123 By 'Ma fille, va prier . . . ' must be understood 'La prière pour tous' in *Les Feuilles d'Automne*, for his borrowings from which in his schoolboy devotional poems, see above, vol. I, pp. 110, 113–14, 118–21. 'Le Faune' is presumably 'Le Satyre' in *La Légende des siècles* (1ère série).

124 'Comme ils n'y ont pas tendu, je l'espère' suggests a veiled allusion. Can it be that Mallarmé is referring slyly to the time when Baudelaire held very different views from those expressed in his article on Gautier? Ideas expressed, particularly, in his introduction to the poems of Pierre Dupont, published in 1851–2. There, such declarations as these can be read: 'Ce sera l'éternel honneur de Pierre Dupont d'avoir le premier enfoncé la porte. La hache à la main, il a coupé les chaînes du pont-levis de la forteresse; maintenant la poésie populaire peut passer. (. . .) Va donc à l'avenir en chantant, poète providentiel, tes chants sont le décalque lumineux des espérances et des convictions populaires' (B., *O.c.*, ii, 34–5).

125 Ibid. 179.

126 In the chapter of *Poésie et Société* on 'la poésie et l'enseignement', as it continues to be discussed today, Georges Mounin makes some interesting observations which he applies to the position taken up by Mallarmé in 'L'Art pour tous': 'Plus profondément toujours, il faut aussi souligner que le slogan de l'école ennemie des poètes se trouve, à l'insu très souvent de ceux qui le colportent, inclus dans une vieille campagne idéologique qui se moque bien du sort de la poésie: la vieille campagne contre la

démocratisation de la culture, déjà sensible dans l'aristocratisme assez cabotin de Théophile Gautier contre les saints-simoniens (dont dérive tout droit l'anathème de Mallarmé)' (op. cit., p. 19). In Mallarmé's case it derived more immediately from Baudelaire, and he appears to have been well aware of the political implications of the position he was taking up.

127 *DSM.* vi, 39. It is remarkable that except for Coligny's acknowledgement that he had received it, there is no mention of 'L'Art pour tous' in Mallarmé's extant correspondence. Even Cazalis, enamoured as he was of the notion that 'les poètes sont des gentilshommes', made no comment. On 25 September, ten days after the date of publication, Mallarmé wrote to Cazalis to answer a letter of a week before that has not survived, and he does not mention the article. It is true that Cazalis was just back from a visit to the Yapps in London, and Mallarmé and Marie were reunited at Sens after a separation of three weeks. So the topics were love and sweethearts, and perhaps on both sides it was thought that a reference to the article would be out of place. Or it may even be that at the end of the summer doldrums, *L'Artiste* of 15 September appeared late. Nothing either from Lefébure, so interested in Mallarmé's publications, who on 25 June had written: 'J'ai retrouvé dans vos vers l'artiste ferme et dédaigneux que je connaissais'. So far as we know the article received no more praise than it deserved, and was mercifully allowed to pass unnoticed. In particular, it won no praise from Baudelaire.

128 *Les Misérables*, IV. i. 5 (in the 1862 Brussels edition, vol. 7, pp. 90–2).

129 Op. cit., pp. 22–3. Hugo's advocations of revolutionary activities and also (in I. i of the novel) the admiring attention lavished on 'le conventionnel G.', may have been a source of private uneasiness for Mallarmé, to whose readers, who would have the same chapters fairly fresh in their memories, the name with which 'L'Art pour tous' was to be signed might suggest that the author had a regicide in his family background. In his very early days he had considered it prudent, and would again much later, to avoid admitting the connection with 'le conventionnel Mallarmé'; see above, vol. I, pp. 6–10. It might seem politic to him, when writing the conclusion to his article for *L'Artiste*, to seize this early opportunity of repudiating publicly all sympathy with democratic ideals. It would be misleading not to add, however, that this political side of his choice appears to have suited his temperament and weathered peaceably, as far from the madding crowd as it was reasonable to expect. In 1895 he reflected on the subject contentedly in the course of an essay on an abstruse politico-aesthetic theme:

> Aristocratie, pourquoi n'énoncer le terme—en face du tant vagi de démocratie: réciprocité d'états indispensable au conflit, national, par quoi quelque chose tient debout, ils se heurtent, se pénètrent, sans vertu si l'un fait défaut.
>
> La pièce de monnaie, exhumée aux arènes, présente, face, une figure sereine et, pile, le chiffre brutal universel ('La cour'; *O.c.*, 415).

130 *Histoire d'un Faune*, p. 64.

131 Ibid. 61.

132 It was in his letter to Cazalis of 25 September that Mallarmé wrote, in high spirits, of finding in railway timetables lines that read like verses: 'Et ces noms divins qui sont mon horizon bleu: Cologne, Mayence, Wiesbaden. C'est là que je voudrais m'envoler avec ma douce sœur, Marie! (. . .) Je suis fou, n'est-ce pas? La preuve, c'est que je vais faire un *poème en prose* sur ces projets de voyage' (*DSM.* vi, 54).

133 Ibid. 34.

134 Vol. I, p. 96.

135 See above, ch. 2, n. 102.

136 My remarks here on 'Les Trois Cigognes' take a little further the brief study of this prose story, above in vol. I, pp. 95–9.

137 *M. lyc.*, 337.

138 *DSM.* iii, 26.

139 In this highly ornamented paragraph, it was noted above (vol. I, p. 96) that the boldest image is borrowed from Hugo, 'Le Parricide' (*La Légende des siècles*, 1ère série). The fanciful detail that precedes it is probably taken from *Gaspard de la nuit*, where it is used twice: 'Si ce n'était que mon aïeul qui descend en pied de son cadre vermoulu' ('La Chambre gothique'); 'Les vénérables personnages de la tapisserie gothique, remuée par le vent, se saluèrent l'un l'autre, et mon bisaïeul entra dans la chambre—mon bisaïeul mort il y aura bientôt quatre-vingts ans!' ('Mon Bisaïeul').

140 It was noted above that 'Ce que disaient les trois cigognes' is not the title of the whole but only of the first section, which could quite well have been one of the additions.

141 This was suggested in ch. 4 of vol. I. Storks do not play a conspicuous part in *Gaspard*, but they are found in the dedicatory piece 'A M. Victor Hugo', and in the opening poem 'Harlem' they attract some attention: 'Et les cigognes qui battent des ailes autour de l'horloge de la ville, tendant le col du haut des airs et recevant dans leur bec les gouttes de pluie.'

Chapter 4

Fruits of the last year at Sens: verse

Though so little is known of Mallarmé's social and family life during his one year in Registry,[1] some information about his poetic activities during the later months of 1861 is available. We owe it partly to the fragmentary but reliable and friendly testimony of three fellow-poets, a little older than himself. The first of them is Emmanuel des Essarts, who in the obituary article already mentioned, published in the *Revue de France* nearly a year after Mallarmé's death, testified with characteristic decorum:

Il faisait volontiers à ses débuts des vers coquets, sortes de tableautins à la Watteau, des stances en octosyllabes gracieuses et mignardes. La fantaisie devançait la poésie.[2]

Of the 'stances en octosyllabes' some have survived and will be commented on later. 'La fantaisie' may well be a prudent reference to verses of a less reputable sort, which Des Essarts seems to have approved of at the time, and of which the second of the friendly testimonies tells a little more. That little is contained in a letter dated by the Pléiade editors 'novembre 1861', bearing the heading 'Revue fantaisiste' and signed by Catulle Mendès, the editor of that lively though short-lived magazine. It is addressed to Mallarmé and reads:

Cher Monsieur,

Je viens de relire attentivement vos *Bals masqués*.

J'ai essayé quelques coupures pour les accom[m]oder au genre de la revue. Je n'ai pas osé; il y en aurait trop à faire, et j'aurais gâté une des plus charmantes choses qu'on puisse lire.

Vous aviez raison. C'est trop petit journal.

Comme vous n'êtes pas embar[r]assé de votre copie, je crois qu'il vous sera indifférent de me faire autre chose: la *Chronique de la quinzaine*, pas pour cette fois, si vous voulez.

Vous êtes de ces gens qui donnent d'assez bonnes choses pour qu'on puisse les attendre.

Bien à vous.

C. Mendès.[3]

The complimentary tenor of this polite refusal may be explainable in part by the fact that Mendès was a friend of Des Essarts, without whose recommendation Mallarmé would surely not have presumed to submit his 'copy'.[4] As to the invitation to deputize for the editor in a later number, it was of little consequence because the *Revue fantaisiste* was about to cease publication. Nevertheless, Mendès was known to be a good judge of poetic talent. His praise would not be altogether perfunctory, and Mallarmé seems to have deemed his letter worth preserving. Its chief interest for us today is that to judge by the title *Bals masqués*, and the reasons given for the refusal, it can be inferred that the poems so entitled (if poems they were, and what else might they be?) involved a play on double meanings too *risqué* for publication in a respectable review. They may for instance have included, to judge again by a title, the one that is named in the last of the three testimonies. It is ventured shyly by Eugène Lefébure in his first letter to Mallarmé, dated 9 April 1862.[5] In the following excerpt from it, what is said of the first of two poems mentioned is intriguing.

Puisque je fais quelques vers, je suppose que vous devez en faire une foule, un poète doit être plus productif qu'un postier. Je vois de temps en temps des articles de vous dans le *Sénonais*, mais comme je ne vois ni le *Papillon* ni l'*Artiste*, il y a une éternité que je n'ai lu de vos vers, et encore, je n'en ai déjà pas tant lu. Je ne connais guère de vous que le rondeau des six Phillis[6] vous savez, et la charmante petite pièce de *l'Enfant à la rose*:

Des pas sur les pierres sonnèrent,
Un pauvre passait dans ce lieu,
Où les blancs lilas s'inclinèrent
Et les oiseaux des bois chantèrent,
Le pauvre étant l'ami de Dieu.

Il priait tout bas la madone, etc. . . .
L'enfant lui présente sa fleur.

The second poem of the two is of a kind so completely different from the other, so innocently pious, that it can only have been composed for some domestic occasion within Mallarmé's family. Lefébure seems particularly to have liked its rhyme-scheme (despite the grammatical endings), for he used it in his own poem, 'Les Asphodèles', which (he said) he wanted to dedicate to Baudelaire, and of which he quoted the first stanza.

Three verse compositions of 1861 have survived in their entirety, though never published in Mallarmé's lifetime: 'A une petite laveuse blonde', 'A un poète immoral', and 'Galanterie macabre'. They were probably written late that year, when with encouragement from Des Essarts the Registry clerk had finally made up his mind to quit the career that had been planned for him, and become a man of letters. They bear witness also to the general direction of his literary sympathies, made more explicit in the essays he was to publish during the following year. The themes of the romantics as well as their rhetoric are largely replaced by more up-to-date sophistications learned from Banville, the later Gautier, and of course the new leader of the modern school, Baudelaire. He probably considered the poems that he wrote as experimental pieces, simply, but those that he did not destroy, however experimental, deserve a rather sharper focusing than they usually receive.

'A une petite laveuse blonde'[7] half-borrows its title and its subject from Banville's 'A une petite Chanteuse des rues' (*Les Stalactites*), and inherits its verse-form (stanzas of four octosyllabic lines in *rimes croisées*) and some of its conceits in the 'Pompadour' convention, from 'La Voyageuse' (*Odes funambulesques*). It is more interestingly indebted to a poem in *Les Fleurs du mal*, differing in verse-form but similar in subject and similarly entitled, 'A une Mendiante rousse'.[8] In the opening stanzas at least of Mallarmé's poem, Baudelaire's adaptation of the tone and rhythms of a sixteenth-century nature poem to the description of a scene in modern Paris is sensitively understood and competently imitated by his young admirer.

The rather shorter poem in the same verse-form, 'A un poète immoral',[9] is addressed by Mallarmé to a poet of his own age, unnamed. The Pléiade editors consider that 'selon toute vrai-semblance' that poet was Des Essarts,[10] but subsequent evidence shows that on the contrary Mallarmé regarded his schoolmaster friend as more conventionally respectable than it was proper for so young a poet to be. The 'poète immoral' is quite likely to have been one of Léon Marc's younger colleagues, since this poem in his praise (vaguely claiming to be a preface to one of his comedies, also anonymous) was written on the eleventh of December, four days after Mallarmé's article on 'Monsieur Besombes et sa troupe' appeared in *Le Sénonais*. The players had been at Sens or in the neighbourhood for a month, and the town had had time to comment on their behaviour on and off the stage. The opening stanzas are written in the manner of Villon and in his honour. This tribute to so obviously suitable a patron, for young poets conscious of being at odds with society, was particularly appropriate in 1861, the fourth centenary of *Le Testament*:

> Escript l'ay l'an soixante et ung . . . [11]

The rest of Mallarmé's poem is in the manner of the *Odelettes* of Banville (poems such as 'A Adolphe Gaiffe'), and his *Odes funambulesques*. There may also be echoes of Glatigny, not unnaturally in view of the subject. The whole poem reads like a fairly light-hearted improvisation, in a style near to Banville's but a shade more familiar. Its general theme and some anti-philistine allusions link it to 'Le Guignon', written one or two months later at most.[12]

'Galanterie macabre' is a Parisian anecdote recounted in the manner of Baudelaire. The author refers to his subject as 'un tableau funèbrement grotesque', and the poem appears to be modelled mainly on those grouped by Baudelaire under the title *Tableaux Parisiens* in the second edition of *Les Fleurs du mal*, published in February 1861.[13] But suggestions from other poems by Baudelaire also went into its making. This undisguised imitation is the earliest proof left by Mallarmé of a keen and active interest in Baudelaire's verse. It is the more significant for his having composed it, in all probability, at the time when he was preparing his bid for the right to be a poet too, not a Registry official. A circumstance not forgotten perhaps by Emmanuel Des Essarts, his principal ally, when two years later, observing that his friend had excluded 'Galanterie macabre' from the selection of his poems that he was circulating among his friends, he expressed surprise and regret. 'C'est un thème saisissant', he protested.[14] It is not however the theme in itself, but the poem's general relation to Baudelaire that entitles it to special notice in this chapter:

Galanterie macabre[15]

Dans un de ces faubourgs où vont des caravanes
De chiffonniers se battre et baiser galamment
Un vieux linge sentant la peau des courtisanes
Et lapider les chats dans l'amour s'abîmant,

J'allais comme eux: mon âme errait en un ciel terne
Pareil à la lueur pleine de vague effroi
Que sur les murs bl[é]mis ébauche leur lanterne
Dont le matin rougit la flamme, un jour de froid.

Et je vis un tableau funèbrement grotesque
Dont le rêve me hante encore, et que voici:
Une femme, très-jeune, une pauvresse, presque
En gésine, était morte en un bouge noirci.

—Sans sacrements et comme un chien,—dit sa voisine.
Un haillon noir y pend et pour larmes d'argent
Montre le mur blafard par ses trous: la lésine
Et l'encens rance vont dans ses plis voltigeant.

Trois chaises attendent la bière; un cierge, à terre,
Dont la cire a déjà pleuré plus d'un mort; puis
Un chandelier, laissant sous son argent austère
Rire le cuivre, et, sous la pluie, un brin de buis . . .

. . . Voil[à].—Jusqu'ici rien: il est permis qu'on meure
Pauvre, un jour qu'il fait sale,—et qu'un enfant de chœur
Ouvre son parapluie, et, sans qu'un chien vous pleure,
Expédie au galop votre convoi moqueur.

Mais ce qui me fit mal à voir, ce fut, la porte
Lui semblant trop étroite ou l'escalier trop bas,
Un croque-mort grimpant au taudis de la morte
Par la lucarne, avec une échelle, à grands pas.

—La Mort a des égards envers ceux qu'elle traque:
Elle enivre d'azur nos yeux, en les fermant;
Puis passe un vieux frac noir et se coiffe d'un claque,
Et vient nous escroquer nos sous, courtoisement.—

Du premier échelon jusqu'au dernier, cet être
Ainsi que Roméo fantasquement volait,
Quand, par galanterie, au bord de la fenêtre
Il déposa sa pipe en tirant le volet.

Je détournais les yeux et m'en allais: la teinte
Où le ciel gris noyait mes songes, s'assombrit,
Et voici que la voix de ma pensée éteinte
Se réveilla, parlant comme le Démon rit.

Dans mon cœur où l'ennui pend ses drapeaux funèbres
Il est un sarcophage aussi, le souvenir.
Là, parmi les onguents pénétrant les ténèbres,
Dort Celle à qui Satan riva mon avenir.

Et le Vice, jaloux d'y fixer sa géhenne,
Veut la porter en terre et frappe aux carreaux; mais
Tu peux attendre encor, cher croque-mort:—ma haine
Est là dont l'œil vengeur l'emprisonne à jamais.

1861.

The imitation starts well enough, as such exercises go, with the liberal assistance of details easily identified, borrowed from *Les Fleurs du mal*, such as:

Souvent, à la clarté rouge d'un réverbère
Dont le vent bat la flamme et tourmente le verre,
Au cœur d'un vieux faubourg, labyrinthe fangeux
Où l'humanité grouille en ferments orageux.

('Le Vin des Chiffonniers')

C'était l'heure où . . .
La lampe sur le jour fait une tache rouge.

('Le Crépuscule du Matin')[16]

The closing section of three stanzas is quite successful too. It follows an example set by several of Baudelaire's poems: the poet-hero's[17] thought moves suddenly from the present scene to a background preoccupation, a mysterious, tragic fate to which he is condemned. Such endings are found in, for instance, 'Duellum', 'Le Flacon', 'A une madone', 'Alchimie de la Douleur' and 'A Celle qui est trop gaie'.[18] 'Alchimie de la Douleur', a sonnet, ends with lines that may well be echoed in the closing (also the most successful) stanzas of 'Galanterie macabre':

> Par toi je change l'or en fer
> Et le paradis en enfer;
> Dans le suaire des nuages
>
> Je découvre un cadavre cher,
> Et sur les célestes rivages
> Je bâtis de grands sarcophages.

The treatment of the 'tableau' itself leaves more to be desired. The interest is confusingly divided between the undertaker's acrobatic performance and what seems to be the theme (burial, or death and the undertaker). The stanza introducing that theme, 'La Mort a des égards . . . ', an accomplished one from the point of view of sound though not of substance, comes too early, interrupting the action and distracting from it. As a result the gruesome incident itself, the 'galanterie macabre', loses pride of place and slips by almost unnoticed. The theme that it should have introduced, being already broached is abruptly silenced, as if considered spent. Added to which, the expression 'par galanterie' does not in any case seize the gruesome irony intended, partly because it is weakened by the use of the word 'galanterie' in the title, and of 'courtoisement' and 'galamment' elsewhere.

These are technical imperfections. What seems quite clear is that this stereotype of a poem by Baudelaire is complimentary in its intention. It is an over-ambitious 'à la manière de', not a critical parody. If any other of Mallarmé's compositions of that year is comparable with it from that point of view, it is the passage in his letter to Des Essarts, dated 23 August 1862, written in the manner of Aloysius Bertrand as mentioned in a previous chapter.[19]

Of the poems composed in 1862—thirteen in number if I am not mistaken—the earliest were probably those that appeared first in print, namely the two sonnets, 'Placet' and 'Le Sonneur',[20] and the relatively long piece in *terza rima*, 'Le Guignon', of which only a fragment was published then.[21] It so happens that 'Placet' and 'Le Guignon' are representative, respectively, of the two strains in which their author would try out his talent during that year, the light-hearted or not very serious on the one hand, the altogether serious on the other. 'Placet' (later revised under the more explanatory title 'Placet futile') is the most pleasing as well as probably the earliest of six short pieces that indulge in smiles or laughter, sometimes satirical and bawdy on occasion. The other five are: 'Soleil d'hiver', '. . . *Mysticis umbraculis*', 'L'Enfant prodigue', 'A un poète parisien', and the sonnet without a title whose first line reads 'Parce que de la viande était à point rôtie', and which was carelessly christened 'Naissance du poète'. 'Le Guignon', on the other hand, and its following of shorter poems, 'Le Sonneur' and two other sonnets, 'Vere novo' and 'Tristesse d'été', then two short pieces in *terza rima* entitled for the time being 'Haine du Pauvre' and 'A un Mendiant', express unquiet moods, a young poet's uncertainties about himself and his art, and also dark thoughts on the subject of Baudelaire, the master whose poetic example he so admired but some of whose attitudes scandalized him. One poem stands apart from the rest, serious and sincere but also joyful, the one poem of young love that Mallarmé has left us, 'Apparition'.[22]

The sonnet 'Placet' appeared on 25 February in *Le Papillon*, the magazine which a few weeks before had published Mallarmé's first review of Des Essarts's *Poésies parisiennes*. Its dedication to Arsène Houssaye did not necessarily mean that its author was personally acquainted with that very influential man of letters. Houssaye was well known as (in Luc Badesco's words) '[un] défenseur intrépide du XVIIIe siècle et de ses "fêtes galantes".'[23] Any young poet who wrote a poem in the Pompadour idiom might therefore quite reasonably dedicate it to him. Few however could have paid him that compliment with such confident skill, as to the manner born:[24]

Placet[25]
A M. Arsène Houssaye

J'ai longtemps rêvé d'être, ô duchesse, l'Hébé
Qui rit sur votre tasse au baiser de tes lèvres;
Mais je suis un poëte, un peu moins qu'un abbé,
Et n'ai point figuré jusqu'ici sur le sèvres.

Puisque je ne suis pas ton bichon embarbé,
Ni tes bonbons, ni ton carmin, ne tes jeux mièvres,
Et qu'avec moi pourtant vous avez succombé,
Blonde dont les coiffeurs divins sont des orfèvres.

Nommez-nous . . . —vous de qui les souris framboisés
Sont un troupeau poudré d'agneaux apprivoisés
Qui vont broutant les cœurs et bêlant aux délires,

Nommez-nous . . . —et Boucher sur un rose éventail
Me peindra, flûte en mains, endormant ce bercail,
Duchesse, nommez-nous berger de vos sourires.

The above is the text that appeared in *Le Papillon*. A little more than twenty years later the poem was re-published, very little altered and with the author's approval, by Verlaine in the study of Mallarmé that figures in his series *Les Poètes maudits*. There, it is presented along with 'Le Guignon' so as to show 'notre cher poète et cher ami dans le début de son talent s'essayant sur tous les tons d'un instrument incomparable'. The comment of the author of *Fêtes galantes*, on 'Placet' read in that context, was made in a terse, bluff style adopted for the occasion:

Hein, la fleur de serre sans prix! Cueillie, de quelle jolie sorte! de la main si forte du maître ouvrier qui forgeait *Le Guignon*.[26]

It is generally and no doubt rightly supposed that it was a copy of 'Placet' that Mallarmé sent to Cazalis on 24 May, in the after-glow of the Sunday at Fontainebleau. He called it 'un sonnet Louis XV' and explained that it was for Nina Gaillard.[27] Perhaps it was Des Essarts's example, particularly the poem 'Une Parisienne de Watteau' in *Poésies parisiennes*, that had tempted his protégé to try his hand in this fashionable genre.[28] For a model to imitate, however, he certainly looked elsewhere, perhaps to Banville's 'La Voyageuse (à Caroline Letessier)' in the *Odes funambulesques*.[29] There he could read and perhaps study such stanzas (of a familiar shape) as these:

Au temps des pastels de Latour,
Quand l'enfant-dieu régnait au monde
Par la grâce de Pompadour,
Au temps des beautés sans seconde;

Au temps féerique où, sans mouchoir,
Sur les lys que Lancret dessine
Le collet de taffetas noir
Lutte avec la mouche assassine;

Au temps ou la Nymphe du vin,
Sourit sous la peau de panthère,
Au temps où Watteau le divin
Frête sa barque pour Cythère.
. . .
Ces bras purs et ce petit corps,
Noyés dans un frou-frou d'étoffes,
Eussent damné par leurs accords
Les abbés et les philosophes.

Vous eussiez aimé ces bichons
Noirs et feu, de race irlandaise,
Que l'on porte dans les manchons
Et que l'on peigne et que l'on baise.

La neige au sein, la rose aux doigts,
Boucher vous eût peinte en Diane,
Montrant sa cuisse au fond du bois
Et pliant comme une liane . . .

But another model, a source even, has been suggested, and indeed it seems certain that in composing 'Placet' Mallarmé had it in mind. It is a sonnet (also 'irrégulier') 'A Madame du Barry', in Privat d'Anglemont's *Paris inconnu* (1861). In intention and general effect it is very different from Mallarmé's, but its quatrains do seem to have provided him with some of the bric-à-brac he used in his own sonnet for local colour. Privat's poem reads:

Vous étiez du bon temps des robes à paniers,
Des bichons, des manchons, des abbés, des rocailles,
Des gens spirituels, polis et cancaniers,
Des filles, des marquis des soupers, des ripailles,

Moutons poudrés et blancs, poètes familiers,
Vieux sèvres et biscuits, charmantes antiquailles,
Amours dodus, pompons de rubans printaniers,
Meubles en bois de rose et caprices d'écailles . . .

Le peuple a tout brisé dans sa juste fureur;
Vous seule avez pleuré, vous seule avez eu peur,
Vous seule avez trahi votre fraîche noblesse.

Les autres souriaient sur les noirs tombereaux,
Et, tués sans colère, ils mouraient sans faiblesse;
Car vous seule étiez femme en ce temps de héros![30]

The most substantial debt of Mallarmé's 'Placet' was of a different kind, however. He owed it to whoever suggested that he should use that title, which brought with it the framework of make-believe on which his elaborate conceit is spread. Both title and framework appear to belong to an earlier phase of preciosity than the description 'sonnet Louis XV' implies. They go back another century, to Voiture and the 'hôtel de Rambouillet'.

Furetière, in his *Dictionnaire universel* of 1690, defines the word *placet* (which he used more seriously than Mallarmé in the titles of some of his own publications)[31] in this way:

Placet, est aussi une requeste obligée, ou prière qu'on présente au Roy, aux Ministres, ou aux Juges, pour lui demander quelque grâce, quelque audience, pour faire quelque recommandation. Ce mot [the final *t* of which, by the way, is silent] vient du Latin *placeat*, à cause qu'on les commence par, Plaise au Roy, à Monseigneur le Président.

The playful use of this procedural convention on which Mallarmé relies in 'Placet' appears to have been of Voiture's own inventing. It is found in four of his poems, all placed under the general heading *Vers burlesques*.[32] Two of them bear the title 'Placet'. One of these begins as follows:

XCVII
Placet

A Monseigneur le Cardinal
Mazarin, pour entrer chez-lui

Prelat passant tous les Prelats passez,
Et les presens, car ce n'est plus trop dire;
Pour Dieu, rendez les souhaits exaucez
D'un cœur dolent, qui de vous voir desire.

The other, nearer to Mallarmé's fiction, begins and ends thus:

LXXXVI
Placet

à une Dame

Plaise à la Duchesse tres-bonne,
Aux yeux tres-clairs, aux bruns cheveux,
Reine des flots de la Garonne,
Dame du Loth, et de tous ceux
Qui virent jamais sa personne.

De laisser entrer franchement,
Sans peine et sans empeschement,
Un homme au lieu de sa demeure:
Qui, s'il ne la voit franchement,
Enragera dedans une heure.
. . .
Il a trop souffert de moitié;
Au nom de sa ferme amitié,
Consolez son ame abbatuë
Ou dittes au moins par pitié,
A vostre Suisse, qu'on le tuë.

How Mallarmé may have been introduced to these gallantries one can only guess. Two new editions of Voiture's poems had appeared during the 1850s and it would be surprising if neither of them had found its way into the library of Émile Deschamps, himself notoriously partial to preciosity in courtly verse. Mallarmé may have read Voiture's *placets* there.

Autres temps, autres mœurs, however. In Mallarmé's frivolous fantasy the burlesque element had to be bolder than it was in Voiture's whimsical fawning. Delicacy, though no less desirable, was correspondingly difficult to maintain. Hence some at least of the corrections made to the text in later versions.[33] The principal flaw in the *Papillon* text is the seventh line. In the one surviving holograph copy, thought to be the one sent to Cazalis for Mademoiselle Nina, it is already altered. 'Et qu'avec moi pourtant vous avez succombé' is replaced by 'Et que sur moi pourtant ton regard est tombé'. (Later the line would be made more intriguingly meaningful: 'Et que sur moi je sais ton regard clos tombé'.) A correction in 'Placet futile', closely related to the change in line seven, attenuates an initial awkwardness in the manipulation of 'tu', 'ton', and 'te', alongside 'vous,', 'votre', and 'vos'—a linguistic acknowledgement presumably of the poet's dual situation, penning a formally humble request ('Nommez-nous', 'Duchesse, nommez-nous'), while still claiming a more intimate relationship: 'au baiser de tes lèvres' and the rest. In the first 'Placet' the 'tutoiement' is used five times, and in 'Placet futile' only three. Thanks to such emending, the 'sonnet Louis XV' has worn well. Were it not for some unruliness in the first tercet—the place for a moment of suspense or repose—it would be the most shapely as well as the most engaging of the early poems. As it is, the Trianon component would be less foolish with the traditional crook and a silvery tinkle, untroubled by the munching and bleating of the lambs.

'Soleil d'hiver' has this in common with 'Placet', that both reflect their author's interest, at the time, in certain French poets of the earlier half of the seventeenth century. As 'Placet' is inspired by Voiture, 'Soleil d'hiver' owes much to Théophile de Viau, and the more robust, though still far-fetched 'precious' imagery with which he flattered his Phillis, his Cloris, or his Corine through the changing seasons. Of these, winter was of course the cruellest. Hence his ode 'Contre l'hiver', and hence also, as a friendly burlesque extension to that complaint, Mallarmé's 'Soleil d'hiver'. For its principal theme, however, he was more obviously indebted to an intermediary, Théophile Gautier, who in an essay in praise of his namesake wrote:

Il proscrivait l'emploi de la mythologie, et voulait qu'on laissât dans leur vieux ciel de papier peint les divinités décrépites de l'ancien Olympe. Il trouvait que l'aurore aux doigts de rose commençait à devenir très-peu récréative et à se couperoser terriblement, qu'il était temps de laisser là Phébus avec sa perruque blonde et sa vielle, et que, à tout prendre, la basse de la pâle sainte Cécile valait bien la trompette de Clio la bouffie . . .[34]

It was on this suggestion that Mallarmé took Phœbus, in two contrasting manifestations, as a subject for a poem: on the one hand the sun-god resplendent in purple and gold, on the other what survived of all that glory when winter came. Nature would be shown giving Phœbus his annual foretaste, as it were, of the fate awaiting him when the Renaissance and its art were over and Christianity truly reigned, in the world of 'la pâle sainte Cécile'.

The poet's design has an obvious weakness, however. To figure Phœbus in his winter shape he has recourse to a comparison which, however amusingly pertinent he might find it, might well prove too recondite for the reader. In the 'Guritan chauve' who occupies all the second half of the poem and all one side of the antithesis on which the whole structure of the poem depends, few were likely to recognize a minor character in Hugo's play *Ruy Blas*:

Soleil d'hiver[35]

A Monsieur Éliacim Jourdain[36]

Phébus à la perruque rousse[37]
De qui les lames de vermeil,
O faunes ivres dans la mousse,
Provoquaient votre lourd sommeil.

Le bretteur aux fières tournures
Dont le brocart était d'ors fins,
Et qui par ses égratignures
Saignait la pourpre des raisins.

Ce n'est plus qu'un Guritan chauve[38]
Qui, dans son ciel froid verrouillé,
Le long de sa culotte mauve
Laisse battre un rayon rouillé:

Son aiguillette, sans bouffette,
Triste, pend aux sapins givrés,
Et la neige qui tombe est faite
De tous ses cartels déchirés![39]

This poem was published on 13 July 1862, at Dieppe in *Le Journal des Baigneurs*, from which oblivion it was retrieved by the critic who signed himself 'Auriant', in an article entitled 'Sur des vers retrouvés de Stéphane Mallarmé'.[40] Mallarmé's editors have left unanswered and indeed unraised the question of its precise date of composition. They appear to have assumed that it was written in view of that publication and at about that time. But that is most unlikely. Its subject was a very ill-chosen one for that season and those readers—a poem on the sun's behaviour in midwinter for a beach-magazine in July. Also, the idea of Phœbus's dwindling into 'un Guritan chauve' would hardly have occurred to Mallarmé at any other time than during the previous winter, when the company of Monsieur Besombes performed *Ruy Blas* at Sens, and Mallarmé expressed in *Le Sénonais* the opinion that Don Guritan was 'fort amusant, sans être peut-être assez grave'.[41] It is reasonable to suppose that 'Soleil d'hiver' was written then, and produced in haste when some six months later, at short notice, an editor asked for copy.[42] Such an editor is confidently identified in Auriant's article, where also the circumstances which led to Mallarmé's becoming a contributor to the *Journal des Baigneurs* are rapidly sketched:

Coligny s'était chargé de donner une tournure à la fois plus mondaine et plus littéraire au *Journal des Baigneurs* . . .

Toute la rédaction du *Papillon* y collaborait . . .

Stéphane Mallarmé? Les baigneurs de Dieppe ne se souvenaient pas d'avoir jamais entendu ce nom-là. Celui d'Éliacim Jourdain, par contre, leur était familier.

Éliacim était célèbre, à Dieppe tout au moins, du mois de juillet au mois de septembre. Coligny l'avait découvert et lancé, histoire de se moquer du monde et de la publicité, qui dispense la gloire littéraire.

Éliacim Jourdain s'appelait de son vrai nom Th.-Étienne-Séraphin Pellican; il était employé à la mairie de Dieppe. Natif d'Angerville, "Ancien secrétaire particulier de feu Dubernay, l'un des quatre inspecteurs de l'Empire", le bonhomme avait la rime facile, et se croyait poète de génie parce qu'il rimaillait des lieux-communs. Sa fécondité était prodigieuse . . . Coligny et ses amis flattaient sa marotte . . .

Stéphane Mallarmé s'était fait, à son tour, complice de la mystification.

Another feature that favours the early date, less cogent but interesting in itself, is the verse-form that is used in the poem, the stanzas of four octosyllabic lines, cross-rhyming. It is the form that served also for 'A un poète immoral', known to have been composed in December 1861, and for 'A une petite laveuse blonde', also dated 1861 and thought to have been written towards the end of that year.[43] After which, if 'Soleil d'hiver' was indeed written later than I suggest, it is the only poem in which Mallarmé used that verse form between the end of 1861 and November or December 1865, when 'Sainte Cécile jouant sur l'aile d'un chérubin' was composed for Cécile Brunet, to celebrate Saint Cecilia's day. The very interesting relationship between the two poems in respect of subject[44] lends significance also to their formal resemblance, which goes beyond the use of the stanza of four octosyllabic lines, cross-rhyming. The number of stanzas is also the same.[45] So far as 'Soleil d'hiver' is concerned, it might be said that its versification was a tribute to Gautier as was its theme, and as on the other hand the use of the alexandrine in 'Galanterie macabre' and nearly all the poems of 1862, was an acknowledgement, however rebellious its context, of Baudelaire's poetic ascendancy.

Two other poems that belong to the more light-hearted class, though only inasmuch as they rely for their effect on a burlesque element, were probably written at some time during the early months of 1862. They are entitled respectively '. . . *Mysticis umbraculis*' and 'L'Enfant prodigue'.[46] Both are dated by their author '1862', and taken together they prove worthy of closer study than they have generally received. They appear to be among the earliest of a series of poems that reveal, more or less darkly, a critical attitude towards Baudelaire.[47]

Until quite recently '. . . *Mysticis umbraculis*' was something of a puzzle, and it still has peculiar features. It is quite exceptionally brief, and unusual in its verse-form (not used elsewhere by Mallarmé, before or since): mono-rhyme stanzas each consisting of three alexandrines. Also, from the simple viewpoint of logical meaning certain of the six lines are curiously lacking in easy, natural cohesion, as if they followed a crooked path, in order to attain the rhyme. As a result, improbable as the suggestion may seem, the poem reads rather like the product of some technical exercise, or friendly contest between young rhymesters, in which certain arbitrary constraints have been imposed, including the use of stated line-endings (say 'améthyste' and 'forêt'). Since the contestant in this case was Mallarmé, and his composition was published for the first time nearly fifty years after his death (in the 1945 edition of the *Œuvres complètes*), it passed muster without much comment as just one more of the youthful efforts of a great-poet-to-be. Such perplexity as was expressed had to do with its title, which seemed to be made needlessly misleading:

Mysticis Umbraculis
(Prose des Fous)

Not until Carl Barbier's 1971 edition of the *Vers et prose d'enfance et de jeunesse* (*DSM*. iii, 13–98) was the true title made known. There the complete poem reads:

. . . *Mysticis umbraculis*.[48]
(Prose des Fous.)

Elle dormait: son doigt tremblait, sans améthyste
Et nu, sous sa chemise: après un soupir triste,
Il s'arrêta, levant au nombril la batiste.

Et son ventre sembla de la neige où serait,
Cependant qu'un rayon redore la forêt,
Tombé le nid moussu d'un gai chardonneret.
1862

When its heading was corrected thus, in conformity with the one holograph copy that had survived among the poet's papers, the poem was relieved of what had been its most perplexing feature. By the restoration of the three dots before *Mysticis umbraculis*, the reader was made aware that the Latin phrase was a quotation, and at the same time that 'Prose des Fous' in brackets (hitherto taken for the sub-title of the poem) was the title of the document from which the phrase was quoted. Since the poet was a young man of Sens, there could be little doubt as to the identity of the document referred to. It may be remembered that it was mentioned above,[49] as helping to explain an echo, in one of the schoolboy poems, of the All Fools' Day tradition at Sens. 'Prose des fous', or 'Prose de l'âne'[50] was the colloquial name for the opening section of the liturgy laid down, in a manuscript believed to go back to the thirteenth century, for the Feast of the Circumcision, celebrated on the first of January.[51] The 'Prose des Fous' proper appears to have been notorious locally because of its ribald associations, inevitable because it appeared from the text itself that in olden times an ass was present in the cathedral, and was supposed to answer with an occasional hee-haw when his praises were sung. But apparently the same title was sometimes given loosely—as easily happens in such situations—to the manuscript of which it was only one part, and which was more usually referred to, colloquially, as *Le Missel des fous*. It is this loose usage that explains Mallarmé's reference, in brackets, to the 'Prose des fous' as part of the title of his poem. For it is not in the 'prose' itself, but in a later, quite separate chant that the words quoted are found. In a *laud* extolling the Blessed Virgin and the miraculous conception (the 'Virgin Birth') of Christ, a totally serious devotional text, the fourth verse reads:

Misticis [*sic*] umbraculis
Olim prefiguratum
Et multis oraculis
Fuit prenunciatum,
Quod nostris in seculis
Gaudemus declaratum.[52]

The fiction that was needed to accommodate the pun, and to give the poem a minimum of substance, was not hard to find. It is borrowed from Banville's 'La Femme aux roses' (*Les Stalactites*). This has been demonstrated by Gardner Davies in a 'Note on Banville and Mallarmé'.[53] His case is argued succinctly:

Both its content and form [those, that is, of Mallarmé's poem] present striking points of resemblance with 'La Femme aux roses' . . . The basic picture is the same: the reclining figure of a woman asleep. In the Banville poem, the only gesture described is that of the 'doigt coquet' which has capriciously scattered the bouquet of roses.—Here [i.e. in Mallarmé's poem], the woman's trembling finger unconsciously rolls up her nightdress, to reveal her naked body. As in 'La Femme aux roses' the final development is an analogical one, in which the whiteness of her stomach is compared with a stretch of snow in the woods . . . (cf. Banville's 'coteaux neigeux'), with the mossy nest of a goldfinch fallen upon it. Some of the details of form are also significantly similar: the laconic 'Elle dormait', in both poems, at the beginning of the line; the 'Et' introducing the final analogy and the use of the verb 'sembler' to establish it; the lengthy interpolation between the auxiliary verbs 'avait' and 'serait' and their past participles 'parsemé' and 'tombé'.

I find this demonstration convincing, but my view differs from that of Dr Davies when he goes on to discuss what he regards as a parallel borrowing, from Baudelaire. The 'Note on Banville and Mallarmé' continues:

While all these similarities could be attributable to an unconscious recollection of Banville's poem, it seems much more probable that Mallarmé has rewritten it, in condensed form, with a view to replacing the unoriginal analogy . . . by one to shock the bourgeois reader. I have drawn attention elsewhere to the technique, borrowed from Baudelaire, which consists of destroying the banal romanticism of an evocation by introducing or implying an unexpected term of comparison—brutal, repulsive or obscene.

It may be that the shock the reader receives in ' . . . *Mysticis umbraculis*' does fall into that same broad category, since it is explainable by the imitation of Baudelaire's technique in this regard. And indeed Dr Davies had specifically placed it there in his earlier remarks on the subject:

L'image de *Mysticis Umbraculis*, comme l'indique le sous-titre *Prose des Fous*, n'a d'autre but que d'outrager le lecteur prude.[54]

But there my agreement with Dr Davies ends. In my understanding, the image has another, more significant aim. In Mallarmé's eyes, the shock to prudery is of secondary importance. A more scandalous result comes about when the words *mysticis umbraculis*—interpreted as meaning something like 'in secret groves' or 'in mystic shades'—enter the equation. The far-fetched pun thus achieved is blasphemous; it vilifies a religious subject and a sacred text. Here Baudelaire is not being imitated in the usual sense of the word, but parodied with critical intent. The most likely particular target is '*Franciscae meae laudes*', the only one of Baudelaire's Latin poems to be published in *Les Fleurs du mal* and, under the linguistic veil, probably the most deliberately, provocatively blasphemous in the whole volume.[55]

The likelihood that it is referred to directly, though prudently, in '. . . *Mysticis umbraculis*' is strengthened by what appear to be signs, vague but very noticeable, of a connection between the two poems. Such are the recourse to Latin and the choice of the mono-rhyme three-line stanza,[56] in both poems. But though for the inquisitive reader these similarities may seem to indicate a surreptitious connection, they do not reveal its nature. To make Mallarmé's attitude and intention clear, plainer evidence must be found, and by sheer good fortune it is not far to seek. It emerges from an unbiased re-examination and comparison of two texts that are quoted in the very interesting commentary devoted to '*Franciscae meae laudes*' in the Crépet-Blin edition of *Les Fleurs du mal*. The first is the very devious Note that Baudelaire appended to his Latin poem in the 1857 edition of the *Fleurs*, but excluded from the second edition, of 1861:

> Ne semble-t-il pas au lecteur, comme à moi, que la langue de la dernière décadence latine—suprême soupir d'une personne robuste, déjà transformée et préparée pour la vie spirituelle,—est singulièrement propre à exprimer la passion, telle que l'a comprise et sentie le monde poétique moderne? La mysticité est l'autre pôle de cet aimant dont Catulle et sa bande, poètes brutaux et purement épidermiques, n'ont connu que le pôle sensualité. Dans cette merveilleuse langue, le solécisme et le barbarisme me paraissent rendre les négligences forcées d'une passion qui s'oublie et se moque des règles. Les mots, pris dans une acception nouvelle, révèlent la maladresse charmante du barbare du nord, agenouillé devant la beauté romaine. Le calembour lui-même, quand il traverse ces pédantesques bégayements, ne joue-t-il pas la grâce sauvage et baroque de l'enfance?[57]

The second document is quoted in a footnote of the same editors, relating to Baudelaire's Note. It reads:

> Il semble bien que Mallarmé se soit souvenu de cette note-là dans *Plainte d'Automne*, l'une des "Divagations" les plus nettement baudelairiennes: '. . . J'ai passé de longues journées seul avec mon chat, et, seul, avec un des derniers auteurs de la *décadence latine*; car . . . j'ai aimé tout ce qui se résumait en ce mot: chute. Ainsi, dans l'année, ma saison favorite, ce sont les derniers jours alanguis de l'été, qui précèdent immédiatement l'automne . . . De même la littérature

à laquelle mon esprit demande une volupté sera la poésie agonisante des derniers moments de Rome, tant, cependant, qu'elle ne respire aucunement l'approche rajeunissante des *Barbares* et ne *bégaie* point le latin enfantin des premières proses chrétiennes.'[58]

To discuss here the general statement that 'Plainte d'automne' is the most Baudelairian of Mallarmé's prose writings would not be relevant. What must be pointed out is simply that the paragraph quoted does not support that statement, as the editors seem to claim. Quite the contrary. For though it is certainly strewn (as is indicated by the italicizing of certain words) with acknowledgements that the author of the prose poem has Baudelaire's note in mind, his intention in ostentatiously borrowing those words is most certainly not to express agreement with what Baudelaire used them to say. The paragraph that the editors quote from 'Plainte d'automne' reads in that context like an interpolation, whose whole purpose is to challenge Baudelaire's perversely eccentric praise of barbarism, and to sustain a contrary view. By this example, I suggest, it is easy to understand that whereas Mallarmé's borrowing from Baudelaire in ' . . . *Mysticis umbraculis*' has hitherto been taken as signifying his admiration, it is in fact to be explained by quite opposite feelings, his desire and intention to condemn or at least to blame.

The Baudelaire parodied in ' . . . *Mysticis umbraculis*' is heavily lampooned in another poem, so close to it in critical purpose that it may be presumed to have been written at about the same time, spring or early summer 1862:[59]

L'Enfant prodigue[60]

I

Chez celles dont l'amour est une orange sèche
Qui garde un vieux parfum sans le nectar vermeil,
J'ai cherché l'Infini qui fait que l'homme p[è]che,
Et n'ai trouvé qu'un Gouffre ennemi du sommeil.

—L'Infini, rêve fier qui berce dans sa houle
Les astres et les cœurs ainsi qu'un sable fin!
—Un Gouffre, hérisseé d'âpres ronces, où roule
Un fétide torrent de fard mêlé de vin!

II

O la mystique, ô la sanglante, ô l'amoureuse
Folle d'odeurs de cierge et d'encens, qui ne sus
Quel Démon te tordait le soir où, douloureuse,
Tu léchas un tableau du Saint-Cœur de Jésus.

Tes genoux qu'ont durcis les oraisons rêveuses,
Je les baise, et tes pieds qui calmeraient la mer[.]
Je veux plonger ma tête en tes cuisses nerveuses
Et pleurer mon erreur sous ton cilice amer;

Là, ma Sainte, enivré de parfums extatiques,
Dans l'oubli du noir Gouffre et de l'Infini cher,
Après avoir chanté tout bas de longs cantiques
J'endormirai mon mal sur votre fra[î]che chair.

The target of Mallarmé's satire can be recognized as, once more, the obnoxious device that Baudelaire apparently enjoys inflicting from time to time on his readers, that of associating a conspicuously unholy subject on the one hand, and on the other, acts, thoughts, words, or symbols that many and indeed a considerable majority of possible readers hold sacred.[61] In 'L'Enfant prodigue' the process is made more blatant, and more bluntly offensive to mid-nineteenth-century Christian susceptibilities, than it is in '. . . *Mysticis umbraculis*', where room is left for a little humour. The poem '*Franciscae meae laudes*' is given no special place in 'L'Enfant prodigue', but bold use is made by the satirist of the two appendages that encumbered, tauntingly, Baudelaire's praise of 'Françoise' in the first edition of *Les Fleurs du mal*. Mallarmé is able, by combining the two, to convert them to his service. The first, the sub-title 'Vers composés pour une modiste érudite et dévote', suggests to him how he may set up a burlesque, purely nominal version of the 'ideal' situation adumbrated in the second, the Note in which Baudelaire calls for a convergence of the poles of the magnet *mysticité-sensualité*. And this time, to make the simulated Baudelairian irreverence the more outrageous, the brunt of the blasphemy would be borne not by an equivocal Latin phrase picked up in a medieval hymn-book of dubious reputation, but by a well-known and much-loved text of the New Testament itself. In the Gospel according to Saint Luke, the prodigal son returns after sowing his wild oats, and receives in his father's house a loving welcome.[62] 'Similarly', in Mallarmé's 'L'Enfant prodigue' the poet-hero, after vainly seeking the Infinite in the brothels,[63] has discovered a convenient way of making his amends. He returns to a life of piety by making a *dévote*, devout to the point of religious mania, his mistress. He thus gains a share, it must be supposed, in the spiritual benefits gained by her devotions. Given this grossly sacrilegious paradox, representing the perversity that Baudelaire did indeed sometimes display in the treatment of religious themes, there can be no doubt that Mallarmé's intention is to caricature harshly this Christian poet's eccentric mockery of Christian teaching and practice. How well his critical faculty had guided that intention is indicated by a document which (as it happens) is often referred to in writings on Baudelaire. It is a paragraph in a letter that he sent on 18 February 1866 to the solicitor Ancelle, under whose financial guardianship he had been placed. It concerns his *Fleurs du mal* and its proper understanding:

> Faut-il vous dire, à vous qui ne l'avez pas plus deviné que les autres, que dans ce livre *atroce*, j'ai mis *tout mon cœur*, toute *ma tendresse*, toute *ma religion* (travestie), toute *ma haine*?

Mallarmé, for his part, had not failed to recognize the '*religion* (travestie)', and it was as such that he chose it for his target. 'L'Enfant prodigue' is his travesty of Baudelaire's own travesty of his own religious beliefs.

It reveals a sudden change in Mallarmé's attitude towards Baudelaire, since the composition of 'Galanterie macabre' not more than a few months before. It may be explained by what he was to tell Henri de Régnier some twenty-five years later:

> Chez le Baudelaire des dernières années s'était développée une manière factice de fumisterie qui montrait que le fond naturel était épuisé.[64]

If Mallarmé's realization of that development took place at the end of his twentieth or beginning of his twenty-first year, the accusations made in 'L'Enfant prodigue', and other poems that were to follow, would be fully accounted for. In the 'fumisterie' he referred to, the young poet had found a good reason for paring down his admiration for Baudelaire, perhaps a chance of reducing it to what was really the older poet's due and so freeing himself from the danger of a paralysing infatuation.

As to the poem itself, its division into the two short sections is interesting. It seems to imply that Mallarmé saw the subject of *Les Fleurs du mal* as a sort of 'Sinner's Progress'. His two first stanzas situate the poet-hero in his self-advertised unending spiritual drama, longing for the Infinite but dreading the Abyss (in other terms, perhaps, the Ideal and the Spleen). The other three stanzas present him perhaps in one vicissitude of his quest. The Baudelairian features that make up so much of the poem are found rather in the substance than the form, but many precise verbal echoes of *Les Fleurs du mal* have also been noted by critics. The general effect is summarized succinctly by Madame Noulet:

Le goût de la profanation, l'abus des parfums, l'oubli . . . des tourments supérieurs dans l'amour vénal, toutes les idées du poème sont baudelairiennes; mais les détails aussi, comme cette comparaison de l'orange qui se trouve dans *Bénédiction* (in 'Au Lecteur' rather, as Mondor points out, but in 'Bénédiction': 'le nectar vermeil').

Comme le vocabulaire: *vin*, *démon* et *fard* qui deviendra un mot mallarméen;

Et les rimes en -ique;

Et même ce beau vers:

O la mystique, ô la sanglante, ô l'amoureuse

qui combine la coupe ternaire et la triple exclamation

O serments, ô parfums! ô baisers infinis! (*Le Balcon*)[65]

To this account of the 'Baudelairisms' in 'L'Enfant prodigue', I would add some further details, situating the expressions referred to line by line:

line 3: *qui fait que l'homme pèche*.—Presumably in his longing to break out of the common limits of human experience. The thought is Baudelairian though not the words. It is expressed in praise of the Lesbians, at the end of the poem 'Femmes damnées (*Comme un bétail pensif* . . .)' the 'poème condamné' that Mallarmé included in his *Glanes*: *O vierges, ô démons, ô monstres, ô martyres, / De la réalité grands esprits contempteurs, / Chercheuses d'infini, dévotes et satyres, / Tantôt pleines de cris, tantôt pleines de pleurs / . . . Vous que dans votre enfer mon âme a poursuivies, / Pauvres sœurs, je vous aime autant que je vous plains . . .*

line 4: the word *gouffre* (not usually with the capital) occurs eighteen times in *Les Fleurs du mal* (see the Crépet-Blin edition, p. 562). The Bonniot facsimile shows that in 'L'Enfant prodigue', lines 4 and 18, it was first written *gouffre*, then corrected to *Gouffre*, perhaps the better to pair with *l'Infini*.

lines 5–6: the description reminds one more of Hugo, or Mallarmé the pantheist, than of Baudelaire.

line 7: Baudelaire seldom describes any one of his abysses physically. He does so however in 'Duellum', and makes it not unfamiliar: *Dans le ravin hanté des chats-pards et des onces, / Nos héros, s'étreignant méchamment, ont roulé, / Et leur peau fleurira l'aridité des ronces. / —Ce gouffre, c'est l'enfer . . .*

line 8: I have found no such torrent (stinking of debauchery?) in any of Baudelaire's *gouffres*.

line 9: *La mystique* and *l'amoureuse* bring together the two poles of the magnet; *la sanglante* brings in self-flagellation, as (again) 'Femmes damnées (*Comme un bétail pensif . . .*)': *Et d'autres dont la gorge aime les scapulaires, / Qui, recélant un fouet sous leurs longs vêtements, / Mêlent, dans le bois sombre et les nuits solitaires, / L'écume du plaisir aux larmes des tourments*. In 'L'Enfant prodigue', the hair-shirt in line 16 has to suffice (except for the suggestion in 'sanglants') as an instrument of self-mortification.

lines 10 and 17: perfumes, particularly of the more exotic kinds, and incense with its religious-sensuous associations, play an important part in Baudelaire's poems, for instance in 'Correspondances' (the two tercets), 'Parfum exotique' (again the two tercets), 'La Chevelure' (stanzas 2 and 7), 'Le Balcon' (closing stanza), 'Le Parfum', 'Harmonie du soir' (first two stanzas), 'L'Invitation au voyage' (second stanza), 'A une Madone' (lines 33 to 36), 'Chanson d'après-midi' (stanzas 3 and 4).

line 11: *Quel Démon . . .* ; cf. in 'Au Lecteur': *C'est le Diable qui tient les fils qui nous remuent*, in 'Ciel brouillé': *agités d'un mal inconnu qui les tord*, and in 'La Destruction': *Sans cesse à mes côtés s'agite le Démon*.

line 12: the two capitals of *Saint-Cœur* (as in *O.c.*, 14) are quite clearly marked in the Bonniot facsimile.

line 14: *tes pieds qui calmeraient la mer*. Madame Noulet (op. cit., p. 371) notes that these words are found also in 'Hérodiade': *Et regardent mes pieds qui calmeraient la mer*.

line 15: there may be a distorted echo here of Baudelaire's 'La Chevelure', *Je plongerai ma tête amoureuse d'ivresse / Dans ce noir océan où l'autre est enfermé*.

line 17: the words *ma Sainte* represent, briefly and mildly, the extravagant praise of this or that woman, in blasphemously religious language, found in such poems as 'Le Possédé', *O mon cher Belzébuth, je t'adore!*, or 'Le Parfum', *Vivant sachet, encensoir de l'alcôve*, or 'A une Madone', *Je veux bâtir pour toi, Madone, ma maîtresse, / Un autel souterrain au fond de ma détresse / . . . Je mettrai le Serpent qui me mord les entrailles / Sous tes talons*, or 'Chanson d'après-midi', *Je t'adore, ô ma frivole, / ma terrible passion! / Avec la dévotion / Du prêtre pour son idole*.

line 20: *J'endormirai mon mal . . .* ; cf. in 'Femmes damnées (Delphine et Hippolyte)', *Et trouver sur ton sein la fraîcheur du tombeau*.

On 6 July, a week before 'Soleil d'hiver', a very different poem had appeared over Mallarmé's signature in the *Journal des baigneurs* at Dieppe:

Contre un poète parisien.[66]

A E. des E. . . . [67]

Souvent la vision du Poète me frappe:
Ange à cuirasse fauve, il a pour volupté
L'éclair du glaive, ou, blanc songeur, il a la chape,
La mitre by[z]antine et le bâton sculpté.

Dante, au laurier amer, dans un linceul se drape,
Un linceul fait de nuit et de sérénité:
Anacréon, tout nu, rit et baise une grappe
Sans songer que la vigne a des feuilles, l'été[.]

Pailletés d'astres, fous d'azur, les grands bohèmes,
Dans les éclairs vermeils de leur gai tabourin,
Passent, fantasquement coiffés de romarin.

Mais j'aime peu voir, Muse, ô reine des poèmes,
Dont la toison nimbée a l'air d'un ostensoir,
Un poète qui polke avec un habit noir.

STÉPHANE MALLARMÉ.

The Flammarion editors date this sonnet 'vers juin 1862'.[68] Their reasons for so doing are presumably the date of its publication and the fact that, writing to Cazalis on 4 June, Mallarmé commented on the interest he had been taking in the sonnet form.[69] Both reasons are directly countered however by circumstances which, taken together, make it seem more probable that the poem was composed not later than the spring of that year. First, the appearance in high summer of a poem about ballroom dancing was almost as unseasonable as that of 'Soleil d'hiver' a week later. It is therefore unlikely that it was composed shortly before its publication. Secondly, as regards the sonnet form, a detail in Mallarmé's review of *Poésies parisiennes* which appeared on 10 January testifies to his lively interest, at this earlier date, not simply in the sonnet form but in that property of the sonnet that is most conspicuously exploited in 'Contre un poète parisien'. The reviewer finds, he says, in Des Essarts's versification:

> une ampleur à outrance, si bien qu'on pourrait avancer en plaisantant qu'il est peu de vers qui ne soient assez vastes et assez frappés pour terminer à merveille un sonnet.[70]

Such a sonnet, that is, as 'Contre un poète parisien', conceived and constructed to prepare, in the quatrains and the first tercet, for the satirical surprise that the ending would spring. Mallarmé, who had read Sainte-Beuve's observations on the subject when he was gathering his *Glanes*, would certainly have taken good heed of examples that Du Bellay had published in his *Regrets*, sonnets he had sent from Rome to friends in France. 'De piquants portraits de la vie romaine', Sainte-Beuve calls them, and he defines them further thus:

> Un bon nombre de sonnets de la dernière moitié des *Regrets* ont la pointe spirituelle, dans le sens français et malin du mot.[71]

He also quotes, from another poet of the sixteenth century, Vauquelin de la Fresnaie, a couplet well known to literary historians:

> Et Du Bellay, quittant cette amoureuse flamme,
> Premier fit le sonnet sentir son épigramme.[72]

A few specimens of closing lines in such sonnets by Du Bellay may serve as illustrations:

> Je n'escris de sçavoir, entre les gens d'église. (*Les Regrets*, LXXIX)

Et pour moins d'un escu dix Cardinaux en vente. (Ibid. LXXXI)

Sans barbe et sans argent on s'en retourne en France. (Ibid. CXXVI)

They by no means put to shame Mallarmé's sardonic snapshot:

Un poète qui polke avec un habit noir.

His whole sonnet is built with that ending in view. Conceptually, it is shaped as an antithesis, one term of which occupies elaborately the quatrains and the first tercet while the other is confined entirely within the closing tercet. Its satiric spice is concentrated in the curt last line.

On the first side of the contrast, the laudatory side, the examples of noble figurations of the poet are several and various. The angel in tawny armour is perhaps in the first place the Hugo of *Châtiments* but may symbolize also great poets in general. One recalls in the schoolboy poem 'Pan' the prayer 'Fais de moi ton archange!',[73] and later, in 1876, the opening lines of the sonnet 'Le Tombeau d'Edgar Poe':

Tel qu'en Lui-même enfin l'éternité le change
Le poëte suscite avec un glaive nu
Son siècle épouvanté . . .

The 'blanc songeur' that follows in the same quatrain is probably a disguised borrowing from Hugo's poem 'Fonction du Poëte' (in *Les Rayons et les Ombres*):

Peuples! Écoutez le poëte!
Écoutez le rêveur sacré!

In their visual aspect, both symbols, the warrior-saint and the spiritual guide, were familiar to Mallarmé as sacred ornaments in the Cathedral of Sens, Saint Michael figuring on a tapestry there[74] and the 'blanc songeur' in statues and stained-glass windows which preserve the memory of a long line of Archbishops of Sens.

The change of model in the second quatrain, to individual poets of past ages, contrasting and both of great renown, is well handled. The naked Anacreon was perhaps suggested by some fanciful frontispiece or vignette in an edition or translation of anacreontic odes.[75] Dante could be one of many pictorial representations inspired by the *Divina Commedia*. Dante with

Homer and Virgil, in Raphael's *Parnassus*, would be very appropriate to the subject of the poem (as also to the idea then taking shape among young poets of a new, contemporary Parnasse). *L'Artiste*, at the beginning of that year, presented a print of that painting to each of its regular subscribers. But the description of Dante in Mallarmé's poem makes it more likely that he had in mind the painting by Delacroix of *Dante et Virgile dans la barque de Caron*, at that time in the Musée Royal (du Luxembourg), later at the Louvre. That is the 'vision of a poet' that could well have inspired the striking line in the second quatrain: 'Un linceul fait de nuit et de sérénité'.

In his first tercet Mallarmé seems to represent in picturesque fashion the poets of his own day. In choosing to depict those of the Bohemian inclination he was influenced by Banville, as the Pléiade editors remark.[76] In portraying them as a wandering group however he made ingenious use of another model too. Described as they are, 'passing by', they have the air of a joyous counterpart of Baudelaire's travelling gypsies, 'Promenant sur le ciel des yeux appesantis / Par le morne regret des chimères absentes'. They are the artists of the 'Vie de Bohème' as extolled by Banville ('La Sainte Bohème) in *Odes funambulesques*):

Avec nous l'on chante et l'on aime,
Nous sommes frères des oiseaux.
Croissez, grands lys, chantez, ruisseaux,
Et vive la sainte Bohème.

Fronts hâlés par l'été vermeil,
Salut, bohèmes en délire!
Fils du ciseau, fils de la lyre,
Prunelles pleines de soleil!

. . .

Nous irons, voyageurs étranges,
Jusque sous les talons des anges
Décrocher les astres du ciel.

Of 'Bohemian' acquaintances in the sense of 'les grands bohèmes', Mallarmé could claim only one, Glatigny,[77] whom he admired, and would later defend and assist on occasion. He was perhaps the representative hero of the first tercet. In the second, to make of ugliness disgraced a positive triumph for beauty, the Muse herself appears. The monstrance effect ascribed to her hair is unexpectedly religious, a sign of sanctity.

One suspects that it is there rather for rhyme than meaning. The salutation 'ô reine des poèmes' is appropriate to the occasion, but it will be suggested presently that it is perhaps a stray echo from *Les Fleurs du mal*.

The Pléiade editors characterize Mallarmé's sonnet as 'une pièce appartenant au genre qu'on appelait jadis "poésies fugitives"'.[78] One would certainly like to suppose that it was not intended for publication, only for insertion as a private jest in friend Emmanuel's album, where indeed it was inscribed by its author. Such intentions can however be foiled. If, as is not unlikely, Mallarmé sent a copy to their mutual friend Coligny, for his own entertainment, one can imagine how it might eventually find its way to Dieppe and the *Journal des Baigneurs*, along with 'Soleil d'hiver'. Such a misadventure would explain why, from the cutting of the printed text which Mallarmé kept, the unfriendly-seeming title was removed. So the Flammarion editors note:

> Peu après la publicaiontion, lorsqu'il range le poème dans ses papiers, Mallarmé élimine l'élément trop circonstantiel, le titre malicieux. Sur une feuille il colle une coupure du texte et écrit au-dessus: Sonnet.—A Emmanuel des Essarts.[79]

Emmanuel, ever-patient, seems to have borne no outward grudge for the unfortunate incident, but he did not forget it. Perhaps it was after opening his album to recall old times that in his obituary article, nearly forty years after, he began his account of his friend Stéphane as he first knew him with the sentence: 'Il évitait les relations mondaines et ne comprenait pas nos ferveurs pour la danse.'[80] Perhaps he had forgotten, or had never realized, how deep the disagreement between them had been. For Mallarmé it was a difference of poetic principle concerning the relationship to be maintained, in poetry, between the ideal and the real. In the closing poem of *Poésies parisiennes* the 'poète parisien' had declared his own conviction, using (rather clumsily) Baudelairian terms that his young companion could not accept and would not forgive:

> Unir dans ses pensers l'action et le rêve,
> Ces frères désunis par la réalité;
> A l'idéal de l'art mêler l'humanité;
> ('Avoir toujours vingt ans', à Charles Coligny)

So in 'Contre un poète parisien' Des Essarts the man about town may indeed have been teased for dancing the polka, no doubt with more fervour than grace. But the serious reproach was for Des Essarts the poet, who in his poem 'La Danse idéale' depicted himself, for posterity and in all seriousness, rising to a heaven of the ideal by way of a mazurka:

O souvenir qui me domine!
Furtive vision que l'extase devine!
C'était la Mazurke divine![81]

The nearest neighbour of 'Contre un poète parisien' is perhaps (though the evidence may seem scanty) another sonnet, excluded likewise by its author from the collections of poems that he himself prepared for publication. Its existence and the greater part of the text were made known by Henri Mondor in his *Vie* (vol. ii, 1942),[82] and the poem was duly admitted to the Pléiade *Œuvres complètes* three years later. Since the one holograph copy to which it owed its survival provided no title, the editors headed it 'Sonnet'. It is commonly designated by its first line or part of it, but sometimes by the pseudonym that Cazalis used on first acquaintance with it, and afterwards Mondor himself on occasion, namely 'La Naissance du poète'. Here, for convenience, it will be referred to as 'Parce que . . .'

['Parce que . . .'][83]

Parce que de la viande était à point rôtie,
Parce que le journal détaillait un viol,
Parce que sur sa gorge ignoble et mal bâtie
La servante oublia de boutonner son col,

Parce que d'un lit, grand comme une sacristie,
Il voit, sur la pendule, un couple antique et fol,
Ou qu'il n'a pas sommeil, et que, sans modestie,
Sa jambe sous les draps frôle une jambe au vol,

Un niais met sous lui sa femme froide et sèche,
Contre ce bonnet blanc frotte son casque-à-mèche
Et travaille en soufflant inexorablement:

Et de ce qu'une nuit, sans rage et sans tempête,
Ces deux êtres se sont accouplés en dormant,
O Shakspeare et toi, Dante, il peut naître un poëte!

This addition to the 'Poëmes d'enfance et de jeunesse' received at first little attention from critics—with the exception of Kurt Wais, who found in it possible thematic relationships with later poems.[84] Then, some twenty years after its publication, the attribution to Mallarmé was challenged, unexpectedly, by a critic of good repute. In an article that appeared on 1 April 1966, in the second number of *La Quinzaine littéraire*, Pascal Pia set out his reasons for believing that the author of the sonnet 'Parce que . . . ' was not Mallarmé, but an almost exact contemporary of his, one Clément Privé, known to students of Mallarmé (thanks to Henri Mondor) as a close friend, and in the early 1860s a prolific collaborator, of Eugène Lefébure.

The case that Pascal Pia argued in support of his thesis may be summarized and assessed as follows. First, he rightly pointed out that the presence among Mallarmé's papers, after his death, of a copy of the sonnet in his own hand ('de la plus belle écriture du poëte' according to the Pléiade editors), but undated and unsigned, could not be deemed to prove that he was its author. The critic believed that it was in fact composed by Privé at about the age of twenty, and copied by Mallarmé when it was shown to him by Lefébure some two years later. At least, that seems to be his surmise when he writes:

> Mondor n'a pas ignoré l'existence de Privé,—dans sa *Vie de Mallarmé*, parue en 1942, il indique même que Lefébure, en 1864, avait montré à Mallarmé trois petits carnets remplis de sonnets écrits en collaboration "avec C. Privé".[85]

Mondor did indeed assume, and it seems most probable, that when in September 1864 Mallarmé stayed for a few days with Lefébure at Charny, near Sens, he read the collection of poems in question, to which nearly a century later Mallarmé's biographer had himself been given access, together with other documents preserved by Lefébure's family. Neatly copied by him in three notebooks, under the title *Sonnets auxerrois*, the collection consisted of about fifty poems, not all sonnets, some of them composed by Lefébure himself, some by Privé but corrected or amended by his friend and elder, and others signed by both.[86] If one of Privé's sonnets took Mallarmé's fancy, it would be natural enough that he should take away a copy of it, as a compliment from one poet to another. But to this easy explanation of the holograph 'Parce que . . . ' found in Mallarmé's file after his death there is a considerable objection. It was before that first visit to Lefébure that Mallarmé had corresponded with him, and also with Cazalis, on the subject of a poem that he must have composed in 1862 and that the editors of the correspondence recognize as being the sonnet in question.

When Cazalis from Strasbourg, wrote to Mallarmé in May 1863, to tell him of his new life there, and new friends, he added a request:

> Emm. me donne souvent de tes nouvelles: m'envoie des vers; et si tu veux m'être agréable, tu m'enverrais [*sic*] tes deux sonnets sur l'aumône (voilà 5 francs va boire) et la naissance du poète (Parce qu'un soir d'avril il lut dans un journal etc); j'en ai donné l'idée à quelques uns de mes amis, et ils ont trouvé cela fort beau.[87]

The untidy epistolary style leaves one uncertain whether Cazalis had learned of the sonnet from Des Essarts's letter or from Mallarmé in person before he left for London. But in either case it will appear to most readers, as it did to Mallarmé's editors, that to judge by what Cazalis says of it the sonnet must be the one that begins 'Parce que de la viande était à point rôtie'. Pascal Pia did not share that opinion, but he was obliged to concede that in one way or another that poem must be involved. Hence his vague and non-commitally off-hand suggestion:

> Mallarmé a probablement écrit un autre *Parce que*, celui dont Cazalis avait retenu l'incipit: *Parce qu'un soir d'avril il lut dans un* journal, mais cette pièce, imitée de Privé ou imitée par Privé, reste à découvrir—.

There are however two other possibilities, each of them more likely than that of a second 'Parce que . . . ' Either Cazalis's recollection, imprecise as it was, enabled him to improvise an alexandrine containing such fragments of the first two lines as he did remember, or alternatively, before sending his poem to Strasbourg Mallarmé had amended its opening stanza. Though the latter hypothesis is in accord with Mallarmé's habits, the former is the more acceptable. How casual Cazalis could be in such circumstances is illustrated by his way of designating, in the same sentence of his letter, the poem he wrongly remembered as another sonnet, 'A un Mendiant': 'voilà 5 francs, va boire'.

As to the suggestion that one of the two poets, Mallarmé or Privé, had imitated the other, it is too far-fetched, and cannot be entertained for either of them. The more obvious, though disagreeable explanation is inescapable: either Mallarmé or Privé has been credited with a sonnet of which the other was really the author. If the one to be thus favoured was Mallarmé, the injustice (as in that case it would certainly be) could bring him no profit. If it was Privé, on the other hand, the advantage to him was considerable. Pascal Pia shows that the attribution to him, rightful or not, won him an enhanced reputation:

> ce sonnet que Mondor croyait inconnu, et qui l'était si peu que, vers 1882, les journalistes y faisaient sans cesse allusion comme on fait allusion encore au sonnet d'Arvers . . . [88] Il est certain en tout cas que *Parce que* . . . fut repris à partir de 1880 dans plusieurs périodiques parisiens, où il me souvient de l'avoir vu au cours de recherches sur Charles Cros et les Zutistes . . . Le nom de Clément Privé figure dans quantité d'ouvrages que Mondor aura au moins feuilletés, s'il ne les a pas lus. Depuis 1912, date à laquelle Edmond Bernard, ancien pharmacien devenu courtier en livres clandestins, publia sous le titre d'*Anthologie hospitalière et latinesque*, une compilation de couplets gaillards et de poèmes plus ou moins libres, tous les recueils de salles de garde ont reproduit, comme avait fait Bernard, le sonnet *Parce que* . . . suivi du nom de son véritable auteur [i.e., of course, Clément Privé].

Much the likeliest hypothesis, therefore, is the following: Privé, who in the early 1880s (the last years of his life) had according to Pia's article fallen on hard times, turned Mallarmé's sonnet to fruitful use on his own behalf. It will be noted that he had not attempted to do so until it had become most unlikely that Mallarmé would publish it himself—even in the *Nouveau Parnasse satyrique*, in the 1878 and 1881 issues of which had appeared his poem 'Les Lèvres roses'. To the impecunious journalist Privé it might seem safe, as well as not really harmful to the rightful author, to publicize the sonnet without discouraging the belief that it was one of his own.

To complete the case in favour of the Pléiade editors, and the Flammarion editors who confirm the attribution of the sonnet to Mallarmé, a miscalculation on the part of Pascal Pia has still to be set right, by adding now to Cazalis's testimony that of Lefébure. When he received from Mallarmé, at some time before 15 April 1864 (the date of his reply) the poems that he hailed with such warm congratulations, he is most unlikely to have kept them hidden from his friend and collaborator Clément Privé. Also, from what Mondor tells us of this 'vaudevilliste de préfecture', it is fairly certain that the poem from Mallarmé that Privé would most admire and of which he would be most desirous therefore to keep a copy, was one of those that Lefébure singled out for special praise in his letter of thanks, from which Pia quotes the following passage:

Je sais maintenant presque tous vos vers par cœur, mais il y en a naturellement qui me plaisent surtout, le sonnet du bourgeois qui crée un poète, la pièce *A un mendiant*, si fière et si belle . . . [89]

It was to Lefébure, we may be sure, and to that occasion, that Privé owed his copy of what Lefébure called 'le sonnet du bourgeois qui crée un poète'—unmistakable when so described. Lefébure's praise also testifies, on the other hand, that in their chronological aspect the critic's assumptions are unsound. When Mallarmé wrote his sonnet he could have no knowledge of either an identical or a similar one by Privé, because it cannot have existed. If it had, whether in *Sonnets auxerrois* or elsewhere, Lefébure would have known of it, and any significant resemblance to it in Mallarmé's 'Parce que . . . ' would have caused him to receive it not with admiration but dismay.

A detail in this curious story that is noted by the Flammarion editors, more precise than their predecessors on this point, is rather puzzling. The sole holograph manuscript of 'Parce que . . . ' is, they say, 'later than the date of composition'. Very much later, it would appear, since they date it speculatively 'vers 1887'.[90] This oddity tempts one to guess that Mallarmé may have learned of Privé's subterfuge (or, to be more lenient, unexpected good fortune), and made a fresh copy of the text he had kept in his file. The occasion of the discovery could have been Privé's death on 15 May 1883. I note in Pascal Pia's article this relevant information:

Gil Blas lui consacra le 17 mai une notice nécrologique dans laquelle Fernand Xau ne manqua pas de rappeler le sonnet *Parce que . . .* dont il cita le premier vers: *Parce que de la viande était à point rôtie.*

The contribution to Mallarmé studies of Pascal Pia's article was not therefore what he had intended, but the revelation of the dual identity (not to say the Jekyll and Hyde existence) of one of Mallarmé's early sonnets was worth the pains. The success he discovered the sonnet to have enjoyed in unexpected circles is a reminder that a well-made poem may be appreciated by a public much wider than the audience of connoisseurs that its author may have had in mind.[91] As to the humorous aspect which was Privé's chief concern ('gras d'humour' is Mondor's compliment to the *Sonnets auxerrois*),[92] Mallarmé had served him the better by passing on a borrowing of his own. For his idea of the 'niais' obediently carrying out nature's laws must owe something to Musset's 'Ballade à la lune':

> Mais monsieur tout en flamme,
> Commence à rudoyer
>   Madame,
> Qui commence à crier.
>
> Ouf, dit-il, je travaille,
> Ma bonne, et ne fais rien
>   Qui vaille;
> Tu ne te tiens pas bien.

The date of composition of 'Parce que . . . ' was probably the winter or early spring of 1862. That he had not sent it to Coligny for publication, like other poems written then, or that Coligny had decided against its publication, the nature of its subject completely explains. My own reasons for believing it to have been written at approximately the same time as 'Contre un poète parisien' are not altogether convincing when considered severally, but stand up better when their coincidence is taken into account. One is that it is another poem about poets. Also, it again pays special tribute to Dante. More strikingly, like the sonnet on the Parisian poet it exploits very successfully the device of the surprise ending (made the more effective here by the no doubt planned absence of a title). Experimentation shows through also in the repetition of the words 'Parce que' in each of the opening lines, following another example set by Renaissance sonneteers. An interest in Baudelaire of a somewhat critical kind, no less characteristic of that phase in Mallarmé's progress, is quite substantially present too. For the subject of 'Parce que . . . ' is a calm contradiction of the most savagely misogynistic of Baudelaire's poems, the one (also without a title) that begins: 'Tu mettrais l'univers entier dans ta ruelle', and (more interestingly for our present purpose) ends:

> La grandeur de ce mal où tu te crois savante
> Ne t'a donc jamais fait reculer d'épouvante,
> Quand la nature, grande en ses desseins cachés,
> De toi se sert, ô femme, ô reine des péchés,
> —De toi, vil animal,—pour pétrir un génie?
>
> O fangeuse grandeur! sublime ignominie![93]

To this—writing with humorous intent rather than in anger—Mallarmé replies by pointing out that nature's mysterious ways of producing a genius involve the other sex too, and indeed the two together. It will be observed that the closeness of 'Parce que . . . ' to 'Contre un poète parisien' gains indirect confirmation from a textual echo that the latter poem contains of that same Baudelairian source. The rather far-fetched hemistich, 'ô reine des péchés', is matched in the sonnet on the Parisian poet by one that is also rather forced, but convenient *qua* hemistich and also for the rhyme: 'ô reine des poèmes'.

Among the poems that quite certainly, or with very little doubt, Mallarmé composed at the beginning of 1862, there is one that stands out as the most serious and also the most important, 'Le Guignon'. It is also, however, the most obscure, and in the patient elucidation that is, I believe, necessary to its understanding, it is useful to take advantage of the variants to be found in several early manuscript copies that have survived. They provide, in addition, a good example of the manner in which, already, the future perfectionist amended details in his poems, continuing the process even as he copied them out to send them to different friends.

A curious feature of the situation of 'Le Guignon' is that what may be called the published text, which appeared with 'Le Sonneur' in *L'Artiste* on 15 March 1862, consists of the first fifteen lines only. Since there is no reason to doubt that the poem was completed before that date and submitted to *L'Artiste* whole, it must be assumed that it was truncated for editorial reasons. But the editor gave no explanation to his readers, and in Mallarmé's correspondence no reference to the anomaly is to be found, at that time or later. The probable reasons for it will be sought (and to my own satisfaction found), in the following pages. The full text, as preserved partly in *L'Artiste* but for much the greater part in manuscript, reads with its most interesting variants as follows:

Le Guignon*[94]

Au dessus du bétail écœurant des humains
Bondissaient par instants les sauvages crinières
Des mendieurs [*A*,D,Y,B²: mendiants] d'azur perdus [*A*,Y,B²: damnés] dans nos chemins.

Un vent mêlé de cendre effarait leurs bannières
Où passe le divin gonflement de la mer,
Et creusait autour d'eux de sanglantes ornières.

La tête dans l'orage, ils défiaient l'Enfer:
Ils voyageaient sans pain, sans bâton [*A*,D,Y,B²: bâtons] et sans urnes,
Mordant au citron d'or de l'Idéal amer.

La plupart ont râlé dans des ravins nocturnes
S'enivrant du plaisir [*A*,D,Y,B²: bonheur] de voir couler leur sang:
La Mort fut [*A*: mort est] un baiser sur ces fronts taciturnes.

*The above composite text takes as its basis the copy of the poem in the *Manuscrit Aubanel*, reproduced by the Pléiade editors (*O.c.*, 1408–9 [1410–11]).

The variants inserted, within square brackets, are found in earlier copies which I refer to by initials, as follows:

A—the earliest text known, restricted to the first five tercets, published in *L'Artiste*, 15 March 1862.

D—the holograph copy of the complete poem, headed 'A Emile Deschamps', in the Deschamps bequest at the Bibliothèque Municipale de Versailles. It is concisely examined in an article ('*Le Guignon* de Stéphane Mallarmé'), contributed in 1968 by the then Librarian, M. Pierre Breillat, to *Humanisme actif, mélanges d'art et de littérature offerts à Julien Cain* (vol. I, pp. 105–10).[101]

Y—a copy of the copy on 'cream-laid paper' sent to Cazalis for 'Mesdames Yapp' on 24 May 1862; see *Corr.* i, 86–9.[102]

B¹— the copy belonging to the dealer Bérès that the Pléiade editors quote from (*O.c.*, 1408 and 1409) [1410 and 1411].

B²—a copy belonging to the same dealer later, of which M. Breillat gives a detailed account in his article.

S'ils sont vaincus, c'est par un Ange très puissant
[*A*,D,Y,B²: S'ils pantèlent, c'est sous un ange très-puissant]
Qui rougit l'horizon des éclairs de son glaive;
L'orgueil fait éclater leur cœur reconnaissant.

Ils têtent la Douleur comme ils tétaient le Rêve,
Et quand ils vont rythmant leurs pleurs voluptueux
Le peuple s'agenouille et leur mère se lève.

Ceux-là sont consolés étant majestueux,
Mais ils ont sous les pieds leurs frères [B¹: égaux] qu'on bafoue,[95]
Dérisoires martyrs d'un hasard tortueux.

Des pleurs aussi salés rongent leur pâle joue,
Ils mangent de la cendre avec le même amour,
Mais vulgaire ou grotesque [D,Y,B²: burlesque] est le Sort qui les roue.

Ils pouvaient faire aussi sonner comme un tambour
La servile pitié des races à l'œil terne,
Égaux [B¹: Frères] de Prométhée à qui manque un vautour!

Non. Vieux, et fréquentant [D,Y,B²: Vieux et jalousant] les déserts sans citerne[96] [Y: citernes]
Ils marchent sous le fouet d'un squelette rageur,
Le *Guignon*, dont le rire édenté les prosterne.[97]

S'ils vont, [D,Y,B²: fuient,] *il* grimpe en croupe et se fait voyageur;
Puis, le torrent franchi, les plonge en une mare
Et fait un fou crotté d'un superbe [D,Y,B²: sublime] nageur;

Grâce à *lui*, si l'un chante en son buccin bizarre
Des enfants nous tordront en un rire obstiné
Qui, soufflant dans leurs mains, singeront sa fanfare:

Grâce à *lui*, s'ils s'en vont tenter un sein [Y: cœur] fané[98]
Avec des fleurs, partout [D,Y,B²: fleurs par qui] l'impureté s'allume,
Des limaces naîtront sur leur bouquet damné;

Et ce squelette nain, coiffé d'un feutre à plume
Et botté, dont l'aisselle [Y: la barbe; B²: le crâne][99] a pour poils [Y: crins] de longs vers,
Est pour eux l'infini de l'humaine amertume.

Et si, rossés, ils ont provoqué le pervers,
Leur rapière en grinçant suit le rayon de lune
Qui neige en sa carcasse et qui passe à travers.

Malheureux sans [B^1: harcelés, sous] l'orgueil d'une austère infortune,
Dédaigneux de venger leurs os de [D,B^2: des] coups de bec,
Ils convoitent la haine et n'ont que la rancune.

Ils sont l'amusement des râcleurs de rebec,
Des putains [D: catins; Y,B^2: femmes], des enfants, et de la vieille[100] [D: maigre] engeance
Des loqueteux dansant quand le broc [D: pot] est à sec.

Les poëtes savants leur prêchent la vengeance,
Et ne voyant leur mal [D,Y: leur plaie; B^1: leurs plaies] et les sachant brisés,
Les disent impuissants et sans intelligence:

"Ils peuvent, sans quêter quelques soupirs gueusés,
"Comme un buffle se cabre aspirant la tempête
"Savourer âprement leurs maux éternisés!

"Nous soûlerons [D,Y,B^2: enivrons] d'encens les Forts [D,Y,B^2: forts] qui tiennent tête
"Aux fauves séraphins du mal [D,Y, B^2: Mal]!—Ces baladins
"N'ont pas mis d'habit rouge et veulent qu'on s'arrête!"
[D,Y,B^2: 'Ne sont pas même ceux que la charité fête!']

Quand chacun a sur eux craché [D,Y,B^2: vomi] tous ses dédains,
Nus, assoiffés de grand[[D,Y,B^2: *grand*] et priant le tonnerre,
Ces Hamlet [D,Y,B^2: Hamlets] abreuvés de malaises badins

Vont ridiculement se pendre au réverbère.

There is of course no doubt that from the point of view of artistry, this 1862 version compares unfavourably with the definitive text published in 1887. If critics mention it, it is usually to point out this inferiority. But if it is compared rather with other examples of Mallarmé's early verse, its contemporaries, it will be found to have an emotional urgency, an imaginative vigour, and sustained rhythmic flow that entitle it to more honour than it receives. Thibaudet did acknowledge its merits, however, and his patient confrontation of one version with the other is prefaced by a reminder that Jules Lemaître considered the earlier one to be 'à peu de chose près un chef-d'œuvre'.[103] Mallarmé himself, twenty years after writing it and now a master craftsman, had enough respect for it to agree to its publication, with only minor amendments, in Verlaine's *Poètes maudits* (1883), in *Le Décadent* (20 November 1886), and in *La Revue rose* (January 1887).[104] Only for the 1887 edition of his collected verse did he compose the new version, with corrections so prolific that it differs from the earlier text, in his own words, 'presque mot après mot'.[105]

Here, only the neglected early version quoted above will be studied, and some attention will be given to the misconceptions that explain the long neglect. Two notions in particular, casually formed no doubt in the first place, have hardened into accepted opinions that I wish to challenge. For the first of them Thibaudet is, I fear, at least partly responsible. It has to do with the subject of the poem, which he defines very succinctly as follows:

> Le *Guignon* est un poème en terza rima. Gautier avait, pour le même sujet, employé le même rythme dans *Ténèbres* (. . .) (Le *Guignon* a été conçu presque certainement comme une suite et une contre-partie de *Ténèbres*.) Il s'agit de ceux qui n'ont pas de chance, et particulièrement des 'poètes maudits'.[106]

This is an over-simplification of the relation between the two poems. It is true that the subject of *Ténèbres* is found again, like its verse-form, in 'Le Guignon', but with this difference that in Mallarmé's poem it is no longer alone. Mallarmé has grafted it, much altered in presentation, into a quasi-surreptitious subject of his own. That will be made clear in the course of this commentary, and at the same time it will become apparent why beyond the fifth tercet the editor of *L'Artiste* could not publish Mallarmé's poem.

The second of the two dubious notions, first expressed by Jean Royère and quoted approvingly by the Pléiade editors,[107] concerns the style. 'Le Guignon' of 1862 was, they say, a Parnassian poem. If they use the word 'Parnassien' precisely and not in vague disparagement, they are mistaken. What the Parnassian poets did, as Mallarmé himself pointed out, was to 'present objects directly' whereas they should only be alluded to.[108]

How far the author of 'Le Guignon' was from falling into that error can be seen by comparing the style of his poem with that of almost any other poem of the time, including that of Gautier (not notably Parnassian) in the representative fragments of 'Ténèbres' quoted below. Seen in the light of that comparison, the elliptical terseness that characterizes a large part of Mallarmé's poem, its exacting demands on the reader's co-operation, the impressionistic manner in which the images are sketched, and the general predominance of indirect over direct expression prove that Jean Royère's comment is unfounded to say the least. Here is Gautier's manner of dealing with his subject:

> Taisez-vous, ô mon cœur! taisez-vous, ô mon âme!
> Et n'allez plus chercher de querelles au sort;
> Le néant vous appelle et l'oubli vous réclame.
> . . .
>
> Et le chaste secret des rêves de vos ans
> Périra tout entier sous votre tombe obscure
> Où rien n'attirera le regard des passants.
>
> Que voulez-vous? hélas! notre mère Nature,
> Comme toute autre mère, a ses enfants gâtés,
> Et pour les malvenus elle est avare et dure.
>
> Aux uns tous les bonheurs et toutes les beautés!
> L'occasion leur est toujours bonne et fidèle:
> Ils trouvent au désert des palais enchantés.
>
> Ils tettent librement la féconde mamelle,
> La chimère à leur voix s'empresse d'accourir,
> Et tout l'or du Pactole entre leurs doigts ruisselle.
>
> Les autres, moins aimés, ont beau tordre et pétrir
> Avec leurs maigres mains la mamelle tarie,
> Leur frère a bu le lait qui les devait nourrir.

S'il éclot quelque chose au milieu de leur vie,
Une petite fleur sous leur pâle gazon,
Le sabot du vacher l'aura bientôt flétrie.
. . .
Sur son trône d'airain, le Destin qui s'en raille
Imbibe leur éponge avec du fiel amer,
Et la Nécessité les tord dans sa tenaille.

Tout buisson trouve un dard pour déchirer leur chair,
Tout beau chemin pour eux cache une chausse-trape,
Et les chaînes de fleurs leur sont chaînes de fer.
. . .
Il est beau d'arriver où tendait son essor,
De trouver sa beauté, d'aborder à son monde,
Et, quand on a fouillé, d'exhumer un trésor;

De faire, du plus creux de son âme profonde,
Rayonner son idée ou bien sa passion;
D'être l'oiseau qui chante et la foudre qui gronde;

D'unir heureusement le rêve à l'action,
D'aimer et d'être aimé, de gagner quand on joue,
Et de donner un trône à son ambition;
. . .
Ceux-là sont peu nombreux dans notre âge fatal.[109]

It is not only the stylistic energy of 'Le Guignon' that is brought into sharp relief by this confrontation with the poem on whose substance it has most conspicuously drawn, but also its lack of clarity. In comparison Gautier seems abundantly explicit, for all his imagery. Indeed, in this first serious treatment by Mallarmé of a subject which was always to be of fundamental importance in his thinking, the situation of artists in the society of his time, exegetists are immediately confronted with a puzzling question. Why is exegesis so necessary for the understanding of a poem on such a subject? If the obscurity could be attributed to a sibylline reticence, it could no doubt be plausibly explained by a statement in the author's article 'L'Art pour tous', published a few months later: 'Toute chose sacrée et qui veut demeurer sacrée s'enveloppe de mystère.'[110] If poetry was sacred, a poem about poets must be sacrosanct and mystery doubly necessary. But in my estimation, for reasons already given, that article has little authority as an expression of Mallarmé's serious thought. For the deliberate obscurity that is certainly met with in some parts of 'Le Guignon' a more specific reason has to be sought. It will emerge in due course, after some laborious dissection.

In remoulding the subject taken from 'Ténèbres' to suit his own purpose, Mallarmé was influenced, visibly, by two of Baudelaire's critical essays, published in 1856 as introductions to the two volumes of his translation of the tales of Edgar Poe. The first of the two passages that I refer to in particular is found in the opening paragraphs of 'Edgar Poe, sa vie et ses œuvres'. It is well known:

Il y a dans l'histoire littéraire des destinées analogues, de vraies damnations,—des hommes qui portent le mot *guignon* écrit en caractères mystérieux dans les plis sinueux de leur front. L'Ange aveugle de l'expiation s'est emparé d'eux et les fouette à tour de bras pour l'édification des autres. (. . .)—Existe-t-il donc une Providence diabolique qui prépare le malheur dès le berceau, qui jette avec *préméditation* des natures spirituelles et angéliques dans des milieux hostiles, comme des martyrs dans les cirques? Y a-t-il donc des âmes *sacrées*, vouées à l'autel, condamnées à marcher à la mort et à la gloire à travers leurs propres ruines? Le cauchemar des *Ténèbres* assiégera-t-il éternellement ces âmes de choix? (. . .)

Un écrivain célèbre de notre temps a écrit un livre pour démontrer que le poète ne pouvait trouver une bonne place ni dans une société démocratique ni dans une aristocratique (. . .)[111] J'apporte aujourd'hui une nouvelle légende à l'appui de sa thèse, j'ajoute un saint nouveau au martyrologe: j'ai à écrire l'histoire d'un de ces illustres malheureux, trop riche de poésie et de passion, qui est venu, après tant d'autres, faire en ce bas monde le rude apprentissage du génie chez les âmes inférieures.[112]

The second passage is part of a paraphrase of Poe's 'poetic principle', in the *Notes nouvelles sur Edgar Poe*:

C'est cet admirable, cet immortel instinct du Beau qui nous fait considérer la terre et ses spectacles comme un aperçu, comme une correspondance du Ciel. La soif insatiable de tout ce qui est au delà, et que révèle la vie, est la preuve la plus vivante de notre immortalité. C'est à la fois par la poésie et *à travers* la poésie, par et *à travers* la musique que l'âme entrevoit les splendeurs situées derrière le tombeau; et quand un poème exquis amène les larmes au bord des yeux, ces larmes ne sont pas la preuve d'un excès de jouissance, elles sont bien plutôt le témoignage d'une mélancolie irritée, d'une postulation des nerfs, d'une nature exilée dans l'imparfait et qui voudrait s'emparer immédiatement, sur cette terre même, d'un paradis révélé.[113]

The two passages were relevant to Mallarmé's intention in 'Le Guignon' for different and indeed opposite reasons. Baudelaire's wilful Guignon came as a valuable substitute for Gautier's abstractions ('notre mère Nature', 'le Destin', 'Fortune', and the like). But on the other hand the Christian doctrine accepted by Poe and Baudelaire, according to which perfection must not be looked for in this life but only beyond the grave, was anathema to Mallarmé and given his subject had to be explicitly denied. It is in his opening tercets that the denial is placed, as part of the introduction to the azure-beggars and their contrary faith.

The beginning of the poem becomes clearer when account is taken of that religious aspect of the author's concern. Without it, the mention of 'l'Enfer' would be hard to understand, as would that of 'un Ange très puissant / Qui rougit l'horizon des éclairs de son glaive'.[114] The azure-beggars, as uncompromising idealists, defy the sword of the angel which would bar the way to paradise, and brave the threat of Hell hereafter in punishment for their pride. This may seem to be inconsistent with their depiction as knights-errant,[115] but these medieval heroes are intended by the author to stand for bold idealists through the ages. Few such remain, Gautier had said, 'dans notre âge fatal'. For Mallarmé, likewise, 'La plupart ont râlé', proud of the privilege of dying in a noble cause.[116]

The modernizing concept of 'les mendieurs d'azur' was suggested by Banville, in two of his prefaces and elsewhere, for instance:

Un immense appétit de bonheur et d'espérance est au fond des âmes. Reconquérir la joie perdue, remonter d'un pas intrépide l'escalier d'azur qui mène aux cieux, telle est l'aspiration incessante de l'homme moderne, qui ne se sent plus ni condamné ni esclave, et qui de jour en jour comprend davantage la nécessité de croire à sa propre vertu et à l'incommensurable amour de Dieu pour ses créatures. (*Les Stalactites*, 'Préface')

Assurément ce temps-ci est un *autre temps* . . . on mourra de dégoût si l'on ne prend pas, de-ci de-là, un grand bain d'azur, et si l'on ne peut quelquefois, pour se consoler de tant de médiocrités, "rouler échevelés dans les étoiles". (*Odes funambulesques*, 'Préface')

Pourquoi donc les chantons-nous,
Cœurs de l'Idéal jaloux,
Qui toujours au ciel obscur
Cherchons l'azur?

(*Odelettes*, 'A Gavarni')[117]

When Houssaye (or Coligny) published with the stirring first four tercets of Mallarmé's 'Le Guignon' a fifth, which does not properly belong to the heroic opening section, he made unavoidable for readers of *L'Artiste* a misunderstanding that is pardonable even today, when we have the whole poem to guide us. The words 'S'ils sont vaincus' appear to refer to 'la plupart', the heroes that are slain. But to make good sense of what follows one must suppose instead that an abrupt shift to new referents is intended. 'S'ils sont vaincus' must mean 'Ceux qui sont vaincus'—those, that is, who on the other hand have surrendered. They are those still living (as the otherwise uninformative variant in *L'Artiste*, 'S'ils pantèlent', confirms) who have yielded to the angel's warning that the Ideal—a new Eden—must not be striven after in this life but only hoped for hereafter. They bow before this law thankfully, even reaping some reward thereby already, here below: 'Et quand ils vont rythmant leurs pleurs voluptueux / Le peuple s'agenouille et leur mère se lève'. It must be understood at this point, and for the rest of Mallarmé's poem, that it is with poets and poets only that the author is really concerned. Furthermore, there are strong suggestions that he has very particularly one poet in mind. The first suggestion is contained in the words 'leur mère se lève'. We are presumably to understand that she rises from her knees, proudly, while the populace kneel down in homage. If that is so, it is fair to suspect a reference here to the first stanza of 'Bénédiction', the first poem in section one of *Les Fleurs du mal:*

Lorsque, par un décret des puissances suprêmes,
Le Poète apparaît en ce monde ennuyé,
Sa mère épouvantée et pleine de blasphèmes
Crispe ses poings vers Dieu, qui la prend en pitié.

The young poet presented by Baudelaire in this poem (himself when young) has a special interest for readers of 'Le Guignon'. He is Baudelaire's own example of a poet 'consoled'. Hated for being a poet, by those who should love him, tormented by his fellow-men in general, he accepts the Christian promise, and endures his present suffering with God-fearing resignation, confident of the supreme reward in a life to come:

> Tous ceux qu'il veut aimer l'observent avec crainte
> Ou bien, s'enhardissant de sa tranquillité,
> Cherchent à qui saura lui tirer une plainte,
> Et font sur lui l'essai de leur férocité.
>
> Dans le pain et le vin destinés à sa bouche
> Ils mêlent de la cendre avec d'impurs crachats;
> Avec hypocrisie ils jettent ce qu'il touche,
> Et s'accusent d'avoir mis leurs pieds dans ses pas.
>
> Sa femme va crier sur les places publiques . . .
> . . .
> Vers le Ciel, où son œil voit un trône splendide,
> Le poète serein lève ses bras pieux,
> Et les vastes éclairs de son esprit lucide
> Lui dérobent l'aspect des peuples furieux:
>
> —"Soyez béni, mon Dieu, qui donnez la souffrance
> Comme un divin remède à nos impuretés
> Et comme la meilleure et la plus pure essence
> Qui prépare les forts aux saintes voluptés!
> . . ."

The tercet in which Mallarmé alludes to this youthful model of a 'poète consolé' has also a more sombre side, by which the reader is reminded of a later Baudelaire, the woeful, tear-laden poet of 'Le Cygne'. The words used by Mallarmé, 'Ils têtent la Douleur . . .', also warned the editor of *L'Artiste* that the last of Mallarmé's tercets that he could publish was the preceding one, the fifth. For they refer directly and unkindly to the lines:

> A quiconque a perdu ce qui ne se retrouve
> Jamais, jamais! à ceux qui s'abreuvent de pleurs
> Et tettent la Douleur comme une bonne louve,[118]

The accusation of making personal misfortune the stuff of his poems was certainly one which Baudelaire would find it difficult to refute, and Mallarmé appears here to make that accusation. 'Ceux-là sont consolés, étant majestueux' was no compliment. Other lines in 'Le Cygne' come to mind. Lines also in such poems as 'Le Masque', which exemplify the solemn grandeur within which the poet can merge his own grief with sorrows famed in story or hallowed in art:

> Andromaque, je pense à vous! Ce petit fleuve,
> Pauvre et triste miroir où jadis resplendit
> L'immense majesté de vos douleurs de veuve.
>
> ('Le Cygne')[119]

> Pauvre grande Beauté! le magnifique fleuve
> De tes pleurs aboutit dans mon cœur soucieux;
> Ton mensonge m'enivre, et mon âme s'abreuve
> Aux flots que la Douleur fait jaillir de tes yeux!
>
> ('Le Masque')[120]

More serious allegations would be made against Baudelaire later in the poem, and already in tercets seven and eight the lines that introduce the subject announced by the title 'Le Guignon' convey an idea of their nature. The same lines reveal that the contrast between the fortunate and the unfortunate, on which the emotive interest of 'Ténèbres' largely depends, has been replaced in 'Le Guignon' by something nearer to a dramatic conflict. Gautier's narrator had compared the misfortunes of the ill-starred majority with the life enjoyed by fortune's favourites. Also, but only momentarily, he had contrasted the commonplace dullness of the ills he complained of with tragic destinies that guarantee for their victims a place in the human story:

> C'est une histoire simple où l'on ne trouve pas
> De grands événements et des malheurs de drame,
> Une douleur qui chante et fait un grand fracas.

This contrast is made much more of, and treated more emotionally, in 'Le Guignon':

> Ceux-là sont consolés étant majestueux,
> Mais ils ont sous leurs pieds leurs frères qu'on bafoue,
> Dérisoires martyrs d'un hasard tortueux.

Des pleurs aussi salés rongent leur pâle joue,
Ils mangent de la cendre avec le même amour
Mais vulgaire ou grotesque est le Sort qui les roue.

Ils pouvaient faire aussi sonner comme un tambour
La servile pitié des races à l'œil terne,
Egaux de Prométhée à qui manque un vautour!

Non. Vieux, et fréquentant les déserts sans citerne,
Ils marchent sous le fouet d'un squelette rageur,
Le Guignon dont le rire édenté les prosterne.

This passage is over-crowded with meanings of which some (but not all) are intentionally veiled. Several details call for comment. The 'consolés majestueux', I have suggested, are poets such as Baudelaire, which really means Baudelaire himself. The victims of the Guignon, 'martyrs' of tortuous chance, proudly refuse to follow the example of the less steadfast, more self-interested and prudent brethren at whose feet they writhe. They share the ills suffered by the Poet in 'Bénédiction' ('Dans le pain et le vin destinés à sa bouche / Ils mêlent de la cendre avec d'impurs crachats'),[121] but scorn to magnify and dramatize their misery—and thus to play the part of Prometheus without the vulture.[122] 'La servile pitié des races à l'œil terne' is puzzling. It may mean the conventional sympathy of the bestial throng, the 'plèbe carnassière' of Leconte de Lisle's poem 'Les Montreurs'.[123] But the reference to drums sounding and awaking a response prompts a bolder guess. The poet may refer to future generations, no less ignorant and weary-eyed, reacting automatically to what poets of past ages tell them. Poets whose ambitious hopes have been fulfilled, hopes such as those expressed in one of Baudelaire's sonnets:

Je te donne ces vers afin que si mon nom
Aborde heureusement aux époques lointaines,
. . .
Ta mémoire, pareille aux fables incertaines,
Fatigue le lecteur ainsi qu'un tympanon . . .

The mention of 'déserts sans citerne' is presumably intended to evoke the death in Algeria of Pétrus Borel, an undoubted azure-beggar *enguignonné* to the end, and a subject of remorse for

Baudelaire his one-time friend.[124] Shortly before Borel died Baudelaire had written an article on this 'génie manqué'. It was so harsh in substance and unfriendly in tone that when it appeared on 15 July 1861, in the *Revue fantaisiste*, it ended with a grudgingly apologetic note added by its author, in meagre reparation:

Comme nous achevions, l'an passé, d'écrire ces notes, trop sévères peut-être, nous avons appris que le poète venait de mourir en Algérie, où il s'était retiré, loin des affaires littéraires, découragé ou méprisant, avant d'avoir livré au public un *Tabarin* annoncé depuis longtemps.[125]

The relevance of this article to Mallarmé's subject is underlined by Baudelaire's return, in its opening paragraphs, to the Guignon theme:

Il y a dans le monde spirituel quelque chose de mystérieux qui s'appelle le *Guignon*, et nul de nous n'a le droit de discuter avec la Fatalité (. . .) Je me suis demandé, dis-je, comment le poète qui a produit l'étrange poème . . . qui sert de préface à *Madame Putiphar*, avait pu aussi en maint endroit montrer tant de maladresse, buter dans tant de heurts et de cahots, tomber au fond de tant de *guignons*.[126]

One-third only of Mallarmé's poem (tercets eleven to seventeen) is devoted to describing the exploits of the Guignon. Though born of Baudelaire's reflections on Edgar Poe, the mischief-maker is animated by other examples, of the hobgoblin kind, most noticeably Puck in *A Midsummer Night's Dream*.[127] Mallarmé's account competes successfully with Gautier's more sober complaining against abstractions like the hand of Destiny and Fortune's wheel. Hidden meanings seem for the time being to be rare, but one pregnant phrase tells the reader that Baudelaire is not forgotten. The line 'Malheureux sans l'orgueil d'une austère Infortune' echoes a very conspicuous instance of his self-glorifyingly dolorous claims:

Ces yeux mystérieux ont d'invincibles charmes
Pour celui que l'austère Infortune allaita!
('Les Petites Vieilles' in *Tableaux Parisiens*)

The final accusation is made in the last four tercets. Certain 'poètes savants' are arraigned for callous heartlessness and a hostile attitude towards their martyred brothers. The most serious satirical shaft of all is reserved for the end-line, with its manifest reference to the suicide of Gérard de Nerval in January 1855,[128] but in the whole of this section the tone of dark insinuation prevails. Study the text as we may, the reading remains conjectural. Who are 'les poètes savants'? Are they the elders who know all, and proclaim their answers to questions young poets ask? If so (and I see no more likely meaning) Baudelaire must occupy a prominent place among them. First, because he is given that title, 'le poète savant', and shown playing that same part, in the section of 'Symphonie littéraire' (written only two years later) in which Mallarmé describes in plain language the emotions he experiences when he reads *Les Fleurs du mal*:

> Alors je me voile la face, et des sanglots, arrachés à mon âme moins par ce cauchemar que par une rare sensation d'exil, traversent le noir silence. Qu'est-ce donc que la patrie?
>
> J'ai fermé le livre et les yeux, et je cherche la patrie. Devant moi se dresse l'apparition du poète savant qui me l'indique en un hymne élancé mystiquement comme un lis. Le rythme de ce chant ressemble à la rosace d'une ancienne église . . . [129]

And what is then described is the sixteenth-century 'paradise' window ('la rose du paradis') in the north transept of Sens Cathedral. 'Qu'est-ce que la patrie?' is still the question, and the answer young poets receive is still the one celebrated in 'Bénédiction' and accepted by Baudelaire in the essay on Edgar Poe: our homeland, the ideal existence that we crave, is the heaven hereafter that we learned of as children, with its crowned heads and angelic music, and voices forever chanting Alleluia! A life beyond the tomb that held no interest for Mallarmé.

The second reason why Baudelaire must figure among 'the poets who know' is his performance in the long poem 'Le Voyage', which in the 1861 edition brings *Les Fleurs du mal* to a despairing close. It elaborates on the answer that experience gives to the same question differently phrased: 'Dites, qu'avez-vous vu?':

> Notre âme est un trois-mâts cherchant son Icarie;
> Une voix retentit sur le pont: "Ouvre l'œil!"
> Une voix de la hune, ardente et folle, crie:
> "Amour . . . gloire . . . bonheur!" Enfer! c'est un écueil![130] . . .

Amer savoir, celui qu'on tire du voyage!
Le monde, monotone et petit, aujourd'hui,
Hier, demain, toujours, nous fait voir notre image:
Une oasis d'horreur dans un désert d'ennui!
. . .
Ô Mort, vieux capitaine, il est temps! levons l'ancre! . . . [131]

Où donc est la patrie? Anywhere, anywhere out of the world. After the Christian answer to children comes the despairing answer of precocious old age and bitter experience, replying to youthful ardour. It is Baudelaire's answer, and it may be noted that there is now no longer room for speculation as to why *L'Artiste* could not publish more than the first few tercets of Mallarmé's poem. Nor, on the other hand, why Baudelaire's disciple should turn thus on his master and in cryptic language call him to account.

As to which of the poets-who-knew preached vengeance to their unfortunate brethren I have no suggestion to make, unless the revenge is stated in the first of the two tercets of direct speech. The poet there depicted as inviting the *enguignonnés*, instead of 'begging a few sighs', to savour proudly and ostentatiously woes whose memory would never fade, is easily identified. He is again the later Baudelaire, who in the second edition of *Les Fleurs du mal* included such lines as these:

Connais-tu, comme moi, la douleur savoureuse,
Et de toi fais-tu dire: 'Oh! l'homme singulier'?
('Le Rêve d'un curieux')[132]

Dans le ravin hanté des chats-pards et des onces
Nos héros, s'étreignant méchamment, ont roulé.
Et leur peau fleurira l'aridité des ronces

—Ce gouffre, c'est l'enfer, de nos amis peuplé!
Roulons-y sans remords, amazone inhumaine,
Afin d'éterniser l'ardeur de notre haine!
('Duellum')[133]

It was to the same Baudelaire that the rebel could attribute the two proclamations in the following tercet, praising (in terms borrowed from 'Bénédiction') the Strong, and dismissing with contempt the failures, 'ces baladins'. The strong who valiantly withstand the 'tawny angels of evil' are presumably none other than Victor Hugo. The praise of his strength and love of all things strong is that expressed by Baudelaire in the article 'Victor Hugo', published in *La Revue fantaisiste* on 15 June 1861 to open the series *Réflexions sur quelques-uns de mes contemporains*. Of the eulogy in which the article largely consists, despite Baudelaire's intense dislike of Hugo and his works, and of the hypocritical sophistry with which the deep aesthetic differences between them are conjured away, the following passages will provide a fair illustration:

Ce serait sans doute ici le cas, si l'espace le permettait, d'analyser l'atmosphère morale qui plane et circule dans ses poèmes, laquelle participe très sensiblement du tempérament propre de l'auteur. Elle me paraît porter un caractère très manifeste d'amour égal pour ce qui est très fort comme pour ce qui est très faible, et l'attraction exercée sur le poète par ces deux extrêmes tire sa raison d'une origine unique, qui est la force même, la vigueur originelle dont il est doué. La force l'enchante et l'enivre; il va vers elle comme vers une parente: attraction fraternelle. Ainsi est-il emporté irrésistiblement vers tout symbole de l'infini, la mer, le ciel; vers tous les représentants anciens de la force, géants homériques ou bibliques, paladins, chevaliers; vers les bêtes énormes et redoutables. Il caresse en se jouant ce qui ferait peur à des mains débiles; il se meut dans l'immense, sans vertige. En revanche, mais par une tendance différente dont la source est pourtant la même, le poète se montre toujours l'ami attendri de tout ce qui est faible, solitaire, contristé; de tout ce qui est orphelin: attraction paternelle. Le fort qui devine un frère dans tout ce qui est fort, voit ses enfants dans tout ce qui a besoin d'être protégé ou consolé. C'est de la force même et de la certitude qu'elle donne à celui qui la possède que dérive l'esprit de justice et de charité (. . .) Il ne s'agit pas ici de cette morale prêcheuse qui, par son air de pédanterie, par son ton didactique, peut gâter les plus beaux morceaux de poésie, mais d'une morale inspirée qui se glisse, invisible, dans la matière poétique, comme les fluides impondérables dans toute la machine du monde. La morale n'entre pas dans cet art à titre de but; elle s'y mêle et s'y confond comme dans la vie elle-même. Le poète est moraliste sans le vouloir, par abondance et plénitude de nature.[134]

Baudelaire's attitude, on the other hand, to 'les baladins' is to be found in yet another article that he published in the same magazine four months later. It was written to serve as a congratulatory foreword to a novel by Léon Cladel entitled *Les Martyrs ridicules*, whose subject was the life of the young

Bohemians of Paris seeking to be men of letters.[135] Between Cladel's 'martyrs' (pilloried much more cruelly in Baudelaire's article than in the novel itself) and the 'martyrs dérisoires', 'ces baladins', that Mallarmé defends, the resemblance is in my estimation so close as to indicate a direct relationship. When in an article I wrote some twenty years ago I gave my reasons for believing that this was so,[136] my opinion was not well received, but two pieces of evidence have since come to light which confirm it. First, the testimony of Henri de Régnier, who had Mallarmé's own authority for stating that the first shock of reading *Les Fleurs du mal* was for him 'une étrange fascination (. . .) quelque chose à rendre fou', but that Baudelaire's eccentricities in his later years ('une manière factice de fumisterie qui montrait que le fond naturel était épuisé') altered his disciple's attitude. Also, and in particular, 'Baudelaire détestait les jeunes gens, avait horreur de ceux qui venaient'.[137]

In his biography of Henri Cazalis, published in 1972, Lawrence Joseph made known a hitherto unpublished part of a letter to Mallarmé which Cazalis must have sent to him at Tournon, at the end of December 1863. It contained an account of an incident involving Baudelaire, which he had himself witnessed and which he clearly knew would be of great interest to his friend. Cazalis had been invited to dinner by his cousin Madame Le Josne, in the company of Baudelaire. He wrote:

> J'ai eu chez ma cousine un bien grand ennui. Je lui avais porté l'article que tu sais. Elle l'avait lu, relu, n'en pouvant croire ses yeux: mais bien entendu n'en avait pas parlé à Baudelaire. Son mari, comme tous les maris, un véritable enfant terrible, et un enfant très maladroit, dès que Baudelaire rentre au salon, lui met cela sous le nez. Grande émotion chez Baudelaire: ma cousine est furieuse, et tout bas le dit à son mari. Baudelaire balbutie, et ne trouve pas de mots pour sa défense. Il finit cependant par dire que ce fut un article de complaisance pour l'éditeur, mais qu'il va paraître une seconde édition, et en tête alors, une seconde préface qui dira tout le contraire de ce que dit la première. Mais qui vous a donné cela, ajoutait toujours le pauvre homme? Il se retira de très bonne heure.[138]

Cazalis does not actually say that it was Mallarmé who gave him the copy of Baudelaire's article, but the expression 'l'article que tu sais' certainly implies some collusion between them in drawing the attention of Madame Le Josne to it. As to its identity, Lawrence Joseph comments:

Nous n'avons malheureusement pas pu identifier avec certitude cet "article" de Baudelaire qui dans la lettre de Cazalis est également désigné sous le nom de "préface". Il s'agit vraisemblablement de celle des *Martyrs ridicules* de Léon Cladel, publiée pour la première fois en 1861 comme article dans la *Revue fantaisiste*. Baudelaire y affiche une attitude hostile à l'égard de la jeunesse littéraire et de son aveugle prédilection pour certaines valeurs romantiques mal comprises, position qui aurait bien pu scandaliser les Le Josne chez qui les auteurs débutants recevaient un accueil chaleureux.

Which completes my case for maintaining that the 'martyrs dérisoires' of 'Le Guignon', some of whom hang themselves, 'ridiculement', in the street, like Baudelaire's erstwhile friend Nerval, are the 'martyrs ridicules' that Baudelaire so derides.

Mallarmé's most important purpose in writing 'Le Guignon' was to avenge them, and who can wonder? The champion of luckless poets, who had written as movingly of Poe as Vigny had of Chatterton, was now (after a virulent diatribe against the younger generation in general) scolding the *enguignonnés* his own disciples, in terms worthy of the Lord Mayor offering Chatterton a living as a servant in his household:[139]

Alpinien, le *martyr* en premier de cette cohorte de *martyrs ridicules* (il faut toujours en revenir au titre) s'avise un jour, pour se distraire des chagrins intolérables que lui ont faits ses mauvaises mœurs, sa fainéantise et sa rêverie vagabonde, d'entreprendre le plus étrange pèlerinage dont il puisse être fait mention dans les folles religions inventées par les solitaires oisifs et impuissants. L'amour, c'est-à-dire le libertinage, la débauche élevée à l'état de contre-religion, ne lui ayant pas payé les récompenses espérées, Alpinien court la gloire, et, errant dans les cimetières, il implore les images des grands hommes défunts; il baise leurs bustes, les suppliant de lui livrer leur secret, le grand secret: "Comment faire pour devenir aussi grand que vous?" Les statues, si elles étaient bonnes conseillères, pourraient répondre: "Il faut rester chez toi, méditer et barbouiller beaucoup de papier!" Mais ce moyen si simple n'est pas à la portée d'un rêveur hystérique. La superstition lui paraît plus naturelle. En vérité, cette invention si tristement gaie fait penser au nouveau calendrier des saints de l'école *positiviste*.

La superstition! ai-je dit. Elle joue un grand rôle dans la tragédie solitaire et interne du pauvre Alpinien, et ce n'est pas sans un délicieux et douloureux attendrissement qu'on voit par instant son esprit harassé—où la superstition la plus puérile, symbolisant obscurément, comme dans le cerveau des nations, l'universelle vérité, s'amalgame avec les sentiments religieux les plus purs,—se retourner vers les salutaires impressions de l'enfance, vers la Vierge Marie, vers le chant fortifiant des cloches, vers le crépuscule consolant de l'Église, vers la famille, vers la mère; la mère, ce giron toujours ouvert pour les *fruits secs*, les prodigues et les ambitieux maladroits. On peut espérer qu'à partir de ce moment Alpinien est à moitié sauvé; il ne lui manque plus que de devenir un homme d'action, un homme de devoir, au jour le jour.[140]

What Baudelaire does not say is that Alpinien, who indeed seeks inspiration from Balzac's tomb, also carries his superstition to the point of following the old and the maimed through the streets of Paris, in Baudelaire's footsteps, reciting 'Les Petites Vieilles' as he goes.

How grave a betrayal this article must have seemed to Baudelaire's disciples can be inferred from what Cladel said himself about his novel, later. In a new preface of his own written in 1880 he confessed that what was said of his former companions in *Les Martyrs ridicules* had been 'violent, injuste, haineux, jaloux'. His daughter, who quotes these words, adds her own commentary:

L'Avant-Propos de Léon Cladel peut donc être considéré comme une sorte d'acte de contrition; car parmi cette faune de cafés et de brasseries, il avait connu plus d'un affamé de liberté et de gloire dont l'existence fut lamentable et la fin tragique. Deux d'entre eux se pendirent, un autre s'asphyxia au gaz . . .[141]

One last paragraph is I hope permissible in this already protracted account of a young poet's rebellion against his master. It appears to be explainable only as a sudden response of that young poet to an exceptional combination of circumstances. His new-found freedom to devote his life to literature must have brought with it a sense of responsibility and at the same time of vulnerability. That moment coincided with the brief heyday of his new and very warm friendship with Léon Marc, an azure-beggar to whom the Guignon was no stranger. Mallarmé's first serious article, published in *Le Sénonais* on 7 December 1861, had been principally concerned with the praise of Marc's victory, as a poet, over 'ce coudoiement perpétuel de l'idéal et de la réalité, ces contraintes ironiques qui interrompent l'Hamlet de province dans son monologue'—a victory, he called it, 'remportée sur le temps et sur toutes les fatalités'.[142] Thus, for Mallarmé, the trials of the azure-beggars were prominent among the moral preoccupations of the moment. We know also, on the other hand, that he was familiar enough with *La Revue fantaisiste* to send for publication there, in November 1861, his 'Bals masqués'. It would not be surprising if on some occasion during that winter, thanks for instance to his other new friend Des Essarts, a copy of the issue of 15 October should have come his way, and revealed to him Baudelaire's sentiments concerning *Les Martyrs ridicules*. What is certainly surprising, however, incensed though he might be, is that he should be so bold as to launch forthwith a personal attack on an illustrious elder. But even there, a particular circumstance should be taken into account. The idea of Baudelaire as a betrayer, a lost leader, was favoured by his decision, at the turn of the year, to stand as a candidate for election to the French Academy.[143]

Of the shorter poems on entirely serious subjects composed by Mallarmé in 1862, the earliest is no doubt 'Le Sonneur'. It was published on 15 March along with the fragment of 'Le Guignon', and it has with that poem some close affinities—underlined, perhaps deliberately, by the reference to escape by suicide in the last line of both. It may be assumed that it was written about the same time, at the beginning of that year. The young Sénonais expresses in it, as in 'Le Guignon', pessimistic fears for his likely fate in the calling he has just won the coveted right to follow. 'Le Sonneur' is an emblematic or allegorical sonnet (in form, like 'Placet', a 'sonnet irrégulier'). In the comparison it develops, after the manner of such poems in *Les Fleurs du mal* as 'L'Albatros' or 'Je suis comme le roi d'un pays pluvieux', the poet himself, as poet, is likened to a church-bell ringer. The subject may have been suggested by Baudelaire's 'La Cloche fêlée', but Mallarmé may also have had in mind poems such as Hugo's 'A Louis B.' (in *Les Chants du crépuscule*), and Lamartine's 'La Cloche du village' and 'La Cloche' (both in *Recueillements poétiques*).[144] It is to be noted however that in all these possible sources of suggestion the comparison is between the poet and the church-bell, not the bell-ringer. As to Hugo's Quasimodo, it is not of course impossible that the deaf dwarf who rang the bells in *Notre-Dame de Paris* helped Mallarmé and his readers to imagine a bell-ringing of a very different kind, but the contribution is not apparent. As published in *L'Artiste*, 'Le Sonneur' reads:

Le Sonneur[145]

Cependant que la cloche enivre sa voix claire
De l'air plein de rosée et jeune du matin,
Et fait à la faucheuse entonner, pour lui plaire,
Un *Angelus* qui sent la lavande et le thym;

Le sonneur essoufflé, qu'un cierge pâle éclaire,
Chevauchant tristement en geignant du latin,
Sur la pierre qui tend la corde séculaire,
N'entend descendre à lui qu'un tintement lointain.

Je suis cet homme. Hélas! dans mon ardeur peureuse,
J'ai beau broyer le câble à sonner l'idéal,
Depuis que la Mal trône en mon cœur lilial

La Voix ne me vient plus que par bribes et creuse.
—Si bien qu'un jour, après avoir en vain tiré,
O Satan, j'ôterai la pierre et me pendrai!

A brief account of this sonnet is given by Pierre-Olivier Walzer.[146] He begins by observing that it is constructed on a traditional plan, 'sur le schéma d'une comparaison très classique, les deux quatrains étant consacrés au sonneur, les deux tercets au poète'. That is so, but the structure is less simple than that statement may suggest. For within each of those two parts a secondary comparison is introduced, not analogical but antithetical. If the bell-ringer and the poet may be likened to each other it is because both are themselves deprived of the rich benefit that they bestow on those they serve. That such is the case so far as the bell-ringer is concerned is confidently and clearly laid before us in the quatrains. M. Walzer continues:

en même temps qu'il [le sonneur] tire sur la corde et que les sons de la cloche se répandent joyeusement dans la fraîcheur du matin, il récite en haletant ses prières latines et ne perçoit, dans la vie des cloches, qu'un tintement étouffé par la distance et les murs.

So far, so good, but M. Walzer then proceeds to explain that in the tercets the poet sees himself as being in the same situation:

Il a beau tirer sur "le cable de l'Idéal", seule une rumeur confuse parvient à ses oreilles; le poète est incapable de capter la voix de l'Idéal et de la faire résonner par le monde. C'est tout le drame de l'impuissance, qui trouve sa solution dans le suicide.

Here, one has to dissent. Such might be the drama of impotence if the poet in question were some poet-prophet prevented by sterility from saving the world, but not when the poet is Stéphane Mallarmé ('Je suis cet homme') at the age of twenty, not listening for a sacred message to be noised abroad but waiting for a breath of inspiration, a stirring of his imagination, an idea for a poetic subject and a poem which would be interesting to compose.

It would seem that the poet was well aware of this flaw in his subject, but thought the difficulty manageable till he had put it to the test. In the tercets, there are indications that he sought to hide the defect or to make it less conspicuous. If the poet's incapacity could be given some religious significance, a parallel with the bell-ringer's situation might be easier to suggest vaguely though not to draw. The silence of the poet's Voice could be made more portentous by giving it a religious meaning.[147] Such thoughts would account for the muddled, hurried character of the tercets, contrasting so strongly with the confident clarity of the quatrains. So might one interpret, for instance, the Christian sin-and-punishment notions that enter a quite alien context to dictate two alternative versions for the last line of the first tercet: 'Depuis que le Mal trône en mon cœur lilial', early amended to 'De froids Péchés s'ébat un plumage féal',[148] to account for the poet's sterility. The sudden emergence also of a diabolic providence, to make a melodramatically Baudelairian last line, can similarly be understood, as a device to avert attention from the crippling logical weakness that cannot be concealed.

Thus a sonnet that began with smiles and graceful dignity ends, through short-sighted planning and despite Baudelairian assistance, in total disarray.[149]

Some consciousness of his partial failure in 'Le Sonneur' may account for the rather deprecatory manner in which Mallarmé presented to Cazalis, in a letter dated 4 June (three weeks after their first meeting), another sonnet, one he had just composed under the title 'Vere novo'. As if to emphasize its private character it was written and sent as an integral part of the letter, which included also a commentary on it. In the following text some early amendments that Mallarmé was to make are added, in italics and between square brackets, to the original version provided by the letter:

Vere novo[150]

Le printemps maladif a chassé tristement
L'hiver, saison de l'art serein, l'hiver lucide[.]
Dans mon être où, dès l'aube, un sang plombé préside
[*Et dans mon être auquel un sang morne préside*]
L'impuissance s'étire en un long bâillement.

Des crépuscules blancs tiédissent sous mon crâne
Qu'un cercle de fer serre ainsi qu'un vieux tombeau;
Et morne, [*Et, triste,*] j'erre après un Rêve vague et beau
Par les champs où la sève immense se pavane[.]

Puis je tombe énervé de parfums d'arbres, las,
Et creusant de ma face une fosse à mon [*ce*] Rêve
Mordant la terre chaude où poussent les lilas

J'attends, en m'abîmant, que le Néant se lève [*mon ennui s'élève*] . . .
—Cependant l'azur rit dans la haie en éveil [*et l'éveil*]
Où des oiseaux en fleur gazouillant au soleil.]
[*De tant d'oiseaux en fleur gazouillant au soleil.*]

The idea of writing a poem about a spring-time spleen may have been born of a recollection of Baudelaire's 'Brumes et pluies', the sonnet with the oddly rhyming quatrains:[151]

O fins d'automne, hivers, printemps trempés de boue,
Endormeuses saisons! je vous aime et vous loue
D'envelopper ainsi mon cœur et mon cerveau
D'un linceul vaporeux et d'un vague tombeau.

Dans cette grande plaine où l'autan froid se joue,
Où par les longues nuits la girouette s'enroue,
Mon âme mieux qu'au temps du tiède renouveau[152]
Ouvrira largement ses ailes de corbeau.

However, despite any relation there may be between the two poems, Mallarmé's sonnet is decidedly very different from his master's.

About his own poem, Mallarmé has things to say in his

accompanying letter that sound interesting, but not all of them are clear, and the obscurity is the more intriguing because it appears to be in part deliberate. The statements are contained in two paragraphs of the letter, one placed immediately before the poem and concerned with its substance, the other placed immediately after it and concerned largely with matters of form. The first of them reads:

As-tu remis mes vers? Puisque tu es si bon que de désirer les garder tous, je t'envoie, pour le joindre au tien, un pauvre sonnet [é]clos ces jours-ci, triste et laid.

Emmanuel t'avait peut-être parlé d'une stérilité curieuse que le printemps avait installée en moi. Après trois mois d'impuissance, j'en suis enfin débarrassé, et mon premier sonnet est consacré à la décrire, c'est à dire à la maudire. C'est un genre assez nouveau que cette poésie, où les effets matériels, du sang, des nerfs sont analysés et mêlés aux effets moraux, de l'esprit, de l'âme. Cela pourrait s'appeler *spleen printannier* [*sic*]. Quand la combinaison est bien harmonisée et que l'œuvre n'est ni trop physique ni trop spirituelle, elle peut représenter quelque chose.[153]

Two details in this commentary are themselves, I believe, in need of comment. First, in the word *éclos* a half-concealed metaphor must I believe be understood and kept in mind. Mallarmé's sonnet is likened to a bird 'newly hatched', still without its feathers and therefore 'triste et laid'. Secondly, 'une stérilité curieuse' sounds rather grand in the circumstances, particularly as Mallarmé had already complained of a sterile period in his first letter to Cazalis, dated 5 May: 'Je sors à peine d'une série de jours brumeux et stériles, et mon premier sourire est à vous'.[154] A literary attitude is probably involved and it is not difficult to identify its source. Since we know that Mallarmé had been acquainting himself with Baudelaire's prose writings,[155] and also that he was taking a special interest in Poe, we may suspect that he had found food for flattering analogies in such remarks as the following: 'Mais la belle saison, la saison du bonheur, pour un homme de rêverie et de méditation comme lui, c'est l'hiver' (*Les Paradis artificiels*, B., *O.c.* i, 475), and the reference to occasions when Poe was 'frappé momentanement d'une de ces stérilités que connaissent les écrivains nerveux' (*Edgar Poe, sa vie et ses œuvres*, ibid. ii, 308). Also such praise as this:

Aucun homme, je le répète, n'a raconté avec plus de magie . . . les fins de saison chargés de splendeurs énervantes, les temps chauds, humides et brumeux, où le vent du sud amollit et détend les nerfs comme les cordes d'un instrument' (ibid. 317).

It must be observed also that Mallarmé had a personal, even a domestic reason for being interested in that side of Poe's talent. He had written to his grandfather, on 17 January 1862, a letter in which the news he gave of his father's health might itself reflect his reading of Baudelaire on Poe:

Je te dirai que mon père (. . .) ne va ni mieux ni plus mal, et qu'on ne sait quel temps souhaiter, les temps humides et doux détendant ses nerfs et le laissant morne et lourd, et les temps froids et toniques l'excitant au dernier point.[156]

The second part of the commentary sent to Cazalis, the part concerned with matters of form, seems at first to promise an explicit account of 'Vere novo', but the author proves to be reticent on the subject. It is not of his own sonnet but the sonnet in general that he writes:

Tu riras peut-être de ma manie de sonnets[157]—non, car tu en as fait de délicieux—mais pour moi c'est un grand poème en petit: les quatrains et les tercets me semblent des chants entiers, et je passe parfois trois jours à en équilibrer d'avance les parties, pour que le tout soit harmonieux et s'approche du Beau.[158]

From which it would appear that the poetic process itself is one by which, after these preliminaries, the sonnet is made beautiful. This process has been experimentally omitted in the case of 'Vere novo', since it is 'triste et laid'. All that its author was prepared to say in its favour is contained in the sentence, vague and finally non-committal:

Quand la combinaison est bien harmonisée, et que l'œuvre n'est ni trop physique ni trop spirituelle, elle peut représenter quelque chose.

Can the poem be said to 'represent' anything other than a spring-time spleen, 'triste et laid'? And has its author had any other intention than to omit, by way of experiment, the poetic process? The answer should perhaps be sought in the frail, seemingly separate theme that begins: 'Et, morne, j'erre après un Rêve vague et beau', and is then interrupted, but emerges again and ends:

Et creusant de ma face une fosse à mon [*ce*] Rêve,
J'attends en m'abîmant que le Néant se lève [*que mon ennui s'élève*] . . .

The element of beauty looked forward to has gone, smothered by the spleen. To return to the original metaphor, the 'pauvre sonnet éclos ces jours-ci, triste et laid' will never put on its feathers and spread its wings. Beauty, which is a special grace, separate even from composition, is in this poem (perhaps to exemplify that principle), deliberately withheld. And the most likely incitement to conduct such an experiment, or test, could well be found in the ideas of Poe as paraphrased by Baudelaire in his *Notes nouvelles sur Edgar Poe*, the preface to the second volume of his translation of the tales.[159]

Paired with 'Vere novo' in several early manuscripts, under a common title which is in some cases 'Soleils malsains'[160] and in others 'Soleils mauvais', is another sonnet—'irrégulier' however in its rhyme-scheme—entitled 'Tristesse d'été. The following version is the one the Flammarion editors have chosen, presumably as likely to be the earliest, of those 'écrites presque certainement en 1862':[161]

Tristesse d'été[162]

Le Soleil, sur la mousse où tu t'es endormie,
A chauffé comme un bain tes cheveux ténébreux,
Et, dans l'air sans oiseaux et sans brise ennemie,
Evaporé son fard en parfums dangereux.

De ce blanc flamboiement l'immuable accalmie,
Me fait haïr la vie et notre amour fiévreux,
Et tout mon être implore un sommeil de momie
Morne comme le sable et les palmiers poudreux!

Ta chevelure, est-elle une rivière tiède
Où noyer sans frissons mon âme qui m'obsède
Et jouir du Néant où l'on ne pense pas?

Je veux boire le fard qui fond sous tes paupières
Si ce poison promet au cœur que tu frappas
L'insensibilité de l'azur et des pierres!

To be accurately read and fairly judged, in the context of the present study, this sonnet must indeed be considered strictly as a poem of 1862, and not as an early version of the poem published under the same title four years later, in *Le Parnasse contemporain*. Its exceptional situation in that regard is recognized by the Flammarion editors, who separate the two poems firmly, despite the genealogical relationship, and set each in its own biographical place.[163]

It is the relationship of 1862 with 'Vere novo', which in my understanding is experimental, that concerns us here. This first 'Tristesse d'été' tells of a summer-time spleen, and was probably written very soon after its spring-time companion, to which it is in substance closely akin. In form, on the other hand, it contrasts with it ostentatiously, returning gratefully as it were to normality after the subjection in 'Vere novo', as an experiment or poetic exercise, to the ban on beauty. In 'Tristesse d'été' the poet regains two means of 'approaching beauty'. One is the presence of an emotional element in which physical beauty is involved, a love affair of sorts. It is substituted for the insubstantial 'Rêve vague et beau', a physical reality ('notre amour fiévreux') replacing in the season of fulfilment the romantic dream of spring.[164] Thus the gloom has been humanized and comforted. The second, more obvious and important aesthetic change is the release of imagination in the manifestation of the summer spleen. Imagery is abundant, artificially so at one point, in the second quatrain. The same part of the poem is rich also in musicality; the first line of the quatrain is sometimes quoted as one of the most beautiful that Mallarmé ever wrote. The alliteration in the lines that follow is partly provided by Musset's 'Rolla',[165] and several features in the general adornment appear to have been gathered from *Les Fleurs du mal*.[166] The spleen mood itself is given a more interesting, dramatic aspect by a definition brought in from Vigny's *Chatterton*, whose poet-hero suffers from a disease described by his Quaker friends as 'la haine de la vie et l'amour de la mort'.[167]

It has been suggested, no doubt on evidence thought to be provided by the poem of 1866, that the lady asleep is Marie Gerhard. In view of the 'cheveux ténébreux', however, whereas Marie had flaxen hair, and given the respectful attitude shown by Mallarmé when he wrote of her to Cazalis on 4–5 August,[168] almost certainly a month or more after composing 'Tristesse d'été', the suggestion seems rather frivolous. It was at the end of October that the young lovers spent together, at Fontainebleau, a day that seems to have been decisive in their courtship, and which they would never forget.[169] The lady asleep in Mallarmé's poem could well signify nothing more than the convenient reappearance of a damsel he had invented for a schoolboy poem three years before, 'Sourire':

Oh! si sur la tiède mousse
Je voyais dormir une sœur!
Oh! si de son haleine douce
Le parfum enivrait mon cœur!
Avril 1859 (classe du soir).[170]

'Le Sonneur', 'Vere novo', and 'Tristesse d'été' are all spleen poems and as such represent an acquiescent response to Baudelaire's example. But the satiric vein of 'Le Guignon' was not exhausted. Two other poems in *terza rima*, 'Haine du Pauvre' and 'A un Mendiant', the former in six tercets, the latter in eight, are clearly related to the longer poem and may be considered as off-shoots from it, in substance as well as form:

Haine du Pauvre[171]

Ta guenille nocturne étalant par ses trous
Les rousseurs de tes [*O.c.*: ses] poils et de ta peau, je l'aime [*O.c.*: aime,]
Vieux spectre, et c'est pourquoi je te jette vingt sous.

Ton front servile et bas n'a pas la fierté blême:
Tu comprends que le pauvre est le frère du chien
Et ne vas pas drapant ta lésine en poëme.

Comme un chacal sortant de sa pierre, ô chrétien,
Tu rampes à plat ventre après qui te bafoue.
Vieux, combien par grimace? et par larme, combien?

Mets à nu ta vieillesse et que la [*O.c.*: ta] gueuse joue,
Lèche, et de mes vingt sous chatouille la vertu.
A bas! . . . —les deux genoux! . . . —la barbe dans la boue!

Que veut cette médaille idiote, ris-tu?
L'argent brille [*O.c.*: brilla], le cuivre un jour se vert-de-grise,
Et je suis peu dévot et je suis fort têtu,

Choisis.—Jetée? alors [*O.c.*: alors,] voici ma pièce prise.
Serre-la dans tes doigts et pense que tu l'as
Parce que j'en tiens trop, ou par simple méprise.

C'est le prix, si tu n'as pas peur, d'un coutelas.

A un Mendiant[172]

Pauvre, voici cent sous . . . Longtemps tu cajolas
—Ce vice te manquait—le songe d'être avare?
Ne les enfouis [*M.*: enterre] pas pour qu'on te sonne un glas.

Évoque de l'Enfer un péché plus bizarre,
Tu peux ensanglanter tes brumeux horizons
D'un rêve ayant l'éclair [*C.*: eclat] vermeil d'une fanfare.

Changeant en verts treillis les barreaux des prisons
Qu'illumine l'azur charmant d'une éclaircie
Le tabac fait grimper de sveltes feuillaisons;

L'opium est à vendre en mainte pharmacie;
Veux-tu mordre au rabais quelque pâle catin
Et boire en sa salive un reste d'ambroisie?

T'attabler au café jusqu'au triste [*M.*: jaune] matin?
Les plafonds sont fardés de faunesses sans voiles,
Et l'on jette deux sous au garçon, l'œil hautain.

Puis quand tu sors, vieux dieu, grelottant sous tes toiles
D'emballage, l'aurore est un lac de vin d'or
Et tu jures avoir le gosier plein d'étoiles!

Tu peux aussi, pour bien gaspiller ton trésor,
Mettre une plume rouge à ta coiffe; à complies,
Brûler un cierge au saint à qui tu crois encor.

Ne t'imagine pas que je dis des folies:
Que le diable ait ton corps si tu crèves de faim,
Je hais l'aumône utile et veux que tu m'oublies:

Et, surtout, ne va pas, drôle, acheter du pain!

Editors and critics have commonly followed Dr Bonniot in supposing these two texts to be successive early versions, or 'states', of the poem published later under the title 'Aumône'.[173] In the following attempt to show that the assumption is mistaken and to establish their actual relationship, the first step will be to establish as far as the evidence permits the date of composition of each. So far as 'Haine du Pauvre' is concerned I see no good reason to question the date usually accepted, though the documentary testimony in its favour is less positive than was until quite recently believed. In 1954 the Pléiade editors, after examining the one early manuscript, repeated Dr Bonniot's assertion that it was 'dated 1862',[174] but this was contested some thirty years later by Carl Barbier, in his edition of Mallarmé's *Vers et Prose d'enfance et de jeunesse*. He described the manuscript as follows:

Encre bleue sur le verso de la feuille qui contient également *Mysticis umbraculis*. (. . .) Le manuscrit est bien de 1862, mais n'est pas daté, quoi qu'en dise Mondor (*O.c.*, p. 1434). Si date il y avait, elle a été coupée lorsque Mallarmé réduisit le format de la feuille pour la coller à une autre afin de cacher *Mysticis umbraculis*.[175]

He did not say on what evidence he nevertheless agreed with Bonniot's dating of 'Haine du Pauvre', but the fact that its chance companion '*Mysticis umbraculis*' does indeed bear the date '1862' is perhaps adequate proof. The sole holograph copy of each of two quite different early poems, neither of them retained by their author for publication, would hardly have been preserved by him with such special care, on the same sheet of paper dated on one side only, if they had not even been composed in the same year.

'A un Mendiant' was for Dr Bonniot a later version of the same poem, written in 1864.[176] The date was shown to be erroneous, however, by Henri Mondor, when he cited in his *Vie de Mallarmé* a letter from Cazalis in Strasbourg to Mallarmé in London, dated May 1863. It contained a request for a copy of

Mallarmé's 'sonnet' (as Cazalis wrongly called it) 'sur l'aumône (voilà cinq francs va boire)'.[177] The poem referred to was clearly 'A un Mendiant', for which the dating must therefore be revised. The Pléiade editors were strangely cautious in their reception of this new testimony. 'Cette seconde version d'*Aumône*', they note, 'remontait peut-être [peut-être!] à l'année précédente'—that is, the year 1863.[178] It is possible to go further. From the uncertainty with which Cazalis repeated the opening words of the poem, it may be inferred, for instance, that Mallarmé had read it, or shown it to him, before leaving for London.[179] There is however another possibility which would make 1862 more definitely the likeliest date of composition. It is quite probable that Cazalis knew of the poem's existence not from Mallarmé himself but through Des Essarts. What he wrote in the letter from Strasbourg seems to suggest as much, and also that he was quoting from memory, in his usual haste, a letter from friend Emmanuel:

> Emm. me donne souvent de tes nouvelles: m'envoie des vers; et si tu veux m'être agréable, tu m'enverrais tes deux sonnets sur l'aumône (voilà 5 francs va boire) et la naissance du poète (Parce qu'un soir d'avril il lut dans son journal, etc); j'en ai donné l'idée à quelques-uns de mes nouveaux amis, et ils ont trouvé cela fort beau.

They were poems that Mallarmé was unlikely to have sent, unsolicited, from London, whether to Des Essarts or to Cazalis, but if they are fruits of his last few months at Sens, Des Essarts might well have been given a copy when he returned there after the summer vacation of 1862. For my part, and as regards the date of composition of 'A un Mendiant', I find that to be the most acceptable hypothesis. As such, it may help in exploring some more general questions later.

Meanwhile, Mallarmé sent Cazalis what he had asked for, and at the same time two of his more recent poems. In the accompanying letter, dated the third of June, he wrote: 'Je joins à ces quelques vers ['Les Fenêtres' and 'L'Assaut'] ceux que tu me demandes'.[180] Ten days later, Cazalis acknowledged all enthusiastically:

> Tes vers m'ont ravi, d'abord les anciens,—qui ont aussi fait l'admiration de quelques amis rares, que j'ai pu découvrir en cette sotte ville: puis *Les fenêtres*.[181]

The terms used to refer to the earlier poems, 'les anciens', complete the case for considering it most likely that 'A un Mendiant' was composed as early as 1862, before the departure for London. By the same token they prompt a question concerning a more important matter than the dating problem itself. If 'Haine du Pauvre' and 'A un Mendiant', generally supposed to be the first two of three early versions of the poem later entitled 'Aumône', were both written, as it now appears they were, within less than a year of each other, why are they so very different?[182]

They have, of course, a similar anecdotal subject, though even in that regard the divergencies are great. Each is a kind of dramatic monologue, addressed to a beggar by an eccentric alms-giver, hatefully cruel in 'Haine du Pauvre' and seductively unrealistic in 'A un Mendiant'. But considered as poems they have little in common except the verse form, the *terza rima* that their author chose also for 'Le Guignon' at the beginning of that same year. Particularly noticeable is the fact that only in one instance does the same rhyme occur in both, a fact that in itself makes very dubious indeed the idea that they are successive early versions of 'the same poem'. Furthermore, the rhyme they do share (rhyme in the technical sense, same-sounding though not necessarily supplied by the same words), gives positive testimony that the so-called two versions are in fact separate compositions. The rhyme is a striking one, 'coutelas' echoing 'que tu l'as' as 'glas' does 'cajolas', but more significant is its placing. One pair adorns the ending of 'Haine du Pauvre', the other the beginning of 'A un Mendiant'. The poems are therefore linked, or hinged as it were, and declared to form a sort of diptych, in the order: (i) 'Haine du Pauvre', (ii) 'A un Mendiant'.

Of their separate identities in this combination assurance is made doubly sure by firm external evidence. Henri Mondor quotes (not in this connection but a propos of 'Galanterie macabre') an instructive query from Des Essarts, in a letter he sent to Mallarmé later, on 3 March 1864, three months after his return to France:

Il m'arrive de reprendre le petit cahier de vers que tu m'as donné, et de le savourer lentement. J'ai aussi lu *Les Fenêtres*. Pourquoi, dans la liste, supprimes-tu l'un des deux *Pauvres*? Pourquoi exclus-tu la *Galanterie Macabre*? C'est un thème saisissant.[183]

The list in question is presumably a list of the poems included in the selective manuscript edition of his poems that Mallarmé sent at the beginning of 1864 to some of his friends and acquaintances. 'A un Mendiant' was included in it, but 'Haine du Pauvre' was not, and was plainly the 'one of the two *Pauvres*' referred to by Des Essarts.[184] In enquiring why Mallarmé was rejecting it, he leaves no doubt that he knew it (and who, of all Mallarmé's friends, was better informed on such matters at that time?) as an individual poem and not an earlier version of 'A un Mendiant'. On that issue, the evidence of his query is to my mind conclusive.

In turning now from such technical considerations to the respective subjects of the two poems and their author's probable intentions, I am aware that some of the suggestions I shall make will seem to be over-influenced by a special interest in Mallarmé's attitude towards Baudelaire and his works. Certainly that attitude, in my understanding, is of fundamental importance in his literary endeavours during the last year at Sens and the year that followed. It is the period, I believe, of which he was thinking when, at two different times later, he made candid statements regarding the adverse reactions to Baudelaire that followed his delirious excitement on first reading *Les Fleurs du mal* in 1860. One of them, made to Henri de Régnier in 1887, I have already quoted, and mentioned more than once because it is not well known:

> Chez le Baudelaire des dernières années s'était développée une manière factice de fumisterie qui montrait que le fond naturel était épuisé.[185]

The other statement is better known, figuring as it does in the *Correspondance*, but it may not have been given as much attention as it deserves. It is an observation in Mallarmé's postscript to a letter he wrote to Cazalis on 14 (or 17?) May 1867. It concerned their fellow-poet Léon Dierx, whose volume of verse *Les Lèvres closes* had just been published:

> Le livre de Dierx est un beau développement de Leconte de Lisle. S'en séparera-t-il comme moi de Baudelaire?[186]

The comparison cannot have been made lightly, appended as it is to the extraordinary letter in which Mallarmé revealed to

Cazalis his secret ambition regarding what he called 'mon œuvre, qui est l'*Œuvre*, le Grand-Œuvre, comme disaient les alchimistes, nos ancêtres.' He must therefore have seen his own separation from Baudelaire not simply—in retrospect—as having been an important phase in his development, but as the culmination of a deliberate process. It had meant a critical examination of some parts of Baudelaire's writings, leading to a clear discrimination between what he admired and what he rejected. He had retained, and always would, a deep appreciation of the master's poetic genius,[187] and to some extent espoused his aesthetic doctrine, but he also accused him, more or less darkly, of fundamental errors and grave moral lapses. Something has been seen of such accusations in 'Le Guignon'; others will be identified later. But nowhere are they so squarely made as they are, I shall now try to show, in the diptych 'Haine du Pauvre' – 'A un Mendiant'.

I know of no evidence, and no reason to assume, that 'Haine du Pauvre' was composed before 'A un Mendiant', but the rhyme-link does invite us as readers to put them in that order. That it is also the more convenient sequence in which to study them, the study itself will confirm. The ostensible subject of 'Haine du Pauvre' is indicated by what appears to be a prosaically objective title. With its assistance, the poem appears to unfold a display of the callous, contemptuous animosity shown by the rich towards the very poor who are obliged to beg for a living. An unlikely subject, one would have thought, for Mallarmé to choose, and treat in so harshly satirical a manner. But his doing so is explained when another theme, more to be expected, is discerned, lurking in the shadows. Two literary reminiscences, closely linked, betray its presence. One of them goes back to Molière's *Dom Juan ou le Festin de Pierre*.[188] The protagonist in 'Haine du Pauvre' imitates, with even more cruelty, the behaviour of Dom Juan during his encounter with the beggar, in Act III scene 2 of the play ('Dom Juan, Sganarelle, le Pauvre'). Molière's text reads as follows:

DON JUAN. (. . .) ah ah, je m'en vais te donner un Louis d'or tout à l'heure pourvu que tu veuilles jurer.

LE PAUVRE. Ah, Monsieur, voudriez-vous que je commisse un tel péché?

DON JUAN. Tu n'as qu'à voir si tu veux gagner un Louis d'or ou non. En voici un que je te donne si tu jures, tiens il faut jurer.
LE PAUVRE. Monsieur.
DON JUAN. A moins de cela tu ne l'auras pas.
SGANARELLE. Va, va, jure un peu, il n'y a pas de mal.
DON JUAN. Prends, le voilà, prends te dis-je, mais jure donc.
LE PAUVRE. Non Monsieur, j'aime mieux mourir de faim.
DON JUAN. Va, va, je te le donne pour l'amour de l'humanité.

In the minds of the readers Mallarmé may have been addressing when he composed 'Haine du Pauvre', the other reminiscence, of one of Baudelaire's earlier poems, would already be associated with that scene. For 'Don Juan aux enfers', first published in 1846 but included in *Les Fleurs du mal*, flaunts its author's unseemly admiration for the cynical 'grand seigneur méchant homme' of Molière's play. It might be remembered by his readers that Baudelaire had depicted in that poem two of the Don's victims, the Beggar and the Commander, sharing an appropriate revenge, conducting their tormentor to an eternity of torments in a Hades more fitting for a fastidious dandy than the inferno into which Molière had cast him. Thanks to which privilege Baudelaire's hero, though bearing himself perhaps a little too much like any officer and gentleman, is able to remain disdainfully apart and defiantly unmoved:

Quand Don Juan descendit vers l'onde souterraine
Et lorsqu'il eut donné son obole à Charon,
Un sombre mendiant, l'œil fier comme Antisthène,
D'un bras vengeur et fort saisit chaque aviron.

. . .

Tout droit dans son armure, un grand homme de pierre
Se tenait à la barre et coupait le flot noir;
Mais le calme héros, courbé sur sa rapière,
Regardait le sillage et ne daignait rien voir.[189]

It seems therefore that 'Haine du Pauvre' is a more hostile portrayal than Molière's of Don Juan in his encounter with 'le Pauvre'. As to its purpose, it might well be intended as a retort to Baudelaire's adulation in 'Don Juan aux enfers', particularly if for some reason that poem had suddenly acquired a topical interest. And so indeed, for Mallarmé at least, it had, the reason being the publication of the first instalment of Baudelaire's

Petits poèmes en prose, as a *feuilleton* in the newspaper *La Presse*, on 26 August 1862. That event would have a good share of the literary talk of the town when, a few days later, the young poet from Sens arrived for his fortnight's stay 'à Paris et à Versailles'.[190] There were also good reasons why, of the nine 'prose poems' in that first instalment, the one that recalled most directly the theme of 'Don Juan aux enfers', namely 'Le Mauvais Vitrier', should be the one that for other reasons attracted most attention. Two of them, the most important from our point of view, are singled out for special mention by Claude Pichois, in the following brief comment:

> Ce poème ['Le Mauvais Vitrier'], qui n'a pas peu contribué à imposer la légende d'un Baudelaire sarcastiquement cruel, est une réplique à *La Chanson du Vitrier* d'Arsène Houssaye.[191]

Each part of this statement is, I believe, of direct interest to the understanding of 'Haine du Pauvre'. First, the effect on Mallarmé of reading 'Le Mauvais Vitrier', at a time when the legend referred to was already taking shape, would be to recall and renew the impression made on him (it would seem) by 'Don Juan aux enfers'. Secondly, as regards Baudelaire's private intention, Arsène Houssaye was not only the literary editor (and for the time being the general editor) of *La Presse*, but also it will be remembered the editor of *L'Artiste*, to which Mallarmé was already a contributor and in which his article 'L'Art pour tous' was about to appear. Gossip comparing Houssaye's glazier (another *pauvre*) with Baudelaire's would therefore be of some personal interest to him. If he did not plan to call on the editor of *L'Artiste* himself, while he was in Paris, he would certainly wish to pay a visit to Coligny, with whom he was in such friendly correspondence. And if he failed to see either, he would be informed on this latest Baudelaire escapade by Deschamps and Glatigny at Versailles. He would also have read the chief documents involved.

There were three of them. The first was Baudelaire's dedicatory foreword to his *Petits poèmes en prose* ('A Arsène Houssaye, Mon cher ami, [. . .] Votre bien affectionné C.B.'), with its insidious remarks about 'Le Mauvais Vitrier' and 'La Chanson du vitrier':

Vous-même, mon cher ami, n'avez-vous pas tenté de traduire en une *chanson* le cri strident du *Vitrier*, et d'exprimer dans une prose lyrique toutes les désolantes suggestions que ce cri envoie jusqu'aux mansardes, à travers les plus hautes brumes de la rue?

Mais, pour dire le vrai, je crains que ma jalousie ne m'ait pas porté bonheur. Sitôt que j'eus commence le travail, je m'aperçus que non seulement je restais bien loin de mon mystérieux et brillant modèle, mais encore que je faisais quelque chose (si cela peut s'appeler *quelque chose*) de singulièrement différent, accident dont tout autre que moi s'enorgueillirait sans doute, mais qui ne peut qu'humilier profondément un esprit qui regarde comme le plus grand honneur du poète d'accomplir *juste* ce qu'il a projeté de faire.[192]

The second document was 'Le Mauvais Vitrier' itself, or rather its narrative part which reads as follows:

Un matin, je m'étais levé maussade, triste, fatigué d'oisiveté, et poussé, me semblait-il, à faire quelque chose de grand, une action d'éclat; et j'ouvris la fenêtre, hélas! (. . .)

La première personne que j'aperçus dans la rue, ce fut un vitrier dont le cri perçant, discordant, monta jusqu'à moi à travers la lourde et sale atmosphère parisienne. Il me serait d'ailleurs impossible de dire pourquoi je fus pris à l'égard de ce pauvre homme d'une haine aussi soudaine que despotique.

'—Hé! hé!' et je lui criai de monter. Cependant je réfléchissais, non sans quelque gaieté, que, la chambre étant au sixième étage et l'escalier fort étroit, l'homme devait éprouver quelque peine à opérer son ascension et accrocher en maint endroit les angles de sa fragile marchandise.

Enfin il parut: j'examinai curieusement toutes ses vitres, et je lui dis: "Comment? Vous n'avez pas de verres de couleur? des verres roses, rouges, bleus, des vitres magiques, des vitres de paradis? Impudent que vous êtes! vous osez vous promener dans des quartiers pauvres, et vous n'avez pas même de vitres qui fassent voir la vie en beau!" Et je le poussai vivement vers l'escalier, où il trébucha en grognant.

Je m'approchai du balcon et je me saisis d'un petit pot de fleurs, et quand l'homme reparut au débouché de la porte, je laissai tomber perpendiculairement mon engin de guerre sur le rebord postérieur de ses crochets; et le choc le renversant, il achevait de briser sous son dos toute sa pauvre fortune ambulatoire qui rendit le bruit éclatant d'un palais de cristal crevé par la foudre.

Et, ivre de ma folie, je lui criai furieusement: "La vie en beau! la vie en beau!"

Ces plaisanteries nerveuses ne sont pas sans péril, et on peut souvent les payer cher. Mais qu'importe l'éternité de la damnation à qui a trouvé dans une seconde l'infini de la jouissance?[193]

The third document was of course Houssaye's 'La Chanson du vitrier'. It is fairly represented, as to substance, tone, and literary quality, by the following three paragraphs or 'verses', out of eleven:

Oh! vitrier!

J'allai à lui. "Mon brave homme, il ne faut pas mourir de faim." Il s'était appuyé sur le mur comme un homme ivre. "Allons! Allons!" continuai-je en lui prenant le bras. Et je l'entraînai au cabaret, comme si j'en savais le chemin. Un petit enfant était au comptoir, qui cria de sa voix fraîche et gaie:

Oh! vitrier!

Je trinquai avec lui. Mais ses dents claquèrent sur le verre, et il s'évanouit;—Oui, madame, il s'évanouit;—ce qui lui causa un dégât de trois francs dix sous, la moitié de son capital! car je ne pus empêcher ses carreaux de casser. Le pauvre homme revint à lui en disant encore:

Oh! vitrier!

. . .

Il retourna à sa femme et à ses enfants, un peu moins triste que le matin,—non point parce qu'il avait rencontré la charité, mais parce que la fraternité avait trinqué avec lui. Et moi, je m'en revins avec cette musique douloureuse qui me déchire le cœur:

Oh! vitrier![194]

Claude Pichois is clearly justified in considering that from a literary point of view a comparison between Houssaye's 'prose poem' and Baudelaire's 'est accablante pour Houssaye'.[195] It seems in fact that to invite that comparison, in the certainty of obtaining that result, was Baudelaire's disloyal intention in referring to 'La Chanson du vitrier' so equivocally in his dedicatory foreword. M. Pichois adds:

Et il n'est pas exclu que, tout en se plaçant sous le patronage de [Houssaye], [Baudelaire] n'ait eu aussi quelque intention ironique.

Suzanne Bernard had expressed the same opinion more

squarely, agreeing with Jacques Crépet that 'Le Mauvais Vitrier' was 'une "assez malicieuse riposte" à la chanson *fraternitaire* de Houssaye'.[196] In September 1862 already, the same thought must have occurred to some at least of Houssaye's friends, among them Stéphane Mallarmé who, if I am not mistaken, thereupon devised a plan to turn the tables on Baudelaire the disloyal friend. In two strongly contrasting short poems in *terza rima* he would reshape the parts played by the protagonists in the two 'prose poems'. They would be so presented that Houssaye's part would sound both nobler and more original than Baudelaire's.

Thus it is that on the one hand, in 'Haine du Pauvre', the protagonist, recognizable as Don Juan, is made more odious than he was in Molière's play and quite as inhumanly cruel as Baudelaire (or the man who says *je*) in 'Le Mauvais Vitrier'. Even the beggar, instead of resisting temptation nobly as in Molière's scene, grovels and betrays his faith for a piece of silver. Thus, in Mallarméan terms, the Real triumphs completely over the Ideal.[197] In 'A un Mendiant' on the other hand, the opposite result must be attained. It was not enough (though it was necessary) to rid Houssaye's protagonist of vulgar sentiment and well-meaning practicality. His performance must be made imaginative and any charity quixotic and paradoxical. Also, he must urge but not constrain. The *pauvre* must be free to make his own choice in the end, and the choice must be philosophical, between (if not quite the Real and the Ideal) at least Reality and Dream. Some light on Mallarmé's intention here may perhaps be found in a remark he was to make two years later in a letter to Cazalis:

> Après tout, tu sais que la seule occupation d'un homme qui se respecte est à mes yeux de regarder l'azur en mourant de faim.[198]

In short, the beggar in 'A un Mendiant' is invited to be a satisfied azure-beggar for a few hours, by buying himself five francs' worth of artificial paradise.

Which of Mallarmé's friends shared the secret of 'les deux *Pauvres*' we can only guess. Des Essarts perhaps, though his query makes it seem doubtful whether he knew all. Coligny almost certainly, and through him possibly Houssaye himself. Coligny was also the one most likely to have advised him, once more, to avoid attacking Baudelaire publicly, and therefore to keep 'Haine du Pauvre' strictly private. The discreet (and unmerited) compliment to Houssaye would suffice. Advice which, whether from friends or his own judgement, appears to have prevailed.[199] Thus, as in the case of 'Le Guignon', a public affront to Baudelaire was avoided. Deprived of its more militant partner, 'A un Mendiant' too would lose its polemic aspect. After which, its original function would be concealed more and more hermetically, revision by revision, under the non-committal title 'Aumône'.

But since the first member of the pair, disfavoured and seemingly discarded, has nevertheless survived, a reader who accepts the hypothesis I have proposed is interested to find in 'Haine du Pauvre' a veiled sign of what its author intended, similar to those in 'Le Guignon' though less emphatic. It is found in the title itself, which ceases to seem inexpressive if one remembers the words used by Baudelaire to introduce his story of 'Le Mauvais Vitrier':

Il me serait d'ailleurs impossible de dire pourquoi je fus pris à l'égard de ce pauvre homme d'une haine aussi soudaine que despotique.[200]

NOTES

1 It amounts to little more than can be vaguely inferred from his grandmother's concern over his religious back-sliding; see vol. I, p. 67.
2 Art. cit., *Revue de France*, 1899; see above, ch. 2, n. 3.
3 *O.c.*, 1626 [1633].
4 When in 1903 Mendès described Mallarmé as he first knew him, he recalled 'un très jeune homme qui m'était adressé par mon ami, l'excellent Emmanuel des Essarts'; see below, p. 295.
5 *Lef.*, 169–70.
6 By its form, the rondel or rondeau lends itself to punning in the refrain line or word. There are several examples of this verse-form in Banville's *Odes funambulesques*, section 'Rondeaux'. Mallarmé's *Bals masqués* were presumably some kind of disguise, as would be the case if they were built on punning rhymes.

The association in the pun 'six Phillis' may have been borrowed from two lines in 'Éveil', another of the *Odes funambulesques*: 'Lesbienne rêveuse, éprise de Phyllis, / Tu n'as pas, il est vrai, célébré S......; 'Passons vite', exclaimed Banville, in his Commentary of 1873.

In love-poems, the name Phyllis (or Phylis, Phillis or Philis) was much used, as the name of the beloved, by poets of the early seventeenth century. Théophile seems to have inherited it from Desportes. In the chapter of *Les Grotesques* devoted to Théophile, Gautier makes good-humoured fun of it: 'Vous savez tous combien Philis était puissante en ce temps-là, comme elle était choyée, encensée, madrigalisée.—Quels innombrables soupirs n'a-t-elle pas fait pousser!' (édition Michel-Lévy Frères, 1853, p. 113).

7 *Fl.*, i. 100–2; *O.c.*, 16–19; *Poésie*, 174–7; *DSM.* iii, 80–3.

8 It appears that Banville and Baudelaire both took the subject from a painting by Émile Deroy, 'La Petite Mendiante Rousse', given to Banville by the artist; see item 108 of the catalogue for the exhibition *Baudelaire* held at the Petit Palais in 1969. Mallarmé had no doubt his early poem in mind when six years later he wrote in his article on 'The Impressionists and Édouard Manet' (*The Art Monthly Review*, 30 September 1867): 'Degas can, nevertheless, be as delighted with the charms of those little washerwomen, who fresh and fair, though poverty-stricken, and clad but in camisole and petticoat, bend their slender bodies at the hour of work.' 'A une petite laveuse blonde' is presumably one of the poems that Des Essarts was to refer to many years later as 'des stances en octosyllabes gracieuses et mignardes'.

9 *Fl.*, i. 104–5; *O.c.*, 19–20; *Poésie*, 178–80; *DSM.* iii, 85–6.

10 *O.c.*, 1388 [1390].

11 A well-known line ('Sur le Noël, morte saison') would add to the anniversary feeling if remembered, but it is unlikely that Mallarmé knew Villon's poem at first-hand. He had probably read, however, Gautier's essay on his life and works (in *Les Grotesques*, 1853), where the date given by Gautier would bring the centenary to mind: 'Il naquit en 1431, le *Testament* ayant été composé en 1461.'

12 See above, pp. 153, 157, 218.

13 There are echoes, in particular, of the poems entitled 'Le Soleil', 'Les Sept Vieillards' and 'Les Petites Vieilles': B., *O.c.* i, 83, 87, and 89.

14 *Vie*, 113; in *Corr.* i, 110 n. 1, the text is unintentionally truncated.

15 *Fl.*, i. 98–9; *O.c.*, 15–16; *Poésie*, 171–3; *DSM.* iii, 77–9.

16 B., *O.c.* i, 106 and 103. It may be that the rhyme *lésine-gésine* in 'Crépuscule du matin' explains the presence of the two words (only one of them at the rhyme) in 'Galanterie macabre'.

17 I borrow this convenient designation (for 'celui qui dit *je*') from Derek Mossop's revealing study of *Baudelaire's Tragic Hero*.

18 B., *O.c.* i, 36, 47, 58, 77, and 156.

19 See above, p. 43 and for the text *Corr.* i, 47.

20 It will be observed that both sonnets are technically 'irréguliers', the rhymes in the quatrains being 'croisées', not 'embrassées'. Mallarmé showed a marked preference for this rhyme-scheme in his early sonnets, and a certain liking later.

21 Five poems were published that year: 'Placet', 'Le Sonneur', a fragment (five tercets) of 'Le Guignon', 'Soleil d'hiver', and 'Contre un poète parisien'. Another three first appeared four years later, in *Le Parnasse*

contemporain: 'A un Mendiant', 'Vere novo' (or 'Spleen printanier', later 'Renouveau'), and 'Tristesse d'été'. Four did not appear in print until after the poet's death: 'L'Enfant prodigue', 'Haine du Pauvre', ' . . . *Mysticis umbraculis*' and 'Sonnet' ('Parce que de la viande était à point rôtie'). The best-known, and most admired, 'Apparition' (almost certainly written in the autumn of 1862 but perhaps in an early version, since lost) and 'Le Guignon' in its entirety were first published in 1883, by Verlaine in his anthology *Poètes maudits*.

22 It is fairly certain that the version of 'Apparition' that has reached us includes some later revisions. In placing it after 'Le Guignon' Verlaine situates it chronologically as going back 'à la même époque environ, mais évidemment un peu plus tard que plus tôt' (Verlaine, *Œuvres en prose complètes*, *NRF.*, Bibliothèque de la Pléiade, ed. Jacques Borel, p. 661). When Mallarmé republished the poem in the 1887 facsimile edition of his poems, he placed it among the 'Premiers poèmes'; see É. Noulet, op. cit., p. 55, and *O.c.*, 1392–3 [1394–5] and 1410 [1412].

23 Op. cit., ii, 760 n. 39.

24 Thibaudet, interested in Mallarmé's preciosity, and his affinity in this regard with poets of earlier centuries, observes (op. cit., p. 74) that he would have made 'un charmant poète de cour'.

25 *Fl.*, i, 110; *O.c.*, 30–1. The text reproduced here is that published, over the signature 'STÉPHANE MALLARMÉ', in *Le Papillon* on 25 February 1862. The variants in successive revisions are closely studied by Carl Barbier under the heading '*Placet*, 1862 et 1883—*Placet futile*, 1887' (*DSM.* iv, 13–18.) He draws attention to the manuscript copy dated 1762, and so placed wittily in context.

26 Verlaine, *Œuvres complètes* (Messein), iv, p. 39. So also in the *Club du Meilleur livre* edition, i, p. 492. Verlaine uses the title both to end the sentence quoted and, at the same time, to head the text of the poem that follows. This droll dual function, intended presumably to emphasize the contrast between the two poems and therefore the diversity of the young poet's talent, is ignored in the Pléiade edition of the *Œuvres en prose complètes*, p. 659; a full stop after the word 'forgeait' corrects the oddity by destroying the sense.

27 'Mlle. Nina m'a demandé des vers, je lui en envoie, c'est un sonnet Louis XV' (letter dated 24 May 1862; *DSM.* vi, 33–4). Nina was a brunette, whence perhaps the further remark, at the end of Mallarmé's letter: 'Dis à Mlle. Nina que ce sonnet ne lui est offert qu'en attendant une pièce plus sérieuse que j'écrirai sur son album'.

28 For an excerpt from 'une Parisienne de Watteau' see above, n. 30 of ch. 3.

29 The sixth in the first section, 'Gaietés'. See the reference to Banville's poem earlier in this chapter, à propos of 'A une petite laveuse blonde'. For a succinct and interesting account of the 'Louis XV' vogue, the participation in it of Gautier, Banville, Houssaye, Glatigny, Des Essarts, and Verlaine in his *Fêtes Galantes*, and its relationship with 'l'art pour l'art', see L. Badesco, op. cit. II, pp. 872–86 and footnotes.

What Mallarmé called the 'Louis XV' style has been much studied in recent years. See for instance J.-B. Barrère, *La Fantaisie de Victor Hugo*

(1949–60), vol. I, pp. 354 ff., vol. II, pp. 279 ff., and vol. III, pp. 112 ff., and J.-H. Bornecque's 'étude verlainienne' justly entitled *Lumières sur les Fêtes Galantes* (1959).

30 This sonnet was brought to the notice of students of Mallarmé by Charles Mauron in *Mallarmé l'obscur*, where he wrote (p. 101): 'M. G. Maurevert, dans l'*Eclaireur de Nice* a donné comme source de 'Placet futile' un sonnet de Privat d'Anglemont "A Madame du Barry". Le fait semble indéniable.' He gave as his immediate authority a notice, including the text of the poem, by R. de Bury [*not* 'Rémy de Gourmont'] in *Le Mercure de France* of 15 September 1923.

It has been suggested that the author of the sonnet was in fact Baudelaire; see L. Badesco, op. cit. II, 886 n. 141.

31 See A. Cioranescu, *Bibliographie de la Littérature Française du dix-septième siècle*, vol. II, p. 933.

32 Vincent Voiture, *Poésies* (ed. Henri Lafay), Didier, 1971, vol. II, poems LXXXVI, LXXXVII, LXXXVIII, and XCVII. Acknowledgement is due here to Littré, who ends his definition of the word *placet* with the note: '4° anciennement. Espèce de petit poëme en forme de placet. Voiture a fait de jolis placets.'

33 They are very numerous, and indicate the interest that Mallarmé found in perfecting this piece of preciosity, which had no other purpose than formal perfection. See *Fl.*, i. 111–12 and 346.

34 'Théophile de Viau', in *Les Grotesques*, 2nd edn. (1853), p. 111. The reference is to lines in 'La Maison de Sylvie', Ode I (*Œuvres complètes de Théophile*, II, p. 194): 'Tout le monde dit qu'Appollon / Favorise qui le reclame, / Et qu'avec l'eau de son valon / Le sçavoir peut couler dans l'ame; / Mais j'estouffe ce vieil abus / Et bannis desormais Phœbus / De la bouche de nos poëtes: / Tous ses temples sont demolis / Et ses demons ensevelis / Dans des sepultures muettes. / Sathan ne nous fait plus broncher / Dans de si dangereuses toiles. / Le Dieu que nous allons chercher / Loge plus haut que les estoilles.'

Théophile had good personal reasons for declaring publicly a distaste for un-Christian notions and practices. His poems are not, however, so purged of pagan mythology as Gautier seems to imply. For example, the line in Mallarmé's poem that exclaims 'O faunes ivres sous la mousse' responds to the presence of satyrs and nymphs and fauns in such poems by Théophile de Viau as the well-known ode on Solitude. It was in that countryside that Mallarmé's Faun first stirred. On the other hand, 'la pâle sainte Cécile' and Gautier's accompanying remarks, as well as suggesting the subject of his poem 'Sainte', written in December 1865, may have provided Mallarmé with food for thought, and led him to a better appreciation of the symbolic strength that abides in Christian images. Cf. for some suggestions on this general subject A. Gill, 'Mallarmé's use of Christian imagery . . . ' in *Order and Adventure in Post-Romantic French Poetry. Essays presented to C. A. Hackett* (1973).

35 *Fl.*, i., 128; *O.c.*, 21; *Poésie*, 182; *DSM*. iii, 93 and (facsimile) opposite 96.

36 For information on the person who went by that name, see the remarks of 'Auriant' on p. 130 (ch. 3, n. 48) above.

37 In a letter of 4 June to Cazalis (*DSM.* vi, 35) Mallarmé refers to 'la perruque rousse d'Harpagon'—oddly, because Molière's Harpagon wears no wig, so as to avoid the expense. He may have had 'perruque rousse' in his mind because he had brought out his own 'Soleil d'hiver' that day to send it to Dieppe, or to Coligny for Dieppe.

38 The whole of stanzas three and four could reflect the manner in which the actor who played Don Guritan at Sens carried out Hugo's intention, expressed in his own words: 'la figure chevaleresque et gravement bouffonne de Don Guritan'; see *DSM.* vii, 184.

39 Don Guritan is in the habit of challenging rivals to a duel. The *cartel* on which the challenge was written would be torn up by the adversary, in scorn or amusement. In the end, melodramatically, he meets a heartless opponent and is killed.

40 *NRF.*, 1 May 1933.

41 See above, p. 74.

42 The same editor, Charles Coligny, writing to Mallarmé on 10 July, added a postscript asking for more: 'Si vous avez quelques sonnets, envoyez-les-moi pour Dieppe' (Bibliothèque Jacques Doucet, MS MVL 411).

43 In his obituary article (see vol. I, ch. 1, n. 22) Des Essarts recollected, no doubt with copies of these early poems to remind him, that Mallarmé, when they first became acquainted, wrote 'des stances en octosyllabes, gracieuses et mignardes'.

44 I had not noted this circumstance when I wrote the article mentioned in n. 74 below.

45 See *Fl.*, i, 198–9; *O.c.*, 53–4; *Poésie*, 64.

46 The fact that the two poems are very close to each other in subject makes it probable that they were written at virtually the same time. On the other hand, the one holograph manuscript of one of them, 'L'Enfant prodigue', is written on the other side of the same sheet of paper as a copy of 'Placet' (see *Fl.*, i, 107), which suggests an early date.

47 I had occasion to express my opinion on this subject some twenty years ago; see the article entitled 'Mallarmé on Baudelaire', in *Currents of Thought in French Literature, Essays in Memory of G. T. Clapton* (1965). I hope now to produce further justification for the same conviction, while still believing that Mallarmé's strictures did not imply a lessening of his admiration for Baudelaire's genius from a strictly poetic point of view. To make that distinction is, to my way of thinking, to interpret fairly Mallarmé's statement to Henri de Régnier many years after Baudelaire's death (see above, vol. I, p. 88): 'Chez le Baudelaire des dernières années s'était développée une manière factice de fumisterie qui montrait que le fond naturel était épuisé'. In so far as *Les Fleurs du mal* is concerned, this distinction between earlier and later poems could have no sound basis. What Mallarmé was more likely to be recalling was the difference between his own reactions, after a first reading and then after further study. Contemporary documentary evidence of his early attitudes to

Baudelaire is unconvincing. In March 1865, Cazalis wrote (*DSM.* vi, 258:): 'Il paraît que ton Dieu Baudelaire te hait, et c'est bien mal récompenser, tu me l'avoueras, la religion, le culte pur de son croyant le plus fidèle.' But in view of their joint indulgence, a little more than a year before, in a plot which put Baudelaire in a very humiliating situation (ibid. 169–70), this statement must surely be ironical. Coligny, the first critic to honour Mallarmé with a mention in one of his articles (in *L'Artiste*, on 15 June 1865), wrote of him: 'Shakespeare et Edgar Poe sont ses dieux, et il dit que ses dieux le conduisent à Charles Baudelaire' (quoted by 'Auriant', art. cit.). But there are reasons, which will be noted below, for considering that Coligny was largely responsible for Mallarmé's equivocal avoidance of open hostility in his attitude towards Baudelaire. As to Mallarmé's expressions of grief when Baudelaire died, they are plainly excessive and could well be diplomatic.

On the other hand, it is clear that Mallarmé greatly admired the author of *Les Fleurs du mal* as a master of poetic form. Two remarks made by him in letters to Lefébure, not suspect of disingenuousness, seem to me to be excellent examples: 'Je ne dis rien du style. Vous ressentirez une sensation à chacun des mots, comme en lisant Baudelaire' (February 1865, on the subject of Villiers de l'Isle-Adam's *Elën*; *Lef.*, 340–1); '*Du fond de son réduit sablonneux, le grillon, / Les regardant passer, redouble sa chanson*, Jusqu'ici, le grillon m'avait étonné, il me semblait maigre, comme introduction au vers magnifique, et large comme l'autre cité: *Cybèle, qui les aime, augmente ses verdures*. Je ne connaissais que le grillon anglais, doux et caricaturiste; hier seulement parmi les jeunes blés j'ai entendu cette voix sacrée de la terre ingénue.' (17 or 27 May 1867, reminded of Baudelaire's sonnet 'Bohémiens en voyage'; ibid. 354.)

48 *Fl.*, i, 108; *O.c.*, 22; *Poésie*; 18, 183; *DSM.* iii, 95.

For the holograph text, see *DSM.* iii, 95 and the accompanying photographic reproduction; also *Fl.*, 108–9, where it is suggested that Mallarmé might not have kept so unsavoury a product of his early talent if his copy had not been written, back to back, on the same paper as his fair copy of 'Haine du Pauvre'. He certainly took pains to keep it very private, but that is not a proof of shame for the poem as such. There is indeed some rather slender evidence, on the manuscript itself, that at some time still to be ascertained he offered it for publication. Although the text has been crossed out, very lightly, in pencil, corrections have been pencilled in too. So has a new title, 'Trumeau d'alcôve', meaning something like 'Chimney-piece for a love-nest'; cf. Shakespeare, *Cymbeline*, II. 4: 'The chimney / Is south the chamber, and the chimney-piece / Chaste Dian bathing' (cited in *OED*). Cf. also Victor Hugo, in a poem 'Dans un vieux château', written in 1861 but not published till 1888 (in *Toute la lyre*; for which poem, see J. B. Barrère, op. cit., vol. III, p. 119, and for the fashionable use of the word in mid-nineteenth-century literary parlance, the whole of that chapter in a remarkable study: 'Fêtes galantes ou "Trumeaux"'.

In his letter to Albert Collignon of 12 December 1863 (*Corr.* i, 98), Mallarmé told him he was sending for publication in the *Revue nouvelle* 'une très-courte *terza-rima*'. The description fits '. . . *Mysticis umbraculis*' better than it does 'Haine du Pauvre' or 'A un Mendiant', Henri Mondor's suggestions. But no short poem of Mallarmé's appeared in that ephemeral review. It appears that it was submitted to Malassis a year later, together with the poem which begins 'Une négresse, par le démon secouée', for inclusion in the *Nouveau Parnasse satyrique du dix-neuvième siècle*. In a postscript to a letter he sent to Cazalis on 15 January 1865 (*Corr.* i, 162) Mallarmé wrote: 'Demande à Armand Renaud des vers que je lui ai griffonnés'. The reference was to 'Une négresse . . . ', but he went on to say: 'Je les destine, avec deux autres poèmes que j'ai en tête, au *Parnasse satyrique* de Malassis sous le nom de "Tableaux obscènes"' (a name that would suit the 'trumeau d'alcôve' quite as well as 'Une négresse . . .' Mondor mentioned this letter in *Vie* (p. 162 n. 3) but assumed that what Mallarmé had sent to Malassis was a pair of 'sonnets', 'Une négresse . . . ' (not in fact a sonnet) which was accepted, and an unnamed piece which was rejected, and subsequently lost. But of this 'lost' second 'sonnet' Mondor was able to quote the final tercet, soon to be recognized (*O.c.*, 1389 [1391]) as the second stanza of '. . . *Mysticis umbraculis*'. Unfortunately, he did not state clearly his reason for believing that the three lines he was able to quote belonged to a poem intended by Mallarmé to be published with 'Une négresse . . . ' The statement in which he introduces the 'tercet' (*Vie*, loc. cit.) reads: 'Je crois, d'après des autographes de collection particulière, que le second tercet du sonnet resté inconnu, et, semble-t-il, si ce texte est authentique, peu regrettable, était celui-ci:

Et son ventre sembla . . . [etc.]'

The same general conclusion is expressed in the Pléiade edition (*O.c.*, 1416 [1418]): the passage in the letter to Cazalis] 'semble indiquer *deux* poèmes, dont l'un doit être celui-ci ['Une négresse . . . '], et dont l'autre nous demeure inconnu'. Henceforth, it could perhaps be agreed that the closing words of this conclusion should read: 'et dont l'autre est presque certainement " . . . *Mysticis umbraculis*".' Also, it can now be acknowledged that neither of the two poems is a sonnet, 'Une négresse . . . ' being (as the Pléiade editors note) a poem of four stanzas each of four alexandrines.

49 Vol. I, p. 258 (n. 3 of ch. 12).

50 Both names were used. In view of Mallarmé's use of the word 'Prose' in the title of one of his most mysterious later poems, 'Prose pour Des Esseintes', it deserves attention here, in what was for him its original context. For the layman, a useful definition of the word *prose*, in relation to that context, is given in the 1954 edition (the Fifth, editor Eric Blom) of *Grove's Dictionary of Music and Musicians*: '*Prose* (Fr[ench].) In a special sense *prose* is another term for a sequence in the medieval meaning of that word: an ornamental interpolation into the plainsong of a mass. After the ninth century, words began to be added to the sequences and these were called *proses* in France. The most famous

example is the twelfth-century *prose de l'âne* sung annually at Beauvais on New Year's Day representing the flight into Egypt—hence the allusion to the ass.' [The prominence given to the Beauvais tradition and the Beauvais version of the text (as against those of Sens which are the most celebrated in France) is probably to be explained by the fact that the Beauvais text can be studied at the British Library (formerly British Museum, Egerton MS 2615).]

51 For a brief but substantial account of the Feast of Fools and the Prose of the Ass, see Grace Frank, *The Medieval French Drama* (1960), pp. 41–2, and for a more detailed treatment E. K. Chambers, *The Mediaeval Stage*, vol. 1, pp. 274–89, and vol. 2, Appendix L (pp. 279–82). He comments (vol. 1, p. 279) on the *Missel des fous* of Sens as follows: 'It is not a missal at all. It is headed *Officium Circoncisionis in usum urbis Senonensis*, and is a choir-book containing the words and music of the *Propria* or special chants used in the Hours and Mass at the Feast.'

The 'Prose des fous' or 'Prose de l'Âne' is studied from the musical point of view (versions of Beauvais and Sens) by H.C C. Greene, 'The Song of the Ass', *Speculum*, VI, October 1931.

It may have been the *Missel des Fous* and the beautiful ivory tablets between which it is kept (now at the Bibliothèque municipale, in the Cathedral until the French Revolution), that Hugo saw and admired when he visited Sens in October 1839, and described in his 'album' as 'un ivoire byzantin, bible naïve et charmante' (Victor Hugo, *Œuvres complètes*, Édition chronologique, Le Club Français du livre, vol. vi, p. 734).

Pierre Larousse's *Dictionnaire universel du XIXe siècle*, vol. 8 (1872), p. 286, describes the Sens manuscript thus: 'On conserve précieusement à la Bibliothèque de Sens le *Missel de la Fête des Fous ou de l'Âne*: . . . ce Missel a pour couverture un diptyque ou double plaque en ivoire sculpté, représentant un Triomphe de Bacchus Hélios: le travail en est merveilleux.'

52 I quote from the edition published in 1907 by the abbé Henri Villetard, under the title: *Office de Pierre de Corbeil (Office de la Circoncision)*.

In 1862 readers had at their disposal a printed copy of the text, published by Félix Bourquelot in the *Bulletin de la Société archéologique de Sens*, vol. VI (1854); it was republished apart, at Sens, in 1856.

As regards the meaning of '*Misticis umbraculis*' in its authentic liturgical context, I understand on excellent authority that 'the words "by mystical foreshadowings" refer to the Old Testament typology of the Virgin Birth.'

53 *AUMLA*, No. 19, May 1963.

54 Gardner Davies, *Mallarmé et le drame solaire* (1959), p. 260. In '. . . *Mysticis umbraculis*' the shock for the bourgeois reader was supposed no doubt to be produced by the last item in the description, softened though it was by the analogy of the bird's nest.

55 It is translated by Jules Mouquet in his *Charles Baudelaire—Vers latins* (1933), pp. 86–8, and his translation is quoted in the Crépet-Blin edition of *Les Fleurs du mal*, pp. 403–4.

The editors comment thus on the general impression made by the poem on Baudelaire's readers: 'Cette savante fantaisie n'avait pas manqué de scandaliser les contemporains' (ibid. 404).

56 The editors (quoting Albert Cassagne) point out that '*Franciscae meae laudes*' is 'le seul poème des *Fleurs* qui soit en latin et en octosyllabes monorimes groupés par tercets' (ibid. 402).

It is noticeable too that the lines in ecclesiastical Latin that provide Mallarmé with his pun would be read most naturally by a French reader not as stanzas composed of seven-syllable lines but rather of fourteen-syllable lines grouped as follows in goliardic fashion:

Mysticis umbraculis olim prefiguratum

Et multis oraculis fuit prenunciatum
Quod nostris in seculis gaudemus declaratum.

—from which arrangement the stanza of three alexandrines is not far removed.

57 Ibid.

58 Ibid., n. 1.

59 As was seen in Chapter 1 (p. 2), the Pléiade editors argued for an earlier date; see *O.c.*, 1386 [1388], though elsewhere, in *M.pl.i.*, p. 19, Mondor gave the date 1862.

We now know that the poem was written in the year 1862. The proof was provided in stages by Carl Barbier. In *DSM.* iii, 87, he stated on the evidence of Dr Bonniot's photographic reproduction that notwithstanding what the Pléiade editors declared, 'le manuscrit est bien daté "1862"'—which on close examination does indeed prove to be clearly the case though the photograph cuts away the lower half of the figures. The question is finally settled in *Fl.*, i, 107: an examination of the holograph manuscript itself, in a private collection, confirms that it is indeed dated '1862'.

60 *Fl.*, i, 106; *O.c.*, 14–15; *Poésie*, 169–70; *DSM.* iii, 88.

61 The deliberate association of the mystical with the sensual is prominent not only in *Franciscae meae laudes* but also in two poems that it follows quite closely in *Les Fleurs du mal*, entitled respectively 'A une Madone, ex-voto dans le goût espagnol' and 'Chanson d'après-midi'. Antoine Adam writes, à propos of the former, in the Garnier edition of *Les Fleurs du mal*, p. 349: 'Il est donc tout à fait impertinent de prononcer, à propos du chef-d'œuvre de Baudelaire, les mots de blasphème et de contre-religion. *A une Madone* est un poème baroque, un admirable poème où la passion emprunte le vocabulaire de la piété la plus fanatique, fait appel aux images les plus somptueuses et les plus raffinées pour dire ses adorations et ses fureurs.' But would those of Baudelaire's readers whose religion he professed to share be of the same opinion, and be as understanding of 'sa volonté d'évoquer, dans une œuvre savante, ce mélange de férocité, de volupté et de mysticisme où il voyait la savoureuse originalité de l'Espagne'? Though not himself one of them, Mallarmé was quite likely to find their objections to be valid on moral and

also aesthetic grounds. In the course of a long 'note critique', in the Crépet-Blin edition of *Les Fleurs du mal* (p. 396), the following excerpt of an article published in 1851 by Baudelaire himself is quoted: 'Il y a une cohue de poëtes abrutis par la volupté païenne, et qui emploient sans cesse les mots de saint, sainte, extase, prière, etc. pour qualifier des choses et des êtres qui n'ont rien de saint ni d'extatique, bien au contraire, poussant ainsi l'adoration de la femme jusqu'à l'impiété la plus dégoûtante.' That is how Mallarmé seems also to regard the practice, to judge by his 'L'Enfant prodigue'.

62 It is possible that Mallarmé was put in mind of the prodigal son by the reference in Baudelaire's 'L'Horloge': '*Remember! Souviens-toi*, prodigue! *Esto memor!*'

63 If I am not mistaken, neither prostitutes nor their consorts are represented by Baudelaire as 'seeking the infinite' (a word synonymous for him with 'ideal', as Derek Mossop points out in *Baudelaire's Tragic Hero*, p. 59). It is in the second of the '*Femmes damnées*': 'Comme un bétail pensif . . . ', and of 'devout' Lesbians, that he writes:

Et d'autres, dont la gorge aime les scapulaires,
. . .
Chercheuses d'infini, dévotes et satyres,
Tantôt pleines de cris, tantôt pleines de pleurs,
Vous que dans votre enfer mon âme a poursuivies . . .

Antoine Adam comments in his edition of *Les Fleurs du mal* (Garnier Frères, 1961), p. 413 (again in defence of Baudelaire as well as in explanation): 'Voilà sans doute le sens que Baudelaire découvrait au saphisme. Non pas vulgaire sensualité . . . Mais insatisfaction, recherche d'un au-delà de l'amour vulgaire.' Of such sympathy and kind sentiments there is no trace in 'L'Enfant prodigue'.

64 See above, vol. I, p. 88 (ch. 3, n. 14).

65 É. Noulet, op. cit. , p. 16.

66 *Fl.*, i. 126; *O.c.*, 20-1; *Poésie*, 181; *DSM.* iii, 90.

67 Thus in the *Journal des Baigneurs*. Over Mallarmé's cutting, and in Des Essarts's album: A Emmanuel des Essarts; (see *Fl.*, i. 127). If it was Coligny, on his own initiative, who sent the sonnet to the *Journal des Baigneurs*, he might very well disguise the name of its victim by keeping only his initials.

68 *Fl.*, i. 774.

69 *DSM.* vi, 38 and *Corr.* v, 189 n.2.

70 *O.c.*, 250.

71 Sainte-Beuve, *Tableau historique et critique de la poésie française et du théâtre français au XVI siècle* (Charpentier, 1869), pp. 347 and 349.

72 Ibid. 349 and note.

73 See above, vol. I, 175.

74 See Plate I in A. Gill, 'Mallarmé's Use of Christian Imagery for Post-Christian Concepts', *Essays presented to C. A. Hackett*, 1973.

75 The best-known statue of Anacreon appears to be the one at Copenhagen

(a Roman copy of a Greek original) a photograph of which is used (Plate 1) in ch. 1 of David Piper's *The Image of the Poet* (1982). The poet is indeed shown naked, but with no such bacchanalian adjuncts as Mallarmé imagined or had somewhere seen.

76 They recognize in the poem 'une certaine tenue littéraire, tout inspirée, assurément, de Banville, particulièrement dans le premier des tercets' (*O.c.*, 1389 [1391]).

77 He is named among the young writers to whom Des Essarts, in his obituary article, recalled introducing his young friend in the early days of their acquaintance; see above, ch. 2, n. 4. It has been noted also that in one of Mallarmé's articles in the *Sénonais* he mentioned Glatigny as if they had met; see above, p. 80.

78 *O.c.*, 1389 [1391].

79 *Fl.*, i. 127.

80 See above, ch. 2, n. 4.

81 Mallarmé's opinion on this subject was (had been, it is fairly safe to say) expressed more diplomatically, tongue-in-cheek, in the review he published in *Le Papillon* (*O.c.*, 250).

82 The claim of 'Parce que . . . ' to be a sonnet by Mallarmé suffered from its first presentation by Mondor, which seemed uncertain. His *Vie de Mallarmé* was written and published under wartime conditions. It heralded a new era in Mallarmé research, but there were imperfections in the editing that have survived. For instance, what was said in vol. I of the sonnet 'Parce que . . . ' was at variance with what was said in vol. II, presumably after further research, and the discrepancy continued in the single-volume edition (and still does perhaps). On p. 90 we may read an excerpt from a letter that Cazalis in Strasbourg wrote to Mallarmé in London, on an unspecified day in May 1863: 'Si tu veux m'être agréable, tu m'enverrais (*sic*) tes deux sonnets sur l'*Aumône* (voilà 5 francs, va boire) et la *Naissance du Poète* (Parce qu'un soir d'avril il lut dans son journal, etc.).' A footnote on p. 91 adds: 'De ce poème, *La Naissance du Poète*, nous n'avons encore trouvé aucune trace.' Then, more than five hundred pages on, the biographer (pp. 642–3) presents his poet selecting, thirty years later, early poems for inclusion in his 'très modeste anthologie' *Vers et Prose* (which appeared in November 1892). Among the poems he rejects, and returns to the cardboard box they have been in those thirty years, is the sonnet 'Naissance du poète', of which Mondor quotes the second quatrain and the two tercets, and promises that it will appear in its entirety 'dans l'édition de la Pléiade des Œuvres Complètes de Mallarmé.' As it did, when the edition was published in 1945.

83 *Fl.*, i. 142; *O.c.*, 22; *Poésie*, 184.

84 *Mallarmé*, pp. 43, 528, and 567 f.

85 Henri Mondor receives less than his due in the article, whose author considers him insufficiently interested in Clément Privé. If I am not mistaken, he is judged by the little he says of Privé in his *Vie de Mallarmé*, while his *Eugène Lefébure* of 1951, naturally more informative on Privé (see pp. 37–40, 47, 63, 78 , 80) , is ignored.

86 See *Vie*, 134, and *Lef.*, 47. From what Mondor says of Privé's verse, it

would seem that he could not have written 'Parce que . . .': 'L'humeur satirique, des [*Sonnets auxerrois*], même s'il vient surtout du vaudevilliste de préfecture qu'était Privé, et le persiflage ricanant ne sont d'ailleurs pas, dans ces vers, sans aboutir à des traits dignes de Laurent Tailhade . . .'; Mondor refers also to Privé's 'truculence rurale'. See *Lef.*, 47.

87 *DSM*. vi, 152–3.

88 *Le Nouveau Petit Larousse*, art. *Arvers* (Alexis-Félix), gives the explanation: 'poète français, né à Paris (1806–1850), immortalisé par un *sonnet* commençant par ce vers: *Mon âme a son secret, ma vie a son mystère*.'

89 For the context see *Lef.*, 177.

90 *Fl.*, i, 142, n.

91 The impact of the dual nature of the sonnet, poetic and pornographic, is very well illustrated in Mallarmé's correspondence with Cazalis and with Lefébure, as annotated by the Flammarion editors. Each of the two fellow-poets, on receiving a copy, praised it highly, as a completely serious poem; see *Fl.*, 142–3, notes (1), (3), and (4). But the remarks quoted from the 'lettre d'un inconnu à un destinataire qui reste également à identifier' read like an informal account, conveyed to Cazalis, of the reactions with which Mallarmé's poems had been received in the group which he had joined at Strasbourg. The sonnet is praised, but in terms in which its two identities are distinguished and the sexual theme given most attention. Of the poems Mallarmé had sent, 'Parce que . . .' was the one preferred; after all, from the *lubrique* point of view Baudelaire was much worse: 'Il y a dans tous les vers de Mallarmé un lyrisme attachant. J'aime beaucoup les lire, plus que Baudelaire, car chez Mallarmé, le dégoûtantisme n'est pas poussé au point extrême.'

Pascal Pia does not express his own opinion as to the merits of 'Parce que . . .', but he quotes with apparent approval the opinion expressed in a letter to him by M. Joseph Bollery: 'Pour parler comme Léon Bloy, si un ange descendait du ciel pour m'affirmer que ce sonnet est de Mallarmé, je lui dirais: Tu mens!' What would be his answer to Claudel, to whom Dr Bonniot had shown the holograph manuscript, and who observed to Valéry: 'Bonniot me montra un sonnet de Mallarmé qui aurait pu être de Rimbaud.' In quoting this remark (*Claudel plus intime* (1960), p. 216) Mondor adds this note: '*La naissance du poète*, voir Edition de la Pléiade, pp. 22 et 1390'.

92 *Vie*, 134.

93 B., *O.c.* i, 27–8.

94 *Fl.*, i. 114–15; *O.c.*, 28–30; *Poésie*, 20–3.

95 B[1] shows an interchange, between this line and the one seven lines later, of the words (here virtually synonyms) *frères* and *égaux*.

96 The *s* at the end of *citernes*, in Y, is a careless slip, making the rhyme imperfect.

97 'Le guignon', traditionally a colloquial though quite respectable word, meaning according to the dictionaries 'la mauvaise chance, surtout au jeu', was acquiring literary connotations from its being used by certain

men of letters in speaking of members of their calling who had been prevented by ill-luck from achieving the success that they had appeared (even if only to themselves) to deserve. Thus Sainte-Beuve (quoted by Antoine Adam in his edition of *Les Fleurs du mal*, p. 287), wrote of 'cette inégalité dans les sorts et dans les chances', 'le *guignon* du hasard', and of circumstances in which 'le *guignon* obscur vous use'. Baudelaire had strengthened this usage in his first essay on 'Edgar Poe, sa vie et ses œuvres', and also in *Les Fleurs du mal* when he altered the title of one of his poems from 'L'Artiste inconnu' or 'Les Artistes inconnus' to 'Le Guignon'. It is Baudelaire's use of the word in these memorable contexts that Mallarmé adopted, when he entitled his own poem 'Le Guignon'.

98 'Cœur' for 'sein', like 'barbe' for 'aisselle' later, both in Y, are probably substitutions made for the sake of etiquette, with the ladies in mind.

99 M. Breillat observes that in B^2 'le crâne' is written over 'la chair'.

100 In Y, the word 'ancienne' is written above 'vieille', in brackets.

101 I am grateful to Pierre Breillat for the excellent photograph of the Versailles manuscript ('à Emile Deschamps') which I owe to his kindness.

102 I do not know the present whereabouts of the copy of 'Le Guignon' on 'cream-laid' paper which we know that Mallarmé (having read the poem to his friends a fortnight before, during the frolics at Fontainebleau) sent to Cazalis for Mrs Yapp on 24 May 1862 (*DSM*. vi, 34). There exists a document, however, which on the one hand makes its survival today in a private collection seem likely, and in any event offers a reliable duplicate of the text. In the British Library's catalogue of printed books, the first item entered under the name Stéphane Mallarmé is a copy of the 1913 edition (Gallimard, *NRF*) of the *Poésies*, to the printed details of which a helpful librarian has added this note: 'p. 172 MS NOTES of variant readings from MSS.' An inquisitive reader who orders the volume is well rewarded for his curiosity. On a fly-leaf, under the name of a previous owner, R. Strete, and in the librarian's hand, is written: 'with collations p. 11 p. 81 from Mss. in the possession of Mme. Filloneau-Yapp of poems by Mallarmé in his own handwriting given to her mother in 1862. They are probably now (1927) in the possession of her son Gen. Filloneau. Mme. Filloneau's—with her mother Mrs. Yapp—house was a centre at that period of young artists and poets interested in English literature, etc.' And indeed, Mr Strete's careful collations, line by line, above the Gallimard text on pp. 11–15 ('Le Guignon') and 81–2 ('Sainte', or rather 'Sainte Cécile jouant sur l'aile d'un Chérubin (image et chanson d'autrefois)') provide us with early states of two of Mallarmé's poems—for which elegant assistance from a generous predecessor Mallarméists are much beholden. In the case of 'Le Guignon', a comparison with the other known versions, lucidly studied by Pierre Breillat in his article '*Le Guignon* de Stephane Mallarmé' (*Humanisme actif, Mélanges d'art et de littérature offerts à Gustave Cain*, 1968, vol. I, pp. 105–10), makes it clear that if the version of 'Le Guignon' presented to us by Mr Strete is not the earliest known, it has only one rival for that distinction, the one numbered here B.

I learned from the Information Service of the Reading Room that the 1913 edition of the *Poésies* was donated to the British Museum in 1927 by Robert Strete, Esq., of 245 Kennington Road, London, SE 11. Misreadings are few and easily identified.

103 Albert Thibaudet, *La Poésie de Stéphane Mallarmé* (1926), pp. 173–4.

104 See É. Noulet, op. cit., p. 519.

105 See Mallarmé's letter to the editor of *Art et critique* in which journal the final version appeared again on 24 August 1889 (*O.c.*, 1406 [1408]).

106 Op. cit., p. 274.

107 *O.c.*, 1408 [1410]: 'Pour Jean Royère, "Le premier texte est d'un Parnassien, le second d'un poëte créateur, d'un maître".'

108 See Mallarmé's reply to Huret in the *Enquête sur l'évolution littéraire* conducted in 1891: he refers to 'Les Parnassiens qui traitent encore leurs sujets à la façon des vieux philosophes et des vieux rhéteurs, en présentant leurs objets directement. Je pense qu'il faut, au contraire, qu'il n'y ait qu'allusion. La contemplation des objets, l'image s'envolant des rêveries suscitées par eux, sont le chant: les Parnassiens, eux, prennent la chose entièrement et la montrent: par là, ils manquent de mystère; ils retirent aux esprits cette joie délicieuse de croire qu'ils créent.' (*O.c.*, 869). It was no doubt still with the Parnassians particularly in mind that he wrote in 'Crise de vers' (*Divagations*, 1897, but the paragraph had appeared in 1892, in *Vers et Prose*, with only minor divergences): 'Abolie, la prétention, esthétiquement une erreur, quoiqu'elle régît les chefs-d'œuvre, d'inclure au papier subtil du volume autre chose que par exemple l'horreur de la forêt, ou le tonnerre muet épars au feuillage; non le bois intrinsèque et dense des arbres' (*O.c.*, 365–6).

109 Thibaudet (op. cit., p. 274) considered that 'Le Guignon' was conceived 'presque certainement comme une suite et une contre-partie de *Ténèbres*'. There is certainly a very close connection. This is the reason for my rather long quotation, which brings out both common elements and great differences between the two poems, considered as variations on the same subject. It helps to show also that Mallarmé's poem is nevertheless more intimately concerned with Baudelaire than with Gautier.

110 See above, p. 94.

111 The poet is Vigny, the book *Stello*.

112 B., *O.c.* ii, 296–7. The tercet of 'Ténèbres' that begins 'Sur son trône d'airain le Destin qui s'en raille' figures as an epigraph to Baudelaire's article. Mallarmé never forgot this presentation of Poe, the *poète enguignonné*. How firmly it remained throughout his life in the thought that he gave to the situation of the poet in the modern age is shown by reminiscences of the passage just quoted in a sentence of his Oxford and Cambridge lecture *La Musique et les Lettres*, delivered in 1894: 'La situation, celle du poète, rêvé-je d'énoncer, ne laisse pas de découvrir quelque difficulté, ou du comique. Un lamentable seigneur exilant son spectre de ruines lentes à l'ensevelir, en la légende et le mélodrame, c'est lui, dans l'ordre journalier' (*O.c.*, 651).

113 Ibid. 334.

114 In the words of *Genesis 2*: 'Il chassa l'homme, et il mit à l'est du jardin d'Éden les chérubins et la lame de l'épée flamboyante, pour garder le chemin de l'arbre de la vie'. But Mallarmé may have been more mindful of Hugo's visions:

> Je voyais, au-dessus du livide horizon,
> Trembler le glaive immense et sombre de l'archange.
> ('Les Malheureux', in *Les Contemplations*, V, xxxvi)
>
> L'ange au glaive de feu, debout derrière toi,
> Te met l'épée aux reins et te pousse aux abîmes.
> ('La Fin', the closing poem in *Châtiments*)

115 At the beginning of the poem there are probably echoes of Hugo:

> La terre a vu jadis errer les paladins;
> Ils flamboyaient ainsi que des éclairs soudains . . .
> ('Les Chevaliers Errants' in *La Légende des siècles*, XV)

and on the other hand:

> Il va, farouche, fauve, et comme une crinière,
> Secouant sur sa tête un haillon de lumière,
> ('Le Poëte', in *Les Contemplations*, III, xxviii)

There is a similar image in Banville's 'La Voie lactée' (*Les Cariatides*):

> Puis nous reconnaissons parmi des spectres vains
> Les inventeurs sacrés, les beaux géants divins,
> Pareils à des lions dont la fauve crinière
> Embrase leurs fronts d'or que baise la lumière.

116 That would seem to be the most likely interpretation of the line 'La mort fut un baiser à ces bouches taciturnes', which echoes perhaps Vigny's 'La Mort du loup': 'Puis après, comme moi, souffre et meurs sans parler' and also Baudelaire's 'Le Vin des chiffonniers': 'De tous ces vieux maudits qui meurent en silence'. On the other hand it contrasts with the ending of Baudelaire's 'La Mort des artistes' which half-promises Poe's 'glories beyond the grave'.

117 The sky-gazing poets in Gautier's poem 'Terza rima' (*Poésies diverses, 1833–1838*) are also forerunners of the 'mendieurs d'azur':

> Les yeux fichés au ciel, ils s'en vont en rêvant . . .
>
> Les anges, secouant leur chevelure blonde,
> Penchent leur front sur eux et leur tendent les bras,
> . . .
> Un auguste reflet de leur œuvre divine
> S'attache à leur personne et leur dore le front,
> Et le ciel qu'ils ont vu dans leurs yeux se devine . . .

In May 1864, Mallarmé would write to Cazalis: 'Après tout, tu sais que la seule occupation d'un homme qui se respecte est à mes yeux de regarder l'azur en mourant de faim' (*DSM.* vi, 211).

118 B., *O.c.* i, 87.

119 Ibid. 85.

120 Ibid. 24.

121 In their edition of *Les Fleurs du mal* (pp. 284–9) J. Crépet and G. Blin provide an illuminating commentary on Baudelaire's poem and its nineteenth-century literary background. They point out that 'Ils mangent de la cendre' in Mallarmé's 'Le Guignon' is probably an echo of 'Bénédiction'. They also quote (after Gonzague de Reynold) Psalm 37: 'Parce que je mangeais la cendre comme le pain, et que je mêlais mes larmes avec ce que je buvais . . . ' It may be that Mallarmé recognized the reference to the psalm since he too brings tears and ashes together: 'Des pleurs aussi salés rongent leur pâle joue, / Ils mêlent de la cendre avec le même amour'. But he knows the bitter truth, and a week later (7 July; *DSM.* vi, 46) consoles Cazalis for Ettie's absence with the words: 'Oui, vraiment heureux ceux qui peuvent souffrir pour quelque chose de grand! Tu te rappelles ma pièce sur le *Guignon*; je suis hélas! parmi les seconds.' And about his own domestic circumstances he complains: 'Tout cela est d'autant plus pénible qu'on souffre sans pouvoir prendre son mal au sérieux.' The subject appears to be on his mind.

122 The poet is himself aware of this danger, and appears to admit falling into it when he changes his comparison in his first letter to Cazalis (5 May 1862; *DSM.* vi, 29): 'Que vous serez désillusionné quand vous verrez cet individu maussade qui reste des journées entières la tête sur le marbre de la cheminée sans penser: ridicule Hamlet, qui ne peut se rendre compte de son affaissement.' Something like the same confession may be intended when he writes to Cazalis again on 1 July 1862 and exclaims: 'Ah! que j'eusse donc voulu accompagner Emmanuel, mais la fatalité, non je me flatte, le guignon, sous forme de pièces d'or absentes, se moque de moi' (ibid. 41).

123 In *Poèmes barbares*: 'Promène qui voudra son cœur ensanglanté / Sur ton pavé cynique, ô plèbe carnassière! / Pour mettre un feu stérile en ton œil hébété, / Pour mendier ton rire ou ta pitié grossière, / Déchire qui voudra la robe de lumière / De la pudeur divine et de la volupté.' It is possible that 'Pour mendier . . . ta pitié grossière', in the third line of this same stanza, is echoed by Mallarmé in a later tercet of 'Le Guignon', by the words 'quelques soupirs gueusés'.

124 In *Pétrus Borel the Lycanthrope* (pp. 149–50), Dr Enid Starkie wrote as follows of Baudelaire's earlier sympathy with Borel: 'Only Baudelaire himself, at that time an artist struggling with lack of means and comprehension, only Baudelaire, with his sympathy and understanding for failures, recognized something most noble and fine in this tragic wreck, in the dark, sad figure who came and went silently in the offices of *L'Artiste*; Baudelaire found him someone after his own heart . . . already knew Borel's work, and in his own early writings modelled himself on him.' She adds: 'Life however eventually broke Borel as it was never to break Baudelaire.' Which, if Borel was indeed one of the luckless

poets that Mallarmé had in mind when he wrote his poem 'Le Guignon', gives meaning to the line: 'Et ne voyant leur mal et les sachant brisés'. More generally, the harshness of Baudelaire's article would itself justify the line: 'Les disent impuissants et sans intelligence'.

125 B., *O.c.* ii, 156.

126 Ibid. 153–4.

127 Mallarmé must have Puck in mind when he brings in the dwarf. In *A Midsummer Night's Dream*, III. 2, 'le pervers' is seen in the hobgoblin side of his part. When Demetrius and Lysander seek to cross swords he leads them away from each other, impersonating each in turn and calling on him to come out and fight. Already in a schoolboy poem Mallarmé refers to the incident (see *DSM.* vii, 153), and he seems to recall it in 'Le Guignon': 'Et si, rossés, ils ont provoqué le pervers, / Leur rapière en grinçant suit le rayon de lune, / Qui neige en sa carcasse et qui passe à travers.'

128 He was found, we are told, 'pendu à la grille d'un escalier, impasse de la Vieille-Lanterne'. The usual version is that he hanged himself from a lamp-post, which explains why Mallarmé, in his letter to Des Essarts of 23 August 1862 (*Corr.* i, 47), referred in grim jest to Nerval's tragic end and his own poem in these terms: 'Voici qu'on met déjà des cordes aux potences des réverbères, et qu'au bout de ces cordes se balancent des pavés en attendant les luminaires ou les poètes enguignonnés.' In other words, it was raining hard: 'Il pleuvait des cordes.'

In an obituary article published in *La Presse* (30 January 1855), Gautier had protested (too much) that his friend was not a victim of a hostile society: 'Qu'on ne vienne pas faire sur cette tombe qui va s'ouvrir des nénies littéraires, ni évoquer les lamentables ombres de Gilbert, de Malfilâtre et d'Hégésippe Moreau . . . '; see Jean Richer, *Nerval par les témoins de sa vie* (1970), pp. 10–11. It was inevitable, however, that Nerval should figure in the literary martyrology. Baudelaire places him there, by the side of Poe, in his introduction to the *Histoires extraordinaires* and in his article on Hégésippe Moreau. In his notes for a letter to Jules Janin he names him as the latest of the martyrs (B., *O.c.* ii, 156–7, 236, and 306; see also ibid. i, 183).

129 *O.c.*, 263–4.

130 This line seems to encapsulate, for Mallarmé, the epitome of the Baudelairian pessimism he rejected. His own calm persistence in the difficult faith of the idealist seems to have been directed later, by a subtle device of mimicry, against Baudelaire. It is to 'Amour . . . gloire . . . bonheur!', so cruelly refuted, that he replies in 'Salut' with 'Solitude, récif, étoile', in 'Au seul souci' with 'Nuit, désespoir et pierrerie' (*O.c.*, 27 and 72). Perhaps in this matter Hugo had been Mallarmé's guide. At the end of the seventh book of Part IV of *Les Misérables*, under the chapter heading 'Les deux devoirs: veiller et espérer', he wrote: 'Faut-il continuer de lever les yeux vers le ciel? Le point lumineux qu'on y distingue est-il de ceux qui s'éteignent? L'idéal est effrayant à voir ainsi perdu dans les profondeurs, petit, isolé, imperceptible, brillant, mais entouré de toutes ces grandes menaces noires monstrueusement amoncelées autour

de lui; pourtant pas plus en danger qu'une étoile dans la gueule des nuages.' The impact of *Les Misérables* on Mallarmé's thinking with regard to the ideal and the real, when it appeared in May–June 1862, will be made apparent in the next chapter.

131 B., *O.c.* i, 134.

132 Ibid. 128.

133 Ibid. 36.

134 Ibid. ii, 136–7. In the two tercets of direct speech the 'poètes savants' become vulgar scoffers, and rather artificially they contrast 'the strong' with 'les baladins'. Their derision seems to make use of Victor Hugo. In *Notre Dame de Paris* (Livre VII, ch. 2) the poet Gringoire is seen by Frollo amusing the crowd for a few coppers. Ashamed at being caught in the red and yellow 'costume de baladin', he braves it out by saying: 'me voilà donc en habit d'histrion, comme saint Genest'. The theme is a not uncommon one, in an age when (as Leconte de Lisle wrote in 'Dies irae'): 'Les Muses, à pas lents, / S'en vont par les cités en proie au rire amer'. Baudelaire himself ended his sonnet 'La Muse vénale' with the lines 'Ou, saltimbanque à jeun, étaler tes appas / Et ton rire trempé de pleurs qu'on ne voit pas, / Pour faire épanouir la rate du vulgaire.' (B., *O.c.* i, 15.) One of the tortures inflicted on Mallarmé's martyrs may have been suggested by two lines in Hugo's 'Sonnez, sonnez toujours . . .' (*Châtiments*, VII, i): 'Et les petits enfants venaient cracher sur l'arche, / Et, soufflant dans leur trompe, imitaient le clairon.'

135 The preface is now included among Baudelaire's articles of literary criticism, under the title '*Les Martyrs ridicules* par Léon Cladel'. *Les Martyrs ridicules* bears the date 1862, but according to Cladel's daughter (Judith Cladel, *Maître et disciple, Baudelaire et Léon Cladel* (1951), p. 33, it appeared before the end of 1861. Mallarmé may well have known the novel as well as Baudelaire's preface to it when he wrote 'Le Guignon'.

136 'Mallarmé on Baudelaire', in *Currents of Thought in French Literature: Essays in memory of G. T. Clapton* (1965).

137 See above, vol. I, p. 88, n. 14.

138 Lawrence A. Joseph, *Henri Cazalis, sa vie, son œuvre, son amitié avec Mallarmé*, p. 62. For the text of the letter, complete so far as the Baudelaire incident is concerned, see *DSM*. vi, 69–70.

139 See Vigny's tragedy *Chatterton*, Act III, scenes 6 and 7.

140 B., *O.c.* ii, 186–7. Judith Cladel (op. cit., pp. 33–4) suggests that when Baudelaire lashed so unmercifully the Bohemian youth of the time he was flagellating himself: 'C'est lui-même que, indirectement, il attaque, c'est lui qu'il frappe avec la cruauté, le besoin morbide de confession et de châtiment dont il donne tant d'exemples dans ses poèmes et dans ses proses.'

141 Ibid. 55.

142 See above, pp. 18–19, and (for the text referred to) *DSM*. vii, 180.

143 Baudelaire's decision was ill-received. François Porché writes that he was 'injurié, raillé comme un rénégat, un transfuge qui, du camp des indépendants, passait à celui des officiels' (*Baudelaire, Histoire d'une*

âme (1944), p. 368. There are earlier, very similar accounts: 'Et cependant, cette démarche, que l'Académie ne prit pas au sérieux, fut unanimement blâmée par la presse. Les amis du candidat l'accusèrent de sacrifier sa dignité, de faire alliance avec les *Philistins*; ses ennemis le traitèrent de présomptueux, de fou, d'impertinent', Étienne Charavay, *A. de Vigny et Charles Baudelaire, candidats à l'Académie Française* (1879), p. 81; 'D'autre part la petite presse railla fort le camarade qui, désertant le camp des irréguliers, passait si effrontément à l'ennemi', E. J. Crépet [et J. Crépet], *Charles Baudelaire* (1907), p. 145.

It is perhaps significant that Mallarmé's rash enterprise did not estrange him from *L'Artiste*. It probably brought him some candid advice from Coligny, but it did not prevent his lightweight article 'L'Art pour tous' from being accepted for publication later that year. The editor received the article from Coligny; see above, p. 90. There appears to be no reason to consider that Houssaye was not himself well disposed towards its author. As has been seen, however, Mallarmé made use of the article to make amends, by treating Baudelaire with due respect—or rather more. Later (in a letter that Mondor dates 'novembre 1863') Des Essarts wrote to Mallarmé 'sois sûr que Houssaye est très-bienveillant pour toi' (*Corr.* i, 95).

144 In 'le câble à sonner l'idéal' there may be a reminiscence of Hugo's 'Voyage de nuit' (*Les Contemplations*):

> Chaque temple, tirant sa corde dans la nuit,
> Fait, dans l'obscurité sinistre et solennelle,
> Rendre un son différent à la cloche éternelle.

Had Millet's picture *l'Angelus* (painted in 1859) been exhibited to the public, one might have surmised that it had suggested the scene in the fields, in the first quatrain, and even the whole poem.

145 *Fl.*, i, 120; *O.c.*, 36; *Poésie*, 36.

146 *Essai sur Stéphane Mallarmé* (1963), pp. 54–5.

147 'Sonner l'idéal' heralds the notion, rather, that religion and art pursue 'the Ideal' each in its own way. Cf. (to anticipate) in 'Les Fenêtres': 'Que la vitre soit l'Art, soit la Mysticité'.

148 The variant is found in the text chosen by the editors of *Fl.*, i and *O.c.* alike.

149 Reference is made in *Fl.*, i to an article on 'Le Sonneur' by Franz J. Nobiling ('Mallarmés "Sonneur"', *Neo-Philologus*, 17 (1931–2), pp. 5–8). I am obliged to the librarian of the Taylor Institute for a photocopy of this interesting commentary. The point of view of the author places it, however, outside the scope and chronological limits of the present study.

150 *Fl.*, i, 130 (under the later title 'Renouveau'); *O.c.*, 34 ('Renouveau'); *Poésie*, 32 ('Renouveau'). The first title 'Vere novo' was no doubt borrowed ironically from Hugo's very different springtime poem, in *Les Contemplations* (I, xii). A not dissimilar ironical borrowing from the same poem may have supplied Mallarmé's 'Soleil d'hiver' with its ending. Hugo makes of the white petals blown on the breeze 'Les petits morceaux

blancs, chassés en tourbillons, / de tous les billets doux, devenus papillons.' The distance is not great to the 'cartels déchirés'.

151 B., *O.c.* i, 100–1.

152 The revised title of Mallarmé's poem, more clearly ironical than 'Vere novo', may have been suggested by this line.

153 *DSM.* vi, 36.

154 Ibid. 27.

155 Whence Cazalis's gesture of sending him a copy of Baudelaire's essay on *Les Misérables*, and Mallarmé's acknowledgement: 'Baudelaire y est Baudelaire.'

156 *DSM.* v, 349.

157 After disagreement between earlier editors as to whether the word should read *sonnets* or *sonnet*, the plural is preferred in the Flammarion edition. It is certainly the more understandable reading of the two.

158 *DSM.* vi, 38.

159 I have in mind such thoughts on poetry and the poet's task as are expressed in the following passages (B., *O.c.* ii, 328–9, 331–2, and 334):

> Pour lui [i.e. for Poe], l'Imagination est la reine des facultés; . . . L'Imagination est une faculté quasi divine qui perçoit tout d'abord, en dehors des méthodes philosophiques, les rapports intimes et secrets des choses, les correspondances et les analogies.

> Le rythme est nécessaire au développement de l'idée de beauté, qui est le but le plus grand et le plus noble du poème.

> Mais, avant toute chose, je dois dire que la part était faite au poète naturel, à l'innéité, Poe en faisait une à la science, au travail et à l'analyse (. . .) Il a soumis l'inspiration à la méthode, à l'analyse la plus sévère (. . .) Tout pour le dénouement, répète-t-il souvent. Un sonnet lui-même a besoin d'un plan, et la construction, l'armature pour ainsi dire, est la plus importante garantie de la vie mystérieuse des œuvres de l'esprit.

Not everything that Poe proclaimed was hailed enthusiastically by Mallarmé, of course. Some parts of the doctrine paraphrased by Baudelaire were later to be anathema to him; in particular, the belief expressed in this passage:

> C'est cet admirable, cet immortel instinct du beau qui nous fait considérer la terre et ses spectacles comme un aperçu, comme une correspondance du ciel. La soif insatiable de ce qui est au-delà, et que révèle la vie, est la preuve la plus vivante de notre immortalité. C'est à la fois par la poésie et *à travers* la poésie, par et *à travers* la musique, que l'âme entrevoit les splendeurs situées derrière le tombeau; et, quand un poème exquis amène les larmes au bord des yeux, ces larmes ne sont pas la preuve d'un excès de jouissance: elles sont bien plutôt le témoignage d'une mélancolie irritée, d'une postulation des nerfs, d'une nature exilée dans l'imparfait et qui voudrait s'emparer immédiatement, sur cette terre même, d'un paradis révélé.

> Ainsi, le principe de la poésie est, strictement et simplement, l'aspiration humaine

vers une beauté supérieure, et la manifestation de ce principe est dans un enthousiasme, une excitation de l'âme,—enthousiasme tout-à-fait indépendant de la passion qui est l'ivresse du cœur, et de la vérité qui est la pâture de la raison.

It may be that for the time being Mallarmé was tolerant of what he could only consider as a mysticization of art. The spice of a critical awareness that Poe's notions were not all acceptable to him might make the admiration for what did seem admirable all the greater.

The relation between art and religion would continue to preoccupy Mallarmé the unbeliever. The subject will be met with again, below, in 'Les Fenêtres' (p. 328). A few years later, he had reached the conviction expressed in 'Toast funèbre', according to which it was part of the modern poet's task to rid the beauties found in nature of all such superstitions as those embraced by Poe; see A. Gill, 'Mallarmé: "La vie et les œuvres"', in *Colloque Mallarmé (Glasgow Novembre 1973)*, Nizet, 1975.

With regard to Mallarmé's interest in Poe (already conspicuous in *Glanes*), the question arises of his ability to read him competently in English. In his so-called 'autobiographical letter' to Verlaine, of 16 November 1885, he would state that when he went to London as a young man it was 'simplement pour mieux lire Poe', and there may be some garbled truth in that claim. When he wrote to Eugène Lefébure in or before February 1862 (see *Lef.*, 169) to ask for a loan of his copy of Poe's poems, it may have been with the idea of obtaining professional help in reading them. He would thus carry out at the same time his undertaking to his grandfather (*DSM.* v, 357) to take English lessons in preparation for his year in London.

160 The title 'Soleils malsains' may be borrowed from Baudelaire's poem 'La Géante' (B., *O.c.* i, 22–3): 'Et parfois en été, quand les soleils malsains, / Lasse, la font s'étendre à travers la campagne . . . '

161 See *Fl.*, i, 135. The Pléiade editors say of this poem (*O.c.*, 1427 [1429]): 'On en connaît trois manuscrits, où il se trouve joint au sonnet *Vere novo*; l'un sous le titre "Soleils Mauvais" (Bibliothèque Jacques Doucet), l'autre sous le titre "Soleils Malsains" (Manuscrit Aubanel), l'autre (sic) sous le titre "Soleils Malsains" (Collection Henri Mondor).' Later, Mondor acquired and published (*Autres précisions*, p. 51) a further copy, under the title 'Soleils Mauvais'.

162 *Fl.*, i, 134; *O.c.*, 36–7; *Poésie*, 37.

163 See *Fl.*, i, 134–5 and 206–7 respectively.

164 Who the dark lady of the sonnet might be (if she was not imaginary) there is no knowing, but the casual character of their 'amour fiévreux' can be surmised from the precepts that Mallarmé dictated to Cazalis in his letter of 24 May 1862 (*DSM.* vi, 32). For the 'Rêve vague et beau' of 'Vere novo' there are of course romantic models, for example Chateaubriand's: 'Je voyais une femme inconnue et les miracles de son sourire; les beautés du ciel me semblaient écloses de son souffle; j'aurais vendu l'éternité pour une de ses caresses. Je me figurais qu'elle palpitait derrière ce voile de l'univers qui la cachait à mes yeux. Oh! que n'était-il en ma puissance de

déchirer le rideau pour presser la femme idéalisée contre mon cœur, pour me consumer sur son sein de cet amour, source de mes inspirations, de mon désespoir et de ma vie!' (*Mémoires d'outre-tombe*, I. vi. 6.)

165 See *O.c.*, 1428 [1430].

166 The attempt to express an outdoor spleen mood in Baudelairian alcove imagery relies on echoes of (for instance) 'La Chevelure', 'Les Bijoux', 'Le Léthé', and 'Le Goût du néant' (B., *O.c.* i, 26, 158, 155, 76.).

167 *Chatterton*, II. 5.

168 *DSM.* vi, 51.

169 Ibid. 55 and n. 7, 88, and 109.

170 *Fl.*, i, 20.

171 Dr Bonniot found a holograph copy of this poem among the poet's papers. He reproduced the text in his article 'Mallarmé et la vie', *Revue de France*, 1 January 1930. He seems to have had no doubt that it was an earlier version of 'A un Mendiant': 'C'est ainsi que nous avons retrouvé, daté de 1862 (. . .) un tout premier état, très différent de ce qu'il fait par la suite, du poème intitulé *Aumône* (. . .) et une seconde version recueillie par lui avec ses tout premiers poèmes dans le petit carnet de cuir de 1864 (. . .) Il n'est pas jusqu'aux changements du titre donné à cette pièce qui ne témoignent chez l'auteur une progression allant de la révolte véhémente et un peu farouche à un apitoiement plus calme sinon moins profond.'

Carl Barbier describes the manuscript in question as follows: 'Le manuscrit autographe fait partie de la Coll. Bonniot. Encre bleue sur le verso de la feuille qui contient également *Mysticis umbraculis* (. . .) Le manuscrit est bien de 1862, mais n'est pas daté, quoi qu'en dise Mondor (*O.c.*, 1434). Si date il y avait, elle a été coupée lorsque Mallarmé réduisit le format de la feuille pour la coller à une autre afin de cacher *Mysticis umbraculis*.' It is likely that Mondor, and Bonniot before him, considered that the '1862' appended to '*Mysticis umbraculis*' dated also the other side of the sheet. One would like to know why it is generally assumed that Mallarmé was himself responsible for such an elaborate concealment of the offending member.

The text of 'Haine du Pauvre' reproduced here is that adopted by Carl Barbier (*DSM.* iii, 97). Except for minor details of punctuation, and one accent, it is identical with Dr Bonniot's, in the aforesaid article. On the other hand it does differ in other details from the text given in the Pléiade edition (*O.c.*, 1432–3 [1434–5]). It must be noted, however, that although the Pléiade editors were able to consult the manuscript (ibid.: 'et dont nous avons pu examiner le manuscrit') the Bonniot version is decidedly more credible.

172 The text of 'A un Mendiant' reproduced here is that of the manuscript now in the Doucet collection—which in the Pléiade notes (*O.c.*, 1433 [1435]) is copied inaccurately in respect of punctuation and the initial letter (a capital in the manuscript) of the word *Rêve* in line six. There are two other early manuscripts, variants taken from which are noted by an initial in square brackets, [C.] standing for Mondor's 'Carnet' (*Autres Précisions* 51–2), and [M.] for the manuscript in the Mondor collection,

referred to in *O.c.*, 1433 [1435]. Differences in punctuation (which may result from editorial slips) are not noted.

173 See *O.c.*, 1432 [1434]. The different view expressed here on the relationship between the two poems was first aired in a note I contributed to the *RHLF.*, Nov.–Dec., 1973: 'Les "deux Pauvres" de Mallarmé'.

174 Again *O.c.*, 1432 [1434].

175 *DSM.* iii, 96.

176 See *O.c.*, 1432–3 [1434–5].

177 Mondor (*Vie*, 90) subjected what Cazalis wrote to some scholarly corrections, which could be considered arbitrarily interpretative and possibly misleading. The text quoted here is that of the Barbier-Joseph *Correspondance avec Cazalis* (*DSM.* vi, 152).

178 *O.c.*, 1434[1436]. Before making this prudent observation the editors had appeared to adopt without question the Bonniot dating. On the previous page, 'A un Mendiant' is introduced as 'une autre version [of 'Aumône'] datant de 1864'.

179 Since then, he had not had the opportunity of doing so. He did not see Cazalis (as he had hoped) when he crossed to Boulogne at the beginning of January 1863, nor when he went to Sens in April; see the letter from Cazalis of 7 January and those from Mallarmé of 1 and 27 April (*DSM.* vi, 103, 142, and 148). During his very brief visit to Paris at the end of January, they spent an evening together, but apparently with the Yapps also, in circumstances very unfavourable to an exchange of poems or conversation about poetry; see below, p. 275.

180 *DSM.* vi, 156.

181 Ibid. 158.

182 Some comparisons may be useful here. Between the first and last versions of 'Le Guignon', written in 1862 and 1887 respectively, and very much altered in the later version, not a single rhyme, out of twenty-two, is changed. Between the 'A un Mendiant' of 1862 and the final version of 1877 ('Aumône'), in spite of at least two complete revisions not one rhyme has been changed and only six rhyming words out of twenty-five.

183 *Vie*, 113. The waywardness of Mondor's copying leaves his more assiduous readers in doubt whether Des Essarts wrote 'l'un des deux *Pauvres*' or as indicated elsewhere (*Vie*, 115 and 116) 'l'un des *Deux Pauvres*', which would imply that the two poems were coupled under that title, as 'Vere novo' and 'Tristesse d'été' were under the title 'Soleils malsains'. What Des Essarts did write was: 'Pourquoi dans la [*or* ta] liste supprimes-tu l'un des deux *pauvres*?'

184 As a result no doubt of Des Essarts's deplorable handwriting, the exact text and meaning of the fragment quoted by Mondor are uncertain. When he requoted it in the 'Notes et Variantes' of the *Œuvres complètes* (*O.c.*, 1387 [1389]), he substituted without comment not only 'Il m'arrive souvent' for 'Il m'arrive' (and 'exclus' for 'exclues') but also 'J'ai ainsi relu *Les Fenêtres*' for 'J'ai aussi relu *Les Fenêtres*'. In the *Correspondance* (*Corr.* i, 110 n. 1), he returned, again without comment, to 'J'ai aussi relu'. (Through a copying error he also left out the reference to 'les deux *Pauvres*', thus concentrating on the suppression of 'Galanterie

macabre'.) To provide for the alternatives 'aussi' and 'ainsi', alternative understandings of the whole fragment are needed. If 'J'ai aussi relu' is the correct reading, a little cautious guesswork allows us to understand that 'le petit cahier de vers' was an early copy that Mallarmé had made of his poems in order to give them to Des Essarts, and that he did so in 1862 before leaving Sens. By the beginning of 1864 the copy was incomplete, lacking the London poems, and Mallarmé had sent these as a complement (whence the remark: 'J'ai aussi relu *Les Fenêtres*'). He had added a full list of the poems he intended to keep for publication, and Des Essarts wondered why, according to that list, 'l'un des deux *Pauvres*' was condemned and also (to his regret) 'Galanterie macabre'. But if it was 'J'ai ainsi relu' that Des Essarts wrote, the poem 'Les Fenêtres' was not sent to him as part of a complement. It was one of the poems contained in 'le petit cahier de vers' itself, which must be one of the notebooks that Mallarmé was at that time giving to poet friends, described by Mendès (see below, p. 296) as 'ces tout petits carnets reliés de carton-cuir et que ferme une bouclette de cuivre'.

It is not in doubt that Mallarmé did indeed eliminate 'Haine du Pauvre' (and with it 'Galanterie macabre') from his up-to-date 1864 copies of his collected poems. See in Mondor's *Autres précisions* (1961), pp. 543–55, the item 'Carnet de la vingt-deuxième année'. In the introduction to it (p. 41) one is given (rather vaguely) to understand that the 'Carnet' reproduced is the one that Mallarmé gave to Théodore Aubanel.

185 See above, vol. I, ch. 3, n. 14.
186 *DSM*. vi, 344.
187 Cf. *Corr*. v, 105: 'Baudelaire, . . . cet extraordinaire et pur génie.'
188 The borrowing was first noted, I believe, by Kurt Wais; see his *Mallarmé* (1952), p. 91.
189 B., *O.c.* i, 19–20.
190 See *DSM*. vi, 52.
191 B., *O.c.* i, 1313.
192 Ibid. 276. Baudelaire deals unfairly or very carelessly with 'La Chanson du vitrier'. It does not claim to be a *chanson*. Its title refers to its subject, the glazier's 'song', 'Oh! Vitrier!'
193 Ibid. 286–7.
194 Ibid. 1309–11. Very helpfully, M. Pichois quotes *in extenso* 'La Chanson du vitrier'.
195 Ibid. 1311.
196 *Le Poème en prose* (1959), pp. 120–1.
197 If piety is, in Rousseau's terms, 'un opium pour l'âme' (*La Nouvelle Héloïse*, Part VI, Letter 8; cf. in Baudelaire's 'Les Phares': 'un divin opium'), to force a man to abandon it for gold is to rob him of his pittance of ideality. The unworthiest act of Molière's Don Juan is this attempt to reduce a poor man to living by bread alone. But he fails. The protagonist in 'Haine du Pauvre' succeeds. In 'A un Mendiant' the beggar is invited to indulge in a night of artificial paradise, that is to prefer the ideal to the real, or at least dreams to reality.

198 *DSM*. vi, 211.

199 It is of course quite possible that it was entirely on his own initiative that Mallarmé withdrew 'Haine du Pauvre'. The author of such a poem might well fear that not all readers would make the right distinction between poet and protagonist. Critics of Molière's *Don Juan* have been unsure, from the time of its first performance, how much of what is said and done in that famous alms-giving scene is part of the depiction of Don Juan and how much can be taken as expressing the sentiments and beliefs of Molière. Readers of 'Haine du Pauvre' might think that Mallarmé's own opinions were involved in the account of what took place. The most that could be confidently assumed of his intention in that regard was (and is, *mutatis mutandis*) what is said of Molière's by one of his editors, Eugène Despois: 'Si l'on voulait chercher, dans cette scène, quelque autre dessein que celui de faire contraster, d'une façon générale, l'immoralité du grand seigneur avec l'honnêteté du pauvre diable [in Mallarmé's case 'avec la moralité chrétienne courante', for instance, since his *pauvre diable* fully merits this name and worse, being ready, for a silver pound to do all his tempter's ungodly bidding] j'y verrais plutôt ce qu'on pourrait appeler de notre temps une intention démocratique, qu'une intention irréligieuse; il est évident que Molière, en mettant ici l'irréligion dans la bouche de Dom Juan ne la recommande point' (*Œuvres de Molière*, 'Les Grands Ecrivains de la France' edition, vol. V, p. 147). Nevertheless, for allowing Don Juan to express himself so freely Molière was obliged to withdraw his play. It is not altogether impossible that part of the answer to Des Essarts' s query had to do with the advisability, in the atmosphere of the Second Empire, of a certain prudence in the expression of political and politico-religious views.

It is not altogether irrelevant therefore to draw attention here to such scraps of information as we possess concerning Mallarmé's political sympathies. It was half-jestingly, no doubt, that he and his friends referred on occasion to his admiration for the great republican hero Garibaldi; see above, p. 62. In London, we shall find him writing seriously to Cazalis of his reasons for not abandoning altogether—though he disliked workmen, they were conceited—his liking for the red flag; see *DSM*. vi, 162. A not dissimilarly equivocal position is reflected in 'Haine du Pauvre'; the tyranny of the lord is odious, but the servility of the *pauvre diable*, in strong contrast with the dignified courage of his predecessor in Molière's play, is contemptible. The same uncomfortable dilemma was to embarrass Mallarmé in later writings; see 'Conflit' and 'L'Action restreinte'. In his 1862 article on 'L'Art pour tous' he had declared that an artist might be a democrat as a man, but as an artist must be an aristocrat; the precept was sometimes difficult to abide by.

200 B., *O.c.* i, 286.

Chapter 5

A Hugolian interlude: 'Apparition'

Apparition[1]

La lune s'attristait. Des séraphins en pleurs
Rêvant, l'archet aux doigts, dans le calme des fleurs
Vaporeuses, tiraient de mourantes violes
De blancs sanglots glissant sur l'azur des corolles
—C'était le jour béni de ton premier baiser.
Ma songerie aimant à me martyriser
S'enivrait savamment du parfum de tristesse
Que même sans regret et sans déboire laisse
La cueillaison d'un Rêve au cœur qui l'a cueilli.
J'errais donc, l'œil rivé sur le pavé vieilli
Quand avec du soleil aux cheveux, dans la rue
Et dans le soir, tu m'es en riant apparue
Et j'ai cru voir la fée au chapeau de clarté
Qui jadis sur mes beaux sommeils d'enfant gâté
Passait, laissant toujours de ses mains mal fermées
Neiger de blancs bouquets d'étoiles parfumées.

It is generally agreed that the most verisimilar way of situating this delightful poem is to suppose that Mallarmé wrote it at Sens, for Marie Gerhard, in the summer or autumn of 1862. Mondor suggests another possibility, however, which he considers more likely though not so obvious. He points out that in the letters that passed between Mallarmé and his friends in 1862 and 1863, there is no mention of a poem entitled 'Apparition', but that on the other hand much is said in the correspondence with Cazalis of a verse-portrait of Ettie Yapp that Mallarmé had promised to compose. Mondor thinks that 'Apparition' may well be that portrait, executed in 1863.[2] The hypothesis has been so favourably received[3] that it cannot be rejected out of hand.

It is based, rather unsteadily, on three passages in the early correspondence between Mallarmé and Cazalis. The first is in a letter dated 1 July 1862, and is Mallarmé's answer to a first request from Cazalis for the portrait. From what he says it appears that the request was accompanied by a portrait in the more literal sense, a photograph of Regnault's drawing of Ettie:

Il y a un mot touchant et qui illumine toute ta lettre, le voici: "reçois, mon cher Mallarmé, le portrait de *notre sœur*." C'est simple, puisque nous sommes frères, et pourtant, c'est bien doux! Oui, elle se rangera dans mes rêves à côté de toutes les Chimènes, les Béatrices, les Juliettes, les Reginas, et, qui mieux est, dans mon cœur à côté de ce pauvre jeune fantôme, qui fut treize ans ma sœur, et qui fut la seule personne que j'adorasse, avant de vous connaître tous: elle sera mon idéal dans la vie, comme ma sœur l'est dans la mort (. . .)

Tu me demandes des vers, frère.

C'était à moi à te demander de m'en laisser faire.

Seulement, je tremble. Vois-tu, c'est mon chef d'œuvre que je veux faire là. Comme je le referai un jour pour ma pauvre sœur dont je n'ai point osé encore rythmer la vision. Laisse-moi donc tout le temps [d]'en faire.

Je comprends combien il serait doux de les lire à ta bien aimée, saintement, avant que l'alouette fatale ne chante l'adieu. Si tu veux faire à la perfection de l'œuvre le petit sacrifice, non, le grand sacrifice de les attendre pour ne les envoyer que plus tard, je te les promets exquis.

Ne crois pas ici que l'amitié soit de la fatuité.

Je te les promets exquis, blancs et or.

D'ici à Samedi, certe[s], je pourrais rimer quelques strophes, jolies même, mais cela ne serait rien, non rien, auprès de ce que je rêve.

Je ne veux pas faire cela d'inspiration: la turbulence du lyrisme serait indigne de cette chaste apparition que tu aimes. Il faut méditer longtemps: l'art seul, limpide et impeccable, est assez chaste pour la sculpter religieusement.

Merci, ami, de me commander et de m'inspirer mes meilleurs vers.[4]

The other passages occur in two letters from Cazalis written respectively in April and June 1863:

Sans cesse à moi-même je me parle d'elle: et je désire, et j'ai besoin que tous mes amis me sachent encore, autant que par le passé, uni à elle; et que son nom soit dit par vous comme si elle était là, la Picciola, à mes côtés. Un jour même, mon Stéphane, quand marié tu seras plus tranquille, je te rappellerai une dette, ces vers, ce portrait que tu m'avais promis: ce sera ton présent de noces pour mon union mystique.[5]

N'essaieras-tu jamais de faire la Vierge, de faire le portrait de notre chère sœur, de celle qui luit sur nous, comme une nuée d'étoiles; (. . .) Un jour, Stéphane, que Marie par un baiser t'aura mis dans l'âme des souffles d'Allemagne, ou qu'en passant près d'un jardin tu auras longtemps regardé un lys, ou qu'une voix d'enfant t'aura ému à force de douceur et de pureté, fais ce portrait, que je te demande.[6]

What can these passages be said to prove? Certainly not that Mallarmé ever wrote a verse-portrait of Cazalis's English sweetheart, but only that he owed him one, and that it was to be as sentimental as the references to her in their correspondence, as ecstatic as if Mallarmé saw her through his friend's eyes. They also contain details which resemble expressions in 'Apparition', so much so as to suggest, according to Mondor, that they are used in praise of the same person. Such are the word 'apparition' in the first passage, and in the third the phrase 'whose light shines down on us like a cloud of stars'. It might be fairly claimed, too, that Cazalis's image of the poet gazing at a lily, in a garden, is very close, rhetorically, to the opening lines of the poem. These are the arguments in favour of Mondor's hypothesis.

Those against it are stronger and to my mind convincing. First, the poem is not a portrait, of Ettie or Marie or anyone else, but an intimate love-poem such as not even Cazalis, for all his need of congratulation, could possibly wish even his best friends to write in praise of his beloved. Secondly, the rhetorical resemblances between praise of Ettie in the letters and praise of the heroine in the poem are at least matched by resemblances of the same kind between the poem and Mallarmé's love-letters to Marie. Marie is as much an angel as Ettie, even in letters that Mallarmé wrote to Cazalis from London in 1863, when she had become his mistress.[7] Moreover, the conceit on which the whole poem is constructed, rather like a Renaissance sonnet,[8] was first used by Mallarmé, in his correspondence, as a compliment not to Ettie but to Marie: 'Il me semble, quand vous tournez la rue, que je vois un fantôme de lumière et tout rayonne.'[9]

'Apparition', then, may fairly be taken as being what it seems, a love-poem to Marie Gerhard. Thoughts of Ettie may, for all we know or are likely to learn, have had some part in its shaping, but we do not need to suppose so to account for rhetorical similarities of the kind pointed out by Mondor. There is a more plausible reason for these. During the summer of 1862, all that Mallarmé wrote about love, whether his friend's adoration of Ettie or his own less ethereal but deepening feelings for Marie, bears the unmistakable stamp of a strong literary influence, that of the love-theme in Hugo's latest novel.

The first three parts of *Les Misérables* had appeared in April and May of that year, and the other two at the end of June, and *Les Misérables* (it may be useful to recall) contains, as well as the story of Jean Valjean, an idealized version of Hugo's first love in the shape of the 'idyll in the rue Plumet'. Mallarmé was so enthralled by it that the loves of Marius and Cosette coloured his thoughts about Cazalis and Ettie and about himself and Marie. This is vouched for by his own letters. On 7 July 1862 he wrote to Cazalis:

> Pauvre Roméo et pauvre Marius, je te plains.
> J'ai pensé à toi toute la semaine en lisant Marius, et à elle, en rêvant de Cosette.[10]

To Marie, on the other hand, he wrote, probably during that same month of July:

> Quand vous m'évitiez tout à l'heure dans la rue, je lisais ces mots, dans l'œuvre nouvelle d'Hugo: "Vous qui souffrez parce que vous aimez, aimez plus encore."[11]

The chapter of *Les Misérables* from which this sentence is taken also belongs to the idyll in the rue Plumet.

The kind of idealization of Ettie and Marie, and the sentiments they inspired, which resulted from this association with Hugo's young lovers, can be illustrated. On 1 July 1862 Mallarmé wrote to Cazalis:

> Frère, voici une journée pluvieuse qui a été traversée de deux rayons de soleil: l'un auroral et blanc, l'autre crépusculaire et flamboyant. Je parle de l'adorable portrait d'Ettie, et d'une centaine de pages philosophiques des *Misérables*.[12]

—and later that month to Marie:

> Ces lettres, je les gardais et je les entassais chaque matin, pensant vous les remettre et osant croire, non pas que vous les liriez toutes, mais simplement que vous jetteriez les yeux au hasard sur quelques

phrases, et que de ces quelques phrases monterait à vous cette clarté qui vous enivre (. . .) Ce rayon devait faire ouvrir en votre cœur la fleur bleue mystérieuse, et le parfum qui naîtrait de cet épanouissement, espérais-je, ne serait pas ingrat. Je le respirerais. On appelle amour, ce parfum.[13]

All these pretty fancies, the white and dawn-like look he sees in Ettie's portrait and the light, and flower, and perfume of love he hopes to find with Marie, are taken from one short passage in *Les Misérables*:

Ce premier regard d'une âme qui ne se connaît pas encore est comme l'aube dans le ciel. C'est l'éveil de quelque chose de rayonnant et d'inconnu (. . .) Toutes les puretés et toutes les ardeurs se concentrent dans ce rayon céleste et fatal qui (. . .) a le pouvoir magique de faire subitement éclore au fond d'une âme cette fleur sombre, pleine de parfums et de poisons, qu'on appelle amour.[14]

Even the letters he speaks of to Marie, letters he says he wrote but never sent, are probably a fiction prompted by Marius's habit of 'writing to' Cosette during their period of separation:

De temps en temps, surtout à cette heure du soir qui attriste le plus les songeurs, il laissait tomber sur un cahier de papier où il n'y avait que cela, le plus pur, le plus impersonnel, le plus idéal des rêveries dont l'amour lui emplissait le cerveau. Il appelait cela "lui écrire".[15]

If the love-talk in the letters to Marie contains so much that is deliberately borrowed from Hugo's novel, what wonder that the love-poem 'Apparition' should also owe a great deal to that rich source, that the idyll in the rue Plumet should indeed be the most important literary influence—though not the only one—discernible in it?

The setting described in the opening lines of the poem is more explicitly paradisal (with its angel music in place of the melody from the lovers' souls) than the garden in which Marius and Cosette make innocent love; nevertheless it is too much like it for the resemblance to be accidental:

Le soir, une vapeur de rêverie se dégageait du jardin et l'enveloppait; un linceul de brume, une tristesse céleste et calme, le couvraient (. . .) La nuit, quand ils étaient là, ce jardin semblait un lieu vivant et sacré. Toutes les fleurs s'ouvraient autour d'eux et leur envoyaient de l'encens; eux, ils ouvraient leurs âmes et les répandaient sur les fleurs.[16]

The time for the happening which the poem celebrates—'C'était le jour béni de ton premier baiser'—is probably suggested by the novel too, for there too there is a blessed, holy hour ('*cette heure bénie et sainte*') when the two souls sealed their love with a kiss.[17] The event itself which the poem describes is very like a phenomenon that Marius experiences several times, and whose recurrence is indeed a sort of *leitmotif*, handled by Hugo with an unexpectedly delicate humour, in the early chapters of the idyll. It occurs first when Marius waits in the Luxembourg gardens, for a sight of the unknown girl who walks there each day with her father:

> Tout en approchant du banc, il tendait les plis de son habit, et ses yeux se fixaient sur la jeune fille. Il lui semblait qu'elle emplissait toute l'extrémité de l'allée d'une vague lueur bleue (. . .) Le lendemain (. . .) il s'y assit comme la veille, considérant de loin et voyant distinctement le chapeau blanc, la robe noire et surtout la lueur bleue (. . .) Un des derniers jours de la seconde semaine, Marius était comme à son ordinaire assis sur son banc (. . .) Tout à coup il tressaillait (. . .) L'auréole venait droite à lui (. . .)
>
> Il contemplait, non pas cette fille, mais cette lumière qui avait une pelisse de satin et un chapeau de velours. L'étoile Sirius fût entré dans la chambre qu'il n'eût pas été plus ébloui (. . .)
>
> Il semblait à Cosette que Marius avait une couronne, et à Marius que Cosette avait un nimbe (. . .) Cosette était une condensation de lumière aurorale sous forme de femme.[18]

To my mind, there is no doubt that Marius's bright angel served as a model for the 'luminous apparition' of Mallarmé's letter to Marie, and for the magic metamorphosis which is the outward, anecdotal subject of 'Apparition'. Further exploration of Hugo's prose idyll reveals a deeper influence too, and in doing so brings into clearer focus the spiritual drama that the anecdote symbolizes, the drama glimpsed in the beautiful lines:

> Ma songerie aimant à me martyriser
> S'enivrait savamment du parfum de tristesse
> Que même sans regret et sans déboire laisse
> La cueillaison d'un rêve au cœur qui l'a cueilli.

Not that this melancholy reflection is borrowed directly from anything that Marius thinks or says of love. He is not afflicted, after Cosette's first kiss, by any such recognition that the plucked flower must die, or in Hugo's dustier metaphor that *L'idéal tombe en poudre au toucher du réel.*[19] But lightly sketched in the story of Marius and Cosette is an analysis of young love which contains hints that the recognition is near. Cosette is shown as still dwelling in, Marius as ripe for leaving, the last phase of the blessed ignorance of childhood, when, however tremulously and precariously, the ideal and the real remain at one with each other.

How congenial to Mallarmé's understanding this analysis of Hugo's was can best be appreciated by relating it, not in the first place to the poem 'Apparition' itself, but to what Mallarmé was to write many years later, about the time of life commemorated by it. The subject of the poem will then be seen to be, in its deeper significance, an episode in the spiritual drama of youth; the lover's imagination, in its role as guardian angel, makes a last effort to ward off the threat to the precious unity of childhood.

At the juncture in the life of Cosette and Marius at which they have only exchanged looks as they passed, Cosette's experience is described thus:

> C'était une sorte d'adoration à distance, une contemplation muette, la déification d'un inconnu. C'était l'apparition de l'adolescence à l'adolescence, le rêve des nuits devenu roman et resté rêve, le fantôme souhaité enfin réalisé et fait chair (. . .) demeuré dans l'idéal, une chimère ayant une forme (. . .) Elle se mit à adorer Marius comme quelque chose de charmant, de lumineux et d'impossible.[20]

Later, when the pair have met, and chastely kissed, and make ethereal love[21] to each other in their garden:

> Donc ces deux êtres vivaient ainsi, très haut (. . .) à peine os et chair, âme et extase de la tête aux pieds; déjà trop sublimes pour marcher à terre, encore trop chargés d'humanité pour disparaître dans le bleu, en suspension comme des atomes qui attendent le précipité; (. . .) émerveillés, pâmés, flottants. Ils dormaient éveillés dans ce bercement. O léthargie splendide du réel accablé d'idéal![22]

Here, on the other hand, are fragments of two critical articles by Mallarmé, 'Ballets' and 'Solitude', published in 1886 and 1895 respectively:

> la crise subie, un laps, au commencement tout à fait de la jeunesse, par

chaque génération—quand l'enfant près de finir jette un éblouissement et s'institue la vierge de l'un ou l'autre sexe.[23]

Au moins, très judicieusement, à l'Éden, ou selon les deux modes d'art exclusifs, un thème marqua l'antagonisme que chez son héros participant du double monde, homme déjà et enfant encore, installe la rivalité de la femme qui *marche* (même à lui sur des tapis de royauté) avec celle, non moins chère du fait de sa voltige seul, la primitive ou fée.[24]

When he wrote these descriptions—definitions almost —Mallarmé was presumably thinking of his own experience of the period of crisis in question. One wonders, however, whether they do not betray some recollection of the reading of Hugo which had helped him to analyse that experience even while he was undergoing it. It has been said that the poetry of young men rarely starts from anything but literature. It would seem that in the case of Mallarmé the influence of literature was strong on life and love as well, but how deeply we can only guess. What his letters of 1862 put beyond doubt is that in his love-making he imitated the angelizing rhetoric of Hugo. How much his emulation of 'pure, seraphic Marius', and Marius's idealizing of love, affected his attitude to Marie in the intimacy of their courtship, or his feelings for her in his heart of hearts, is another matter. But it does seem clear that the reflections on young love which begin in 'Apparition', and which will be seen to continue in poems of 1863, reflections whose conclusion is formulated in the passages quoted from 'Ballets' and 'Solitude', are in the first place inspired or assisted by Hugo's descriptions and analyses. From this point of view, and in particular (to return to the main concern) as an aid to the understanding of 'Apparition', one more passage from *Les Misérables* deserves attention. It is one in which ideal love is seen as a prelude to the sensual love which will very soon take its place:

"Faire des compliments" à celle qu'on aime (. . .) c'est quelque chose comme le baiser à travers le voile. La volupté y met sa douce pointe, tout en se cachant. Devant la volupté le cœur recule, pour mieux aimer. Les cajoleries de Marius, toutes saturées de chimère, étaient, pour ainsi dire, azurées (. . .) C'était ce qui se dit dans la grotte, prélude de ce qui se dira dans l'alcôve; une effusion lyrique, la strophe et le sonnet mêlés, les gentilles hyperboles du roucoulement,

tous les raffinements de l'adoration arrangés en bouquet et exhalant un subtil parfum céleste, un ineffable gazouillement de cœur à cœur.[25]

'Apparition' is the most formal of the compliments paid to Marie by her lover, probably not very long before she became his mistress. There is much lyrical effusion in it, but it is a thoughtful poem, skilfully fashioned to symbolize the last effort of adolescence to escape the awareness that ideal love and real love cannot live together—an effort that is momentarily successful. When the beloved comes down from the ideal world to become the woman who walks and kisses, the hero of the poem is able, by a ruse of his imagination, to identify her with 'the fairy' and so to restore her to her former status. He thus contrives ('a man already yet still a child') to bring together again, precariously, the real and the ideal.

The talented critic Jean-Pierre Richard, who first pointed out the very close relationship between the fairy in 'Apparition' and the fairy in the article 'Ballets',[26] interprets the poem differently. He sees it as symbolizing Mallarmé's rejection of Marie, the woman of flesh and blood, in favour of a creature of his dreams. The interpretation is too much at variance with the plain biographical facts to be acceptable. In 1862 (if the poem was written in that year) Mallarmé wooed Marie and won her, and in 1863 (which Jean-Pierre Richard takes to be the date of composition)[27] he was living with her—and marrying her—in London.

It is odd that the celestial being in whose semblance the beloved appears should be a fairy. One would have expected it to be an angel, in view of the love-rhetoric of Mallarmé's letters (and of its model in Hugo's novel), in view even of the opening lines of 'Apparition' itself: *Des séraphins en pleurs* . . . One would have expected it also because in the poem by Banville which is the fairly obvious source for the visual image at the end of the poem, the luminous apparition is an angel, not a fairy:

> Je la revis, c'était bien elle! dans un rêve.
> Oh! si belle toujours! sa chevelure d'Ève,
> Comme une vapeur d'or, voltigeait à l'entour
> De son front (. . .)
> Mes sens plus compliqués et qui percent les voiles
> Perçoivent dans l'éther le parfum des étoiles.
> (. . .)

Et que je sentirai, dans un rêve inouï,
Cet Ange glorieux, vainqueur des épouvantes,
Secouer sur mon front des étoiles vivantes.
('Le cher Fantôme')[28]

Are we then to suppose that fairy for angel is a deliberate choice, explainable by anti-Christian sentiments (though these had seemed in the interests of love-making to be in abeyance)? Or had Mallarmé's childhood dreams really been haunted by a fairy as well as by angels? A poem written three years earlier suggests an affirmative answer to both these questions. It is the one entitled 'Viens!', included in the first section of *Entre Quatre Murs* and already mentioned above as one of the pieces in that collection which express the hesitations of an adolescent freeing himself from Christian bondage.[29] It represents a rhetorical struggle for the soul of a child, between a guardian angel and a Puck-like spirit whose name is Ohl-le-follet, and whose kinship with 'la fée au chapeau de clarté' in the young poet's imaginings is clear from the opening stanza:

Un enfant dormait blond et rose.
L'œil rêveur, un ange frôlait
De l'aile sa paupière close:
Sur son front des feuilles de rose
Pleuvaient des doigts d'Ohl-le-follet!

Ohl-le-follet in his turn has a forerunner in Mallarmé's even earlier writings, for the first of these that we know is the short essay on The Guardian Angel written at the age of twelve, in which the angel (learnedly identified by the author as the Christian counterpart of the tutelary gods of antiquity) struggles with the devil for the souls of the dying.[30]

It is noteworthy, however, that if a gradual process of transformation in a young imagination might in itself explain the choice of a fairy in place of the expected angel in Mallarmé's love-poem, there is further strong support for this choice in one of Hugo's poems. There is in *Odes et Ballades* a poem entitled 'Une Fée' which begins and ends with the refrain-stanza:

Que ce soit Urgèle ou Morgane,
J'aime, en un rêve sans effroi,
Qu'une fée au corps diaphane,
Ainsi qu'une fleur qui se fane,
Vienne pencher son front sur moi.

And as an appropriate reminder that the poetry of young men, however much it is fed by their dreams, commonly draws even more on literature, this youthful poem bears as epigraph a fragment of a translation by Émile Deschamps (alas! poor Mercutio) of *Romeo and Juliet*:

> La Reine Mab m'a visité. C'est elle
> Qui fait dans le sommeil veiller l'âme immortelle.

That 'Viens! (Ballade)' is partly imitated from 'Une Fée' ('Ballade première' in Hugo's collection) is certain, since the same five-line stanza of octosyllabic lines and the same rhyme scheme are used, as well as some of its fairy lore. Indirectly, therefore, through Ohl-le-follet, or directly from a persisting reminiscence (but the distinction is a dubious one), the fairy of 'Apparition' also owes something to 'Une Fée' and thus provides one more indication that if Mallarmé's thoughts about love were 'bathed in azure' it was azure from a literary heaven, whose most bountiful god was Victor Hugo.[31] Only when the spleen returned, several months later, was Baudelaire to become once more the dominating influence and the master to be admired and fought with.

NOTES

1 *Fl.*, i, 290; *O.c.*, 30; *Poésie*, 24. The Pléiade editors note (*O.c.*, 1412 [1414]) that some details of punctuation were changed in the later editions. The version given here follows the punctuation of the Flammarion edition. The Pléiade text differs from it in placing a comma after 'archet au doigt' in the second line, and a full stop at the end of the fourth. The comma is found in *Vers et prose* too; the full stop is probably a misprint pure and simple.

2 See *Vie*, 54 n. 1 and (less confident) 264; also, *O.c.*, 1410–11 [1412–13]. The Flammarion editors (*Fl.*, i, 291) accept a compromise.

3 In particular by Charles Mauron, in his *Introduction à la Psychanalyse de Mallarmé* (1950), p. 88. (A major weakness of this work, compared with the excellent *Mallarmé l'obscur* which the same author published in 1941, is the uncritical alacrity with which he accepts doubtful suggestions when they are compatible with his psychoanalytical conjectures.)

4 *DSM*. vi, 40–1. A sentence in the same letter makes it clear that 'le portrait de notre sœur' was Regnault's drawing: 'Rappelle aussi à Piccolino, en le

félicitant de ce charmant portrait, que je lui ai dernièrement demandé sa carte et qu'il a la mienne.' Regnault's drawing is signed 'Piccolino'; see the reproduction opposite p. 290 in *DSM*. vi.

5 *O.c.*, 1411 [1413], *DSM*. vi, 146, and *Corr.* i, 88 n. 1.

6 *O.c.*, 1411 [1413], and *DSM*. vi, 158.

7 In Mallarmé's references to Ettie the most persistent theme is that of the lovers being in paradise: 'une taille d'ange qui reploierait ses ailes sous son corsage' (*DSM*. vi, 32), 'ce galbe séraphique, avec des cheveux qui, dénoués, frissonneraient le long de son dos comme deux ailes de lumière' (ibid. 39), 'Ettie . . . faisait les honneurs de façon à vous emparadiser dans chacune de ses questions . . . l'air d'une séraphine qui se serait fait [*sic*] quakeresse et se souviendrait du ciel' (ibid. 95). Cf., dans *Les Misérables*: 'Cosette était retombée dans le profond amour séraphique. L'abîme Éden venait de se rouvrir' (IV. iv. 5), 'deux êtres . . . débordant de toutes les félicités du ciel, plus voisins des archanges que des hommes . . . ' (IV. viii. 1), 'Il était dans le ciel, il était tout simple qu'il oubliât la terre' (IV. viii. 2), 'Elle était dans l'âge où la vierge porte son amour comme l'ange porte son lis' (IV. viii. 3).

The compliments to Marie are less ethereal. At the philandering stage, during which the courtship is a more earthy, somewhat burlesque emulation of Cazalis's wooing of Ettie (see the letter to Cazalis dated 7 July 1862, *Corr.* i, 41 and *DSM*. vi, 46), the angel rhetoric is used with a cynical purposefulness: 'Vous êtes adorable et vous voulez qu'on vous trouve détestable, car il faudrait vous trouver détestable pour ne pas vous aimer—vous qui êtes un regard divin et un sourire céleste! Vous êtes punie d'être un ange: je vous aime. Pour me punir à mon tour de vous aimer, il faudrait n'être plus un ange, et vous ne le pouvez pas. Donc laissez-moi vous contempler et vous adorer—et espérer' (*Corr.* i, 38), 'Et comment vous comprendre sans vous aimer? Il fallait n'être pas l'ange que vous êtes, ne point avoir le sourire dont vous souriez. Vous deviez bien savoir qu'on n'est pas céleste impunément et qu'une enchanteresse enchante!' (ibid. 39). The same rhetoric is later used in earnest in letters to Cazalis: 'Comme elle a pleuré quand elle m'a revu et nous sommes restés cinq bonnes minutes, le soir, elle pleurant, moi baisant ses larmes—sans nous dire un mot. Je sais un ange. Il s'appelle Marie.' / 'Ce qui m'attire vers elle, c'est quelque chose de magnétique et qui n'a pas de cause apparente. Elle a un regard à elle qui m'est une fois entré dans l'âme, et qu'on ne pourrait en retirer sans me faire une blessure mortelle'. / 'Oui, elle est noble, oui, elle est une sainte. La pauvre âme exilée a tout donné à celui qui l'a aimée (. . .) Je la respecte, comme je respecte ma sœur morte (. . .) Non, elle n'a pas été ma maîtresse. Elle a été mon ange gardien, et elle devrait être ma femme.' (Ibid. 51–2, 54, 64–5; *DSM*. vi, 55–8, 87–8.)

8 The poem seems to be modelled on a common type of sixteenth- and early seventeenth-century love sonnet, the type in which the mistress appears and puts the sun to shame. Thus in sonnet LXXXIII of Du Bellay's collection *L'Olive*, the tercets run thus:

Quand d'Occident, comme une étoile vive,
Je vy sortir dessus ta verde rive,
O fleuve mien! une Nymphe en riant.

Alors voyant cete nouvelle Aurore,
Le jour honteux d'un double teint colore
Et l'Angevin et l'Indique orient.

9 *Corr.* i, 38 and n. 1. The editors of the *Correspondance* note the resemblance between this compliment and the end of the poem.
10 Ibid. 41 (and *DSM.* vi, 45).
11 Ibid. 38.
12 Ibid. 34 (and *DSM.* vi, 39).
13 Ibid. 37.
14 III. vi. 3. The 'rayon auroral et blanc' in Mallarmé's letter may not seem necessarily to echo this 'premier regard . . . comme l'aube dans le ciel', but my suggestion is confirmed by further echoes, one in another chapter of *Les Misérables*: 'Cosette était une condensation de lumière aurorale en forme de femme' (IV. viii. 1), the other in the same letter to Cazalis: 'bien que vous ayez encore dans le regard l'aube du commencement, vous êtes tous deux, enfants, bien loin dans la vie déjà, et bien haut dans la gloire puisqu'il ne vous manque qu'un Shakespeare pour être les deux noms que tous les amants murmurent dans un baiser' (*Corr.* I, 35). A Shakespeare or, of course, a Hugo. There are other references, direct and indirect, to Romeo and Juliet in the *Correspondance*, but during the summer of 1862 far more to Marius and Cosette. Hugo, for his part, does not fail to compare his idyllic pair with Shakespeare's star-crossed lovers.
15 IV. ii. 2.
16 IV. iii. 3; IV. viii. 1. The seraphs with their viols, who in 'Apparition' mingle their music with the incense from the flowers, are not found in Cosette's garden. They appear to have come down from the 'concert of angels' in a window in Sens cathedral, a window that figures in the prose poem 'Symphonie littéraire'; see below, p. 349.
17 'A partir de cette heure bénie et sainte où un baiser fiança ces deux âmes, Marius vint là tous les soirs' (IV. viii. 1).
18 III. vi. 4; III. vi. 5; III. vi. 6; III. viii. 10; IV. viii. 1.
19 For the context (in *Feuilles d'Automne*, xxvii), see below, ch. 7 n. 45.
20 IV. iii. 6.
21 'Cosette était heureuse, et Marius était satisfait. Ils vivaient dans ce ravissant état qu'on pourrait appeler l'éblouissement d'une âme par une âme. C'était cet ineffable premier embrassement de deux virginités dans l'idéal' (IV. viii. 1).
22 IV. viii. 2.
23 *O.c.*, 406.
24 *O.c.*, 306. The very expression 'La femme qui marche' is reminiscent of Hugo's observation: 'Le jour où une femme qui passe devant vous dégage de la lumière en marchant, vous êtes perdu, vous aimez' (IV. v. 4).
25 IV. viii. 1.

26 *L'Univers imaginaire de Mallarmé* (1961), p. 147. See also A. Gill, 'Mallarmé et "L'Être aux ailes de gaze"', in *Studi in onore di Italo Siciliano*, Firenze, 1966.

27 J.-P. Richard, op. cit., p. 123.

28 This poem is included in *Les Exilés* (1867), but it had appeared in the *Revue européenne* in 1860; see M. Fuchs, *Théodore de Banville*, p. 212. (It probably played its part in consecrating the theme of the dead sister, the 'poor little spectre', in Mallarmé's letters and poetry. This suggestion may seem offensive to the sentimental psychologists who prefer to overlook the very conscious character of Mallarmé's memories of Maria and his highly literary treatment of them.)

In Baudelaire's 'La Mort des Pauvres' it is again an Angel who watches over the sleeper:

> C'est un Ange qui tient dans ses doigts magnétiques
> Le sommeil et le don des rêves extatiques.

So also is the heavenly being in a poem in Hugo's *Les Contemplations*, which is entitled, like Mallarmé's, 'Apparition', and whose verse-form is almost identical (eighteen lines in *rimes plates*, compared with Mallarmé's sixteen). Mallarmé either knew this poem very well or re-read it at the beginning of 1862. When in a letter dated 4 June (*DSM*. vi, 36) he calls Cazalis 'le papillon à travers l'aile de qui on voit le soleil' he is surely referring to its closing lines:

> Et je voyais, dans l'ombre où brillaient ses prunelles,
> Les astres à travers les plumes de ses ailes.

29 Vol. I, pp. 255–6.

30 On this school exercise see above, Vol. I, pp. 83–4, 103–4, 92–5, and 122, and for the text, *O.c.*, 1381 [1383].

31 Thibaudet notes (*La Poésie de Stéphane Mallarmé*, p. 165, n.) that a line ending with *Mains mal fermées* is rhymed with *parfumées* in the tenth poem of *Les Chants du Crépuscule*. Another possible reminiscence of Hugo may have merged with, or recalled, the image in Banville's poem; in *Les Misérables* (IV. V. 5) Cosette learns what love is by reading the pages that Marius 'wrote to her': 'C'était comme une main qui se serait ouverte et lui aurait jeté subitement une poignée de rayons'.

Concerning Mallarmé's deep and lasting admiration for Hugo there is no more striking testimony than that of Claudel, recorded by Henri Guillemin ('Claudel et Hugo', *Le Monde*, 11 May 1955); it concerns an incident which happened at one of Mallarmé's Tuesday evenings, in the early 1890s presumably and which Claudel still remembered sixty years later and narrated thus: 'Mallarmé était d'une politesse exquise, vraiment d'une grande bonté. Il était très gentil avec moi, avec tous. Je ne l'ai jamais vu discourtois et, ma foi, brutal qu'une seule fois; avec moi, précisément. Rue de Rome, j'avais l'habitude de me taire. J'écoutais de toutes mes oreilles mais je me taisais. Un jour, pourtant, je me suis risqué à une réflexion, à une interjection, plutôt; Mallarmé venait de prononcer le nom de Victor Hugo, et j'ai sorti je ne sais plus quoi d'assez violent, d'assez gros, contre le bonhomme. Alors Mallarmé a pivoté sur les talons et m'a demandé, carrément, si j'étais malade. Comme ça, devant tout le monde. Je n'ai plus pipé mot (. . .) Il l'aimait, lui, Hugo. Il l'admirait profondément.'

Chapter 6

The trial year

The experimental marriage was to prove a sterner test than young love had bargained for. The blithe honeymoon period was to last for some three weeks and end with a sudden crisis. The first of two separations followed. Twice Marie would wrench herself away from her Stéphane, taking refuge first in Paris then in Brussels. Twice she would resist for a month or more his entreaties and her own longing before returning to his arms. Return she did however, and the second time, in April 1863, it was to stay. They had proved to themselves their mutual devotion. They married without haste, in August. Why the way to the altar had not been smoother is a searching question, the answer to which must be sought in the letters exchanged between Mallarmé and Cazalis during that troubled winter and spring. They tell a puzzling story.

Stéphane's first letter to Henri, dated 14 November 1862,[1] was all youthful exuberance, and very different from the dutifully woeful missive he had sent to the Desmolins on arrival.[2] He was delighted with London, perhaps because it was as he had expected it to be. He told Cazalis (after admitting that the fog was asphyxiating, and he had been swindled out of forty francs, and called a fool by the magistrates into the bargain) what it was that he liked:

Nous demeurons dans un square qui donne dans Coventry Street. J'ai Londres à deux pas, et, ici, je suis en province. Je n'entends pas un chat—mais, en revanche, c'est le rendez-vous de tous les orgues de barbarie, les singes en casquette rouge, les nègres gratteurs de guitare, les bandes du Lancashire; Polichinelle y donne chaque jour une représentation. Je suis une averse de pence et de farthings, mais aussi que de joie, et que j'aime cela. Je gronde Marie parce qu'en fille sage et grande elle n'admire pas Polichinelle. Si tu voyais notre chambre! Nous nous sommes montés un vrai ménage anglais, si bien que je sens déjà le besoin d'écrire à mon notaire. Je lis, j'écris, elle brode, tricote, et quitte à chaque instant son ouvrage pour venir m'embrasser, me caresser, et me dire des choses bleues. Mets des théières et des pots à bière avec un grand lit au second étage du paradis, et tu as notre chambre.

J'aime ce ciel toujours gris, on n'a pas besoin de penser. L'azur et les étoiles effrayent. On est chez soi, ici, et Dieu ne vous voit pas. Son espion le soleil n'ose y ramper.[3]

Marie too wrote to Cazalis, whose knowledge of the German language was helping to make him on slight acquaintance her good friend. Her impressions of London were less favourable than Stéphane's. She could never grow accustomed to the dark, dismal clouds, and the fog that engulfed you and crept in everywhere and made the house so dark that you had to keep the lamp lit all day. What she did like was evenings together at home.[4]

She found it more difficult than Stéphane to banish uneasy thoughts about their precarious situation. He was rather put out by this, and said so in a postscript which he added to her letter:

Elle a été souffrante et elle a encore fort mal à l'estomac. Joins à cela qu'étant désœuvrée elle pense beaucoup à Camberg, à sa famille qu'elle n'oserait revoir si l'on se doutait de rien, à son père qui ignore encore son séjour à Londres. Tu sais combien elle est impressionnable; ses maux d'estomac qui sont purement des indigestions lui font croire qu'elle est enceinte. Sur cela, elle pleure. Voilà de quoi me chagriner beaucoup n'est-ce pas: et cette semaine a été fort pénible pour moi.[5]

Less so than for Marie, one may be sure. Stéphane was perhaps right in thinking that it was for want of something to do that she fretted, but he might have added also that she was too often alone, for a reason she could not find reassuring. He had Cazalis to think of, as well as her. The Yapps were still in London, and without their knowing of her existence Stéphane must call on them as they expected. His duty to friend Henri required that he should send him news of them as often as he could.[6] During the first week in London he went to see them at least three times, and he found pleasant company in the person of Ettie's elder sister. He so reported to Cazalis in the letter of 14 November:

Lundi, Kate seule était à la maison. J'ai passé la soirée avec elle et le frère de Miss Mary. Elle est ce que tu me l'as peinte, *forte* dans toute l'extension et dans tous les sens du mot. Elle arrivait le matin de Brighton. Je jouerai souvent avec elle comme on met un lambeau de pourpre devant les grilles d'une jungle. Cela m'amusera.[7]

So not all the evenings that Marie looked forward to were spent with Stéphane in their second-floor paradise. Perhaps significantly, it was on his return home after a visit to Katie that Marie told him she must leave him and go back to France.[8]

That was on the third of December: they had been in London less than a month. Stéphane's letter to Cazalis announcing this development, written on 4 and 5 December, is a curious document. It consists of three long gushes of lamentation, of which the tenor probably quite pleased Henri, relieving his uneasiness on both Stéphane's and Marie's account; from a friend's point of view, it was so much better that they should part. The manner of writing, on the other hand, he must have found disconcerting. Not only was such a display of emotion out of character.[9] The style in which the emotion was expressed was quite extraordinary in its tearfulness. The early part of the letter is so bestrewn with references to Stéphane's weeping that one is reminded of his first love-note to Marie, with its counterfeit stains. It may be that the epistolary tears are no less spurious, and that the letter or some part of it was intended to be read by Marie before it was dispatched to Paris. In the first page and a half of the printed text, the tears rain thick and fast:

O mon pauvre ami! j'ai tant pleuré depuis hier que j'en suis malade, et ma pauvre Marie n'a plus de larmes (. . .) Je pleure, je sanglote sans trêve. Elle, tâche de rester ferme devant moi pour ne point me peiner et va pleurer dehors (. . .) Je sanglote à la seule pensée de ne la plus sentir auprès de moi (. . .) Oh! je pleure, je pleure, mon pauvre ami, en t'écrivant tout cela! Je pleure depuis ce matin; je n'ai pas un instant de répit: dès que je la regarde, j'éclate.[10]

It is unlikely that Cazalis, reading his friend's outpourings when Marie decided to leave him, would make the unkind comparison with the seducer's *billet doux* of six months before.[11] He may well have remembered, however, that in a more recent letter Mallarmé had quite unashamedly, perhaps indeed boastfully, used the device of reported tears, with a view to the same effect though for a less cynical purpose. The letter itself was apparently judged, by its writer, too likely to give an impression of cool rationality, and it was to avoid that danger that a postscript was added. 'Ce que j'ai au cœur', it declared, 'je ne le raisonne pas; j'aime mieux pleurer, souvent'. And as if to suit the action to the word there followed a passage in the tear-drenched style of writing. So successful a demonstration of it indeed that its author decided not to waste its effect on his male correspondent, who received in its stead a note explaining that it had been removed, and why:

[Les larmes me coulaient le long] des joues et je t'ai écrit d'un trait tout le temps qu'elles ont coulé. Les larmes étaient pour Marie, les lignes que je griffonnais se sont trouvées être pour elle aussi.[12]

It seems very likely that the same was true of the tearful paragraphs in the letter from London of 4 and 5 December. They were intended to be read by Marie, and touch her heart, before the letter was sent to Cazalis.

That, however, was not all. The terms in the letter of December were charged also, and perhaps primarily, with another function. They had to salve the writer's conscience, which was sorely troubled. The tearful style gave a tender, generous colouring to a half-intention that was selfish and faithless. For the true purport of the letter was Stéphane's agreement to Marie's departure, and acceptance of their separation. It may seem at first reading that the writer is (to use his own expression) 'weeping instead of reasoning'. But in fact some cool reasoning does go on under the cover of tears. The letter argues in favour of Marie's decision by glorifying it with sobbing tributes to her virtue, her devotion to her lover, her noble selflessness. The argument is sketched tentatively at the beginning of the letter, as follows:

Juge ce que la pauvre enfant a dû souffrir et combien elle a d[û] penser, pour arriver, elle qui ne vit que par moi, à une telle résolution. Est-ce en songeant à elle qu'elle en est venue là? Est-ce en se rappelant que sa pauvre mère, qui l'aimait particulièrement, lui avait confié, l'an dernier, en mourant, ses plus jeunes sœurs? Est-ce en se disant que son père, qu'elle adore, la renierait et rougirait d'elle s'il la savait près de moi? Est-ce en pensant à sa vie que je brise chaque jour, à son honneur que j'efface heure par heure, elle chaste, honnête et qui ne se serait jamais douté autrefois de l'état où l'amour la conduirait? Non, mon ami, non, c'est pour moi, et elle me fait ce sacrifice comme elle m'a fait tous les autres. Elle voit que je suis pauvre—le notaire me manque de parole—et que la vie est dure: elle est navrée de voir que je me prive de tout. Elle voit que sa présence m'empêche de recevoir les personnes qui pourraient m'être utiles et que je suis forcé de me cacher d'elles. Elle a deviné—et cela est—que ma mère était informée de tout en ce moment, et elle a craint de me mettre mal avec ma famille. Alors, elle s'est dit "Je suis de trop ici. Je vais, après lui avoir tout sacrifié, sacrifier encore le bonheur que j'ai d'être avec lui; ma vie!"

Et rien ne peut l'ébranler (. . .) Je n'ose vraiment, moi qui me sens déjà à moitié mort de douleur, la dissuader. Ce serait de l'égoïsme, Henri. Qui sait? il n'y a peut-être rien de perdu jusqu'ici pour elle. Son père ne sait encore rien, ni les personnes qui la connaissent. Elle peut encore se présenter le front haut quelque part, ce qu'elle ne pourrait plus plus tard (. . .) il me semble que le devoir me commande de la laisser partir avant qu'il ne soit plus temps. Horreur! je dois être mon propre bourreau! (. . .)

Ce qu'elle endure en son cœur pour pouvoir, malgré mes larmes et mes baisers, ne pas fléchir dans sa résolution, est effrayant. A sa p[â]leur je vois qu'il y a en elle des luttes affreuses! Pauvre Marie! Mon ami, elle a poussé le dévouement et le sacrifice jusqu'à ses dernières limites. Elle fait plus que de se tuer pour moi. Elle est grande, sainte: je ne devrais parler d'elle qu'à genoux.[13]

'Et rien ne peut l'ébranler', he declared. But did he really try to persuade her, with facts and arguments instead of tears and kisses? Did he tell her, as he told Cazalis later in strict confidence, that he was not poor as she supposed, but quite well-off?[14] And that whatever his stepmother had learned of their affair, she did not know that Marie was with him in London?[15] Above all, did he renew his promise to marry her? It seems clear that he was careful not to do so.[16] Even to Cazalis, in the first half of this intimate letter of some 2,500 words, the only mention of marriage is this hypocritical-sounding bid for Henri's complicity, unlikely to be refused:

Et moi, que faire? Conseille moi, mon frère. Après qu'elle s'est toute sacrifiée à moi, il y a de la lâcheté, n'est-ce pas? à l'abandonner ainsi, seule—avec des remords, peut-être,—à la laisser ainsi briser toute sa vie! Et d'un autre côté, en me sacrifiant—comme elle s'est sacrifiée pour moi—c'est-à-dire en ouvrant guerre ouverte à ma famille, je ne

me sacrifie pas seul. Mon père et mon grand père ne survivraient point à ce qu'ils ne comprendraient pas. Suis-je maître de ces vies là[?]
Oh! enseigne moi un moyen de me sacrifier seul à elle![17]

In the second section of the letter, written on the following day, the subject is approached more directly but still in guarded terms, and as if Marie's noble silence concerning his promise of marriage was a kind of absolution annulling it. I doubt, however, whether this part of the letter too was to be read by Marie. It was probably intended for Henri and himself:

Écoute combien elle est noble et délicate. Outre qu'elle ne m'a jamais adressé un reproche, et que, quand je la regardais tristement, elle me disait parfois "Crois-tu que je t'aime moins? tu me perdrais à jamais que je ne te reprocherais jamais rien, même en pensée", elle ne m'a jamais dit un mot de ces imprudentes conversations où je lui parlais de mariage. La pauvre âme souriait mélancoliquement, mais au fond n'y croyait pas. Hier, avant-hier, ce matin, elle aurait pu me dire "Mais—tu m'avais dit que nous nous marierions, si tu le pouvais, un jour:" et, bien que je ne lui aie parlé de cela qu'après que le voyage de Londres fut convenu, et que, par conséquent, cela ne fût pour rien dans sa décision, elle aurait pu en souffler une parole, elle s'est tû [*sic*]. J'ai même vu à l'expression de ses yeux et de son visage qu'elle n'y a pas pensé une minute. Oh! que c'est grand et beau! Tout ce qu'il y a de trésors dans ce cœur personne ne le saura jamais.[18]

Cazalis, of course, welcomed wholeheartedly Marie's decision and Stéphane's acceptance of it. His reply appears to have gone astray; he had sent it to Panton Square, not knowing that they had moved. But he obtained from Des Essarts (who had it from Anne Mallarmé) their new address, 16 Albert Terrace, Knightsbridge,[19] and wrote again, on 24 December. But now his letter was mainly devoted to bitter reflections on Ettie, who was too busy with amateur dramatics and other childish, bluestocking games to write to him and send him her photograph. He railed against the Yapp family, and more generally the national characteristics of the English ('de continuels mensonges, d'éternelles injustices, d'impitoyables duretés, un implacable égoïsme, une cupidité sans mesure and enfin une générale et immense hypocrisie'). He did however turn for a moment from these preoccupations to give Stéphane the advice he was counting on:

Je crois qu'il faut vous résigner tous deux, mon Stéphane, à cette grande douleur: il le faut pour vous deux et il faut que tu ne sois pas toujours lâche. Un malheur pourrait vous perdre, et j'y pense parfois, et j'en ai souvent peur: qu'elle soit enceinte demain, que devenez-vous tous les trois? Ce qu'elle t'a dit était d'une inspiration sublime, une sainte inspiration de son cœur: il faut la suivre, et je regrette beaucoup que ce ne soit pas fait encore. Sache-le, mon bon Stéphane, s'il faut qu'elle parte, elle doit partir, tout de suite, et il faut qu'elle parte. Je ne comprends pas que tu n'aies pas vu que ce qu'elle te disait était vrai, que tu la perdais pour toujours en restant avec elle, que tu la sauvais, que tu pouvais la sauver encore en lui permettant de te quitter. Oui, je comprends quelle douleur pour toi: mais quelle douleur plus grande si tu la voyais brisée par toi, par la colère de son père, qui est chose grande en Allemagne.[20]

Henri's regret that they were still together is not surprising. He might well suppose, from Stéphane's letter, that Marie's departure was imminent. Perhaps she had first to find employment in Paris. Whatever the reason, she stayed on for over a month, during which time presumably their way of life remained unchanged. On the Feast of Stephen, Boxing Day, Stéphane went to a party at the Yapps', and sent Henri a tantalizing description of Ettie at her most angelic:

Je quitte le brouillard pour le ciel, le gris pour le bleu. Vendredi soir, il y a eu une charmante petite soirée chez les Yapp. Ah! que tu manquais! Ettie était, comme toujours, d'une simplicité adorable: elle faisait les honneurs d'une façon à vous emparadiser dans chacune de ses questions. L'absence de crinoline outrée, sa délicieuse robe brune montante, qui découpait excellemment sa taille grecque, tout cela, et de plus la fierté douce et la bonté profonde de son regard bleu sombre, lui donnait l'air d'une séraphine qui se serait fait [*sic*] quakeresse et se souviendrait du ciel. Quakeresse est un peu fort: cela serait vrai si les quakers avaient pour tremblement le frisson des étoiles. Elle m'a dit si cordialement, quand nous étions seuls: "Si Monsieur Cazalis vous parle de moi et pour moi, vous me le direz, n'est-ce pas[?]" A quoi je lui ai répondu que cent fois oui et que ce serait le soir même de sa lettre.[21]

The parting between Marie and Stéphane took place a fortnight later, but not in London. They crossed the Channel together on 9–10 January, in very stormy weather, and spent a last fond weekend recovering at Boulogne.[22] Then Marie took the midnight train to Paris, where Cazalis was to meet her (and she was to hand him a contraband copy of Hugo's *Châtiments*).[23] Stéphane's boat left Boulogne an hour later than Marie's train, and when he wrote to Cazalis two days later he described the state of mind in which he went aboard after bidding her goodbye:

Puis j'ai gagné mon bateau en cognant les murs du port de ma tête comme un ivrogne. Henri, le convoi n'était pas parti. Pendant cet horrible trajet qui fut mon calvaire, je l'ai entendu siffler deux fois. J'ai encore ce sifflet[-]là dans la tête, il me harcèle. Il n'y a pas de fer froid qui en m'entrant dans le cœur m'e[û]t fait ce mal-là.

Oh! j'ai senti alors pour la première fois, devant cette ombre immense du ciel et cette mer d'encre, moi, pauvre enfant abandonné par tout ce qui fut ma vie et mon idéal, combien était vaste ce mot *seul*.[24]

His main concern in this letter however was not to bewail their separation. It was to retract the arguments on which his agreement to it was founded, those he had woefully but diligently put together when Marie first declared that they must part. While she was still by his side, for nearly a month, he had presumably abided by them, since part they did. But two days of actual separation had demolished the case he had argued in its favour. Not without some histrionics of the kind that Henri liked, and even tears from time to time (used now for weeping, not for devious thought), Stéphane examined his conscience anew and told his friend calmly and honestly what he now saw very clear-sightedly to be the truth:

Et comment se fait-il qu'elle soit loin de moi et qu'elle soit vivante? Voilà le crime. C'est parce que je l'ai trompée. J'ai des remords, mon ami. La première fois que je lui ai parlé de Londres, elle se laissait dire par moi—c'était à Fontainebleau—que je l'épouserais. Je sais bien qu'elle n'y comptait pas et qu'elle disait "Je t'aime, voilà tout!" Mais cependant je devais tenir ma promesse.

Quand, un jour, elle a senti que nous ne pourrions vivre plus longtemps ensemble de la sorte sans nous nuire à tous deux, elle s'est généreusement sacrifiée et moi j'ai accepté le sacrifice comme un lâche. C'est alors que je l'ai trompée. Quand même je ne l'eusse plus aimée, je devais me sacrifier et l'épouser. Je le devais, Henri; dis oui, car tu es honnête. Or, je l'aimais, et j'avais non pas à me sacrifier, mais à l'empêcher de se sacrifier, et à faire son bonheur en faisant le mien.

Et j'ai reculé, et j'ai hésité, parce qu'il y avait à lutter et que cela serait difficile! (. . .)

Je me regarde comme un mauvais père qui a abandonné sa fille.

Non, cela ne sera pas. Je vais lui [é]crire, et elle va revenir. C'est assez de ce dernier sacrifice; il est sublime, car elle l'a fait sans savoir si elle me reverrait jamais. Je vais la récompenser; elle va venir chercher sa couronne de martyre. Elle a tant souffert jusqu'ici en se donnant à moi, car elle avait toutes les délicatesses. Et moi, je n'ai fait que jouir de cela. A mon tour maintenant de lutter, de souffrir s'il le faut. (. . .) Nous allons nous marier: ce sera cela de gagné, et après cela, nous lutterons. Je suis sûr que ceux qui d'abord seront contre elle l'aimeront. Est-ce que ce que je fais là, Henri, n'est pas noble? et le désavoues-tu? me renies-tu?

Je suis ton conseil, mon ami. Dans une lettre de toi que j'ai toujours gardée, tu me disais: "Fais l'essai du mariage, et, si tu l'aimes toujours, tu l'épouseras". Or, chaque jour je l'ai plus aimée. Chaque jour je découvrais un trait noble de plus en elle, chaque jour mettait une plume de plus à ses ailes d'ange. Son dernier sacrifice est sa dernière épreuve. Je l'épouserai. Sois sûr que, de toutes les luttes que j'aurai à soutenir pour cela, je suis assez gentilhomme, étant poète, pour me tirer noblement et sans une faute. Henri, va auprès de Marie, dis-lui tout cela: encourage[-]la. Sois moi auprès d'elle. Que dirais-tu si je l'abandonnais? Et quand tu m'objecterais que c'est me sacrifier à elle que de l'épouser—ce qui n'est pas, tu le sais—ne dois-je pas le faire? Telle est la voix de mon honneur: c'est ce que dit ma conscience. La tienne, ami, ne te parle-t-elle pas ainsi?[25]

This acknowledgement of Marie's deserts, and his own duty towards her on that account, is too long-winded to ring altogether true. The duty of 'sacrificing himself' by marrying her might be as clear to him as he said, but he viewed it with some reluctance. The idea that he would be marrying below his station was not easily dismissed, for all his insistence on duty. There is irresolution, and a half-invitation to Cazalis to disagree with his high purpose, in the question: 'Et quand tu m'objecterais que c'est me sacrifier que de l'épouser—ce qui n'est pas, tu le sais—ne dois-je pas le faire?' Cazalis was more than willing to express a contrary opinion. No, he wrote, it was not Stéphane's duty to marry the girl who had sacrificed herself to him. No, he had not deceived her, for Passion does not deceive: 'C'est la Vie qui nous trompe, qui nous promet la joie, puis nous rit au nez.'[26] But the argument that Henri used to clinch his case was ill-chosen. Coming down from abstract rhetoric to practical matters, he urged Stéphane to look at the facts. He and Marie could not wed, because neither had the money needed to bear the expense of married life. But that was not really so. The facts as Stéphane knew them, and must now acknowledge them to be, made his duty clear. Calmly, and even with a hint of complacency, he revealed his true financial position:

Mon enfant, tu as raison, car tu supposes que je suis pauvre : mais je ne le suis pas. Depuis une première lettre où je te disais que le notaire m'avait abandonné, j'ai reçu de lui exactement mon argent. Henri, je parle ici avec des chiffres, sache la vérité : je reçois à Londres de 3600 à 4000 f par an—j'ai ici un appartement de 1200 f—Combien d'employés mariés à quarante ans n'ont pas plus! Au mois de Mars, le 19, je touche 20 000 francs.[27] Cela me mènera bien jusqu'au jour où je serai professeur. Alors je joindrai cette petite rente à mon traitement. Mon grand père et ma grand mère *m'amassent une assez jolie fortune*, et mon père a de NOMBREUSES propriétés dont quelque chose me reviendra. Tu vois que Beaucoup seront plus pauvres que nous.

Nous n'avons été dans la charmante misère dont tu parles à Londres que quand, comme de vrais moineaux étourdis, nous avions fait mille petites folies au commencement du mois. (. . .)

Tu peux donc le dire à Marie à qui je n'avais jamais voulu parler d'argent.[28] Du reste, comme on ne s'entend pas par lettres, j'en causerai avec vous un de ces jours. (. . .)

Adieu, embrasse ma Marie dont les lettres sont sublimes. C'est un ange.[29]

The visit that Stéphane promised ('J'en causerai avec vous [i.e. Marie et toi] un de ces jours') took place a few days later. He went to Paris for a single day, probably Monday 26 January,[30] and seems, from the little we know, to have done none of the things we may suppose he intended to do. Instead of 'talking things over with them', and winning Henri over to the idea that Marie and he should now be wed, he actually promised under oath that he would not ask her to return to London. Marie herself (perhaps this was part of the oath) he did not even see, though she was only 'five minutes away'.[31] Instead, he went with Henri to spend the evening with the Yapps, also newly arrived.[32]

However, this weakening of his resolve while in Henri's company was short-lived. Once he was back in London and

alone, his sense of duty was restored. Heroically so, in his own esteem:

Mon bon Henri, voici deux jours que je suis arrivé. (. . .)

Je ne puis plus pleurer: je me suis mis à réfléchir longuement et voici ce que j'ai à faire. (. . .)

Je pensais cette nuit à la mère de Marie. Comme cette morte, si les morts nous voient, doit me maudire d'avoir *défloré* son enfant et de la jeter avec les vieux bouquets.

Ce ne sont pas l[à] des mots: le devoir existe.

Or je sens que le mien est de ne pas abandonner Marie. (. . .)

Ce n'est donc pas en aveugle que je l'épouserai, mais avec la fierté de celui qui obéit à sa conscience.

Je sens mon sacrifice, il est entier, immense,—mais je le *dois* faire. (. . .) Je le dois et je le ferai. Et je serai fier, parce que, sans fausse modestie cela est beau et rare. Je sais que je fais une chose noble. Si tu savais, mots à part, comme cela fait du bien. Tu me relèves de mon serment, n'est-ce pas?

J'écris à Marie qu'elle revienne, sans lui parler de mariage, exprès, parce qu'elle ne consentirait pas, autrement.

Si tu savais comme je sens déjà une joie aurorale illuminer ma conscience: oui, le bien existe. J'ai eu bien des petitesses, j'ai fait de vilaines choses jusqu'ici, cela me relève. J'aurai les morts,—ma mère, ma sœur—qui voient les choses de haut, et mes amis, qui me comprennent, pour moi: c'est assez.[33]

Here was a style to which Cazalis was partial. Also, he was caught in a sanguine mood, as his relations with Ettie had suddenly improved after the misunderstanding. He was prepared to raise anew Stéphane's drama of duty and sacrifice to an exalted, Cornelian plane. He withdrew his opposition to Marie's returning to London, and apologized for his previous objections: 'Oui fais ce que dois, et sois fier de ton âme. (. . .) Ta parole t'est rendue: et j'ai honte de te l'avoir prise. Tu as atteint si haut que je suis jaloux de toi.'[34] But when this admiring acquiescence reached London, Stéphane's noble plan was in disarray. He had received an answer from Marie, and she had refused. 'La seule chose belle que je pusse peut-être faire au monde jamais, elle m'a empêché de la faire. Pourquoi? pourquoi? pourquoi? . . . ' Such was his complaint to Cazalis, in a letter that describes the thoughts and feelings, of chagrin, dismay, outrage, self-pity, and self-derision, which assailed him. He had resolved to act with a noble generosity, and

here was Marie, a mere woman, seeming to outdo him in nobility:

Mon ami, Marie refuse. Je ne puis croire qu'elle le fasse avec désintéressement. Elle se figure que ce mariage ne vaudrait rien sans doute. Non, je ne puis croire à tant de sublime chez une femme. (. . .) Non, la plus noble des femmes ne vaut pas un homme. Peut-être est-elle trop sublime. Mais c'est niais d'être trop sublime.[35]

The following day, after further searching, he was still asking why, and the sense of his questioning was becoming clearer. He was rigorously applying to Marie's conduct the criterion of self-sacrifice:

Tâche de voir *pourquoi* elle n'a pas voulu venir se marier. Et, si tu ne vois pas cela, demande-lui comme une question indifférente *si elle reviendrait bien ici sans que je l'épousasse*? Par ce qu'elle te répondra à cela, je verrai jusqu'où va son désintéressement. Car ce doute m'accable. Demande-lui cette dernière chose surtout, sans avoir l'air de vouloir la faire revenir. Ce sera là ma pierre de touche.[36]

The fanatical persistence with which he pressed these abstruse questions, worthy of a medieval court of love, forced Cazalis to react sharply on Marie's behalf. Perhaps he realized that Stéphane was pushing to its furthest limit, beyond all reason, the test of Marie's worthiness to be his wife. On 14 January he had written: 'Son dernier sacrifice est sa dernière épreuve. Je l'épouserai', but he had now become more exacting, as will be seen. It was at this juncture that Cazalis showed himself at his best, and perhaps in the truest light, as Stéphane's faithful and patient comrade and at the same time Marie's protector and advocate, fair-minded and humane: to both, a true friend in need. What his letters tell of Marie's sentiments and behaviour amounts to an eloquent and convincing tribute to her selfless devotion. He replied on 5 February to Stéphane's letter of the day before and upbraided him for his inhumanity as an elder brother might:

Mon Stéphane, tu m'épouvantes: tu es fou. Je viens de voir Marie: elle est sublime, et tu la tueras si tu continues. Oui, elle reviendrait, pour toi et non pour elle. Elle me l'a dit, dit avec une admirable passion; et tu as douté d'elle! Si elle t'a refusé le mariage, c'est pour toi: c'est pour qu'un jour, toi *si jeune*, tu n'aies pas à regretter d'avoir fait si noblement ton devoir, tu n'aies pas en un mot à la moins aimer.

Si elle ne t'a pas répondu, c'est qu'elle est morte aujourd'hui, toute étendue, toute brisée par toi, par ta lettre qui l'a accablée. *Elle est à ta discrétion*: tu feras d'elle ce que tu voudras. (. . .) mais en ce moment, mon Stéphane, tu n'es pas un homme. Tu es livré à ton mauvais génie: tu as la passion de l'enfant, non celle de l'homme: et tu veux te marier.[37]

The long reply that Stéphane sent by return of post showed no relenting, no sign that on his side of the argument too, feeling had got the better of calculation. With pedantic obstinacy he made it still clearer that what he required, and was still not satisfied he had received, was proof of Marie's absolute 'uncalculating' love. It appears that—for reasons he expounds, not very convincingly—he had not even promised to marry her if she returned:

Au lieu de lui dire: "Marie, viens que je t'épouse!" je lui ai dit, sachant qu'à cette première prière elle m'eût répondu non, et voulant après tout le sacrifice que je faisais pour elle voir si elle m'aimait à se perdre entièrement pour moi, je lui ai dit: "Marie, viens auprès de moi et sois encore ce que tu étais auparavant, mon bon ange, sans être ma femme." Je me disais: "Par noblesse et générosité, elle refuse de se marier, mais elle ne refusera pas de se perdre. Il y a l[à] un sacrifice d'elle-même à faire, il y a à se jeter dans un abîme pour moi,—elle n'hésitera pas—." Or, elle m'a répondu non.[38]

He would, he said, leave it to her to decide whether, and on what conditions, she would return. He enumerated the courses open to her. She might: (i) stay in Paris, (ii) come to London to talk things over, (iii) come back to him unconditionally, or (iv) come back to get married. Cazalis tried once more to reason with him:

Non, tu n'as pas un reproche à faire à Marie: il n'y a pas, comme tu le crois, à choisir entre trois ou quatre décisions: il faut qu'elle soit ta femme ou qu'elle reste. (. . .) Marie, avant[-]hier n'a pas cessé de me le répéter: elle veut te sauver, te sent trop jeune, a peur, mon Stéphane, de te prendre ta vie, fût-ce même pour l'entourer d'amour; elle sent que ton sacrifice est trop grand; et elle t'aime, et ne veut pas de ton sacrifice. (. . .) Je vais la voir: et si elle persiste dans son très noble refus, je l'admire encore et je me tais. Si elle veut partir, je ne la retiens pas et elle te rejoint demain.[39]

But he did not see her. Undecided until the very last moment, and perhaps not daring to face another discussion with Cazalis, Marie stole away and returned to London. Stéphane wrote on 10 February: 'Ma Marie est arrivée ce matin; toute malade. (. . .) Je suis dans l'extase de la voir, voilà tout ce que je sais. (. . .) Écris à Emmanuel: gagne-le à elle, à moi, à nous—de sorte que, dans l'abandon, je puisse encore compter sur son approbation comme sur la tienne.'[40] Which seems to mean that he was ready, if necessary, to risk being disowned by his family.

Yet though reunited, they still remained unmarried, no doubt to Marie's private dismay. On 5 March Stéphane wrote to Cazalis to tell him that she had left him once more:

Mon bon Henri, je suis seul. Marie est partie hier pour Bruxelles. Tout est fini. Je sens que je ne la reverrai plus jamais. Pourtant elle était ma sœur et ma femme. (. . .)

Nous étions convenus que nous aurions beaucoup de courage: et en effet, nous nous sommes longtemps embrassés et regardés sur le bateau sans pouvoir pleurer tellement nous étions fous de douleur. Longtemps nous avons agité nos deux mouchoirs, et, quand je n'ai plus vu le sien, j'ai sangloté à travers les rues. (. . .)

Je crois que nous avons fait, ou que nous faisons—car je ne puis dire que je l'aie fait encore—un des plus grands sacrifices qui se soient vus. Plein[s] de vie et d'amour, à l'instant où nous sommes plus unis que jamais, étant une même chair comme une même âme, nous séparer et nous vouer à l'oubli, violemment. A qui faisons-nous ce sacrifice? A ma famille qui, si elle me parlait de Marie, la calomnierait. (. . .)

Marie est partie bien malade et la poitrine très oppressée; elle est méconnaissable. Je crois que le chagrin la tuera. Dans ce cas, je la suivrais, et c'est ce qui serait le plus heureux pour nous deux.

Ne pouvant être unis ici, il est presque sûr que nous le serons autre part.

Tu vois, pauvre fou que je suis, je ne puis me résoudre à ne pas espérer. Ne pouvant plus le faire pour cette vie, je le fais pour une autre.[41]

This was the letter Stéphane later described as 'une longue lettre, où je pleurais à mon aise'. Cazalis did not reply to it. There was nothing for him to say that he had not urged before, in vain. Besides which, overburdened with misfortunes of his own, he was about to leave Paris and seek relief from love's sickness in a long stay at Strasbourg, far from Ettie. No more letters passed between the two friends for nearly a month, and the silence coincided with a change in Stéphane's situation which, together with Henri's departure, can be considered as bringing to a close the first phase of their friendship, in which the bond so rapidly formed between them had proved its worth. By active assistance as well as sympathy and understanding, and from Henri salutary advice, they had served each other loyally. Their intimacy had matured as their mutual respect and trust had been confirmed. Since they were destined to live far from each other for some years still, and seldom meet, their relations continued perforce to be embodied in a written correspondence most of which, very fortunately, has survived. It would quickly change its character, however, as literature, and thoughts of the kind on which literature thrives, established their rightful ascendancy over problems of the heart.

Its temporary suspension in March 1863, marking the first lull in their exchanges, was broken by Mallarmé, writing on the first of April not from London but (for reasons he explained) from Versailles. Des Essarts had given him Henri's address at Strasbourg, together with news just received from him, the first since his departure. It appeared that all was over between him and Ettie. In consequence, Stéphane began his own letter with the gentlest of reproaches, quickly dispelled by expressions of affectionate commiseration. A quiet, succinct account of the changed state of his own affairs followed:

Oui, pauvre ami, tu as été cacher ta blessure bien loin!

Et tu ne veux donc pas que même tes amis en voient la traînée sanglante car tu souris dans ta lettre [a letter sent to Des Essarts] et tu affectes la sérénité. Je t'ai compris, Henri. (. . .)

Parle-moi de ton âme. Songes-tu encore à la blanche vision qui l'a traversée? Lui as-tu élevé une petite chapelle dans ton souvenir, où tu puisses l'adorer comme un Rêve que la fatalité sociale te défend d'étreindre? . . . Ou as-tu rompu même avec le souvenir? (. . .)

Quant à moi, je suis comme il y a trois mois—ou plutôt, non, j'ai une résolution. J'épouse Marie. Cela se fera peut-être avant Mai. J'ai assez réfléchi—trop, même: je n'avais pas besoin de tant.

En venant à Paris,—a Sens,—pour affaires de famille,[42] je suis passé par Bruxelles où je n'ai eu que le temps d'embrasser la chère enfant.

Ma mère sait tout. J'ignore comment. La seule chose qu'elle n'ait pas apprise est que Marie a été à Londres: tant mieux. Je lui ai avoué, pressé de questions amicales, que si elle ne m'en eût pas parlé, j'aurais épousé Marie sans le lui dire. Elle se croit obligée, par devoir, de dire quelques mots à ma grand mère pour que la nouvelle, tombant des nues, de mon mariage ne la saisisse pas trop. Elle vient ce matin à Versailles et je verrai avec elle jusqu'où elle doit parler. Après, elle semblerait disposée à nous laisser marier silencieusement, et feindrait, je crois, de ne l'apprendre que par lettres; c'est bien bon de sa part.

La pauvre femme montre en cela une délicatesse inouie et une grande amitié. J'ai été souvent ingrat envers elle, et l'ai méconnue: elle était sous l'influence inquisitrice de ma grand mère, voilà tout. Les hommes sont brutaux.[43]

This acknowledgement of his debt to Anne Mallarmé was certainly overdue. But her stepson did not yet realize, perhaps, even now, how much he owed to her good offices and forethought. As to his grandmother, whatever her first reaction may have been to the news of Stéphane's intended marriage, all her love and compassion responded to the sudden misfortune that had delayed his return to London. She announced it to Mélanie Laurent on 13 April, with details of his reasons for being in France. Without revealing the nature of the latest and deepest disappointment she had suffered on Stéphane's account, she confessed that he was in great need of their prayers:

Chère Mélanie, j'ai de bien tristes nouvelles à t'apprendre, car notre pauvre cher Stéphane est maintenant complètement orphelin, son pauvre père a été enlevé Dimanche par une nouvelle congestion, mortelle cette fois. Par une suite de circonstances vraiment providentielles, le cher enfant avait dû venir en France, pour assister à la révision, où il a été réformé, ce qui n'était pas un grand avantage, ayant été assuré d'avance.[44] Ses 21 ans étant accomplis, on avait profité de son séjour pour régler ses comptes de tutelle; toutes ces formalités terminées, il avait quitté Sens Vendredi, laissant son père assez bien, quoiqu'un peu faible, ce qu'on attribuait à la saison. Prêt à partir Samedi de Paris pour Londres, une dépêche l'a rappelé en toute hâte, son père venait d'être frappé à l'instant. Arrivé près de lui, il l'a bien retrouvé encore, mais sans sa connaissance, paraît-il, et [il] s'est étaint Dimanche (. . .)

Voilà donc notre pauvre enfant privé de ce dernier appui, qui, tout frêle qu'il était, servait pourtant de lien à la famille. Certes, sa belle-mère est excellente, mais elle se doit à ses propres enfants[.] Stéphane, ayant ce qui lui revient légitimement n'a plus *droit de chez lui*, au nom de la loi, et ne peut le tenir que de sa bienveillance; enfin, ce n'est plus ce refuge paternel, où tous les enfants sont égaux. Il lui faut donc redoubler d'efforts, ou plutôt commencer à les faire sérieusement, pour se créer une carrière, et son caractère à la fois apathique et confiant est un grand obstacle. Prie donc pour lui, avec sa pauvre mère et nous, chère Mélanie, il en a bien plus besoin qu'on ne peut le supposer.[45]

His father's death kept Stéphane at Sens for another week or so before he went to join Marie at Brussels and take her to London. On the way back he appears to have spent at least a day in Paris and called on the Yapps. Between Brussels and London he and Marie went on what he called 'a pilgrimage' to Antwerp. They were in London by 27 April. The authority for these fragments of information is the letter to Cazalis bearing that date and a new address, 6 Brompton Square.[46] It is mainly devoted to explaining the marriage that Cazalis had persistently advised against, and Stéphane had himself—partly no doubt for the same reasons—so long delayed. Marie had passed the sacrificial test, and Stéphane's turn had now come. There was reason and responsibility in what he wrote, but in a letter to Henri the subject called for some heroics too:

Dès que je saurai comment m'y prendre, nous serons mariés. Position étrange, il ne nous manque qu'une chose,—c'est d'être instruits des formalités.

Le voilà donc venu, mon bon Henri, ce jour que, dans ta fraternelle sollicitude, tu redoutais. Oui, il est assez près pour que je voie clairement ce qu'il y a derrière. Depuis deux mois, j'ai beaucoup plus vécu qu'autrefois, et peut-être suis-je un peu plus mûr.

Voici la façon dont je vois l'avenir.

Si j'épousais Marie pour faire mon bonheur, je serais un fou.

D'ailleurs, le bonheur existe-t-il sur cette terre? Et faut-il le chercher, *sérieusement*, autre part que dans le Rêve? C'est le faux but de la vie; le vrai est le Devoir. Le Devoir, qu'il s'appelle l'Art, la Lutte, ou comme on veut.

Je ne me dissimule pas que j'aurai affreusement à combattre parfois—et de grands désenchantements qui deviennent plus tard des tortures. Je ne me cache rien. Seulement, je veux tout voir avec un regard ferme, et invoquer un peu cette Volonté dont je n'ai jamais connu que le nom.

Non, j'épouse Marie uniquement parce que je sais que sans moi elle ne pourrait pas vivre, et que j'aurais empoisonné sa limpide existence.

Si donc je souffre dans l'avenir, toi, qui seul reçois ces épanchements profonds et intimes de mon cœur, ne me dis pas, frère—"Tu t'es trompé, en dépit de mes sages exhortations." mais bien: "Tu accomplis, en souffrant, le but élevé que tu as assigné à ta vie,—Courage, ne reste pas au-dessous." (. . .)

Non, Henri, je n'agis pas pour moi—mais pour elle seulement. Toi seul au monde sauras que je fais un sacrifice: aux yeux de mes autres amis, je ferai semblant de croire que je cherche dans cette union à échafauder mon bonheur,—afin que Marie grandisse à leurs yeux.

Brûle mes lettres, toi seul verras jusqu'au fond de mon âme.[47]

In the event, he was to be spared the dire misfortunes so stoically awaited. Indeed, it is not clear what consequences of his marriage he had to fear, now that there was no danger of his family disowning him.[48] Perhaps the histrionic posture should be understood as no more than an over-dramatized recognition that to marry was to dwindle—in his case rather early, it is true—into a husband. The context does suggest however a deeper significance, an awareness that to make Marie his wife, socially ineligible as she was in the eyes of his kith and kin though 'droite, pure, loyale, noble et dévouée' as from the first he had found her to be,[49] was part and token of the fundamental choice he was committing himself to, between the pursuit of material well-being and the nobler values and commitment of the artist. In his homage to Duty ('qu'il s'appelle l'Art, la Lutte, ou comme on veut'), the allusion to the Struggle is respectful to political ideals, but three months later, as if to make his own position in that regard clear, he returned to the subject and declared:

Tu sais que toutes mes illusions politiques se sont effacées une par une, et que si j'arbore un drapeau rouge c'est uniquement parce que je hais les gredins et déteste la force.

Henri, tu le verras, il n'y a de vrai, d'immuable, de grand, et de sacré, que l'Art.[50]

So the plans he had laid for his future at the beginning of the previous year remained virtually unaltered. Cazalis offered irresponsibly rosy suggestions about possible employment in Switzerland, but Mallarmé declined them gracefully and reasserted in plain terms the resolution that had brought him to London: 'La vie de professeur dans un Lycée est simple, modeste, calme. Nous y serons tranquilles; J'y vise.'[51]

Meanwhile, considered as a preparation for that peaceful future, the stay in London had not been well employed. Stéphane's domestic situation when Marie was with him, and his agitation on her account when she was not, had been altogether unfavourable to the task of 'perfecting' his knowledge of the English language. When Henri wrote enthusiastically of the friends he had made at Strasbourg, and urged Stéphane to seek out among the English poets 'ceux qui se rapprocheraient de Poe, les poètes au parfum puissant, mortel à certaines heures',[52] he replied dejectedly, with a touch of literary melancholy for the benefit of Henri's friends:

Heureux! Je t'envie bien, étant si seul ici. Je n'ai personne avec qui causer d'Art, des poètes, de l'Idéal. Je ne connais pas un artiste sérieux et jeune à Londres. Presse les mains à tes amis, que j'aimerais à ce seul titre, de la part d'un esprit bohémien toujours dégoûté de la pla[ce où] il a campé et qui voudrait se reposer dans leur calme et noble entretien.[53]

The self-portrait is unconvincing, but he was probably not exaggerating his isolation. It may well be that he was choosing his terms quite carefully. The one artist he is known to have had any conversation with during his nine months in England was a writer who was neither young nor 'serious'—in any likely sense of that word. He was a Frenchman, who settled in England for political reasons after 1830 and was naturalized British in 1848. His strongest claim to be considered an artist was his productivity as a translator of English poetry into poor French verse. Mallarmé mentioned him later, in a letter written from Tournon on 11 April 1864 to Albert Collignon, the editor of the ephemeral *Revue nouvelle*. 'Le Chevalier de Chatelain,' he wrote, 'mauvais poète français habitant Londres, m'a promis de s'abonner à la *Revue*, l'a-t-il fait?'[54] It is not known when exactly, or in what circumstances, Mallarmé made the acquaintance of Jean-Baptiste François Ernest Le Chatelain, of Castelnau Lodge, 20 Warwick Crescent, Westbourne Terrace Road, Paddington, calling himself in England 'le Chevalier de Chatelain'. The most likely possibility is that he had called on him with a letter of introduction from their mutual friend, Émile Deschamps.[55] For Mallarmé it was a fortunate meeting. The eccentric, well-to-do gentleman, forty years his senior, was to be a generous friend for nearly twenty years, and a considerable benefactor when he died in 1881.[56] It appears to have been during Marie's second absence, just before Stéphane's visit to Sens and Versailles 'on family business', in March 1863, that he discussed with Chatelain translations into French—including presumably their own—[57] of poems by Edgar Allan Poe. As a freak consequence of which, the name of Stéphane Mallarmé was made known to the best-known of all translators of Poe's tales by a letter dated 26 March and headed: 'Le Chevalier de Chatelain Correspondant des journaux étrangers à M. Charles Baudelaire'. It read as follows:

Monsieur,
Je n'ai pas l'honneur de vous connaître personnellement, mais grâce à un jeune ami,—Stéphane Mallarmé,—je viens de lire votre belle traduction des contes de Poe, et je l'admire beaucoup. Votre introduction dans le premier volume et vos notes nouvelles dans le second forment un travail très remarquable; et si ma bonne fortune me fait un jour faire votre connaissance personnelle—ce qui, hélas! est fort aléatoire—j'aimerais à causer à ce sujet avec vous longuement.

Aujourd'hui, voici le but de ma lettre, c'est de vous demander si vous voudriez bien échanger avec moi vos deux volumes contre ma traduction (2e édition) des "Beautés de la Poésie Anglaise" dans lesquelles se trouvent le *Raven* et les *Cloches* du grand poète?

Si vous aviez l'occasion de me faire passer votre ouvrage, je ferais en sorte de vous faire tenir le mien. En attendant, je copie *for your acceptance*, comme on dit ici, une traduction des cloches—que trouverez sous ce pli.

Agréez, Monsieur, l'assurance de ma haute considération.

Le Chevalier de Chatelain[58]

Whether Baudelaire replied, and whether he took note of the name Stéphane Mallarmé, are questions unlikely to be answered.

If the acquaintance with Chatelain was the fruit of one of the letters of introduction from Versailles, that letter was the exception. In general, Mallarmé appears to have been wary of using the recommendations that the Desmolins had collected for him.[59]

Truth to tell, such company as his grandparents had hoped he would seek, and even discussions with young and serious artists, were not essential to the task for which Stéphane was supposed to be in London, but congenial English company of some kind would surely have helped. Yet the only contacts of which there is any evidence are those with Chatelain, the Yapps before they went back to Paris (and with whom as with the Chevalier he may well have spoken French), and two friends of the Yapp girls who were sometimes with them when he called. They were Mary Green (the third young lady of the picnic at Fontainebleau, the 'Anglaise aux airs de reine A qui Diane porte un toast'),[60] and her brother. Stéphane seems not to have been interested in 'Miss Mary' ('Sicy' or 'Sissy'), but her brother he would have liked to see more of, if only for the sake of Cazalis who looked on him as a possible rival.[61] He hesitated to do so however, on account of Marie's presence in his life and his home:

Je n'ose voir le frère de *Sicy*: donne-moi ton avis. Je le connais peu, dois-je le mettre au courant de notre vie. Je ne peux lui ouvrir la porte de ma chambre sans lui ouvrir celle de la confiance. Si, dans la pruderie anglaise ou prenant Marie pour ce qu'elle n'est pas, il me perdait dans l'estime des Yapp! Je suis très-embarrassé.[62]

By the time summer came round, Stéphane and Marie had resumed their life together, peacefully and in good earnest. With the uncertainties of the winter months behind them and Stéphane's firm intent renewed, they seem to have been content to remain in their seclusion. Stéphane's letters to Cazalis were now less frequent, and more concerned with intellectual than personal matters, whether Henri's or their own. Apart from Des Essarts with whom there are signs that relations were improving,[63] friends are hardly so much as mentioned. In such glimpses of their own activities as the letters afford, no acquaintances appear. June was delightful, and they enjoyed its pleasures together as if in a world of their own:

Ne t'étonne pas de voir l'enveloppe de cette lettre [é]crite au crayon. Nous avons fait hier une magnifique promenade en bateau à travers les bois enchantés de Richmond, et nous voulions amar[r]er quelques instants et te dater une bonne lettre du tronc de quelque bouleau penché sur l'eau verte et sombre. Mais le courant nous a emportés. Depuis bien longtemps le courant m'emporte à travers les jours et je vis je ne sais comment.[64]

Perhaps they thought of Fontainebleau that day. Marie picked forget-me-nots to send to Henri, 'dans un de ces petits coins d'ombre et d'eau verte où Ophélia a d[û] se noyer' (but before she could send them, a stupid housemaid threw them away).[65]

July came, and made Stéphane homesick. He was physically ill also, and the examination was beginning to look near:

J'ai été malade, et, maintenant, j'ai énormément à travailler en vue de mes examens.—Malade, pas dangereusement, mais d'une façon ennuyeuse. Le soleil de Londres n'est pas ce gai soleil de Paris qui fait [é]clore le long des boulevards toute une verdure charmante de tables à bière et verse la gaîté dans sa lumière. Ici les rayons semblent avoir pris quelque chose de blafard aux pauvres murs d'hôpitaux où ils se sont endormis et dont ils ont chauffé le plâtre malade. L'air malsain se charge de toutes les exhalaisons de la misère que la lourde chaleur putrifie, et pour les pauvres, l'été n'est que la saison où la vermine, attiédie, grouille le plus dans leurs loques. Je hais Londres quand il n'y a pas de brouillards: dans ses brumes, c'est une ville incomparable. (. . .) Mon mal a été une éruption, et, depuis, je suis tout jaune—comme un envieux—comme un coing. Sang jaune, yeux jaunes, face jaune—et pensée jaune. Est-ce ennui? Est-ce appauvrissement du sang?[66]

It sounds like what the English would call shingles followed by jaundice. The trial year was taking its toll.

Mallarmé had of course formed his own opinion on 'les Anglais', or rather Londoners, seen in the mass. They were 'like the rooms at the Grand Hotel', they all looked alike.[67] Also, they were all snobs, even the labouring class:

Hier, cependant, je me suis rendu à un meeting populaire en faveur de la Pologne. Ce qui m'a surtout frappé c'est que tous ces ouvriers applaudissaient frénétiquement quand on les appelait gentlemen. Je n'aime pas les ouvriers: ils sont vaniteux.[68]

He called 'les Anglaises', Ettie excepted (he did not say on what experience he judged the others), 'ces anges de cuisine qui rêvent aux rayons de leurs casseroles, sans se douter de l'étoile Astarté'.[69]

The examination he had to sit for in August[70] is mentioned a second time in the same letter. He was thinking of it, and studying for it, as a matter of 'set books' rather than of the English language: 'c'est à grand peine que je puis préparer mon examen—Roméo et Juliet, pourtant!'[71] He intended to take

Marie to Paris as soon as they were married. That could not be before the tenth of August as the banns must be published first.

The wedding took place on that date as planned, in Kensington at the Oratory, now known as Brompton Oratory, between Étienne Mallarmé, Artist, of 6 Brompton Square, and Christina Maria Gerhard of 19 Montpellier Square.[72] Two details in the marriage documents suggest that more careful planning than the circumstances would seem to call for had been involved. The first is in the register at Brompton Oratory, where it is stated that the religious ceremony had been performed under a special dispensation, *Obtenta dispensatione apostolica*.[73] Why this was necessary I have not been able to discover. The banns had been published in England though not in France,[74] and both parties were baptized Catholics as were their parents. It may be that the religious authorities were informed of their having lived together before marrying, and that this was an impediment that had to be removed by papal dispensation. The second peculiarity, more disturbing, is found in the civil registration. A marriage certificate, from Somerset House, records that 'Christina Maria Gerhard' declared her age to be twenty-three.[75] She appears to have produced as evidence a counterfeit birth certificate, preserved thereafter by Mallarmé in his 'Mariage de Londres' file.[76] Again one can only guess at the explanation. Perhaps Stéphane had lied to his stepmother and grandparents on the subject of Marie's age, and decided he must keep up the deception.[77] Or perhaps she herself had procured the document for occupational purposes, because employment as a governess was easier to obtain at twenty-three than at twenty-eight.

It was in mid August therefore that Stéphane returned with his bride to France. Until the beginning of December they lived, the editors of the *Correspondance* tell us, 'in Paris and at Sens'.[78] When, or for how long, they were at Sens is not known. It seems likely that Anne Mallarmé would wish them to stay with her for some time as soon as they were free to do so, that is in late August when Stéphane's examination was over. For the rest, what we do know is that from late October to the beginning of December they were resident in Paris, at 25 rue des Saints-Pères, near Saint-Germain-des-Prés.[79]

Stéphane had two important tasks to attend to. The one that

must have seemed the more urgent from Marie's point of view was to obtain legal recognition in France for the 'English marriage'. Progress towards that end would be slow, for reasons that will be seen and explained later. The other task, which kept the young couple in Paris or at least made it reasonable for them to stay on there, was that of ensuring a livelihood by Stéphane's qualifying for an appointment and securing one. This was done without undue delay. Stéphane faced his examiners on the appointed days, was informed on 15 September that he had passed (though it seems with little to spare),[80] and was certified 'apte à l'enseignement de la langue anglaise' in a state school. On 19 September he sent in his application for a teaching post, if possible at the Lycée de Saint-Quentin (whose new headmaster was Monsieur Clément, formerly at Sens).[81] Six weeks later, by a ministerial order dated 3 November 1863, he was appointed 'temporary assistant master', not at Saint-Quentin but at Tournon in the Ardèche department.[82] 'Bien loin, derrière Lyon', he complained.[83] And indeed it was nearly three hundred and fifty miles south of Paris, two hundred and seventy beyond Sens.

His initial salary was to be two thousand francs a year, as he had assured his doubting grandparents it would.[84] The letter of 3 or 4 November in which Anne Mallarmé sent this and other news to the Desmolins at Versailles is the one document I know that presents the young couple in their family circumstances at this juncture, with Anne in her role as intercessor. As well as with Stéphane's first task, now accomplished, the letter deals with the one that remained, of legalizing the English marriage by having it registered at Sens. Apparently, the necessary consent of the grandparents to the union was now half-promised, and Fanny Desmolins had complained of the time that Stéphane was taking to send them the certificates from London that were needed to satisfy the French authorities that he and Marie were properly wed though in the English manner. Anne Mallarmé wrote:

Je trouvais le temps long sans lettre de Stéphane, chère madame, lorsqu'hier j'ai reçu une qui m'apprenai[t] non pas sa nomination mais une indisposition bien grave causée par une [a]ngine des plus mauvaises qui a beaucoup effrayé le médecin et sa pauvre Marie souffrant elle-même de la jaunisse. Un mieux sensible s'est fait sentir après l'opération et une seconde lettre reçue ce matin est tout à fait rassurante. Je viens de causer de cette indisposition avec Monsieur des Essarts qui venait de l'apprendre par son ami Cazalis ami aimé de Stéphane et qui dépeignait bien les tristesses qui avaient déjà visité ce jeune ménage, et aussi le dévouement et les soins incessants de la pauvre Marie. Comme contre poid[s] à cette nouvelle peine, M^r des Essarts m'annonçait la nomination de Stéphane à Tournon, notre proviseur venait de l'apprendre par le journal. Le pauvre garçon l'ignorait encore sans doute à cause de sa réclusion. Il va être bien loin de nous[;] de Paris, ce n'est pas un mal assurément mais de toutes nos affection[s] il n'en est pas de même. Sa maladie l'excuse de "point vous avoir envoyé les papiers désirés". Je prends la partie de vous expédier ceux que j'ai[,] ou Marie[,] y joignant une lettre de Londres reçue hier, voyez ce que vous pourrez faire de tout cela[;] quelques jours de lit encore, un départ, tout cela ne permettra gu[è]res au pauvre garçon de s'occuper de cela lui-même. Il s'agira de trouver un traducteur juré puisqu'on le demande ainsi. Allons ne nous laissons pas décourager. Voilà une position de 2.000 au moins sans compter les répétitions, elle pouvait se faire désirée [*sic*] beaucoup plus longtems. Ce départ à une si grande distance et pour longtems peut-être ne se fera pas sans que vous permettiez au pauvre prodigue de venir à vous comme à son cher bon papa, ah s'il fallait vous en faire la demande à genoux je n'hésiterais pas tant j'ai à cœur qu'il entende votre pardon! Vous le laisserez venir n'est-ce pas et vous ne le repousserez point (. . .)[85]

The affectionate manner in which Stéphane and particularly Marie are referred to in this letter suggests that they had been Anne's guests at Sens for more than a few days after their return to France, and been helped by her loyal support to brave the hostile opinion of a bourgeoisie unlikely to show lenience to her erring stepson and his guilty wife. This subject is touched on in a letter received by Stéphane from Des Essarts, probably about the middle of October when Emmanuel returned to Sens after the long vacation, and reported to Stéphane on the situation there. It is partly paraphrased, partly (but very briefly) quoted from, in the first volume of the *Correspondance*: Emmanuel, in the editor's words:

'ne songe plus à contester le mariage avec une "jeune femme digne de toi et qui mérite tous nos respects", mais Sens est un peu scandalisé, au point que le proviseur n'eût pas été favorable à une nomination au lycée de la ville: 'Le fait n'en est pas moins là, jugé comme jugent les hommes et de nature à te nuire quelque temps. Ta mère envisage la situation chrétiennement avec l'idée qu'elle se fait de la sainteté du mariage, somme toute avec une grande noblesse. Tu la connais maintenant cette femme que j'ai devinée, et tu peux voir quelle âme haute . . .'[86]

It was not ungenerous on the part of the Desmolins to be impatient with their grandson. He had been back in France for over two months when Anne sent on to them such papers as she and Marie had been able to muster. The one particularly mentioned, the 'lettre de Londres, reçue hier', must have confirmed their impression that he had done very little to put an end to what they naturally saw as a most unsatisfactory situation. It was almost certainly the following reply from the Consul-General in London, dated 28 October, to Stéphane's request of the 26th for a certificate satisfying all the requirements of French law:

Il n'est pas de la compétence du Consulat Général de délivrer un certificat, comme celui que vous demandez par votre lettre du 26 de ce mois. La seule chose que vous ayez à faire c'est de prier Mme Wright, votre amie, de lever un extrait de votre acte de mariage et de faire ensuite légaliser la signature du R. P. Morris à la Chancellerie du Consulat. De cette façon vous serez parfaitement en règle.[87]

At the same time, however, this friendly letter from a high official may have reassured the Desmolins, and helped them to make up their minds. So also did legal advice obtained confidentially within the family.[88] On 19 November they declared 'devant notaire' their intention not to oppose the legalization, after the event, of their grandson's marriage.[89]

The occasional references in the correspondence between Mallarmé and Cazalis during the next three months give the impression that between them they bungled badly the part of the legalities that they were supposed to be attending to. But when the documents in his 'Mariage à Londres' file, published by Carl Barbier in 1976, are also taken into account, a new likelihood takes shape which, in so far as it can be confirmed, puts a different complexion on Mallarmé's performance if not his friend's. The seeds of the hypothesis were sown many years ago in Henri Mondor's *Vie de Mallarmé*. There, at the end of the ninth chapter and beginning of the tenth, in terms that leave his reader uncertain whether he is stating fact as well as weaving whimsical fancies, he sends Stéphane and Marie on a brief nostalgic visit to London before they left for Tournon.[90] Whatever reason he had for entertaining such a notion, the documents from London that eventually found their way to Sens seem to bear it out. The dates appended to the official signatures, testifying to their authenticity,[91] tempt one strongly to conjecture that Stéphane, perhaps with Marie, perhaps alone since she had been unwell, did make that quick trip to London. It was not however simply to revisit that city, without compare in its autumn mists, but on urgent business. Those dates, together with the advice in the Consul-General's answer of 28 October, suggest that after a first brief appearance that Mallarmé had to put in at Tournon on 23 November, to swear his oath of allegiance to the Emperor and be installed in his functions,[92] he returned to Paris (with perhaps a halt at Sens) and then went on to London. He was there on Tuesday the first of December to do what the Consul-General had told him, a month before, might be done on his behalf by Mistress Wright, the witness at the wedding. That is, he obtained a marriage certificate and a certificate of custom, and handed them in at the Consulate-General for transmission to Paris, explaining his needs and his intentions and paying in advance the several dues. He then hastened back to Paris with his conscience at ease. The documents needed at Sens would be sent to the Ministry of Foreign Affairs in Paris, for more signatures, and thence, in accordance with his instructions, forwarded to Cazalis. By 3 December he was back at 25 rue des Saints-Pères. Three days later the new English master and his wife arrived at Tournon, where for the next few years they were to dwell.[93]

As to the benefit of a literary nature that Mallarmé must have derived from his first prolonged stay in the French capital, our knowledge is limited. There is evidence, however, of his seeking and finding some of that companionship with other young poets which in London, to his chagrin, he had neither found nor sought.[94] A notable feature of his success in this regard is that his literary associations (perhaps because he was still the protégé of Des Essarts) continued to be with men a little older than himself. With Emmanuel, friendship was renewed, and deepened, as Marie won his esteem and warm affection.[95]

Cazalis was back from Strasbourg but could not give them so much of his time as they had hoped.[96] Émile Roquier seems to have rejoiced at their being in Paris, and to have paid them several visits.[97] It is probable that Mallarmé took up again his good relations with Coligny, but I know of no proof that he did.

There were new friends, young poets for the most part, and it happens that those amongst them who were to count in Mallarmé's life were all concerned in the one literary enterprise with which, it appears, he endeavoured to associate himself during that autumn. For that reason he names them in two short letters, the first written a few days after he left for Tournon, the second some two months later. Both were sent to Albert Collignon, a young lawyer with literary interests and intentions, by three years Mallarmé's senior, for good relations with whom poets of his own generation were vying. For he was to edit *La Revue nouvelle*, which during Mallarmé's stay in Paris was busily preparing, with much publicity, to make an ambitious début. (Who could suspect that before six months had passed it would be no more?)[98]

It was to congratulate Collignon enthusiastically on the quality of its opening number that Mallarmé wrote the first of the two letters, from Tournon on 12 December.[99] He also told Collignon that he had not had time to finish the translations he had promised to send for publication, of three poems by Edgar Poe. He was sending him instead, 'en attendant', a very short poem in *terza rima*, in the hope that it might appear in the second number of the review.[100] He reminded him furthermore of services he had rendered and would continue to render, at home and particularly abroad, in making the *Revue nouvelle* known:

> Comptez sur ma propagande, à Londres en particulier. La réclame que je vous avais promise dans *la Gazette des étrangers* y a paru deux jours après mon départ.[101] Armand Renaud ne m'a pas écrit, et je ne sais si celle qu'il devait faire éclore dans la *Revue contemporaine* n'est pas bien en retard. Voyez cela.

Two other names, of greater avant-garde prestige than Renaud's, occupy a postscript that seems to have no other purpose than to display them:

Je ne vous dis rien pour Mendès ni Glatigny, à qui je compte écrire ce soir.

The second letter, dated 21 February [1864], begins with a complaint, courteously but explicitly stated. Mallarmé had not been sent complimentary copies of the two February issues of the *Revue*. No doubt he would soon receive them, as he would of course future numbers as they appeared. (Clearly, following the example of Des Essarts, he was already sensitive to signs that Paris ceased to be interested in you when you were elsewhere.) A further disappointment was more diplomatically conveyed, then followed by a reminder that (though now a provincial) the writer was on excellent terms with three distinguished contributors to the *Revue nouvelle*:

Vous ne recevrez rien de moi aujourd'hui encore, parce que depuis quelques mois je ne fais guère que des vers; or vous en avez déjà tant, je pense, sans compter ceux que je vous ai envoyés en décembre, et tant de beaux, que je m'abstiens. Je vous demanderai toutefois, quand le volume de vers de notre ami Glatigny paraîtra, de me laisser quelques pages pour l'étudier amoureusement.

Quand vous verrez Mendès et Villiers, serrez-leur bien la main, très fort, en leur disant que je ne les oublie pas.

Je serre la vôtre d'abord, et vous prie de croire à ma sympathie qui voudrait devenir une amitié.[102]

To see in these claims to good literary connections only self-interested name-dropping would be unjust. For some three months the young poet had enjoyed the excitement and satisfactions of living among his peers, and it was understandable that he should cling to the friendships he had made or strengthened, now that he found himself far away, in what he already called 'ce hideux trou de Tournon (. . .) , le noir village où je suis exilé'.[103]

In this he was to prove successful. All the friendly relations mentioned in the two letters were to ripen and endure. In the years that followed Renaud was to prove a loyal, unassuming *confrère*, and more than once a friend in need.[104] Glatigny the poet–actor, the disciple of Banville and Baudelaire, with whom Mallarmé had once paid Léon Marc the compliment of comparing him, was his elder by three years. They had already met, it would seem, at Versailles in the summer of 1862, when Émile

Deschamps was the first and Glatigny the second to honour Mallarmé's album with a poem. There had also been a brief correspondence. In this case it was the younger man who would be called on sometimes, and would not fail, to be a generous friend.[105]

Of greater consequence, however, was his meeting during that same autumn with Catulle Mendès and his close friend Villiers de l'Isle-Adam. Its importance in Mallarmé's life can be judged from his letter of November 1885, known as his Autobiography and made use of as such in a previous chapter.[106] He declares in the most intimately personal sentence it contains:

Mes grandes amitiés ont été celles de Villiers, de Mendès, et j'ai, dix ans, vu tous les jours mon cher Manet, dont l'absence aujourd'hui me paraît invraisemblable.[107]

Precisely how the earlier of these his greatest friendships began (Manet he met ten years later) is less well known today than it was thought to be when Henri Mondor wrote his biography, and could quote with confidence Mendès's own account of Mallarmé's first visit to him and Villiers, themselves at the time close friends. It was published and presumably written—with the help no doubt of earlier notes—forty years after the event. In the last thirty years its authority has in some respects been questioned, but it is still a document of considerable biographical interest if accompanied (or, as here, followed) by some attention to the critical observations that have revealed its shortcomings. It reads:

Vers l'année 1864,—je crois cette date exacte,—Villiers de l'Isle-Adam et moi, qui habitions à Choisy-le-Roi, chez mon père, nous reçumes la visite d'un très jeune homme qui m'était adressé par mon ami, l'excellent Emmanuel des Essarts. Après le déjeuner, Villiers de l'Isle-Adam s'enferma dans sa chambre,—il travaillait alors à *Elën*,—et j'allai me promener avec Stéphane Mallarmé, (c'était ce jeune homme), le long de la Seine. Il était peu grand,[108] chétif, avec sur une face à la fois stricte et plaintive, douce dans l'amertume, des ravages déjà de détresse et de déception. Il avait de toutes petites mains fines de femmelette et un dandysme (un peu cassant, et cassé) de gestes. Mais ses yeux montraient la pureté des yeux des tout petits enfants, une pureté de lointaine transparence, et sa voix, avec un peu de fait exprès dans la fluidité de l'accentuation, caressait. D'un air de n'attacher aucune importance aux choses tristes qu'il disait, il me conta qu'il avait assez longtemps vécu très malheureux, à Londres, pauvre professeur de français; qu'il avait beaucoup souffert, dans l'énorme ville indifférente, de l'isolement et de la pénurie, et d'une maladie, comme de langueur, qui l'avait, pour un temps, rendu incapable d'application intellectuelle et de volonté littéraire. Puis, il me donna des vers à lire. Ils étaient écrits, d'une écriture fine, correcte et infiniment minutieuse, sur un de ces tout petits carnets reliés de carton-cuir et que ferme une bouclette de cuivre. Je lus, tout en marchant au bord de l'eau, les premières poésies de Stéphane Mallarmé. Et je fus émerveillé. Car ils existaient déjà, ces miracles de rêve, de sensibilité, de charme et d'art: *Les Fenêtres*, *Les Fleurs*, *Le Guignon*, *L'Azur*, d'autres encore, que nous avons tant admirés, qu'on ne cessera pas d'admirer. On conçoit la joie, ou, pour mieux dire, l'extase de ma surprise. Incontestablement, un poète, rare, exquis, parfait, se révélait à moi. (. . .) Très vite, je ramenai Stéphane Mallarmé à la maison, je lus ses vers à Villiers de l'Isle-Adam, qui partagea tout de suite mon enthousiasme, et de ce jour s'établit, entre Mallarmé et nous, une profonde affection faite,—j'ai gloire à le dire,—d'estime réciproque, de mutuelle confiance, et que rien, pas même les différentes directions d'existence, que rien, pas même la mort, n'a rompue. Hélas! je survis à mes chers préférés.

Cependant Stéphane, nommé professeur d'anglais en province, partit pour Tournon; puis, ce fut à Avignon qu'on le relégua; nous fûmes, Villiers et moi, près de sept années sans le voir.[109]

The first serious doubt as to the reliability of this account had to do with its rather hesitant opening assertion: 'Vers l'année 1864—je crois cette date exacte'. It was Alan Raitt, in the course of an article published in 1955,[110] who drew attention to the significance, in this regard, of a detail in Mallarmé's second letter to Collignon, the one dated 21 February 1864, published for the first time in 1952.[111] He pointed out that it contained a friendly message for Mendès and Villiers which was not consistent with the dating by Mendès, in his *Rapport*, of their first meeting with Mallarmé:

Quand vous verrez Mendès et Villiers, serrez-leur bien la main, très fort, en leur disant que je ne les oublie pas.

Either the visit described by Mendès took place not in the autumn of 1864 but a year earlier (and this, the critic added, was materially possible), or, alternatively, it did take place in 1864 but was not their first meeting.

The matter is taken up again by Luc Badesco, in the chapter on Villiers de l'Isle-Adam which concludes the first volume of *La Génération poétique de 1860*. He seeks to take the argument further, raising doubts as to the accuracy of the narration itself of Mallarmé's visit. He begins by accepting, without explanation but apparently unhesitatingly, the second of the two alternatives: the meeting at Choisy did take place in 1864, but Mallarmé had met Villiers before. Whether he had already met Mendès is left uncertain, but they knew each other in the sense that they had exchanged letters in November 1861.[112] Into this situation M. Badesco introduces a new element. He refers to the long and interesting letter that Mendès sent, in October 1864,[113] replying to one from Mallarmé now lost. Both Mendès and (in a postscript) Villiers thanked their friend for poems he had sent them:

> Cher ami [Mendès wrote], nous avons été tout à fait touchés de votre excessive gracieuseté. *Fanfarlo*[114] nous a valu une charmante matinée, et vos poèmes n'ont point fini de nous rendre des services contre l'ennui . . .

> Mon cher Mallarmé [added Villiers], Je vous suis bien reconnaissant pour ma part de l'envoi que vous avez fait à Catulle, car j'en ai profité. C'est fort admirable, décidément; et j'espère que de tels vers ne resteront pas longtemps impunis. Merci de vous être souvenu de moi: nous avons bien parlé de vous, aussi et avec une amitié vraie . . .[115]

From which M. Badesco concludes that some of the recollections published by Mendès in his *Rapport* are not fact but fiction:

> Par conséquent "les premières poésies de Stéphane Mallarmé", que Mendès dans sa réponse commente avec beaucoup de sagacité, il ne les lut pas "émerveillé", "tout en marchant au bord de l'eau", "le long de la Seine" pendant la visite de leur ami à Choisy-le-Roi, et il ne ramena pas Mallarmé à la maison pour les lire aussi "à Villiers de l'Isle-Adam qui partagea tout de suite mon enthousiasme", comme il le prétend, de bonne foi, dans son rapport où il confond les deux dates.[116]

This cheerfully iconoclastic proposition is, however, easily refuted. What Mendès says of the poems that Mallarmé brought to Croisy is perfectly reconcilable with his receiving other poems from him by post, if this happened a year later. They were not the same poems (and that is why Mendès used the plural when he expressed the wish 'à voir se gonfler vos petits paquets de poésie'). In other words it is the first and not the second of the chronological alternatives that best fits the evidence available (as Dr Raitt seemed quietly to suggest in the first place).[117] The visit to Croisy was made in the autumn of 1863, and the poems that Mendès read as he walked with Mallarmé on the banks of the Seine were those, or some of those, that were written at Sens or, it will be suggested later, in London. They were such poems as 'Le Guignon', 'Le Sonneur', 'Vere novo', 'A un Mendiant', 'Haine du Pauvre', 'Les Fenêtres', 'Le Château de l'Espérance'. Those, on the other hand, that he sent from Tournon a year later, after again seeing Mendès if not Villiers in Paris,[118] would be the ones he wrote or finished during his first months at Tournon, including such poems as 'A une Putain', 'L'Azur', 'Las de l'amer repos', and 'Les Fleurs' (from which Villiers quoted to Mendès, who was writing his letter of thanks, a line sumptuous enough for his own pen, 'Où rougit la pudeur des aurores foulées'[119]. Mendès had no reason in his *Rapport* to keep the two sets separate, and he did not.

But that is, momentarily, to anticipate. The partial rehabilitation of the description by Mendès of Mallarmé's visit to Croisy-le-Roi brings the present chapter to its close. None of the friendships nurtured during the stay in Paris would so decisively serve Mallarmé's career during the next few years as that with Catulle Mendès, and no friendship formed then or later would have on his poetic ambition an influence comparable with that of Villiers de l'Isle-Adam. For the time being, it seems to be Mendès who interests him. The enthusiasm for the extraordinary promise that Villiers showed would be expressed when *Elën* was published. Not until 1865, it would seem, did Mallarmé begin to know Villiers himself well enough to be fascinated by his personality and to make him his literary hero.

NOTES

1 He explained why he had not written before: 'Je n'ai pas pu encore écrire à Emmanuel, je compte le faire demain. J'avais tant à écrire à mes parents!' (*DSM.* vi, 68).
2 See above, ch. 2, n. 117; also, *DSM.* v, 388–9: Mme Desmolins's version of her grandson's arrival in London.
3 *DSM.* vi, 67.
4 Ibid. 75–6 (Marie's letter), and n. 1, 76–7 (translation into English).
5 Ibid. 77–8.
6 The story of Henri and Ettie has been told by Lawrence Joseph in *Henri Cazalis, sa vie, son œuvre, son amitié avec Mallarmé*, 1972. Only in so far as they appear to affect his friend's attitude and behaviour will Mallarmé's interventions be recounted here. In that regard, what is notable in his first few letters from London, is that his mission is clearly to give news of the Yapp family, not simply of Ettie. The comments that were probably most weighty from that point of view were the following, on Ettie's younger sister Flo: 'Florence est ravie de sa martyre [*sic*]. Elle te porte en son cœur. Elle est ravissante, j'aimerais lui voir un peu moins d'argot littéraire. La poésie aux femmes, le métier aux hommes' (*DSM.* vi, 66). The effect on Cazalis can be judged by the opinion on bluestockings that he expressed in his reply (ibid. 72). Hence perhaps, in Mallarmé's letter to him of 14 January (ibid. 111) the passage: 'Toi aussi, ton rêve est [é]croulé. Et j'ai été l'un de ceux qui l'ont démoli. Mon ami, je ne me le reproche pas, parce que je l'ai fait loyalement d'abord, et aussi parce qu'il valait mieux que tu fusses prévenu de ce qui était vrai avant qu'Ettie ne v[î]nt à Paris. Tu aurais été trop navré de voir cela de près'. Ettie's absorption in her amateur dramatics while Cazalis waited for news from her and her portrait seems to have convinced him that Mrs Yapp was right when she told them that Ettie was still a child.

The account provided here of Mallarmé's stay in London is confined rather closely to events and developments within his personal situation. This restriction seemed reasonable because the story had been told in a broader social context by Cecily Mackworth, in the second chapter ('The Young Mallarmé') of *English Interludes*—published like Lawrence Joseph's *Henri Cazalis* in 1972.
7 Ibid. 66.
8 Ibid. 82: 'Hier, je revenais de voir Katie, qui est un peu souffrante. Ettie et sa mère étaient chez un photographe. Quand j'embrassai Marie en rentrant, elle était toute triste. Je lui demandai la cause de son chagrin, et je compris qu'elle avait réfléchi longuement durant mon absence. "Il faut que je parte!" me dit-elle doucement.'
9 His grandmother, writing to Mélanie in April 1863, referred to 'son caractère à la fois apathique et confiant' (*DSM.* v, 400). A cool customer she had found him, particularly in their discussions of the previous year. Cazalis too, a little later, confessed that he found him rather unfeeling:

'Sais-tu dans ta lettre, ce qui m'a le plus étonné, et le plus ému. C'est ce que tu m'as dit de ta mère (. . .) Je crains, je te sais un peu froid, que tu ne lui montres pas assez comme tu as été touché de tant de délicatesses' (*DSM*. vi, 146). No doubt Cazalis remembered how Stéphane had written about her a very few weeks before: 'Avec ces indications, elle croira que j'ai été joué par une rouée. Si je pleurais devant elle, elle me plaindrait comme une pauvre dupe. Elle ferait tout contre Marie—criminelle de m'avoir trop aimé' (ibid. 87).

10 Ibid. 82–3.

11 Ibid. 46: letter of 7 July 1862.

12 Ibid. 61. It was as if the author of both these letters was demonstrating his emotion rather than simply yielding to it. One is put in mind of a much earlier incident in his life (already given some prominence above, vol. I, p. 18), when as a boy of five, on his mother's death, 'embarrassé de son manque de douleur qui ne lui donnait pas une contenance due [il] prenait le parti de se rouler sur une peau de tigre étendue et agitait ses longs cheveux qui lui battaient les yeux'.

In narrating the incident to Régnier, Mallarmé made it quite clear that the cause of his behaviour was his failure to feel the grief the occasion called for. Otherwise one might think he was conscious rather of failing to manifest in the adequate and appropriate way the deep sorrow he felt, like Tolstoy in the story he tells of his own behaviour when his beloved mother died (*Boyhood, Adolescence, Youth*, ch. 11, 'My Grief').

13 *DSM*. vi, 82–3.

14 See above, p. 275.

15 See above, p. 280.

16 A month later he confessed frankly to Cazalis that he had really made that promise, and not simply 'talked of marriage'; see above, p. 271. In the meantime, when Marie arrived in Paris Cazalis wrote: 'Il faudrait qu'elle s'habituât à cette vie nouvelle, à ce veuvage; qu'elle fût forte, et ne te perdît pas dans sa douleur. Sois prudent dans tes lettres: ne risque aucun mot, mon Stéphane, qui te lie, qui te mette une pierre au cou. C'est pour toi la vie, la vie sortant de la mort' (ibid. 107).

17 Ibid. 85.

18 Ibid. 88.

19 Ibid. 91. They seem to have moved in the third week of December, to what must have been a much more salubrious neighbourhood.

20 Ibid. 93.

21 Ibid. 95.

22 In a letter from Boulogne, Mallarmé described to Cazalis the wild conditions, and their need for rest. He added: 'Je m'accroche à ce bout de planche avec extase, et je veux me donner encore pendant deux jours l'illusion de notre douce vie à deux' (ibid. 104).

23 It was the second copy he had given, or lent, to Cazalis; see ibid. 31. Perhaps it was yet another he tried to retrieve on 3 December 1863 and again on 8 January 1864. See *Corr*. i, 102, and ii, 309 n. 2 and 310 n. 2. It is clear from a letter to Armand Renaud published in *DSM*. vii (pp. 213–16), also dated 8 January 1864, that those in which Mallarmé asked for

the copy of *Châtiments* were not addressed to him. They were presumably therefore sent to Maurice Dreyfous, which according to the editors of the *Correspondance* was the other possibility.

Dreyfous's concern over Mallarmé's rashness in sending this prohibited publication to his friends (as recounted in *Ce qu'il me reste à dire*) appears to have been excessive. Hugo's book was still contraband, but the last case of a prosecution for its clandestine importation that Pierre Angrand could find (*Victor Hugo raconté par les papiers d'état*, 1961, pp. 116–19) occurred in May 1869. I note in Georges Mounin's *La Poésie et la Société*, 2ème édition revue, 1965, p. 10, a reference to the time when 'les *Châtiments* clandestins de l'édition de Stockholm étaient colportés par les marchands ambulants de mercerie dans la France entière'.

24 *DSM*. vi, 108.

25 Ibid. 109–11.

26 Ibid. 113.

27 On 19 March he would be twenty-one, and 'of age'. It appears from two legal documents analysed by Carl Barbier (*DSM*. v, 67 and 70) that on coming of age he inherited about 7,000 francs, and after his father's death a further 13,500 francs, making up the 20,000 he had expected on coming of age. Its value at the time can be judged by comparing it with the salary of 2,000 francs a year he believed he would earn as a *chargé de cours*.

In view of his admission to Cazalis of his financial position, it is interesting to note the manner in which he still postponed repayment of fifty francs that Cazalis had lent him. The loan may have been made on the occasion of the brief visit to Paris at the end of January 1863, or made to Marie at about the same time. The fact that her address was 'chez Mme Koch, une dame qui place les gouvernantes' (*DSM*. vi, 127) suggests that she had not found employment. On 14 January Mallarmé had asked Cazalis to lend Marie the fare to London and (an improbable suggestion) collect the twenty francs from Mme Desmolins (ibid. 110). However that may be, Cazalis had to ask for his fifty francs about the end of February (ibid. 138): 'les 50 francs m'ont été réclamés, et je n'ai pas un sou'. Mallarmé replied on 5 March (ibid. 141): 'J'attends de l'argent de mon notaire demain, et je t'enverrai de suite cinquante francs. Je suis bien pauvre. Le voyage de Marie m'a ruiné. Pardon, mon pauvre ami.' On 1 April, at Versailles, he was still apologizing (ibid. 144). But he promised then that as soon as his financial business on coming of age was finished he would send the money if he had to do so by instalments, on his return, when he was back in London (ibid. 144). Presumably he did so, since nothing more is heard of the fifty francs, even when, from Strasbourg, Cazalis wrote of his impecunious state.

28 If he wanted her to know, why not tell her himself? It was unlikely that Cazalis would do so.

29 Ibid. 120–1.

30 A letter from Cazalis to his aunt Valentine Le Josne, full of information on the part Mallarmé played in healing a breach between Cazalis and the Yapps, was published by Lawrence Joseph (unfortunately not in its

entirety) in his article 'Mallarmé et son amie anglaise' (*RHLF.*, Jul.–Sept. 1965). In it, Cazalis mentions a visit to the Yapps in terms that situate Mallarmé's day in Paris: 'Hier où je finissais ma lettre arrive Stéphane de Londres; pour un jour; je vais hier soir avec lui chez les Yapp'. In *Henri Cazalis* (p. 37 n. 11), L. Joseph further states that the date on the letter 'Lundi neuf heures' can be interpreted as meaning, no doubt, 26 January. Which means that Stéphane arrived in Paris on the 25th or (if Monday was itself 'hier' by the time the letter was finished) the following day.

31 In a letter dated 3 February written to Cazalis when he was back in London, Mallarmé made this brief reference to his visit: 'je vais encore être ballotté de pensées en pensées—cela me tuait déjà à Paris où je t'avais et où je pouvais lui parler et avoir la réponse en cinq minutes, qu'est-ce ici, où je suis seul' (*DSM.* vi, 126). I take 'je pouvais lui parler' to mean that he could but did not.

32 See n. 30 above. In a letter written on 14 January, Cazalis had mentioned 'l'arrivée dans quelques jours d'Ettie, de Mad. Yapp, de Katie' (ibid. 107). Two days later he was still asking Mallarmé to call on them, however (ibid. 114), and Mallarmé obliged, though not to much purpose. He reported (not, as the different editors state, on 30 or 31 January, but on the 23rd): 'J'ai passé la soirée d'hier avec Madame Yapp: je n'ai pas pu parler. Il y avait là tous les acteurs de la Tragédie' (ibid. 121). The Yapps must have travelled to Paris on the 24th, 25th, or 26th.

33 Letter of 29 or 30 January; ibid. 117–19. It is interesting to see how easily the young unbeliever, confronted with a serious question of right and wrong, has recourse to the habits of thought of a Christian boyhood.

34 Letter of 2 February; ibid. 122.

35 Letter of 3 February; ibid. 124–5.

36 Fragment of a letter dated by the editors 'peut-être le 4 février 1863'; ibid. 127.

37 Ibid. 128.

38 Ibid. 129.

39 Ibid. 133–4.

40 Ibid. 135–6.

41 Ibid. 139–40. The belief in an afterlife again shows its tenacity.

42 See the opening paragraph of Madame Desmolins's letter of mid-April to Mélanie Laurent, p. 281 above, and n. 44 below.

43 Ibid. 142–3.

44 This seems to mean that he had been bought out of military service, as one would expect. The price was one thousand francs; see in Carl Barbier's *Chronologie de Mallarmé jusqu'en 1863* the item 'Liquidation de Mallarmé', dated 11 February 1864: '1000 fr. en principal pour exonération de service militaire' (*DSM.* v, 70).

45 Ibid. 399–400.

46 *DSM.* vi, 148–9.

47 The situation was that the matter of Stéphane's inheritance on coming of age had already been attended to before his father died. After his death, his son's presence was required not only for the funeral ceremony but for

the business of providing for Numa's second family and the disposal of his estate. Stéphane was present, for instance, at a meeting of the 'family council' held on 14 April, at which Émile Mallarmé was appointed subrogate guardian to Anne Mallarmé's children; see *DSM*. v, 68.

48 More than anything else, it seems to have been this fear that had made him put off the decision for so long. He appears to have found understandable, and not to have entirely disagreed with, his family's objections to his marrying Marie. When all the difficulties were over and done with, when they were married and assured of the legalization of their marriage in France, he was still wondering, as if jealously, how his stepmother came to accept it: 'Tu comprends comme elle s'est d'abord opposée à l'idée de mariage. En effet, en elle-même et pour qui ne voit que son côté extérieur, cette idée est absurde. Surtout, quand l'aimée est une personne que la société étiquette d'une classe inférieure, n'a pas d'argent, et lui est inconnue. Toutefois elle a compris mes sanglots intérieurs. Je m'étonne même—et cela est dû à la seconde vue qu'ont les femmes—qu'elle ne refuse pas absolument. Ce mariage ne peut être compris que de moi' (ibid. 143–4). He did not intend to forego, in his own esteem at least, the credit for self-sacrifice that he considered to be his due.

49 Ibid. 57. He had known Marie for two months, and seen little of her, when he wrote of her thus. But his subsequent correspondence, in so far as it is known today, contains no suggestion that he ever really wavered in the opinion he expressed then.

50 Ibid. 162. The political illusions are presumably those for which Mallarmé was referred to by his friends and himself, jokingly, as a Garibaldian.

51 Ibid. 155.

52 Ibid. 153.

53 Ibid. 156.

54 *Corr.* i, 114.

55 Deschamps and Chatelain appear to have been old friends. Vol. 3 of the latter's *Beautés de la Poësie anglaise*, published in 1863, opens with a dedicatory poem 'A mon ami Émile Deschamps', lavish in his praise. On the other hand, in the *Œuvres complètes* of Deschamps (2me partie, 1873), there is a sonnet 'à Mistress C. de Chatelain'.

56 I ventured some comments on the subject in the course of a review, in *MLR*, July 1976, p. 682.

57 When in 1885 Mallarmé told Verlaine that he went to London as a young man in order to read Poe there was a modicum of truth in what he said. See above, p. 285. He went there, apparently, equipped with the two volumes of Baudelaire's translation of the tales, which he lent to Chatelain. That he was still interested in translating the poems seems to be suggested by his letter to Cazalis dated 24 July 1863; he quotes in it, perhaps from memory, several lines of a translation of 'Ulalume' (*DSM*. vi, 161).

58 This document was published in E. J. Crépet's *Baudelaire, Étude biographique*, revue et complétée en 1907 par Jacques Crépet (1907), pp. 342–3.

59 In a letter to Mélanie Laurent dated 21 January 1863, Fanny mentioned Stéphane's having written to congratulate his grandfather on his promotion to the rank of Officer in the Legion of Honour. She wrote: 'Notre pauvre Stéphane a pris sa part de la satisfaction de famille, et l'a exprimée chaudement à son grand père; mais le pauvre garçon est pour nous le revers de la médaille, et le triste côté de notre vie présente; son avenir est si chanceux, et le présent si peu utile, et si nuisible à ses intérêts pécuniaires, que nous ne pouvons y songer sans regret et sans crainte; il a trouvé, jusqu'ici, peu de ressources pour alléger ses frais, qui sont nombreux; et il n'a pas assez de raison pour se présenter chez les personnes pour qui nous lui avions obtenu les lettres de recommandation, par une paresse ou une sauvagerie coupables, puisqu'elles le privent de l'appui qu'il eût pu trouver près d'elles, pour se procurer des élèves' (*DSM*. v, 393). Her earlier account of these recommendations (ibid. 388) shows how unlikely it was that Stéphane would make the contacts she had hoped (also how well he had contrived to conceal the real facts of his life in London).

60 See above, p. 62 (n. 77).

61 See *DSM*. vi, 122–3 and 137.

62 Ibid. 136.

63 We know enough of the correspondence between them to gather that during the earlier part of his young friend's absence Des Essarts had been unsympathetic. Perhaps his continuing friendship with Anne Mallarmé inclined him to be more Stéphane's mentor than his comrade. The long letter Mallarmé wrote to Cazalis on 4 and 5 December 1862, when Marie first announced her intention to leave him, ended with a request that Des Essarts should read it too. He appears to have written to Emmanuel on the 3rd and already received a rather callous reply: 'Cette fois je devais écrire au cher Emmanuel, de qui j'ai reçu dernièrement deux petits billets dans les lettres d'un de nos amis communs. Le cher ami, que j'aime parce qu'il est franc et croit me parler pour mon bien, verra par cette lettre la blessure que me fait ce qu'il appelle en riant "un coup d'état de ménage" et combien profondément ce qu'qu'il dit des "billevesées" était ma vie et mon bonheur. Envoie-lui cette triste lettre. (. . .) Emmanuel, quand je serai seul à Pâque[s], si j'ai le courage de rester à Londres, tu vi[endras]' (ibid. 90). After Stéphane's stay at Sens and Versailles in April 1863 they probably exchanged letters frequently. In May Cazalis wrote from Strasbourg: 'Emm. me donne souvent de tes nouvelles' (ibid. 152), and on 14 June: 'Est-ce donc par un jour de brouillard que tu as écrit à Emmanuel: ta lettre, m'a-t-il dit, était d'un homme qui se va noyer, et se noyer tristement, comme un sot ou comme un athée' (ibid. 157). That is, no doubt, a letter similar to the one in which he opened his soul to Cazalis (p. 283 above). At the beginning of August Des Essarts sent Mallarmé two letters that have been published, a very senior-sounding testimonial commending Stéphane, 'ce bon jeune homme', to the priest who was to officiate at his wedding, accompanied by a formal covering letter apparently intended to be read by the priest too, but so avuncular ('Mon cher enfant,' . . .) that if the sender had not

been Des Essarts one would suspect a practical joke (ibid. 164 and 165). The correspondence seems not to have been seriously interrupted during the whole of that year.

64 3 June 1863; ibid. 154.

65 Ibid. 163.

66 23 or 24 July 1863; ibid. 160–1.

67 Ibid. 161.

68 Ibid. 162. It is quite probable that the workers at that meeting did show themselves lacking in the humility proper to their station. The following year, under the guidance of a studious comrade whose name was Karl Marx, they would be so bold as to found the International Working Men's Association. As to 'gentlemen', it was perhaps one of the few words in the speeches that the young Frenchman easily recognized, and how was he to know it did not mean 'gentilshommes'? His reaction to the word is interesting. He went on: 'Pour qui donc ferait-on une république? pour les bourgeois? Contemple[-]les en foule, dans les parcs, dans les rues. Ils sont hideux, et il est évident qu'ils n'ont pas d'âme. Pour les grands? c'est[-]à[-]dire les nobles et les Poètes? Tant qu'il y aura de l'or pour les uns et de beaux marbres pour les autres, tout ira bien. Henri, est-ce que l'homme qui a fait la Vénus de Milo n'est pas plus grand que celui qui sauve un peuple, et ne vaudrait-il pas mieux que la Pologne succombât que de voir cet éternel hymne de marbre à la Beauté brisé?' Cazalis would probably understand that his paradoxical evaluation was not unrelated to Mallarmé's own situation. It was as a poet, as an artist, that he had taken his honourable decision to respect his promise to Marie. In doing so he was acting in accordance with Henri's judgement of six months before, when he wrote: 'Les poètes sont des gentilshommes, Stéphane: la parole d'un gentilhomme, ce me semble, doit être, comme celle de Dieu, chose sacrée' (ibid. 63).

69 Ibid. 160. There is a literary reference here, as well as perhaps a critical comment on the Englishwoman Mrs Yapp, who had once earned Mallarmé's disdain (see ibid. 56) by expressing the hope that Cazalis, in his attentions to her daughter, would come to terms with 'les réalités de la vie'. In a very different context (*Profils et Grimaces*, 1856, pp. 248–9) Auguste Vacquerie wrote: 'Et cependant, c'est vrai, il y a des artistes qui croient que l'art se suffit à lui-même, et pour qui tout l'art est dans la forme. (. . .) Ils ont horreur de retomber du ciel à la cuisine, de l'astre à la casserole. Il leur semble impie de faire servir l'idéal à nos besoins journaliers'. Cazalis would no doubt recognize in this discreet reference to a literary heresy a homage to the ideality of his love for Ettie.

70 Henri Mondor is mistaken when he states (*Vie*, 96 and *Corr.* i, 369) that the examination was held on 17 September. The *épreuves préliminaires* with which it began took place on Monday 17 and Tuesday 18 August; see the *Bulletin administratif de l'Instruction publique*, XIV (1863), pp. 100 and 166. The Mallarmés presumably returned to Paris therefore, as Stéphane had intended, immediately after their marriage on the tenth, and not at the end of the month.

On 24 July he wrote to Cazalis: 'Je hume d'avance Paris où je retournerai dans les premiers jours du mois prochain' (*DSM*. vi, 160). By 'premiers jours' he meant, presumably, 'as soon as marriage permits'.

71 Ibid. 161–2. The prescribed books ('choix de textes à expliquer en 1863') were Shakespeare's *Romeo and Juliet* and Sheridan's *School for Scandal*; see *Bull. admin.*, XIII (1862), p. 238.

72 When he returned to London after his father's death, Mallarmé admitted to Cazalis that though they had now decided to be married, neither he nor Marie knew how to go about it. Perhaps it was for that reason that they again changed their residence and went to live near the Oratory, at 6 Brompton Square (where an enamel plaque affixed by London County Council tells the passer-by that 'Stéphane Mallarmé, 1842–98—Poet—stayed here in 1863'). At the Oratory they would get the advice they needed, including no doubt the information that they must reside at separate addresses before the banns could be put up. Hence Marie's removal to Montpellier Square, a few hundred yards from Brompton Square. The witnesses were Leonia Wright and Charles William Rooke, both 'of Brompton'. In a document referred to in n. 79 below, published *in extenso* by Carl Barbier (*DSM*. v, 409), and quoted in the present chapter (p. 291), the French Consul-General in London mentions 'Mme Wright, votre amie'. A long note in Mallarmé's own hand, quoted by the editors of the *Correspondance* (*Corr*. i, 106 n. 1), contains with other information on 'the English marriage' the following details: 'les témoins . . . ont été: "Mme Vve. Léonie Wright, rentière, à Londres, demeurant: Burleigh House, Old Brompton Road, S.W. London et Charles William Rooke, frère, demeurant à l'Oratoire, Brompton Road, S.W. London ".'

73 *DSM*. v, 402.

74 In a postscript to his letter of 24 July 1863 (*DSM*. vi, 163) Mallarmé told Cazalis: 'Nous ne pouvons pas nous parier avant le dix Août: les bans se publient. Un l'est.' They were published, that is, at the Oratory on 19 and 26 July and 2 August. The non-publication of the banns at Sens proved to be one of the possible hindrances to the legalization of the marriage in France.

75 *DSM*. v, 403.

76 Ibid. 401.

77 The first authentic birth certificate produced for or by Marie ('Christine Gerhard'), at this time or later, appears to be the one of which a sworn translation, dated 20 October 1898, is preserved among the documents collected by the Ministry of Education to establish Marie's entitlement to a pension, after Mallarmé's death; see A. Gill, 'Mallarmé fonctionnaire', *RHLF*., Jan.–Feb. 1968, p. 6 and note. (There I assumed that Stéphane and Marie were present at the Desmolins's declaration of consent to their marriage, but that now seems to me unlikely. I know of no evidence that Stéphane even paid his grandparents a visit between his return from London and his departure for Tournon.)

The sworn translation of the authentic certificate is reproduced in *DSM*. v, 121–2. It reveals that Christine Gerhard was born on 19 March 1835, seven years (almost to the day) before Mallarmé. He had known from the first that her age would be a main argument against their marrying. He wrote to Cazalis in December 1862: 'Ce qui me fait mal encore quand j'y pense, c'est qu'on doit la maudire dans ma famille. Ma mère en a entendu parler depuis, par mes ennemis de Sens, comme d'une personne fine, habile, ayant de l'éducation, et beaucoup plus âgée que moi' (*DSM.* vi, 87).

78 *Corr.* i, 369 ('Chronologie de Mallarmé. 1863'): 'Fin août. Mallarmé et sa femme quittent l'Angleterre. Ils habitent à Paris (rue des Saints-Pères) et à Sens'.

79 The letter from the French Consul-General in London, referred to in n. 72 above, dated 28 October and replying to one sent by Mallarmé two days before, is addressed to Monsieur Stéphane Mallarmé at that address; see *DSM.* v, 409. Similarly one from Émile Deschamps dated 10 November; see *Vie*, 97 for the letter and 149 n. 2 for the address. Mallarmé himself, writing to Maurice Dreyfous on 3 December (*Corr.* ii, 309) gave him that address and told him they would be leaving it to go to Tournon three days later.

80 In order of merit, he was ninth of the eleven candidates that passed; see the ministerial order of 15 September (*Bulletin administratif de l'Instruction publique*, XIV (1863), pp. 279–80), where he figures as 'Mallarmé (Etienne), professeur libre'.

81 Presumably they had corresponded with each other on the subject. It will be remembered that M. Clément had promised to recommend his former pupil to one of Stéphane's examiners, whom he knew; see above, p. 55 (n. 37). In later years he would continue to take a watchful interest in Mallarmé's career as a teacher.

82 For the text of the *arrêté*, see *DSM.* v, 410. He was considered for the time being as a *suppléant*, replacing temporarily one M. Wright, who had a year's leave of absence. This gentleman was the candidate '*Bight* (sic), Maysson-Guillaume Édouard, chargé du cours d'anglais au lycée de Tournon', who obtained the *certificat d'aptitude* at the same time as Mallarmé, and was fifth on the list. He appears to have been transferred to Rodez, then to Nevers.

83 In the letter to Maurice Dreyfous referred to in n. 79 above, he wrote: 'Je suis nommé professeur bien loin, derrière Lyon à Tournon'. A year and a half later Émile Roquier, writing to Mallarmé, remembered his reaction to the news of his appointmnent: 'Que deviens-tu à ce Tournon qui te faisait si peur, et où, j'en suis convaincu, tu t'ennuies moins que tes prévisions te le faisaient craindre' (*DSM.* vii, 204).

84 See above, p. 20.

85 *DSM.* v, 411–12. Marie's jaundice and recovery from it are commented on to Cazalis, in two of Mallarmé's early letters from Tournon. On 9 December he wrote: 'Marie va beaucoup mieux; c'est déjà une rose-thé', and in his New Year's letter of 30 December: 'Marie est devenue rose et grasse, ne la vois plus jaune' (*DSM.* vi, 166 and 173). It was presumably during their respective illnesses that Stéphane and Marie were befriended by a doctor who was to remain their benefactor. He tried to help them again, a year later, when Mallarmé was seeking transfer to a

more congenial post; see the letter dated by its first editors (*Corr.* i, 141) 'jeudi [novembre] 1864', but in *DSM.* vi, 261, for good reasons, 'Jeudi [Mars 1865]': 'Le vieux docteur qui nous soigna, pour rien presque, rue des Saints Pères, est resté notre ami. Cet excellent vieillard ayant appris, par mes compliments de bonne année, que nous languissions dans une contrée sauvage, a été voir un de ses clients qui est un des gros bonnets de *mon* ministère, et a intercédé pour moi.'

86 *Corr.* i, 95 [–6], n. 1. One suspects that extracts from Des Essarts's letters of this period would be met with more frequently and would be less fragmentary (and indeed that the early letters might by this time have been published as later ones are in vol. IV of the *Correspondance*) if his handwriting had been less difficult to decipher. Mallarmé commented on it to Cazalis in these terms: 'J'ai pu lire, dans son mystérieux grimoire qui m'aveuglera un jour, que tu lui avais lu des poèmes en prose merveilleuse' (*DSM.* vi, 179–80).

As to the opinion of Sens on the subject of the flight to London, it will be remembered that Mallarmé had feared that his stepmother had heard about Marie 'from his enemies at Sens'; see note 77 above. Of the curiosity that would be excited, and the kind of rumours that would go the rounds, some indication is given in a document that has survived—ironically, in view of the non-survival of Mallarmé's letters to Lefébure, for it is a letter to Lefébure from Privé. During his brief stay at Sens in April 1863, Mallarmé had told Courtois something of his adventure. More or less faithfully, Courtois had repeated it to Privé, who passed it on to Lefébure: 'Courtois me charge de vous serrer la main. Il m' a raconté que Mallarmé est maintenant à Sens. Son père est mort, et il a été forcé d'y venir. Il va y rester quelque temps pour régler ses affaires et puis retournera en Angleterre d'où il vient. Courtois m'a raconté une aventure à ce propos. A Sens, chez les bourgeois, il y avait une jeune institutrice anglaise. Mallarmé en devint amoureux. Les bourgeois l'apprirent et le dirent à la jeune miss qui ne resta pas longtemps à Sens et retourna à Paris où elle se trouva dans une position très précaire. Mallarmé le sut et lui fit passer de l'argent anonymement, puis, peu après, fila à Paris et alla déposer son amour aux pieds de la fille de la blonde Albion et passa deux mois avec elle à Paris. Ils partirent tous deux ensuite pour Londres, où le goddam féminin le lâcha d'un cran et le laissa plongé dans le désespoir. Mallarmé fut alors atteint du spleen et n'en guérit qu'au bout de deux à trois mois. Son père mourut sur ces entrefaites. S. Mallarmé revint à Sens sans avoir travaillé en Angleterre. Tel est le récit de Courtois, si vous voulez lui écrire il est à Sens. Je ne sais s'il fait toujours des vers. Courtois ne m'en a pu rien dire' (*Lef.*, 78–9).

87 *DSM.* v, 409.

88 See the letter from Achille Pinson to his cousin Desmolins, ibid. 405. Anne Mallarmé too had taken advice, perhaps from the mayor of Sens (himself a lawyer) and her list of the steps that must be taken has survived. It may well be one of the papers she sent to the Desmolins on 3 or 4 November 1863. The third item in her list would explain the reference in her accompanying letter to 'un traducteur juré' (payment for

whose services all concerned seem to consider a very unpleasant necessity). The fourth shows the wisdom of the precaution she had taken several months before, when she took Stéphane to Versailles to inform his grandmother of his intention to marry: 'Déclaration devant notaire par les ascendants qui reconnaissent que si le mariage a eu lieu sans publications, et sans justifier de leur consentement, ils renoncent à attaquer le mariage; une expédition de cette déclaration sera délivrée par le notaire' (ibid. 407).

89 The official 'transcription du mariage' at the *Mairie de Sens*, dated 8 February 1864, includes the 'consentement des aïeuls maternels', signed by M. André Marie Léger Desmolins and 'Madame Louise Étienne Magnien son épouse' on 19 November 1863 at Versailles. For the complete text of the document, see ibid. 417–21.

90 *Vie*, 98–100.

91 In the terms of the sworn translation the marriage certificate, like the certificate of custom, was declared 'Vu au Consulat Général de France en Angleterre pour légalisation de la signature d'autre part de M. C. R. Barnes Registrar des Actes de l'Etat Civil dans le District de Kensington comté de Middlesex en cette Ville Londres le deux décembre 1863 (L.S.) Le Consul Général de France signé Fleury. Le Ministère des Affaires Étrangères certifie véritable la signature de M. Fleury. Paris le huit décembre 1863' (*DSM.* v, 418). (Certificates handed in on the first of December would be signed by the Consul-General the following day.)

92 See *DSM.* v, 413. It may be remembered that he was officially appointed from that date; see ibid. 410, n. 1.

93 The editors of *Corr.* ii (p. 309) date convincingly 'Jeudi matin [3 décembre 1863]' a letter to Maurice Dreyfous (see n. 79 above). In it Mallarmé, in the midst of 'les mille tracas d'un départ', asks his correspondent to return to him, at 25 rue des Saints-Pères, the copy of Hugo's *Châtiments* that he had borrowed, and to do so '*ce soir* ou *demain matin* sans faute'. He adds that he is leaving for Tournon on Saturday morning. That would allow Stéphane and Marie to spend the evening and perhaps the night at Sens and arrive at Tournon as they are believed to have done (*O.c.* , XVIII), on Sunday the sixth of December.

94 See above, pp. 284–6.

95 He had been against the marriage (though not against the London experiment, which according to the letter from Cazalis to Mallarmé of 17 November 1862 (*DSM.* vi, 70) seemed to him to have proved a great success). When he got to know Marie in Paris, towards the end of his summer vacation in 1863, he became (like Cazalis) her devoted friend. The fragment quoted from his mid-October letter to Mallarmé, on pp. 290–1 above, is evidence of good intentions that reflect the generous attitude of Anne Mallarmé towards the young couple, though he was sceptical, as she was not, concerning the validity, in France, of their union.

96 That would seem to be the sense of the remark in his 'lettre jourdelanesque' of 31 December 1863 to Cazalis: 'Ah! que nous aussi nous regrettons le temps perdu, vilain qui nous as si peu vus' (*DSM.* vi, 173). On 24 July, when he wrote to Cazalis from Brompton Square and

told him they would be back in Paris 'dans les premiers jours du mois prochain', he had asked his friend if he too would be there (back from Strasbourg), and added: 'Je tremble d'y aller sans t'y voir. Paris serait vide sans Cazalis. Marie l'a dit et je le pense' (ibid. 160 and 163).

97 See Roquier's letters to Mallarmé of 5 April 1865 and 14 May 1866 (*DSM.* vii, 204 and 208–9): 'Tu as là-bas (*i.e.* at Tournon) tous les éléments du bonheur qu'on puisse rêver: ta charmante femme si douce, si bonne et si aimante qui a conquis si vite les personnes de ma connaissance qui l'ont vue et au bon souvenir de laquelle je te prie instamment de me rappeler (. . .)'; 'Présente donc à Madame Mallarmé mes meilleures sympathies et mes souvenirs reconnaissants pour l'accueil si bon qu'elle voulait toujours bien me faire lorsque vous habitiez Paris.'

98 Luc Badesco devotes the greater part of a chapter to the *Revue nouvelle*, the reasons for its appearance and early disappearance, and the intellectual flutter that attended the birth of this 'revue des jeunes, et pour les jeunes, et de tous les jeunes pour tous les jeunes' (op. cit. II, p. 910). Of its editor, later known as a literary critic, he writes: 'Né à Metz en 1839, juriste de formation libérale, inscrit au barreau de cette ville, professeur à Strasbourg, il avait débuté par un poème: *Exposition universelle* (1861) "à MM. les membres de l'Acad. Impériale de Metz," (. . .) qui le couronnèrent (. . .) Il n'en écrira point d'autre' (ibid. 916 n.). It seems that for his acquaintance with Collignon it was not to Des Essarts that Mallarmé was beholden. It was perhaps with a sense of his growing independence that he received in January 1864 a letter in which Emmanuel told him he had met Collignon: 'Je suis *enchanté* de Collignon, le directeur de la *Revue nouvelle*—Je lui ai parlé de toi. Il m'a dit qu'il avait reçu de toi des vers et qu'il les publierait' (*DSM.* vi, 175). The Strasbourg connection may suggest that the intermediary was perhaps Cazalis. But it was more likely to be Glatigny. If it was through him that he knew Collignon, it would be natural that Mallarmé should ask the editor (in vain, as will be seen) to let him review for the *Revue nouvelle* the volume of poems (*Les Flèches d'or*) by 'notre ami Glatigny', which was about to be published.

99 *Corr.* i, 98–9. Mallarmé was enthusiastic on the subject, and claimed discreetly the advantage of being a friend of the contributors to such a result: 'Ce premier numéro est aveuglant: que de noms aimés et que de belles choses!' He had already sung its praises to Cazalis, in his letter of 9 December: 'Abonne-toi (pour cinq francs par an) à la *Revue nouvelle* (17 rue St-Benoît), ou lis-la au café, ce qui coûte plus cher. C'est la vraie revue des Jeunes. Il y a dans le premier numéro des merveilles de Banville, Cladel, Mendès, Glatigny, etc.—' (*DSM.* vi, 167). The editors of the Pléiade *Correspondance* (*Corr.* i, 97 n. 1) provide details: 'Ce premier numéro avait paru le 1er décembre. Il contenait entre autres, un poème de Banville, intitulé *Le Pays latin*, des *Rondeaux parisiens*, de Mendès, un conte de L. Cladel: *L'Enterrement d'un îlote*, des articles de Glatigny (*Poètes et Vaudevillistes*) de Villiers (sur le *Philomèle* de Mendès), et de Mendès lui-même (*Revue dramatique*)'. In view of the

quite unique admiration that Mallarmé was to express later for Villiers (whom he had met as will be seen), Henri Mondor is right to find it worthy of note that his article should not be included by his young admirer among the marvels of the first number of the *Revue nouvelle*; see *Vie*, 100 and n. 2.

100 Regarding the 'très courte *terzarima*', the editors of the first volume of the *Correspondance* (*Corr.* i, 98 n. 4) make this suggestion: 'Peut-être s'agit-il de *Haine du pauvre* ou *A un mendiant*'. But why call a poem of nineteen lines, or in the other case twenty-five, 'très courte'? Is it not more likely to be '. . . *Mysticis umbraculis*', six lines long? The term *terza rima* would need to stretch its meaning of course, but not too much, to cover a poem of two tercets, each on a single rhyme.

101 Luc Badesco notes (op. cit. II, p. 916 note—13 of the previous page, continued) that Mallarmé 'avait fait de la "réclame" pour la prospérité de la revue, avant son départ pour Tournon', in *La Gazette des étrangers*. That was certainly what Mallarmé told Collignon, but I can find no trace of a periodical appearing under that title at that time, either in France or across the Channel. However, the fact that on another occasion (see *Corr.* i, 114) Mallarmé also assured Collignon that the Chevalier de Chatelain had promised to subscribe to the *Revue nouvelle*, suggests that he may have asked Chatelain for his assistance in publicizing it in England. (He was to call on him for such help in similar circumstances later; see *Corr.* iv, 369 n. 2, and 370 n. 1). And one is reminded that among Henri Mondor's suggestions concerning the half-asserted, half-imagined brief return to London is the following one for which he probably had some documentary support: 'Peut-être au cours de ce voyage, Mallarmé a-t-il vu ou retrouvé cet étranger Chevalier de Chatelain' (*Vie*, 99). If Mallarmé did make that visit to London before moving to Tournon (and that idea gains some support from the possibility I now entertain), he may well have taken with him, promising to have it published in England, a copy of Collignon's 'prospectus' for the *Revue nouvelle*. *Gazette des étrangers* would then be a carelessly misremembered title for a periodical with which Chatelain was associated. One such was *Le Courrier de l'Europe* (an incomplete set of which was one of the items in the bequest Chatelain told Mallarmé, years later, that he was making him in his will.) The Newspaper department of the British Library has a full set or something near it, and one can note therefore that in the issue of 28 November 1863, among its many miscellaneous advertisements between one for 'Nettoyage et Teinture' and one for Norwich Union Fire Insurance, figure the following literary items: 'Chaucer in French—3 vols. with 15 Illustrations, £1 15s 0[d], Contes de Cantorbéry traduits en vers français, par le Chevalier de Chatelain [and given high praise in accompanying excerpts from a review]' followed by 'Shakespeare in French. Hamlet, tragédie en cinq actes de Shakespeare. Traduite en vers français, par le Chevalier de Chatelain, Member of the Shakespeare National Committee'. If on Chatelain's suggestion or through his good offices, Mallarmé sent Collignon's *prospectus* of the *Revue nouvelle* to the *Courrier de l'Europe*,

to appear in the following number on 5 December, Mallarmé might indeed inform Collignon that it had appeared two days after his departure *from London*—too late, that is, for him to bring back a copy. In actual fact, however, the 'prospectus' did not appear there, though Chatelain's advertisements continued to do so. Mallarmé, on these indications, had tried, but in vain.

102 *Corr.* i, 109–10.

103 Those are the terms he used in the first of the letters to Collignon (ibid. 98 and 99).

104 In July 1864, when Cazalis was hesitating over the choice of a career, and was considering the possibility of finding employment for the time being in office-work, Mallarmé advised him as follows: 'L'hôtel de ville serait la meilleure chose . . . Comme je connais ce chemin-là, j'ai tant de fois été voir Armand Renaud—qui dormait ou faisait des vers, deux choses également divines, sur son pupitre vide' (*DSM.* vi, 219). (Renaud was not in fact a casual employee. He was on the way to a distinguished career, leading to the post of 'Inspecteur en chef des Beaux-Arts et des Travaux historiques de la Ville de Paris'.)

In a footnote to the first letter to Collignon, the editors of the *Correspondance* state that 'Armand Renaud était un disciple d'Émile Deschamps (*Corr.* i, 98 n. 3). If that was so, it might well lead to his meeting Mallarmé, perhaps even as early as 1860. It is very probable that he had at least profited from the poetic experience and advice of Deschamps, living as he did at Versailles. Writing to Renaud on 8 January 1864, Mallarmé added a postscript: 'Mes compliments affectueux à Émile Deschamps. Dites-lui qu'il n'aurait pas dû me répondre étant si malade.' Renaud knew the Desmolins also, since in the same postscript Mallarmé added: 'Qu'on ne sache pas *rue Neuve* que Glatigny viendra bientôt chez moi' (*DSM.* vii, 215). It would indeed have seemed to his grandparents extravagance on his part.

105 See his defence of Glatigny against Cazalis, in *Corr.* i, 126.

106 The first chapter of Volume I.

107 *O.c.*, 664.

108 Charles Mauron (*Mallarmé par lui-même* (1964), p. 24, notes: 'Ses élèves, beaucoup plus tard, garderont le souvenir d'un petit homme, grandi par de hauts talons'. He adds: 'Quand Mallarmé prit sa retraite, il mesurait 1m.63' (that is, a little over 5′ 4″).

109 Catulle Mendès, *Le Mouvement poétique français de 1867 à 1900* (1903), pp. 135–6. Henri Mondor quotes the passage in *Vie* (pp. 136–7), and G. Jean-Aubry with no less confidence in *Une Amitié exemplaire: Villiers de l'Isle-Adam et Stéphane Mallarmé* (1942), p. 13.

110 'Autour d'une lettre de Mallarmé', in the *Revue des sciences humaines* of January–March 1855 (Special number: 'Autour du symbolisme, Villiers de l'Isle-Adam et Stéphane Mallarmé').

111 It was published in the second of the two special 'Stéphane Mallarmé' numbers of *Empreintes* (Sept.–Oct. 1952).

112 See *Vie*, 52, n. 2.

113 For the date, 'octobre 1864', see G. Jean-Aubry, op. cit., p. 17, and for

the text, ibid. 17–20, or the *Correspondance générale de Villiers de l'Isle-Adam* (ed. Joseph Bollery, i. 75–7).

114 G. Jean-Aubry notes (op. cit. , p. 17 n. 3): '*Fanfarlo*. S'agit-il de la nouvelle de Baudelaire? Mallarmé avait-il retrouvé le *Bulletin de la Société des gens de Lettres* de janvier 1847, ou les *Veillées littéraires* de 1849 où cette nouvelle avait paru?'

115 G. Jean-Aubry, op. cit., pp. 17–18 and 21.

116 Luc Badesco, op. cit. I, p. 664.

117 There is really no doubt about the date of the visit. What Mendès says his visitor told him of his life in London (not dissimilar to the tale he told Courtois at Sens, in April of the same year, though now—for good reasons—no mention is made of its heroine, 'la fille de la blonde Albion'; see above, p. 308) was much more likely to be Mallarmé's theme a few weeks after his return to France than after a first year of married life and teaching at Tournon. And on the other hand, the statement with which Mendès opens the next paragraph, 'Cependant Stéphane, nommé professeur en province, partit pour Tournon', surely tells of what took place soon after the visit, not a year before it. The 'nearly seven years' that were to pass before the three came together again in comparable circumstances (though not literally, as will be seen, before they met again) also indicate the year 1863, not 1864, since the reference is certainly to their reunion in August 1870, at Avignon. It is a date that Mallarmé's letters (which Mendès said he had kept and had before him) would provide him with, if his own memories of that dramatic year did not. For the circumstances, see A. W. Raitt, 'Villiers de l'Isle-Adam en 1870', *French Studies*, October 1959.

118 That he saw Mendès is testified in the post-script to Mallarmé's letter of 'jeudi matin [octobre 1864]' to Théodore Aubanel (*Corr.* i, 136): 'J'ai donné ton volume de la *Miougrano* à Catulle Mendès qui en raffolait: serais-tu assez charmant pour ne pas m'en vouloir et m'en renvoyer un?' Villiers on the other hand, in the postscript he added to Mendès's letter to Mallarmé, writes as it were from a distance, as if he had not seen him since the previous year: 'Merci de vous être souvenu de moi: nous avons bien parlé de vous, aussi et avec une amitié vraie' (G. Jean-Aubry, op. cit., p. 21).

Mendès added (ibid.) a postscript of his own, after that of Villiers and as if on a private matter: 'J'aurais dû vous renvoyer depuis longtemps ce que vous savez. Une suite de misères m'en a empêché. Je ne ferai point d'*insistance* pour que vous *m'excusiez*. Bientôt, huit jours sans doute. Pourvu que ce retard ne vous gêne point!' This loan too (which Villiers also mentions, discreetly, in his postscript) favours the idea that the visit to Croisy took place in 1863, and that Mendès and a Mallarmé no longer the waif from London but a young schoolmaster, in funds, met again in Paris the following year, when we know that Mallarmé spent part of his summer vacation there.

I note two more details in Mendès's letter that are of interest. The first is his assurance that 'Villiers partage absolument mon affection pour vos poèmes: il a, d'ailleurs, malgré la coutume que nous avons de vivre seuls à deux une très grande sympathie pour vous-même'. The other is in the first postscript: 'Veuillez remercier Madame Mallarmé de son aimable souvenir. Assurez-la de mes respectueuses sympathies.' It would appear from this greeting that Mendès met Marie before she left Paris for Tournon in December 1863. Perhaps he returned Mallarmé's visit to Choisy by calling at 25 rue des Saints-Pères. The two poets may well have met more than once the following summer, when Mallarmé had planned to stay in Paris during the last half of September and the first few days of October. He wrote to Des Essarts and Cazalis on 30 August: 'Je dis donc que je vous verrai vers le dix septembre en allant à Versailles, et qu'à mon retour de cette ville lointaine j'aurai trois semaines à vous donner à Paris, jours et nuits' (*DSM*. vi, 232–3). He returned to Tournon on 4 October; see ibid. 237 n. 1. The visit to Versailles is an interesting piece of news. Was it his first since returning from London? He had no doubt legal matters with a financial aspect to attend to there, whence his ability to help Mendès out of a temporary difficulty.

119 G. Jean-Aubry, op. cit., p. 20. With regard to Mallarmé's poems Mendès would be in the same position as Des Essarts had been a few months before. Each had two batches. Des Essarts wrote to Mallarmé on 3 March 1864: 'Il m'arrive souvent de reprendre le petit cahier de vers que tu m'as donné et de le savourer lentement. J'ai ainsi relu *Les Fenêtres*.' Then 'J'ai fort aimé tes derniers vers. Le sonnet que tu m'envoies est splendide d'exécution, profond de pensée, d'une clarté parfaite, ce dont je te félicite' (*Corr.* i, 110, n. 1; also, more complete, *Vie*, 113). The correction, *ainsi* for *aussi*, confirmed by the manuscript at the Bibliothèque littéraire Jacques Doucet, is made in *O.c.*, 1387 [1389].

Chapter 7

London poems and a discerning homage in prose

The first letters that Mallarmé wrote to Cazalis from England were, as has been seen, on the whole happy and eager, auguring well for poetry. His first vivid impressions of London town are recognizable as the stuff of which some of his prose poems are made. But these would be written a year later, from recollection in tranquillity. That winter was not to be one of those he had celebrated in the well-turned line 'L'hiver, saison de l'art serein, l'hiver lucide'.[1] During the two months that followed Marie's return to France in mid January 1863, there is in his correspondence no serenity, not much lucidity, and silence on the subject of poetry.[2] However, two of his early short poems do seem to have been written at that time. Both are expressions of the anxiety and despondency he was obsessed with in his solitude.

The first is entitled, diversely, 'A une Putain', 'A celle qui est tranquille', 'Angoisse' (titles it is useful to remember and call into service on occasion), and by Des Essarts euphemistically 'A une dame d'honneur de la reine de Naples' or (elsewhere in the same letter) 'de la reine Victoria'.[3] It is an irregular sonnet like 'Tristesse d'été', with which it shares other features too though in subject and tone it is much more sombre:

A une Putain[4]

Je ne viens pas ce soir vaincre ton corps, ô bête
En qui vont les péchés d'un peuple, ni creuser
Dans tes cheveux impurs une triste tempête
Sous l'incurable ennui que verse mon baiser.

Je demande à ton lit ce [D and C: le] lourd sommeil sans songes
Planant sous ses [C: les][5] rideaux inconnus du remords,
Et que tu peux goûter après tes noirs mensonges,
Toi qui sur le néant en sais plus que les morts.

Car le vice, rongeant ma native noblesse
M'a comme toi marqué de sa stérilité,
Mais tandis que ton sein de pierre est habité

Par un cœur que la dent d'aucun crime ne blesse,
Je fuis, pâle, défait, hanté par mon linceul,
Ayant peur de mourir lorsque je couche seul.[6]

This Baudelairian-sounding poem is usually supposed to have been composed at the beginning of 1864, when Mallarmé first sent it to his friends, but there are three reasons (at least) for preferring the earlier dating here proposed. First, a line in the first quatrain, 'En qui vont les péchés d'un peuple', reads much more like an impression of vice in a foreign capital than of prostitution somewhere in France.[7] Secondly, when Des Essarts substitutes, in his politer title for the poem, 'la reine Victoria' for 'la reine de Naples', it is very likely to be because he knows that he is naming a London poem. The third reason is more weighty. It concerns the subject, not the words used. Only at certain moments in that phase of the London drama—which can be taken to extend with intermissions from mid January to March—can the Mallarmé portrayed in the correspondence be imagined turning, or imagining himself turning, to a prostitute for relief in his anguish. The similarity between the moral preoccupations of the hero of the poem (i.e. 'celui qui dit *je*') and those of the loquacious correspondent of Henri Cazalis at that juncture is most clearly underlined by their common recourse to two nouns as keywords in their dilemma: 'le remords' and 'le crime'. For instance (and some of these fragments from the correspondence will be remembered from previous quotations), on 14 January, accusing himself of abandoning his beloved like a father deserting his child: 'Il y a là une faute. Il y a un vrai crime (. . .) Voilà le crime. C'est parce que je l'ai trompée. J'ai des remords, mon ami'; again on 30 January: 'Il serait *malhonnête, criminel* de ne pas l'épouser (. . .) je n'agis pas par la crainte du remords. Le remords ne dure pas dans ce siècle'; then, as Henri had complained of the Yapps, and wondered whether Ettie and he should part, it is evident that Stéphane compared his friend's situation with his own when he gave his advice: 'Je ne peux que te dire oublie, parce que tu peux le faire sans remords'; on 3 February, he

repeated his desire to forget his misfortune, a desire never satisfied because 'quand je veux oublier, j'ai des remords'. He depicted his wretchedness in terms that expressed a state of mind very similar to that of the hero of his poem: 'Maintenant, je veux dormir! Je vais avoir une affreuse période à traverser. Je vais dormir pendant ce temps-là. Avec du gin, avec de l'opium, avec tout.'[8] (In the poem another means is tried, not admitted in the letter.)

If despite this evidence it is still maintained that the poem was composed a year later, in the too great peace of Tournon, 'A une Putain' must be considered as no more than another exercise in Baudelairian verse, more mature in feeling and technique than those he wrote two years before—which would be a most improbable hypothesis, certainly not entertained by Mallarmé's most intimate friends when they first read the poem. Their exceptionally high praise of its poetic quality was conveyed in terms that signified also respect for the suffering to which it bore witness. In the case of Lefébure, the best judge amongst them, that respect was explicit:

> Ce qui me frappe surtout, dans vos vers éclatants et sombres, c'est une singulière puissance de concentration. Il est probable que les causes en remontent très loin dans votre vie, et qu'ils ont abouti comme corollaire au spleen qui fait votre force comme poète et votre douleur comme homme. Je sens si bien cela, moi qui vous suis fraternel, qu'il m'est impossible de vous lire sans que cela me fasse de la peine. Je pense surtout à votre *Sonnet à une putain*, un vrai chef-d'œuvre, qui contient un puits de douleur. Et moi aussi, j'ai été hanté par mon linceul! . . .[9]

This is not to say there is not much borrowing from Baudelaire in this poem. At this juncture, Mallarmé seems to have much frequented *Les Fleurs du mal*, and found there ideas and images that help him to express poetically his own thoughts and feelings. If the Hugo who told the story of Marius and Cosette had been the right literary model for his pseudo-Romantic courtship, one can understand that Baudelaire should bring Mallarmé assistance in the spleen-time that followed. Several reminiscences of *Les Fleurs du mal* that are perceptible in 'A une Putain' have been enumerated by such scholars as Madame Noulet and L. J. Austin.[10] For instance, one of its titles recalls

(perhaps deliberately) 'A celle qui est trop gaie', and there are undoubted echoes of such lines as these:

> Si ce n'est, par un soir sans lune, deux à deux,
> D'endormir la douleur sur un lit hasardeux.
>
> ('Brumes et pluies')
>
> Tombeaux et lupanars montrent sous leurs charmilles
> Un lit que le remords n'a jamais fréquenté.
>
> ('Les Deux Bonnes Sœurs')
>
> J'ai cherché dans l'amour un sommeil oublieux.
>
> ('La fontaine de sang')
>
> Je veux longtemps plonger mes doigts tremblants
> Dans l'épaisseur de ta crinière lourde;
> . . .
> Je veux dormir! dormir plutôt que vivre!
> Dans un sommeil aussi doux que la mort,
> J'étalerai mes baisers sans remords
> Sur ton beau corps (. . .)
> Je sucerai, pour noyer ma rancœur,
> Le népenthès et la bonne ciguë
> Aux bouts charmants de cette gorge aigüe
> Qui n'a jamais emprisonné de cœur.
>
> ('Le Léthé')[11]

Not all the echoes of *Les Fleurs du mal* in Mallarmé's sonnet are to be regarded as 'imitations', however, comprehensive as the word may be. For instance, the dominant metaphor in the following lines of Baudelaire's 'La Chevelure' is certainly borrowed for the first stanza of 'A une Putain':

> Fortes tresses, soyez la houle qui m'enlève!
> Tu contiens, mer d'ébène, un éblouissant rêve
> De voiles, de rameurs, de flammes et de mâts:
> . . .
> Je plongerai ma tête amoureuse d'ivresse
> Dans ce noir océan où l'autre est enfermé;
> Et mon esprit subtil que le roulis caresse
> Saura vous retrouver, ô féconde paresse,
> Infinis bercements du loisir embaumé!

But the lines in 'A une Putain' read:

ni creuser
Dans tes cheveux impurs une triste tempête
Sous l'incurable ennui que verse mon baiser.[11]

That is, what is significant is not the borrowing but the negation and disfigurement of what is borrowed. If we discern this debasement, at the beginning of Mallarmé's poem, in a *guignon*-haunted parody of Baudelaire's sumptuous imaginings, we shall I believe be reading it as he intended. In situation and tone of voice, his hero is markedly different from him that speaks in any of the Baudelaire fragments echoed by him. He does not accuse, revile, perversely admire, or ironically exalt the woman he addresses. He compares her with himself and envies her. Both are guilty of odious crimes ('noirs mensonges') but she, 'celle qui est tranquille', remains free from remorse and unafraid. He, for his part, confesses to a weakness directly opposite to her strength:

Je fuis, pâle, défait, hanté par mon linceul,
Ayant peur de mourir lorsque je couche seul.

My suggestion here is that Mallarmé's borrowing from 'La Chevelure' is in his intention a clear reference to it, such that the reader is made aware that what might have been an echo of melodious lines telling of voluptuous pleasure is here deliberately soured, at the very beginning of the poem, by the attitude of self-disparaging, lacklustre heaviness of flesh and spirit which is Mallarméan *ennui*. From which we may know that some at least of the poems in *Les Fleurs du mal* are presumed by Mallarmé to be part of the context in which his own poems will be read and understood. Another example of that presumption is found at the end of the poem, but it is one that will perhaps be seen more clearly when the earlier subject, the relationship between the substance of Mallarmé's poem and his personal experience, has been pursued further.

A good lead to follow in returning to that subject is provided by Madame Noulet, who remarks concisely, in her brief study of 'Angoisse':

Que l'expérience personnelle soit à la base de tels vers, ce n'en est pas moins le vocabulaire de Baudelaire qui sert à l'exprimer.[12]

This is written with particular reference to 'l'idée du vice, cause de l'impuissance', expressed in the lines

> Car le vice, rongeant ma native noblesse
> M'a comme toi marqué de sa stérilité.

Since the publication of the first volume of the *Correspondance* in 1959, it has been possible to see more clearly how pertinent Madame Noulet's example is. For Mallarmé's suspicion that his barren periods were attributable to youthful over-indulgence in the 'vice' referred to is made explicit in a letter to Cazalis dated 21 December 1864:

> Pour les vers, je suis fini, je crois: il y a de grandes lacunes dans mon cerveau qui est devenu incapable d'une pensée suivie et d'application. J'expie cruellement, par un réel abrutissement, toi seul le sais, mon ami, le priapisme de ma jeunesse.[13]

The 'toi seul le sais' is probably explained by a remark in an earlier letter, the second sent to Cazalis, of 24 May 1862:

> Je ne sais vraiment si je pourrai aller à Meudon. Il y a deux cornes diaboliques qui passent trop souvent à travers mon portefeuille.[14]

This example bears out neatly Madame Noulet's contention. How Mallarmé's readers are expected to understand the lines she quotes is a quite different question, however. They are presumably not supposed to penetrate as far as Cazalis into those very private recesses of the poet's experience and self-analysis. In any case, the comparability between a poet's sterility and a prostitute's ('M'a comme toi marqué de sa stérilité') is dubious and artificial, however elastic the term. The two lines in question weaken the sonnet's structure.

On the other hand, this defect is perhaps compensated for by the strength of the other, more important component of that structure, the contrast that outweighs the similarity, the antithesis *angoisse–tranquillité*. Immunity from remorse, considered as the moral characteristic of women of easy virtue, is a familiar convention in Baudelaire's world of promiscuous loving. For that reason, no doubt, it is made the symbol on which the opposition between poet and prostitute in Mallarmé's sonnet depends. The poet, obsessed by remorse for his betrayal of the woman he loves, hopes to share the benefit of the prostitute's privilege, the absence of remorse that she enjoys, when he comes to share her bed. It is clearly advantageous from the reader's point of view, and therefore the sonnet's, if we can remember, even indistinctly, the closing lines of Baudelaire's poem 'Allégorie':

> Elle ignore l'Enfer comme le Purgatoire,
> Et quand l'heure viendra d'entrer dans la Nuit noire,
> Elle regardera la face de la Mort,
> Ainsi qu'un nouveau-né, sans haine et sans remords.[15]

The likelihood that these lines were in the background of Mallarmé's sonnet clarifies not only the poem itself but the poet's moral problem, the very serious 'cas de conscience' which is its subject. A few months before, he had written to Cazalis, à propos of Ettie:

> Le bonheur est fait d'amourettes, comme d'amours (. . .) un cœur vierge peut apprendre ce que c'est qu'être blasé. *Apprendre* et *jouir*, tout est là.[16]

It was in this spirit, or so he said and perhaps thought, that he had started to woo Marie, and their London venture itself was to be an experiment. But that summary philosophy had proved inadequate when put to the test, and recourse had been necessary to an earlier moral sense conditioned by a Christian upbringing, and apparently still active. Thus conscience had made a coward of the would-be cynic. That, at least, is what the sonnet 'A une Putain', with some help, deviously obtained from Baudelaire, seems to tell.

The other poem that seems more likely to have been composed at the beginning of the period of solitude in London than at any other time is 'L'Assaut', or 'Le Château de l'Espérance'. It is a delicate allegory, and a poem less dramatically sombre than 'A une Putain'. When he sent it to Cazalis on 3 June 1863, Mallarmé said that it was 'vague et pâle comme une Rêverie',[17] and it does possess a dream-like quality. The allegory it sketches is fairly transparent. The poet's attempt (prefigured in 'Apparition') to make of his mistress 'his life and his ideal', both the woman to set up with him 'a real English home' in London and a pure, angelic creature to be worshipped,[18] had failed. 'L'Assaut' acknowledges that failure:[19]

L'Assaut
or
Le Château de l'Espérance[20]

Ta pâle chevelure ondoie
Parmi les parfums de ta peau
Comme folâtre un blanc drapeau
Dont la soie au soleil blondoie.

Las de battre dans les sanglots
L'air d'un tambour que l'eau défonce,
Mon cœur à son passé renonce
Et, déroulant ta tresse en flots,

Marche à l'assaut, monte,—ou roule ivre
Par des marais de sang,—[C: no dash] afin
De planter ce drapeau d'or fin
Sur ce [C: un] sombre château de cuivre

Où, [C: —Ou,] larmoyant de nonchaloir,
L'Espérance rebrousse et lisse
Sans qu'un astre pâle jaillisse
La Nuit noire comme un chat noir.

Although Mallarmé never published 'L'Assaut', it is one of the few poems of this period on which we have his own comments. When he sent it to Cazalis, he also sent him this explanation:

D'une chevelure qui a fait naître en mon cerveau l'idée d'un drapeau, mon cœur, pris d'une ardeur militaire, s'élance à travers d'affreux paysages et va assiéger le Château fort de l'Espérance pour y planter cet étendard d'or fin. Mais l'insensé, après ce court moment de folie, aperçoit l'Espérance qui n'est qu'une sorte de spectre voilé et stérile.[21]

A very different phantom from the bright fairy of 'Apparition', and opposite in meaning. There are links with other poems of the previous year too; analogy is strengthening its patterns in the poet's thought. The knight-errant with his golden banner is surely one of 'les mendiants d'azur, leurs pieds dans nos chemins'. The castle that proves to be of brass, and not 'pure gold' like the banner, recalls (with an ironical inversion of the real and the ideal) the medal in 'Haine du Pauvre', prone to verdigris as the golden louis is not.

Of the reminiscences of other authors in this poem, the one most easily discernible is one already recognized in 'Le Guignon'. Even more clearly than in the earlier poem, the sanguine idealist in 'L'Assaut' is, like Poe's knight errant, 'in search of Eldorado'.[22] The echoes of Baudelaire are less distinct, but not I think less sure. We may assume that it was Marie Gerhard's hair that had (to recall the poet's own words) put the idea of a flag into his head. But certain lines in Baudelaire's 'La Chevelure' no doubt helped. For instance, the conceit 'Je la veux agiter dans l'air comme un mouchoir' is likely to have prompted the more heroic idea of a banner streaming in the wind. As symbols, Mallarmé's 'chevelure' and Baudelaire's are opposites. Marie's hair speaks of heroic ventures and noble hopes, whereas the dark tresses of the mistress in Baudelaire's poem are a 'tent of darkness drawn', a refuge of indolent pleasure that shuts out both ugliness in this world and the heaven of the ideal:

> Cheveux bleus, pavillon de ténèbres tendues,
> Vous me rendez l'azur du ciel immense et rond . . .[23]

The image of Hope as a veiled spectre, 'larmoyant de nonchaloir' (one of Baudelaire's words)[24] and stroking the black cat, night—in vain for not a spark is seen—probably has its source in Baudelaire too. A clue to it is found in an early letter to Cazalis, on whose love for Ettie Mallarmé commented thus: 'Oh! Espérance—"une folle charmante", comme dit mélancoliquement ce grand Baudelaire'.[25] The reference is to an item in 'Les Litanies de Satan':

> O toi qui de la Mort, ta vieille et forte amante
> Engendras l'Espérance,—une folle charmante![26]

The lugubrious figure of Despair posing as Hope in Mallarmé's poem must surely be related to that 'charming, crazy' daughter of Satan and Death.[27]

The London thoughts which this Baudelairian fancy may have helped to shape into 'Le Château de l'Espérance' can be recognized, I believe, like those in 'Angoisse', in the letters that Mallarmé sent to Cazalis at the end of January and beginning of February 1863. For instance, in his letters of 30 January and 3 February, which contain such details as these:

Mon ami, sur terre l'amour ne peut avoir qu'une fin digne de lui, *la mort*. Les autres fins sont le désenchantement ou l'indifférence. Que c'est affreux! . . .

Je suis seul, tout seul avec un chat noir. Et cela est affreux.[28]

Perhaps it was that evening, as he ruffled and smoothed the black cat's fur, and wondered what hope remained, that he imagined Baudelaire's 'folle charmante', like himself disconsolate and tearful, absently ruffling and smoothing the sable robe of night.

One of Mallarmé's best-known sonnets, usually supposed to have been written in 1864, is so closely related to 'L'Assaut' in subject, and so similar to it in general shape, that one may be fairly sure it was written at about the same time.[29] The poet continues his despondent reflections on love, changing however his point of view. The theme is not now the frailty of a lover's hope of happiness, but the punishment of the artist who has been faithless to the Muse:

Le Pitre châtié[30]

Pour ses yeux,—pour nager dans ces lacs, dont les quais
Sont plantés de beaux cils qu'un matin bleu pénètre,
J'ai, Muse,—moi, ton pitre,—enjambé la fenêtre
Et fui notre baraque où fument tes quinquets.

Et d'herbes enivré, j'ai plongé comme un traître
Dans ces lacs défendus, et, quand tu m'appelais,
Baigné mes membres nus dans l'onde aux blancs galets,
Oubliant mon habit de pitre au tronc d'un hêtre.

Le soleil du matin séchait mon corps nouveau
Et je sentais fraîchir loin de ta tyrannie
La neige des glaciers dans ma chair assainie,

Ne sachant pas, hélas! quand s'en allait sur l'eau
Le suif de mes cheveux et le fard de ma peau,
Muse, que cette crasse était tout le génie!

The love-adventure has taught the poet a bitter truth about his art, or rather brought home to him a truth half-apprehended already, and intimated more vaguely in 'Le Sonneur'. He has discovered that poetry really is, as Poe said, fiction, a matter of histrionics, cock's feathers, greasepaint, and beauty-patches.[31] Let the poet once plunge into real life and all this make-believe which was his private world will desert him. When he seeks to return to his art he will find himself unfitted to pursue it, left as he is with only cold reason and experience of the world—plain truth instead of dreams. Life (and therefore love) is inimical to art. As Balzac had once put it: 'Les caresses d'une femme font évanouir la Muse.'[32] This blunter formulation is relevant to Mallarmé's experience and indicates the place of 'Le Pitre châtié' in the chain of his introspective thought. The rivality between the woman and the fairy, eluded in 'Apparition', has now assumed its final shape. The Muse has taken the place of the fairy, or the fairy has been identified as the Muse.[33] The choice is still however between life and dream.[34]

The link between 'Le Château de l'Espérance' and 'Le Pitre châtié' is as plain in the symbolism as in the thought. In the one the beloved's hair is a banner that should fly proudly on the Castle of Hope, and in the other her eyes are lakes which offer the joy of living, after long exile from life in the stifling artificiality of the Muse's tent.[35] In both, it should be observed, the hero is a clown who escapes from his booth at the fair. In this respect, the sonnet appears as a well-constructed extension of a metaphor which had been left in a vague and shapeless condition in 'Le Château de l'Espérance' (where indeed it hangs loose, not integrated in the main fiction):

> Las de battre dans les sanglots
> L'air d'un tambour que l'eau défonce,
> Mon cœur à son passé renonce . . . [36]

All these resemblances do not however prove that the two poems are near-contemporary. Emotions can be recollected, and images elaborated, after some time has passed. But the letters to Cazalis once more provide some corroboration. The one written on 3 June 1863, mentioned above, not only expresses ideas on reality and dreams which provide the best psychological context for 'Le Pitre châtié', but also contains hints that some of the poem's symbols were still—or already—in the poet's mind when he wrote the letter:

Nous avons fait hier une magnifique promenade en bateau à travers les bois enchantés de Richmond, et nous voulions amarrer quelques instants et te dater une bonne lettre du tronc de quelque bouleau penché sur l'eau verte et sombre. Mais le courant nous a emportés. Depuis bien longtemps le courant m'emporte à travers les jours et je vis je ne sais comment . . . Tu me parles de la Suisse. Il y a tant de bleu là bas, autre que le ciel,—et les yeux de Marie qui m'y suivrait,[37]—que ce rêve est un de ceux dont je caresse le mieux la crinière et que je chevauche avec le plus de joie . . . Si je ne songeais à la Suisse que pour ses glaciers vierges et la neige qui y est une fleur comme les lys, je partirais sans un penny dans ma bourse . . . Presse les mains à tes amis . . . de la part d'un esprit bohémien toujours dégoûté de la place où il a campé et qui voudrait se reposer dans leur calme et noble entretien.[38]

In the absence of any evidence in favour of another date, therefore, there are good reasons for believing that 'Le Pitre châtié' not only expresses some of Mallarmé's London thoughts but was composed in London, in the late spring or early summer of 1863.

The main symbol of the poem, which makes of the poet the Muse's buffoon—clown and showman combined—whose task is to attract the public, by his antics and his patter, into the booth in which the Muse is on show, was to play an important part in Mallarmé's work.[39] The clown is clearly the luckless poet of 'Le Guignon ' in a new guise, and I have already suggested that the idea for the new guise seems to come from Poe's description of the stage properties that constitute the stock-in-trade 'in ninety-nine cases out of the hundred, . . . of the literary *histrio*'. Perhaps there are also reminiscences of Banville's 'Pauvres Saltimbanques' and Baudelaire's 'Le Fou et la Vénus':

Saltimbanques et pauvres saltimbanques, en effet, ces poëtes inspirés, ces comédiens ivres de passion, ces voix éloquentes, ces joueurs de violons et ces joueurs de lyre, ces marionnettes de génie qui ont pour état de pleurer d'abord, comme le veut Horace, et après de faire pleurer la foule et de la faire rire . . . [40]

Aux pieds d'une colossale Vénus, un de ces fous artificiels, un de ces bouffons volontaires .. . . . affublé d'un costume éclatant et ridicule, coiffé de cornes et de sonnettes, tout ramassé contre le piédestal, lève des yeux pleins de larmes vers l'immortelle Déesse.[41]

Lines in Baudelaire's 'La Béatrice' may have helped to quicken the image of the *poète enguignonné* as the debased actor:

—"Contemplons à loisir cette caricature
Et cette ombre d'Hamlet imitant sa posture,
Le regard indécis et les cheveux au vent.
. . .
Ce gueux, cet histrion en vacances, ce drôle, . . . "[42]

'Le Pitre châtié' is a poem in the *guignon* convention, and it is in accordance with that convention that the clown's escapade ends in dismal disillusionment. In itself, the understanding that art is make-believe is not necessarily ruinous to the artist. That life and art contradict each other might be a melancholy truth for the lover , but for the poet it was a promise of rebirth. It is not in 'Le Pitre châtié' that the general conclusion is expressed concerning the reflections on life and art pursued by Mallarmé during the early months of 1863; it is rather in 'Les Fenêtres', sent to Cazalis with 'Le Château de l'Espérance' on 3 June, the first of three poems in a verse-form Baudelaire had used for several of his longer poems, four-alexandrine stanzas with alternate rhymes:

Les Fenêtres[43]

Las du triste h[ô]pital, et de l'encens fétide
Qui monte en la blancheur banale des rideaux
Vers le grand crucifix ennuyé du mur vide,
Le moribond, parfois, redresse son vieux dos,

Se traîne, et va, moins pour chauffer sa pourriture
Que pour voir du soleil le long d'un mur, coller
Les poils longs et les os de sa blême figure
Aux fenêtres qu'un beau rayon clair veut hâler.

Et sa bouche, fi[é]vreuse et d'azur bleu vorace,
Comme un luxurieux dont la lèvre s'endort
En savourant la fleur d'une peau jeune, encrasse
D'un long baiser amer les tièdes carreaux d'or;

Ivre, il vit, oubliant l'horreur des saintes huiles,
Les tisanes, l'horloge, et le lit infligé,
La toux. Et quand le soir saigne parmi les tuiles,
Son œil, à l'horizon de lumière gorgé,

Voit des galères d'or belles comme des cygnes
Sur un fleuve de pourpre et de parfums dormir
En berçant l'éclair fauve et riche de leurs lignes
Dans un grand nonchaloir chargé de souvenir!

Ainsi, pris du dégoût de l'homme à l'âme dure
Vautré dans le bonheur, où tous ses appétits
Mangent, et qui s'entête à chercher cette ordure
Pour l'offrir à la femme allaitant ses petits,

Je vais [in other early manuscripts: 'Je fuis,'] et je m'accroche
à toutes les croisées
D'où l'on tourne le dos à la vie, et, béni,
Dans leur verre lavé d'éternelles rosées
Que dore le matin chaste de l'Infini

Je me mire et me vois ange! Et je meurs, et j'aime
—Que la vitre soit l'Art, soit la Mysticité—
A renaître, portant le Rêve en diadème,
Au ciel antérieur où fleurit la Beauté.

Mais hélas! *Ici bas* est le roi: sa hantise
Vient m'écœurer encor jusqu'en cet abri s[û]r
Et le vomissement infect de la Bêtise
Me force à me boucher le nez devant l'azur.

Est-il moyen, mon Dieu qui savez l'amertume,
D'enfoncer le cristal par ce monstre insulté
Et de m'enfuir, avec mes deux ailes sans plume,
—Au risque de rouler pendant l'éternité?

'Les Fenêtres' is an eloquent declaration of the philosophy on which the young poet intended to found not simply his aesthetic but his life as an artist. Cazalis, when he received a copy, wrote from Strasbourg on 14 June and proclaimed it 'quasi un chef-d'œuvre'. There is no doubt that it is the most important and the most impressive of the London poems. Mallarmé was to make it his frontispiece, explicitly so entitled, in his manuscript 'Carnets' of 1864; and two years later, in *Le Parnasse contemporain*, it again had pride of place.

It is a profession of faith addressed to his early readers, just as the sonnet 'Salut', placed at the head of his collected poems in the 1899 and later editions, is a profession of faith addressed to posterity. Fundamentally, the faith is the same, the radical idealism of the 'azure-beggar'.

How seriously and completely Mallarmé had embraced that faith by the summer of 1863, his letters to Cazalis have already shown. Among them, the one dated 3 June is of particular relevance to the reading of 'Les Fenêtres' for it contains the following passage:

Il [Emmanuel] . . . confond trop l'Idéal avec le R[é]el. La sottise d'un poète moderne a été jusqu'à se désoler que "l'Action ne fût pas la sœur du Rêve".—Emmanuel est de ceux qui regrettent cela. Mon Dieu, s'il en était autrement, si le Rêve était ainsi défloré et abaissé, où donc nous sauverions-nous, nous autres malheureux que la terre dégoûte et qui n'avons que le Rêve pour refuge. O mon Henri, abreuve-toi d'Idéal. Le bonheur d'ici bas est ignoble—il faut avoir les mains bien calleuses pour le ramasser. Dire: "Je suis heureux!" c'est dire: "Je suis un lâche"—et plus souvent: "Je suis un niais." Car il ne faut pas voir au-dessus de ce plafond de bonheur le ciel de l'Idéal, ou fermer les yeux exprès. J'ai fait sur ces idées un petit po[è]me "*Les Fenêtres*", je te l'envoie (. . .) Adieu, mon Henri; oui, ici-bas a une odeur de cuisine.[44]

As well as shedding light on the meaning of the poem, this summary of the ideas embodied in it helps to place the ideas themselves in relation to the French tradition. They are central in the early romantic creed, and were luminously expressed a hundred years before ('Art and Mysticity' included) by Rousseau's Julie:

'L'illusion cesse où commence la jouissance. Le pays des chimères est en ce monde le seul digne d'être habité; et tel est le néant des choses humaines que hors l'Être existant par lui-même il n'y a rien de beau que ce qui n'est pas.[45]

In Mallarmé's own time, Julie's belief had nowhere been echoed more seductively than in the writings of Baudelaire. No one had proclaimed with more apparent conviction the supremacy of dreams and their divorce from life and action:

Des rêves! toujours des rêves! et plus l'âme est ambitieuse et délicate, plus les rêves l'éloignent du possible. Chaque homme porte en lui sa dose d'opium naturel, incessamment sécrétée et renouvelée, et, de la naissance à la mort, combien comptons-nous d'heures remplies par la jouissance positive, par l'action réussie et décidée?[46]

Le bon sens nous dit que les choses de la terre n'existent que bien peu, et que la vraie réalité n'est que dans les rêves. Pour digérer le bonheur naturel, comme l'artificiel, il faut d'abord avoir le courage de l'avaler; et ceux qui mériteraient peut-être le bonheur sont justement ceux-là à qui la félicité, telle que la conçoivent les mortels, a toujours fait l'effet d'un vomitif.[47]

Du sein d'un monde goulu, affamé de matérialité, Poe s'est élancé dans les rêves. Etouffé qu'il était par l'atmosphère américaine, il a écrit en tête d'*Euréka*: "J'offre ce livre à ceux qui ont mis leur foi dans les rêves comme dans les seules réalités!"[48]

In his letter to Cazalis Mallarmé so nearly echoes Baudelaire's affirmations that he may well have had them in mind as he wrote. He was not expressing agreement with Baudelaire, however, but, once more, condemning his recent betrayal of ideals and beliefs he had formerly espoused.[49] Without any doubt, Baudelaire is the modern poet whose foolishness is referred to so harshly, though some critics are curiously loth to believe that admiration does not necessarily exclude critical disagreements. It was he who had written, in 'Le Reniement de saint Pierre':

—Certes, je sortirai, quant à moi, satisfait
D'un monde où l'action n'est pas la sœur du rêve;
Puissé-je user du glaive et périr par le glaive!
Saint Pierre a renié Jésus . . . il a bien fait![50]

In 'Les Fenêtres', as in the letter to Cazalis, Mallarmé is once more using Baudelaire's own tenets to confound him. In this particular case, it seems ungenerous of him to do so, if not wilfully unjust. 'Le Reniement de saint Pierre' was one of the poems he had copied, as a schoolboy, from the first edition of *Les Fleurs du mal*. He must therefore have read the note (not included in later editions) in which the charge he was laying had been anticipated by Baudelaire, and dismissed:

Parmi les morceaux suivants, le plus caractérisé a déjà paru dans un des principaux recueils littéraires de Paris, où il n'a été considéré, du moins par les gens d'esprit, que pour ce qu'il est véritablement, le pastiche des raisonnements de l'ignorance et de la fureur. Fidèle à son douloureux programme, l'auteur des *Fleurs du Mal* a dû, en parfait comédien, façonner son esprit à tous les sophismes comme à toutes les corruptions. Cette déclaration candide n'empêchera pas sans doute les critiques honnêtes de le ranger parmi les théologiens de la populace et de l'accuser d'avoir regretté pour notre Sauveur Jésus-Christ, pour la Victime éternelle et volontaire, le rôle d'un conquérant, d'un Attila égalitaire et dévastateur.[51]

This surely is the very accusation contained in Mallarmé's letter to Cazalis, against 'un poète moderne'. Now, as in 'Le Guignon' a year before, his complaint is that because the ideal and the real are incompatible, because their values are irreconcilable, the poet who was the champion of the idealists has turned against them and thrown in his lot with the realists. Not that he has given up one ideal in order to serve another, but he has acknowledged that the Ideal is unattainable in this world.

The accusation is now more detailed than in 'Le Guignon', and the mention of Emmanuel des Essarts, coupled unexpectedly with Baudelaire,[52] has implications that reveal another aspect of Mallarmé's criticism. It will be remembered that he had written, in his article on Des Essarts's poems, contemporary with 'Le Guignon':

Théodore de Banville . . . , qui décoche contre la Réalité la flèche d'or de son arc divin, l'Idéal, fait juste le contraire d'Em. des Essarts, lequel prend le Réel au sérieux et le *lyrise*.[53]

The tone of approving interest in which this observation was made is deceptive. Mallarmé was very politely reproaching his friend with an aesthetic error into which Banville never fell. When therefore, a year later, he names Des Essarts as one who, *like Baudelaire*, regrets that action is not sister to the dream, he is accusing the author of 'La Chevelure' of 'taking reality seriously' and lyricizing it, like Des Essarts. That appears to be the general sense of the commentary Mallarmé sent to Cazalis, sketching the thoughts that had gone to the making of 'Les Fenêtres'. It would be wrong, however, to assume that the thoughts actually expressed in the poem are identical with those in its author's commentary, or altogether reducible to them. They can be accurately discerned only in a critical reading of the poem itself, taking account of literary interferences.

In rhetorical shape, 'Les Fenêtres' is an extended simile, of the same general type as 'Le Sonneur', or Baudelaire's

'L'Albatros'. The first term of the simile, the vehicle, the sick man near to death, looking for a ray of sunshine and beholding a glorious sunset, through the windows of a hospital ward, occupies the first five stanzas. The other term, the tenor, the poet's seeking after the ideal, takes up the next three, and in the last two the vehicle and the tenor merge.

The first half of the poem holds no difficulties that cannot be quickly removed. Its secrets, so far as the substance is concerned, amount to no more than a few literary reminiscences (some of which the Pléiade editors have noted) of Sainte-Beuve and Baudelaire. The borrowing from Sainte-Beuve is considerable. The whole idea of Mallarmé's simile is provided by the 'Sonnet imité de Bowles' in *Notes et sonnets*:

> Comme, après une nuit de veille bien cruelle,
> Un malade en langueur, affaibli d'un long mal
> . . .
> Se lève enfin, et seul où le rayon l'appelle,
> Se traîne: il voit le ciel, l'éclat oriental
> . . .
> Et son front se ressuie, et son âme est sereine:
> Ainsi, douce Espérance, après l'âpre saison
> Tout mon cœur refleurit: j'ai senti ton haleine!

The following contributory lines occur in Baudelaire's poem 'Réversibilité':

> Ange plein de santé, connaissez-vous les Fièvres,
> Qui, le long des grands murs de l'hospice blafard,
> Comme les exilés, s'en vont d'un pied traînard,
> Cherchant le soleil rare et remuant les lèvres? . . . [54]

And these in 'Les Phares':

> Rembrandt, triste hôpital tout rempli de murmures,
> Et d'un grand crucifix décoré seulement . . . [55]

The Baudelaire passage which probably inspired Mallarmé's stanzas on the sick man's sunset is the description, in 'La Vie et l'œuvre d'Edgar Poe', of the experience of opium-eating:

> L'espace est approfondi par l'opium; l'opium y donne un sens magique à toutes les teintes, et fait vibrer tous les bruits avec une plus significative sonorité. Quelquefois des échappées magnifiques, gorgées de lumière et de couleur, s'ouvrent soudainement dans ses

paysages, et l'on voit apparaître au fond de leurs horizons des villes orientales et des architectures, vaporisées par la distance, où le soleil jette des pluies d'or.[56]

If this fragment is indeed the source of the sunset in stanzas four and five, it has made possible in 'Les Fenêtres' some fine Baudelairian lines,[57] but at considerable cost. The simile that sustains the poem is intended to compare experiences at two quite different levels, and its effect depends on this distance, as much as on the similarity. But the magic sunset that the sick man is favoured with abolishes the distance and at the same time all verisimilitude. Instead of the moment of humble human pleasure he aspires to ('voir le soleil le long d'un mur'), he is given the triumph for which an azure-beggar might long—the poet himself for instance ('celui qui dit *je*'). The balance of the simile and therefore of the whole poem is seriously disturbed.

It is possible that stanzas six and seven need no other explanation than that provided in the letter to Cazalis, but here too some attention to the immediate literary background will not be found superfluous. The eighth and following stanzas on the other hand require attentive reading almost line by line.

Ainsi, pris du dégoût de l'homme à l'âme dure
Vautré dans le bonheur, où tous ses appétits
Mangent . . .

One may wonder who represented, in Mallarmé's life at that time, such men as these. People in London he only saw from a distance. His memory needed to go back only a few weeks, however, to his stay at Sens, and the meetings held with his uncles to discuss the material consequences of his father's death. Such was the impression they had made on him that when he wrote to Cazalis from Versailles, on the first of April, he had called them 'un tas d'égoismes ventrus qui sont mes oncles',[58] and Cazalis had expressed his sympathy by adding his own contempt: 'Tes oncles vont bien rire: tes oncles avec leur gros rire. Et comme leur gros mépris va faire fi de toi maintenant. Passe avec fierté sous leur mépris Stéphane, et ne daigne même pas les mépriser à ton tour.'[59] It is as the opposites of such creatures that the artists figure in this correspondence, those that Cazalis had found in Strasbourg, those that Mallarmé had failed to find in London, whence the ending of Stéphane's letter of 3 June, quoted above.[60] Thus there is recent personal experience, keenly felt, behind stanza six of 'Les Fenêtres'.

> *Je fuis, et je m'accroche à toutes les croisées*
> *D'où l'on tourne le dos à la vie . . .*

This description of the poet's reactions to his situation, and the magic casements that offer him release from it, is better understood if we suppose it to have been written under the influence of Poe, whose idealistic conception of art is less aggressively theological and pessimistic than Baudelaire's (as formulated for instance in 'Les Phares') and whose pleasing presentation of his beliefs makes it possible for artistic delight and religious ecstasy to be compared even by an unbeliever. We know that Mallarmé had with him in London Baudelaire's translation of Poe's tales (since he lent it to Chatelain),[61] and therefore the two essays on Poe that served as prefaces to the two volumes. In the second of them Baudelaire repeats his paraphrase of the passage of Poe's 'The Poetic Principle' that begins: 'An immortal instinct, deep within the spirit of man, is thus, plainly, a sense of the Beautiful':

> C'est cet admirable, cet immortel instinct du Beau qui nous fait considérer la terre et ses spectacles comme un aperçu, comme une correspondance du Ciel. La soif insatiable de tout ce qui est au delà, et que révèle la vie, est la preuve la plus vivante de notre immortalité. C'est à la fois par la poésie et *à travers* la poésie, par et *à travers* la musique que l'âme entrevoit les splendeurs situées derrière le tombeau; et quand un poème exquis amène les larmes au bord des yeux, ces larmes ne sont pas la preuve d'un excès de jouissance, elles sont bien plutôt le témoignage d'une mélancolie irritée, d'une postulation des nerfs, d'une nature exilée dans l'imparfait et qui voudrait s'emparer immediatement, sur cette terre même, d'un paradis révélé.
>
> Ainsi le principe de la poésie est, strictement et simplement, l'aspiration humaine vers une beauté supérieure, et la manifestation de ce principe est dans un enthousiasme, une excitation de l'âme,—enthousiasme tout à fait indépendant de la passion qui est l'ivresse du cœur, et de la vérité qui est la pâture de la raison.[62]

Much as there is in Poe's belief that Mallarmé could not accept, there is also much that he need not reject, and (to anticipate) I know of no more likely source than this passage for the image that makes of Art and Mysticity windows *through* which (as in Poe's essay *through* the poem and *through* the music) we may have access to *le ciel antérieur où fleurit la Beauté*. Even if in this I am mistaken, a comparison between the two texts indicates the direction which Mallarmé's thoughts on poetry were apparently taking. The Ideal and the Real are separate, and alien in nature one to the other, but the joys of the Ideal (Poe notwithstanding) are accessible to those who have not yet departed from this world.

Je me mire, et me vois ange!

The window-pane that becomes a mirror is an enigma which we can solve, I believe, by looking not for highly metaphysical subtleties but for more borrowings, and not for esoteric symbolism but for over-elliptical expression. The sources are again in Baudelaire. The condition to which the poet of 'Les Fenêtres' says he aspires appears to be that described in the section of *Le Poème du haschisch* originally entitled 'L'Idéal artificiel' and later 'Le Goût de l'Infini':

Il est des jours où l'homme s'éveille avec un génie jeune et vigoureux. Ses paupières à peine déchargées du sommeil qui les scellait, le monde extérieur s'offre à lui avec un relief puissant, une netteté de contours, une richesse de couleurs admirables. Le monde moral ouvre ses vastes perspectives, pleines de clartés nouvelles. L'homme gratifié de cette béatitude, malheureusement rare et passagère, se sent à la fois plus artiste et plus juste, plus noble, pour tout dire en un mot. Mais ce qu'il y a de plus singulier dans cet état exceptionnel de l'esprit et des sens, que je puis sans exagération appeler paradisiaque, si je le compare aux lourdes ténèbres de l'existence commune et journalière, c'est qu'il n'a été créé par aucune cause bien visible et facile à définir . . . C'est pourquoi je préfère considérer cette condition anormale de l'esprit comme une véritable grâce, comme un miroir magique où l'homme est invité à se voir en beau, c'est-à-dire tel qu'il devrait et pourrait être; une espèce d'excitation angélique, un rappel à l'ordre sous une forme complimenteuse.[63]

It is an experience given to the sinner as to the saint. So in the poem 'L'Aube spirituelle':

Quand chez les débauchés l'aube blanche et vermeille
Entre en société de l'Idéal rongeur,
Par l'opération d'un mystère vengeur
Dans la brute assoupie un ange se réveille.

Des Cieux Spirituels l'inaccessible azur
Pour l'homme terrassé qui rêve encore et souffre,
S'ouvre et s'enfonce avec l'attirance du gouffre . . .[64]

For his part Mallarmé declares:

[Je me mire, et me vois Ange,] et je meurs (in the Vacquerie Manuscript 'je songe'), et j'aime
—Que la vitre soit l'Art, soit la Mysticité—
A renaître, portant le Rêve en diadème,
Au ciel antérieur où fleurit la Beauté.

The analogy between Art and Mysticity, aesthetic delight and religious exaltation, is insinuated by extending an image frequently used of the one in such a way that it extends to the other as well. Aesthetic rapture, like religious fervour (and like immortality in the Christian doctrine) is a dying in the world of the flesh in order to live according to the spirit. The analogy that at first was suggested only by *renaître* became more explicit when *je meurs* was substituted for *je songe*.

The window of Art and the window of Mysticity[65] give access to paradises that are artificial in the sense that they are man-devised, fabricated; they are natural in the sense that they are enjoyed with the help of no other drug than the natural opium of the imagination.[66] The windows are mirrors inasmuch as there is a secret correspondence between us and the environment created for us by (for instance) the paintings of Leonardo as Baudelaire describes them:

Léonard de Vinci, miroir profond et sombre,
Où des anges charmants, avec un doux souris
Tout chargé de mystère, apparaissent à l'ombre
Des glaciers et des pins qui ferment leur pays.[67]

If 'Les Fenêtres' were read as a purely personal confession of the poet's own beliefs, his recognition that religious exaltation provides one of two alternative escapes into the ideal would be puzzling. This compliment to religion would be at variance with his previous anti-Christian attitude and directly in conflict with the emphatic declaration, sent to Cazalis only a few weeks after this poem, that 'nothing is great, true, changeless and holy but Art'.[68] Moreover, it would be contradicted by poems written a little later ('Symphonie littéraire' in particular'), in which the criticism of Baudelaire is taken up again and aimed specifically at his 'mysticity'.[69] To explain such apparent inconsistencies one would have to consider whether 'Les Fenêtres' does not bear witness to some otherwise unrecorded vicissitude of the London ordeal, some momentary revulsion against the bleakness of unbelief. But if the poem is read as a profession of faith in 'azure-begging', in general, no such hypothesis need be entertained since there is no inconsistency. The recognition of religion is abstract and theoretical, and a requirement of the subject. It is also in the spirit of the time. In a very similar sense Flaubert had written to Louise Colet, in letters dated respectively 12 October 1853 and 4 September 1852, of 'Art and Religion, those two great manifestations of the idea', and of his own faith as 'a sort of aesthetic mysticism'. The notion that art was, as it were, taking over from religion was very much in the air. Renan was beginning to spread persuasively the doctrine that one of his opponents summarized as follows:

Les religions sont la forme la plus touchante et la plus naïve de l'art; mais elles appartiennent à l'art; à leur source, elles ne s'en distinguent pas. C'est ce que déclare expressément l'auteur: "La religion est certainement la plus haute et la plus attachante des manifestations de la nature humaine; entre *tous les genres de poésie*, c'est celui qui atteint le mieux le but essentiel *de l'art*." (. . .) A mesure que la raison se développe et que la lumière de la réflexion grandit, les fantômes divins que créait la jeune imagination de l'homme décroissent, pâlissent, et s'effacent. Ces grandes ombres, suspendues entre le ciel et la terre, s'évanouissent dans les nuages. L'art se substitue, dans sa pureté, au culte de ces simulacres invraisemblables et vieillis, et devient l'universelle religion de l'humanité réfléchie. "L'art seul est infini." (. . .) Ainsi la religion, forme imparfaite du culte de l'idéal, fait retour à son principe et vient s'absorber dans l'art; telle est la conclusion suprême des *Études d'histoire religieuse*.[70]

Seen in the light of these ideas, 'Be the window Art or be it Mysticity' is not inconsistent with Mallarmé's aesthetic idealism. More than once in the following years he repeats the admission that religion is a sort of passive substitute for poetry. Writing to Cazalis on 14 May 1867, he refers to 'ce paradis, que la pauvre humanité n'espère qu'en sa mort, par ignorance et par paresse';[71] and in the stilted, dogmatic, obscure conclusion to an article on Leon Dierx he writes, in 1872:

L'âme, tacite et qui ne [se] suspend pas aux paroles de l'élu familier, le poète, est, à moins qu'elle ne sacrifie à Dieu l'ensemble impuissant de ses aspirations, vouée irrémédiablement au Néant.[72]

Which would seem to mean that spiritually, outside of art, which is the experience of beauty, and religion which is the pathetic hope that we shall have that experience hereafter, there is nothing.

[A renaître,] portant mon Rêve en diadème,
Au ciel antérieur où fleurit la Beauté!

The analogy is pursued, but with a bias better served by the variant '*je songe*' than it is by *je meurs*. *Rêve* and *Beauté*, like *je songe*, point to art, and not to religion as Christians understand it. This is well brought out, and at the same time the poet's intention in this and the following stanzas is clarified, by a comparison with two poems by Baudelaire. They are 'Les Phares' and 'Bénédiction', both of which were in Mallarmé's mind when he wrote 'Les Fenêtres'. The fact that he has chosen to use the same verse-form makes the contrast between his conception and Baudelaire's the more striking. In 'Les Phares', after symbolizing in eight stanzas the worlds opened to us by the works of eight modern artists, from Leonardo to Delacroix, Baudelaire ends his poem with the magnificent *de profundis* hymn which places the significance of all art ultimately in man's tragic relationship to God:

Ces malédictions, ces blasphèmes, ces plaintes,
Ces extases, ces cris, ces pleurs, ces *Te deum*,
Sont un écho redit par mille labyrinthes;
C'est pour les cœurs mortels un divin opium!

C'est un cri répété par mille sentinelles,
Un ordre renvoyé par mille porte-voix;
C'est un phare allumé sur mille citadelles,
Un appel de chasseurs perdus dans les grands bois!

Car c'est vraiment, Seigneur, le meilleur témoignage
Que nous puissions donner de notre dignité
Que cet ardent sanglot qui roule d'âge en âge
Et vient mourir au bord de votre éternité![73]

Similarly, poetry is a form of prayer for the poet of 'Bénédiction':

Vers le Ciel, où son œil voit un trône splendide,
Le Poète serein lève ses bras pieux,
Et les vastes éclairs de son esprit lucide
Lui dérobent l'aspect des peuples furieux:

—"Soyez béni, mon Dieu, qui donnez la souffrance
Comme un divin remède à nos impuretés
Et comme la meilleure et la plus pure essence
Qui prépare les forts aux saintes voluptés!

Je sais que vous gardez une place au Poète
Dans les rangs bienheureux des saintes Légions,
Et que vous l'invitez à l'éternelle fête
Des Trônes, des Vertus, des Dominations.

Je sais que la douleur est la noblesse unique
Où ne mordront jamais la terre et les enfers,
Et qu'il faut pour tresser ma couronne mystique
Imposer tous les temps et tous les univers.

Mais les bijoux perdus de l'antique Palmyre,
Les métaux inconnus, les perles de la mer,
Par votre main montés, ne pourraient pas suffire
A ce beau diadème éblouissant et clair;

Car il ne sera fait que de pure lumière,
Puisée au foyer saint des rayons primitifs,
Et dont les yeux mortels dans leur splendeur entière,
Ne sont que des miroirs obscurcis et plaintifs!"[74]

Different as they are from each other in mood, these two poems in praise of art both celebrate the power and glory of God. 'Les Fenêtres', on the other hand, is a hymn to Beauty. The contrast, and at the same time the affinity with Mallarmé's poem, is particularly clear in 'Bénédiction'. The young poet who is its hero no doubt served as a model for the dreamer in 'Les Fenêtres'. Like him he turns away from the horrors of here below. Like him he sees himself in the heavenly choirs. But whereas the diadem of the one (*ce beau diadème éblouissant et clair*) is a martyr's crown, won by suffering and to be worn hereafter, the other's is the emblem of the dreamer, and belongs not to a future heaven of ecstatic adoration but to a world of beauty that can be enjoyed this side of the grave. A spiritual

climate such as is described in Baudelaire's 'L'Invitation au Voyage' (*Spleen de Paris*):

Fleur incomparable, tulipe retrouvée, allégorique dahlia, c'est là, n'est-ce pas, dans ce beau pays si calme et si rêveur, qu'il faudrait aller vivre et fleurir? Ne serais-tu pas encadrée dans ton analogie, et ne pourrais-tu pas te mirer, pour parler comme les mystiques, dans ta propre correspondance?[75]

In some sense a *former* heaven, the innocent paradise of childhood, which only art can open up anew. Whether Mallarmé was tempted also, as were other poets of the time, by the idea of a golden age which was the childhood of mankind, when paradise really was on earth, is a question that need not be answered here. In the meantime, if we are dubious about the 'ciel antérieur', we may note that at least it dispenses, usefully from the poet's point of view, with the need for Poe's 'ecstatic prescience of the glories beyond the grave'.

Mais hélas! Ici-bas *est le roi: sa hantise*
Vient m'écœurer parfois jusqu'en cet abri sûr
Et le vomissement impur de la Bêtise
Me force à me boucher le nez devant l'azur.

This is one of those stanzas against which Mallarmé's friends were soon to begin warning him, too packed with meaning to be clear or even comprehensible.[76] In these four lines of close-knit metaphor the terms of the original simile are refocused and elaborated. The analogy is made more complex. The dying man at the window, *d'azur bleu vorace*, gazes gratefully at the blue sky, but the smell of sickness is in the air he breathes and he has to hold his nose. So it is with the dreamer. His ideal atmosphere is sometimes fouled by a nauseating obsession with reality (*sa hantise*), 'the impure vomit of Stupidity'. He too, to continue his azure-gazing, must keep the stench from his nostrils as best he can.

Only an inattentive or impatient reader could take this stanza to mean simply, and quite uninterestingly, that thoughts of here below (like a smell of cooking) sometimes call the dreamer back to earth. His aesthetic pleasures are not impaired by any care of his own for the real, but by the failure of certain artists to free themselves from its tyranny, the 'stupidity of the modern artist' who takes reality seriously for its own sake, the heresy of which Mallarmé accuses Des Essarts and which sometimes disfigures even works he delights in. Works like *Les Fleurs du mal*, soiled by such poems as 'Le Reniement de saint Pierre'. In other words, in this penultimate stanza the subject of 'Les Fenêtres' has narrowed. What is in question now is realism in art. It is scathingly condemned, in a harsh image which Mallarmé was not the first to employ. It had already been used at Baudelaire's expense in an article published by the *Figaro* on 12 December 1861, praising *Les Fleurs du mal* but making some outspoken reservations which culminate in the sentence: 'Il faut lire ses *Fleurs du mal* d'une main—et se boucher le nez de l'autre':[77]

> *Est-il moyen, mon Dieu qui savez l'amertume,*
> *D'enfoncer ce cristal par le monstre insulté*
> [De casser le cristal par le monstre empesté]
> *Et de m'enfuir, avec mes deux ailes sans plume,*
> *—Au risque de rouler pendant l'Eternité?*

Since on this side of the window of art there is no sure protection from the obsession with reality, is it possible to burst through to the other side, and dwell there? This appears to be the broad general sense of the last stanza, but in the detail the meaning is blurred, as if continuity of theme and even consistency of tone were sacrificed to the need for a dramatic ending.[78] The announcement that the hero has some Icarus-flight in mind, with its attendant perils, is unexpected. The Christian prayerfulness with which it is proclaimed is even more so, and needs explanation.

It was suggested above, with reference to the eighth stanza, that the admission of Mysticity, alongside Art, as an alternative way to the ideal, might be attributed to the requirements of the subject. But the same cannot be said of the tone of Christian fervour that dominates the last stanza. It is very unlikely that purely for dialectical or dialectico-rhetorical convenience Mallarmé (who is no Baudelaire, 'shaping his mind to every sophistry') would express in such accents sentiments abhorrent to him. To explain them one has to note that during his months of ordeal in London, such sentiments do appear to have become for a time less uncongenial to his heart and imagination, though not (so far as the evidence goes) to his reason. His letters occasionally suggest that the emotional stress he underwent, if it did not alter his convictions, did soften considerably his anti-Christian attitude. That he should call Marie a saint, a martyr, an 'angel good and serene' can be put down to common figurative usage, but there are expressions less easy to dissociate from belief or at least from nostalgia for belief. 'Lama Sabactani!' he exclaimed, when the return to the loneliness of London appalled him, and 'Si elle était morte . . . ce serait la faute de Dieu.' Then, when he had resolved to brave the disapproval of his family and marry her, 'J'aurai les morts—ma mère, ma sœur—qui voient les choses de haut, et mes amis, qui me comprennent, pour moi.'[79] This occasional indulgence in childhood habits of thought and speech shows clearly enough how the poet might without much straining, if the Muse required it, write out of past rather than present convictions.

The first line of the final stanza of 'Les Fenêtres' compares the idealist's present plight with Christ's on Golgotha, when the wine mixed with gall was pressed to his lips. It recalls directly the exclamation 'Lama sabactani! why hast thou forsaken me?' It is in accord therefore with the feelings of the London experience as represented, outside the poems, in the correspondence. It is in particularly close accord with the reflections on 'Le Reniement de saint Pierre', which are also in the poem's background. Within the poem, it is relevant to the analogy with the dying man in his hospital, under the *grand crucifix ennuyé du mur vide*. For the exclamatory first line, therefore, there is adequate justification. The only other line that relies much on Christian notions and sentiments, the last line of the poem, though less easy to justify, is not difficult to explain. Its vaguely metaphysical and strongly melodramatic character is presumably a toning-down of Baudelaire's romantically desperate endings. That of 'Le Voyage':

> Plonger au fond du gouffre, Enfer ou Ciel, qu'importe?
> Au fond de l'Inconnu pour trouver du *nouveau*!

That of 'Le Mauvais Vitrier':

> Mais qu'importe l'éternité de la damnation à qui a trouvé dans une seconde l'infini de la jouissance.

Unfortunately the Baudelairian rhetoric, if it gives an air of urgency to the question asked in the last stanza, does so at the cost of obscuring its purport. So unconvincing is the question 'Est-il moyen . . . ?' in this context, if we take it as a question about despair, or about pride and its punishment, that this Christian tone can be little more than a disguise for what is really a question about art. In its substance, this question is not inspired by Baudelaire, but by Banville, the poet whose art does indeed awaken thoughts of an earthly paradise, of *la terre heureuse*.[80]

Banville's 'Le Saut du tremplin' has been referred to already, several times, as having probably influenced such poems as 'Le Guignon', 'Le Sonneur', and 'Le Pitre châtié'. Its hero, like the hero of 'Les Fenêtres', seeks to escape from the here-below. He succeeds by excelling in his humble art:

Le clown sauta si haut, si haut,
Qu'il creva le plafond de toiles
Au son du cor et du tambour,
Et, le cœur dévoré d'amour,
Alla rouler dans les étoiles.

This best-known of Banville's symbols for 'the attraction of the abyss above' is not the only one to be reflected in the ending of 'Les Fenêtres'. An earlier poem, 'A Méry', one of the *Odelettes* that accompany *Les Stalactites*, had celebrated the accomplishments of a famous tightrope walker, comparing her explicitly and at length with the poet, who likewise moves high above the rest of men and—like Icarus, it will be noticed, but this analogy is left unexplained—runs the risk of a disastrous fall:

Dans les nuages vermeils,
Au beau milieu des soleils
Qu'elle touchait de la tête
Et parmi l'éther bravé,
Elle songeait au pavé.
Tel est le sort du poète.

Il trône dans la vapeur,
Beau métier s'il n'avait peur
De tomber sur quelque dalle
Parmi les badauds sereins,
Et de s'y casser les reins
Comme le fils de Dédale.

If these promptings by Banville are taken as pointers to Mallarmé's meaning, they suggest that the question asked in the last stanza of 'Les Fenêtres', is whether the hero, unready as he is, all 'unfledged', can shut himself off from the real, dying to the flesh in order to live in an ideal world of art, and daring to risk the fall which would be to a living death.

The question is more understandable if we suppose that the hero asks it not as a consumer of works of art, mirroring himself in other artists' creations, but as a producer, an artist himself. His ambition will then be not simply to live (as Flaubert expressed it) 'in an aesthetic state from morning to night',[81] but to fashion a work that is pure, absolute art, unsullied by any hankering after reality and action, a refuge for dreamers, and for the poet himself, 'a region in which to live',[82] like God in his universe. Interpreted thus, the question with which 'Les Fenêtres' ends is our first glimpse of what was to be Mallarmé's lifelong passion, the ambition to create the Work that would be the final, crowning achievement of the absolute, the Work in view of whose creation the world exists.[83] More immediately, it signifies his refusal of an alternative answer, the stock answer, to the problem of the relation, in art, of the ideal and the real. The answer, that is, accepted by Des Essarts (take reality seriously and lyricize it) and by Vacquerie, to whom 'Les Fenêtres' was originally dedicated and who had written:

> Il n'y a de vrai chef-d'œuvre que celui qui satisfait l'artiste et le philosophe. L'art complet, c'est l'utile et le beau mêlés; c'est l'unité du terrestre et de l'idéal, du progrès et de l'infini . . . Et c'est pourquoi les artistes purs ne rêvent pas seulement une chose inhumaine, ils rêvent une chose impossible. Heureusement pour eux, il n'est au pouvoir d'aucun homme de s'abstraire de l'humanité. Ils servent le progrès malgré eux; seulement, ils se retirent le mérite.[84]

This doctrine is Baudelaire's too, as Mallarmé wilfully interprets him. And the quarrel is still above all with Baudelaire, as the letter to Cazalis clearly indicates. Mallarmé castigates his master, once the idealist who placed 'true reality' in dreams, for seeking (for instance) in 'Le Mauvais Vitrier' not magic casements looking away from life but coloured glass to enhance it, and for placing among the seductive suggestions of 'L'Invitation au voyage' the old-fashioned cliché that makes of art a selective imitation of nature: 'Pays singulier, supérieur aux autres, comme l'Art l'est à la Nature, où celle-ci est réformée par le rêve, où elle est corrigée, embellie, refondue.'[85] Thus the poem that Mallarmé sent to Cazalis on 3 June 1863 is not simply a poetic transposition of the ideas expressed in the letter he sent with it. In choosing for his hostile comment to Cazalis a line from 'Le Reniement de saint Pierre', he might seem to be fretting still over his master's moral betrayal, but in the poem the emphasis is different. The reflection on Baudelaire has progressed since 'Le Guignon'. What he is charged with now is backsliding to the doctrine he had preached many years before in an article on Pierre Dupont. There Baudelaire had dismissed contemptuously from the modern literary scene, and banished to fairy lands forlorn, all the progeny of Chateaubriand's romantic heroes (and Sénancour's and Goethe's, but it is Chateaubriand's style that is ironically parodied):

> Disparaissez donc, ombres fallacieuses de René, d'Obermann et de Werther; fuyez dans les brouillards du vide, monstrueuses créations de la paresse et de la solitude. Comme les pourceaux dans le lac de Génézareth, allez vous replonger dans les forêts enchantées d'où vous tirèrent les fées ennemies, moutons attaqués du vertige romantique . . . Le génie de l'action ne vous laisse plus de place parmi nous.[86]

To which Mallarmé replied: '[If literature were thus allied to action] where should we poor unfortunates go, who are sickened by this world and for whom dreams are the only refuge?' This conception of 'the ideal' not as 'true reality' but as an escape from reality, does not express simply a passing mood or a conviction of the moment. It is the foundation of his philosophy, the aesthetic idealism whose permanent symbols one can now see taking shape. They are symbols that owe more to the poems and the example of Banville than to those of Baudelaire. An instance of this is seen in a stanza of the 'odelette' 'A Méry', quoted from above; after the reference to Icarus, Banville continues his comparison between the funambulist and the poet as follows:

> Et, sylphe au ventre changeant,
> Couvert d'écailles d'argent,
> Il se penche vers la place
> Du haut des deux irisés,
> Pour envoyer des baisers
> A la vile populace.

Many years later this poet-sylph was still a part of Mallarmé's thinking and dreaming, about the poet who would break free (*Est-il moyen, mon Dieu?*) from the earthward pull of the real. It inspired the beautiful sonnet, published in 1887 in *La Revue indépendante*, of the sylph held prisoner (like the ice-bound swan) by its own paralysing horror of life: *Moi, sylphe de ce froid plafond*.[87] It inspired on the other hand the reflections on Banville, the sylph that is free, first in the article 'Solennité', published a few weeks after the sonnet in the same journal:

> Personne, ostensiblement, depuis qu'étonna le phénomène poétique, ne le résume avec audacieuse candeur que peut-être cet esprit immédiat ou originel, Théodore de Banville et l'épuration, par les ans, de son individualité en le vers, le désigne aujourd'hui un être à part, supérieur et buvant tout seul à une source occulte et éternelle . . .[88]

Then five years later, in the article 'Théodore de Banville':

> J'attends que, chauve-souris éblouissante et comme l'éventement de la gravité, soudain, du site par une pointe d'aile autochtone, le fol, adamantin, colère, tourbillonnant génie heurte la ruine; s'en délivre, dans la voltige qu'il est, seul. Théodore de Banville parfois devient ce sylphe suprême.[89]

Praise such as this, for Banville, from a poet so very different from him, has puzzled critics more than it should. It is explained by Mallarmé himself in an early writing that is not forgotten. To judge by the references to it in Mallarmé's correspondence with friends, it was composed in a first version early in the spring of 1864, and finished to its author's provisional satisfaction by about the middle of April.[90] Having failed to get it published, under the title 'Trois poèmes en prose', he revised it stylistically to very good effect and it appeared in *L'Artiste* in February 1865, more attractively though dubiously entitled 'Symphonie littéraire'. The Pléiade editors have consigned it to the section *Proses de jeunesse*,[91] but they make some amends in their interesting annotation. In particular they quote a sentence from an article by Henry Charpentier written in 1926, which summarizes a view of 'Symphonie littéraire' that is perhaps fairly generally accepted still:

> Mallarmé publie, en 1865, dans l'*Artiste*, un important article où il rend à Baudelaire, à Gautier et à Banville, les honneurs qu'il leur doit, mais qui sonne comme un adieu.[92]

Meaning, presumably, a last farewell to the time when a youthful Mallarmé had read with wonder and admiration the poems of those masters, learning from them precious secrets in the art of poetry. In other words, a last farewell to the early Mallarmé. As such, 'Trois poèmes en prose' (not 'Symphonie littéraire', written less than a year later but decidedly more mature and outside our subject) claims some attention here. It offers an interesting piece of self-portraiture by the poet, in the situation in which we are to leave him, reaching adult status but dismayed at finding himself suddenly deprived of the exhilaration of Paris, an outcast from civilized society. That situation is reflected in the 'three prose-poems' more directly than it may seem.

'Ce hideux trou de Tournon', he called their new abode, and 'le noir village où je suis exilé', when he wrote on 12 December 1863, a week after their arrival, to Albert Collignon,[93] the editor of *La Revue nouvelle* it will be remembered. It was to that same Paris contact that he had recourse some four months later when he wrote again, on 11 April 1864, and sent Collignon the three prose poems for publication.[94] He introduced them as 'quelques poèmes en prose dont vous aimez les *inspirateurs*'. One may assume that his purpose in underlining this word was to draw Collignon's attention to the special use he was putting it to, designating thus the three poets who would more naturally be considered as his *subjects*,[95] Gautier, Baudelaire, and Banville. He implied that a reading of their poems had provided the inspiration for the 'Trois poèmes en prose'. And indeed the word appears appropriate enough when one reads the 'introduction' with which his composition begins:

Muse moderne de l'Impuissance qui m'interdis depuis longtemps le trésor familier des Rythmes, et me condamnes (aimable supplice) à ne faire plus que relire—jusqu'au jour où tu m'auras enveloppé dans ton irrémédiable filet, l'ennui, et tout sera fini alors—les maîtres inaccessibles dont la beauté me désespère; mon ennemie, et pourtant mon enchanteresse, aux breuvages perfides et aux mélancoliques ivresses, je te dédie, comme une raillerie ou—le sais-je?—comme un gage d'amour, ces quelques lignes vécues et écrites dans les heures clémentes où tu ne m'inspiras pas la haine de la création et le stérile amour du Néant. Tu y découvriras les jouissances d'une âme qui n'est que femme encore, et qui demain sans doute sera bête.

(This complaint has been allowed to run over, as it were, into the accompanying letter to Collignon, perhaps as a further explanatory comment on the poems:

> Je me sens cependant bien mort: l'ennui est devenu chez moi une maladie mentale et mon atonique impuissance me rend douloureux le plus léger travail. (. . .) Mon ami, ma vivante antithèse, Emmanuel Des Essarts—qu'une prodigieuse activité écarte de la tristesse, et que la solitude, loin de lui permettre de s'affaisser, fortifie—vous a remis quelques vers de moi.[96] Je ne saurais plus les faire.)

On this evidence 'inspiration', and more particularly the lack of it, would seem to be the general topic of the 'Trois poèmes', and the three poets honoured are seen as having provided, respectively, the inspiration necessary for their admirer to write the three prose-poems in their praise. If they are considered from that point of view they lead us back to our first concern, with Banville. The author is at pains to make it clear that the inspiration engendered by a reading of Banville differs conspicuously from that created by the other two—also different from each other in their way, of course, but not essentially. The effects of the three readings are described in turn. First, the poet–reader's response to Gautier:

> Toutefois au bord de mes yeux calmes s'amasse une larme dont les diamants primitifs n'atteignent pas la noblesse—est-ce un pleur d'exquise volupté? ou peut-être tout ce qu'il y avait de divin et d'extra[-]terrestre en moi a-t-il été appelé comme un parfum par cette lecture trop sublime? De quelle source qu'elle naisse, je laisse cette larme, transparente comme mon âme lucide, raconter que c'est à l'aide de cette poésie, née d'elle-même et qui exista de tout temps dans le répertoire éternel de l'Idéal avant sa moderne émersion du cerveau d'un impeccable artiste, qu'il est donné à une âme, dédaigneuse du banal coup d'aile de l'enthousiasme humain, d'atteindre la plus haute cime de sérénité où nous puisse ravir la Beauté.

The reward for reading Baudelaire is very different, but no more stimulating for the reader *as Poet*:

> Enfin des ténèbres d'encre ont tout envahi où l'on n'entend voleter que le crime, le remords et la Mort. Alors je me voile la face et des sanglots, arrachés à mon âme moins par ce cauchemar que par une amère sensation d'exil, résonne dans le noir silence.

The only consolation offered by Baudelaire for all this grief is the Christian faith that Mallarmé has abjured:

Devant moi se dresse l'apparition du poète savant qui me l'indique en un hymne élancé mystiquement comme un lys. Le rythme de ce chant ressemble à la rosace d'une ancienne église . . . Il y a toujours du baume en Galaad.

When he turns then to Banville, Mallarmé presents himself less guardedly as the seeker after poetic (not philosophical or religious) inspiration. A young poet has a right to it. His elders owe it to him, but only Banville provides it. We are allowed at this point a brief, plain glimpse of the contrast that until now the flow of rhetoric had kept concealed;[97] here is Banville:

Avec lui je sens la Poésie m'enivrer—ce que tous les peuples ont appelé la Poésie—et, souriant, je bois le nectar dans l'Olympe glorieux du Lyrisme.

Et quand je ferme le livre, ce n'est plus serein [clearly, as with Gautier] ou tourmenté [as with Baudelaire], mais fou d'amour et débordant, (. . .) et plein d'un nouvel orgueil d'être homme. Tout ce qu'il y a d'ambrosien en moi et de bonté musicale, de noble et de pareil aux dieux, chante et j'ai l'extase de la Muse! J'aime les roses, j'aime l'or du soleil, j'aime les harmonieux sanglots des femmes aux longs cheveux et je voudrais tout confondre dans un poétique baiser. Une radieuse sympathie envers toutes les choses me transporte. (. . .)

C'est que cet homme résume tout ce qu'il y a de grand et de rythmique en nous: il est le Poète, l'éternel et classique Poète, fidèle à sa Muse, et vivant parmi le chœur oublié des Dieux et des Déesses. Son chant est sans cesse un chant d'enthousiasme où se mêle la Musique: c'est le cri de l'âme ivre de toute la gloire de la terre.

Here is the inspiration the young poet seeks. Here is the elder passing on the torch to his disciple. A disciple far from modest in his expectations, we do well to reflect. When only three provincial years had passed, at Tournon and Besançon, he would be writing to Cazalis in another mood:

Pour moi, la Poésie me tient lieu de l'amour, par ce qu'elle est éprise d'elle[-]même et que sa volupté d'elle retombe délicieusement en mon âme; mais j'avoue que la Science que j'ai acquise, ou retrouvée au fond de l'homme que je fus, ne me suffirait pas, et que ce ne serait pas sans un serrement de cœur réel que j'entrerais dans la Disparition suprême, si je n'avais pas fini mon œuvre, qui est l'*Œuvre*, le Grand-Œuvre, comme disaient les alchimistes, nos ancêtres.[98]

NOTES

1 It may be remembered that this line is the second in the poem 'Vere novo'.

2 Between the beginning of December 1862, when Marie first told her lover they must part, and the following June when she was back in London to stay, there is with one exception barely a whisper of interest in poetry to be found in the letters to Cazalis. The exception is that when Marie was on her way to Paris Mallarmé told his friend she was bringing him a copy of Hugo's *Châtiments*; see *DSM*. vi, 105.

3 See *Corr*. i, 114 n. 2, and *Vie*, 117. It is surely to 'A une Putain' that Des Essarts refers by these titles, and not to an unknown poem as Mondor supposed. He was probably embarrassed by Mallarmé's title. I take it that 'dame d'honneur de la reine de Naples' was a current polite synonym for *putain*, 'terme grossier et malhonnête' according to Littré, who adds: 'On évite d'écrire ce mot entier; on l'indique par p . . . , ou on le fait deviner' (*Dictionnaire*, t. III, p. 1391).

4 This is the title in the early manuscript copies, Doucet, Aubanel, and Carnet (D, A, and C), for details in which I rely on the reproduction and notes in *O.c.*, 35 and 1424–5 [1426–7]. The fact that in Doucet the poem shares a folded sheet with a very early state of 'Les Fenêtres' may be deemed to support my dating, since 'Les Fenêtres' was certainly written by June 1863. The poem was included in *Le Parnasse contemporain*, with no further variants except that a capital V is given to the word *vice*, a colon substituted for the full stop at the end of the first quatrain, and the title changed to 'A celle qui est tranquille'. In the 1887 *Revue indépendante* edition of the poems, and in all editions since, the text is as in *Le Parnasse contemporain*, but the title has again been changed, to 'Angoisse'.

5 In Doucet, *tes* has been altered to *ses*.

6 The Pléiade editors note (*O.c.*, 1425 [1427]) that 'dans ses *Notes sur Mallarmé* (Paris, Publication de la *Vogue*, 1886) note p. 8, Teodor de Wyzewa dit avoir vu un premier texte de ce sonnet dont le dernier vers était: *Et j'ai peur de penser lorsque je couche seul*.' This would be another close link with the early versions of 'Tristesse d'été'; see the first tercet in these versions, pp. 212–14 above.

7 Corresponding expressions are found in *Les Fleurs du mal*: 'Tu mettrais *l'univers entier* dans ta ruelle' and 'Elle appelle des yeux *la race des* humains', in 'Tu mettrais . . . ' and 'Allegorie' respectively; B., *O.c.* i, 27 and 116.

8 *DSM*. vi, 109, 118, 119, and 124–5.

9 *Lef.*, 176. For comments from other friends, see *O.c.*, 1424 [1426], and *Corr*. i, 107 n. 2; also, for a fuller quotation, *DSM*. vi, 195(–6) n. 1. Cazalis called the poem faultless, Des Essarts said it was 'splendide d'exécution, profond de pensée, d'une clarté parfaite', and added later (7 April 1864, *Corr*. i, 114 n. 2) 'Mon père est fou de ton sonnet'.

Lefébure, the most perspicacious, considered it 'un vrai chef-d'œuvre qui contient un puits de douleur'.

10 See the latter's article on 'Mallarmé disciple de Baudelaire', in *RHLF*, April–June 1967 (special Baudelaire number).

11 B., *O.c.* i, pp. 101, 114, 115, and 155–6.

12 É. Noulet, *L'Œuvre poétique de Stéphane Mallarmé*, 1940, p. 58.

13 *DSM*. vi, 247.

14 Ibid. 34.

15 B., *O.c.* i, 116. In other editions, 'remord' for the rhyme—as also in 'Le Léthé'.

16 *DSM*. vi, 32.

17 *DSM*. vi, 156.

18 Letters to Cazalis, 14 November and 14 January respectively (ibid. 67 and 108): 'Nous nous sommes monté un vrai ménage anglais'; 'moi, pauvre enfant abandonné par tout ce qui fut ma vie et mon idéal'. For the sentimental idealizing, the clearest evidence is the extravagant language in some of the letters—such expressions as: 'Du reste . . . Marie me fera planer au-dessus dans ses ailes d'ange' (letter to Cazalis dated 30 January 1863; ibid. 118).

19 Much of what is said here of 'L'Assaut' repeats in substance a more elaborate account in 'An Allegory of Love: Mallarmé's "L'Assaut"', which I contributed to a volume in honour of A. R. Chisholm (*Australian Journal of French Studies*, vol. VI, nos. 2–3).

The failure of the romantic attempt to make of the mistress a muse is the subject of a note in Banville's commentary (published in 1873) on his own *Odes funambulesques*: 'En 1830 (c'est toujours à cette date qu'il faut remonter), les poètes voulurent, comme Byron, amalgamer leur vie idéale et leur vie réelle, être vraiment dans la vie ce qu'ils étaient dans le livre et, dans la double extase de leur inspiration et de leurs amours, la femme pour eux devint muse, et la muse femme. On voit dans mes satires le dernier reflet de cette tradition, morte déjà'.

20 Although in his letter to Cazalis Mallarmé used the title 'L'Assaut', in the manuscripts the poem is entitled 'Le Château de l'Espérance'. The Pléiade editors surmise that Mallarmé may have refrained from publishing this poem because Cazalis commented on it unfavourably (see *O.c.*, 1391 [1393]). They also point out, however, that Mallarmé included it in the little collection of his poems which he copied in 1864 for his close friends, and that when it was omitted from *Le Parnasse contemporain* of 1866 Aubanel expressed his disappointment and therefore his liking for the poem. If it was Mallarmé who withheld it from the *Parnasse* publication, it was perhaps because of the intimate personal confession it contained, thinly veiled.

The text was published by Dr Bonniot in the May 1919 number of *Littérature*. The text given by the Pléiade is supplied by the manuscript that Bonniot had reproduced (see *O.c.*, 1390 [1392]), reproduced here. The text published by Mondor in the *Carnet* (*Autres précisions*, pp. 52–3) contains a fairly obvious error: *Dans* for *Dont* at the beginning of the fourth line.

21 *DSM.* vi, 156.

22 See above, p. 323. One detail which does not come from Poe is curiously persistent in Mallarmé's conception of knight-errantry. In 'Le Guignon'

> La plupart ont râlé dans des ravins nocturnes
> S'enivrant du plaisir de voir couler leur sang

while in 'L'Assaut' the hero

> Marche à l'assaut, monte—ou roule ivre
> Par des marais de sang—

It is possible that there are echoes here of *chansons de geste*, *La Chanson de Roland* for instance.

23 B., *O.c.* i, 27.

24 The word is also used by Gautier; it is the title of one of his 'Premières Poésies'. But the line in 'Les Fenêtres' (as L. Lemonnier points out in his *Enquêtes sur Baudelaire*, p. 67) is a direct reminiscence of Baudelaire's 'Ô boucles! Ô parfum chargé de nonchaloir'.

25 7 July 1862; *DSM.* vi, 43. (For the date, see *Corr.* i, 42. Emmanuel had had time to give Stéphane news of the excursion of Sunday 6 July.)

La Rochefoucauld's maxim also comes to mind: 'L'espérance toute trompeuse qu'elle est, sert au moins à nous mener à la fin de la vie par un chemin agréable.'

26 B., *O.c.* i, 124.

27 He had written to Cazalis, who was sighing after his 'Sperata': 'Emparadise-toi le mieux possible dans ta folie. Et le plus longtemps', and 'Ah! que l'amour est fort qui fait regarder l'avenir en souriant' (24 May and 1 July 1862; *DSM.* vi, 34 and 40). In the juvenilia, hope is practically synonymous with requited love—as for instance in the 1859 poem 'Donnez' (*DSM.* vii, 134).

28 *DSM.* vi, 119 and 125.

29 So far as I can see, the only reason why 'Le Pitre châtié' is generally supposed to have been written early in 1864 is the fact that the first mention of it in Mallarmé's correspondence is found in Lefébure's letter of 15 April 1864, the first since his young friend returned from London (*Lef.*, 177). It seems to me much more likely to be a London poem, for reasons I have touched on and will develop further.

The Pléiade editors begin their comments on 'Le Château de l'Espérance' (*O.c.*, 1390 [1392]) by referring to Dr Bonniot's presentation of that poem when he published it in the review *Littérature* in May 1919. They quote his interesting observations on the manuscript which had provided the text: 'Sur la feuille de garde du petit carnet relié de carton-cuir où sont renfermés, manuscrits, les vers que Mallarmé, venant à Paris, jadis montra à Mendès, 1864 [1863 rather], on lit, écrite au crayon postérieurement de la main de l'auteur, l'annotation: "Vers publiés dans le Parnasse de 1866, sans les corrections. *Trois poèmes n'ont pas été publiés: Le Guignon, Le Pitre châtié, Le Château de l'Espérance*, qui font partie de

l'Œuvre Enfantine."' The reason given for the non-publication of these three poems is unconvincing, and does not even correspond with the place given to them in the *carnet* itself. The real reason, in the case of 'Le Guignon', is much more likely to be the one that prevented *L'Artiste* from publishing more than the first five tercets. As to 'Le Pitre châtié', and 'Le Château de l'Espérance'—like 'Apparition' which is not even admitted to the *carnet*—they were much too intimately concerned with his life and love to be made public, for Marie's sake as well as his own.

On the other hand (to return to the poem under discussion) to put 'Le Pitre châtié' in the 'Œuvre Enfantine' and at the same time date it 1864 is not reasonable. In the *carnet*, the sonnet is placed next to 'Le Château de l'Espérance', between 'Le Guignon' and 'Le Sonneur'. When the poem was published for the first time (radically altered in the *Revue indépendante* edition of 1887, Mallarmé again set it among the earliest poems. These facts in themselves outweigh the very flimsy evidence advanced in support of the later date.

30 This early version was made known by Dr Bonniot in an article which appeared on 15 April 1929 in *La Revue de France*. It is reproduced in the notes of the Pléiade edition (*O.c.*, 1414 [1416]). The text in the Mondor *carnet* is identical with Bonniot's, except that the word *hélas* in line 12 is followed by a comma instead of the exclamation mark.

31 Poe's doctrine is only new in its 'shock-the-bourgeois' absoluteness. This was congenial to Mallarmé, whereas Lefébure (for instance) could not accept it, for he wrote on 15 April 1864: 'Ah! j'ai une observation à vous faire: je ne comprenais pas d'abord le pitre châtié, parce que vous disiez que la crasse était tout le génie: le suif et le fard dont vous parlez correspondent évidemment à ce que l'on nomme l'*acquis*. En relisant j'ai vu que vous aviez d'abord écrit mon génie: il me semble en effet, que l'on peut dire cela de soi en se méprisant (bien que je vous conteste le droit de le penser de vous).' (*Lef.*, 177.)

32 After Wenceslas married Hortense, in *La Cousine Bette*, 'Hortense et Wenceslas se livrèrent aux adorables enfantillages de la passion légitime, heureuse, insensée. Hortense fut alors la première à dispenser Wenceslas de tout travail, orgueilleuse de triompher ainsi de sa rivale, la Sculpture. Les caresses d'une femme, d'ailleurs, font évanouir la Muse, et fléchir la féroce, la brutale fermeté du travailleur'. In 'Le Pitre châtié', the lover has found that 'a life of sensation rather than thought' is not much more than was promised in 'Tristesse d'été':

> Ta chevelure, est-elle une rivière tiède
> Où noyer sans frissons mon âme qui m'obsède
> Et jouir du Néant où l'on ne pense pas?

But the disillusionment of the lover, who had fondly seen in his mistress's hair a banner for ideal hopes, had been told in 'L'Assaut'. The subject of 'Le Pitre châtié' is the disillusionment not of the lover but the poet, when his art is revealed as being a denial, not an idealizing, of life.

33 In an article already referred to, on 'Mallarmé et "l'Être aux ailes de gaze"'

(*Studi in onore di Italo Siciliano*), I suggested that in the conversion from the fairy of childhood to the fairy who is the Muse, Baudelaire's poem 'L'Irréparable' played a part. So perhaps did Gérard de Nerval's *Sylvie*, at some point or points in a rather complex story (for Baudelaire may have thought of Gérard too if he wrote his poem after *Sylvie* appeared in 1853, and particularly if he read *Sylvie* while Marie Daubrun was playing in her 'théâtre banal' as Jenny Colon had played in hers). I note at the beginning of *Sylvie* the following details: 'A la seconde ou à la troisième scène d'un maussade chef-d'œuvre d'alors, une apparition bien connue illuminant l'espace vide . . . Nous étions ivres de poésie et d'amour. Amour, hélas! des formes vagues, des teintes roses et bleues, des fantômes métaphysiques! Vue de près, la femme réelle révoltait notre ingénuité; il fallait qu'elle apparût reine ou déesse, et surtout n'en pas approcher . . . C'est ainsi que, sortant du théâtre, avec l'amère tristesse que laisse un songe évanoui . . . '

34 Over thirty years later Mallarmé was preaching, more wittily, the same doctrine. In 'L'Action restreinte' (*O.c.*, 370) he wrote: 'Le droit à rien accomplir d'exceptionnel ou manquant aux agissements vulgaires, se paie chez quiconque, de l'omission de lui et on dirait de sa mort comme un tel. Exploits, il les commet dans le rêve pour ne gêner personne.'

35 For swimming as a symbol of living, cf. Lefébure's poem 'Le Pingouin' published in 1866, in *Le Parnasse contemporain*:

> Et moi, je suis un être abruti qui ne peut
> Nager dans l'action ni planer dans le rêve.

36 The importance of this impression of passing through day after day in haphazard living, and as it were of the evanescence and passivity of 'action', is clearer in the later, revised version:

> De ma jambe et des bras limpide nageur traître,
> A bonds multipliés, reniant le mauvais
> Hamlet, c'est comme si dans l'onde j'innovais
> Mille sépulcres pour y vierge disparaître.

37 Eyes as blue as the lake at Geneva is a familiar image to Mallarmé. He had used it in praise of Ettie: 'Le fait est que les [A]nglaises sont d'adorables filles. Cette blondeur douce; ces gouttes du lac Léman, enchassées dans de la candeur et qu'elles veulent bien appeler leurs yeux . . . ' (letter to Cazalis, 24 May 1862; *DSM*. vi, 32). The metaphor 'yeux, lacs' is a commonplace of the poetry of the time. See for instance how Gautier exploits it in 'Caerulei oculi' (*Emaux et Camées*) or Banville in 'L'Attrait du gouffre' (*Les Exilés*), to say nothing of Baudelaire's 'Semper eadem'. Gautier reverses it when in *España* he calls mountain lakes 'les yeux bleus de la montagne'.

38 *DSM*. vi, 154–5.

39 It is most fully developed in 'La Déclaration foraine'.

40 Quoted in the Crépet-Blin edition of *Les Fleurs du mal*, p. 308.

41 B., *O.c.* i, 283–4.

The influence of Banville's 'Le Saut de tremplin' is not apparent in the early version of Mallarmé's poem, but certain details in the later version ('J'ai troué dans le mur de toile . . . ' and the cymbals) were probably suggested by it.

42 Ibid. 117.

43 In his edition (or 'history') of 'Les Fenêtres' (*DSM.* v, 439–74) Carl Barbier rates as probably the earliest state known the one that has reached us in a manuscript that belonged to Armand Renaud. It is the one, therefore, that is reproduced here, without variants save one (between square brackets) that clarifies the meaning, but with some accents supplied where they are omitted in the manuscript.

All the early states of the text, dating presumably from late 1863 or early 1864, are for a Mallarmé poem of that period unusually close to the final version.

44 *DSM.* vi, 155–6. It will have been noted that in the quotation from 'Ténèbres' Gautier refers to the Ideal and the Real in the same terms as Baudelaire, but with a more restricted pessimism. For him, it is ill-luck that interferes with the noble aim 'D'unir heureusement le rêve à l'action'.

In view of the fact that in a very early manuscript (*DSM.* v, 440) 'Les Fenêtres' is dedicated 'à Auguste Vacquerie', one wonders if he was not one of the realists Mallarmé was answering. In a letter to Cazalis dated 24 July 1863 (ibid. 160) he had occasion to describe 'les Anglaises' as 'ces anges de cuisine qui rêvent aux rayons de leurs casseroles, sans se douter de l'étoile Astarte'—in which is surely involved, as well as Poe's 'Ulalume', a detail in *Profils et grimaces*, published by Vacquerie in 1856. In ch. viii Vacquerie had attacked the conception of art that Mallarmé was to uphold, expressing surprise that there should be 'des artistes qui croient que l'art se suffit à lui-même (. . .), que le beau, c'est le ciel entr'ouvert, c'est la face de Dieu entrevue. Ils ont horreur de retomber du ciel à la cuisine, de l'astre à la casserole'. Vacquerie's theory was Hugo's theory ('le beau est serviteur du vrai'), as to Mallarmé's horror the master would set it out in *William Shakespeare*; see *DSM.* vi, 204–5.

45 *La Nouvelle Héloïse*, sixième partie, lettre viii; another passage from the same letter is quoted above, ch. 2, n. 7. Chateaubriand quoted these words in *Le Génie du christianisme* (deuxième partie, livre troisième, ch. 4) and the sentiment they express became a commonplace during the romantic period. No author of the time repeated it more lustily than George Sand, in laments like the following in her novel *Lélia*: 'Aussi à quoi m'a servi de voyager? Ai-je jamais rien vu qui ressemblât à mes fantaisies? Oh! que la nature m'a semblé pauvre, le ciel terne et la mer étroite, au prix des terres, des cieux et des mers que j'ai franchies dans mon vol immatériel!' (Deuxième partie, ch. XXIX, 'Solitude'.) Baudelaire is quieter, more cunning and more poetical:

> Ah! que le monde est grand à la clarté des lampes!
> Aux yeux du souvenir que le monde est petit!
>
> ('Le Voyage'; B., *O.c.* i, 129.)

Even Hugo acknowledged this disillusionment that experience brings, and being Hugo put it into an alexandrine:

> Restons loin des objets dont la vue est charmée,
> L'arc-en-ciel est vapeur, le nuage est fumée,
> *L'idéal tombe en poudre au toucher du réel.*
> ('A mes amis L.B. et S.-B.'; *Les Feuilles d'Automne*, xxvii.)

46 'L'invitation au voyage' (*Spleen de Paris*); B., *O.c.* i, 303.

47 Preface to *Les Paradis artificiels*: 'A J.G.F.', ibid. 399.

The example of Baudelaire is all-important for Mallarmé at this time. Were that not so, and if one were more interested in spiritual than literary affinities, one might wish to compare Mallarmé's intuitions rather with Flaubert's than Baudelaire's. In some of Flaubert's letters (which Mallarmé did not of course know) there are expressions which are strikingly close to those used in the letter to Cazalis we are considering. Flaubert wrote to Maxime du Camp on 7 April 1846: 'C'est étrange comme je suis né avec peu de foi au bonheur. J'ai eu, tout jeune, un pressentiment complet de la vie. C'est comme une odeur de cuisine nauséabonde qui s'échappe par un soupirail', and to Louise Colet on 29 November 1853: 'au-dessus de la vie, au-dessus du bonheur, il y a quelque chose de bleu et d'incandescent, un grand ciel immuable et subtil dont les rayons qui nous arrivent suffisent à ranimer des mondes. La splendeur du génie n'est que le reflet de ce Verbe caché'. In his very interesting account of the intellectual background of 'Les Fenêtres' (*Life and Letters in France*, 3. *The Nineteenth Century*, Nelson, 1965, p. 138), Dr A. W. Raitt quotes, in this connection, a letter written by Flaubert to Mlle Leroyer de Chantepie on 18 March 1856: 'La vie est une chose tellement hideuse que le seul moyen de la supporter, c'est de l'éviter. Et on l'évite en vivant dans l'art.' On 3 October 1846 he wrote to Louise Colet: 'Pour moi, je ne sais pas comment font pour vivre les gens qui ne sont pas du matin au soir dans un état esthétique'. A passage in *Madame Bovary* comes to mind also: 'Toute l'amertume de l'existence lui semblait servie sur son assiette, et, à la fumée du bouilli, il montait du fond de son âme d'autres bouffées d'affadissement'.

48 *Notes nouvelles sur Edgar Poe*, ii, 321.

49 Cf. above, the pages on 'Le Guignon' in ch. 4.

50 Ibid. i, 122.

51 Ibid. 1075–6.

52 It is the more unexpected as Mallarmé considered the poetry of Des Essarts to be lacking in precisely those qualities for which he never ceased to admire Baudelaire's poems—whatever fault he might find with his ideas.

53 See above, p. 255.

54 B., *O.c.* i, 44.

55 Ibid. 13.

56 Ibid. ii, 318.

57 At least one other reminiscence of Baudelaire is recognizable, the 'Ô parfum chargé de nonchaloir!' in 'La Chevelure' (ibid. i, 26).

58 *DSM*. vi, 144.
59 Ibid. 147.
60 Ch. 6, n. 53.
61 See above, p. 334.
62 B., *O.c.* ii, 334. The passage is quoted also in the first of Baudelaire's two essays on Théophile Gautier (ibid. 113–14) in which Mallarmé had shown some interest earlier.
63 Ibid. i, 401–2. In the long development that follows, the following fragment is noteworthy from the point of view of 'Les Fenêtres': 'Cette acuité de la pensée, cet enthousiasme des sens et de l'esprit, ont dû, en tout temps, apparaître à l'homme comme le premier des biens. C'est pourquoi . . . il a . . . cherché . . . sous tous les climats et dans tous les temps, les moyens de fuir, ne fût-ce que pour quelques heures, son habitacle de fange, et, comme dit l'auteur de *Lazare* "d'emporter le paradis d'un seul coup"' (ibid. 402).

For the mirror of art in Mallarmé's writings, see A. Gill, 'Le symbole du miroir dans l'œuvre de Mallarmé' (*Cahiers de l'Association des Études Françaises*, July 1958).
64 B., *O.c.* i, 46.
65 The word *mysticité* may well be borrowed from Baudelaire, who uses it in a note to 'Francescae meae laudes' mentioned above in connection with '. . . *Mysticis umbraculis*', and again below with reference to 'Plainte d'automne'. Baudelaire's note, which was suppressed after the first edition of *Les Fleurs du mal*, places *la mysticité* in an antithesis very much in line with Mallarmé's separation of the ideal from the real: 'La mysticité est l'autre pôle de cet aimant dont Catulle et sa bande, poètes brutaux et purement épidermiques, n'ont connu que le pôle sensualité'. More privately, Baudelaire writes of his childhood thus (*Journaux intimes*): 'Dès mon enfance, tendance à la mysticité. Mes conversations avec Dieu' (*Mon cœur mis à nu*, ibid. 706). Perhaps Mallarmé remembered also Chateaubriand's very suggestive use of the word: 'On demande quelle est cette plénitude de bonheur céleste promise à la vertu par le christianisme; on se plaint de la trop grande mysticité: "Du moins dans le système mythologique, dit-on, on pouvait se former une image des plaisirs des ombres heureuses; mais comment comprendre la félicité des élus?".' Robert's *Dictionnaire alphabétique et analogique de la langue française* (t. I, p. 721) quotes the example from Chateaubriand and gives the meaning of the word as being 'caractère, extase, pratique mystique'. He gives a second, more modern meaning: 'Foi, devotion intuitive et intense'. In 'Les Fenêtres' the word has very much the same associations ('Je me mire et me vois ange') as in Chateaubriand, and we may understand it as meaning a religious exaltation that tells of heavenly bliss, something like the ecstatic adoration figured in Baudelaire's 'Bénédiction'. It has been found possible to speak of 'mysticité religieuse et mysticité poétique'.
66 In 'Les Phares' art and mysticity are merged and called 'un divin opium'.

Littré quotes in his dictionary, under 'opium', on the one hand Rousseau's 'La dévotion est un opium pour l'âme' (*La Nouvelle Héloïse*, vi, 8), which admirers of Karl Marx should note, and on the other hand Lamartine's 'Ils [*les bardes saints*] versent aux soucis cette molle langueur, / Cet opium divin que dans sa soif d'extase / Le rêveur Orient puise en vain dans son vase' (*Jocelyn*, Sixième Epoque).

67 The second stanza of 'Les Phares' (B., *O.c.* i, 13).

68 Letter dated 24 July 1863 (*DSM.* vi, 162).

69 See above, p. 337.

70 Elme Caro, *L'Idée de Dieu et ses nouveaux critiques*, 2nd edition (1864), pp. 72, 78, and 79.

71 *DSM.* vi, 343.

72 *O.c.*, 694.

73 B., *O.c.* i, 13. The relation to poetry of this idea of correspondence is expressed most felicitously by Mallarmé in a description of the experience of reading a beautiful poem; it is in the article 'Solennité', published in 1887: 'Ce spirituellement et magnifiquement illuminé fond d'extase, c'est bien le pur de nous-mêmes par nous porté, toujours, prêt à jaillir à l'occasion qui dans l'existence ou hors l'art fait toujours défaut' (*O.c.*, 334).

If the following translation of a passage in Hölderlin's *Hyperion* had appeared before 'Les Fenêtres', and not four years later, one would have thought Mallarmé had read it: 'Le premier-né de la beauté est l'art; dans l'art, l'homme *se rajeunit et se reflète* [my italics]: il veut se sentir lui-même, et c'est pourquoi il pose en face de lui sa propre beauté . . . La seconde fille de la beauté est la religion, car l'amour de la beauté est religion . . . ' (Challamel-Lacour in *Revue des deux mondes*, 15 June 1867).

74 Ibid. 8–9. In the word *antérieur* there may be a suggestion similar to that developed by Gautier in a passage of *Spirite*, quoted by Léon Cellier (*Mallarmé et la Morte qui parle*, p. 99): 'Il semblait à Guy qu'il écoutait de la musique pour la première fois. Un art nouveau se révélait à lui, et mille idées inconnues se remuaient dans son âme; les notes éveillaient en lui des vibrations si profondes, si lointaines, si antérieures, qu'il croyait les avoir entendues dans une première vie, depuis oubliée.'

75 B., *O.c.* i, 303.

76 See the letter from Armand Renaud of 12 February 1864 (*DSM.* vii, 216–17), and the more discreet observations of Lefébure (*Lef.*, 176) and Des Essarts (*Corr.* i, 110 n. 1).

77 The relevant passage, quoted by W. T. Bandy and Claude Pichois (*Baudelaire devant ses contemporains*, 1957, p. 188), from '*Lettre de Junius*, écrite en collaboration par Alphonse Duchesne et Alfred Delvau, *Figaro*, 12 décembre 1861 . . . ' reads: 'M. Charles Baudelaire, encore un poète, mais un poète nerveux, qui a l'âpreté d'Agrippa d'Aubigné et la crudité de Mathurin Régnier; si le mot n'avait pas déjà servi, je dirais qu'il a des truculences de langage qui sentent l'abattoir d'une lieue: il faut lire ses *Fleurs du mal* d'une main—et se boucher le nez de l'autre. Les Caprices de Goya ne sont pas plus funèbres! Et cependant je donnerais soixante Arsène Houssaye pour un Baudelaire'. It will be noticed that the

article first appeared in the *Figaro* at a time when Mallarmé was particularly likely to be attentive to criticism of Baudelaire. It was in the issue dated 12 December 1861, and Mallarmé's poem 'A un poète immoral' bears the date of 11 December 1861. 'Le Guignon' was written not much later.

J. Crépet and G. Blin in their 1948 edition of *Les Fleurs du mal* (p. 504) recall a story told by Robert de Bonnières. Baudelaire was reading his poem 'Un Voyage à Cythère' to the critic Monselet. At the line *Ses intestins pesants lui coulaient sur les cuisses*, Monselet did not conceal his distaste. 'Et qu'eussiez-vous mis à ma place?' Baudelaire asked, and Monselet answered: 'Une rose'.

78 In a letter to Cazalis, written on 21 May 1866 (*DSM*. vi, 320), Mallarmé points out that his friend has 'stolen' for one of his own poems the line *Au risque de rouler pendant l'éternité*! The terms he uses make it clear that he prized the line for its dramatic effect at the end of the poem: 'Sais-tu que je suis furieux contre toi? tu m'as volé, Monsieur, le dernier vers des *Fenêtres*, mouvement et situation, dans le dernier vers de *A la nature*. Je t'entends rire d'ici!' *Au risque du Néant, dont tu m'avais tiré* is the line complained of.

79 Letters to Cazalis, 10, 14, and 30 January 1863 (*DSM*. vi, 105, 109, and 118–19). In the letter written to an unidentified friend on 3 December 1863, already referred to, is a sentence to whose conventionally Christian character the editors of the *Correspondance* call attention: 'voici six mois à peine que Dieu a rappelé à lui mon pauvre père' (*Corr.* ii, 309). The Desmolins idiom is recognizable here; Mallarmé's using it in referring to his father's death is probably significant of nothing more than his willingness to conform socially in such matters.

80 See the section of 'Symphonie littéraire' written in praise of Banville (*O.c.*, 265).

81 See Flaubert's assertion to Louise Colet, quoted above, n. 47.

82 In the poem 'Le vierge, le vivace et le bel aujourd'hui' the line 'pour n'avoir pas chanté la région où vivre' must be interpreted, so far as I can see, as an expression of sorrow that the Work is still uncreated, even in the poet's imagination. Later, Mallarmé referred more optimistically to this private world. In 'La Musique et les Lettres', for instance, when he describes the situation of an imagined 'civilisé édennique' (*O.c.*, 646), and in the closing sentence of the article 'Bucolique' (*O.c.*, 404–5): 'je dis combien, sur les remparts, tonne, peu loin, le canon de l'actualité pour qui coupe, en imagination, une flûte où nouer sa joie selon divers motifs celui, surtout, de se percevoir, simple, infiniment sur la terre'.

Camille Mauclair, in his novel *Le Soleil des morts* (1898), puts into the mouth of his hero Calixte Armel (a portrait of Mallarmé) words to the effect that men may be able one day to live in beauty without even the help of works of art: 'j'ai souvent rêvé . . . qu'un jour viendrait où l'homme serait assez complet, assez habitué à penser avec une beauté constante, pour se passer de cet exercice améliorant' (quoted by J. Lethève in his article 'Mallarmé sur les chemins de des Esseintes', *Bulletin de la Société J.-K. Huysmans*, No. 43, 1962.

83 The Work considered as the poet's duty is formulated in the well-known sentence reported by the journalist Huret, who quotes it as the concluding remark of an interview with Mallarmé in 1891: 'Au fond, voyez-vous, *me dit le maître en me serrant la main*, le monde est fait pour aboutir à un beau livre' (*O.c.*, 871). The remark is repeated in the article of 1895, 'Le Livre instrument spirituel' (*O.c.*, 378): 'Une proposition qui émane de moi—si, diversement, citée à mon éloge ou par blâme—sommaire veut, que tout, au monde, existe pour aboutir à un livre.'

The poet was referring to the same ambition when he alluded, in a letter to Calixte Rachet (18 May 1887; *Propos* 154), to 'mon manque d'hésitation à me jeter au gouffre du rêve apparu, quand je pourrais rester aux jardins anciens, parmi les fleurs ordinaires et certaines'; the terms used show the close relation, in Mallarmé's mind, between the temptation of the Work and the danger of falling into the abyss that the Dream might become.

84 *Profils et grimaces*, pp. 249 and 250. In a more authoritative, theoretical formulation of prevailing notions on this subject, Edgar Quinet uses images which are strikingly similar to the one used in the last line of 'Les Fenêtres': 'De ce principe conclurons-nous que l'art se confond avec la philosophie? Nullement. Celle-ci peut oublier la forme des objets pour ne s'occuper que des idées. L'artiste, au contraire, a deux mondes à régir, le réel et l'idéal; il ne peut ni les détruire l'un par l'autre, ni les résoudre l'un dans l'autre. Il faut qu'ils les laisse également subsister, et qu'il fasse sortir l'harmonie de leurs apparentes contradictions . . . *Tu n'iras pas plus loin.*'

85 B., *O.c.* i, 302.

86 Ibid. ii, 34.

87 'Surgi de la croupe et du bond' (*Fl.*, i, 324; *O.c.*, 74).

88 *O.c.*, 332–3.

89 Ibid. 521.

90 The flair or good luck of Henri Mondor, or good relations in the second-hand book trade, acquired for him not simply an early manuscript copy of 'Trois poèmes en prose' but the very copy that Mallarmé sent to Collignon for publication in *La Revue nouvelle*. With it were two letters, also from Mallarmé to Collignon, the one dated 11 April 1864 that accompanied it and another sent some two months later, lamenting the early demise of the journal in question and requesting—in vain it would seem—the return of his poems. Mondor published 'Trois poèmes en prose' in *Mélanges d'histoire littéraire et de bibliographie offerts à Jean Bonnerot* (Nizet, 1954), and again as the second item in *Autres Précisions*. It is from this text that I shall quote here. The two letters obtained with it are published in their due place in the *Correspondance* (*Corr.* i, 113–14 and 119–20).

91 *O.c.*, 261–5.

92 Ibid. 1538 [1545]. It is notable that Lefébure, whose judgement on such matters was usually sound, regarded 'Trois poèmes en prose' as written in honour (excessive in his opinion) of the three poets named. His letter to Mallarmé of 13 May 1864 is for the most part concerned with the three prose-poems, which he praised highly. He commented on them thus:

'J'en trouve l'idée originale et juste: la forme en est fouillée d'une manière exquise, comme tout ce que vous écrivez: vous avez partout de rares bonheurs d'idées et de mots[.] Baudelaire en paysages surtout est neuf, étrange et puissant. (. . .) Oui, Gautier est bien la perfection grecque, Baudelaire le parfum du péché, et Banville la poésie jeune. Toutefois, il me semble qu'en peintre ami vous avez un peu flatté vos portraits. Banville surtout se trouvera grandi . . .'. Among recent writers on Mallarmé, the one who perhaps pays most attention to 'Symphonie littéraire', Pierre-Olivier Walzer, sees it in much the same light as Lefébure. He entitles his account 'Adieu à trois maîtres', referring perhaps to Henry Charpentier's suggestion but without pursuing it further (op. cit., pp. 86–8).

93 *Corr.* i, 98–9.

94 Ibid. 113–14.

95 Thus Lefébure, in his letter on the subject (see above, n. 92), remarks that Mallarmé's compliments to the three poets are 'vrais pour les lecteurs et flatteurs pour les sujets'.

96 The comparison with Des Essarts was meaningful. He was a particularly stark example of the Parisian banished to the deep south, recently transferred from Sens to Avignon. The poems he had taken for Mallarmé to Collignon were 'L'Azur' and 'A une Putain'; see Mondor, *Autres Précisions*, 19, but Mondor failed to recognize the second poem under the title bestowed on it by Des Essarts, 'A une Dame d'Honneur de la Reine Victoria'—which suggests that Emmanuel knew or guessed that it was a London poem.

97 I should hesitate to make this assertion so confidently were it not that in seeking positive support for it I find that when Des Essarts received from Mallarmé two parts of the composition, the 'introduction' and the poem in praise of Banville, he replied with this appreciation, in a letter dated 18 April 1864 (*Corr.* i, 117 n. 1): 'Je l'ai beaucoup aimé ce poème et il me fait bien augurer des deux autres [on Gautier and Baudelaire]; beaucoup aimé aussi la dédicace à l'Impuissance. C'est très original et très nouveau. Impossible de mieux rendre ce duel de l'inspiration avec le découragement si moderne et si vrai, hélas!' It was perhaps in response to this enthusiastic tribute that Mallarmé added a postscript to his letter to Cazalis of 25 April (*Corr.* i, 117 and *DSM.* vi, 206–7): 'Demande à Emmanuel une *introduction à Trois poèmes en prose* et le *po*[*è*]*me sur de Banville* que je lui ai envoyés. J'ai horreur de recopier cela. Les poèmes 1er et 2e sont sur Th. Gautier, et Baudelaire.' Mallarmé sent to Banville, and perhaps to Gautier and Baudelaire, a copy of 'Trois poèmes en prose'. The letter of grateful thanks that Banville sent him is quoted by the Pléiade editors (*O.c.*, 1538 [1544]).

98 The letter was written on 14 or 17 May 1867; see *Corr.* i, 243–4 and *DSM.* vi, 343.

BIBLIOGRAPHY

Ambrière, F. 'Deux ouvrages inconnus de Stéphane Mallarmé' ['Le Carrefour des Demoiselles' is one], in the *Bulletin du Bibliophile*, 20 Nov. 1935.

Angrand, D., *Victor Hugo raconté par les papiers d'état*. Paris 1961.

Annuaire de l'Instruction publique.

Art et Critique.

Art Monthly Review.

L'Artiste.

'Auriant'. 'Sur des vers retrouvés de Mallarmé' ['Contre un poète parisien' and 'Soleil d'hiver'], in *NRF*., 1 May 1933.

AUMLA (Journal of the Australasian Universities Language and Literary Association).

Austin, L. J. 'Les "Années d'apprentissage" de Stéphane Mallarmé' in *RHLF*., Jan.–Mar. 1956.

——'Mallarmé disciple de Baudelaire', in *RHLF*., Apr.–June 1967.

Badesco, L. *La Génération poétique de 1860*. Paris 1971.

Bandy, W. T. and Pichois, Cl. *Baudelaire devant ses contemporains*. Monaco 1957.

Banville, Th. de. *Les Stalactites*. Paris 1846.

—— *Les Pauvres Saltimbanques*. Paris 1853.

—— *Odelettes*. Paris 1856–7.

—— *Odes funambulesques*. Paris 1857.

—— *La Sainte-Bohême*. Paris 1858.

—— *Esquisses parisiennes*. Paris 1859.

—— *Critiques*, ed. V. Barrucand. Paris 1917.

Barbier, C. P. *Documents Stéphane Mallarmé* (7 vols). Paris 1968–80.

—— (ed.) *Vers et prose d'enfance et de jeunesse, 1854–62*, in *DSM*. iii (1971), 13–98.

—— (ed.) 'Mallarmé et E. des Essarts: *Le Carrefour des Demoiselles*', in *DSM*. iv (1973), 21–36.

—— (ed.) *Chronologie de Mallarmé jusqu'en 1863* and *Lettres et documents de familles, 1765–1864*, in *DSM*. v (1976), 29–436.

—— (ed., in collaboration with L. A. Joseph) *Correspondance avec Henri Cazalis, 1862–1897*, *DSM*. vi (1977).

—— (ed.) *Entre quatre murs*, in *DSM*. vii (1980), 31–165.

—— 'Mallarmé, Léon Marc et Émile Roquier', ibid. 167–209.

Barrère, J.-B. *La Fantaisie de Victor Hugo* (3 vols.). Paris 1949–60.

Baudelaire, Ch. *Œuvres complètes*, ed. Cl. Pichois (2 vols., *Bibl. de la Pléiade*). Paris 1975–6.

—— *Les Fleurs du mal*, ed. J. Crépet and G. Blin. Paris 1942.

—— *Les Fleurs du mal*, ed. A. Adam. Paris 1961.

—— *Correspondance Générale* (vols. I-VI of *Œuvres complètes de Charles Baudelaire*, ed. J. Crépet and Cl. Pichois). Paris 1947–53.

—— *Petits poèmes en prose*, ed. M. Zimmerman. Manchester 1968.

—— 'Pierre Dupont (I)', the earlier of two articles on the poet of that name, first published as the preface to the first volume of his poems, *Chants et Chansons*. Paris 1851.

—— 'Théophile Gautier', in *L'Artiste*, 13 March 1859.

—— 'Victor Hugo', in *La Revue fantaisiste*, 15 June 1861 (opening Baudelaire's series *Réflexions sur quelques-uns de mes contemporains*).

—— 'Théophile Gautier', in *La Revue fantaisiste*, 15 July 1861 (figuring as No. IV in the same series as the 'Pierre Dupont (I)').

—— '*Les Martyrs ridicules* par Léon Cladel', in *La Revue fantaisiste*, 15 Oct. 1861.

—— '*Les Misérables* par Victor Hugo', in *Le Boulevard*, 20 Apr. 1862.

Bénichou, P. 'Mallarmé et le public', in *Cahiers du Sud*, 2e semestre 1949. (Re-published in his *L'Écrivain et ses travaux*. Paris 1967.)

—— *Le Temps des prophètes*. Paris 1977.

Bernard, S. *Le Poème en prose de Baudelaire à nos jours*. Paris 1959.

Bertrand, Aloysius (or Louis). *Gaspard de la nuit*. Paris 1842.

Boileau-Despréaux, N. *L'Art poétique*. Paris 1674.

Bollery, J. (ed.) *Correspondance Générale de Villiers de l'Isle-Adam*. Paris 1962.

Bonniot, E. 'Trois poèmes de jeunesse inédits de Mallarmé [one being 'L'Enfant prodigue']', in *Le Manuscrit autographe*, May–June 1926.

—— 'Le Château de l'Espérance', in *Littérature*, May 1919.

Borel, P. *Madame Putiphar*. Paris 1838.

Bornecque, J. H. *Lumières sur les 'Fêtes Galantes' de Paul Verlaine*. Paris 1959.

Le Boulevard.

Breillat, P. '*Le Guignon* de Stéphane Mallarmé', in vol. I of *Humanisme Actif*, Mélanges d'art et de littérature offerts à Gustave Cain. Paris 1968.

Bourquelot, F. 'Office de Pierre de Corbeil', in the *Bulletin de la Société archéologique de Sens*, vol. VI (1854).

Le Bulletin administratif de l'Instruction publique.
Le Bulletin de la Société archéologique de Sens.
Le Bulletin du Bibliophile.

Les Cahiers de l'Association Internationale des Études Françaises.
Les Cahiers de Sud.
Calmels, F. 'Louis (Aloysius) Bertrand', in *La Revue fantaisiste*, 15 Oct. 1861.
Caro, E. *L'Idée de Dieu et ses nouveaux critiques*. Paris 1864.
Cassagne, A. *La Théorie de l'art pour l'art en France*. Paris 1906 (reprint 1959).
Cazalis, H. *Lettre aux Français*. Brussels 1862.
Cellier, L. *Mallarmé et la Morte qui parle*. Paris 1959.
Chambers, E. K. *The Mediaeval Stage*. Oxford 1903 (reissued in 1925).
Chapon, Fr. *Mystère et splendeurs de Jacques Doucet*. Paris 1984.
Charavay, E. *Alfred de Vigny et Charles Baudelaire, candidats à l'Académie Française*. Paris 1879.
Charpentier, H. 'De Stéphane Mallarmé', in the special Mallarmé number of the *NRF.*, 1 Nov. 1926.
Chateaubriand. *Le Génie du christianisme*. Paris 1802.
—— *Mémoires d'Outre-Tombe*. Paris 1949–50.
Cladel, J. *Maître et disciple, Baudelaire et Léon Cladel*. Paris 1950.
Cladel, L. *Les Martyrs ridicules*. Paris 1961.
Le Courrier de l'Europe.
Crépet, E. *Les Poètes français*, vol. iv ('Les Contemporains'). Paris 1862.
Crépet, E. J. *Charles Baudelaire, étude biographique*, revue et complétée par J. Crépet. Paris 1907.
Currents of thought in French Literature. Essays in memory of G. T. Clapton. Oxford 1965.

Davies, G. *Mallarmé et le drame solaire*. Paris 1959.
—— 'Note on Banville and Mallarmé', in *AUMLA*, 19 May 1963.
Dennery, A. P. and Dumanoir, Ph. *Le Capitaine Roquefinette*. Paris 1843.
Deschamps, Em. *Œuvres complètes*. Paris 1862–94.
Des Essarts, E. *Les Poésies parisiennes*, Paris 1862.
—— 'Souvenirs littéraires: Stéphane Mallarmé', in *La Revue de France*, 14 July 1899.
—— 'Stéphane Mallarmé, professeur d'anglais', in *L'Intermédiaire des chercheurs et curieux*, 20 Oct. 1906.
Dreyfous, M. *Ce que je tiens à dire*. Paris 1912.

—— *Ce qu'il me reste à dire*. Paris 1913.
Du Bellay, J. *Les Regrets*. Paris 1558.
Dumas, A. (the Elder). *Souvenirs dramatiques*, ii. Paris 1881.

Empreintes 9–10 (Sept.–Oct. and Nov.–Dec. 1952: special numbers: 'Stéphane Mallarmè'.
Europe.

Frank, G. *The Medieval French Drama*. Oxford 1960.
Fuchs, M. *Théodore de Banville*. Paris 1912.
Furetière, A. *Dictionnaire universel*. La Haye and Rotterdam 1690.

Gautier, Th. *Mademoiselle de Maupin*. Paris 1835.
—— *Les Grotesques*. Paris 1844.
—— 'François Villon' and 'Théophile de Viaud' (chapters i and iii in *Les Grotesques*).
—— *España*, in *Poésies complètes*. Paris 1845.
—— *Caprices et Zigzags*. Paris 1852.
—— *Émaux et Camées*. Paris 1852.
La Gazette.
La Gazette des Étrangers.
La Gazette rose.
Gély, Cl. 'Les Misérables' *de Victor Hugo*. Paris 1975.
Germain, E. *Riens mis en vers*. Sens 1862.
Gil Blas.
Gilman, M. *The Idea of Poetry in France from Houdar de la Motte to Baudelaire*. Cambridge, Mass. 1958.
Gill, A. 'Le symbole du miroir dans l'œuvre de Mallarmé', in *Cahiers de l'Association Internationale des Études Françaises*, July 1958.
—— 'Les vrais bosquets de la 'Prose pour des Esseintes, ibid., March 1963.
—— 'Mallarmé et "L'Être aux ailes de gaze"', in *Studi in onore di Italo Siciliano*. Florence 1966.
—— 'Mallarmé fonctionnaire', in *RHLF*., Jan.–Feb. and Mar.–Apr. 1968.
—— 'Mallarmé's use of Christian imagery for post-Christian concepts', in *Order and Adventure in Post-Romantic French Poetry: Essays presented to C. A. Hackett*. Oxford 1973.
—— 'Mallarmé: "La Vie et les Œuvres"', in *Colloque Mallarmé* (Glasgow, November 1973). Paris 1975.
Girard, H. *Un Bourgeois dilettante à l'époque romantique. Émile Deschamps 1791–1871*. Paris 1921.
Glatigny, A. *Les Flèches d'or*. Paris 1864.

Le Globe.

Goncourt, E. et J. de. *Journal, mémoires de la vie littéraire*. Paris 1891–1902.

Greene, H. C. 'The Song of the Ass', in *Speculum* vi, Oct. 1931.

Grove's Dictionary of Music and Musicians, ed. E. Blom, London–New York, 1954.

Houssaye, A. 'Chanson du Vitrier', published in his *Œuvres poétiques*. Paris 1857. (The text is quoted *in extenso* by Claude Pichois, B., *O.c.* i, 1309–11.)

Hugo, V. *Œuvres complètes, édition chronologique* (Le Club français du livre). Paris 1969.

—— *Odes et ballades*. Paris 1822.

—— *Les Orientales*. Paris 1829.

—— *Hernani*. Paris 1829.

—— *Les Feuilles d'automne*. Paris 1831.

—— *Les Chants du Crépuscule*. Paris 1835.

—— *Les Voix intérieures*. Paris 1837.

—— *Ruy Blas*. Paris 1838.

—— *Les Rayons et les Ombres*. Paris 1840.

—— *Châtiments*. Brussels 1852.

—— *Les Contemplations*. Paris 1856–7.

—— *La Légende des siècles*. Paris 1859–83.

—— *Les Misérables*. Brussels and Paris 1862.

—— *William Shakespeare*. Paris 1864.

—— *Toute la lyre*. Paris 1888–93.

Huret, J. 'Réponses à des enquêtes sur l'évolution littéraire. M. Stéphane Mallarmé.'

Jean-Aubry, G. *Une Amitié exemplaire: Villiers de L'Isle-Adam et Stéphane Mallarmé*. Paris 1942.

Joseph, L. A. 'Mallarmé et son amie anglaise', in *RHLF*., July–Sept. 1965.

—— *Henri Cazalis, sa vie, son œuvre, son amitié avec Mallarmé*. Paris 1972.

—— (ed. in collaboration with C. P. Barbier) *Correspondance avec Henri Cazalis*. *DSM*. vi. (1977).

Journal des Baigneurs à Dieppe, 1862.

Karr, A. *Une Poignée de vérités*. Paris 1853.

Lamartine, A. de. *Recueillements poétiques*. Paris 1839.

Larousse, P. *Grand dictionnaire universel du XIXe siècle*. Paris 1864–90.

Lefébure, E. and Privé, C. *Sonnets auxerrois* (1862). (Unpublished.)

Lemer, J. *Les Poètes de l'amour*. Paris 1850 and 1858.

Lemerre, A. (publisher) *Le Parnasse contemporain*, recueil de vers nouveaux. 3 vols. Paris 1866, 1869, and 1876.

Lethève, J. 'Mallarmé sur le chemin de Des Esseintes', in *Bulletin de la Société J.-K. Huysmans*, No. 43 (1962).

Littérature.

Mackworth, C. *English Interludes*. London and Boston 1974.

(a) Editions of his works

Mallarmé. *Œuvres complètes*, ed. H. Mondor and G. Jean-Aubry (*Bibl. de la Pléiade*). Paris 1945 and 1951.

—— *Œuvres complètes*, I. *Poésies*, ed. C. P. Barbier and C. G. Millan (Flammarion). Paris 1983.

—— *Vers et prose* (Perrin). Paris 1892.

—— *Poésies* (Gallimard 'Éditions, *NRF*'). Paris 1913.

(Successive Gallimard 'editions' have produced the less restricted 'Collection *Poésie*' edition, now dated 'achevé d'imprimer 1981'.)

—— *Correspondance*. Recueillie, classée et annotée par Henri Mondor et Lloyd James Austin (Gallimard). Paris 1959–85.

—— *Vers et prose d'enfance et de jeunesse (1854–1862)*, ed. C. P. Barbier in *DSM*. iii, 13–98.

—— *Entre quatre murs* (the schoolboy poems) was published by Mondor in *M.lyc.* (121–225), then edited by C. P. Barbier in *DSM*. vii (1980), 31–165. The text of the 'scie', 'Le Carrefour des Demoiselles', printed at Sens by Ph. Chapu for private circulation with the signatures of Mallarmé and Des Essarts, and dated 18 May 1862, is admitted very oddly to the volume *Poésies*, as is C. P. Barbier's edition of *Entre quatre murs*.

The prose tale 'Ce que disaient les Trois Cigognes' was published by Mondor, first in *M.pl.i.* (22–42) then in *M.lyc.* (338–56). *Glanes*, the schoolboy anthology, is described analytically in *M.lyc.* (295–328).

(b) The Poet's own Publications, Poems excepted

'Les Poésies parisiennes', in *Le Papillon*, 10 Jan. 1862.

'La Milanaise et l'Autrichien', in *Le Sénonais*, 19 Mar. 1862.

'Les Poésies parisiennes', in *Le Sénonais*, 22 Mar. 1862.

'Hérésies artistiques: 'L'Art pour tous', in *L'Artiste*, 15 Sept. 1862.

'Symphonie littéraire, in *L'Artiste*, 1 Feb. 1865.

'Le Phénonème futur', in *La République des lettres*, 20 Dec. 1875.

'The Impressionists and Edouard Manet', in *The Art Monthly Review*, 30 Sept. 1876.

'Villiers de l'Isle-Adam', in *L'Art moderne* (Brussels), 23 Feb. 1890.
'Théodore de Banville', in *The National Observer*, 17 Dec. 1892.
'Le Mystère dans les lettres', in *La Revue blanche*, 1 Sept. 1896.

Marc, L. *La Fin d'un rêve*. Verviers 1860.
Mauclair, C. *Le Soleil des morts*. Paris 1898.
—— *Oiseaux des tempêtes*. Brussels 1871.
Mauron, Ch. *Mallarmé l'obscur*. Paris 1941.
—— *Introduction à la psychanalyse de Mallarmé*. Neuchâtel 1950.
—— *Mallarmé par lui-même*. Paris 1964.
Mendès, C. *Le Mouvement poétique français de 1867 à 1900*. Paris 1903.
—— *La Légende du Parnasse*. Paris 1884.
Michaud, G. *Mallarmé, L'Homme et l'œuvre*. Paris 1953. (Then, with minor revisions, under the simplified title *Mallarmé*, new editions in 1958 and 1971.)
—— *Message poétique du symbolisme*. 3 vols. Paris 1947.
Le Missel de la fête des Fous: a medieval choir-book improperly so called, at the *Bibliothèque municipale de Sens*.
The Modern Language Review.
Molière. *Œuvres* ('Les grands écrivains de France'), ed. E. Despois and P. Mesnard. Paris 1873–89.
—— *Don Juan, ou le Festin de Pierre*. 1665.
Mondor, H. *Vie de Mallarmé*. Paris 1941–2.
—— *Mallarmé plus intime*. Paris 1944.
—— *Histoire d'un Faune*. Paris 1948.
—— *Eugene Lefébure*. Paris 1951.
—— *Propos sur la poésie*. Monaco 1953.
—— *Mallarmé lycéen*. Paris 1954.
—— 'Léon Marc et Mallarmé', in *La Voix des poètes*, Jul.–Sept. 1959.
Montel, F. and Monda, M. *Bibliographie de Mallarmé*, in *Bulletin du Bibliophile*, 1925–6. (In volume form, Paris 1927.)
Morris, D. H. *Stéphane Mallarmé, twentieth-century criticism, 1901–1971*. Mississippi (University Romance Monographs No. 25) 1977.
Mossop, D. *Baudelaire's Tragic Hero*. Oxford 1961.
—— *Pure Poetry*. Oxford 1971.
Mounin, G. *Poésie et Société*. (Revised edition) Paris 1968.
—— 'Mallarmé et le langage', in *Europe*, Apr.–May 1976.
Mouquet, J. *Charles Baudelaire—Vers latins*. Paris 1933.
Musset, A. de. *La Confession d'un enfant du siècle*. Paris 1836.

The National Observer.
Neophilologus.

Nerval, G. de. *Sylvie*. Paris 1853.

Nobiling, F. 'Mallarmé's "Sonneur"', in *Neophilologus* 17 (1931–2).

Noulet, Ém. *L'Œuvre poétique de Stéphane Mallarmé*. Paris 1940.

Le Nouveau Parnasse Satyrique, 1878 and 1881.

Order and Adventure in Post-Romantic French Poetry. Essays presented to C. A. Hackett. Oxford 1973.

Le Papillon.

Piper, D. *The Image of the Poet*. Oxford 1982.

Poe, E. A. *Works*, ed. E. C. Stedman and A. E. Woodberry. London 1895.

Porché, F. *Baudelaire, histoire d'une âme*. Paris 1944.

La Presse.

Prévost, J. *Baudelaire*. Paris 1953.

Privat d'Anglemont, *Paris inconnu*. Paris 1861.

Programme pour l'examen du Baccalauréat ès-Lettres, 1852.

Proust, M. 'Contre l'obscurité, in *La Revue blanche*, 15 July 1896.

Raitt, A. W. *The Nineteenth Century* (in the series *Life and Letters in France*) London 1965.

—— 'Autour d'une lettre de Mallarmé', in *La Revue des Sciences humaines* (Special number: *Autour du symbolisme*. I. *Villiers de l'Isle-Adam, Stéphane Mallarmé*), Jan.–Mar. 1955.

—— 'Villiers de l'Isle-Adam en 1870', in *French Studies*, Oct. 1959.

Renan, E. *Études d'histoire religieuse*. Paris 1857.

La République des lettres.

La Revue blanche.

La Revue contemporaine.

La Revue de France.

La Revue de l'histoire de Versailles.

La Revue Européenne.

La Revue Indépendante.

La Revue Nouvelle.

Richard, J.-P. Pour un Tombeau d'Anatole. Paris 1961.

—— *L'Univers imaginaire de Mallarmé*. Paris 1961.

Roquier, E. and Pied-Guérin, C. *Les Sénonaises, Chansons*, printed by Ph. Chapu. Sens 1863.

Rousseau, J.-J. *La Nouvelle Héloïse* (1761).

Sainte-Beuve, Ch. A. *Tableau historique et critique de la poésie française et du théâtre français au XVIe siècle*, with its complement *Les Œuvres choisies de Ronsard*. Paris 1828.

—— *Portraits contemporains*. Paris 1846.

—— 'Victor Hugo en 1831', dated by its author July 1832. It was included in *Portraits contemporains*, with a note to the effect that in its first form it was an anonymous notice published by the newspaper *Le Globe* with one of Hugo's early odes.

Sand, G. *Elle et Lui*. Paris 1859.

Sardou, V. *Nos Intimes*. Paris 1862.

Le Sénonais ('Journal de l'Yonne').

Shackleton, R. (ed.) *Fontenelle, Entretiens sur la pluralité des mondes*. Oxford 1955.

Shakespeare. *A Midsummer Night's Dream*.

—— *Cymbeline*.

Sheridan. *The School for Scandal* (1777).

Starkie, E. *Petrus Borel the Lycanthrope*. London 1953.

Théophile. See *Viaud*.

Thibaudet, A. *La Poésie de Stéphane Mallarmé, étude littéraire*. Paris 1912. (New edition, Gallimard. Paris 1926.)

Thieme, H.-P. *Bibliographie de la littérature française, de 1800 à 1930*. Paris 1953. (To which vast work the author of this modest bibliography is much indebted.)

Tolstoy, L. *Childhood, Boyhood and Youth* trans. Louise and Aylmer Maude (Centenary edition). London 1928.

Vacquerie, A. *Profils et grimaces*. Paris 1856.

Vauquelin de la Fresnaye. *Art poétique françois*. Caen 1605.

Verlaine, P. *Œuvres complètes*. Messein. Paris 1911–13.

—— *Œuvres complètes*. Club du meilleur livre. Paris 1959–60.

—— *Œuvres en prose* complètes, ed. J. Borel (Bibl. de la Pléiade). Paris 1972.

—— *Les Poètes maudits:* 'Stéphane Mallarmé' (*Lutèce*, 17 Nov. 1883–5 Jan. 1884.

—— *Les Fêtes galantes*. Paris 1869.

Viaud, Théophile de. *Œuvres complètes* (ed. Ch. Alleaume), Paris 1855–6.

Vigny, A. de. *Chatterton*. Paris 1935.

Villetard, l'abbé H. de. (ed.) *L'Office de Pierre de Corbeil (Office de la Circoncision)*. Improprement appelé 'Office des Fous'. Paris 1907.

Villiers de l'Isle-Adam, A. *Elën*. Paris 1862.

Villon. *Le Testament*. 1461.

Vivier, R. *L'Originalité de Baudelaire*. Brussels 1952.

La Vogue.

Voiture, V. *Poésies*, ed. Henri Lafay. Paris 1971.

La Voix des poètes.

Wais, K. *Mallarmé: Dichtung, Weisheit, Haltung*. Munich 1952.

Walzer, P. O. *Essai sur Stéphane Mallarmé*. Paris 1963.

Weightman, J. 'Mallarmé and the language obsession', in *Encounter*, Oct. 1978.

Reference is made also to the following unpublished documents:

Régnier, H. de. '*Journal*. Annales psychiques et oculaires' (7 vols. of typescript). Bibliothèque Nationale, Nouvelles acquisitions françaises 14976–80.

Cahier d'Honneur du Lycée Impérial de Sens. Lycée de Sens.

Lefébure, E. and Privé, C. *Sonnets auxerrois*. 1862, unpublished.

Glanes (the anthology put together by Mallarmé during his last year at school). Bibliothèque Littéraire Jacques Doucet. MNR. MS 1168.

Barthelme, M. M. *Formation et mise en œuvre de la pensée de Mallarmé sur le théâtre* (an unpublished Dissertation for the University of Paris 1959). *Bibliothèque de la Sorbonne*.

Index

(a) The Mallarmé Family*

(b) General

* It is hoped that this *Mallarmé* section of the index, given first place, may serve in some modest measure as a sketch of Stéphane's early family background, to complete which, however, it is essential to pay attention also to the entries below that concern the *Desmolins*, his maternal grandparents.